LEGAL PHILOSO
RUSSIAN LIBE

Legal Philosophies of Russian Liberalism

ANDRZEJ WALICKI

UNIVERSITY OF NOTRE DAME PRESS

NOTRE DAME   LONDON

Copyright © 1992 by
University of Notre Dame Press
Notre Dame, Indiana 46556
All Rights Reserved
Manufactured in the United States of America

Library of Congress Cataloging-in-Publication Data

Walicki, Andrzej.
  Legal philosophies of Russian liberalism / Andrzej
Walicki.
    p.   cm.
  Originally published: Oxford : Clarendon Press : New
York : Oxford University Press, 1967.
  Includes bibliographical references and index.
  ISBN 0-268-01298-9
  1. Law—Philosophy—History. 2. Liberalism—
Russia—History. 3. Law—Russia—Philosophy—
History. I. Title.
K218.S65W35   1992
340′.1—dc20   92-50407
                                                    CIP

∞ *The paper used in this publication meets the minimum requirements*
of the American National Standard for Information Sciences—Permanence of Paper
for Printed Library Materials, ANSI Z39.48-1984.

IN THE MEMORY OF
SERGIUS HESSEN

Acknowledgements

T H I S book could not have been written without my first teacher, Sergius Hessen, to whom its last chapter is devoted. His works and his lively image in my mind were a constant source of inspiration.

Secondly, I owe a debt of gratitude to two British scholars of Russian–Jewish background, both convinced liberals: Sir Isaiah Berlin and the late Leonard Schapiro. Sir Isaiah never ceased to give his moral support to my studies in Russian thought and often expressed his wish that I should not neglect 'the unfortunate liberals, victims of history and historians alike'. A similar wish was expressed by Leonard Schapiro who strongly encouraged me to write the present volume.

Finally, I should mention the History of Ideas Unit of the Australian National University in which this book was written. I owe a great deal to its congenial atmosphere and excellent working conditions. Several parts of this book benefited from discussion at the weekly seminars organized by the unit. The Head of the unit, Professor Eugene Kamenka, often showed his friendly interest in my work and his conception of the 'three paradigms of law' proved very useful for conceptualizing some of my main ideas.

The style of this book owes very much to the corrections made by Mrs Elizabeth Y. Short, the research assistant of the unit. Of course, the responsibility for the remaining mistakes or awkward expressions is entirely mine.

Canberra   ANDRZEJ WALICKI
November 1984

Contents

Introduction

RUSSIA is rarely associated with liberalism and law; hence a book on the legal philosophies of Russian liberalism might seem to be dealing with a rather insignificant subject. However, my choice of this subject was deliberately provocative: I wanted to show that the liberal intellectual tradition in pre-revolutionary Russia was in fact much stronger than is usually believed, that the main concern of Russia's liberal thinkers was the problem of the rule of law, and that the most precious legacy of Russian liberalism was precisely its contribution to the philosophy of law, as well as to what might be called the controversy about law, the debate in which the value of law as such was seen as a controversial issue, something in need of defence, and not something to be taken for granted. That is why I have chosen to concentrate on those Russian thinkers, whether professional jurists or not, who combined their work in legal philosophy with wider philosophical, religious, and social interests.

Does it change the widely accepted picture of the Russian intellectual tradition as hostile both to liberalism and law, bound up with different negative attitudes, both left-wing and right-wing, towards law? Not entirely. In a sense it even confirms the truth of this widespread view, since the liberal thinkers with whom I deal here were bitterly aware of the existence, in Russian thought, of a deeply rooted tradition of anti-legal prejudice—a tradition which they wanted to overcome and which was a constant frame of reference for their attempts to vindicate the value of law. On the other hand, the truth of this view is made relative, since to show the strength and high quality of the intellectual opposition to the dominant tradition censuring law introduces a change in the overall view of the legacy of pre-revolutionary Russian thought. In addition, a closer examination of traditional Russian anti-legalism, as presented in my first chapter, leads to the conclusion that its distinctively Russian features should not be exaggerated. Enmity towards, or at least a deep suspicion of rational law, is to be found to a greater or lesser extent in all backward and peripheral societies, especially in those which experience modernization as westernization and thus tend to see modern law as something

alien to their native culture, peculiar to the West. In pre-revolutionary
Russia such a tendency was, perhaps, especially marked. But is it
justifiable to attribute this to an inherent enmity between the Russian
nature and the spirit of law? I prefer to remain sceptical of this. A
closer examination of nineteenth-century Russian thought indicates
rather that in many cases its characteristic anti-legalism was derived
from Western sources. Russian intellectuals were exposed to the
powerful influence of the Western critique of capitalism, in both its
left- and right-wing forms, and it was only natural that this greatly
strengthened their anti-liberal and anti-legal prejudices. It was one of
the tragic consequences of Russia's retarded development.

The legacy of negative attitudes towards law is still alive among the
Russians. Solzhenitsyn, the greatest Russian writer today and the
forceful prophet of Russia's moral regeneration, has spoken of the
'juridical form of life', typical of the West, in the spirit of Slavophile
censure of law.[1] But there are also other voices, heard both in Soviet
Russia and in the Russian diaspora. In fact, even Solzhenitsyn should
not be seen as unequivocally hostile to law and other liberal values. In
his preface to the Russian edition of Leontovich's *History of Liberalism
in Russia* he stressed the value of civil rights guaranteed by law,
pointing out their fundamental importance for human freedom. True,
he also set them against *political* rights, emphasizing that freedom as
active participation in politics must be preceded by winning and *legally
safeguarding* those human rights which are not directly political.[2] But
this is no longer in the Slavophile tradition. The view that individual
freedom under the rule of law is more important than the principle of
popular sovereignty is, of course, fully compatible with liberalism (in
the European sense of this term). As we shall see, Solzhenitsyn's stand
in this matter is very similar to the position of Boris Chicherin, a
staunch defender of the classical liberal conception of law and a sworn
enemy of Slavophile anti-legalism.

There are many reasons for thinking that the ideas of the Russian
liberal legal philosophers presented in this book, have a chance of
being seen as relevant to contemporary Russian problems. They
deserve serious consideration in contemporary discussion of Russia's
future.

---

[1] See A. L. Solzhenitsyn, 'Raskolotyi mir', speech delivered at Harvard University on
8 June, 1978, in *Novyi Zhurnal (New Review)*, vol. 131, 1978, pp. 307–10.

[2] See V. V. Leontovich, *Istoriia liberalizma v Rossii 1762–1914*, Paris, 1980, pp. iii–iv.

I would also like to think that the subject of this book might be of some interest *not only* to people concerned with Russia. The six thinkers here presented were keenly aware of the crisis in legal ideas and the general crisis of liberalism—a crisis that is still with us. Their problems were often so like ours that it seems reasonable to feel that their ideas might be of interest not just to intellectual historians, or historians of Russia, but to legal philosophers and political scientists as well, that they deserve to be known to all who are concerned with the fate of liberalism and of law, with the place of liberal values in the world in which we live today.

My analyses of these ideas confirm the view that 'the modern developments in law and the modern crisis in legal ideas consist of a half-conscious confrontation between three great paradigms of social ideology, social organization, law, and administration—each of them representing a complex but potentially coherent view of man, social institutions and their place in society'. These paradigms have been called 'the *Gemeinschaft* or organic communal-familial, the *Gesellschaft* or contractual commercial-individualistic, and the bureau-cratic-administrative paradigms'.[3] In accordance with the mainstream tradition of European liberalism, Russian liberals saw the *Gesellschaft* type of law as proper, the closest approximation to the idea of law. They knew its limitations but they defended it as the necessary foundation of individual freedom, as the safeguard of personal inviolability, as a means of protecting human personality not only against the arbitrary commands of the government but also, sometimes above all, against the mechanism of social conformity or the moral pressures of the community. Human personality, insisted one of them, contains a 'supra-social kernel' impenetrable for the group;[4] law protects this 'impenetrability' against external compulsion exercised by the state and legal consciousness helps the individuals in defending

---

[3] Eugene Kamenka and Alice Erh-Soon Tay, 'Social traditions, legal traditions', in *Law and Social Control*, E. Kamenka and A. Tay (eds.), London, 1980, p. 7. See also E. Kamenka and A. E.-S. Tay, 'The Sociology of Justice', in *Legal Change: Essays in Honour of Julius Stone*, Sydney, 1983, pp. 107–22.

The ease with which I accept the conception of the three paradigms of social ideology and law is due to the fact that I used the *Gemeinschaft–Gesellschaft* typology in my previous works on Russian intellectual history. See *The Slavophile Controversy*, Oxford, 1975, pp. 168–78 and 265–6, *The Controversy over Capitalism*, Oxford, 1969, pp. 74–5, and *A History of Russian Thought from the Enlightenment to Marxism*, Oxford, 1980, pp. 107–9 and 285.

[4] See below, Ch. VII, 4.

their moral autonomy and not yielding to collective pressure. With such views on the essence of law it was easy and natural to identify the cause of law with the cause of liberalism, to present law as the core value in the liberal view of the world.

The Russian enemies of liberalism were inclined to share this view of law, to see the rule of law as the ideal of Western individualism and, therefore, to oppose it in the name of communal values, i.e. the values of *Gemeinschaft* which might be given a conservative-traditionalist, a populist, or an anarchist interpretation. On the other hand, the liberal conception of law was opposed in Russia by supporters of bureaucratic absolutism who believed in bureaucratic-administrative regulations and did not want to submit them to the higher authority of general, aim-independent legal rules. There was nothing peculiarly Russian in this pattern of opposites. The specificity of the situation can be reduced to the fact that the liberal conception of law was constantly under attack, that its supporters were in a minority and that its institutional bulwark, the new judiciary, was too weak, safeguarded neither by a written constitution, nor by the historical tradition of the country. Yet it was precisely because of this that Russian liberals were so ardent in their vindication of the higher value of law, so committed to the ideal of the rule of law and so deeply convinced of the centrality of law for the political and social regeneration of Russia.

This book does not attempt to deal with *all* the legal philosophies which originated in Russia and were related to liberal values. Instead of covering the entire field of my subject in a superficial way I have selected the six most outstanding, representative thinkers and analysed their ideas in depth, showing them as typifying different schools of legal philosophy and, at the same time, different stages in the evolution of liberalism. Despite the great political differences in their theories of law these thinkers had certain features in common. All were aware of the general crisis in legal ideas and saw glaring evidence of this crisis in the dominance of legal positivism—a theory of law which they regarded as misinterpreting the very notion of law, demoralizing the legal profession, and betraying liberal values. They accused legal positivism of putting political authority, 'the sovereign', above law and thus paving the way for tyranny. Though carefully distinguishing between morality and law, they refused to agree with the legal positivists that law should be completely separate from morality (since legal rules, as Kelsen put it, 'can have any content whatsoever') and that jurisprudence should be concerned only with positive law, *ius qua iussum*, dismissing the problem of just law, *ius qua iustum*.[5] All tried to develop a theoretical justification for the subjective rights of man, which would limit the scope of political power, including the power of a democratic majority. All placed law within the context of a general, often metaphysical, philosophy of man and a philosophy of values, trying to avoid the cynical relativism inherent, as they saw it, in positivism and to find an independent criterion by which the value of existing positive laws could be judged and which could serve as a guide for future legislation. In this way Chicherin and Soloviev took the first steps towards the revival of natural law which the younger thinkers, Petrażycki and Novgorodtsev, openly proclaimed.

Another common feature was their emphasis on the autonomy of law from politics, on the logical and axiological priority of the rule of law over political freedom. All the thinkers to whom I have devoted separate chapters in this book were concerned to build a legal culture and defend it against excessive politicization. They were quite clear that the rule of law was conceivable without full political freedom, but not the reverse; they wanted political struggles to be waged within a strong legal framework, in other words, they opted for a rule-bound society, one in which political decisions could not be arbitrarily made, in which law would set the rules for politics, and not vice versa. This aspect of their views seems especially relevant today, since hostility towards the law, stemming from the realization that law interferes with political processes, has become widespread among supporters of social planning and also among adherents of so-called 'interest-group liberalism' who conceive of politics as bargaining and see law as creating unnecessary obstacles to the freedom of political decision-making.[6]

It should be stressed that Russian liberal theorists were much more conscious of the possibilities of conflict between law and politics than

---

[5] The best defence of legal positivism is to be found in M. Maneli, *Juridical Positivism and Human Rights*, New York, 1981.

[6] 'At least some of the current hostility to law', wrote Alice Erh-Soon Tay, 'is based on the belief that this elevation of an impartial, rule-bound, conflict-resolution-oriented judiciary interferes with social planning and social reform, that it protects existing and entrenched interests against the requirements of the future.' (A. E.-S. Tay, 'Law, the citizen and the state', in E. Kamenka, R. Brown and A. E.-S. Tay (eds.), *Law and Society*, London, 1978, p. 8). For 'interest-group liberalism' see T. J. Lowi, *The End of Liberalism: Ideology, Policy, and the Crisis of Public Authority*, New York, 1969. According to Lowi 'liberalism is hostile to law . . . Interest-group liberalism has little place for law because law interferes with the political process' (p. 125).

the leadership of the Kadet party. This explains why Petrażycki and Novgorodtsev—both members of the Kadet Central Committee—were less inclined to sacrifice liberal principles and the long-range interests of law to purely political considerations. They thus found themselves on the right wing of the party, although their respective visions of ultimate goals were probably more left-wing than the ideals of the average Russian liberal. This dichotomy between scepticism of left-wing politics and commitment to left-wing ideals was even more striking in the case of Bogdan Kistiakovsky, who associated himself with right-wing critics of the politicized Russian intelligentsia while at the same time sympathizing with socialism.

Political and doctrinal differences between the six legal philosophers reflect different stages in the development of Russian liberalism. From this point of view they may be seen as links in a remarkably continuous process: that of transforming classical liberalism, as represented by Chicherin, first into a 'new liberalism' and then, with Kistiakovsky and Hessen, into 'rule-of-law socialism'. The fact that the principal legal theorists of the Kadet party, Novgorodtsev and Petrażycki, were so willing to accept the tenets of the new, social liberalism, corroborates Miliukov's view that this party was 'the most left-wing of all analogous political groups in Western Europe'.[7] The possibility of Russian liberalism developing into liberal socialism provided, in turn, additional testimony of 'the close historical relationship between Russian liberalism and socialism'.[8] (Chicherin was in this respect an important exception.) The originality of the conception of rule-of-law socialism, as elaborated by Kistiakovsky and Hessen, consists in seeing liberal socialism not simply as an extension of the democratic principle of popular sovereignty (through its application to the economic sphere), but rather as a higher stage in the development of the distinctively liberal concept of the rule of law, that is, as a further extension of the scope of human rights. Thus it was not a concession to populist democracy but a fusion of socialist and classical-liberal principles, emphasizing subjective rights and safeguarding them against all forms of arbitrary political power, including that of unlimited democracy.[9] It was an effort to preserve liberal values in a changing world by creating

---

[7] P. Miliukov, *Political Memoirs, 1905–1917*, Ann Arbor, 1967, p. 48.

[8] Cf. G. M. Hamburg, *Politics of the Russian Nobility 1881–1905*, New Brunswick, NJ, 1984, p. 222.

[9] On 'unlimited democracy' see F. A. Hayek, *Law, Legislation and Liberty*, London, 1982, vol. 3, pp. 138–9, 145–6, 172.

an alternative to the increasing government regulation and control. This alternative—*legal* regulation and *legal* control—was to bring about a partial socialization of economic relations without abandoning the classical-liberal principle of limited government.

This book is a historical study and does not pretend to solve theoretical problems. It analyses Russian legal philosophies in their historical and comparative context without attempting a thorough evaluation on the theoretical level. Nevertheless, I feel strongly that the problems under discussion are very much alive today. If so, it is justifiable to claim that the intellectual heritage of Russian liberalism should be recognized as being relevant and of value to us today.

I

The Tradition of the Censure of Law

1 Introductory remarks: the 'Russian soul' and the 'spirit of law'

THE idea of the 'Russian soul', once very fashionable, is today
deservedly unpopular among serious scholars. I am not going to try to
revive this obsolete notion, but would prefer to concentrate, in this
book, on a tradition in Russian thought which has little in common
with the traditional image of the 'Russian soul' but which should yet be
treated as deeply rooted in specifically Russian problems. It is an
expression of some specifically Russian yearnings, showing how the
Russians could free themselves from the fatal heritage of their history,
and thus contradicting the view that the Russian mind was predetermined by an allegedly immutable 'Russianness'.

Nevertheless, the notion of the 'Russian soul' is a stereotype which,
like most stereotypes, contains a grain of truth and, if used with due
caution, may be useful for a better understanding of Russian
intellectual history. Its relative truth is a result of its reflection, however
one-sided, of certain features of the historically-formed Russian
national character. It is profoundly false in its eternalization of these
features and in ignoring the fact that national character is always
historically shaped and historically changing. Even false ideas,
however, if significant enough, can be of great historical interest.
Cyprian Norwid, a great nineteenth-century Polish poet, rightly
pointed out that national history cannot be reduced to bare facts, that
views concerning it, however false, also play a part; a part, moreover,
that may be of great significance in shaping national myths or the
national self-image.[1] The fate of the idea of the 'Russian soul',
I believe, corroborates this perceptive judgement.

Wladimir Weidle, in his stimulating book *Russia: Absent and Present,*[2]

---

[1] C. K. Norwid, *Pisma wszystkie* (*Collected Works*), Warsaw, 1971–3, vol. 7,
pp. 85–92. A similar view underlies M. Cherniavsky's book *Tsar and People: Studies in
Russian Myths*, New York, 1969.

[2] See W. Weidle, *Russia: Absent and Present*. A. Gordon Smith (trans.) New York,
1952, pp. 129–53.

gives a good summary of traditional views of the 'Russian soul'. In his opinion its main features are: 'the family connection', a fear of law, a hatred of forms, and a spirit of humility, all of course supporting and supplementing one another. The exaltation of the organic quality of family life and relationships, of being bound in a close community with the members of one's primary group (or groups), resulted in a strong commitment to collectivism of the *Gemeinschaft* type and a fear of the cold, impersonal, legalistic *Gesellschaft*.[3] Hence arose the preference for spontaneous relationships between people and a deeply rooted fear of law, related to a general hatred and distrust of all forms, whether in society, where social conventions were felt to be a species of hypocrisy, or in thought, where this distrust produced a lack of logical discipline, or even in art. 'The largeness of soul on which a Russian prides himself', Weidle writes, 'gives him a feeling of being cramped when he is compelled to depend on rule of law'.[4] But this anarchical instinct 'is not due, as might be thought, to an unbridled desire for individual freedom; quite the opposite. It comes from the fact that he is accustomed to a collective way of life in which relations between members of a group are less clearly defined and regulated, more warm and homely than would be possible in a modern State'.[5] Legal logic is alien to both his mind and his moral feeling. For example he hardly distinguishes between lending money and giving it; similarly, he censures an offence against the rules of property 'merely in so far as it is prejudicial to a person' and 'would readily exculpate a thief on the ground of his poverty or even on the ground of his victim's wealth'.[6] His deprecation of law and logic may place him either above them, or beneath them. The same is true of another, closely related, feature of his psyche, a certain effacement of personality, which at its worst is hardly distinguishable from servility but which can also manifest itself as the spirit of charity and humility.[7]

In spite of his obvious sympathy for certain features of the 'Russian soul', Weidle does not mean to idealize it but wants, rather, to remain within the sphere of the descriptive. Russian intellectual history, however, provides many instances of the unbridled idealization of similar images of 'true Russianness', the 'Russian soul', or the 'Russian idea'. It was an image easy to romanticize and many Russian thinkers, from the Slavophiles to Berdyaev, from Bakunin to the twentieth-century mystical anarchists, indulged in doing just that. As

---

[3] Ibid., p. 134.   [4] Ibid., p. 139.   [5] Ibid., p. 136.
[6] Ibid., pp. 136–7.   [7] Ibid., pp. 144–5.

we shall see, such romanticization also embraced a negative attitude towards the cold formalism of law. The 'spirit of law' was perceived as something peculiarly Western, or peculiar to capitalism, and condemned for various reasons and from different quarters: in the name of autocracy or in the name of freedom, in the name of Christ or in the name of Marx, for the sake of higher spiritual values or for the sake of material justice. In this way both conservative and radical thought in Russia became strongly affected by a disparagement of law, or even by a kind of 'legal nihilism'. (I put this convenient term in inverted commas because the phenomenon so called was much broader than a consistent negation of all law, which was characteristic only of radical anarchists, including Tolstoy.)

The idealization of the 'Russian soul' was at one time also quite widespread in the West, especially in Germany, where it found a congenial atmosphere in the neo-romantic anti-capitalism of the early years of this century. It occurs in Thomas Mann, who was strongly influenced by Merezhkovsky's well-known book on Dostoevsky and Tolstoy, and in the young Lukács, who succeeded in interesting Max Weber in the 'Russian spirit' as a consistent and meaningful rejection of the 'spirit of capitalism'.[8] Ferenc Fehér has reconstructed Lukács's project of a work on Dostoevsky, in which the author of *The Brothers Karamazov* was to be presented as the harbinger of a new man, the portrayer of a new community.[9] As a recent book on Lukács summarizes it:

The planned work, of which *The Theory of the Novel* was to be only an introduction, was to involve far more than a book on Dostoevsky. Envisioned was a world-historical confrontation between objective spirit (the state, the church, law, formal ethics, the German war, Western civilization) and soul (community, religion, morality, substantive ethics, the Russian idea). The vision projected the radical supplanting of the first by the second.[10]

There was also another and, in the West, more influential tradition dealing with the problem of the peculiar quality of 'Russianness'. In Russia it was started by the lonely thinker, Petr Chaadaev, a religious Westernizer who saw his country as excluded from participation in universal history, abandoned by divine Providence and, therefore,

[8] See A. Arato and P. Breines, *The Young Lukács and the Origins of Western Marxism*, New York, 1979, p. 51.
[9] Ibid., p. 69. Cf. F. Fehér, 'Am Scheideweg des romantischen Antikapitalismus', in Agnes Heller *et al.*, *Die Seele und das Leben*, Frankfurt am Main, 1977.
[10] Ibid., p. 70.

strangely amorphous, lacking the discipline of forms, that is, the discipline of logic, of law, and of social conventions; a country of infantile people, who grew up but did not mature and who knew little about 'the ideas of duty, of justice, of right, of order'.[11] His ideas influenced the marquis de Custine, who, in his *La Russie en 1839*, depicted the proverbial largeness and shapelessness of the Russian nature as the obverse, and the inner cause, of a totally repressive autocracy and an instinctive urge for external expansion. Jules Michelet, who knew the works of both Chaadaev and Custine, added a peculiar emphasis on the Russian disparagement of law, combined with an idolatrous cult of the state. In his *Légendes démocratiques du Nord* he made the following accusation against the Russians:

The tendency of such a State is to become less and less a State, and more and more a religion. Everything is religious in Russia. Nothing is legal, nothing is just. Everything seeks to be holy . . . What an undertaking! You cannot even organize in your realm the world of civil order, the inferior world! And you aspire to the superior world of religion! Enemies of the Law, you want to place yourself higher than the Law, you seek the realm of Grace! Unable to perform the work of man, you call yourselves Gods.[12]

In our times criticism of Russian 'legal nihilism' has often been used, and sometimes abused, by those Western historians who have tried to explain the totalitarian character of the Soviet state by the totalitarian features of pre-revolutionary Russia and by corresponding traits in the traditional Russian mentality. An extreme example of such an approach is provided by Tibor Szamuely's *The Russian Tradition*. Following Chicherin, Szamuely treats the 1649 Code of Russian laws as 'the final and complete subjugation of society to the State' and quotes with approval Berdyaev's statement that 'the Orthodox Tsardom of Muscovy was a totalitarian State'.[13] Passing to the nineteenth century Szamuely concentrates his attention on the Russian intelligentsia which he sees as a 'curious stratum' that 'contributed more than any other group to the downfall of the old order and the establishment of the Soviet regime'.[14] He wrote:

[11] See P. Chaadaev, 'Philosophical Letters', in J. M. Edie *et al.*, *Russian Philosophy*, Chicago, 1965, vol. 1, p. 113.
[12] J. Michelet, *Légendes démocratiques du Nord*, Paris, 1968, pp. 203, 205. Quoted from A. Besançon, *The Intellectual Origins of Leninism*, S. Matthews (trans.), Oxford, 1981, p. 80.
[13] T. Szamuely, *The Russian Tradition*. R. Conquest (ed.), London, 1974, pp. 50, 55.
[14] Ibid., p. 177.

The rule of law was for them a meaningless abstraction, and the whole libertarian, legalistic and constitutionalist approach was irritably regarded as a red herring which could only divert attention from the issues that really mattered. No other ideological feature demonstrates more convincingly than this the extent to which the Russian intelligentsia and their leaders, for all the radicalism and revolutionism, were moulded by the Russian tradition. Throughout the centuries the ideas of legality and liberty, of the rule of law and the rights of the individual, had been outside the compass of Russian experience. They were to remain beyond the perception of the class uniquely dedicated to the transformation of Russian society. In this connection it is worth mentioning that the whole voluminous corpus of Russian political literature, from Radishchev to Lenin, contains not a single work on legal theory, constitutionalism, the rights of man, the natural law, or kindred subjects. This was all considered to be so utterly irrelevant and unimportant that no progressive man would ever give it a thought (characteristically, the only people who ever did take an interest in these problems were a handful of zealous State officials like Speransky, Pogodin or Chicherin).[15]

The passage quoted contains some errors which reveal serious flaws in Szamuely's knowledge of Russian intellectual history. Radishchev was a firm believer in the rule of law, a theorist of natural law and of the rights of man, an enthusiastic worshipper of the American Constitution and of the entire Anglo-Saxon tradition of freedom under law; thus, to associate him with the deprecation of law is completely unjustified. Treating Chicherin as a 'zealous State official' is equally wrong and curious. To assert that the whole corpus of pre-revolutionary Russian political literature did not contain *a single work* on legal theory, the rights of man, or the natural law, is also wrong as the voluminous legacy of Chicherin and the works of other authors dealt with in this book conclusively demonstrate. In his sweeping generalizations on the Russian intelligentsia Szamuely closely followed Kistiakovsky's classic essay 'In the Defence of Law',[16] but was not cautious enough to avoid over-statement. For instance, Kistiakovsky complained that Russian political thought had produced nothing like *L'Esprit des lois* or *Le Contrat social*. This is true, but it is not at all the same as the wider assertion discussed above.

Nevertheless, in spite of its obvious oversimplification, Szamuely's conception of the 'Russian tradition' contains some important truths, though no more than Weidle's image of the 'Russian soul'. In a sense these conceptions complement each other, but for scholarly purposes

[15] Ibid., pp. 171–2.   [16] See Ch. VI, 5.

they must be submitted to radical demystification. It is necessary to be clearly aware that what they define or describe is not a permanent quality but something relative, historically produced and historically changing; something relatively autonomous, able to exert influence on historical events as a relatively independent factor, but not something predetermining these events; something characteristic of Russia but not peculiar to it and entirely unknown to the rest of the world. To put it differently, we should be aware that all the components of the 'Russian soul', or the 'Russian tradition', occur in the history of other countries as well, although, of course, in somewhat different historical configurations.

An important contribution to a better understanding of the role of law in the Russian tradition was recently made by Richard S. Wortman.[17] Among other things, he succeeds in showing the Western sources of Russian antilegalism and in carefully distinguishing its modern, post-Petrine variety from the abhorrence of juridical rationalism characteristic of the ideologies of the different opponents of modernization. He reminds us that the post-Petrine Russian autocracy consciously modelled itself on the absolute 'police' state of the West[18] and that this involved both a belief in rational legislation and a deep suspicion of law and lawyers. 'To western rulers and thinkers', Wortman writes, 'the legal profession had come to represent a residue of traditional habits and attachments acting to thwart the will of the rational legislator. An antilegalist spirit animated Frederick the Great to try to abolish lawyers in Prussia, and Jeremy Bentham to find a rational legislation that would eliminate the need for lawyers' obfuscation.'[19] This view of lawyers was fully shared by Russian monarchs. Catherine II wrote: 'Lawyers depending on when they are paid and who pays them now defend what is true, now what is false; now what is just, now what is unjust.'[20] Nicholas I was so terrified of lawyers that in his reign the word *lawyer* (*advokat*) was banned from the press.[21] His view of lawyers was defended by Count V. N. Panin (the future Minister of Justice) who believed in an inquisitorial system with written procedure; the chief merit of which, for him, was that it dispensed with the need for lawyers, who 'try to bias the court, not by law, but by eloquence, and the case is decided not according to justice

[17] R. S. Wortman, *The Development of a Russian Legal Consciousness*, Chicago and London, 1976.
[18] Ibid., p. 9.
[19] Ibid., p. 10.   [20] Ibid., p. 12.   [21] Loc. cit.

(*po pravde*) but according to the transports of the moment'.[22] Similar views found expression in Dostoevsky's works and thus became associated in the West with the 'Russian soul'. In fact, however, there was nothing peculiarly Russian in them. They reflected the attitude towards law characteristic of the 'well ordered police state',[23] that is, of a state which stressed the need for detailed legal regulation of all spheres of life while rejecting the view of law as a limitation of executive power; a state which emphasized legality while seeing the monarch as sole creator and interpreter of the law, thereby subordinating judicial authority to the executive power and inevitably confusing laws with administrative rulings. What was really peculiar to Russia was not the Russian mind, not the *ideas* of law and lawyers current in court and bureaucratic circles, but a peculiar historical development.

In Russia, unlike the West, no rising class of jurists, specially trained in rational law,[24] had prepared the way for eighteenth-century absolutist rule and modernization. Therefore Russian absolutism adopted the ethos of rational legislation and the policy of the *état bien policé*, while preserving many features of a traditional patriarchal autocracy, and did not have to concern itself with an organized legal profession. The institution of the Bar only appeared in Russia with the judicial reforms of 1864.

Of course, lawyers were criticized in Russia not only by administrators and rulers by also by the common people. This criticism from below sprang, as a rule, from attitudes characteristic of a pre-modernized society, based upon immediate relationships and unreflective traditionalism. But this phenomenon was not unknown in the West, as the German saying *Juristen böse Christen!* shows.[25]

Another Western source of Russian 'legal nihilism' was the ideological breakdown of the belief in rational legislation—a belief which characterized not only eighteenth-century monarchs but also, and to a greater extent, eighteenth-century revolutionaries. Widespread disappointment with the results of the French Revolution produced an almost universal rejection of the rationalist approach to social change and, also, of the rationalist theory of human rights. Constitutionalism was criticized by both right and left. Socialists entirely agreed with

[22] Ibid., p. 176.
[23] Cf. M. Raeff, *The Well-Ordered Police State. Social and Institutional Change through Law in the Germanies and Russia, 1600–1800*, London, 1983.
[24] Cf. *Max Weber on Capitalism, Bureaucracy and Religion*. S. Andreski (ed.), London, 1983, p. 28.
[25] See A. P. d'Entrèves, *Natural Law*, London, 1970, pp. 154–5.

feudalist conservatives that a 'written constitution' was a 'mere scrap of paper' (in the famous phrase of Frederick William IV), and that what really mattered was not legal form but social content. The newly emergent science of sociology concentrated on showing that social processes are independent of the human will, that man is always a product of history, a member of a particular society, and that the notion of an abstract individual, holder of inalienable rights, is merely a fiction whose appearance and function is subject to sociological explanation. At this point we again see the possibility of essential agreement between conservatives and socialists: both (with some exceptions, of course) were equally convinced that the fiction of 'inalienable human rights' was serving the interests of the bourgeoisie. Sociology, we are told, 'arose in an atmosphere characterized by the conservative reaction to revolution'.[26] True, but it is equally justifiable to say that it arose in the atmosphere created by the socialist reaction to bourgeois domination.

The impact of these facts on the Russian intelligentsia was partially realized by Bogdan Kistiakovsky, the author of the essay 'In the Defence of Law', mentioned above. He pointed out in one of his earlier articles that the outlook of the Russian intelligentsia had developed in the 'socio-centric' nineteenth century and that this was one reason why mainstream Russian thinkers paid little attention to the problem of individual rights and to the normative significance of law (as distinct from its social function).[27] He did not, however, develop this important idea further for he was more interested in overcoming the Russian derogation of law than in explaining its ideological genesis; quite probably, he was not even fully aware of the importance of his observation.

Historical hindsight enables us to understand the problem more clearly. We ourselves are constantly grappling with difficulties arising from the uneven development of the world, from the unintended results of the ideological influence of advanced countries, which have undergone successive phases of economic and cultural development, upon underdeveloped or unevenly developed countries. György Lukács has shown how the Western critique of democracy—a critique stemming from 'a certain disappointment with democracy on the part of the masses and their ideological spokesmen'[28]—helped to engender

[26] Don Martindale, *The Nature and Types of Sociological Theory*, 2nd edn., Boston, 1981, p. 130.

[27] B. Kistiakovsky, *Sotsial'nye nauki i pravo*, Moscow, 1916, pp. 498–9.

[28] G. Lukács, *The Destruction of Reason*. P. Palmer (trans.), London, 1980, p. 68.

'the ideology of aggressive German imperialism, the doctrine of the German "Mission" to signpost the future of mankind, and this on the very basis of a conserving of all the retrograde institutions of the "German misery"'.[29] In this way socialist criticism of bourgeois democracy helped to pave the way for the victory of Nazism. Lukács attributed this to Germany's retarded capitalist development. It is hardly possible to agree with his wholesale and brutal condemnation of the mainstream intellectual tradition in Germany but his general thesis is, none the less, quite convincing: Germany's retarded development explains the weakness of German liberalism and thus the weakness of German resistance to totalitarian temptations.

Despite Lukács (who thought that in the case of Russia retarded capitalist development had brought about beneficial results)[30] a similar reasoning may be applied to Russia. Its retarded development created conditions in which the powerful influence of Western criticism of capitalism, and its 'formal freedom', merged with certain important elements in the national heritage and called into being an intellectual tradition deeply suspicious of law and hostile to liberal values. In this sense it may truly be said that the Russian nineteenth-century intellectual tradition helps to explain the weakness of Russian liberalism and the relatively easy victory of totalitarian dictatorship. It does not, however, follow that the nineteenth-century Russian intelligentsia deserved nothing better, or that the Russian tradition as a whole made totalitarianism inevitable. Szamuely's efforts to present the entire Russian tradition as inherently and incurably hostile to freedom are no more acceptable than Lukács's views on the mainstream intellectual tradition of Germany.

The present book deals with thinkers who reacted against Russian 'legal nihilism' and thus distanced themselves from the mainstream Russian intellectual tradition. But to react against something is itself a significant relationship, a participation in the same discourse and, in that sense, in the same tradition. I shall try to show that the passionate Russian denigration of law, or, rather, the effort to understand and overcome it, determined the direction 'of thought of the six liberal Russian legal philosophers, whose views are presented and analysed

[29] Ibid., p. 717.
[30] According to Lukács, 'it was precisely as a result of its retarded capitalist development that the Russian nation managed to transfer its bourgeois-democratic revolution to the proletarian one, thereby sparing itself sorrows and conflicts which still exist in the German nation today.' (ibid., p. 37). These words were written at the height of Stalinist totalitarianism.

below. It was no accident that the best, although not sufficiently known, intellectual achievements of Russian liberalism were in the field of legal philosophy; this was because liberal thinkers in Russia had had to come to grips with the questions asked by those Russian thinkers representing right- or left-wing varieties of 'legal nihilism'. For them, Russian 'legal nihilism' was not only a negative frame of reference but, whether acknowledged or not, a precious vantage point from which they could view their subject, that is law, from outside as it were, and place it in a much broader philosophical and cultural context than was possible for contemporary Western legal philosophers. The seriousness of the Russian accusations gave strength to their defence of law; the depth of Russian scepticism towards 'legal forms' fed their desire to overcome it and thus lent conviction to their cherished ideal of the rule-of-law state (*pravovoe gosudarstvo*); the usual Russian condemnations of law in the name of morality caused them to examine with special care the complex relationship between morality and law; the Russian tradition of subordinating law to force, as in the case of the defenders of autocracy, or of identifying law with force, as in the case of anarchist and other Russian rebels against the state, determined their efforts to disentangle law from power and their unanimous opposition to legal positivism. We are entitled to say, therefore, that the tradition of the Russian critique of law helps us to understand the best intellectual achievements of Russian liberalism, which also belong to the 'Russian tradition', and show the direction in which it might have developed under more favourable political circumstances.

2   *The 'juridical world-view': its emergence and breakdown in Russia*

The eighteenth century, unlike the nineteenth, firmly believed in 'institutional change through law', that is, in the omnipotence of rational legislation.[31] This aspect of the Age of Enlightenment, common to the ideologies of enlightened absolutism and of the rising bourgeoisie, has been aptly called 'juridical rationalism', by Max Weber, or the 'juridical world-view'. The last term was used by Engels, who contrasted the 'juridical world-view' with the theological world-view of the Middle Ages. He wrote:

In England religion was extolled for the last time in the seventeenth century, and barely fifty years later the new world-view made its debut in France—the

---

[31]   Cf. Raeff, *The Well-Ordered Police State.*

world-view that was to become the classical one for the bourgeoisie, namely, the juridical world-view.

This was the secularization of theology. Human justice replaced the divine law, or God's justice; the state assumed the role of the church. Economic and social circumstances, formerly sanctioned by the church and thus believed to be established by the church and its dogma, were now regulated by the state and held to be based on equity. On a societal scale the exchange of commodities, with all its sophisticated implications of advance payments [loans] and credit, requires mutual contracts and universally valid rules. Only society could feasibly provide these instruments—legal norms enacted by the state. This led to the general assumption that such norms were the result of formal acts of state, rather than having emerged from economic reality. And because competition, the fundamental form of business of free manufacturers, is one of the strongest equalizers, the main battle cry of the bourgeoisie became 'equality before the law'. Every class struggle is political, and because possession of the state was the goal of this new class in its struggle against feudal landlords and the absolute monarchy they supported, their struggle had to be waged around legalistic demands. This solidified a world view based on legal rights.[32]

This long quotation shows that Engels's notion of the 'juridical world-view' combines two quite different categories of belief in rational law: the belief in rational legislation by the state, bound up with the ideology of state absolutism and giving rise to the doctrine of legal positivism,[33] and the belief in universally valid and legally claimable rights of man, which formed the foundation of the liberal version of natural-law doctrine. It is obvious that, while these two ideologies might join forces in the struggle against feudal privilege and irrational traditionalism, they would have to part company thereafter. Engels emphasized the replacement of the church by the state, but strangely underestimated the modernizing role of absolute monarchy, seeing it only as the ally of feudal landlords. He did not pay enough attention to the fact that an exaggerated belief in rational legislation was characteristic not only of the progressive bourgeoisie but also of an absolutist monarchy and that the latter often supported free manufacturers rather than a reactionary nobility. He also failed to see that a 'world-view based on legal rights' could provide arguments against all forms of state absolutism, not only the monarchical, that human rights

[32] F. Engels and K. Kautsky, 'Juridical Socialism'. Piers Beirne (int.), *Politics and Society*, 7, 1977, p. 204. (Originally published under the title 'Juristen-Socialismus' in *Die Neue Zeit*, 1887, no. 2.)

[33] Cf. W. A. Luijpen, *Phenomenology of Natural Law*, Pittsburgh, Pa., 1967, pp. 43, 79.

might be seen as pre-existent, not enacted by the state, and that the legal interpretation of the rights of man might therefore contradict the doctrine of the sovereign authority of the state; in other words, that human rights might be treated as inalienable, thus setting definite limits to the will of rational legislators.

Nevertheless, the notion of a juridical world-view seems a useful characterization of the epoch in which the new socio-economic order, capitalism, was developing under the protection of the 'well-ordered police state'. It is also useful as an explanation of certain peculiarities of post-Petrine Russia.

The reforms of Peter the Great provide the most spectacular example of institutional change through law. His successors were also committed to rational legislation and the idealization of their enlightened absolutism was the dominant motif in eighteenth-century Russian thought and literature. Kantemir, Trediakovsky, Sumarokov, Lomonosov, and Derzhavin wrote poems on the theme of the 'Northern Rome', in which they praised the modernization achieved by the emperors and the splendours of St Petersburg, the new capital symbolizing the Westernization of Russia and the miraculous power of Peter's will.[34] All enthusiastically supported the legal regulation of life and proclaimed the need for further reforms, to be achieved through law. All shared the view that, as Helvetius put it, 'la législation fait tout'. And all eulogized Russian autocracy as the form of government most suited to breaking the traditional inertia, crushing the resistance of conservative forces and realizing the ideal of rational legislation. (This view is known to have been shared by quite a few Western thinkers.)[35] Thus, if we conceive the belief in rational legislation to be an important part of the juridical world-view, we must acknowledge that in this respect the latter, far from being absent in eighteenth-century Russia, was on the contrary spectacularly present, affecting almost all the intellectual life of the country.

[34] This tradition found a splendid continuation in Pushkin's poetry, especially in his *Bronze Horseman*. See W. Lednicki, *Pushkin's Bronze Horseman*, Berkeley and Los Angeles, 1955, pp. 43–57.

[35] The enthusiasm of some western thinkers (Voltaire, Diderot, M. Grimm, and others) for the legislative activity and, even more, for the declared aims of Catherine II is well known. Less well known is the fact that Russia was sometimes conceived as a country where nothing had as yet been accomplished and where, therefore, everything remained to be done by a rational legislator. Diderot put forward this view in his *Essai historique sur la police*, written for Catherine II (cf. G. V. Plekhanov, *Sochineniia*, vol. 22, Moscow–Leningrad, 1925, p. 144). Leibniz voiced a similar opinion in connection with the Petrine reforms. (See L. Richter, *Leibniz und sein Russlandbild*, Berlin, 1946.)

The Russian reception of the juridical world-view was, however, peculiarly one-sided. The police state in the West encouraged initiative and independent action in the economic, social, and cultural spheres, whereas Peter the Great, to quote Raeff, 'in fact stifled these qualities by resorting to force and by focusing exclusively on the needs of the central establishment'.[36] Catherine II tried, somewhat half-heartedly, to stimulate independent social activity by legislative fiat, but her efforts really benefited only the nobility.[37] Eighteenth-century Russia lacked a social class like the western bourgeoisie which could effectively combat feudal privilege and formulate its aims as legal demands. Therefore, if we conceive the juridical world-view as based on legal rights, we must concede that in this respect it did not take strong root in Russian soil. We might even say that the promotion of state authority at the expense of the authority of religion and tradition, which characterized the juridical world-view, entailed a general identification of law with the will of the head of state, which in fact blatantly contradicted 'the spirit of law', as understood by Montesquieu. Those most aware of this were the spokesmen of the conservative nobility who urged that laws and legally sanctified priviliges should be protected against arbitrary change.[38] But the very fact that this view of law, as independent of the state and as something to be discovered rather than made, was defended by conservative critics of the post-Petrine autocracy only made the progressives more suspicious of it than ever. In other words, constitutional dreams in Russia were for a long time monopolized by a faction of the old hereditary aristocracy, and this explains why the lesser nobility, the servants of the state, and the intellectual elite, which owed its position to the state-promoted modernization of Russia, were so hostile to these dreams, setting all their hopes on an enlightened absolute monarchy.

A striking exception to this rule was Aleksandr Radishchev, the first Russian thinker openly to question the legitimacy of autocracy by referring to the concept of the inalienable rights of man. He wrote:

Autocracy is the system most repugnant to human nature . . . if we relinquish part of our rights and our innate sovereignty in favour of an all-embracing law, it is in order that it might be used to our advantage; to this end we conclude a tacit agreement with society. If this is infringed, then we too are released from

[36] Raeff, *The Well-Ordered Police State*, p. 216. [37] Ibid., pp. 236–45.
[38] Their best known ideologist was Prince Mikhail Shcherbatov. See Walicki *The Slavophile Controversy: History of a Conservative Utopia in Nineteenth-Century Russian Thought*, Oxford, 1975, pp. 20–32.

our obligations. The injustice of the sovereign gives the people, who are his judges, the same or even greater rights over him than the law gives him over criminals. The sovereign is the first citizen of the people's commonwealth.[39]

A poetic illustration of these words is to be found in Radishchev's 'Ode to Liberty', which contains a sublime defence of tyrannicide.

In his famous *Journey from St Petersburg to Moscow* (1790), Radishchev developed his concept of revolutionary justice and also applied it to extreme cases of social exploitation and oppression. 'Every man', he reasoned,

is born into the world equal to all others . . . If the law is unable or unwilling to protect him, or if its power cannot furnish him immediate aid in the face of clear and present danger, then the citizen has recourse to the natural law of self-defence, self-preservation, and well-being . . . No matter in what estate heaven may have decreed a citizen's birth, he is and will always remain a man; and so long as he is a man, the law of nature, as an abundant wellspring of goodness, will never run dry in him, and whosoever dares wound him in his natural and inviolable right is a criminal.[40]

The conclusion drawn from this was that peasants who killed a cruel landowner were not guilty, since their oppressor fully deserved his fate.

Nevertheless Radishchev cannot be accused of contempt for positive law. He agreed that 'the law, however bad it is, is the bond that holds society together';[41] he postulated the improvement of existing laws by means of rational legislation, allowing direct recourse to natural law only in cases of extreme violation of natural justice. He was no anarchist, and realized that there could be no return to the original pre-social state of mankind in which people were not subject to hierarchical pressures. Human imperfection made it impossible for this state to continue; people formed nations and thus entered the social state. Thenceforth they belonged to history and shared the vicissitudes of historical progress. But Radishchev had no doubt about the general direction of this progress: people, he thought, having lost their natural freedom, should regain as much of it as possible in the form of political freedom, freedom under law. The two countries he approved of most warmly were England and the United States, both of

[39] Quoted in D. Blagoy, *Istoriia russkoi literatury XVIII veka*, Moscow, 1951, p. 539. (The quotation is from Radishchev's first work—the notes to his translation of Mably's *Observations sur l'histoire de la Grèce*.)
[40] A. N. Radishchev, *A Journey from St. Petersburg to Moscow*, Leo Wiener (trans.), Cambridge Mass., 1958, pp. 102–3.
[41] Ibid., p. 120.

which he praised for assuring their citizens the widest range of civil rights and political liberties. This preference even led him to make the unusual suggestion that the first foreign language taught to children should be not French but English, since English shows 'the elasticity of the spirit of freedom'.[42]

In his conception of the nation Radishchev was a typical representative of the juridical world-view. He saw the nation as a 'collection of citizens' rather than as a supra-individual whole endowed with a collective soul. A nation, as he put it, is a 'collection of individuals', a political society composed of people who 'have come together in order to safeguard their own interests and security by their collective efforts; it is a society submitting to authority.'[43] As this quotation shows, 'nation' for Radishchev was a juridico-political concept indistinguishable from society, which in turn was indistinguishable from the organized state. Radishchev even attempted a juridical definition of 'fatherland' as a set of people linked together by mutually binding laws and civic duties. Only a man enjoying civic rights could be a son of his fatherland, he argued. It followed from this that peasants living under serfdom, that is, the vast majority of the population of Russia, were deprived of their fatherland. The revolutionary implications of this view were well understood. It has been suggested that Radishchev's essay 'On What It Means to Be a Son of the Fatherland' caused Emperor Paul to include the word 'fatherland' in a list of banned words and to demand its replacement by the word 'state'.[44]

Radishchev's thought, emphasizing human rights rather than enlightened legislation from above, represented a quite sophisticated form of the liberal-democratic variant of the juridical world-view. He was a solitary figure, whose influence was much less than Soviet scholars would like us to believe, but, none the less, it is important to note that his ideas marked the beginning of the liberal-democratic tradition in Russia.[45] It is no contradiction that they also marked the

---

[42] Ibid., p. 115. Cf. Max M. Laserson, *The American Impact on Russia—Diplomatic and Ideological, 1784–1917*, New York, 1950, pp. 54–71.

[43] A. N. Radishchev, *Polnoe sobranie sochinenii*, Moscow–Leningrad, 1938–52, vol. 1, p. 188.

[44] See A. Gorshkov, *Istoriia russkogo literaturnogo yazyka*, Moscow, 1961, pp. 124, 128. Cf. W. Peltz, *Oświeceniowa myśl narodowa w Rosji na przełomie XVIII–XIX wieku*, Zielona Góra, 1980, p. 24.

[45] This was emphasized by P. Miliukov in his essay 'Intelligentsiia i istoricheskaia traditsiia', in *Intelligentsiia v Rossii. Sbornik stat'ei*, St. Petersburg (hereafter referred to as SPb), 1910, p. 138. Miliukov praised Radishchev's liberalism for what he saw as its 'sobriety, broad-mindedness and practicality'.

beginning of Russian revolutionary radicalism. Like Thomas Paine, for example, Radishchev typified, though in a version reflecting Russian conditions, the radical current of the European Enlightenment— a current which managed to combine revolutionary radicalism with deep commitment to liberal-democratic values.

Another, much less politically radical form of the liberal variant of the juridical world-view was to be found in the Free Association of the Lovers of Literature, the Sciences and the Arts, which existed in the reign of Alexander I and was especially active in the years 1801–7. Its most outstanding members were Ivan Pnin, author of *An Essay on Enlightenment Concerning Russia* (1804) and Vasily Popugaev, whose main work bears the title *On the Firmness of Constitution and Laws*. Like Radishchev, both also wrote poetry. Soviet scholars often treat these men as Radishchev's disciples,[46] but they may more justifiably be seen as continuing and developing some of the ideas of Semyon Desnitsky, the first theoretical jurist in Russia, who studied in Glasgow under Adam Smith and was greatly influenced by the Scottish Enlightenment.[47] In his *Juridical Discourse on the Views of Various Nations Concerning Property and Various Forms of Social Relationships* (1781) he followed Adam Smith and Adam Ferguson in developing the conception of a 'commercial society', based upon private property and representing the highest stage of social evolution. Pnin and Popugaev took up this idea and specially emphasized that a necessary precondition of the commercial stage of universal progress was the emergence of a 'civil society' (*grazhdanskoe obshchestvo*), with a developed system of private law and legally safeguarded rights of man. They warmly supported the constitutional projects of the young Emperor, urging him thereby to complete the transformation of Russia from a military to a commercial state.[48] They did not dare to elaborate their own constitutional blueprint but their minimum programme included such demands as the universalization of private property, equality before the law, the inviolability of the person, ruling in accordance with the law and setting legal limits to the scope of political power, and, finally, the gradual introduction of representative government by extending the rights of the existing Senate. The first of these demands meant

---

[46] See V. Orlov, *Russkie prosvetiteli 1790–1800kh godov*, Moscow, 1953.
[47] For a presentation of his views see Walicki, *A History of Russian Thought From the Enlightenment to Marxism*, Stanford, 1979, Oxford, 1980, pp. 11–14.
[48] I. P. Pnin, 'Opyt o prosveshchenii', in *Russkie prosvetiteli (ot Radishcheva do dekabristov)*, Moscow, 1966, vol. 1, p. 192.

essentially the abolition of serfdom and the transformation of the Russian peasantry into a class of free smallholders, with full property rights to their land.

Pnin's *Essay on Enlightenment* was confiscated and destroyed, sharing in this the fate of Radishchev's *Journey from St Petersburg to Moscow*. This was because the Emperor's ostensible commitment to liberal principles was more apparent than real. Prince Adam Czartoryski, the Polish aristocrat who at the beginning of the century was a close personal friend of Alexander I, an influential member of his 'secret council' and Russia's Minister of Foreign Affairs, commented:

The Emperor liked forms of liberty as he liked the theatre; it gave him pleasure and flattered his vanity to see the appearances of free government in his Empire; but all he wanted in this respect was forms and appearances; he did not expect them to become realities. In a word, he would willingly have agreed that every man should be free, on condition that he should voluntarily do only what the Emperor wished.[49]

Pnin's place in the history of Russian liberalism is well-defined: together with Popugaev and other Russian 'Enlighteners' (*prosvetiteli*) of the early nineteenth century, he was a link between Radishchev's liberal ideas and the liberal ideology of the first Russian revolutionists —the Decembrists.[50]

True, the ideology of the Decembrist movement, named after the ill-fated uprising of December 1825, was neither coherent nor socially homogeneous. It was divided into two main trends, that of the Southern Society, headed by Colonel Pavel Pestel, who was a Jacobin rather than a liberal, and that of the Northern Society with its liberal-aristocratic conception of freedom, combining the ideas of Adam Smith and Benjamin Constant with an idealization of former feudal liberties and a belief in the role of the aristocracy as a 'curb on despotism'. Both these trends are of interest in the present context, since both may be seen as variants of the juridical world-view. Both held that societies are shaped, or even constituted, by legal and political forms, not vice versa, and, accordingly, both found their fullest expression in constitutional projects.

There is no need here for a detailed presentation of these projects.[51]

[49] Prince A. Czartoryski, *Memoirs*. A. Gielgud (ed.), vol. 1; repr. Academic International, 1968, p. 325.
[50] See A. A. Kizevetter, *Istoricheskie ocherki*, Moscow, 1912; repr., The Hague, 1967, pp. 59 and 87.
[51] See Walicki, *History of Russian Thought*, pp. 57–70.

It suffices that Pestel's constitution, called *Russian Justice*, favoured a strong central government while the draft constitution prepared by Nikita Muraviev of the Northern Society was committed to federalism and consciously modelled in this respect on the constitution of the United States. The former was much more democratic, indeed republican, in tone, advocating universal suffrage while yet, in a bureaucratic-étatist spirit, outlawing all independent societies and associations; the latter was monarchist, more liberal in that it offered more freedom from government control but still insisting on property qualifications for citizenship, granting full voting rights only to landowners and capitalists, and revealing a rather conservative approach to the peasant issue. What united the authors of these two different blueprints for Russia's future was not liberalism but their juridical world-view in the form of an extreme juridical rationalism. Both Muraviev and Pestel were strongly inclined to identify social ties with juridical relationships and to think of society in terms of abstract, atomic individuals and their rational-utilitarian aims. Because of this Muraviev's proposal for dividing Russia into fourteen autonomous states was not a concession to any actual, or at least possible, decentralizing tendencies; the boundaries of these states were arbitrarily determined, with no concern for different ethnic territories or different historical traditions. Pestel defined the nation as an 'association of all those members of one and the same state who form a society of citizens in order to ensure the realizable well-being of each and all'.[52] This utilitarian definition, echoing the Jacobin view of the nation as voiced by Abbé Sieyès,[53] made no distinction between a 'nation' and the population of a given state, totally ignoring internal linguistic or cultural divisions. The revolutionary implications of this were obvious: if the foundations of society (or a nation) rest on the political will, on an act of association for the sake of achieving a certain goal, then this society or nation can be dissolved and a new association formed on different and superior principles thought up by revolutionaries.

To sum up, neither the ideology of the post-Petrine Russian autocracy nor that of its first challengers could be accused of 'legal

[52] *Izbrannye sotsiyal' no-politicheskie i filosofskie proizvedeniia dekabristov*, Moscow, 1952, vol. 2, p. 80.
[53] Sieyès formulated this definition in his famous words: 'Qu'est-ce que c'est qu'une nation?—un corps d'associés vivant sous une loi commune et représentés par la même legislature'. (Quoted from H. Kohn, *Prelude to Nation States: The French and German Experience, 1789–1815*, Princeton, 1967, p. 21.)

nihilism'. The almost universal disrespect for law in Russian life was not a subject of idealization in the eighteenth and early nineteenth centuries. The tsars, committed to the Western ideal of a well-ordered police state, differed both from the liberal reformers and from the revolutionaries in their attitude to the problem of civil and political rights, but all of them—the monarchs, the reformers and the revolutionaries—enthusiastically accepted the other side of the juridical world view: a belief in the need to extend the legal regulation of life and exaggerated optimism concerning the possibility of social change through rational legislation.

The Decembrist revolt was in all respects a failure but, none the less, its impact on Russian thought was tremendous. It completed the rupture of the alliance between the educated élite of Russian society and the Russian autocracy and marked the breakdown of the juridical world-view in Russia, in the minds both of the Russian élite and of Russia's rulers. In other words, both the élite and the rulers lost faith in the abstract reason of the Age of Enlightenment. The élite, deeply shocked by the spectacular defeat of the attempted revolution, withdrew from politics and tried to blame the defeat on the abstract rationalism of the Decembrists' juridical world-view. The new ruler, Nicholas I, alarmed that the educated élite had dared to take up arms against the Russian autocracy, realized that the danger of abstract rationalism was inherent in the belief in rational legislation which characterized the post-Petrine autocratic tradition. This dual reaction to the Decembrist uprising closely resembled some Western responses to the tragic vicissitudes of the French revolution and its aftermath. Both in Russia and in the West the juridical world-view had been deeply undermined, whether as a belief in rationally devised revolutionary blueprints or as a belief in rational legislation from above, that is, both as revolutionary constitutionalism and as the ideology of enlightened absolutism.

The impact of the Decembrist uprising upon the ideology of the Russian autocracy has been set out by Wortman, in his book cited above. He writes

The Decembrist Revolt showed Nicholas the danger of the abstract universal concepts of justice that had influenced previous attempts at codification. Instead, he adopted historistic and national views that simplified the task of codification and did not threaten the monarch's monopoly of authority. This approach, argued in Russia by Karamzin, and formulated by Savigny and the German historical school of jurisprudence, presented the laws of each nation as expressions of that nation's particular characteristics and needs. It banished the notion that law had to conform to universal natural norms, and consecrating the statutes issued by the autocrat, exempted them from outside judgement.[54]

In accordance with these views 'courses in natural law were banished from the law curriculum and the students were to occupy themselves instead with the mastery of the details of Russian legislation'.[55] The study of specific 'laws' (*zakony*) was encouraged while the general subject of 'law' (*pravo*) became suspect.[56]

This change of attitude towards the law did not entail a rejection of the ideal of the well-ordered police state. Nicholas firmly believed in the legal regulation of society and never manifested a contempt for law; on the contrary, he felt considerable respect for even those laws which he could not wholeheartedly accept, as was shown in his brief constitutional reign in Poland.[57] There is no doubt that he wanted to be a European emperor rather than an ancient Russian tsar. He put a bust of Peter the Great on his desk and declared: 'This is the model I intend to follow throughout my reign.'[58] In spite of this, however, he was obviously unable and unwilling to promote the further modernization of Russia. Unlike Peter, he was afraid of modernization and resolutely opposed to the imitation of Western models. He wanted a stabilized autocracy but no longer believed in its progressive mission. Therefore, it is rather misleading to call his reign the 'apogee of autocracy'.[59] It seems more proper to stress that the beginning of his reign coincided with the Decembrist uprising, the first grave symptom of crisis in the post-Petrine Russian autocracy, and that this crisis, despite appearances, continued and deepened under his rule.

Thus, Nicholas's view of law was equally far removed from the juridical world-view of the Enlightenment and from conservative-romantic antilegalism. Two aspects of this view can be distinguished, each giving rise to different consequences.

First, Nicholas stressed legality, the strict, precise execution of written positive laws. This tendency of his thought, combined with his conviction that the law was the best way to combat revolution, helped

[54] Wortman, *Russian Legal Consciousness*, p. 43. Karamzin's views are discussed in Walicki, *The Slavophile Controversy*, pp. 32–44.
[55] Wortman, *Russian Legal Consciousness*, p. 45.   [56] Ibid., pp. 45–6.
[57] Cf. A. A. Kizevetter, 'Imperator Nikolai I kak konstitutsionnyi monarkh', in Kizevetter, *Istoricheskie ocherki*, pp. 402–18.
[58] Quoted from Wortman, *Russian Legal Consciousness*, p. 42.
[59] Cf. A. Presniakov, *Apogei samoderzhaviia, Nikolai I*, Leningrad, 1925.

him to overcome 'the autocrat's traditional distrust of specialized legal expertise'.[60] Hence he tended to approve of the faculties of law in the universities of Petersburg and Moscow, and even agreed to the establishment of an élite school of law—the Imperial School of Jurisprudence, opened in 1835. The aim of this school was to train legal officials wholly devoted to the service of the autocratic state, but in fact, it produced a somewhat different result: the 'emergence of a legal ethos' (to quote Wortman) among the higher levels of the Imperial bureaucracy.[61] It educated an élite of jurists endowed with the 'moral identity' of a professional group, with a sense of mission, loyal to the Emperor but devoted to the cause of law and legal reform in their country.

Secondly, Nicholas saw Russian rulers as the only legitimate source and the only authoritative interpreters of Russian law, a view which led him to make important concessions to the traditional, patriarchal view of the administration of justice. This aspect of his views is illustrated in the following extract:

The advantage of autocratic power consists precisely in the fact that the autocratic sovereign has the possibility of acting according to conscience and, in certain cases, is even obliged to put law aside and complete the case as a father decides a dispute among his children; for laws are a creation of the human mind, and they could not and cannot foresee all of the devices of the human heart.[62]

As we shall see, identical or similar views were voiced by the Slavophiles and other Russian critics of the cold legalist formalism of the West. But the above quotation was taken from a different source, from a report of Nicholas's secret police.

In the development of Russian philosophical and social thought the failure of the Decembrist uprising marked the end of the rationalist approach to social change and of the juridical conception of the nation. At the same time, it marked the beginning of the 'philosophical epoch' in Russia,[63] an epoch in which the most talented people escaped from practical political problems to speculative philosophy, seeing the latter as a way of personal and collective secular salvation. This was because,

---

[60] Wortman, *Russian Legal Consciousness*, p. 44.
[61] Ibid., pp. 197–234.
[62] Ibid., p. 180. (Quoted by the author from 'Otchet III otdeleniia za 1842g.', pp. 201–2.)
[63] For a detailed discussion see Walicki, *The Slavophile Controversy*, chs. 7–8, and *A History of Russian Thought*, ch. 7.

as in Germany, philosophical speculation concerning man and history had a compensatory function for people of intellectual vigour whose energy could find no outlet in an almost completely paralysed public life, and who had no faith in the efficacy of political action. It is hardly surprising that they ceased to be 'Francophile' or 'Anglophile', becoming instead enthusiasts for the 'land of the ancient Teutons'.[64] This German orientation dominated Russian intellectual life until the end of the 1830s and continued to play an important part in the 1840s. Vissiarion Belinsky wrote in 1837: 'Germany is the Jerusalem of the modern generation and that is where they should turn their eyes in hope and expectation; thence a new Christ will come, not a persecuted Saviour bearing wounds and a martyr's crown, but one surrounded by a halo of glory.'[65]

In the 1820s the main centre of German-style philosophy was the Moscow circle of the Lovers of Wisdom, established in 1823. After the Decembrist uprising it was formally disbanded, but in fact continued to exist until the early 1830s, developing its ideas in conscious opposition to the Decembrists' style of thought. Its leading thinker was Prince Vladimir Odoevsky who, among other things, transplanted the social philosophy of German conservative romanticism to Russia. He opposed the juridical world-view, which defined the nation in terms of citizenship and social contract, setting against it a view of the nation as a whole transcending its individual parts, a unique collective individuality which evolved historically according to its own distinctive principles.[66] National unity, he stressed, is based not upon rational laws but upon irrational factors, such as religion, tradition, and the poetic imagination and it finds expression in the national mythology. Genuine nations develop organically, and not through mechanical changes introduced by rational legislators, no matter whether these are victorious revolutionaries or enlightened absolute monarchs.

Similar views were widespread in the influential Stankevich Circle, which was active in Moscow in the 1830s. They were voiced most forcefully by the two leading members of the circle—the young Bakunin and the young Belinsky, in the period of their so-called

---

[64] The 'Germanophile' tendency in Russian thought was already manifest in the almanac *Mnemosyne*, published in 1824, but became dominant after the Decembrist uprising. The words quoted are those of Prince Vladimir Odoevsky. See P. N. Sakulin, *Iz istorii russkogo idealizma: Kniaz' V. F. Odoevskii*, Moscow, 1913, vol. 1, pp. 138–9.

[65] V. G. Belinsky, *Polnoe sobranie sochinenii*, Moscow, 1953–9, vol. 11, p. 152.

[66] Cf. Walicki, *The Slavophile Controversy*, pp. 67–82.

'reconciliation with reality'.[67] Unlike the Lovers of Wisdom they were inspired not by Schelling, Franz von Baader, and other romantic thinkers, but by Hegel, although at first, in their reconciliation period, they interpreted him in a conservative-romantic way. Characteristically, they ignored Hegel's philosophy of law, concentrating instead on his criticism of the abstract rationalism of the Enlightenment. Law was not central to their interests and they were not looking for positive solutions to legal problems. They refused, however, to accept the notions of the social contract, inalienable rights and universal justice, seeing them as socially disruptive fictions, creations of the abstract, ahistorical *Verstand* (*rassudok*), as opposed to the historical and dialectical *Vernunft* (*razum*). Belinsky went so far as to extol the organic social ties of 'blood and soil', stressing that the tribal and national unity based upon such ties had logical and historical priority over the merely institutional and juridical unity of the state. Nations, he argued, could not be called into existence by constitutional fiat. The United States, therefore, was only a state, not a nation, and might become a nation only if it succeeded in preserving and developing its English national heritage. If national ties depended upon legal contract rather than upon 'flesh and blood' the notion of a betrayal of one's fatherland would make no sense; to change one fatherland for another would not be an act of treason, or a disaster, but merely a matter for rational calculation of profits.[68]

Belinsky's condemnation of juridical rationalism did not lead him to take a critical view of Peter's reforms; in this respect he was a convinced Westernizer even during his reconciliation period. But his interpretation of the Hegelian view that 'everything that is real, is rational' made him hostile to the idea of imitating the advanced countries of the West by legally limiting the power of the Russian emperors. In a letter of 1837 he wrote:

The achievements of Peter are the best proof that Russia will never create her existence and freedom as a state by herself, but will receive both from her rulers . . . We have as yet no rights, we are still slaves, but this is because we still have to be slaves. Russia is still a child which needs a loving nurse with a birch in her hand to punish her ward for its pranks. To give full freedom to a child is to bring about its destruction. To give present-day Russia a constitution would be to bring about her destruction. Our people (*narod*) understand freedom as will (*volya*), and exercising their will as indulging in

[67] Cf. Ibid., ch. 8. Cf. also I. Berlin, *Russian Thinkers*, London, 1978, pp. 114–209.
[68] See V. G. Belinsky, *Polnoe sobranie sochinenii*, vol. 3, pp. 327–32.

licence . . . Civic freedom should grow from the inner freedom of each
member of the nation, and this inner freedom is to be achieved by developing
consciousness. This is the beautiful way by which Russia will arrive at
freedom.[69]

This letter was written very early in Belinsky's 'reconciliation'.
When he had fully developed his conservative and nationalist
interpretation of Hegelianism, he gave his views on Russia's freedom
at once a more philosophical and more extreme expression:

In the word 'Tsar', there is a marvellous fusion of the consciousness of the
Russian people, to whom this word is full of poetry and mysterious meaning.
And this is not an accident but the most rigorous and rational necessity,
revealing itself in the history of the Russian nation . . . The Tsar is our *freedom*,
because from him comes our new civilization and our enlightenment as well as
our life . . . absolute submission to the will of the Tsar is not simply useful and
necessary for us, but is the highest poetry of our lives—is our *nationality* . . . it
is time to recognize that we have a *rational* right to be proud of our love for the
Tsar, of our boundless devotion to his sacred will, just as the English are proud
of their political institutions, of their civil rights, just as the United States of
America are proud of their liberty. The life of every nation is a rationally
necessary form of the universal idea, and within this idea is contained the
significance, the power, the might, the poetry of the national life, while the
living, rational consciousness of this idea is both the goal of that life and its
inner motive force. Peter the Great, by bringing European life to Russia, gave
Russian life a new and greatly broadened form but by no means changed its
substantial foundation . . . We shall not forget that the attainment of the goal
[of universal history] is possible only through the *rational* development not of
any alien or external principle, but of the substantial *native* principle of our
national life, and that the mysterious seed, the root, the essence, and the vital
pulse of our national life is expressed in the word 'Tsar'.[70]

In the years 1840–1 Belinsky underwent the painful and liberating
experience of outgrowing his 'reconciliation with reality'. At a certain
stage this involved a re-examination of his negative attitude to the
French Enlightenment and Voltaire, the Encyclopaedists and the
Jacobins became rehabilitated in his eyes, as part of his general
rehabilitation of the 'destroyers of the old'. Nevertheless he made it
clear that this was not a return to anti-historical Enlightenment
rationalism.[71] Although he had become a radical democrat, he did not

[69] Ibid., vol. 11, pp. 140–56.
[70] Ibid., vol. 3, pp. 246–8. Quoted from Edie *et al.*, *Russian Philosophy*, vol. 1,
pp. 296–9.
[71] See Walicki, *A History of Russian Thought*, pp. 123–6.

cease to be a historicist; he rejected the conservative variety of historicism, espousing instead a left-wing interpretation which emphasized dialectical negation rather than historical continuity. He continued to think in terms of the laws of history, rather than in terms of universal natural law, or the inalienable rights of man. Thus, his democratic radicalism and his commitment to 'the idea of personality' did not entail acceptance of the liberal-democratic version of the juridical world-view.

Belinsky's case, although extreme, may be helpful, I think, in understanding why the nineteenth-century Russian intelligentsia, whose spiritual father he was, tended to be indifferent (if not hostile) to the idea of law; why, in Kistiakovsky's words, it had 'never been wholly possessed by ideas of the rights of the individual or of the rule-of-law state'.[72] This was because there was no direct continuity between the contemporary Russian intelligentsia, which had emerged in Belinsky's time, and the earlier radicals, like Radishchev, or revolutionary constitutionalists (the Decembrists) who had been wholly committed to the juridical world-view. The classical Russian intelligentsia, a specific stratum of mixed social background, seeing themselves as society's natural leaders and the bearers of the progressive tradition,[73] emerged *after* the breakdown of the juridical world-view in European thought, at a time when such ideas as the social contract, the natural rights of man, and so forth, sounded anachronistic and unscientific, if not hypocritical, and when law was increasingly identified with the

[72] B. Kistiakovsky, 'In the Defence of Law: The Intelligentsia and Legal Consciousness', in *Landmarks: A Collection of Essays on the Russian Intelligentsia*. M. Schwartz (trans.), B. Shragin (ed.), New York, 1977, p. 116. (I have corrected the translation because *pravovoe gosudarstvo* means 'rule-of-law state', and not just 'legal government'.)

[73] The literature on the Russian intelligentsia is too vast to be cited here. Many authors treat the intelligentsia as a peculiarly Russian phenomenon—a view which I cannot endorse. It is more correct to say that the nineteenth-century intelligentsia was a phenomenon characteristic of all backward, or relatively backward, European countries and that a similar phenomenon emerged, in our own time, in other underdeveloped countries in the world. Karl Mannheim saw the intelligentsia as a peculiarly German phenomenon (see K. Mannheim, 'Conservative Thought', in *Essays on Sociology and Social Psychology*, London, 1953, p. 125); some Polish authors described it as a phenomenon of which the classical form emerged in nineteenth-century Poland and Russia (see A. Hertz, 'The Case of An Eastern European Intelligentsia', *Journal of Central European Affairs*, 1, no. 11, 1951, and A. Gella, 'The Life and Death of the Old Polish Intelligentsia', *Slavic Review*, 30, no. 1, 1971). The widespread belief that the word 'intelligentsia' was coined in Russia in the 1870s (cf. M. Malia, 'What is Intelligentsia?', *Daedalus*, Summer 1960) is groundless; in fact it was already being used in Poland in the 1840s (see A. Walicki, *Philosophy and Romantic Nationalism: The Case of Poland*, Oxford, 1982, p. 177).

positive laws of existing states. It was difficult for the Russian intelligentsia to be inspired by the idea of law, because historicism and, later, legal positivism severed the cause of law from the cause of universal justice, thereby depriving the idea of law of its lofty, inspiring meaning.

There was yet another aspect of the debased status of law in the intellectual life of the nineteenth century. The juridical world-view was part of the eighteenth-century belief in the 'kingdom of reason' but the nineteenth century became generally aware, to quote Engels, that 'this kingdom of reason was nothing more than the idealized kingdom of the bourgeoisie'.[74] In a backward country, lacking experience of the advantages of freedom under law, a premature awareness of this could easily lead to a general disillusionment with law and give rise to its disparagement and denigration. As we shall see, this was precisely what happened in Russia.

3   The censure of law by the right

The most interesting Russian example of the conservative-romantic reaction to the juridical world-view was that of a group of thinkers known as 'Slavophiles', a name which indicated their opposition to Western influences. The main ideologists of this group were Ivan Kireevsky (1806–56), Aleksei Khomiakov (1804–60), Yury Samarin (1819–76), and Konstantin Aksakov (1817–60), of whom the first and the last were the most significant.

The Slavophiles' protest against Westernization was in fact a protest against the rationalization of social life, so magnificently described by Max Weber.[75] Their romantic criticism of rationalism, in the name of immediate, living, and integral knowledge, was in fact a defence of immediate, unreflective, emotional, and time-honoured social ties, which were endangered by the progressive rationalization of human conduct. One can say, therefore, paraphrasing Mannheim's words about German conservative thought, that Slavophilism was an ideological defence of the *Gemeinschaft* against the *Gesellschaft*.[76] The Slavophiles saw pre-Petrine Russia as a *Gemeinschaft* type of community, based upon social ties which were organic and integral, not merely mechanical and rational, and which embraced the whole man—a

---

[74] See F. Engels, *Socialism: Utopian and Scientific.* Quoted from K. Marx and F. Engels, *Selected Works*, Moscow, 1977, vol. 3, p. 116.
[75] Cf. Walicki, *The Slavophile Controversy*, pp. 174–7 and 265–6.
[76] Cf. Mannheim, 'Conservative Thought', p. 89.

community betrayed by the westernized upper classes but, happily, kept alive in the Russian Church and in the peasant commune. In spite of their roots in the ancient hereditary nobility they were reluctant to stand up for their own class; they attempted rather to sublimate and universalize traditional values and to create an ideological platform that would unite all the classes and social strata representing the true, ancient Russia, as opposed to a westernized Russia. This led them to sharp criticism of the westernized Russian elite, including the landowning nobility, and to idealization of the non-westernized Russian peasantry.

The Slavophiles' views on law were determined by their opposition to juridical rationalism, which they saw as peculiar to the West. They were inclined to treat juridical rationalism as inherent in legal thinking as such and were apt too readily to attribute it to all professional jurists. Their views, therefore, may be described as romantic antilegalism. In fact, however, juridical rationalism is not necessarily involved in all law. It is absent from the so-called *Gemeinschaft* paradigm of law, characteristic of organic societies which are held together by internalized tradition, religion, and custom. It became an essential feature of legal thinking with the emergence of the so-called *Gesellschaft* paradigm of law, which assumes a society made up of atomic individuals and private interests, modelled on commercial contracts and sharply distinguishes the legal and the moral; it was developed even further in the bureaucratic-administrative paradigm of law which emphasizes legislation and rational planning.[77] It is clear, nevertheless, that juridical rationalism permeated Roman civil law, which served as a model for modern civil codes, and that its role steadily increased with the progress of modernization. The Slavophiles had therefore many reasons for seeing it as an expression of the spirit of *modern* law, namely, of that law which was an essential element of the advanced bourgeois societies of the West.

Romantic antilegalism was a pan-European trend of thought which consciously opposed modernization. Its representatives—from Joseph de Maistre to the German historical school of law—emphasized that laws could not be simply devised, but had to grow from traditions and popular custom, and that this growth should be spontaneous and organic, free both from indirect external influences and from

---

[77] See Introduction, p. 13. For the most recent formulation of this conception see Alice Erh-Soon Tay and Eugene Kamenka, 'Public Law—Private Law', in *Public and Private in Social Life*, S. I. Benn and G. F. Gauss (eds.), London, 1983, pp. 67–92.

mechanical interference from above. Therefore they took the part of 'historical law' and sharply attacked 'rational' or 'theoretical' law, which generally meant idealizing and defending customary law of the *Gemeinschaft* type. The same can be said of the Slavophiles, although in their case an additional element was involved: that of interpreting the controversy about rationalism as essentially a controversy about the West and seeing non-rationalized forms of social unity as something peculiar to non-westernized Slavdom.

According to Kireevsky, the main difference between Russia and the West lay in the fact that Russia lacked the heritage of ancient Roman rationalism, most perfectly embodied, in his eyes, in Roman law. Its logical perfection, he thought, was the reverse of the inner atomization of Roman society. Its spirit had infected western Christianity and paved the way for modern 'logical and technical civilization', based upon the idea of a legal contract between isolated, rational individuals. In such a society everything must be based upon formalized legal conventions, because the inner, organic social ties no longer exist. The legal safeguards of individual liberty, extolled by Western liberals, only appear to contradict the principle of external legal compulsion, since both legal rights and legal constraints express the spirit of external, formal, legality, as opposed to informal inner unity, stemming from moral convictions and internalized traditions of community.

All these ideas anticipate the views of Ferdinand Tönnies, the creator of the *Gemeinschaft–Gesellschaft* typology. He stressed that 'the assimilation of Roman Law has served and still serves to further the development of *Gesellschaft* in a large part of the Christian–German world',[78] because this type of law was intrinsically incompatible with an organic community. The same was true of modern natural law and natural rights theory: in its 'disintegrating and levelling sense, general and natural law is entirely an order characteristic of *Gesellschaft*, manifested in its purest form in commercial law'.[79] Tönnies developed this view in words strongly reminiscent of the social philosophy of German conservative romanticism in the first half of the nineteenth century:

A rational, scientific and independent law was made possible only through the emancipation of the individuals from all the ties which bound them to the

[78] F. Tönnies, *Community and Society*. Charles P. Loomis (trans. and ed.), East Lansing, 1957, p. 203.
[79] Ibid., p. 202.

family, the land, and the city and which held them to superstition, faith, tradition, habit and duty. Such a liberation meant the fall of the communal household in village and town, of the agricultural community, and the art of the town as a fellowship, religious, patriotic craft. It meant the victory of egoism, impudence, and cunning, the ascendency of greed for money, ambition and lust for pleasure. But it brought also the victory of the contemplative, clear and sober consciousness in which scholars and cultured men now dare to approach things humane and divine . . . Arbitrary freedom (of the individual) and arbitrary despotism (of the Caesar or the State) are not mutually exclusive. They are only a dual phenomenon of the same situation.[80]

The same view was developed by Adam Müller, a classical representative of German early nineteenth-century conservatism, for whom the spirit of Rome, personified in Roman law and the Roman empire, was the primary source of capitalism, industrialism, the French revolution, social atomization, and centralized despotism of the Napoleonic type.[81] Other conservative romantics in Germany wrote in similar vein and Kireevsky, formerly a member of the circle of Lovers of Wisdom, was well acquainted with German thought. He attributed his views to his recovery of religious faith and to the spirit of Orthodox Christianity; in fact, however, he owed much more to contemporary German thinkers than to the Fathers of the Eastern Church.

In Kireevsky's eyes ancient Russian law was the antithesis of rational law. It was a customary law, based on usage and tradition, subordinated to religion and morality, organically rooted in history. It

grew out of life and its evolution had nothing to do with abstract logic. In Russia the law was not drawn up in advance by learned jurists; it was not the subject of profound and eloquent discussions in any legislative assembly and did not later fall like snow on the heads of the surprised public, breaking up some established arrangement in social relations. In Russia the law was not drawn up but was in fact only written down on paper when it had taken shape by itself in the minds of the people, had become accepted as the custom and part of popular tradition. The logical development of law is only possible where society itself is based on artificial conventions.[82]

The same conservative understanding of historical continuity and the same deep suspicion towards all rational legislation characterized the historical school of German jurisprudence. Its first theorist, Friedrich Carl von Savigny, was, somewhat paradoxically, a Romanist and idealized the medieval Roman law tradition in Germany; his

[80] Ibid., pp. 202–3.   [81] Cf. Mannheim, 'Conservative Thought', p. 105.
[82] I. V. Kireevsky, *Polnoe sobranie sochinenii*, Moscow, 1911, vol. 1, p. 208.

successors, however, developed his thought in a consistently romantic and nationalist spirit, concentrating on the distinctively national principles in law and founding the Germanist school of legal philosophy.[83]

Thus, Kireevsky's reaction to juridical rationalism and the juridical world-view could not be called 'legal nihilism'. He protested against the 'juridicization' of social ties, but did not see law as such as inherently evil. It was Konstantin Aksakov who put forward this view and defended it with great inventiveness and energy. His anti-legal tirades were ridiculed in the following satire of B. N. Almazov:

> For reasons entirely organic
> We have not been endowed with at all
> That quality wholly satanic—
> Common sense in the matter of law.
>
> Russian natures broad and wide
> Seeking truths eternal,
> Cannot be constrained inside
> Lawyers' rules infernal.[84]

To understand Aksakov's view of law it is necessary to dwell a little longer on the Slavophile image of pre-Petrine Russia. The Slavophiles' favourite periods of Russian history were (1) the period before the absolutism of Ivan the Terrible and (2) the seventeenth century, the time of the 'Assemblies of All the Land' (*Zemskie sobory*) and a considerable weakening of absolute central power. We must remember, of course, that in the Slavophile view absolutism emerged in Russia only as a result of Peter's reforms. In pre-Petrine Russia, they insisted, the term 'autocracy' meant not a power which was absolute but merely one which was indivisible in its own limited sphere. Even with this distinction, however, it was clear that they preferred those periods of Russian history in which the scope of tsarist autocracy had been relatively limited and different forms of self-government had been allowed to exist. Sometimes the Slavophiles stressed the principle of self-government in Old Russian life so strongly that their doctrine may seem akin to the historical constructions of the

[83] Cf. C. J. Friedrich, *The Philosophy of Law in Historical Perspective*, Chicago, 1963, pp. 138–40.

[84] Quoted from L. Schapiro, 'The *Vekhi* Group and the Mystique of Revolution,' *Slavonic and East European Review*, 34, no. 82, Dec. 1955, p. 62. For a different translation see Kistiakovsky's essay in *Landmarks*, p. 117. (Cf. above, n. 72.)

Decembrists, who saw Old Russia as a country ruled by essentially republican principles. In fact, however, this similarity is quite superficial. The Decembrists treated the peasant communes with their self-governing *mir* as 'tiny republics', a living survival of ancient Russian liberty,[85] while the Slavophiles totally rejected such views. And it was Aksakov who formulated most clearly the fundamental difference between republican principles and the principles of the *mir*. The first, he claimed, were principles of the struggle of all against all and of the rule of a mechanical *legal* majority; the second were *moral* principles of unanimity and concord. In the republican order, society was atomized; there was no real organic community, only isolated individuals in a state of continuous tension with one another. In the Russian *mir* there existed a 'free unity' based on common beliefs and customs, regulating the behaviour of individuals *from within*, and hence there was no need for legal compulsion. The same applied to the Slavophile image of pre-Petrine Russia, according to which all of holy Russia was one great *mir*, one great community of land, custom and faith. We may conclude, therefore, that the difference between the Western-republican and the Slavophile view of self-government boiled down to different attitudes towards the law.

Konstantin Aksakov was the most radically outspoken in this respect. For him the contrast between pre-Petrine Russia and the West was a contrast between internal and external truth. By 'internal truth' he meant the voice of conscience and a living tradition freely expressed in community life; by 'external truth' he meant juridical and political forms. In his view law and the state represented the sphere of society's self-alienation. They demanded obedience irrespective of moral convictions, under the threat of physical coercion and were therefore incompatible with morality, which they tried to replace with mere legality. In law, he wrote, 'man's inner nature is externalized',[86] the dictates of conscience are codified, human relations become depersonalized and free moral bonds are replaced by constraints. This path is destructive of human spirituality but much easier than the path of internal truth and therefore very tempting. Aksakov concluded:

Formal or rather external law requires an *act* to be moral within the meaning of

---

[85] See S. S. Volk, *Istoricheskie vzgliady dekabristov*, Moscow–Leningrad, 1958, p. 303. The Decembrists were influenced in this respect by some Polish historians, especially Joachim Lelewel and Zorian Dołęga-Chodakowski, who developed the conception of ancient Slavonic communalism, or republicanism, (ibid., pp. 314–18).

[86] K. S. Aksakov, *Polnoe sobranie sochinenii* vol. 1, Moscow, 1861, p. 249.

the law, but cares not in the least whether the man himself is moral or what motives inspire the act. On the contrary, the law aspires to a perfection that would in fact make it unnecessary for a man to be moral provided he acts in accordance with legality. Its aim is to establish a system perfect enough to render the soul superfluous, so that even without it men could act morally and be decent human beings. [That is why] the domination of external law in society undermines man's moral worth and teaches him to act without an inner moral impulse.[87]

It is clear that this romantic antilegalism was not levelled against law of the *Gemeinschaft* type. But it must be added that in Aksakov's eyes only modern rational law represented the true essence of law, 'law as a principle'. In this he was a more radical critic of law than Kireevsky. He would have agreed with the anarchist view that in a truly good society there is no need for written laws at all. It is worthwhile to note in this connection that Mikhail Bakunin, the father of Russian anarchism, frankly confessed that his condemnation of law had been inspired, originally, by Aksakov's ideas.[88]

When applied to the judicial sphere, Aksakov's antithesis between internal and external truth corresponds to Weber's differentiation between 'substantially rational justice', that is, judgement according to conscience, backed by ethical and religious norms, and 'formally rational' justice, implying a rational judicial system based on general and codified rules. The model for settling disputes according to conscience was in his eyes the peasant *mir*.

Another principle of external truth was, in Aksakov's view, the principle of statehood. Because of human imperfections, he argued, the state is a necessary evil; being an evil, however, it should be separated from society as much as possible. This strange logic becomes comprehensible if we remember that the Slavophiles conceived of freedom not as political freedom but as *freedom from politics*, and such a freedom, of course, could exist only under an autocratic ruler who would carry the entire burden of politics on his own shoulders. In a similar way Aksakov explained the Norman origins of the Russian state. The ancient Russians *had* to invite Varangians to rule over them. They saw the sad necessity of statehood but they did not want to become a state themselves and so, in order to avoid self-alienation, they preferred to be ruled by foreigners; having accepted

[87] Ibid., pp. 52, 249.
[88] See E. Lampert, *Studies in Rebellion*, London, 1957, pp. 145, 156.

external truth they wanted to make it as external to their life as possible.[89]

In this manner Aksakov managed to combine a kind of Christian anarchism with an apologia for autocracy. This was possible because by autocracy he meant absolute power in the *political* sphere only, which was for him only a small part of social life. In Muscovite Russia, he thought, the autocratic State was neatly separated from the Land (*Zemlya*), that is, from people living in accordance with internal truth. Relations between Land and State were based on agreement and trust, and on the principle of mutual non-interference; the people never tried to rule and the tsars in return did not interfere with the communal life of the land. (To this view Ivan the Terrible was of course an exception.) The people could present their case at the Land Assemblies but the final decision was left in the monarch's hands. Thus people could be sure of complete freedom to live and think as they pleased, while the monarch had complete freedom of political action.

This idyllic state of affairs was destroyed by a 'revolution from above', namely, by the Petrine reforms. In the person of Peter the Great the State betrayed the Land and, from being a 'necessary evil', became a principle that tried to force the people into brutal submission. It invaded the people's moral freedom, tradition, and customs. The upper class of society, the 'servants of the state', became divorced from the 'people of the Land', adopted foreign dress, and even ceased to use their native tongue. The tsar, who had assumed the foreign title 'Emperor', no longer needed ancient Moscow and built a new capital, St Petersburg, populated by people who were either completely alienated from their own nation or simply foreigners. The Land could now be compared to conquered territory and the State to an occupying power. The westernized sector of society, especially the nobility, became affected by political ambition and this gave rise to a series of palace revolutions culminating in the Decembrist uprising, the logical outcome of the Petrine reforms. In order to avoid further revolutions, which, sooner or later, would bring about complete catastrophe, Russia must 'return to herself' by re-establishing the pre-Petrine relationship between the State and the Land.[90]

[89] Cf. Aksakov, *Polnoe sobranie sochinenii*, pp. 7–17.

[90] Aksakov developed these views in his detailed memorial *On the Internal Affairs of Russia* which he submitted to the new emperor, Alexander II. This memorial is to be found in L. N. Brodsky, *Rannie slavianofily*, Moscow, 1910, pp. 69–97.

In Aksakov's eyes the greatest merit of this peculiar relationship consisted in the fact that it involved no legal guarantee; in other words, that the people's freedom was not safeguarded by the law. He insisted:

A guarantee is not required. A [legal] guarantee is an evil. Where it is necessary, good is absent; and life where good is absent had better disintegrate rather than continue with the aid of evil. The whole power is in the idea. What good are conditions and contracts when the inner authority is missing? No contract can restrain men where there is no inner inclination. That is the treasure possessed by Russia, for she has always believed in it and has never had recourse to contracts.[91]

Another inalienable part of the Old Russian ideal of society was the 'principle of unanimity', a principle which had survived Peter's reforms in the peasant communes of Russia. If society was to retain a spiritual and moral unity, Aksakov argued, all important decisions should be unanimous; to accept the 'principle of the majority' would be to treat disunity as something normal, to sanction discord and conflict in society. It would be equivalent to conceding that society is merely the sum of individual views. Aksakov extolled the ancient Slavs who (according to the chronicle of Dietmar) preferred rather to enforce unity than to accept disunity by raising the rule of the 'mechanical majority' to the status of a principle. He wrote:

Unanimity is a complicated issue; however, it is always difficult to attain the heights of moral achievement, and most difficult of all to be a Christian; and yet this does not mean that men should give up reaching for the moral heights or renounce Christianity . . . This is not the right place to recall how from the earliest times the Slavs tried to preserve the cherished principle of unanimity; how, when unable to reach agreement, they preferred rather to do battle, to inflict punishment upon themselves, as it were, for their imperfection; how, in order to wrest agreement from a few, they had recourse to violence, and all this to avoid recognizing majority decisions as legally valid, as a principle; in order not to destroy the principle of universal concord on which rested a unity of a higher order—the unity of the commune.[92]

Aksakov was not sufficiently aware that the principle of unanimity was not peculiar to Slavdom.[93] And he was quite unaware of the fact

[91] Aksakov, *On the Internal Affairs of Russia*, pp. 9–10.   [92] Ibid., pp. 292–3.
[93] It is widely acknowledged that the view that mutually binding decisions should be unanimous was once universal. As Max Weber wrote: 'Once the magical and charismatic means for the discovery of the right law had disappeared, there could be and did arise the idea that the right law was the one produced by the majority and that, therefore, the minority had the duty to associate itself with it. But before the minority did so,

that the old Polish gentry, whom he condemned for their 'betrayal of Slavdom', should have been accounted among the most stubborn and consistent defenders of this principle. After all, the notorious *liberum veto* was nothing but the converse of the principle of unanimity. This was fully realized by the great Polish poet, Adam Mickiewicz, who compared the Diet of the Polish–Lithuanian Commonwealth to the cardinals' conclave and to the English jury. He even quoted the same anecdote about the ancient Slavs which Aksakov had taken from Dietmar's chronicle, commenting:

> The veto was not an invention of the Poles but goes back to the beginning of Slavonic history. The right of veto existed in all Slavonic communities, where property, the law, and duties were common to all; every man benefited from a part of the supreme laws. The communities, however, safeguarded themselves against the veto by force, coercing opponents with sticks to vote in line with majority opinion. The veto also existed in Russian and Czech communities.[94]

Bringing together Mickiewicz's and Aksakov's views provides an interesting example of two different grounds for romantic idealization of the unanimity principle: one based on freedom and one on the moral cohesion of the collective. Mickiewicz emphasized the right of veto as an expression of respect for the individual; Aksakov, on the other hand, interpreted the principle of unanimity as recognition that the individual should accept his moral dependence on the community by giving up his separate views in the name of unity and concord. Nevertheless, on closer examination the affinity between these two interpretations turns out to be more important than might appear at first sight. Aksakov, like Mickiewicz, recognized an individual's right of secession from his community; Mickiewicz, like Aksakov, opposed the principle of majority rule in the name of the moral, and not merely 'mechanical', unity of society. Both refused to sanction inner conflicts and a pluralism of opinion in social life; in both cases unanimity was conceived of as the guardian of national tradition, a device against innovation.[95]

We can add to this that in both cases the principle of unanimity was

---

occasionally under drastic compulsion, the majority resolution was not law and no one was bound by it. (*Max Weber on Law in Economy and Society*, Max Rheinstein (ed.), New York, 1954, pp. 155–6). Weber refers in this connection to W. Konopczyński, *Liberum veto*, Cracow, 1918).

[94] A. Mickiewicz, *Dzieła*, Warsaw, 1955, vol. 10, pp. 66.

[95] For a comparative analysis of the relationship between Mickiewicz's Messianism and Russian Slavophilism see Walicki, *Philosophy and Romantic Nationalism*, pp. 269–76.

embraced in conscious opposition to modern law of the *Gesellschaft* type. Unanimity as a form of the corporate will is obviously incompatible with the notion of 'abstract individuals', whose votes can simply be counted. It implies mutual understanding (consensus) and concord stemming from a deep agreement on core values. Using the terminology of Tönnies one therefore can say that unanimity expresses the organic will of the *Gemeinschaft* (*Wesenwille*), as opposed to the rational will of the *Gesellschaft* (*Kürwille*). From this point of view the differences between Mickiewicz's image of unanimity in the old Polish–Lithuanian Diet and Aksakov's view of the principle of unanimity in the Old Russian way of life (and in the peasant *mir*) can be reduced to a common denominator.[96]

To sum up, the Slavophile critique of law was linked to an idealized image of the past, a 'conservative utopia', in Mannheim's term.[97] Their hostility to modern law of the *Gesellschaft* type, which they often identified with 'law as a principle', stemmed from their abhorrence of individualism and rationalism, which they correctly saw as closely connected with the rational juridicization of social ties. Their idealization of the ancient Russian autocracy had nothing to do with endorsement of unlimited state power; on the contrary, they stressed that the power of the Muscovite tsars had in fact been strictly limited, not by law but by religious and moral convictions, tradition, and customs.

A different type of right-wing denigration of law was represented by those Russian thinkers who idealized the Russian autocracy as the highest embodiment of the omnipotent state, or of sovereign and unlimited personal power. Their disrespect or outright contempt for law was simply an expression of their reverence for force and of their belief that only the strongest possible government could save Russia

---

[96] One should remember, of course, that Mickiewicz romanticized the archaic features of the Polish 'democracy of the gentry'. In reality the case of the Polish–Lithuanian Commonwealth was much more complicated. Cf. the view of the Belgian Slavist, Claude Backvis: 'After all, this society was a *Gemeinschaft*, because it was organic, embracing people in the wholeness of their existence and consciousness, based upon mutual understanding and agreement, *Eintracht, concordia* . . . It is clear, however, that it owed its achievements not to a unifying faith but to listening to different individual views and to the pressures of public opinion, and therefore could be treated as a product of activities characteristic of the *Gesellschaft*. It was inspired by *Wesenwille* [organic will]. But it would be ridiculous to ignore that it applied *Kürwille* [rational will] in many matters and circumstances.' (See C. Backvis, 'Individu et société dans la Pologne de la Renaissance,' in *Individu et société à la Renaissance*, Bruxelles–Paris, 1967. Quoted from C. Backvis, *Studia o Kulturze staropolskiej*, Warsaw, 1975, p. 552).

[97] Cf. K. Mannheim, *Ideology and Utopia*, New York–London, 1952.

from imminent disaster. As Konstantin Leontiev (1831–91), the most original thinker of the extreme right in nineteenth-century Russia, put it:

With us a man of the people is governed far more by the feeling he has for the person of the Sovereign (anointed by the Lord), and by the secular habit of obeying the officers of that Sovereign, than by any natural virtues or a vague respect for legal fictions. It is well known that Russia is impervious to common sense. It is naturally inclined to extremes. *Thus, if the power of the Monarchy were to lose its absolute significance; and if the people were to grasp that they were no longer ruled by a Sovereign, but by deputies elected according to a system of voting they did not understand (less even than the workers of other countries); then these people would reach the stage of believing that they had outgrown obedience.* At this very moment, the people are weeping in the Churches for their assassinated Emperor [Alexander II]. They believe that tears are *salutary for the soul.* Not only would they not weep for their elected deputies, but they would claim *as much soil and wealth as possible,* and the minimum of taxes . . . They would certainly not fight for the freedom of the press or for Parliamentary debates.'[98]

The final outcome of such a course of events was foreshadowed by Leontiev in another passage, often quoted as evidence of his prophetic insight:

It is no small undertaking to teach our people the *spirit of the laws* ; it might well take a century to do so. Unfortunately, great events will not wait to see the outcome. And besides, our people love and understand authority better than laws. In their eyes an army general is not only a more familiar but also a more sympathetic figure than a paragraph of the civil code. A constitution, which would undermine Russian authority, would not have time to teach the people *a devotion such as the English have for the observance of law.* And our people are right. I can see no other practical solution of the contemporary problem of capital and labour except in a well-established monarchical system, sanctified by the Church and limited only by its conscience. We should forge ahead of Europe and show her an example . . . *Our people have greater need of affirmations of faith and of an assured* material life than of jurisprudence and true science . . . Only that which will satisfy both the material and the religious wants of the Russian people, can rescue future peasant generations from the claws of the Nihilist Minotaur. Otherwise we shall fail to crush the Revolution, *and the triumph of Socialism will be assured sooner or later.*[99]

---

[98] Quoted from N. Berdyaev, *Leontiev*, Orono, Maine, 1968, pp. 186–7. I have slightly modified the translation.

[99] Ibid., pp. 187–8 (cf. G. Meier, *U istokov revolutsii*, Frankfurt am Main, 1971, pp. 29–30). I have slightly modified the translation.

Leontiev was sometimes very pessimistic about the chances of avoiding this outcome, but consoled himself with his conviction that the liberals, whom he hated bitterly and whom he held responsible for the general decay, would not be spared by the socialist revolution of the future. The victorious revolutionaries, he wrote, would despise liberals, and rightly so.

However hostile these people [the socialists] are to the conservatives themselves and to the forms and methods of their conservative activity, nevertheless all the essential aspects of conservative doctrine will prove useful to them. They will require terror, they will require discipline; traditions of humility, the habit of obedience, will be of use to them; nations who (let us suppose) have already managed successfully to reconstruct their economic life but have nevertheless failed to find satisfaction in earthly life, will blaze up with renewed enthusiasm for mystical doctrines.[100]

Like the Slavophiles, Leontiev found his social ideal in the romanticized past and, in this sense, represented a version of conservative utopianism. But he consciously distanced himself from the Slavophiles, whom he saw as half-liberals, given to one-sided moralism, unable to understand the need for strict, severe government or the aesthetic aspect of the great cruelties of history.[101] He wanted a return to the Byzantine heritage of Russia and had no esteem for purely Slavonic values. On the contrary, he sharply ridiculed such traditional values as 'mildness' and a 'peace-loving nature', and praised instead what he saw as the Russian inclination to brute force (*nasil'stvennost'*) and love of armed conquest. Without Byzantism, the Russians and the Slavs in general were to him raw 'ethnographical material', lacking any distinct, cultural identity. From a purely tribal point of view what he prized in the Russians was not their Slavonic characteristics but rather the fusion of Asiatic (Turanian) elements and the 'Orthodox *intus-susceptio* of strong and imperious German blood'.[102]

---

[100] K. Leontiev, *Sobranie sochinenii*, SPb, 1912–14, vol. 7, p. 217.

[101] Cf. Walicki, *The Slavophile Controversy*, pp. 523–30.

[102] Leontiev, *Sobranie sochinenii*, vol. 7, p. 323. The theory of the Turanian origin of the Russians was put forward and developed by the Polish ethnographer F. H. Duchiński (1816–93), who wrote in French and had considerable influence in France (cf., for example, H. Martin's *La Russie et l'Europe*). He wanted to prove that the Russians, because of their Turanian origin, were given to despotism and aggression, while the true Slavs, including Ukrainians and Belorussians, were characterized by a love of peace and freedom. Thus his view of the Turanian impact on the national character of the Russians was the same as Leontiev's, although his values and intentions

Leontiev's views were too extreme to be officially recognized in Russia. The role of chief ideological prop of autocracy in the reactionary reign of Alexander III fell to the lot of the influential journalist Mikhail Katkov (1818–87). There were at least three stages in his ideological evolution. Early in his career he was a liberal Westernizer of the Anglophile type; the Polish uprising of 1863 transformed him into the mouthpiece of chauvinist nationalism; still later, the development of the revolutionary movement in Russia turned him into a conservative hard-liner, a supporter of and apologist for the reactionary counter-reforms of Alexander III. In the present context, only the last need concern us.

Unlike the Slavophiles or Leontiev, Katkov, a man of humble social background, did not indulge in conservative-romantic utopianism. He supported the Russian autocracy in its contemporary form, putting emphasis not on archaic social ties (as the Slavophiles did), nor even on the charismatic authority of the tsar, but on the centralization of political power and the necessity of exercising it through the bureau-cratic machinery of state. He saw centralization and concentration of power as the most important criteria of political progress, which led him to proclaim that unlimited autocracy was a more developed and more progressive form of government than constitutional monarchy, let alone a parliamentary republic.[103] His contempt for law was not linked to the usual conservative respect for 'organic growth' and criticism of arbitrary legislation; on the contrary, he praised autocratic power as a means of consciously shaping the course of history and criticized the law and lawyers as obstacles in the enforced submission of the people for the sake of higher political aims.[104] In other words, he emphasized the incompatibility between the law and the sovereign political will, condemning the first in the name of the second.

Ivan Aksakov, Konstantin Aksakov's younger brother, who made it his mission to spread Slavophile ideology at a time when its founders were no longer alive, reacted negatively to Leontiev's views, labelling them a 'lascivious cult of the truncheon'.[105] More complicated was his attitude to Katkov, for, although he found him too servile in his

were diametrically opposite. His 'Turanian theory' was used in France and England to warn the West against the Russian danger.

[103] See V. A. Tvardovskaia, *Ideologiia poreformennogo Samoderzhaviia* (*M. N. Katkov i ego izdaniia*), Moscow, 1978, p. 202.

[104] Ibid., p. 269.

[105] See M. D. Chadov, *Slavianofily i narodnoe predstavitel'stvo*, Kharkov, 1906, p. 45.

relations with the court and too fond of the soulless bureaucracy, he shared his obsessive fear of revolution in Russia, and this made him very critical of the liberal reforms of the 1860s. As Aleksandr Koshelev, another and more liberal-minded adherent of Slavophilism, commented: 'What I found particularly distasteful were Aksakov's outbursts against the liberals, against the juridical system, representative institutions, the new courts, etc. These pronouncements of his were openly aimed at us, supporters of the new reforms, and he thus stood, as it were, under the banner of Katkov.'[106]

As we can see from this quotation, there were people who considered themselves Slavophiles but yet wholeheartedly supported the cause of modernizing reforms. Most of these played an active part in the newly created local self-government (the *zemstvos*), seeing the creation of the *zemstvos* (1864) as a return to the pre-Petrine pattern of self-government of the Land. Koshelev even postulated the convention of a *Duma*, presenting this, too, as a return to ancient Russian traditions. He insisted that the introduction of a *Duma*, while helping the tsar to recognize the true needs of his people, would have nothing in common with Western constitutionalism or the parliamentary system. Some Slavophiles, however, refused to accept these arguments. Yury Samarin campaigned to rouse the nobility against Koshelev's 'childish ideas',[107] in the belief that only a social 'people's monarchy', making full use of its absolute power, could ensure a peaceful solution to Russia's problems.

At the turn of the century the Slavophile-inspired current in the *zemstvo* movement grew stronger and more obvious. It was headed by Dmitry Shipov (1851–1920), the chairman of the Zemstvo Council for the Moscow province. In the early twentieth century he was widely recognized as the moral leader of the right-wing reform movement. Like other *zemstvo* leaders, he tried to increase the role of independent social organizations, to unite the forces of the local *zemstvos* and to ensure for them a real influence in national affairs. Where he differed from the majority, led by Ivan Petrunkevich, was in refusing to endorse constitutional demands. He wanted popular representation at only an advisory level, modelled on the Assemblies of the Land in pre-Petrine Russia, rather than on Western parliaments. Because of this he could neither join the Kadet party nor support the repressive government of

---

[106] A. I. Koshelev, *Zapiski* (1812–83), Berlin, 1884, pp. 249–50.
[107] See R. Wortman, 'Koshelëv, Samarin and Cherkassky, and the Fate of Liberal Slavophilism', *Slavic Review*, 21, 1962, p. 261.

Stolypin. Like his Slavophile mentors, he believed in the moral unity of society and set his hopes on a moral regeneration of Russia. It is no wonder, therefore, that he strongly opposed all forms of violence, both revolutionary and counter-revolutionary, deeply deplored all forms of divisive hatred and wrote about universal reconciliation. His political views were full of a somewhat naïve idealism but also contained a significant and very realistic insight into the destructive logic of political conflict in a situation in which both sides are unable, or unwilling, to arrive at an honestly acceptable compromise solution.[108]

An important element in Shipov's views was his traditionally Slavophile distrust of law, and he distanced himself from the constitutionalists because he considered that they idolized the law and underestimated the importance of moral foundations to the community. He wanted no legal limitation of autocracy because he did not believe in external restraints on power. He also liked the term 'autocracy' (*samoderzhavie*), which for him denoted not state absolutism but merely a truly independent power;[109] autocracy, he argued, is a Christian concept, compatible with the view that nothing can be absolute on earth, whereas state absolutism in all its forms is a dangerous kind of idolatry. Shipov held that every state was based upon two principles, that of law and that of authority (*vlast'*).[110] Both these principles were necessary evils, stemming from the imperfection of man, and both had only relative significance. The absolutization of law was for him no less dangerous than state absolutism because in both cases the necessary evil suppressed the higher, religious, and moral principles of social cohesion. Especially dangerous was the combination of a legalist mentality with the struggle for popular sovereignty: it led to an emphasis on rights for all and the neglect of moral duties, to a sharpening of existing conflicts instead of seeking their peaceful solution.[111] The legalist mentality, he believed, made people egoistic, uncompromising, unable to sacrifice individual and group interests to the common good and totally lacking the Christian spirit of love and humility. The very slight development of legal consciousness among the Russian people was to Shipov an advantage, as helping to preserve Christian virtues.[112]

[108] For a sympathetic account of Shipov's views see L. Schapiro, *Rationalism and Nationalism in Russian Nineteenth-Century Political Thought*, London, 1967, pp. 143–67.
[109] Cf. D. I. Shipov, *Vospominaniia i dumy o perezhitom*, Moscow, 1918, p. 147. According to Shipov, the Russian autocracy was very similar to the British monarchy since both were limited not by law, but by consciousness of moral duty (ibid., p. 271).
[110] Ibid., pp. 142–3.   [111] Ibid., p. 144.   [112] Ibid., p. 272.

It is not surprising that Shipov repeatedly accused the Kadet party of a boundless faith in the importance of legal forms and of a passionately ambitious commitment to political struggle.[113] He even criticized the constitutional (or semi-constitutional) principles of the Imperial Manifesto of October 1905 as defining the relationship between the tsar and his people in terms of rights, rather than moral duties: in other words, as an attempt to solve Russia's problems through law, rather than through moral regeneration.[114] He accepted the October Manifesto (even becoming a co-founder and first Chairman of the Octobrist party) only because he saw it as the lesser evil, and he deeply deplored the fact that the Russians could not arrive at a true compromise, based upon firm *moral* grounds. According to his friend, N. A. Khomiakov, he became a constitutionalist against his will, in obedience to the Imperial command.[115] Since he took the newly acquired freedom very seriously, defending it against Stolypin's government, he soon abandoned the pro-government Octobrist party, and joined the Party of Peaceful Renovation, which was trying to mediate between the government and the Kadets. But he was never a genuine, convinced supporter of constitutionalism, holding that the Fundamental Laws of 1906 created legal grounds for increasingly bitter political conflict, which, he predicted, would bring catastrophe to his beloved Russia.

As we can see, the negative attitude towards law was represented in Russia by very different types of conservative thinker, from ultra-reactionaries like Leontiev, to liberal conservatives like Shipov. It had deep roots in Russian history but was also shaped, or strengthened, by influences from the West, especially by the powerful influence of German conservative thinkers. Unlike the denigration of law by the left, it did not amount to 'legal nihilism' in the literal meaning of this term. Even Konstantin Aksakov, the most utopian conservative thinker, preached a kind of 'legal nihilism' only in developing his views on the social *ideal*; when he wrote about social *reality* he recognized the corruptness of human nature and reluctantly agreed that a minimum of legal regulation had to be accepted. The left-wing thinkers, rejecting the Christian dogma of original sin and ardently believing in salvation on earth, as a rule went much further in their critique of law. Some of them developed a truly nihilist attitude towards law and took this to its logical conclusion.

[113] Ibid., p. 393.
[114] Ibid., pp. 329–33.
[115] Ibid., p. 447.

4   The censure of law by the left

The first outstanding representative of left-wing antilegalism in Russia was Aleksandr Herzen—a thinker who forms a natural link between the so-called 'superfluous men' of the 1840s and the radicals of the 1860s and 1870s.[116] He saw himself as continuing the radical tradition of the Decembrists although his views on law had nothing in common with their 'juridical world-view'. Seen from this perspective he resembles rather his close friend, Mikhail Bakunin, the father of Russian anarchism. Both were originators of a revolutionary tradition which in fact differed completely from that of the Decembrists—a tradition deeply suspicious of 'the spirit of law', programmatically rejecting the struggle for constitutionalism and dismissing 'merely political' democracy as a bourgeois fraud or, at best, a bourgeois illusion.

In Herzen's case rejection of belief in law was part of his general disillusionment with the West and of his break with Russian Westernism. The distinctive feature of his intellectual career was that from the very beginning he conceived of his time as an epoch of crisis out of which—according to the laws of social 'palingenesis'—a new, regenerate world would be born. In the opposition student circle which he had organized together with his friend Nikolai Ogarev, and during his exile in Perm', Viatka and Vladimir (1834–40), he studied, in addition to German philosophy, the works of the French social romantics (the Saint-Simonians, Leroux, Ballanche), and, under their influence, compared contemporary European civilization to the dying civilization of ancient Rome and the European socialists to the ancient Christians. This way of thinking led him to ask whether the Russians, and the Slavs in general, were not destined to play the role of the new barbarians. In the early forties, he was already considering the possible validity of some of the ideas and insights of Slavophilism and of the Paris lectures of Adam Mickiewicz.[117]

Nevertheless, in his philosophical works of 1843–5, among the best products of Russian Left Hegelianism, Herzen remained a Westernizer. His final break with Westernism took place a little later, as the result of the direct confrontation of his image of the West with the social reality of Western countries, particularly France.

At the beginning of 1847 Herzen was at last allowed to realize his

[116] For a detailed characterization of the Russian 'superfluous men' see Walicki *Slavophile Controversy*, pp. 337–63.

[117] Ibid., pp. 580–2.

old project of a journey to the West. He had never been an uncritical admirer of the bourgeois West but the France of Louis-Philippe seemed to him even worse than he had expected. In his 'Letters from France and Italy' (1847–52) he expressed his feelings in an aesthetic, somewhat aristocratic, criticism of western bourgeois civilization, which he presented as an ugly kingdom of trivial mediocrity. The victory of the bourgeoisie in the revolution of 1848 was for him a violent shock, causing him to lose faith in an inevitable, teleologically conceived progress. In his book *From the Other Shore* (1850) he finally broke with Hegelianism: history, he asserted, has no 'Reason', it is but a blind play of chances, an eternal improvisation which never repeats itself. His break with the concept of the 'Reason of History' was thus a result of his loss of faith in Europe. He embraced instead the idea of the decline of the West, exclaiming: 'Farewell, departing world, farewell, Europe!'[118] These views, however, did not prevent him from appreciating the individual freedom which he found in the West. In the preface to *From the Other Shore* he defended his moral right to emigrate in the following words, addressed to his friends in Russia:

... I have become accustomed to free speech and I cannot accept serfdom again, not even for the sake of suffering with you. If it had been necessary to restrain oneself for the common cause, perhaps one might have found the strength to do so; but where at this moment is our common cause? At home you have no soil on which a free man can stand. How after this can you summon us? ... If it were to battle—yes, then we would come: but to obscure martyrdom, to sterile silence, to obedience—no, under no circumstances. Demand anything from me, but do not demand duplicity, do not force me again to play at being a loyal subject; respect the free man in me.

The liberty of the individual is the greatest thing of all, it is *on this and on this alone* that the true will of the people can develop. Man must respect liberty in himself, and he must esteem it in himself no less than in his neighbour, than in the entire nation. If you are convinced of that, then you will agree that to remain here is my right, my duty; it is the only protest that an individual can make amongst us; he must offer up this sacrifice to his human dignity. If you call my withdrawal an escape and will forgive me only out of your love, this will mean that you yourselves are not wholly free.[119] ...

In Europe a man who lives abroad has never been considered a criminal, nor one who emigrates to America a traitor. We have nothing similar. With us the individual has always been crushed, absorbed, he has never even tried to

---

[118] A. Herzen, *From the Other Shore and The Russian People and Socialism*. Isaiah Berlin (int.), London, 1956, p. 150.

[119] Ibid., pp. 11–12.

emerge. Free speech with us has always been considered insolence, independence—subversion; man was engulfed in the State, dissolved in the community. The revolution of Peter the Great replaced the obsolete squirearchy of Russia—with European bureaucracy; everything that could be copied from the Swedish and German codes, everything that could be taken over from the free municipalities of Holland into our half-communal, half-absolutist country, was taken over; but the unwritten, the moral check on power, the instinctive recognition of the rights of man, of the rights of thought, could not be and were not imported.[120]

Despite this moving tribute to Western freedom Herzen, in the same book, argued that the difference between Europe and Russia was not very important from the point of view of the popular masses, since the right to free speech was not enough to achieve their social, political, and moral emancipation. Political revolutions in France and the intellectual revolution in Germany had not fulfilled their promises. Herzen wrote:

German science is a speculative religion, the republic of the Convention is the absolutism of the Pentarchy and at the same time a Church. In place of the creed there appeared civil dogmas. The Assembly and the Government officiated at the mystery of the people's liberation. The legislator became the priest, the seer, and enunciated benevolently and without irony eternal, infallible judgements in the name of popular sovereignty.

The people, of course, remained, as before, the *laity*, the *governed*. For them nothing was changed and they attended the political liturgies understanding nothing, just as they had the religious ones.[121]

It is worthwhile to point out the close similarity between this passage from Herzen and Engels's characterization of the 'juridical world-view', quoted above.[122] Both thinkers treated the bourgeois faith in law as the secularization of theology and both stressed that this change had little in common with genuine human emancipation. What is striking is the fact that Herzen saw no connection between individual freedom, which he so much enjoyed in the West, and its political and legal safeguards. His appreciation of the moral check on power, the instinctive recognition of the rights of man, was the obverse of his belittling of the importance of the political and legal conditions of individual freedom, including, of course, freedom of speech; his praise of respect for human dignity as something deeply rooted in the whole of European history was paralleled by his indifference to the positive

[120] Ibid., p. 120. [121] Ibid., p. 148. [122] See above, n. 32.

contribution of recent, 'bourgeois' progress, achieved by change through law.

For Herzen the failure of the revolutions of 1848 sealed the fate of Europe: the countries of the West, he thought, had found their equilibrium in a bourgeois structure and even Western socialists had become imbued with bourgeois traits—which was why they had failed to seize their great chance. This left Slavdom—and above all Russia—as the last hope of mankind. To substantiate this hope he set forth his doctrine of Russian Socialism. We find here some characteristic ideas of Petr Chaadaev, the author of the famous 'Philosophical Letter' on Russia,[123] of the Slavophiles, and of the liberal and democratic Westernizers of the forties. Like Chaadaev, Herzen asserted that Russia was a country without history, a country where no 'burden of the past' would hinder the introduction of a new and better social organization. Like the Slavophiles, he saw Russia's immense superiority over the West in the peasant commune but thought that the commune should be permeated by the 'idea of personality', which had been introduced to Russia from the West and was represented by the Russian intelligentsia, especially the educated Russian gentry. Individual freedom, he reasoned, had been developed most fully in England, but this development had been achieved at the cost of complete loss of the communal principle; the Russian peasant, on the contrary, preserved his commune but was swallowed up by it. The task of Russian Socialism was therefore to reconcile the values of the westernized Russian intelligentsia with the communism of the Russian peasantry: 'to preserve the commune and to render the individual free'.[124]

In his open letter to Jules Michelet, entitled 'The Russian People and Socialism' (1851), Herzen developed not only the idea that absence of a firm juridical tradition of private property in Russia was a positive good, but also the idea of the advantages of lawlessness. The Russian peasant, he wrote, 'is, quite literally, outside the law: the law contrives to offer him absolutely no protection whatsoever'.[125] Because of this a respect for law and the courts is completely unknown to most Russians; the same is true of moral condemnation of convicted criminals. The Russian peasant 'leaves the court in the same wretched

---

[123] See Walicki, *Slavophile Controversy*, ch. 3 and *History of Russian Thought*, ch. 5.
[124] A. Gertsen [Herzen], *Sobranie sochinenii* (30 vols., Moscow, 1954–65), vol. 12, p. 156.
[125] Herzen, *From the Other Shore*, p. 181.

state whether he has been condemned or whether he has been acquitted. The difference between the two verdicts seems to him a matter of mere chance or luck . . . In the eyes of the Russian people, there is no stigma attached to a man merely because he has been found guilty in a court of law. Convicts and those who are sentenced to transportation are in popular parlance called *"unfortunates"*.' This is because the peasant 'has no real knowledge of any form of life but that of the village commune: he understands about rights and duties only when these are tied to the commune and its members. Outside the commune, there are no obligations for him—there is simply violence.'[126] This explains why Russian peasants have no scruples whatsoever in lying to judges. But *within* the commune 'they very rarely cheat one another. An almost boundless good faith prevails amongst them: contracts and written agreements are quite unheard of.'[127]

In this way the general lawlessness had helped to preserve something better than law: a morality which 'flows quite instinctively and naturally' from communal life.[128] In Herzen's view, this was a precious legacy which made Russia better prepared for the advent of socialism than any other country in the world. 'The organic life of the commune', he wrote, 'has persisted despite all the attempts on it by authority, badly mauled though it has been at times. By good fortune it has survived right into the period that witnesses the rise of socialism in Europe.'[129]

Another advantage of Russian disregard for law, for Herzen, lay in the attitudes prevailing among the educated, westernized strata of Russian society. The emancipated Russian, he argued, is 'the most independent creature in the world', not restrained and enslaved by the respect for law.[130] His disrespect for law is not confined to Russia; he is almost equally contemptuous of the praetorium in which the French administer their 'Barbaro-Roman justice'.[131] Addressing Michelet, Herzen summed up his views on law as follows:

It is quite clear that any difference there may be between your laws and our Ukases lies almost entirely in the wording of their preambles. Ukases start with a painful truth—'The Tsar commands . . . '—whereas your laws start with an insulting lie, the triple Republican motto, the ironical invocation in the name of the French people. The *Code Nicholas* is intended to be unreservedly against mankind and in favour of authority. The *Code Napoléon* seems really no different. There are already enough impositions that we are forced to endure,

[126] Ibid., pp. 182–3.   [127] Ibid., p. 183.   [128] Ibid., p. 184.
[129] Ibid., p. 186.   [130] Ibid., p. 198.   [131] Ibid., p. 200.

without our making the position worse by imposing new ones on ourselves of our own free will. In this respect our situation is exactly like that of the peasantry. We bow to brute force: we are slaves because we have no way of freeing ourselves: but whatever happens, we shall accept nothing from the enemy camp.

Russia will never be Protestant.

Russia will never be *juste-milieu*.

Russia will never stage a revolution with the sole aim of ridding herself of Tsar Nicholas only to replace him by a multitude of other Tsars—Tsar deputies, Tsar-tribunals, Tsar-policemen, Tsar-laws.[132]

The defeat of Russia in the Crimean War, together with the unexpected and enigmatic death of Nicholas I, created a situation in which important political and social changes were unavoidable. The new Tsar, Alexander II, realized that some reforms, notably the emancipation of the serfs, could not be further delayed, that some relaxations of the autocratic system of Nicholas I was necessary. Though half-hearted, his liberalism stirred up hopes, created a 'thaw', and permitted the rise of a relatively strong public opinion with clear-cut political divisions. In this atmosphere Herzen became more willing to compromise: he appealed to the new emperor to seize the chance of furthering 'bloodless progress', declaring, on his own behalf, a readiness to accept the continued existence of the monarchy provided the most urgent reforms were put into effect. Thanks to this change of front, his influence reached a far wider cross-section of society. His *émigré* journal *The Bell* was eagerly read not only by radicals, but also by moderate liberals, including people who were close to the Russian court.

However, in the domain of social and political thought the most important event was the emergence of a new radicalism. It expressed the ideas and attitudes of the non-conformist elements among the *raznochintsy*, the intelligentsia not of gentle social background, the educated commoners, who had begun to figure prominently in Russian intellectual and social life. The chief organ of the new trend was Nekrasov's journal *The Contemporary*, and its ideological leaders were both sons of provincial priests: Nikolai Chernyshevsky, a journalist with a scholarly, encyclopaedic mind, and his disciple, the literary critic Nikolai Dobroliubov. Feeling themselves sharply distinguished from the 'men of the forties', they claimed to represent the 'new men', different in all respects from the weak and wavering liberal gentry,

[132] Ibid.

whom they found faithfully portrayed in Russian literature in the type of 'superfluous man'.[133] Especially significant, from this point of view, was Dobroliubov's article 'What is Oblomovism?' (1859), a long review of Goncharov's novel *Oblomov*: the 'men of the forties' were here accused of idle day-dreaming and paralysis of will resulting from their failure to break with the mentality and parasitic way of life of the privileged class.

The severity of this attack evoked many protests. It is significant that Herzen, too, hastened to the defence of the 'superfluous men'. In his article 'Very dangerous!' (title in English, 1859) he even suggested that by criticizing the liberal press and the liberal traditions of the Russian intelligentsia the 'buffoons' of *The Contemporary* were abetting the tsarist regime and deserved to be decorated for their services to absolutism. The editors of *The Contemporary* were taken aback to find themselves the target of an attack from such a source—even Dobroliubov had always regarded Herzen, and Belinsky too, as superior natures whom his criticism did not concern. Chernyshevsky thought it essential to go to London in order to clear up the misunderstanding in person. He returned with little to show for his pains, convinced that Herzen was a man of the past. The misunderstanding had been cleared up, but the difference of opinion remained.

In spite of this, there was in fact a remarkable community between Herzen's and Chernyshevsky's views on 'merely political' democracy and on the liberal idea of law. As I have tried to show, Herzen was never a liberal in the sense of believing in the rule of law, the parliamentary system, and economic freedom. Even the radicals of the 1860s did not see him as such; when they accused him of liberalism they used this term in its very broad and specifically Russian sense, meaning simply a lack of radicalism, the search for a middle way, and faith in non-revolutionary social change.

Obviously, if 'liberalism' is identified with belief in, or desire for, non-revolutionary social change, it is not incompatible with support for unlimited autocracy. On the contrary, in a country like Russia, it was quite natural to believe that only a strong autocratic power could break the resistance of the privileged social classes and introduce the necessary reforms. Russian autocracy was contrasted with constitutionalism as being a political power not bound up with the vested interests of the propertied and, therefore, more likely to protect

---

[133] For a detailed discussion of this conflict between the two generations of Russian intelligentsia see E. Lampert, *Sons Against Fathers*, Oxford, 1965.

the interests of the common people. (We must remember that the advocates of Russian autocracy tended to present constitutionalism as a mask for the oligarchic rule of the privileged.) People who held such views, as for instance the influential statesman Nikolai Miliutin, were called liberals and the habit of so calling them persists in Soviet historical writing. It is interesting that a classical formulation of liberalism so conceived may be found in the *Diary* of the young Chernyshevsky: 'It does not matter whether there is a Tsar, or not, whether there is a constitution, or not; what really matter are the social relations, that is how to prevent a situation in which one class sucks the blood of another.' And he concludes:

It would be best if absolutism could retain its rule over us until we are sufficiently permeated with democratic spirit, so that, when a popular form of government comes to replace it, political power could be handed over—*de jure* and *de facto*—to the most numerous and the most unhappy class (peasants + hirelings + workers) and thus we could skip all the transitional stages.[134]

It should be noted that Chernyshevsky himself used the word 'liberalism' in its Western sense, associating it above all with individual and political freedom. What was peculiarly Russian in his use of the term was his sharp contrast between liberalism and democracy, which he defined in his articles on the political history of France. Liberalism, he explained, aims at merely political reforms while the only aim of democracy is the real welfare of the people. In this manner the notion of democracy became de-politicized and made compatible with any form of government. Chernyshevsky drew from this his famous paradox about Siberia and England: 'For a democrat our Siberia, in which the common people enjoy well-being, is far better than England, where the majority of the population endures great want.'[135]

Chernyshevsky's critique of liberalism contained some deep insights and, therefore, deserves closer examination. This is what he wrote on the liberal conception of individual freedom:

Freedom is a very pleasant thing. But liberalism understands freedom in too narrow and formal a way: it is conceived in terms of abstract rights, as a paper dispensation, as absence of legal restriction. Liberals will not understand that juridical freedom has value for man only when he possesses the material power

---

[134] N. G. Chernyshevsky, *Polnoe sobranie sochinenii*, Moscow, 1939–53, vol. 1, p. 110.
[135] Chernyshevsky, *Polnoe sobranie sochinenii*, SPb, 1906, vol. 4, p. 156. Quoted from Szamuely, *The Russian Tradition*, p. 176.

to take advantage of it. Neither you, reader, nor I are debarred from eating off a golden dinner-service. Unfortunately, neither you nor I are likely to have the means of assuring such a refined prospect. I must frankly say, therefore, that I do not in the least cherish my right to possess a golden dinner-service and am ready to sell this golden right for one silver rouble, or even for less. The same could be said of all the rights for the people about which our liberals fuss.

This critique of 'negative freedom', that is, freedom from external restriction or coercion, was supplemented by a similar critique of the liberal view of political freedom, freedom as a formal right to participate in political affairs:

> Participation in the exercise of political power, or influence on social affairs depends not on whether certain people or certain classes have obtained the formal right to share in the formal acts of government: it depends on whether such people and such classes are so situated in the life of society as to be able to have real significance in it . . . The point is not to provide formal conditions for exercising one's influence on political life, but to have the power to exercise such influence.[136]

For many people such reasonings are convincing even today, particularly in those countries where people have grown accustomed to liberal freedom, take it for granted, as it were, and, therefore, are inclined to underestimate its value. Because of this it is necessary to show the weakness of Chernyshevsky's views on freedom and the profound misunderstanding upon which they were founded.

Lack of freedom should not be confused with lack of ability, lack of power. If I want to run but cannot, perhaps because of a broken leg, this is an accident of fate, misfortune, but not servitude; lack of freedom, servitude, would be at issue when I could run but was not allowed to do so. This can be seen even from Chernyshevsky's ironical remarks about freedom to eat off a golden dinner-service. Quite unwittingly Chernyshevsky has proved more than he wanted to do, showing not only the weakness but also the strength of the classical liberal conception of freedom. One only needs to reverse the situation he describes and imagine someone who can afford to purchase a gold dinner-service but is forbidden to do so because the ownership of such things is the monopoly of the ruling caste. It is easy to agree, I believe, that such a situation, because of the arbitrary nature of the prohibition,

---

[136] Chernyshevsky, *Polnoe sobranie sochinenii*, 1939–53, vol. 5, pp. 106, 217. Quoted from Lampert, *Sons Against Fathers*, p. 199.

would violate one's sense of freedom and dignity far more painfully than the situation described by Chernyshevsky.

The same criticism applies to Chernyshevsky's view of political freedom. We may not be able to exercise a real influence on political events but, none the less, it is a matter of great moment whether we are allowed to try or not. Having observed the bureaucratic methods used in preparation for the abolition of serfdom in Russia, Chernyshevsky himself came to the conclusion that it would have been much better if the reform had been handled not by bureaucrats but by freely elected representatives of social forces—even if the latter were in practice confined to the gentry. With this conclusion he abandoned his contemptuous attitude towards constitutionalism; in his 'Letters Without Addressee' (1862) he sided with the liberal gentry of Tver, who demanded a constitution for Russia.[137]

Tsarist censors, however, banned publication of the 'Letters' and Chernyshevsky, exiled to Siberia, could no longer influence the ideology of the Russian revolutionary movement. But he did not again change his views. His fellow-prisoners, according to one of them, the author of a memoir, were taken by surprise when they heard from him the following credo:

> You repeat that political freedom cannot feed a hungry man. But let us take, for example, the air, and let us ask: can it feed a man? Of course not. And yet, without food man can survive for a few days, whereas without air he cannot live more than ten minutes. As the air is necessary for the life of the human organism, so political freedom is necessary for the normal functioning of society.[138]

The evolution of Chernyshevsky's political views anticipated, as it were, the evolution of revolutionary Populism in the seventies.

In the broad sense of the term Chernyshevsky supported Populist theories though he was not primarily a Populist. In spite of his advocacy of non-capitalist development in Russia he saw himself as a Westernizer and insisted that the Westernization of Russia should be

---

[137] In fact the addressee of the 'Letters' was Alexander II whom Chernyshevsky wanted to persuade of the necessity of further reforms, both social and political. The *zemstvo* of Tver was to become a stronghold of the constitutional movement in Russia which culminated in the emergence of the constitutional Democratic Party (the Kadets). Seen in this perspective Chernyshevsky's support for the liberals of Tver acquires a symbolic meaning.

[138] Memoirs of S. Stakhevich, quoted in Iu. Steklov, *N. G. Chernyshevskii, ego zhizn' deiatel'nost'*, Moscow–Leningrad, 1928, vol. 1, pp. 448–9.

completed by the eradication of 'Asiatic conditions, the Asiatic social structure, and Asiatic habits'.[139]

Populism proper, on the other hand, saw capitalism as its primary target and stressed the dangers of the further Westernization of Russia, identifying it, as a rule, with that capitalist development whose cruelties were vividly described by Marx.[140] We may say, therefore, that the Populists in the narrower sense were also disciples of Chernyshevsky who, having perceived (with the help of Marx) the painful contradictions of capitalist development, lost their confidence in European progress, recognizing only the regressive aspects of capitalism, and combined their democratic opposition to everything feudal with the backward-looking ideals of peasant socialism.

The specifically Populist revolutionary movement emerged at the beginning of the 1870s. Its most peculiar feature was a deep prejudice against constitutionalism and liberal parliamentarianism, which were seen as mere instruments of bourgeois domination. In contradistinction to the first 'Land and Freedom' party (1861), whose aims were democratic rather than socialist, the revolutionaries of the seventies— the participators in the great 'Go to the People Movement' of 1873–4 and the members of the second 'Land and Freedom' party (1876)— thought it necessary to cut themselves off from bourgeois democracy to emphasize the socialist character of the movement and to ensure that it should not pave the way for capitalist development. This emphasis was made clear in their insistence on the priority of the 'social' revolution over a 'merely political' one—a theory which became the hallmark of classical revolutionary Populism. The 'political' revolution, that is the revolutionary transformation of the existing political structure, was conceived as merely a bourgeois revolution, with which true socialists should have nothing to do. In short, Russian revolutionaries, having realized that changes in the form of government could not solve the painful social problems, took care to ensure that they were not 'bourgeois revolutionaries', that *their* revolution, in contrast to Western political revolutions, would not further the interests of the bourgeoisie. Their preoccupation with the anti-bourgeois character of their movement became a real obsession. This accounts for the curious fact

[139] Chernyshevsky, *Izbrannye filosofskie sochineniia*, Leningrad, 1950–51, vol. 2, p. 668.

[140] For a discussion of the different meanings of the term Populism and for an analysis of Marx's impact on Populist thought see Walicki, *The Controversy Over Capitalism: Studies in the Social Philosophy of The Russian Populists*, Oxford, 1969, pp. 1–28, 59–63, 132–53.

that revolutionaries in Russia, a country which had suffered greatly from its autocratic political structure, became so intransigent and stubborn in their scorn of constitutional safeguards for human rights and the 'fraudulent' political freedom of the West.

It is undeniable that such a viewpoint was grateful to Russian national sentiment, greatly diminishing the Russian inferiority complex *vis-à-vis* the West, since the Western political systems no longer looked superior to the Russian autocracy. Even more: if social relations were all that really mattered, then Russia, with its village communes, seemed superior and better prepared for the advent of socialism than the Western countries with their capitalist economy and their legal systems sanctifying atomistic individualism and absolute private property. From this point of view Russian Populism can be seen as the left wing of Russian anti-Westernism. Its critique of the liberal idea of the rule of law, of bourgeois constitutions and the parliamentary system, echoed the views of conservative Russian thinkers.

A distinctively Populist component of this attitude to legal rights and political freedom was the peculiar masochistic psychology of the 'conscience-stricken gentry', who together with the *raznochintsy* played an important part in the Russian revolutionary movement. The rejection of political struggle meant for these young men an act of self-renunciation on behalf of the peasants, for whom political freedom and formal rights were completely abstract and worthless matters. This intense ethical spirit of self-sacrifice, together with an ardent belief in the great progressive mission of the intelligentsia in history, found expression in Petr Lavrov's *Historical Letters* (1869). This little book owed its enormous popularity among democratic youth mainly to one chapter, 'The Price of Progress'. The possibility of talking about progress, declared Lavrov, has been dearly bought by the human race. The personal development of some members of the privileged classes has been purchased with the blood and sweat of many generations of heavily exploited ordinary people. The 'conscious minority'—the intelligentsia—should never forget its debt and should make every effort to discharge it.

Another Populist thinker, Nikolai Mikhailovsky, has forcefully shown the direct connection between Lavrov's appeal for the discharge of the social debt and the view that economic and social aims should have absolute priority over individual and political freedom. He wrote:

Freedom is a wonderful and seductive thing, but we do not want freedom if, as has happened in Europe, it will only increase our age-old debt to the people.

By saying this I am giving expression to one of the most deep-seated and heartfelt sentiments of our time . . . European history and European science have convinced us with the utmost clarity that freedom as an absolute principle is a bad guide . . . We have become convinced that so-called full economic freedom in reality means nothing but unrestrained licence for the large economic forces and veritable slavery for the small forces. As for political freedom, we have discovered that it really is a sun, but only a sun, and although this may be of immense importance in the economy of the terrestrial world, it stands only for very little in the peculiar economy of human ideals. Political freedoms are incapable of changing the relationships between the existing forces within society.[141]

In Mikhailovsky's view, this rejection of freedom meant the victory of conscience (a sense of moral duty) over honour (a feeling for one's rights). He appealed to the intelligentsia's sense of social guilt and recommended self-effacement for the sake of the welfare of the people. He did so for moral reasons, with full awareness of how much was at stake:

For a man who has tasted the fruit of the general human tree of knowledge nothing is more attractive than political freedom, freedom of conscience, freedom of speech and freedom of the press, free exchange of ideas, free political meetings and so on. And, naturally, we want all this. But if the rights, which this freedom will give us, are to prolong our role as a coloured, fragrant flower—in that case we reject these rights and this freedom! Curse upon them, if they only increase our debt to the people, instead of enabling us to discharge it! . . . By giving the highest priority to *social* reform we renounce the increase of our rights and our freedom, since we see these rights as instruments for the exploitation of the people and the multiplication of our sins.[142]

The sad conviction that an increase of the political and civil rights of the intelligentsia could be achieved only at the expense of the people was derived, mostly, from Marxism: from Marx's description of the atrocities of primitive accumulation and from his theory of the close interconnection between political emancipation and capitalist develop-ment. Marx's *Capital* (vol. 1) had been widely known in Populist circles even before its Russian edition appeared (1872); almost all Populist thinkers, both revolutionaries and reformists, referred to Marx in their denunciations of liberal political economy and their unmasking of the nature of capitalist exploitation. True, Marx himself never neglected

---

[141] N. K. Mikhailovsky, *Sochineniia*, SPb, 1896, vol. 4, pp. 949–50. Quoted from Szamuely, *The Russian Tradition*, p. 174.
[142] N. K. Mikhailovsky, *Polnoe sobranie sochinenii*, vol. 1, SPb, 1911, pp. 870–2.

the political struggle, but the Russian Populists put their own interpretation on his words. Marx's thesis that the political superstructure always serves the interests of the ruling class, his angry tirades against bourgeois hypocrisy, his description of liberal freedom as 'the liberty of capital freely to oppress the workers'—all these could be interpreted as powerful arguments for the priority of social and economic over political change.

The most peculiar feature of Populist 'a-politicism' was their naïve belief that their own policy of indifference towards forms of government would somehow neutralize the tsarist government and prevent its active defence of the propertied classes. This, of course, proved to be an illusion and when they realized this, revolutionary Populists concluded that the cause of social revolution was inseparable from political struggle. But the latter, in turn, could be understood in many different ways. Its first form was revolutionary terrorism, as practised by the 'innovators' within the second 'Land and Freedom', who went on to found a new party under the name 'The Will of the People'. Terrorism, however, was only one choice among the possible methods of political struggle, and left open the problem of its aim. In the beginning it was conceived as a defensive measure, or as a means of exerting pressure on the government. 'The Will of the People' adopted a more ambitious political aim—the overthrow of the Tsarist government—but was not clear what should be done after achieving this end. Broadly speaking, there were two possible answers to this question: either to seize power and establish a long-term revolutionary dictatorship, or to seize power for a short time only, in order to pave the way for a constitutional system based upon the sovereignty of the people and guaranteeing full political freedom. Within 'The Will of the People' the first position was represented, though not consistently, by Lev Tikhomirov who was strongly influenced by the Blanquist (Jacobin) current of Russian revolutionary thought; the second position was that advocated by Andrej Zheliabov, for whom the movement's switch to political struggle meant a striving for alliance with all the social forces working for the overthrow or limitation of Russian absolutism, that is, primarily the liberals. Paradoxically enough, theoretical justification of this position was provided by Mikhailovsky in the series of 'Political Letters of a Socialist', published anonymously in the journal *Will of the People* (1879). He opposed the views which till recently he himself had preached, arguing that under Russian conditions political freedom might become a weapon of anti-bourgeois forces, since the Russian bourgeoisie was, happily, still too weak to impose its rule after the breakdown of the Russian autocracy.

The most consistent spokesman for the Jacobin current within Russian revolutionary Populism (broadly conceived) was Petr Tkachev. His revolutionary élitism was incompatible with the principle of action *through* the people and *among* the people which characterized the classical Populism of the seventies. He urged that the revolutionary movement should operate through a conspiracy of professional revolutionaries who would strive, first of all, for the seizure of political power. He saw the 'movements to the people' as only a tremendous waste of energy, setting against them the legacy of the revolutionary conspiracies of the first half of the century and recommending, above all, the tradition of Babeuf and Buonarroti. He was also deeply sceptical of the potential of revolutionary spontaneity. Even after the overthrow of the tsarist autocracy, he reasoned, the people alone would not be able to create a dynamic, progressive society; it would not even be able to remain true to its old communalist ideals and defend them against hostile social forces. The task of the revolutionary vanguard could not, therefore, be confined to crushing the tsarist regime; it must take over and strengthen the absolute power of the Russian State in order to make it a powerful instrument of revolutionary dictatorship capable of a thorough transformation of the whole of social life. The authority of the revolutionary party running the revolutionary state would replace, for the Russian people, the authority of its 'mythical tsar'. Needless to say, this dictatorial power would not be limited by any laws. It would follow the principles of justice defined as promoting the welfare of the people, but would not respect the people's will, since the people might be wrong in understanding what was good for them. It would reject the very notion of the inalienable rights of man, as a legal expression of the poisonous principle of individualism, and would be guided, instead, by the principle of anti-individualism, as formulated by Plato in his idealized image of ancient Sparta.[143]

The mainstream Populist thinkers, deeply attached, as they were, to Herzen's ideal of uniting peasant communalism with the 'principle of individuality', were horrified by these views. In spite of this, however, some of them, especially those who were associated with 'The Will of the People', were more and more inclined to think that it would be necessary to pass through a phase of revolutionary dictatorship.

---

[143] Cf. Tkachev's article 'Utopicheskoe gosudarstvo burzhuazii', 1869 in Tkachev, *Izbrannye sochineniia*, vol. 2, Moscow, 1932.

Petr Lavrov, whom Tkachev severely criticized for a lack of true revolutionary spirit, was among those Populists who remained opposed to revolutionary tyranny and tried to find an alternative solution. But it was typical of traditional Populist distrust of law that he sought in every way to avoid constitutional safeguards of liberty. He proposed, instead, to rely on the moral integrity of the members of the revolutionary government, on the one hand, and on the 'direct people's summary justice', on the other, even going so far as to suggest that this 'direct summary justice' might be modelled on the lynch law of the American Wild West. Lynch law, he argued, though repugnant to a capitalist society, would under socialism be fulfilling different functions, thus acquiring impeccable moral justification.[144]

Against this background it is clear that the constitutional tendency within 'The Will of the People' represented by Zheliabov was a very promising new development. It was, however, foolish to think that Russia's path to a constitutional order lay through the assassination of the tsar. The killing of Alexander II by a bomb thrown by a member of 'The Will of the People' produced a consolidation of autocracy and a considerable strengthening of reactionary forces. The Executive Committee of the party, or, rather, those members of it who had managed to escape arrest, sent the new tsar a letter in which they exhorted him to summon the representatives of all Russian people in order to rebuild the existing political system, thereby avoiding a bloody revolution in the future. This letter contained a solemn declaration that the revolutionary party would unconditionally submit to the decisions of a freely elected National Assembly. But it was unrealistic to think that Alexander III would accept conditions set by his father's assassins.

Despite many set-backs the Populist-inspired revolutionary movement was gradually overcoming its anti-legal prejudices. It is symbolic that Victor Chernov, the chief theorist of the neo-Populist movement and one of the main leaders of the Socialist Revolutionary party, had begun his revolutionary career in the party of the 'People's Right'—a party organized in 1893 by those who wanted to continue the tradition of 'The Will of the People' with emphasis on 'revolutionary constitutionalism'.[145] Equally significant is the fact that he became

[144] See Szamuely, *The Russian Tradition*, pp. 310–12.
[145] See A. Egorov (Martov), 'Zarozhdenie politicheskikh partii i ikh deiatel'nost'', in L. Martov, P. Maslov, and A. Potresov (eds.), *Obshchestvennoe dvizhenie v Rossii v nachale XX-go veka*, SPb, 1909, vol. 1, pp. 372–5 and F. Dan, *Proizkhozhdenie bolshevizma*, New York, 1946, pp. 298–300.

Chairman of the Constituent Assembly which met in Petrograd in January 1918 and was dispersed by the Bolsheviks for its adamant defence of constitutional principles.

Such a development was not possible in the case of another product of socialist thought in nineteenth-century Russia—that of revolutionary anarchism. For the Populists the chief enemy was capitalism; they attacked the existing state as supporting Russian capitalism, but also realized that the power of the state might be used to secure a non-capitalist way of development. (This might apply not only to the future revolutionary state but to the tsarist state as well.)[146] For the Anarchists the chief enemy was the state; capitalism, in their eyes, was a by-product of statism, and not vice versa. Their intransigent hostility towards the state was bound up with an equally strong hostility towards the law. They contrasted 'the "organic", communal quality of the people with the organized body politic of the nation';[147] law, in their view, was a phenomenon inseparable from the state and serving as a mere instrument of the state. Many Populists shared these views, but it was possible to be a Populist without stressing free communalism. In fact an increasing number of Populist thinkers, both revolutionists and reformists, postulated a radical increase of state interference in social and economic life, in the full awareness that it would entail a marked increase in the legal regulation of human relationships. To the Russian Anarchists such a development was, of course, completely unacceptable.

It should be stressed that hostility towards law *is not* something inherent in the very notion of anarchism. Anarchy means the rejection of the authority of man over man, but not necessarily the rejection of law. 'We should not be surprised to find an interesting strain of anarchist theory, perhaps best represented by Proudhon (and the utopian socialists who preceded him), able to support the Aristotelian model of political association'—an association based upon the profoundest *respect* for law.[148] Indeed, we read in Proudhon that anarchy is 'the absence of a master, of a sovereign', but not the absence of law.[149] On the contrary, Proudhon was fully aware of the value of law

---

[146] Cf. the discussion of the views of the so-called 'legal Populists' in Walicki *Controversy Over Capitalism*, pp. 107–31.

[147] E. Lampert, *Studies in Rebellion*, London, 1957, p. 142.

[148] Lisa Newton, 'The Profoundest Respect for Law: Mazor's Anarchy and the Political Association', in *Anarchism*. J. Roland Pennock and John W. Chapman (eds.), Nomos 19, New York, 1978, p. 164.

[149] P. J. Proudhon, *Qu'est-ce que la Propriété?*. Quoted from G. Woodcock, *The Anarchist Reader*, Glasgow, 1980, p. 67.

for human freedom. 'Law', he wrote, 'resulting from the knowledge of facts, and consequently based upon necessity, never clashes with independence . . . Liberty is infinite variety, because it respects all wills within the limits of the law.'[150]

Inevitably, such a view of law was incompatible with legal positivism, which derived all laws from the will of the sovereign. The difference between the Russian Anarchists and Proudhon can be explained, partially at least, by the fact that in nineteenth-century Russia legal positivism was the dominant legal theory while in France the notion of law was not necessarily associated with positive laws laid down by the state. It reflected the difference between a country accustomed to unlimited autocracy and one in which the will of the sovereign could be challenged in the name of law, in which the notion of law was still strongly associated with the tradition of Natural Law, both in its Catholic version and in the form of modern 'natural rights' theory.

The social theory of the greatest thinker of Russian Anarchism, Mikhail Bakunin, revolves around two oppositions: the opposition between society and the state, on the one hand, and the opposition between natural and man-made laws, on the other. He argued:

Society is the natural mode of existence of the human collective, and is independent of any contract. It is governed by customs and traditional usages and never by laws . . . There are many laws which govern society without the latter being aware of their presence, but these are natural laws, inherent in the social body, just as physical laws are inherent in material bodies . . . Those laws therefore should not be confounded with the political and juridical laws which, promulgated by some legislative power, are deemed to be, according to the social contract theory, logical deductions from the first compact knowingly formulated by men.[151]

This theory was grounded in a philosophical conception of freedom—a conception which emphatically rejected the notion of free will, *liberum arbitrium*, stressing that freedom was the opposite of external constraint, not of internal necessity. Man, Bakunin reasoned, was a product of nature and society; the natural/social laws to which he

[150] Ibid., p. 68. Another important theorist of anarchism who held such views was H. Read. 'Anarchism', he explains, 'means literally a society without an *arkhos*, that is to say without a ruler. It does not mean a society without law and therefore it does not mean a society without order. The anarchist accepts the social contract, but he interprets that contract in a particular way, which he believes to be the way most justified by reason'. (H. Read, *A Coat of Many Colours*, 1947, pp. 59–60.)

[151] *The Political Philosophy of Bakunin: Scientific Anarchism*. Compiled and edited by G. P. Maximoff, Glencoe, Ill., 1953, p. 166.

must submit were, therefore, the laws of his own being, against which it would be absurd to revolt. Freedom should be opposed not to determinism but to coercion and different forms of alienation, as represented by religion and the state. There is nothing humiliating in dependence on the laws of nature (or on social laws, as a special variety of the laws of nature); this cannot be called slavery, for 'there is no slavery without a master, a lawgiver who is external to the being to whom the commands are given'.[152] But it is deeply humiliating to be dependent on authority, whether human or divine. This is why the Church and the state are the greatest enemies of freedom. Every religion, and especially Christianity, implies the 'impoverishment, subjugation, and annihiliation of humanity in favour of divinity'.[153] The same is true of the state which is nothing less than organized coercion. There is no real difference between the absolutist and the liberal conceptions of the state: the first claims that the state is a divine creation, the second sees it as created by man's free and conscious will, but in both cases the state 'dominates society and tends to absorb it altogether.'[154]

On closer examination it turns out that Bakunin accepted the involuntary and inevitable obedience to all natural laws while rejecting all forms of dependence on the conscious will, since the very notion of being controlled by conscious will (as opposed to inner impulses, or internalized traditions of the collective) carried for him the connotation of external constraint, or unfreedom. Hence he was opposed to law not only as the commands of a political authority but also as the conscious contracts between independent individuals. In this respect he differed from Proudhon and was fully aware of it. 'How ridiculous', he wrote, 'are the ideas of the individualists of the Jean-Jacques Rousseau school and of the Proudhonian mutualists who conceive society as the result of the free contract absolutely independent of one another and entering into mutual relations only because of the convention drawn up among them.'[155]

There were two reasons for Bakunin's rejection of the contractual model of society. First, it assumed a pre-social state in which each individual had been an isolated, self-sufficient monad:

As if these men had dropped from the skies, bringing with them speech, will, original thought, and as if they were alien to anything on the earth, that is,

---

[152] M. Bakunin, *Izbrannye sochineniia*. Petrograd–Moscow, 1919–22, vol. 2, p. 164.   [153] Ibid., p. 159.   [154] Maximoff, *Scientific Anarchism*, p. 167.   [155] Ibid.

anything having social origin. Had society consisted of such absolutely independent individuals, there would have been no need, nor even the slightest possibility of them entering into an association; society itself would be non-existent, and those *free individuals*, not being able to live and function upon the earth, would have to wing their way back to their heavenly abode.[156]

But another reason is more important in the present context. For Bakunin the idea of individual freedom, freedom as independence *from society*, was inseparable from the acceptance of external constraints, since only such constraints, backed by sheer force, could curb individual licence. True freedom, for him, was spontaneity, fully compatible with the natural laws of collective life but not with man-made laws. From such a viewpoint the difference between laws as commands of the sovereign and laws as freely agreed contracts between independent individuals was of secondary importance.

The result of Bakunin's thinking about law was a consistent legal nihilism. He condemned all man-made laws—'authoritarian, arbitrary, political, religious, and civil laws which the privileged classes have created in the case of history.'[157] He described them as laws whose sole aim was to enable the exploitation of the masses, curbing the liberty of the masses; laws 'which under the pretext of a fictitious morality, have always been the source of the deepest immorality.' And he concluded:

Thus we have involuntary and inevitable obedience to all laws which constitute independently of all human will, the very life of Nature and society; but on the other hand, there should be independence (as nearly unconditional as it is possible to attain) on the part of everyone with respect to all claims to dictate to other people, with respect to all human wills (collective as well as individual) tending to impose not their natural influence but their law, their despotism.[158]

Another leading theorist of Russian and international anarchism, Prince Petr Kropotkin, was equally consistent in his rejection of law. In his article 'Law and Authority' (1886) he ridiculed 'the religion of law' and tried to persuade his readers that treating 'servility before the law' as a virtue was a telling testimony to the abnormal condition of society.[159] It was not true, he argued, that society could not exist otherwise than under the reign of law: 'Law is a product of modern times. For ages and ages mankind lived without any written law . . . During that period, human relations were simply regulated by

---

[156] Ibid.   [157] Ibid., p. 168.   [158] Ibid.
[159] *The Essential Kropotkin.* Emile Capouya and Keitha Tompkins (eds.), London, 1976, pp. 27–8.

customs, habits and usages, made sacred by constant repetition, and acquired by each person in childhood.'[160] These customs and usages were not established by law; they preceded all law. Customs are 'absolutely essential to the very being of society' but law is not;[161] on the contrary, law hinders the normal evolution of society since its distinctive trait is a tendency to immobility, 'a tendency to crystallize what should be modified and developed day by day.'[162] Like individual capital, which was born of fraud and violence, law has no title to the respect of men.[163]

In his views on the origins of law Kropotkin tried to represent the standpoint of scientific evolutionism and was careful enough to avoid the pitfalls of crude legal positivism. He wanted to show 'how law originated in established usage and custom, and how from the beginning it has represented a skilful mixture of social habits, necessary to the preservation of the human race, with other customs imposed by those who used popular superstition as well as the right of the strongest for their own advantage.'[164] Thus law has two faces, as it were: it is a compendium of customs useful for the preservation of society and, at the same time, a 'guarantee of the results of pillage, slavery and exploitation'.[165] During the growth of political organization the second face of law developed at the expense of the first. With the emergence of the modern codes of law, protecting private property and backed by the entire machinery of the modern state, law became 'nothing but an instrument for the maintenance of exploitation of the toiling masses by rich idlers'.[166] Because of this the imminent communist revolution should proclaim the slogan: 'No more laws! No more judges!'[167]

In his historical views Kropotkin was strongly inclined to idealize the primitive human communities, based, as he saw it, upon principles of mutual help and communal property. At this stage, he asserted, people 'have perfectly understood that the man who is called 'criminal' is simply unfortunate; that the remedy is not to flog him, to chain him, or to kill him on the scaffold or in prison, but to help him by the most brotherly care, by treatment based on equality, by the usages of life among honest men.'[168]

Kropotkin saw the development of history as a constant struggle between the communal spirit of free co-operation and the politico-

---

[160] Ibid., p. 31.   [161] Ibid., p. 34.   [162] Ibid., p. 30.
[163] Ibid., p. 34.   [164] Ibid.   [165] Ibid., p. 35.
[166] Ibid., p. 38.   [167] Ibid., p. 43.   [168] Ibid.

legal spirit of hierarchical subordination. The first was represented by
the rural communes and medieval towns, the second found expression
in the modern state, consciously based upon the model of ancient
Rome. The victory of absolutism in the sixteenth century meant the
invasion of free cities by 'new barbarians'—royal officials, prelates and
lawyers, all of them representing the Roman tradition. The bourgeois
revolutions against absolute monarchies did not change this trend, but
rather strengthened it by attacking what was left of the corporate spirit
of the Middle Ages. In the post-revolutionary period the *étatist* spirit
penetrated deeply into even those social and political movements that
questioned the existing system and were opposed to the class rule of
the bourgeoisie. The contemporary radical, Kropotkin declared, 'is a
centralizer, a state partisan, a Jacobin to the core, and the socialist
walks in his footsteps'.[169]

Despite this diagnosis Kropotkin was convinced that the natural
bent towards free co-operation and mutual aid had not died out in the
masses but was only buried deep in their unconscious. He hoped,
therefore, that the conflict between the two traditions—one Roman
and authoritarian, the other popular and free, had not been settled,
and that the Anarchists would be able to secure the victory of popular
freedom.

As I have written elsewhere,[170] Kropotkin's contraposition of two
traditions and two types of human relationships may be compared to
the two contrasting types of social bonds—'community' and 'society'—
posited by Ferdinand Tönnies, who was mentioned earlier in
connection with the Slavophiles. Tönnies, like Kropotkin, contrasted
organic communal bonds based on mutual co-operation (*Gemeinschaft*)
with bonds based on the assumption that society is an aggregate of
conflicting individuals whose relations must be regulated by law and
the State (*Gesellschaft*). Like Kropotkin, he regarded the rural
commune and medieval cities as examples of the former, organic type,
and Roman civilization and capitalism (based on competition, synony-
mous with conflict) as classic examples of the latter. This comparison
cannot, of course, be taken too far. Kropotkin, for instance, tried to
base his views on the natural sciences and, unlike Tönnies and the
Slavophiles, did not emphasize the role of religion in the formation of
communal bonds. In the present context, however, it is important to
stress that there was a significant similarity between the Slavophiles'

---

[169] P. Kropotkin, *The State, Its Historic Role*. London, 1943, p. 41.
[170] Cf. Walicki, *A History of Russian Thought*, p. 285.

and Kropotkin's views on law: both identified the ideal model of law with the '*Gesellschaft* paradigm of law', and both opposed legal relationships in the name of the moral bonds characteristic of a true community. This shows that in their attitudes towards law there was considerable and significant agreement between some left-wing and some right-wing Russian thinkers.

5 Fyodor Dostoevsky and Lev Tolstoy

Even a brief survey of the nineteenth-century Russian attitudes to law should not omit the greatest Russian writers—Fyodor Dostoevsky and Lev Tolstoy. Both of them also count as prophets of universal moral regeneration and are seen as great representatives of the 'Russian idea'. Both are known, too, for their negative attitude to the cold legalistic spirit of the West. The young Lukács reflected a widespread view when he described Dostoevsky as 'harbinger of the new man', as a thinker who defended the living soul and the authentic, brotherly community against alienation, against the tyranny of the 'objective spirit' embodied in law and the state.[171] Even more widespread, as well as more correct, is the view of Tolstoy as one of the greatest enemies of law in modern times. Indeed, his violent diatribes against law are unsurpassed in strength, although the intellectual content of his critique is not very subtle.

However, in spite of this broad common denominator, the differences between the two writers in their views on law are in fact very important, more important than the similarities.[172] Dostoevsky, in sharp contrast to Tolstoy, was neither an anarchist nor a pacifist: he wanted the Russian state to be as strong as possible, extolled 'national vigour',[173] ardently supported Russia's *Drang nach Osten*, praising the salutary moral influence of wars and stubbornly repeating that Constantinople must be Russian.[174] He did not believe in the abolition of law, describing this idea as completely utopian and commenting as follows: 'all the Utopias will come to pass only when we grow wings and all people are converted into angels'.[175] He strongly believed that crimes must be punished whereas Tolstoy preached that men have no

[171] See above, p. 11.
[172] For a presentation of other differences between the two writers see ch. 15 ('Two Prophetic Writers') of my *History of Russian Thought*.
[173] See F. M. Dostoevsky, *The Diary of a Writer*. Boris Brasol (trans.), London, 1949, p. 843.
[174] Ibid., pp. 554–6, 661–5, 902–8.   [175] Ibid., p. 870.

right to judge other men, that each crime is its own punishment while each punishment imposed by law is a crime.[176]

Lukács's view of Dostoevsky derived from Dostoevsky's Anti-Westernism, as expressed, for instance, in his *Winter Notes on Summer Impressions* (1864)—a report of his first journey to the West. In this impressive Slavophile critique of the West Dostoevsky takes as his target the famous slogan of the French revolution: *liberté, égalité, fraternité*. It is not surprising that he attacks primarily the juridicization of human relations, as implied in the notions of freedom under law and equality before the law. In an eloquent passage he writes:

What is *liberté*? Freedom. What freedom? Equal freedom for each and all to do as they please within the limits of the law. When may a man do all he pleases? When he has a million. Does freedom give each man a million? No. What is the man without a million? The man without a million is not one who does all that he pleases, but rather one with whom one does all that one pleases. And what follows from this? It follows that besides liberty there is still equality, or more precisely equality before the law. Only one thing can be said about this equality before the law: that as it is now put into practice, each Frenchman can, and ought to, consider it a personal insult.[177]

Equally sharp is his critique of the bourgeois conception of fraternity. The Westerners, he argues,

do not understand that it is impossible to obtain fraternity if it does not exist in reality . . . But in French nature, and in Occidental nature in general, it is not present; you find there instead a principle of individualism, a principle of isolation, of intense self-preservation, of personal gain, of self-determination of the I, of opposing this I to all nature and the rest of mankind as an independent autonomous principle entirely equal and equivalent to all that exists outside itself. Well, fraternity could scarcely arise from such an attitude. Why? Because in fraternity, in true brotherhood, it is not the separate personality, not the I, which should be concerned with its rights to equality and equilibrium with everything else, but rather this *everything else* which comes *of its own volition* to the individual who is demanding his rights, to that individual I, and of itself, without his asking, should recognize him as possessing the same value and the same rights as it does, i.e. as everything else on earth. And what is more, this demanding, rebellious individual ought first of all to offer

---

[176] A. A. Goldenweiser reminds us in this connection of the title of an essay on Tolstoy's *Resurrection*, written by his father A. S. Goldenweiser: 'Crime as Punishment, and Punishment as Crime'. Tolstoy had read and highly approved this essay. See A. A. Goldenweiser, *V zashchitu prava. Stat'i i rechi*. New York, 1952, p. 19.

[177] F. M. Dostoevsky, *Winter Notes on Summer Impressions*. Lee Renfield (trans.), New York, 1955, pp. 109–10.

the I, to offer himself entirely to society, not only without demanding any rights but, on the contrary, offering these up unconditionally to society.[178]

Against the bourgeois ideal of a society based upon the legally guaranteed rights of man and thereby sanctifying the principle of egoism, Dostoevsky set the ideal of the authentic fraternal community; a community in which the individual does not demand his rights but voluntarily submits himself to the collective, and the collective, for its part, does not demand great sacrifices but grants the individual freedom and safety, guaranteed by fraternal love. A community of this kind must 'happen of itself', it cannot be invented or made: 'If there is to be a foundation for brotherhood and love, there must be love. One must be drawn instinctively toward brotherhood, community, and harmony; one must be drawn despite the nation's age-long sufferings, despite the barbaric coarseness and ignorance rooted deeply in it, despite slavery since time immemorial, despite the invasions of foreigners.'[179]

It is clear that Dostoevsky attributed these characteristics to the long-suffering Russian nation. Although he probably arrived at his views independently of the Slavophiles, they bear a striking similarity to Slavophile ideas, especially to Khomiakov's conception of the 'free unity' of *sobornost'*.

To throw additional light on Lukács's view of Dostoevsky another similarity should be stressed, that between Dostoevsky's views, presented above, and Marx's condemnation of the rights of man. Like Dostoevsky, Marx saw these rights as 'the rights of egoistic man separated from his fellow men and from community',[180] as 'boundary markers which separate competing egoists'.[181] He shared with the Slavophiles and Dostoevsky the assumption that an authentic community can dispense with legal rights, that a system of rights to *guarantee* individual freedom is needed only in a seriously flawed society.[182] This assumption well illustrates the interesting similarities between the conservative and socialist critiques of law and rights in nineteenth-century social thought.[183]

Of course, the scope of this similarity is limited, as Dostoevsky's

---

[178] Ibid., pp. 110–11.   [179] Ibid., pp. 112–13.
[180] K. Marx, 'On the Jewish Question', in K. Marx, F. Engels, *Collected Works*, vol. 3, London, 1975, p. 164.
[181] A. E. Buchanan, *Marx and Justice: The Radical Critique of Liberalism*. London, 1982, p. 163.
[182] Ibid., pp. 51, 64.   [183] Cf. Walicki, *The Slavophile Controversy*, pp. 547–51.

case very clearly shows. The peculiarity of his attitude to law and rights, which distinguished him not only from the socialist critics of law but from the Slavophiles as well, consisted in a strange combination of a negative view of law as the determination of rights with a positive view of it as a system of commands to be obeyed or, to put it differently, as an instrument of social control enforced by the state. Because of this he was always inclined, both as publicist and as writer, to sympathize with investigating magistrates and public prosecutors while, at the same time, being deeply suspicious of barristers whom he accused of hypocrisy or, even, of simply lying for money.[184] He quoted with approval the popular saying 'Advocate means hired conscience', and commented: 'A lawyer is never able to act in accord with his conscience ... he is a man doomed to dishonesty'. 'The most important and most serious point in the whole matter' was for him the fact that 'this sad state of affairs has been, as it were, legalized by somebody and something, so that it is regarded not as a deviation at all but, on the contrary, as a most normal condition.'[185]

These words, from Dostoevsky's *Diary of a Writer* (1876), suggested that it might be desirable to abolish the institution of the Bar, an idea not entirely unfeasible since the Bar was introduced to Russia only in 1864. Dostoevsky did not, however, dare to say this openly. In the next entry in his *Diary* he hastened to modify his comments. But he persisted in claiming that the Bar is 'a sad institution'; an institution which might easily be used for 'distorting every sane feeling whenever occasion calls for such a distortion'.[186] In his novels he always suggested that the very existence of professional defenders implied moral cynicism, that barristers were in fact 'modern sophists' who relativized all moral principles and did so for money.

In his great novel *The Brothers Karamazov* Dostoevsky satirized Włodzimierz Spasowicz, the famous Russian lawyer of Polish descent, under the ridiculous-sounding name Fetyukovich. As an advocate of liberal, humanitarian views on the criminal law Spasowicz was so hateful to Dostoevsky that he did not hesitate to call him 'the corruptor of thought'.[187] He also described him in the pages of his *Diary*, in connection with the Kronenberg case—the father who had

---

[184] Dostoevsky, *The Diary of a Writer*, 1876, p. 215.
[185] Ibid.   [186] Ibid., p. 237.
[187] This is the title of ch. 13 of Book 12 of *The Brothers Karamazov* in Constance Garnett's translation. In Russian it sounds even stronger, closer to the 'fornicator of thought' (*preliubodei mysli*).

cruelly beaten his seven-year-old daughter but, thanks to Spasowicz, was acquitted by the jurors. Dostoevsky was particularly incensed by the fact that Spasowicz, in pleading for his client, had invoked the 'sanctity of the family', an idea particularly dear and sacred to Russian conservatives. Similarly, in *The Brothers Karamazov* he satirized Fetyukovich's attempts to appeal to Russia's 'glorious history' and to the specifically Russian sense of justice. Dostoevsky's notes highlight the reason for his anger: in his view Spasowicz, both as lawyer and as Pole, could not understand that, for Russians, something sacred could never be raised to the level of an abstract principle, or that the very habit of appealing to such principles was characteristic of the legalistic mentality of the West. Let me quote some excerpts:

> To Spasowicz. Sanctity of the family. We, thank God, are still Russians, and not French bourgeois who defend their family and property beyond anything you can imagine, simply because they are family and property and they comprise for them 'l'ordre'. No, we keep account for ourselves and even when it is 'necessary' we will act sooner by conscience than by necessity. Plenty, Mr. Spasowicz, plenty, come to your senses, what banknotes! . . . true, you are in that kind of position . . . The family. Raise these things to the level of principles abroad. But in Russia none of our sacred objects is afraid of being questioned openly, did you know that, Mr. Spasowicz. Well, now you know. We Russians are also proud of our unique characteristics. Our Orthodoxy will translate the Bible on its own. We do not have sacred objects *quand-même* . . . No, Mr. Spasowicz, don't introduce these rotten rules to us.[188]

It is true that Dostoevsky did not advocate cruel punishments; in particular, he never supported capital punishment.[189] On the other hand, he never ceased to stress that crimes must be followed by harsh punishments (such as imprisonment and penal servitude), that easy acquittals are irresponsible and immoral.[190] He strongly condemned the fashionable theory that 'crime is a pathological condition resulting from poverty and unhappy environment',[191] and he was furious when exponents of this theory alleged its affinity with the traditional Russian

---

[188] *The Unpublished Dostoevsky. Diaries and Notebooks (1861–81)*, Ann Arbor, 1973–6, vol. 2 (1975), pp. 136–40.

[189] Cf. 'Dostoevsky i problema nakazaniia', in Goldenweiser, *V zashchitu prava*, pp. 67–73.

[190] In Dostoevsky's view, severe punishments would be good for the criminals themselves. He wrote: 'I would not wish my words to sound cruel. Nevertheless, I shall venture to speak frankly. I will say plainly: by harsh punishment, by prison and penal servitude, perhaps, you would have saved half of them.' (*The Diary of a Writer*, p. 16).

[191] *The Diary of a Writer*, p. 337.

view that crime is a misfortune and criminals are sufferers.[192] In fact, he contended, the popular view and the 'doctrine of environment' were in sharp contrast, because the first stemmed from the Christian conviction that everybody was guilty while the second was based upon the assumption that most criminals were not guilty and consequently should not be punished. The doctrine of environmental influence, he argued, is incompatible with Christianity: 'Making man responsible, Christianity *eo ipso* also recognizes his freedom. However, making man dependent on any error in the social organization, the environmental doctrine reduces man to absolute impersonality, to a total emancipation from all moral duty, from all independence; reduces him to a state of the most miserable slavery that can be imagined.'[193]

His meaning here is splendidly illustrated in his 'Legend of the Grand Inquisitor', describing a social order which might be called 'benevolent totalitarianism'. Knowing that all men are weak, the Inquisitor, consciously acting against the spirit of Christ's teaching, relieves them of the burden of freedom, conscience, and personal responsibility; he replaces freedom by external authority, and the unity of free consent by a unity based upon compulsion. In this way the Church transformed into State unites all 'in one unanimous and harmonious ant heap'.

The idea of the Church transforming itself into an omnipotent state, giving bread to the people, indeed, but at the cost of depriving them of their inner freedom, was for Dostoevsky a danger peculiar to the West, inherent in its Roman heritage. Like the Slavophiles, he thought that Roman Catholicism and Western socialism were significantly related to each other, as two variants of 'unity without freedom'. Russia, in his view, represented a completely different world since the Russian Orthodox Church was not permeated by the pernicious influence of the juridical rationalism of ancient Rome.[194] Because of this, he argued, Russian autocracy should not be regarded as a menace to personal freedom. On the contrary:

Civil liberty may be established in Russia on an integral scale, more complete than anywhere in the world, whether in Europe or even in North America, and precisely on the same adamant foundation. It will be based not upon a written sheet of paper, but upon the children's affection for the Czar, as their father, since children may be permitted many a thing which is inconceivable in the case of contractual nations; they may be entrusted with much that has nowhere

---

[192] Ibid., pp. 13–15.
[193] Ibid., p. 13.   [194] Ibid., pp. 1004–6.

been encountered, since children will not betray their father, and, being children, they will lovingly accept from him any correction of their errors.'[195]

The introduction of the system by the juridical reform of 1864 was, for Dostoevsky, a good illustration of how freedom can flourish under autocracy. He stressed that his criticism of the new courts of law was not directed against the jury system: 'I am not attacking the institution; I have no idea of attacking it; it is a good institution, infinitely better than those courts in which public conscience did not participate.'[196] His sharp criticism of the reformed courts should be seen as criticism of barristers rather than jurors, as criticism of liberal-minded lawyers trying to use the institution of the jury for their own purposes. Above all, it was an attempt to interpret the jury in such a way as to prevent its development on the lines of the Western ideal of the 'rule of law'.

Like Dostoevsky, Tolstoy condemned the idea 'that personality has its inalienable rights'; he described it as an idea totally alien to the common people, invented by 'intellectual, pampered, idle persons' who had distorted their reason by thinking 'not merely of insignificant, trifling matters, but also of such as are improper for a man to think of'.[197] In all other respects, however, he differed radically from Dostoevsky. While Dostoevsky extolled military glory, 'national vigour', and an expansionist government policy Tolstoy, a radical Christian anarchist, proclaimed that the state was merely a system of organized violence, that the concept of a 'Christian state' was a contradiction in terms, that 'a Christian cannot be a military man, that is, a murderer',[198] and that all forms of patriotism, including that of subject nations, were instruments of oppression, leading to the renunciation of human dignity, reason, and conscience. While Dostoevsky advocated severe punishments, Tolstoy believed that a criminal ought to be answerable only to his own conscience, and that the very existence of law courts contradicted the Gospel warning, 'Judge not, that you may not be judged' (Matthew 7:1). The judge, sentencing people to death, was in his view much worse than the executioner. The executioner, he explained, is a hateful figure, he

---

[195] Ibid., pp. 1033–4.   [196] Ibid., p. 917.

[197] L. N. Tolstoy, *The Complete Works*, vol. 16 (*My Religion. On Life. Thoughts on God. On the Meaning of Life*), London, 1904, pp. 315–16. For a comparative study of Dostoevsky's and Tolstoy's views on law see B. Sapir, *Dostoewsky und Tolstoy über Probleme des Rechts*, Tübingen, 1932. For a discussion of the metaphysical impersonalism underlying Tolstoy's view of the inalienable rights of personality see Walicki, *History of Russian Thought*, pp. 332–5.

[198] Tolstoy, *Complete Works*, vol. 22, 1904, p. 526 ('On the Relation to the State').

knows that himself and feels guilty in the depths of his soul, while the judge responsible for the executions feels innocent and claims to be worthy of public respect.[199] The same is true of good and bad law courts: the former are in fact worse, because they can claim respect and, as a rule, succeed in getting it.[200]

Equally extreme were Tolstoy's views on law. Unlike Dostoevsky, he did not think that the idea of abolishing law was unrealizable on earth but saw it as part of Christ's teaching in the Sermon on the Mount, and thought that this teaching was in fact very practical, easy to implement. In his eyes law was merely a weapon of the state.[201] Its main function was simply to provide a crude justification for all those acts of brutal violence by which some people rule over and exploit others. Even if the law were truly impartial and dedicated to the common good (which, in practice, is never the case), it would still be utterly defective and detrimental to morality. The reason for this, Tolstoy argued, is very simple: even the most idealistic, the most noble interpretations of the essence of law are not free from the mortal sin of juridical thinking—the belief 'that there are relations in which men may be dealt with without love'. For a Christian, however, 'there are no such relations'.[202]

The best summary of Tolstoy's views on law is to be found in his 'Letter to a student concerning law' (1909). It was written as a reply to a letter by one of Petrażycki's students, I. Krutik, who was deeply impressed both by Petrażycki's legal philosophy and by Tolstoy's negation of law. Confused and hesitating, he wrote to Tolstoy, setting out Petrażycki's theory of law and asking what he thought of it. Tolstoy used this occasion to sum up his views on law and to persuade the young man that the so-called 'science of law' was nothing but intellectual rubbish serving very concrete and dirty interests. The crucial passage in Tolstoy's argument is worth quoting in its entirety:

Law? Natural law, state law, civil law, criminal law, catechetical law, law of war, international law, *das Recht, le Droit, pravo*. What does it mean, what is defined by this strange word? If we are thinking not in accordance with

---

[199] Cf. 'Tolstoy i nakazanie', in Goldenweiser, *V zashchitu prava*, p. 45.
[200] Ibid., p. 44.
[201] See Tolstoy, 'What I Believe' (1844), in Tolstoy, *Polnoe sobranie sochinenii*, 1st series, vol. 23, Moscow, 1957, pp. 328–34.
[202] Tolstoy, 'The Law of Violence and the Law of Love' (1909), quoted in G. Radbruch, 'Legal Philosophy', in *The Legal Philosophies of Lask, Radbruch and Dabin*, Cambridge, Mass., 1950, p. 80.

'science', i.e. not in terms of [Petrażycki's theory of] imperative-attributive experiences, but in accordance with universal common sense, then the answer to this question is very simple and clear: for those in power law means the authorization, which they have given themselves, to do everything which is advantageous to themselves while for those subject to them law means permission to do whatever is not forbidden to them. [For the rulers] state law is the right to deprive people of the fruits of their labour and to force them to commit murders which are called wars, while for those who are being deprived of the fruits of their labour and forced to wage wars law means the right to use those fruits of their labour which have not been taken away from them and to enjoy peace until they are forced to wage war. Civil law is the right of some to own land, even tens of thousands of *dèssiatinas*, as well as other means of production, while for those who are deprived of land and other means of production it is the right to sell (upon threat of dying of poverty and hunger) their labour and their lives to the owners of land and capital. Criminal law is the right of some to send others into penal servitude, to put them in prisons, or to hang them, while for those who are subject to penal servitude, imprisonment or execution it is only their right to avoid these things until those who are in power decide otherwise. The same is true of international law: it is the right of Poland, India, Bosnia and Herzegovina to enjoy independence from foreign rule but only until those people who have great armies at command decide otherwise. This is clear to everyone who thinks not in terms of imperative-attributive experiences but in accordance with general human common sense. For such a man it is clear that what is covered by the term 'law' is nothing but the most brutal justification for all acts of violence committed by the people in power.

But, the 'scholars' say, laws are determined by statutes [*zakony*]. By statutes? Yes, but these statutes are invented by the same people, by emperors, kings, royal advisers or members of parliament, that is by those who live by violence and, therefore, introduce statutes to protect their exercise of violence. The same people implement these statutes and continue to do so only as long as it is advantageous to them; when particular statutes cease to benefit them, they invent new ones, in accordance with their current needs.

You can see how simple it is: there are the oppressors and the oppressed, and the former want to justify themselves.[203]

The intellectual content of these strong words may be described as combining the view of law as commands by a sovereign authority (i.e. the command theory of law characteristic of, although not identical with, legal positivism)[204] and the anarchist-socialist critique of law.

---

[203] Tolstoy, *Polnoe sobranie sochinenii*, 1st series, vol. 38, Moscow, 1936, pp. 55–6.

[204] 'It is necessary to point out', writes Dennis Lloyd, 'that positivism [in legal philosophy] is by no means necessarily linked to the command theory of law, though the

Interestingly, Tolstoy refused to pay serious attention to Petrażycki's radical critique of all variants of legal positivism; he took for granted that all law is reducible to positive law and that positive law boils down in practice to rules formulated by those who are in power. He thus endorsed the command theory of law, carrying it to its logical conclusions and interpreting it in the light of the socialist critique of law as an instrument of oppression, and derived from this a powerful, although crude, justification of his consistent legal nihilism.

We can see from this how legal positivism, especially the command theory of law and also Ihering's 'jurisprudence of interests',[205] could be used to support negative attitudes to law. It was no accident that these attitudes flourished in Russia at the time when legal positivism enjoyed almost universal acceptance in all branches of jurisprudence. At the beginning of the nineteenth century, that is at the time when the classical liberal idea of law as controlling government was still alive and when the word 'law' was still associated rather with the limitation of power than with its manipulation, Russian writers were much less inclined to oppose or to challenge the 'spirit of law'. For the greatest Russian poet, Alexander Pushkin, the rule of law was the foundation both of the genuine social order and of individual freedom; in this respect he was close to Radishchev and very different from both Dostoevsky and Tolstoy.[206] His case provides additional proof of the inadequacy of sweeping generalizations about the eternal hostility between 'the Russian soul' and 'the spirit of law'.

6 *The problem of law in Russian Marxism: Plekhanov and Lenin*

Let us pass now to the Russian reception of Marxism, the most eventful chapter in the history of pre-revolutionary Russian thought. There is no need to discuss in this book all the complexities of this subject and all the different currents in Russian Marxism. The problems of law in pre-Soviet Marxist thought in Russia can be sufficiently highlighted by concentrating on two great figures: Georgy Plekhanov, 'the father of Russian Marxism', and Vladimir Lenin, the creator of the Soviet State.

---

combining of these by Austin has often mistakenly created this impression . . . We may, for instance, adhere to the basic tenet of positivism and still reject the command theory, as Kelsen does.' (Dennis Lloyd, *The Idea of Law*, Penguin Edition, 1981, p. 175.)

[205] See below, Ch. IV, 3.

[206] See 'Zakon i svoboda. Problema prava v mirovozzrenii Pushkina', in Goldenweiser, *V zashchitu prava*, pp. 95–113.

Bogdan Kistiakovsky saw early Russian Marxism as a theoretical support for a 'new wave of Westernism' and attributed to it the merit of beginning 'to refine somewhat the Russian intelligentsia's legal consciousness'.[207] He had in mind the view that Russia had to follow the countries of the West in passing through the capitalist phase of development—a view which was the main tenet of Plekhanov's Marxism, sharply distinguishing it from the populist tradition and placing it on the right-wing of the Russian revolutionary movement. For Plekhanov 'passing through the capitalist phase' included not only the maximum capitalist development of productive forces but also developing the proper 'superstructure' in the form of a constitutional and parliamentary state. Hence, turning from Populism to Marxism meant for him choosing 'the long and difficult capitalist way'.[208] The future socialist revolution, he reasoned, should be separated from political revolution (i.e. from the overthrow of tsarist absolutism) by a period of time long enough to enable the fullest capitalist development of the country and to educate the Russian proletariat in the school of political freedom, by means of legal activity in a law-observing parliamentary state. This period might be shorter than in the West because in Russia (owing to the influence of the West) the socialist movement was organized very early, when Russian capitalism was still in its initial stage. On the other hand, however, it should not be artificially shortened; it must follow the natural pattern of development, as exhibited by the history of the advanced countries of the West. In this sense Russian Marxism was indeed a new wave of Russian Occidentalism. This was made explicit by Plekhanov's words that the great mission of the Russian working class was to complete the Westernization of Russia, to finish the work of Peter the Great.[209]

For a long time Plekhanov's views on the necessary and desirable development of Russia for the 'orthodox' interpretation of Marxist theory in its application to Russian conditions. The further development of Russian Marxism consisted in different deviations and departures from this Plekhanovite 'orthodoxy'. The boldest departure was Trostky's conception of the permanent revolution—a conception which completely denied the necessity, and even the possibility, of separating the bourgeois revolution from the socialist one. Lenin was

---

[207] See *Landmarks* (n. 72 above), p. 123.

[208] G. V. Plekhanov, *Sochineniia*, 2nd edn., Moscow–Petrograd, 1923–27, vol. 2, p. 325.

[209] Ibid., vol. 3, p. 78.

initially reluctant to embrace it, among other reasons, because of his sensitivity to the demands of the Russian peasantry which caused him to emphasize the 'bourgeois' nature of the Russian revolution of 1905–6. But it cannot be denied that in 1917 he behaved in accordance with Trotsky's scenario.

From his interpretation of Marxism Plekhanov drew the conclusion that Russian socialists had to support the Russian liberals in their struggle for 'bourgeois freedom'. In defending this view he often referred to the *Manifesto of the Communist Party*. He was especially fond of quoting from it the sarcastic remarks about the German 'true socialists' who refused to support the German liberals in their fight for political freedom.[210] He levelled these remarks against populist 'apoliticism' and, later, against Lenin's intransigent anti-liberalism. The relevant quotation ran as follows:

> This German socialism, which took its schoolboy task too seriously and solemnly, and extolled its poor stock-in-trade in such mountebank fashion, meanwhile gradually lost its pedantic innocence.
>
> The fight of the German and, especially of the Prussian bourgeoisie, against feudal aristocracy and absolute monarchy, in other words, the liberal movement, became more earnest.
>
> By this, the long wished-for opportunity was offered to 'True' Socialism of confronting the political movement with the Socialist demands, of hurling the traditional anathemas against liberalism, against representative government, against bourgeois competition, bourgeois freedom of the press, bourgeois legislation, bourgeois liberty and equality, and of preaching to the masses that they had nothing to gain, and everything to lose, by this bourgeois movement. German Socialism forgot, in the nick of time, that the French criticism, whose silly echo it was, pre-supposed the existence of modern bourgeois society, with its corresponding economic conditions of existence, and the political constitution adapted thereto, the very things whose attainment was the object of the pending struggle in Germany.
>
> To the absolute governments, with their following of parsons, professors, country squires and officials, it served as a welcome scarecrow against the threatening bourgeoisie.
>
> It was a sweet finish after the bitter pills of flogging and bullets with which these same governments, just at that time, dosed the German working-class risings.[211]

Plekhanov did not intend (or, perhaps, did not dare) to accuse the

---

[210] Ibid., vol. 13, pp. 169–70 ('O nashei taktike po otnosheniiu k bor'be liberal'noi burzhuazii s tsarizmom').

[211] K. Marx and F. Engels, *Selected Works*, Moscow, 1977, vol. 1, pp. 131–2.

Bolsheviks of representing reactionary interests. But, like Lenin, he did so in respect of the Populists, whom he saw as representing ('objectively') the reactionary standpoint of the backward-looking small producers—the petty-bourgeoisie and peasantry. From this point of view the parallel between the 'true socialists' in Germany and the Populist socialists in Russia was complete, since, to quote Marx and Engels, ' "True" Socialism directly represented a reactionary interest', the interest of the German petty-bourgeoisie.[212]

Even more. Under Russian conditions, Plekhanov thought, the peasantry, with its communal ownership of land, was a pillar of Asiatic despotism, a class whose aspirations were reactionary in a deeper sense than the aspirations of the small producers in the West. The revolution of 1905 was, in his view, the joint work of two completely different forces: the 'Asiatic Russia' of the peasantry and the 'European Russia' of the industrial proletariat. The first force was essentially conservative, even in its violent revolutionary activities, while the second was revolutionary to the bone, even when refraining from revolutionary violence.[213] Owing to the peculiar dialectics of historical development the counter-revolutionary nobility, who had succeeded in restoring their political power, cut their own roots by legislating against the peasant commune and thereby undermined the very foundation of the 'old order' in Russia. The nobility wanted to kill the old agrarian tradition which provided the peasants with a ready-made justification for expropriating the big landowners. In fact, however, the destruction of communal ownership of land would strike the final blow to oriental despotism in Russia. 'It is doubtful', Plekhanov concluded, 'whether it will be in the interest of the nobility but it is quite certain that it will be in the interest of the proletariat . . . Anyway, this counter-revolutionary measure is a step towards the Europeanization of our socio-economic relationships, although the people have paid for it a higher price than would be the case in other political conditions'.[214]

Thus, paradoxically, 'the father of Russian Marxism' was able to see the progressive side of Stolypin's agrarian reform much more clearly than the mainstream Russian liberals, the leaders of the Kadet party, who treated Stolypin as merely a counter-revolutionary henchman and thought that political expediency demanded the wholesale condemnation of everything he did.[215]

Plekhanov's attitude towards Stolypin's reform perfectly harmonized

[212] Ibid., p. 132. [213] Plekhanov, *Sochineniia*, vol. 20, pp. 112–15.
[214] Ibid., pp. 126–7. [215] Cf. below, Ch. II, 3 and Ch. VI, 6.

with his critique of Lenin's ideas on the nationalization of land.[216] He proposed instead the municipalization of land or, if this proved impracticable, the division of land among individual peasants. In Russian conditions, he argued, the nationalization of land would strengthen both the 'Asiatic' mentality of the masses, seeing themselves as slaves of the state, and the despotic psychology of the rulers, seeing themselves as owners of the country. In an article of 1906 be summed up his position as follows:

A division of land among the peasants unquestionably would have many inconveniences from our point of view. But as compared with nationalization it would have the enormous superiority of striking the definite blow at the old order under which both the land and the tiller of land were the property of the state, and which was nothing else but a Muscovite edition of the economic order lying at the base of all the great Oriental despotisms. But nationalization of land would be an attempt to restore in our country that order which first received some serious blows in the eighteenth century and has been quite powerfully shaken by the course of economic development in the second half of the nineteenth century'.[217]

As we see, Plekhanov was indeed strongly committed to Westernism. He radically cut himself off from the Populist tradition of condemning 'bourgeois freedom' and summoned the Russian socialists to ally themselves with the Russian liberals in the struggle for constitutional order and parliamentary government. His attitude to Stolypin's agrarian reform also reveals his understanding, quite unusual for a Russian intellectual of his time, of the political progressiveness of consistently 'bourgeois' changes in the sphere of civil law, his ability to avoid the common error of reducing all political problems to the single question: who wields political power?

Yet, it would be a great mistake to conclude from this that Plekhanov's Westernism implied a real understanding of the intrinsic value of law or a genuine commitment to the rule of law. True, his Westernism was an integral part of his Marxism because he interpreted Marxism as a theory of history which made Western-type capitalist development a necessary precondition of socialism. But his acknowledgement of the necessity and progressiveness of capitalist development did not entail endorsement of the 'juridical world-view' of the bourgeoisie. On the contrary: Marxism, as Plekhanov saw it, was the culmination of the nineteenth-century reaction against the

[216] See S. H. Baron, *Plekhanov, the Father of Russian Marxism*, London, 1963, p. 305.
[217] Plekhanov, *Sochineniia*, vol. 15, p. 31, as quoted in Baron, *Plekhanov*, p. 305.

'abstract rationalism' of the Enlightenment, with its belief in natural rights and rational legislation. It was the scientific form of dialectical historicism, equally merciless in unmasking the class content of bourgeois illusions and in demonstrating the ahistorical and unscientific character of socialist utopias. As such, it could not lead to a genuine vindication of the autonomous value of law. Neither could it provide a theoretical justification for treating the rule of law as irreducible to the class rule of the bourgeoisie.

Like other Marxist theorists of the Second International Plekhanov was strongly inclined to interpret Marxism in the spirit of the positivist evolutionism of his days.[218] He was also strongly influenced by Hegel from whom he took the idea of a 'rational necessity' governing the development of history.[219] A similar mixture of naturalistic evolutionism and Hegelianism was to be found in Engels who, we should remember, was at that time considered 'a philosopher of even greater importance than Marx'.[220] It is no wonder therefore that Plekhanov's views on law were entirely dependent on Engels to whom law was essentially an instrument of class domination. We may say that, like Engels, he in fact endorsed the dominant theory of legal positivism or, to be more precise, the command theory of law, differing from its non-Marxist representatives in emphasizing the class content of legislation and the administration of justice. Obviously, this was not a good position for combating Kropotkin's view that law was 'nothing but an instrument for the maintenance of exploitation of the toiling masses by rich idlers'. And indeed, this view of law is not criticized in Plekhanov's influential brochure on anarchism. Instead, he criticizes the Anarchists as '*decadent* Utopians',[221] defining a Utopian as '*one who, starting from an abstract principle, seeks for a perfect social organization*',[222] and claiming that International Social Democracy, in contrast to Utopianism, is based not upon any abstract principle but 'upon a scientifically

[218] For a presentation of Plekhanov's philosophy see Walicki, *History of Russian Thought*, pp. 413–27.

[219] Hence he was greatly impressed by Belinsky's 'reconciliation with reality'. On his interpretation the period of reconciliation was the most fruitful of Belinsky's entire intellectual development. In his rejection of the abstract ideal Belinsky was a precursor of the Russian Marxists, whose rejection of the Populist ideal of a direct transition to socialism was also a kind of 'reconciliation with reality'. See ibid., pp. 417–20.

[220] See *A Dictionary of Marxist Thought*, T. Bottomore (ed.), Oxford, 1983, p. 151 ('Engels').

[221] G. Plechanoff, *Anarchism and Socialism*, Eleanor Marx Aveling (trans.), London, 1895, p. 82.

[222] Ibid., p. 4 (italics mine).

demonstrable economic necessity'.[223] He accused the Anarchists of many other things, such as · a propensity to violence, excessive individualism and even immoralism,[224] but paid little attention to their views on law. He seemed to be unaware of the difference between Bakunin and Kropotkin, who rejected all laws, and Proudhon, who saw law as 'the expression of the sovereignty of the people' and believed that 'the Contract solves all problems'.[225] Characteristically, he devoted much space to criticizing Proudhon's positive view of law while passing over in silence Bakunin's and Kropotkin's legal nihilism. His general definition of anarchism explains this emphasis: Proudhon's positive view of law was for Plekhanov clear proof of the utopian nature of anarchist thought, of its utopian belief in a perfect legislation,[226] while the view of law as an instrument of class rule, held by the Russian Anarchists, was in his eyes a realistic, Marxist-inspired element in anarchist doctrine.

With such views on law it was logical to see state power as standing above the law; that is, as a dictatorship. 'In politics', Plekhanov argued, 'he who holds state power is the dictator'.[227] He added, of course, that all forms of state power should be explained in terms of the dictatorship of a given class, defining such dictatorship as 'the domination of that class which enables it to use the organized force of society in defence of its interests and for the suppression of all social movements which directly or indirectly endanger these interests'.[228] He stressed that the bourgeois revolution would have been impossible without establishing dictatorship of the bourgeoisie and that, likewise, the social emancipation of the workers was impossible without proletarian dictatorship.[229] Thus, he fully shared Engels's and Lenin's view that law is merely an instrument of political power and that all forms of political power are class-bound and dictatorial in nature. The differences dividing him from Lenin lay elsewhere. First was his belief in the necessity of a neat separation in time between the bourgeois and the socialist revolutions in Russia (as in all other backward countries). Second was his conviction that the best form of dictatorship of the proletariat is a democratic republic. In this respect he emphatically agreed with Engels.[230] What he would have thought of the communist

[223] Ibid., pp. 12–13.
[224] Ibid., pp. 92–3 and *Sochineniia*, vol. 4, pp. 249–57 ('Sila i nasilie').
[225] *Anarchism and Socialism*, pp. 40–3.   [226] Ibid., p. 1.
[227] See *Leninskii sbornik*, vol. 2, Moscow–Leningrad, 1924, pp. 60, 95.
[228] Plekhanov, *Sochineniia*, vol. 11, p. 319.
[229] Ibid., vol. 12, pp. 226–7.   [230] Ibid., p. 239.

dictatorship in the USSR (had he lived long enough to see it) can be easily deduced from his general view on the results of the premature seizure of power by a socialist party. He had already expressed this view in his first Marxist work, *Socialism and the Political Struggle* (1883), pointing out that a seizure of power by revolutionary socialists in a backward country would bring about a historical disaster. Authentic socialism, he argued, can only be established when economic development and proletarian class consciousness have attained a sufficiently high level. Political authorities trying to organize socialist production from above in an underdeveloped country would have 'to seek salvation in the ideals of "patriarchal and authoritarian commun-ism", only modifying those ideals so that national production is managed not by the Peruvian "sons of the sun" and their officials but by a socialist caste'. 'There is no doubt', Plekhanov added, 'that under such a guardianship the people, far from being educated for socialism, would even lose all capacity for further progress or would retain that capacity only thanks to the appearance of the very economic inequality which it would be the revolutionary government's immediate aim to abolish.'[231]

It is worth noting that Plekhanov never abandoned these views. He was not exaggerating when he wrote a quarter of a century later that on tactical issues his standpoint had not changed in any important particular, and that in the controversies between Bolsheviks and Mensheviks he remained firmly committed to the ideas worked out by him in the early 1880s.[232] His favourite idea of a rational historical necessity was directed against two opposing tendencies within the Russian working-class movement: the 'economist' tendency (which he saw as yet another version of the old 'apolitical' Populism) and the 'Blanquist' (or 'Jacobin') tendency, which exaggerated the 'subjective factor' in history and showed a dangerous inclination towards revolutionary voluntarism. Of course, he accused the Bolsheviks of being heirs to this latter tendency.

Plekhanov's critique of both 'economism' (and other forms of reliance on the spontaneity of the masses) and 'Blanquism' might appear, on the whole, quite reasonable and convincing. But one must not overlook the danger inherent in his own position. He assumed that

---

[231] G. Plekhanov, *Selected Philosophical Works*, vol. 1, Moscow, 1977, p. 99 ('Socialism and Political Struggle').

[232] Plekhanov, *Sochineniia*, vol. 19, p. 283.

his interpretation of Marxism provided the only correct knowledge of the necessary laws of history and that the possessors of such knowledge had a right, even a duty, to ignore the opinions of the ignorant majority; that they ought to shape reality in accordance with their 'scientific theory' of what was to be done, disregarding all moral scruples and other 'bourgeois prejudices' because the legitimation of their deeds derived from their correct understanding of history, and not from the legally expressed popular will. This aspect of Plekhanov's thought came out with drastic clearness in a conversation between the old Engels and the Russian social-democratic writer Alexei M. Woden, as recorded by the latter. Let us quote from Woden's notes:

Engels asked what Plekhanov's personal position was with regard to the dictatorship of the proletariat. I had to admit that Plekhanov had frequently said to me that, when 'we' were in power, 'we' would naturally allow freedom to none but 'ourselves' . . . But, in order to give the Russian Social Democrats some reason for striving for power, it would in his (Plekhanov's) opinion be extremely desirable for the Russian Social Democrats to make use of the experience of their German comrades. In answer to my question as to who should logically be recognized as the monopolists of liberty, Plekhanov replied: the working classes, under the leadership of comrades who had properly understood Marx's teaching and had drawn from it the correct conclusions. When I asked whether there was an objective criterion for the proper understanding of Marx's teaching and for the correct conclusions to be drawn from it, Plekhanov confined himself to the comment that all this was 'sufficiently clearly' set out in his (Plekhanov's) works.[233]

The exactness of this report cannot be guaranteed but it is undeniable that it fits very well the peculiar quality of Plekhanov's mentality—the arrogant self-confidence of a possessor of the 'only correct knowledge' of the objective laws of history.

To legitimize one's political position by referring to a mandate derived from the faultless understanding of historical necessity could not be combined with a genuine commitment to the rule of law or popular sovereignty. Plekhanov made this explicit in his famous 'Jacobin speech' at the Second Congress of the Russian Social Democrats (August 1903).

Every given democratic principle, he said, should be examined not on its own

[233] M. Rubel (ed.), 'Gespräche über Russland mit Friedrich Engels. Nach Aufzeichnungen von Alexei M. Woden', in *Internationale wissenschaftliche Korrespondenz*, Berlin, April 1971, pp. 22–3.

merits in the abstract, but in its bearing on what may be called the basic principle of democracy, namely, on the principle that says: *salus populi suprema lex*. Translated into the language of the revolutionary this means that the success of the revolution is the highest law. If it were necessary for the success of the revolution to restrict the effect of one or another democratic principle, it would be criminal to stop at such a restriction. As my own personal opinion I would say that even the principle of universal suffrage should be regarded from the point of view of this basic principle of democracy I have just mentioned. Hypothetically it is conceivable that we, Social Democrats, may have occasion to come out against universal suffrage . . . The revolutionary proletariat could restrict the political rights of the upper classes the way these classes once restricted the political rights of the proletariat. The fitness of such a measure could only be judged by the rule: *salus revolutionis suprema lex*. The same point of view should be adopted by us on the question of the duration of parliaments. If, on an impulse of revolutionary enthusiasm, the people were to elect a very good parliament, a sort of Chambre Introuvable, we should try and make it a long parliament; and if the elections turned out to be unfavourable, *we should try and dismiss it not in two years' time, but if possible in two weeks*.[234]

No wonder that Lenin thought it convenient to recall these words in January 1918, in connection with Plekhanov's objections against the Bolshevik terror. On the eve of the dispersal of the freely elected Constituent Assembly he reprinted the quoted passage in full, commenting that it 'might have been written specially for the present day'.[235]

Plekhanov's last article was an attempt to disclaim responsibility for having laid an ideological foundation for the Bolshevik terror and the dispersal of the Constituent Assembly. But his arguments had nothing to do with the defence of law and political democracy as a principle. On the contrary, he based his reasoning on his favourite conception of historical necessity, claiming simply that under Russian conditions the Constituent Assembly was a progressive force and that the time was not ripe for replacing it by a dictatorship of the proletariat. He did not deny that the Assembly stood for 'bourgeois' democracy nor did he forget that, for Marxists, bourgeois democracy meant capitalism, that is, a new form of the enslavement of the working classes, but he countered this by pointing out that even ancient slavery was historically justified since, as Engels put it, 'without ancient slavery modern

---

[234] Plekhanov, *Sochineniia*, vol. 12, pp. 418–19. English translation in Lenin, 'Plekhanov on terror', *Collected Works*, vol. 42, London, 1969, pp. 47–8.

[235] Lenin, *Collected Works*, vol. 42, p. 47.

socialism would have been impossible'.[236] The rejection of historical necessity in the name of an 'abstract ideal' was characteristic of Russian Populism, as opposed to Marxism, and he therefore concluded that the Bolsheviks should be seen not as his (Plekhanov's) children but rather as half-brothers of Victor Chernov, the Chairman of the dispersed Assembly.[237]

True, Plekhanov must have realized that Russian workers might not sympathize with the Constituent Assembly merely on the grounds of its alleged historical necessity. He therefore added a phrase saying that the members of the Assembly stood firmly 'for the interests of the toiling people of Russia'.[238] But the real thrust of his argument lay in defending bourgeois democracy as a necessary stage of progress, as something good from the point of view of the ideal norm of the rational development of history, and not as an expression of the class interests of the workers.

Indeed, Plekhanov's tragedy was that of a Russian Westernizer who wished for his country a 'normal', 'European' development, following a rational sequence of phases and always perfectly in tune with 'inner', economic and cultural growth. On the one hand, his Marxism assumed that it was necessary to develop the class antagonism between proletariat and bourgeoisie; on the other hand, it proclaimed the need to educate Russian workers in the spirit of 'scientific socialism', to prepare them to accept, for a generation or two, the rule of their class enemy. The psychological impossibility of an equal commitment to each of these two aims should have been obvious but, amazingly, Plekhanov fully realized it only in the last days of his life, when he was tormented by the question: 'Did we not begin the propaganda of Marxism too early in backward, semi-Asiatic Russia?'[239] He died in the painful consciousness that his life-long activity had helped to produce results other than those he had anticipated; in other words, that he had been deceived by his idol, History.

The difference between Plekhanov and Lenin was considerable from the very beginning, although for some time neither man was fully conscious of its root. Briefly, it was the difference between Marxism interpreted as technological determinism, seeing history as an

---

[236] Plekhanov, *God na rodine*, vol. 2, Paris, 1921, p. 260 (for the quotation from Engels see Engels, *Anti-Dühring: Herr Eugen Dühring's Revolution in Science*, Moscow, 1954, pp. 250–1).

[237] Ibid., p. 268.

[238] Ibid., pp. 265–6. [239] Quoted from Baron, *Plekhanov*, p. 358.

objective process, independent of the human will, determined by the development of productive forces (Plekhanov's case), and Marxism interpreted as a theory of class struggle, seeing history as a battlefield and explaining it in terms of struggle, stressing the nature and intensity of fundamental class antagonisms, the strength and militancy of the organized proletarian vanguard and the nature and respective strengths of other class forces (Lenin's case). It is obvious that the second of these interpretations involved more consideration for 'subjective factors' and less reliance on 'objective' impersonal historical processes. Already in his early works on Populism Lenin had rejected not only Populist 'subjectivism' but also the 'objectivism' that in those years seemed to be an intrinsic part of historical materialism. 'When demonstrating the necessity for a given series of facts', he argued, 'the objectivist always runs the risk of becoming an apologist of these facts' while the materialist 'discloses the class contradictions and in so doing defines his standpoint'.[240] Objectivism gives a survey of the process as a whole, presenting it as an 'objective course of events', while materialism obliges its protagonist to stand up simply and openly for the standpoint of a definite social class. These sharply critical remarks were directed against Peter Struve and other 'legal Marxists' but they applied also to Plekhanov's variety of 'objectivism'.

Equally important was the difference between Plekhanov and Lenin in the controversy over capitalism. Plekhanov saw capitalism as Russia's future while Lenin saw it as Russia's present, as something which had not only gained a foothold in Russia but was already 'definitely and irrevocably established'.[241] Plekhanov maintained that capitalism in Russia had irrevocably entered its initial stage but stressed the necessity of further capitalist development, defining the full development of capitalism in terms of productivity and seeing it as necessarily bound up with a 'properly capitalist superstructure', that is, with a constitutional and republican form of state. Lenin agreed with Engels that a democratic republic was 'the best political shell for capitalism'[242] but did not conclude from this that fully-fledged capitalism was impossible under autocracy; neither did he define the level of capitalist growth in terms of the development of productive forces. He emphasized the question of the prevailing *relations* of

---

[240] Lenin, *Collected Works*, vol. 1, p. 401.
[241] Ibid., p. 495. See also J. Frankel (ed.), *Vladimir Akimov on the Dilemmas of Russian Marxism, 1895–1903*, Cambridge, 1969.
[242] Lenin, *Selected Works*, Moscow, 1977, vol. 2, p. 247.

production and the nature of the fundamental class contradiction. By the total and irrevocable establishment of capitalism he meant the establishment of commodity production based on the exploitation of hired labour, a point of view which enabled him to see Russia as a backward but yet fully capitalist country. In other words, he defined capitalism in terms of class struggle and thus made its fate depend on the intensity of this struggle, on the will and consciousness of the working class and on the able leadership of its vanguard. Accordingly, for him 'passing through the capitalist stage' did not inevitably involve the highest possible development of capitalist production.[243]

An analysis of the different phases of Lenin's thought is, clearly, beyond the scope of this book. Let us discuss instead his views on law and the state, compared with those of Plekhanov. A good starting point for such a discussion is provided by Lenin's definition of the dictatorship of the proletariat: 'Dictatorship is rule based directly upon force and unrestricted by any laws. The revolutionary dictatorship of the proletariat is rule won and maintained by the use of violence by the proletariat against the bourgeoisie, rule that is *unrestricted by any laws*'.[244]

To understand all the implictions of this definition it is necessary to put it into a wider context. Like Plekhanov, Lenin saw law as merely an instrument of the state, namely, as an instrument of class rule. In his famous pamphlet *The State and Revolution*, written on the eve of the Bolshevik seizure of power, he developed a consistent theory of the state—a theory which claimed to add nothing new to Marx's and Engels's views on the state but which was in fact sufficiently original to be seen as distinctively Leninist. Its relative novelty consisted in a complete disregard of law, in a tendency to reduce state power to its repressive function and to stress that this function is, as a rule, exercised directly, without the mediation of law.

'According to Marx', Lenin argues, 'the state is an organ of class *rule*, an organ for the *oppression* of one class by another'. Its power, as Engels put it, consists mainly 'of special bodies of armed men having prisons, etc. at their command'; in other words, 'a standing army and police are the chief instruments of state power'.[245] If so, every state is

---

[243] For a fuller discussion of Lenin's early works within the Populist–Marxist controversy see Walicki, *Controversy over Capitalism*, pp. 176–9 and *History of Russian Thought*, pp. 440–8.
[244] Lenin, *Selected Works*, vol. 3, p. 23 (italics mine).
[245] Ibid., vol. 2, pp. 242–3.

based ultimately upon naked force. It was no accident that law was not even mentioned in this context. The main thrust of Lenin's theory of the state was directed against the view of law as an important, indispensable element in the state or, at least, in modern statehood. Unlike Plekhanov, he was not content to assert that state power stands above the law and that every law is *in fact* a command of those in power, but wanted to add that the holders of political power could easily dispense with law, that there is no inherent necessity to give their commands legal form. The state, as the organized power of a given class, was for him, essentially, not a legal structure but, rather, a phenomenon similar to the army. The same was true, in his view, of the revolutionary party; it could not be otherwise since he saw class struggle as a kind of warfare and deeply admired the military form of organization. He accused Western socialists of being 'degraded and stultified by bourgeois legality', contrasting Social-Democratic organiz-ations with his cherished vision of 'organizations of *another* kind', consciously modelled on the army.[246] Let me quote:

Take the army of today. It is a good example of organization. This organization is good only because it is *flexible* and is able at the same time to give millions of people *a single will* . . . When, in the pursuit of a single aim and animated by a single will, millions alter the forms of their communication and their behaviour, change the place and the mode of their activities, change their tools and weapons in accordance with the changing conditions and the requirements of the struggle—all this is genuine organization.[247]

From the point of view of such an ideal legal forms were, of course, not flexible enough, not able to direct the collective will, creating unnecessary obstacles to its direct expression and obscuring the common aim. It followed from this that a truly revolutionary class struggle demanded an organization based upon the principle of direct command, animated by a single will and using all possible means for the attainment of its aim, that is for 'the total defeat, the elimination, the extermination of the enemy'.[248] This was the ideal which Lenin tried to have embodied in his party and later, in the revolutionary Soviet state.

As might be expected, Lenin was delighted by Marx's and Engels's critique of 'bourgeois freedom' and did everything possible to push it to extremes. He stressed that under capitalism universal suffrage was

[246] Lenin, *Collected Works*, vol. 21, p. 252. [247] Ibid., p. 253.
[248] Cf. Alain Besançon, *The Intellectual Origins of Leninism*, Oxford, 1981, p. 221.

not capable of revealing the will of the majority of the working people and thus deserved to be called an instrument of bourgeois rule.[249] He was fond of referring to Marx's phrase about 'deciding once in three or six years which member of the ruling class was to misrepresent the people in parliament', taking them out of their specific context and, in fact, falsifying this quotation by attributing to Marx much stronger words: 'To decide once every few years which member of the ruling class is *to repress and crush the people through parliament*—this is the real essence of bourgeois parliamentarianism, not only in parliamentary-constitutional monarchies, but also in the most democratic republics'.[250] This definition amounted to taking an essentialist position on the issue of parliamentarianism, that is to assuming that the parliamentary form of the modern state was inseparable from its bourgeois content and that parliamentary institutions were by their very essence a form of bourgeois dictatorship.[251] To support this claim Lenin referred to Engels's view that every state is a 'special force' of oppression and to Marx's criticism of the notion of a 'free state' as presented in his *Critique of the Gotha Programme*, but his logic clearly betrayed him. First, the view that every state is an apparatus of oppression was not the same as seeing every state as an instrument of the propertied class— the very notion of the dictatorship of the proletariat contradicted such a conclusion. Second, Marx's criticism of the idea of a 'free state' was based not on the assumption that the very existence of the state excluded freedom but on the view that 'freedom consists in converting the state from an organ superimposed upon society into one completely subordinate to it' and that 'the forms of state are more or less free to the extent that they restrict the "freedom of the state" '.[252] Consequently, Marx wanted to say that the 'freedom of the state' in fact means the absolute power of the state and that such a freedom should be restricted for the sake of more freedom for society. He made it explicit that from this point of view a democratic republic was greatly preferable to a monarchy. He criticized the German workers' party for the illusion that its democratic programme could be realized within 'the present-day national state', that is, within the 'Prusso-German

---

[249] Lenin, *Selected Works*, vol. 2, p. 247.
[250] Ibid., p. 270 (italics mine). Cf. K. Marx, F. Engels, *Selected Works*, vol. 2, p. 221.
[251] Barry Hindness writes in this connection of 'the essentialism of Lenin's analysis of democratic forms' and 'Lenin's essentialist rejection of parliamentary institutions'. See B. Hindness, 'Marxism and Parliamentary Democracy', in *Marxism and Democracy*, Alan Hunt (ed.), London, 1980, pp. 34–5.
[252] K. Marx and F. Engels, *Selected Works*, vol. 3, p. 25.

Empire', but did not imply that even in a democratic republic parliamentary institutions could serve only the interests of the bourgeoisie.[253]

True, Lenin's attitude towards 'bourgeois political freedom' was not entirely negative. He remembered that recognition of the relative value of political freedom was a characteristic of early Russian Marxism, sharply distinguishing it from the Populist tradition; he was also aware that the nihilist attitude to political freedom involved a danger of coming too close to the position of the reactionary Black Hundreds. Hence his view of political freedom was not wholly consistent. Many good analyses of his contradictory views on this matter are to be found in the book by Marcel Liebman, an author very sympathetic to Leninism. Liebman concludes:

Lenin has no difficulty in exposing the formalism of political freedoms, of their *de facto* concentration in the hands of the bourgeoisie. But the biting accuracy of his criticism does not alter the fact that there is a contradiction in his analysis. On the one hand Lenin said that 'the most democratic bourgeois republic is no more than a machine for the suppression of the working class by the bourgeoisie, for the suppression of the working people by a handful of capitalists'; that 'freedom in the bourgeois democratic republic was actually freedom *for the rich* . . . In fact, the working masses were, as a general rule, unable to enjoy democracy under capitalism'. And he concluded in his writings on *The Revolution and the Renegade Kautsky*, that bourgeois democracy is 'democracy for the rich and a swindle for the poor', 'a paradise for the rich and a snare and a deception for the exploited, the poor'. At the same time, Lenin considered that 'it is incumbent on us to make use of the forms of bourgeois democracy', adding that 'We ought not in any way to give the impression that we attach absolutely no value to bourgeois parliamentary institutions. They are a huge advance on what preceded them'. On this point Lenin never made himself clear: how could the revolutionary workers' movement hope to use to its own advantage a regime in which the freedoms provided were 'only for the rich'?[258]

Nevertheless, the contradictions in Lenin's views are not as deep as Liebman seems to think. Broadly speaking, Lenin did not deny the possibility of using 'bourgeois parliamentary institutions' against the bourgeoisie (which distinguished him from the 'Leftists') while at the same time denying their *inherent* value for the workers, in which he sharply differed from Plekhanov. The 'father of Russian Marxism'

[253] Ibid., pp. 26–7.
[254] M. Liebman, *Leninism under Lenin*, London, 1975, p. 428.

played at the beginning with the idea of a 'direct popular legislation' but this concession to participatory democracy,[255] as he himself later explained, was for him only a minor point. He changed his views on this matter under the influence of Kautsky's work *Der Parlamentarismus, die Volksgesetzgebung und die Sozialdemokratie* (1893)[256] and thereafter firmly defended parliamentary democracy, seeing it as the best political school for the working class, a school in which Russian workers were to 'Europeanize' themselves and learn to distinguish between force and violence (a distinction obliterated by the anarchists), to wage their class struggle in a civilized way, within the framework of 'those juridical institutions which constitute the natural, legal complement of the capitalist development of production'.[257] We may say therefore that Plekhanov, in spite of some obviously cynical elements in his class theory of law and the state, attributed a certain inherent value to the role of 'bourgeois freedom' in the historical education of the working class, while Lenin saw its value as purely instrumental and laid stress on the educative influence of all forms of capitalist class struggle, without paying special attention to its legal forms, let alone attributing to them any particularly positive significance. Both men ignored the problems of legal theory (which they saw as a kind of bourgeois scholasticism) but yet differed markedly from each other in their attitude towards law. Plekhanov understood the cultural value of thinking in terms of the general rules provided by law (although he stressed that the formality of such rules suits the interests of the bourgeoisie) while Lenin thought only in directly utilitarian terms—in terms of class aims, to be realized irrespective of means, through the resolute and violent struggle. Plekhanov's Marxism was a part of the general historicist reaction against the 'juridical world-view'; he saw this world-view as a classical example of the utopian belief in an 'abstract ideal' but, nevertheless, treated it seriously, as an expression of the genuine aspirations, or honest illusions, of the progressive bourgeoisie, and as an important dialectical phase in the unfolding of Historical Reason. To Lenin any belief in universal legal justice was simply absurd. He was deeply convinced that intelligent human beings could not honestly dispute the view that law, by its very nature, serves the interests of the stronger; therefore, he was inclined to treat the

---

[255] See 'Programme of the Social-Democratic Emancipation of Labour Group', in Plekhanov, *Selected Philosophical Works*, vol. 1, p. 360.
[256] Plekhanov, *Sochineniia*, vol. 12, p. 215.
[257] See *Leninskii sbornik*, vol. 2, p. 18.

lofty image of law as merely a contemptible expression of cowardly bourgeois hypocrisy. This explains why he 'always showed a certain tenderness for Anarchists',[258] criticizing them severely but, unlike Plekhanov, treating them seriously, as brave and honest in their convictions, devoid of the cowardly spirit of bourgeois liberalism.

In 1917 Lenin and Plekhanov found themselves on opposite sides of the barricade. Plekhanov, whom Lenin was by then calling 'the ill-famed renegade from Marxism'[259] saw the tragedy of the revolution in the inability of the Russian socialists to ally themselves firmly with the liberals. He criticized the Mensheviks, whom he treated as 'half-Leninists', for the inconsistency of their views on the revolution and their task in it: in accordance with their theoretical credo, they stressed its bourgeois character while rejecting alliance with the liberals, let alone liberal leadership, as if a bourgeois revolution could be carried on without bourgeois parties, as if capitalism were possible without capitalists.[260] He accused Kerensky's government of lack of energy in combating the 'waves of anarchy',[261] even the Kadet party was in his eyes too soft on the radical left, permeated with 'Zimmerwald-Kienthal spirit' and not resolute enough in defence of the fatherland.[262] Lenin's 'April Theses' were for him the ravings of a madman.[263] His position was so adamant and well known that shortly after Lenin's seizure of power he was invited to occupy a ministerial post in a counter-revolutionary coalition. He rejected the offer but this gesture reflected only his personal tragedy: 'I have given forty years to the proletariat, and I will not shoot it down when it is going along the wrong way'.[264] In the depth of his heart he was convinced that the Bolshevik revolution was a historical catastrophe.

Lenin's position in 1917, before his seizure of power, may be described as a flirtation with the idea of direct democracy, as expressed in the Soviets. He stressed that a socialist revolution was impossible without a certain reversion to 'primitive democracy',[265] that its final aim

---

[258] See Liebman, *Leninism under Lenin*, pp. 261–2.
[259] Lenin, *Selected Works*, vol. 2, p. 263.
[260] Plekhanov, *God na rodine*, vol. 1, p. 233.   [261] Ibid., vol. 2, p. 198.
[262] Ibid., p. 193.   [263] Ibid., vol. 1, p. 21.
[264] Quoted from Baron, *Plekhanov*, p. 259. According to R. M. Plekhanova General Krasnov asked Plekhanov to become Premier. A few months earlier, before the Bolshevik revolution, General Kornilov had wanted to appoint Plekhanov to a ministerial post in the Cabinet with which he proposed to replace the Kerensky government (see Baron, *Plekhanov*, p. 351).
[265] Lenin, *Selected Works*, vol. 2, p. 269.

coincided with the anarchist ideal of a stateless society, and that his disagreement with the Anarchists concerned only the *means* of struggle ('We do not at all differ with the anarchists on the question of the abolition of the state as the *aim* ').[266] He harshly condemned 'the venal and rotten parliamentarianism of bourgeois society institutions', setting against it his vision of a 'democracy without parliamentarianism',[267] whose institutions would combine executive and legislative functions. He saw it as dictatorship of the proletariat and, at the same time, as 'a state so constituted that it begins to wither away immediately';[268] a state whose functions 'can be reduced to such exceedingly simple operations of registration, filing and checking that can be easily performed by every literate person';[269] a state in which all officials are elected and subject to recall at any time, and in which there is no place for 'special bodies of armed men', since all power is placed in the hands of 'the armed vanguard of all the exploited and working people'.[270]

It would be too easy to dismiss these declarations of intent as merely *mala fide* tactical manœuvres. But the fact remains: as soon as Lenin became aware that direct democracy did not work, that workers control brought chaos and inefficiency, he drastically changed his course. He proclaimed not only the necessity of terror against counter-revolutionary elements but also the necessity for coercion in industry, claiming that there was 'absolutely *no* contradiction in principle between Soviet (*that is*, socialist) democracy and the exercise of dictatorial powers by individuals'.[271] He argued that

Dictatorship presupposes a revolutionary government that is really firm and ruthless in crushing both exploiter and hooligans [i.e. undisciplined workers A.W.], and our government is too mild. Obedience, and unquestioning obedience at that, during work, to the one-man decisions of Soviet directors, the dictators elected or appointed by Soviet institutions, vested in dictatorial powers (as is demanded, for example, by the railway decree), is far, very far from being guaranteed as yet . . . The proletariat must concentrate all its class consciousness on the task of combating this petty-bourgeois anarchy.[272]

In this way the former apologist of a direct participatory democracy became an ardent advocate of 'iron discipline' and 'the exercise of dictatorial powers by individuals'. It is not surprising that he supported

---

[266] Ibid., p. 281.   [267] Ibid., p. 272.   [268] Ibid., p. 254.
[269] Ibid., p. 269.   [270] Ibid., p. 273.
[271] Ibid., p. 610 ('The Immediate Tasks of the Soviet Government').
[272] Ibid., p. 622.

Trotsky's demand for the 'militarization of labour'.[273] The fact that this demand was almost unanimously rejected proves only that Lenin's evolution in this direction was too rapid to be immediately accepted and that some elements of democracy had not yet been eliminated from the Bolshevik party.

The idea of direct popular democracy in the administration of justice shared the same fate. Lenin's seizure of power was followed by the Decree of 7 December 1917, which abolished 'all existing general legal institutions' and instituted popular courts with elected judges. These new courts were to act in accordance with the dictates of 'revolutionary consciousness', or the 'class consciousness of the working people', which meant, among other things, taking into account the class background of the offender and the class character of the offence ('was it or was it not committed with a view to restoring the oppressor class to power?').[274] Very soon, however, it turned out that the socialist character of the improvised courts could not be guaranteed, that their verdicts were very different from the expectations of the party leadership. Very often popular judges were too indulgent; in other cases they were barbarically severe but, at the same time, far removed from the socialist hierarchy of values. (Thus, for instance, in the rural areas 'the death penalty was invoked for mere cases of theft and sometimes carried out on the spot').[275] In view of this, their subsequent development was easily predictable: 'popular courts' gave way to a highly repressive centralized system of the administration of justice; a directly politicized system subordinated to the commands of the party leadership.[276] There was, however, a common platform uniting the theorists of this system with the theorists of a decentralized 'popular justice': both emphatically rejected the independence of the judiciary and both stressed that the classical bourgeois notions of law, let alone the rule of law, were not applicable to Soviet conditions.

Thus, the difference between Plekhanov and Lenin in their attitudes towards law and the state may be defined as the difference between the view that law is an instrument of class dictatorship (dictatorship in the sense of social domination) and the view that class

[273] See I. Deutscher, *The Prophet Armed*, London, 1954, p. 493 and Liebman, *Leninism under Lenin*, p. 326.

[274] See Liebman, *Leninism under Lenin*, p. 326.   [275] Ibid.

[276] E. Pashukanis, the chief Soviet legal theorist of that time, commented: 'For us revolutionary legality is a problem which is 99 per cent political.' See E. Pashukanis, *Selected Writings on Marxism and Law*, Pierce Beirne and Robert Sharlet (eds.), London, 1980, p. 29.

dictatorship can and should be *unlimited by law*; between the view of the state as an apparatus of oppression and the view that the necessity for proletarian statehood justifies *the complete elimination* of freedom (since, after all, 'so long as the state exists there is no freedom. Where there is freedom, there will be no state').[277] Plekhanov did not succeed in overcoming the Russian tradition of legal nihilism but at least moved in this direction; Lenin went far in the opposite direction, returning to the revolutionary tradition of Russian legal nihilism, both in its anarchist and in its Jacobin (Tkachevian) varieties.[278] We can understand why, to Plekhanov, the victory of Leninism was the victory of Bakunin and Nechaev, the victory of Asian over Western Russia.[279] We may prefer to use other words, but we must agree that this victory was a terrible blow to legal culture in Russia.

Of course, this conclusion makes sense only if we assume that a legal culture did exist in pre-revolutionary Russia. True, there are many authors, Szamuely for example, who have tried to prove that it was not so, that legal culture in the Western sense had always been alien to the Russians. But it seems much more just to point out that after the reform of 1864 legal culture in Russia, in spite of many setbacks, was on the increase and that, in some respects at least, its advances were truly impressive. Goldenweiser wrote about it as follows:

The first [new] courts were opened in Petersburg in 1866, and in December 1917 the People's Commissar of Justice signed the Decree closing all judiciary institutions and abolishing the Bar. How much has been done in this short time! The collection of decisions of the Civil Court of Appeal of the Senate can favourably withstand comparison with collections of decisions of the high courts in France, Germany, Britain or America. And our Bar, in the persons of its best representatives, was certainly no worse if no better, than the Bar in any of the Western countries.[280]

A similar judgement occurs in the memoirs of Wacław Lednicki, son of Aleksander Lednicki, a famous Russian lawyer (of Polish background) and a prominent member of the Kadet party. At the end

---

[277] Lenin, *Selected Works*, vol. 2, p. 308.

[278] Cf. Alfred L. Weeks, 'Peter Tkachev: the Forerunner of Lenin', in *Lenin and Leninism: State, Law and Society*, B. W. Eissenstat (ed.), Lexington, Mass., 1971.

[279] Cf. Plekhanov, *God na rodine*, vol. 2, p. 267. Plekhanov called the peasant uprisings, which paved the way for the victory of Bolshevism, 'barbarian reaction against the reforms of Peter the Great' (ibid., p. 209).

[280] Goldenweiser, *V zashchitu prava*, pp. 211–12.

of the nineteenth and at the beginning of the twentieth century Russia was

> a law-abiding state—in spite of the frequent misdemeanours of its bureaucracy, the abuses of power by this or that imperial government, and the misdeeds of some of its lower or higher officials. Its courts represented high standards of honesty and justice and they were independent.
>
> While criticism of the Russian autocratic system as such is well-founded yet obedience to law did exist there, and not only in theory; it had become an efficient and effective factor in Russian life.[281]

This is, perhaps, a somewhat over-idealized picture, but it cannot be denied that the foundations of legal culture in Russia had been laid, although not yet firmly secured. Even in the last decades of its existence imperial Russia was far from being a 'rule of law state'. Nevertheless, it was moving in this direction.

It is not my aim to present and analyse this historical process. This book deals with intellectual history and, therefore, discusses only intellectual achievements. But since intellectual history is a part of general history it is justifiable to claim that a knowledge of Russia's achievements in the philosophy of law may provide additional arguments in the dispute over whether Russia possessed a legal culture or not.

As I have tried to show, the mainstream intellectual tradition of nineteenth-century Russia reflected strong doubts about the Western 'spirit of law', doubts which often hardened into resentment and conscious resistance. Many Russian thinkers, including Lenin, were not able to understand freedom under the law; they defined freedom in anarchist terms and so were often caught in Lenin's dilemma: either freedom, or the state. Bakunin opted for freedom, Lenin for the state, but in both cases the alternatives were the same: either anarchism or authoritarianism, with liberal solutions dismissed as merely slavery in disguise. It is possible to explain this without resorting to the concept of an eternal 'Russian soul' but it is still broadly true that the development of Russian thinking about law lagged behind the development of Russian judicial institutions and hampered their educative influence upon Russian society. On the whole, the role of ideas, even the most radical ones, was strangely conservative in this respect.

Nevertheless, this is only a part of the truth. Russian intellectual

---

[281] W. Lednicki, *Pamiętniki*, London, 1963, vol. 1, p. 309.

history provides evidence that this state of affairs was also changing in a commendable way. The six thinkers discussed below bear testimony to the fact that the dominant Russian tradition of censure of law was opposed by an increasingly strong strain of thought, extolling law and stressing the need to transform Russia into a rule-of-law state. The strength of this movement cannot be measured by the number of its followers but, rather, by the level of its intellectual achievements. As we shall see, this level was very high—too high, perhaps, to be easily understood by and popularized among the general public, including the people who called themselves liberals. In other words, it was a movement confined to a rather narrow intellectual élite but yet one whose very existence was historically significant. It seems justified to say that the high level of its intellectual achievements would not have been possible without considerable advances in the general level of legal culture in the Russian Empire.

II

Boris Chicherin: the 'Old Liberal' Philosophy of Law

1 Introductory remarks

BORIS Chicherin (1828–1904) occupies a very unusual place in Russian intellectual history. There is little doubt that he was 'one of the most outstanding intellects of the Russian nineteenth century'.[1] Vladimir Soloviev paid homage to him as 'the most universal and the most knowledgeable among contemporary Russian and, perhaps, among contemporary European scholars as well';[2] this high estimate, it must be added, did not stem from a spiritual affinity—the reverse, rather, was true. The two thinkers sharply criticized each other and the quoted words were in fact a prelude to Soloviev's energetic, almost brutal reply to Chicherin's criticism of his views on law and morality. Soviet scholars, too, treat Chicherin with great respect, emphasizing his intellectual calibre and personal integrity, while at the same time regarding him as a staunch class enemy of progressive forces. The Soviet editors of his memoirs called him 'the most remarkable Russian liberal',[3] one of the most outstanding representatives of political thought on the European scale, a man whose scholarly output was 'something absolutely exceptional' in the Russian social sciences of his time.[4] The same view has been voiced by such *emigré* Russian scholars as the well-known historian of Russian liberalism, V. Leontovich, who

---

[1] L. Schapiro, *Rationalism and Nationalism in Russian Nineteenth-Century Political Thought*, New Haven and London 1967, pp. 89–90.

[2] V. S. Soloviev, *Sobranie sochinenii*. Phototype edition. Brussels 1966, vol. 8, p. 671.

[3] V. Nevskii, 'Reaktsionnaia sushchnost' liberala', preface to B. N. Chicherin, *Vospominaniia: zemstvo i moskovskaia duma*, Moscow, 1934 (republished Cambridge, 1973), p. 16 (hereafter referred to as *Vospominaniia* 4).

[4] S. Bakhrushin, Preface to B. N. Chicherin, *Vospominaniia. Moskovskii Universitet*, Moscow, 1929 (republished Cambridge, 1973), p. 6 (hereafter referred to as Vospominaniia 3).

A similar appraisal of Chicherin as a scholar is to be found in V. D. Zor'kin, *Iz istorii burzhuazno-liberal'noi politicheskoi mysli Rossii vtoroi polviny XIX—nachala XXV (B. N. Chicherin)*, Moscow, 1975, p. 14.

hailed Chicherin as 'the greatest theoretician of Russian liberalism'.[5]

Nevertheless, it is almost always stressed that Chicherin was an isolated thinker, a 'solitary figure' whose ideas have not exerted any real influence.[6] The most extreme judgement is Nicolai Berdyaev's. In his *Russian Idea* he mentions Chicherin as *the only* philosopher of Russian liberalism and accusingly describes him as a thinker completely alien to everything Russian: 'In Chicherin there can be studied a spirit which was opposed to the Russian Idea, as it was expressed in the prevailing tendencies of Russian thought in the nineteenth century.'[7] Such a view of Chicherin was quite natural in the case of a philosopher whose intellectual development was so heavily influenced by Slavophile-inspired romantic anti-legalism. Indeed, Berdyaev's attitude towards classical liberalism and its idea of law was always, as he himself confessed, one of outraged hostility; to oppose 'formal law' in the name of 'freedom of spirit' was for him a moral duty.[8]

Chicherin's isolation was equally insisted upon by Prince E. Trubetskoi, a moderate liberal who, unlike Berdyaev, saw this fact as tragic and regrettable. Chicherin's life was in his eyes 'the story of a man who was ill-suited to Russia and was thrown overboard by life, because he was too crystal-clear, too granite-firm, too whole-hearted'.[9] He was equally alien to all currents in Russian philosophical and political thought. Being a Hegelian in the second half of the nineteenth century condemned him to be seen as 'a man from another planet'. He despised positivism as a testimony of philosophical ignorance, but, at the same time, sharply distanced himself from the anti-positivist crusade of Soloviev, whom he accused of undisciplined mysticism, leading to the annihilation of science. He was opposed in principle to the reactionary politics of Alexander III, but was adamant in his

---

[5] V. Leontovich, *Geschichte des Liberalismus in Russland*, Frankfurt am Main, 1957, p. 129. See also S. V. Utechin, *Russian Political Thought: A Concise History*. London, 1963, p. 105.

[6] Being 'solitary' (in the sense of having no followers) does not exclude being 'typical' (in the sense of holding views which are typical for a certain group). This has been properly understood by G. Fischer who called Chicherin a 'solitary figure' but, none the less, saw him as a typical gentry liberal, 'akin to the *Rechtsstaat* liberals of Bismarck Germany'. (G. Fischer, *Russian Liberalism: From Gentry to Intelligentsia*, Cambridge, Mass. 1958, p. 19.)

[7] N. Berdyaev, *The Russian Idea*, London, 1947, pp. 144–5.

[8] See N. Berdyaev, *Samopoznanie: opyt filosofskoi avtobiografii*, Paris, 1949, p. 103.

[9] E. Trubetskoi, *Vospominaniia*, Sofia, 1921 (reprinted Newtonville, Mass. 1976), p. 125.

condemnation of the radical movements, which he held responsible for destroying the chances of liberalism and for paving the way for the victory of reaction. He was relatively isolated even among people who called themselves liberals: in his view they were making too many concessions to populism or state socialism, while in their view he was too doctrinaire and unrealistically inflexible. He wanted a 'pure' liberalism, 'liberalism without any amalgams', and such a liberalism did not exist in Russia.[10]

A similar explanation of Chicherin's isolation, although in the context of quite a different evaluation of his thought, was given by Peter Struve. His article on Chicherin was written in 1897, at the time when he was still a 'legal Marxist'. He classified Chicherin as an 'uncontaminated liberal', or a 'liberal of the bourgeois-doctrinaire type', and argued that such a position could satisfy no one in a society in the early stages of capitalist modernization.[11] It was quite normal that the German liberalism of the 1840s should have a distinctively 'social' tinge; it was equally normal and understandable that nineteenth-century Russian liberalism should be permeated by some elements of populism, as in the case of Kavelin. Chicherin, exceptionally, never made a single concession to populism, but neither could he claim to be ahead of his times, since he stubbornly clung to the obsolete economic liberalism of the Manchester school. At the end of the nineteenth century much of his writing resembled a kind of 'literary fossil'.[12]

However, a few years later Struve's view of Chicherin changed radically. Having abandoned 'legal Marxism' he became, first, a 'liberal on the Left' and, later, a 'liberal on the Right'.[13] In this last stage he defined himself as a 'liberal-conservative', a political philosophy he saw as best exemplified in the thought and activities of Chicherin.[14] The same view was expressed by V. Maklakov, the leader of the right wing of the Kadet party, who deeply regretted that

[10] Ibid., p. 120.
[11] P. Struve, 'G. Chicherin i ego obrashchenie k proshlomu', in P. Struve, *Na raznye temy*, SPb 1902, p. 94.
[12] Ibid., pp. 94–5.
[13] See the two books by R. Pipes: *Struve, Liberal on the Left, 1870–1905* (Cambridge, Mass. 1970) and *Struve, Liberal on the Right, 1905–1944* (Cambridge, Mass. 1980).
[14] See Pipes, *Struve, Liberal on the Right*, pp. 375–6. As other representatives of conservative liberalism in Russia Struve named N. Karamzin, I. Turgenev, D. Shipov, and P. Stolypin. This association was not very convincing: Shipov, for instance, had little in common with Stolypin and his views on law were diametrically opposed to Chicherin's.

Chicherin had never influenced the mainstream of the Russian liberal movement.[15]

To complicate the picture further it should be stressed that, unlike Struve, Chicherin's views evolved from a right-wing position to one more on the left. In his brochure *Russia on the Eve of the Twentieth Century* (published anonymously in Berlin in 1900) he argued forcefully that the only solution of Russia's problems would be 'a change from absolute to constitutional monarchy'. This programme, although still quite moderate, was welcomed by Plekhanov as supporting his views on the possibility and desirability of an alliance between Russian Marxists and Russian liberals in the common struggle for political freedom. It is interesting to note that in his long review of Chicherin's brochure (whose authorship, of course, was no secret to him) Plekhanov did not stress Chicherin's isolation, but rather treated him as a representative figure.[16] The abstract character of Chicherin's thought, his somewhat doctrinaire emphasis on principles, typified the mentality of those Russian liberals of gentle birth whom Russian writers, notably Turgenev, represented as 'superfluous men'. They felt themselves to be superfluous and alienated, and were seen by others as 'foreigners in their own country', because they lacked a social base for the realization of their ideals. Thus, Chicherin as an individual was not atypical because alienation, together with the resulting impracticality of thought, was in fact characteristic of all liberal Westernizers in Russia. Plekhanov felt that the social alienation and consequent helplessness of this group would disappear with the success of the Russian workers' movement. In a review of another political brochure of Chicherin's he concluded: 'A serious liberal movement can emerge in our country only as a result of the workers' movement. This is one of the most interesting peculiarities of our society.'[17]

A certain qualified sympathy for Chicherin was quite natural to Plekhanov. As the most consistent and doctrinaire Westernizer among the Russian Marxists, he was bound to feel a certain sympathy for the most consistent and doctrinaire Westernizer in the liberal camp. This feeling was given a rational colour by his theory of stages and his view

---

[15] See V. Maklakov, 'Iz proshlogo', *Sovremennye zapiski*, vol. 40, Paris, 1929, pp. 308–10.
[16] G. V. Plekhanov, *Sochineniia*. D. Riasanov (ed.), 2nd edn., vol. 12, Moscow (n.d.), pp. 183–5.
[17] Ibid., p. 187.

of the necessity for an alliance between Russian liberals and Marxists. It could, however, not be reciprocated. In Chicherin's eyes socialism as such, incuding its Marxist variety, was not a harbinger of a further stage in the development of Western civilization but a dangerous symptom of its illness and decay.

In the context of this book Chicherin's importance in Russian intellectual history is clearly very great. His writings prove that classical liberalism, in spite of its social weakness, was represented in the history of Russian thought and that it achieved a high degree of sophistication and self-awareness.[18] In the heyday of Russian 'legal nihilism' he was ably and energetically defending the '*Gesellschaft*-paradigm' of law. His ideas were diametrically opposed to all variants of 'legal nihilism' and for this reason his importance in the controversy over law in Russian intellectual history can hardly be exaggerated.

2 Biographical note

The decisive influence on Chicherin's intellectual development was undoubtedly the spiritual climate of the 'remarkable decade', 1838–1848;[19] because of this he always felt himself to be a 'man of the forties'. At the end of 1844 he came to Moscow to prepare himself for university studies. His private teacher was T. Granovsky, professor of European history at Moscow University, a former member of Stankevich's circle and one of the intellectual leaders of liberal Westernism. Following Granovsky's advice, young Chicherin chose the faculty of law and tried to combine jurisprudence with historical studies. Apart from Granovsky, whom he always treated as his 'master', his main teacher in history was the liberal Westernizer K. Kavelin, founder of the *étatist* school of Russian historiography. His

---

[18] The view of Chicherin as a liberal has been passionately challenged by Aileen Kelly, in whose opinion 'the term liberal is wholly inapplicable' to Chicherin's political philosophy (A. Kelly, 'What is Real is Rational: the Political Philosophy of B. N. Chicherin', *Cahiers du monde russe et soviétique*, XVIII (3), July–Sept. 1977, p. 196). The arguments for this thesis, however, are unconvincing. As we shall see, it is not true that Chicherin idolized the State, still less that he was a rigid determinist. In fact he emphatically rejected determinism (which he tended to identify with mechanical determinism) and argued that Hegelianism properly understood had nothing in common with it. More important still is the fact that determinism, however rigid, is perfectly compatible with liberal political philosophy (cf. for example Spencer or social Darwinism). Struve, who criticized Chicherin's emphasis on the freedom of the will, was perfectly right in maintaining that free will and civil/political freedom are completely different things. (See Struve, 'G. Chicherin', p. 102.)

[19] See ch. entitled 'A Remarkable Decade' in Isaiah Berlin, *Russian Thinkers*, New York, 1978.

main teacher in law, P. Redkin, a right-wing Hegelian, was a man of lesser abilities but compensated for this by his great enthusiasm for philosophy and by his vivid memories of Germany where he had studied under Savigny, Gans, and other celebrities. In a sense Granovsky was at that time also a Hegelian, so it was natural for Chicherin to immerse himself in the study of Hegel. He supplemented his education in the Pavlovs' literary salon, listening to the heated discussions between the Slavophiles and the Westernizers. There he used to meet the leading figures of the 'remarkable decade': Chaadaev, Herzen, Khomiakov, I. Kireevsky, K. Aksakov, and others.

His political views had been formed early in life. The influence of his father, in whose study hung the portraits of Franklin, Washington, and Canning,[20] prepared him for an easy acceptance of Granovsky's liberal Westernism. Like many Moscow students he enthusiastically welcomed the 1848 revolution in France and the introduction of a republican system. But he could not accept the 'June Days': the insurrection of the Parisian workers, cruelly suppressed by Cavaignac, was in his eyes a nonsensical event, thwarting the designs of 'Historical Reason'.[21]

The Tsarist government reacted to revolutionary events in Europe by the severest administrative control of intellectual life. Philosophy was banished from universities and the new censorship rules made it impossible even to mention in print the names of Hegel or Feuerbach. For Chicherin these measures represented the enthronement of 'oriental despotism' in Russia[22] and rendered the thought of a career in government completely antipathetic to him. Therefore, after passing his final university examinations, he settled on his family estate near Tambov, where he concentrated on his philosophical studies and on writing his master's dissertation, the equivalent of a Western doctorate.

The title of his dissertation was *Regional Institutions in Seventeenth-Century Russia*. It was completed by the end of 1853 but the dean of the faculty of law of Moscow University refused to accept it on the grounds that it gave too unfavourable a picture of seventeenth-century Russian administration. Granovsky hoped that Petersburg University might be more liberal, but in vain; Chicherin did not receive his master's degree

---

[20] See S. Bakhrushin, Preface to B. N. Chicherin, *Vospominaniia: Moskva sorokovykh godov*, Moscow, 1929 (reprinted Cambridge, 1973), p. XVII (hereafter referred to as *Vospominaniia* 1).
[21] B. N. Chicherin, *Vospominaniia* 1, p. 76.   [22] Ibid., p. 158.

till 1857, at the height of the political 'thaw' which followed the death of Nicholas I and Russia's humiliating defeat in the Crimean war. His dissertation, published in 1856, soon became a classic of Russian legal history.

Like other Russian liberals, Chicherin had fully realized that a Russian victory in the Crimean war would strengthen the repressive régime; consequently, like Granovsky, he preferred Russia's defeat, although all his sympathies were with the heroic Russian soldiery.[23] In a manuscript written during the war (before the death of Nicholas) and circulated in liberal circles he postulated a radical regeneration: 'We must regenerate ourselves from head to foot, reform all our institutions, liberate Poland, repudiate our past and choose an entirely new road.'[24] According to a Soviet historian this programme represented 'the highest level of [liberal] political opposition' in the 1850s.[25]

At the beginning of the new reign Chicherin was eager to collaborate with Herzen who, by then, was also basing his hopes on the liberal intentions of Alexander II. Chicherin contributed some important articles to Herzen's *Voices from Russia*, a series published in London which provided a free forum for independent public opinion in Russia. In the first issue of *Voices* (1855) an open letter signed 'Russian liberal' appeared, written jointly by Chicherin and Kavelin. It proclaimed: 'We are ready to gather behind any liberal government and support it with all our strength, for we are profoundly convinced that we can act, and achieve results, only through the government.'[26] This emphasis on the role of the government was in accordance with the main thesis of the *étatist* school, which claimed that in Russia the state had always been the leading organizer of society and the indispensable agent of progress.

The Russian journals, although restricted by censorship, acquired enough freedom to become more outspoken in support of various ideological positions. Liberal Westernizers started to publish their own journal, the *Russian Messenger*, and Chicherin became one of its leading contributors. His first article for the *Russian Messenger* dealt with the problem of the origin of the peasant commune in Russia. It enraged

---

[23] Ibid., pp. 149–50.
[24] Quoted from V. A. Kitaev, *Ot frondy k okhranitel'stvu: Iz istorii russkoi liberal'noi mysli 50–60 kh godov XIX veka*, Moscow, 1972, p. 39.
[25] See V. N. Rozental, 'Narastanie krizisa verkhov v seredine 50-kh godov XX veka', in *Revolutsionnaia situatsiia v Rossii v 1859–1861 gg.*, Moscow, 1962, p. 45.
[26] Quoted from D. P. Hammer, 'Introduction: Chicherin and Russian Liberalism' (Preface to Chicherin, *Vospominaniia* I), p. ix.

the Slavophiles and initiated a long-drawn-out controversy between
the *Russian Messenger* and the Slavophile *Russian Conversation*. The
radicals who, following Herzen, were inclined to see the commune as a
precious heritage of ancient Russia, immediately recognized the
importance of this debate. Nikolai Chernyshevsky, the leading figure
in the radical camp, openly sympathized with the Slavophiles,
condemning Chicherin's 'fossilized Westernism' and stressing that in
Slavophilism 'there are healthy and valid elements deserving of
support'.[27] The controversy was by no means purely academic, since
the problem of the origin of the commune was closely bound up with
the problem of its future: was it to continue to function as before or
should it be abolished together with serfdom.

Another topical issue was the problem of the proper organization of
the apparatus of state. On this issue liberal Westernizers were divided.
The Anglophile group opted for maximum decentralization, and the
Francophiles stressed the progressive role of a centralized state.
Curiously enough, the editor of the *Russian Messenger*, M. Katkov, who
later became the most intransigent defender of a centralized absolute
monarchy, was at this time a radical Anglophile, while Chicherin, a
prominent member of the *étatist* school of historiography, represented
the Francophile or *étatist* version of liberalism. These differences
became so pronounced that Chicherin's group had to break away from
the *Russian Messenger* and start to publish their own journal,
Ateneum.[28]

In the spring of 1858 Chicherin went abroad. In Vienna he engaged
in serious discussion with Lorenz von Stein, one of his mentors in
political science. In Turin he was greatly impressed by a session of
parliament and by the freedom of the press. Soon afterwards he
travelled to France and for some time joined the court of the Grand
Duchess Elena Pavlovna, by then living in Nice. In the autumn he
came to London. His main aim there was to meet Herzen, whose
growing scepticism about liberal reforms in Russia was in his eyes a
dangerous symptom. He hoped to be able to influence Herzen, to
persuade him that the true mission of the Russian *émigré* press was to
push the government in the direction of reforms while, at the same
time, prudently restraining the increasing impatience of the radicals.[29]

[27] Cf. N. G. Chernyshevsky, *Poln. sobr. soch.*, vol. IV, Moscow, 1948, p. 760. For a
more detailed account see Walicki, *The Slavophile Controversy*, pp. 464–7.

[28] Cf. V. A. Kitaev, *Ot frondy k okhranitel'stvu*, ch. 2.

[29] B. N. Chicherin, *Vospominaniia: puteshestvie za granitsu*, Moscow, 1932 (reprinted
Cambridge, 1973), pp. 49–50 (hereafter referred to as *Vospominaniia* 2).

However, it was not possible to achieve this. In fact, Chicherin's discussions with Herzen, described in detail by both of them, brought about the final severance of their tactical alliance. Chicherin summed up their differences in an open letter which, in December 1858, appeared in the pages of Herzen's *Kolokol*.[30] He accused Herzen of relying on the 'poetic caprices' of history (instead of on Historical Reason), of listening to the voice of unbridled passion and of appealing to brute force. He warned Herzen that a lack of moderation and rational control was most dangerous for the cause of liberal reform in a young, immature society and insisted that revolutionary impatience could only play into the hands of reaction.

Herzen in his turn wrote to Chicherin a private letter which he later printed in *My Past and Thoughts*. He attributed to Chicherin a Hegelian belief in a rational sequence of historical phases ('if the past was thus and thus, the present is bound to be thus and thus, and is bound to lead to such and such in the future')[31] from which he entirely dissociated himself, seeing in it 'the geometrical dryness', 'the algebraic impersonality' of dogma.[32] Accusing Chicherin of replacing faith in God with worship of the State, he confessed: 'Your secular, civic and legal religion is the more frightening for being deprived of all that is poetical, imaginative, of all that is child-like in its nature'.[33] Elsewhere in the book he described Chicherin's views as the 'philosophy of bureaucracy'.[34] We shall see how far from the truth this description was.

Many Russian liberals sided with Chicherin, but a large group was reluctant to part with Herzen. In Kavelin's eyes Chicherin's 'Open Letter' amounted to a betrayal of the political opposition and support of the government.[35]

From London Chicherin went to many other places in Europe. He came to know a number of scholars and statesmen, including A. Thiers and H. Passy. His general impressions of the West were very favourable: he did not notice any symptoms of decline, which strengthened his faith in historical progress.[36]

Chicherin's trip to Europe lasted three years; when he returned, the Manifesto emancipating Russian peasants had already been signed and enacted. He saw this reform as the best achievement of Russian

---

[30] Reprinted in B. N. Chicherin, *Neskol'ko sovremennykh voprosov*, Moscow, 1862.
[31] A. Herzen, *My Past and Thoughts*, vol. 2, New York, 1968, p. 627.
[32] Ibid., p. 628.   [33] Ibid., pp. 628–9.   [34] Ibid., p. 625.
[35] See Chicherin, *Vospominaniia* 2, pp. 54–67.   [36] Ibid., p. 126.

legislation and felt indignant at the radical left's attacks on it. He was horrified by revolutionary proclamations, especially by Zaichnevsky's 'Young Russia'—a proclamation which combined a revolutionary appeal for the extermination of the ruling classes, including the entire royal family, with a communist demand for the wholesale nationalization of the economy. He was aware that Chernyshevsky did not approve of such extremism but still felt that Russian radicalism as a whole was to blame for endangering the success of reforms. With this awareness he placed himself on the right wing of Russian liberalism which soon led to a final break with Kavelin.

At the beginning of 1861 the Academic Council of Moscow University offered Chicherin the position of extraordinary professor of State Law. He accepted this proposal and immediately became involved in the political tensions created by the continuing student disturbances. Though critical of the authorities he insisted that no concessions to the students should be made before order was fully restored. His favourite maxim was: 'liberal measures and strong government'.[37] His long political letters to his brother, a government employee in St Petersburg, were reported to the young Tsar and his entourage. He hoped to influence the government but, characteristically enough, did not want to compromise himself in the eyes of public opinion. His letters were highly valued in government circles though the rewards they attracted were not to his taste. He was invited to publish in the semi-official organ of the Ministry of Internal Affairs (which he, of course, refused to do) and the censors received instructions prohibiting any criticism of his inaugural lecture.[38] He was dismayed by this lack of understanding that independence was a necessary condition of his public influence.

He accepted, however, one peculiar favour and agreed to become one of the tutors of the Heir Apparent, Nikolai Alexandrovich. In 1864 he accompanied this young prince on his travels to the West, travels which ended with Nikolai's illness and death. Chicherin himself suffered a serious illness abroad, during which he experienced a kind of religious enlightenment. He became convinced that Christianity was not 'a religion of the past', as he had previously thought, but an eternal truth, an indispensable element of Absolute Spirit.[39]

[37] *Vospominaniia*, pp. 28–9.
[38] Ibid., pp. 49–51. In spite of his wish Chicherin could not avoid being protected by censorship: in 1862 the Russian censors received secret instructions prohibiting criticism of his political articles, published in the journal *Our Times* (*Nashe vermia*). See M. Lemke, *Epokha tsenzurnykh reform*, 1904, p. 95.   [39] Ibid., pp. 148–9.

In spite of his rather unpopular political views Chicherin was remarkably successful in upholding his authority among the students: if not loved, he was certainly deeply respected by them. Much less enjoyable were his relations with his colleagues, who could not stand his frankness, his intolerance towards careerist mediocrities, and his emphasis on the observance of the law. Following his principle of obedience to the law rather than to men, he placed the authority of the law above the specific commands of one's superiors and above majority opinion. This led to a serious conflict with the majority of the University Council and to his ostentatious resignation from his chair at the beginning of 1868.

After his resignation Chicherin settled on his estate, wrote books and participated in the activities of the Tambov *Zemstvo*. His withdrawal from political life was never complete since all his books contained a political message; thus, for instance, as he himself confessed, the two volumes of his *Property and State* (written in the 1870s) were conceived as a means of promoting liberal reforms and counteracting the socialist ideas of the revolutionary movement.[40] After the assassination of Alexander II he decided once more to engage in active politics. In order to influence the new Tsar, to ensure that he would follow his father along the path of 'liberalism from above', he wrote an article, 'The Tasks of the New Reign', and handed the manuscript to the powerful Minister for Internal Affairs, Count Loris-Melikov. This article, expressing a philosophy of 'liberal measures and strong government', was in fact the most comprehensive conservative-liberal political programme of the time.[41] It argued that political freedom must be accepted as a remote ideal and that the Russian government and the Russian people had to be prepared for its gradual introduction. As the first step in this direction Chicherin proposed to supplement the composition of the State Council by elected representatives of the *zemstvo*s, thus establishing a 'living link' between government and society.

Among his other proposals was that of liberating the Russian peasants from the tutelage of the village communes, thus making them equal before the law with the rest of the population.[42] It was in effect a demand that the Russian peasantry be transformed from a closed

[40] *Vospominaniia* 4, p. 108.
[41] A detailed summary, with generous quotations, is contained in Chicherin, *Vospominaniia* 4, pp. 123–30.
[42] Ibid., pp. 127–8.

estate, living under its own separate laws, into a class of free farmers, fully-fledged members of civil society.

Characteristically enough, Loris-Melikov was interested mainly in Chicherin's proposal for restraining the freedom of the press, while securing freedom for academic expression; he even considered the possibility of entrusting Chicherin with this rather thankless task.[43] However, his own days were numbered. Alexander III chose to listen to the extreme reactionaries, Pobedonostsev and Katkov.

Another important episode in Chicherin's public life was his election (at the end of 1881) to the post of Mayor of Moscow. He held this office with great dignity, never yielding to bureaucratic pressures, relying instead on the active support of the elected City Council, but his term turned out to be unexpectedly short. His speech on the occasion of the tsar's coronation on 16 May 1883 contained an appeal for uniting the forces of local self-government in Russia; this was immediately misinterpreted as a call for the constitutional limitation of bureaucratic absolutism and Chicherin was compelled to resign.[44]

The years which followed were years of reaction, of deliberate attempts to cancel, or at least minimize, the effect of the 'great reforms' of Alexander II. For Chicherin it was a bitter disappointment. He was determined to defend the principle of local self-government, represented by the *zemstvo*s. Without abandoning his view of the progressive role of centralization he proposed the decentralization of certain functions of the state and went so far as to defend this not only against the centralist inclinations of the bureaucracy but also against the provincial *zemstvo*s, ambitious themselves to control the activities and finances of district *zemstvo*s. (This, indeed, was the reason for his conflict with the head of the Moscow Zemstvo, D. Shipov.)[45] At the end of his life he came to the conclusion that it was not possible to limit the power of the bureaucracy without limiting the absolute power of the tsar, that no form of the rule of law was compatible with arbitrary personal rule. In this conviction he proclaimed the necessity of transforming Russian absolutism into a constitutional monarchy.[46] At the same time, however, he grew more and more pessimistic. He predicted great catastrophes, revolutions and wars, the victory of brute force in international relations (instancing Bismarck's Germany), the

---

[43] Ibid., pp. 133–4.   [44] Ibid., pp. 233–43.

[45] See B. N. Chicherin, *Voprosy politiki*, 2nd edn., Moscow, 1905, pp. 102–15. Cf. D. N. Shipov, *Vospominaniia i dumy o perezhitom*, Moscow, 1918, p. 52.

[46] See [B. N. Chicherin], *Rossiia nakanune XX-go stoletiia*, Berlin, 1900, p. 180.

degeneration of democracy and the inevitable triumph of socialist despotism.[47] Trubetskoi has aptly remarked that Chicherin was then a Hegelian without the Hegelian faith in the final victory of reason: 'He gave the impression that for him universal reason was wholly a thing of the past'.[48]

Chicherin's scholarly output is very impressive indeed. Apart from his valuable works on Russian history he wrote on a vast variety of topics. His strictly philosophical books include *Science and Religion* (1879), *Mysticism in Science* (a criticism of Soloviev, 1880), *Positive Philosophy and the Unity of Science* (1892) and *Principles of Logic and Metaphysics* (1894, translated into German as *Philosophische Forschungen*, Heidelberg, 1899). His political, legal and economic views were developed in the big volume *About Popular Representation* (1866, 2nd edn., 1899), in the two volumes of *Property and State* (1822–3) and in the three volumes of *A Course of Political Science* (1894–8). The link between his metaphysics and his theory of law was made explicit in his masterly *Philosophy of Law* (1900). The five volumes of his *History of Political Doctrines* (1869–1902) belong to the best works of this kind produced in the nineteenth century.[49] All these works, however, were too difficult and too academic to arouse a lively interest among the Russian intelligentsia; they seemed, often mistakenly, to be too detached from topical problems of the day, they demanded too much intellectual effort, and their ideas were almost always against the current. At the end of his memoirs Chicherin sadly reflected upon this:

The writing of scholarly books is the most thankless kind of work in Russia, especially if one resists dominant currents of thought and tries to preserve unbiased standards of scholarship. My books appeared one after another without evoking any response or gratitude. I never had the satisfaction of seeing my thoughts, sometimes completely original, assimilated and developed.[50]

Hindsight enables us to modify this bitter conclusion. In the 1890s, at a time of mounting reaction to the dominance of legal positivism and of increasing interest in the philosophical approach to law, Chicherin's works came to be read more widely, even if he failed to notice it. According to M. N. Pokrovsky, Pavel Novgorodtsev—soon to be the

---

[47] B. N. Chicherin, *Vospominaniia* 4, pp. 300–1.
[48] E. Trubetskoi, *Vospominaniia* p. 122. Quoted from V. V. Zenkovsky, *A History of Russian Philosophy*. G. L. Kline (trans.) vol. 2, London, 1953, p. 609.
[49] This view is shared, among others, by V. D. Zor'kin, *Iz istorii*, pp. 15–16.
[50] B. N. Chicherin, *Vospominaniia* 4, pp. 310–11.

leading figure in the neo-idealist school of legal philosophy—had in
the early nineties a deep reverence for Chicherin's works.[51] Pokrovsky's
view, that Chicherin was by then as important for the liberal publicists
as Plekhanov for the social democrats,[52] seems to be an exaggeration.
Chicherin's conservative liberalism, as I have shown, never became
popular, let alone dominant, in the Russian liberal movement. It is
undeniable, however, that his legal philosophy became the starting-
point for the peculiarly Russian anti-positivist tradition in the liberal
philosophy of law, which is the subject of the present book.

3 Russian history and Russia's future

Despite appearances, Chicherin's legal philosophy, together with his
historical views, can be seen as part and parcel of the great debate on
the national identity and future development of Russia. Such a
perspective provides a useful corrective to seeing him as a pure
theorist, whose views were, allegedly, not related in any meaningful
way to the central problems of Russian intellectual history.

As historians of Russia, Kavelin and Chicherin were the founders of
the so-called *étatist* school of Russian historiography. They claimed
that in Russia the state had had greater autonomy and had been much
stronger in its relations with social forces than in the West; so much
stronger, in fact, that it had become the chief agent in Russian history.
In the West the estates had been strong and independent of the state
even under an absolute monarchy, whereas in Russia they had been
created from above, for state purposes, and had no autonomy of their
own. In Kavelin's view this constituted a qualitative difference, a sharp
contrast, between the ways of European and of Russian historical
development in the past. In the West, he maintained, everything had
been done 'from below', while in Russia everything had been done
'from above'. Thus, Kavelin combined Westernization as a programme
for Russia's future with insistence on the distinctiveness of Russian
history.[53]

Chicherin's position in this regard is a matter of dispute. Some
historians of Russian historiography stress his basic agreement with
Kavelin,[54] others, however, insist that in his view Russia's distinctive-

[51] See M. Pokrovsky, *Istoricheskaia nauka i bor'ba klassov*, vol. 2, Moscow, 1933,
pp. 175–6.   [52] Ibid.
[53] See K. D. Kavelin, *Sobr. soch.*, vol. I, SPb 1897, pp. 566–8.
[54] Cf. N. L. Rubinstein in *Russkaia istoriografiia*, (Moscow–Leningrad, 1941) and in
'Gosudarstvennaia shkola', *Sovetskaia istoricheskaia entsiklopediia*, vol. 4, Moscow, 1963,
p. 621.

ness was only relative and that, in fact, he saw Russian history as a variant of the European pattern of historical development.[55] There are indeed good reasons for such an interpretation. It suffices to quote Chicherin's own words:

> The entire course of Russian history offers a remarkable parallel with the history of the West. In both areas development starts with the appearance of Germanic warriors subjugating the native population. In both areas the rule of a princely retinue (*druzhina*) is followed by the development of the patrimonial principle, when society is fragmented into a multiplicity of unions based upon property rights. In both areas, together with the patrimonial system, free communes, considered as states or semi-states, appear. In both areas, almost simultaneously, patrimonial fragmentization and free communes give way to monarchical rule which wipes out medieval particularism and unites the entire country into a single state. Finally, both Russia and the West pass through a period of assemblies of the land, which is followed by the establishment of absolute monarchy.
>
> This parallelism, without equivalent in ancient or modern history, shows clearly that Russia is a European country, one which does not elaborate any previously unknown principles but develops like others, under the influence of the dominant forces in modern [European] history.[56]

A general account of Chicherin's historical views does not fall within the scope of this book. Therefore, I must limit myself to pointing out that there was a tension between two tendencies in his view of Russian history—a tendency to stress its parallelism with the history of the West and a tendency to concentrate on its distinctive features, often contrasted with the corresponding aspects of Western development. It was this second tendency which prevailed in Chicherin's views of the history of Russian law, legal culture, and legal consciousness. Looking at Russian history from this point of view he came to the conclusion that it differed sharply from the Western model. Because of this his general statement (quoted above) about Russia as a country belonging to the European family was followed by an analysis of important differences, all reducible to the contrast between the principle of law and the principle of unlimited authoritarian power. This contrast is to be found in almost all his works. Thus, for instance, in his *Course of Political Science* (based upon his lectures at Moscow University)[57] we

---

[55] This view has recently been voiced by Zor'kin, *Iz istorii*, pp. 89–96.

[56] B. Chicherin, *O narodnom predstavitel'stve*, Moscow, 1866, pp. 355–6.

[57] See Zor'kin, *Iz istorii*, p. 15.

read: 'From time immemorial the cornerstone and foundation of the edifice of the Russian state has been authoritarian power (*vlast'*), and not the law'.[58]

This was not because of any innate qualities in the Russian character but for geographical and historical reasons. Russia was a vast country with a small, scattered, semi-nomadic population; it had no natural boundaries, was remote from Europe and exposed to invasions from the East. Under such conditions it was difficult to develop strong corporate ties and, in view of the paramount importance of defence, it was necessary to compensate for this weakness of the inner organization of society by the development of an exceptionally strong external organization of social forces, namely, by militarization and increasing state autonomy. The principle of law, always strong in the West as a result of powerful self-generating social forces and their energetic struggle for rights, gave way in Russia to the principle of total subordination of all social elements to the authoritarian power of government, acting as an independent force, superimposed, as it were, upon society and shaping it in accordance with its own needs and aims.[59] The culmination of this development was the enserfment of all social classes: 'the notion of law completely disappeared' and even the landed aristocracy became 'serfs of the tsars',[60] compulsory 'servitors of the state', deprived of personal freedom and of hereditary right to their estates (since ownership of land became conditional on state service).

The Tartars played an extremely important role in this process. Centralized states in the West took law-abiding ancient Rome as a model; in Russia the model was provided by the oriental despotism of the Khans.[61] After the Tartar invasions, anything resembling law was replaced by enforced obedience to an arbitrary and unrestrained power.[62] The basic right of Western estates—the right to have a say in matters of taxation—could not develop in a country accustomed to paying arbitrary tribute to the Tartars. No wonder, therefore, that the Russian Assemblies of the Land never remotely aspired to political rights.[63]

It should be stressed that Chicherin did not see this development as

[58] B. Chicherin, *Kurs gosudarstvennoi nauki*, vol. 3—*Politika*, Moscow, 1898, p. 403.
[59] B. Chicherin, *O narodnom predstavitel'stve*, pp. 356–62.
[60] B. Chicherin, *Kurs*, vol. 3, p. 403.
[61] B. Chicherin, *O narodnom predstavitel'stve*, pp. 360–1.
[62] B. Chicherin, *Kurs*, vol. 2—*Sotsiologiia*, Moscow, 1896, p. 368.
[63] B. Chicherin, *O narodnom predstavitel'stve*, pp. 361–2.

the evolution of a 'rational necessity' in the Hegelian sense. He saw it as a purely empirical necessity, a necessity in terms of adaptation to unfavourable external conditions, but not in terms of Hegelian Historical Reason. As a consistent Westernizer, he looked for the normal pattern of development in the West; seen from this point of view, Russian history appeared an anomaly, a sad deviation from the norm, but he regularly said that there was nothing fatalistic about it, that it could have been otherwise. Kievan Russia had had a highly developed legal system. The ancient city-states, Novgorod and Pskov, showed that 'principles of law and political freedom had not been alien to the Russian people'.[64] Even later, after the Tartar invasions, Chicherin believed that history had offered Russia the possibility of an alternative course of development, in the decision of the Boyar Duma, in 1610, to offer the Russian crown to Vladislav, son of the King of the Polish-Lithuanian Commonwealth, on condition that he accept a formal, contractual limitation of his power. If this plan had materialized (i.e. if Vladislav, the Tsar-Elect, had become enthroned), the history of Russia would have taken an entirely different shape.[65]

History, however, did not favour the cause of law and freedom in Russia and consequently the Russian national character, moulded by events, had become equally unsympathetic to it. On this point Chicherin was very pessimistic indeed. He was bitterly aware that legal consciousness was alien, as a rule, to his contemporaries and that, as he put it, their national character was uncongenial to freedom.[66] The Russian people, he asserted, lacked individual energy and initiative, preferred tutelage to self-reliance, had no awareness of their rights and, in fact, liked to be ruled in an authoritarian way; even their virtues, such as patience, endurance, readiness to sacrifice themselves for the sake of 'tsar and fatherland', were not conducive to individual liberty. On the other hand, unlike the Asian peoples, they could not offer a truly disciplined obedience: the 'principle of individuality' was too weak in them to generate independence and self-reliance but strong enough to foster anarchic leanings.[67] They understood obedience and anarchy, but not freedom under the law; they had no feeling for 'measure and limits', no respect for relative values.[68] Because of this it was a great mistake to see so-called Russian

---

[64] Ibid., p. 359.   [65] Ibid., p. 368.   [66] Ibid., p. 412.
[67] Ibid., pp. 412–13.
[68] B. Chicherin, 'Mera i granitsy', in Chicherin, *Neskol'ko sovremennykh voprosov*, Moscow, 1862, pp. 77–81.

'nihilism' as an import from the West. In fact nihilism was an expression of another side of the Russian's 'nature broad and wide', an expression, on the one hand, of a hidden desire 'to be on the loose', free of restraints, and on the other, of a striving for an earthly Absolute, characteristic of people who have passed through the school of disciplined, self-restrained freedom.[69]

National character is not immutable although it changes only slowly. Chicherin concluded from this that, while there was no reason to despair of the final victory of freedom in Russia, it could not be achieved quickly, by means of a sudden change. Political freedom in Russia must be preceded by the introduction and full utilization of civil freedom, under which the Russian people could develop the spirit of economic self-help and the ability for self-government at the local level.[70]

According to Chicherin, Russian history was already moving in this direction. Peter the Great had based the machinery of power on general rules rather than on specific commands, which was a big step forward towards absolutism of the Western type. The enserfment of all social classes was gradually dismantled: the first milestone on the road was the Manifesto on the Liberty of the Gentry (1762), freeing landowners from compulsory state service, and a further decisive step was the emancipation of the peasants. Finally came the reforms of 1864, which created the legal framework for genuine local self-government for all classes (*zemstvo*) and introduced independent courts, the jury system and the organization of lawyers into a formal Bar. Chicherin felt strongly that before the 'crowning of the edifice', before the transformation of autocratic into constitutional monarchy, Russian society needed to mature by making full use of these reforms.

This cautious approach to political change explains Chicherin's attitude towards the landowning nobility. In his view the nobility was the class in Russian society with the longest tradition of independence from the state, the only class having its own elective institutions and some awareness of its rights.[71] Because of this, Chicherin did not share the widespread view, voiced among others by I. Aksakov and M. Katkov, that corporate organization of the nobility should have

[69] B. Chicherin, *O narodnom predstavitel'stve*, p. 414.
[70] Ibid., pp. 415–17.
[71] B. Chicherin, *Neskol'ko sovremennykh voprosov*, pp. 89–132. The author felt, however, that even among the Russian nobility the awareness of rights was not sufficiently developed, especially by comparison with the Western aristocracy (cf. *Kurs*, vol. 2, p. 209).

been abolished together with serfdom. On the contrary, he thought that the lack of a strong and organized Russian bourgeoisie created a vacuum which could be filled either by the nobility, that is, by an independent social force, or by a bureaucracy, which would strengthen the government's control of society, thus creating an additional obstacle to the coming of age of the Russian people. His articles in defence of the nobility were attacked from many sides, and even the elected representatives of the nobility were sometimes embarassed by them.[72] But it should be remembered that Chicherin saw the nobility as the vanguard of the independent forces of society, that his aim was not to preserve but to universalize privileges and thus to transform them into rights. As he himself said: 'Privileges should give way to universal rights. The significance of privileges consists in their role in the elaboration of general laws; so, if the privileged classes descended from their high place without gaining rights for all, they would not have fulfilled their historical mission.'[73]

Chicherin fully realized, of course, that to support some relics of the corporate privileges of the nobility could only be a temporary measure. He saw the great mission of absolute monarchy as the transformation of feudal society into a society of 'universal citizenship' (*obshchegrazh-danskii stroi*), based upon equality before the law, thus preparing the way for its own replacement by constitutional order.[74] The great reforms of Alexander II had almost completed this task but the principle of autocracy had remained untouched. Under absolutism, however, the only mainstay of freedom, the only means of limiting the power of bureaucracy, were, in Chicherin's view, the special rights of the privileged classes.[75] Without them absolutism would be transformed into 'democratic Caesarism', a system combining the worst features both of absolute monarchy and of democracy.[76] There would be no

[72] Thus, for instance, Count P. P. Shuvalov, a marshal of the nobility to whom Chicherin was presented and recommended as 'un des rares défenseurs de la noblesse', commented on this recommendation: 'Je trouve, que Monsieur nous défend trop' (Chicherin, *Vospominaniia* 3, pp. 70–1).

[73] *Vospominaniia* 4, p. 39.

[74] See B. Chicherin, *O narodnom predstavitel'stve*, p. 426. Cf. Zor'kin, *Iz istorii*, pp. 106–9.

[75] Cf. B. Chicherin, *Kurs*, vol. 2, p. 204–5.

[76] B. Chicherin, *Sobstvennost' i gosudarstvo*, vol. 2, Moscow, 1883, pp. 350–1. The same idea was developed by Chicherin in his illegally published brochure *Konstitutsionnyi vopros v Rossii*, 1878. (Cf. Zor'kin, *Iz istorii*, p. 160.) Its conclusion was that a gradual transition to constitutionalism was in Russia the only alternative to 'democratic Caesarism'.

place for law and freedom in such a system since in it everything would be subordinated to the arbitrary commands of an unrestrained centralized power, legitimizing itself, more or less sincerely, by promoting the social welfare of the uneducated masses. To avoid this the most independent and best organized social force in Russia, the nobility, should temporarily preserve its separate identity; it should disappear with the demise of autocracy, but not before.

These considerations explain Chicherin's political strategy. From the very beginning it was clear to him that Russian autocracy was bound to be transformed into constitutional monarchy, so he was concerned mainly with the question of proper timing. In the sixties he vigorously supported the reforming government. After the assassination of Alexander II he proposed a moderate step in the direction of political freedom—the co-option of the elected representatives of society (of the *zemstvo*s and of the nobility) to the State Council. He saw this, of course, as merely a temporary measure since he himself had defined such a consultative body as a palliative, unable to satisfy any real-needs and useful only as a transition to more developed forms of political participation.[77] In subsequent years the reactionary policies of the government, especially the series of 'counter-reforms', meant to limit the changes introduced by the great reforms of the sixties, led him to conclude that absolute monarchy had become incompatible with further progress. At the same time the advances in capitalist modernization of Russia, especially conspicuous in the nineties, made him more confident of the maturity of Russian society and its ability to dispense with government guidance.[78] Therefore, on the eve of the twentieth century he decided to proclaim that the time had finally come for limiting the power of the tsar, for transforming Russian autocracy into a constitutional monarchy.[79]

In his American lectures on 'Russia and Its Crisis' Miliukov quoted the relevant words from Chicherin's *Russia on the Eve of the Twentieth Century* and called them 'the minimum programme of contemporary [Russian] liberalism'.[80] In fact, however, the Kadet Party never committed itself to such a programme—it was much too moderate for its ideas. What Chicherin had in mind was constitutionalism but not

---

[77] Cf. B. Chicherin, *O narodnom predstavitel'stve*, p. 106.
[78] See B. Chicherin, *Vospominaniia* 4, p. 266. According to Zor'kin (*Iz istorii*, p. 166) this part of Chicherin's memoirs was written in 1894.
[79] See above, n. 46.
[80] P. Miliukov, *Russia and Its Crisis*, New York, 1962, p. 242.

yet political freedom, *limited*, but not representative, parliamentary, government. He had no doubts that political freedom is the highest form of liberty under law, he was outspoken in declaring that the stronger and higher a political system is, the freer it could and should be.[81] But he did not think that for a country like Russia a direct transition to full political freedom would be desirable. Under constitutional order without representative government people would get used to defending their civil liberties, local self-government would flourish and the rule of law would have a chance to become entrenched in the traditions and mental habits of the nation. Despite appearances, under representative government it would not be so: legal considerations would be less important than the struggle for a share in political power, the pursuit of different substantive aims would overshadow the values represented by the rule of law, and the development of legal consciousness, a necessary condition of true freedom, would be hindered or distorted.

It seems difficult to deny that what was to happen in Russia was precisely what Chicherin wanted to avoid.[82] Whether his own programme was realistic enough, that is, whether the possibility of a smooth transition through limited government to full political freedom really existed in Russia, is, of course, quite a different question.

In the above account of Chicherin's views of Russia's past and future one important problem has been deliberately left for separate analysis: the problem of the peasant commune. In this respect Chicherin was a truly exceptional figure in the history of nineteenth-century Russian thought. He was the only major thinker of his time whose attitude towards the peasant commune, so much idealized, both on the left and on the right of the Russian ideological spectrum, was consistently negative, who saw in it an institution hindering economic progress and, even more importantly, completely incompatible with the legal order of 'universal citizenship'.

First of all, Chicherin's historical works threw a new light on the origin of the commune. Working on his master's thesis he was struck by the number of documents showing that peasants in the ancient Russia had held their land by individual households and at their own disposal, being able to sell it, to bequeath it to a monastery, and so forth. Further work on this problem led him to very interesting

[81] B. Chicherin, *Kurs*, vol. 1 (1894), *Obshchee gosudarstvennoe pravo*, p. 214.
[82] Cf. D. W. Treadgold, *Lenin and His Rivals: The Struggle for Russia's Future, 1898–1906*, London, 1955, 555, 55–72.

conclusions. The peasant commune, he claimed, had not existed in Russia before the enserfment of all social classes by the Muscovite autocracy; it was not a product of spontaneous growth, a relic of ancient communalism, but had been deliberately created by the government to simplify the collection of taxes and to impose on the peasants a 'collective liability' (*krugovaya poruka*) for their financial obligations.[83] Like serfdom, it was also meant to attach peasants to the land and thus to cure them of their nomadic leanings, to ensure that they served their masters who, in turn, were obliged to serve the government. Therefore it was part of the peculiarly Russian pattern of serfdom, peculiar in that it had been a deliberate creation of the government and thus, in contrast to the medieval West where serfdom had belonged to the sphere of private law, a part of the public law of the country.[84] It had been so convenient for the government that its forcible imposition on the peasants continued until the last decades of the eighteenth century.

A long and well-documented exposition of Chicherin's view of the origins of the Russian commune appeared in 1856, in the first issues of the *Russian Messenger*.[85] The Slavophiles, to whom Chicherin's views amounted to outright slander, asked a professional historian, I. D. Beliaev, for help, but his reply to Chicherin turned out to be rather inconclusive. Subsequent historical studies (including those of V. O. Kliuchevsky and P. Miliukov) gave more substance to Chicherin's arguments, while not denying the existence of genuinely archaic communalism in Russian history.[86] But this was not denied by Chicherin himself: what he was concerned with was the modern peasant commune, such as existed in the nineteenth century, and not its archaic ancestor or prototype. In later years he explicitly agreed with Maine, Maurer, Morgan, and other scholars who saw primitive communalism as a stage of the universal development of mankind; he emphasized, however, that primitive tribal communalism had disappeared in Russia by the fifteenth century and that the later,

[83] B. Chicherin, *Vospominaniia* 1, pp. 262–3.

[84] Cf. Zor'kin, *Iz istorii*, 102–4. Chicherin's views are fully shared by V. Leontovich (cf. *Geschichte des Liberalismus in Russland*).

[85] See B. Chicherin, 'Obzor istorii razvitiia a sel'skoi obshchiny v Rossii', *Russkii Vestnik*, 1856, I, pp. 373–86 and 579–602.

[86] The opinion of Western scholars has been summed up as follows: 'Contemporary opinion holds that the commune of the imperial period was indeed a modern institution, as Chicherin claimed, there being no solid evidence of its existence before the eighteenth century'. (R. Pipes, *Russia Under the Old Regime*, Penguin Edition, 1977, p. 18.)

modern form of the peasant commune was forcibly imposed on the peasants together with serfdom.[87] He did not deny that there might be some links between the archaic and the modern commune, sometimes even defining the latter as an artificial *restoration* of the former.[88] What was really important to him was to show that the peasant commune known to him owed its existence to autocracy and serfdom and, by the same token, could not claim to be meaningfully related to the ideals of 'ancient freedom' and 'ancient equality'. Where there was no autocracy, that is in the territory of Kievan Russia which had become a part of the Polish–Lithuanian Commonwealth, the archaic form of the commune disappeared completely, without being replaced by a new form of communal land-tenure;[89] where there was no serfdom it was the same, except for such cases as the free peasantry of the north who at the end of the eighteenth century were forced by the government to introduce the commune and thereby lost a significant part of their freedom.[90]

Emancipatory reform could have abolished the commune together with serfdom but Chicherin had not sought such a solution. He thought that the commune should neither be abolished nor be sanctioned by the new legislation, that its fate should be left to spontaneous development. Other liberals were more cynical. Kavelin, for instance, fully realized that 'in its present form the communal ownership of land is a heavy yoke on the peasant's back', a chain which 'fetters him to the soil and deprives him of his liberty'; nevertheless he saw it as a 'talisman' offering protection against social upheavals, as an institution that would strengthen the position of the gentry in face of

[87] B. Chicherin, *Sobstvennost' i gosudarstvo*, vol. 1, Moscow, 1882, pp. 446–9. It is interesting to note that an almost identical view of the Russian peasant commune was set forth by a Polish revolutionary Henryk Kamieński, who had spent several years in Russia as a political exile. In his book on Russia, unknown in the West and undeservedly forgotten in Poland, he treated the commune as an institution bound up with serfdom and peculiarly convenient for autocracy. From this point of view he criticized the idealization of the commune in Herzen's 'Russian Socialism'.

On Kamieński see Walicki, *Philosophy and Romantic Nationalism: The Case of Poland*, Oxford, 1982, pp. 190–206. The title of his book on Russia was *Rosja i Europa: Polska. Wstęp do badań nad Rosją i Moskalami* (*Russia, Europe, and Poland: An Introduction to the Study of Russia and the Muscovites*, Paris, 1857). A shortened version of this book was published in French under the title *La Russie et l'avenir* (Paris, 1858).

[88] Cf. B. Chicherin, *Kurs*, vol. 1, p. 209.

[89] Cf. B. Chicherin, *Voprosy politiki*, p. 199.

[90] Cf. B. Chicherin, *Vospominaniia* 1, p. 265. Chicherin referred in this connection to the book of his former opponent I. D. Beliaev, *Krest'yane na Rusi* and to the study of A. Efimenko, *Krest'anskoe zemlevladenie na krainem severe* (1884).

social change, and for that reason strongly advocated its preservation.[91] There is no evidence for attributing the same reasoning to Chicherin, but it is certain that he was apprehensive of too many drastic changes introduced at the same time. He wanted to avoid destabilizing processes in the countryside and therefore thought it preferable to allow the commune to disintegrate by itself, from below, instead of being abolished by government decree. In his interpretation the Emancipation Act of 1861 was conceived precisely in this way: it contained articles which not only gave individual peasants the right to purchase land of their own (from outside the commune) but also the right to demand their own share of communal land, provided that they paid their share of redemptive payments (article 165).[92]

In the following decades Chicherin became more and more convinced that the continued existence of the commune was one of the greatest obstacles to liberal progress. The commune preserved the existence of the peasantry as a separate, isolated estate, subject to separate administration and customary law (one, moreover, allowing physical punishment), which was absolutely incompatible with the spirit of law and with the principles of the great reforms of the sixties.[93] Constant and all-pervasive control by a closely-knit small collective, supervised in its turn by a bureaucracy, supported the sad legacy of serfdom—the infantile mentality of the peasant, which prevented the development of self-reliance, consciousness of one's rights, and personal responsibility.[94] This was precisely what was desired by the Russian conservatives who wanted to save the peasants from 'corruption' by isolating them from the rest of the population and making them, as it were, wards of the state, enclosed in a 'patriarchal legal *apartheid*'.[95] On the other hand, the commune was also supported by Russian populist socialists, who praised it for keeping alive the ideal of distributive justice (although in fact, as Chicherin repeatedly pointed out, the periodic redistributions of land prevented only the growth of the productivity of labour, but not the growth of social inequality). This remarkable agreement in support of the commune was in Chicherin's

---

[91] See K. D. Kavelin, 'Krest'anskii vopros', *Sobr. soch.* (SPb 1897), vol. 2, pp. 461–5. Cf. N. A. Tsagolov, *Ocherki russkoi ekonomicheskoi mysli perioda padeniia krepostnogo prava* (Moscow, 1956), pp. 333–42.

[92] Cf. B. Chicherin, *Voprosy politiki*, pp. 54–6.   [93] Ibid., p. 54.

[94] B. Chicherin, *Sobstvennost' i gosudarstvo*, vol. 1, p. 457.

[95] The quotation, from an analysis of Chicherin's views, is by L. Schapiro. See L. Schapiro, 'The Pre-revolutionary Intelligentsia and the Legal Order', in R. Pipes (ed.), *The Russian Intelligentsia*, New York, 1961, p. 25.

eyes a 'paradox of post-reform Russia': a paradox consisting in the fact that the Emancipation Act of 1861, although conceived in the spirit of liberal Westernism, did not strengthen the forces of liberal Westernism in Russia. On the contrary: both on the right and on the left almost everybody in Russia called for more tutelage, and almost nobody wanted more freedom.[96]

Chicherin's negative attitude to the peasant commune was made clear in his programmatic manuscript 'The Tasks of the New Reign', mentioned above. The addressee of this memorial, Alexander III, decided, however, to embark on a completely different policy. In 1889 the communes were put under the direct bureaucratic control of so-called 'land-captains', special officials endowed with vast judicial and administrative powers; this effectively wiped out any resemblance between the peasant *mir* and genuine self-government. Another counter-reform, introduced in 1893, made the commune compulsory for all peasants: the right of individual peasants to buy out their land allotments was cancelled (except by unanimous agreement of the *mir*) and the redistribution of land every twelve years was enforced. Chicherin saw it as a deliberate effort to restore serfdom, with the difference that now the peasants were enserfed not to the nobles but directly to the state (which was, otherwise, consistent with the view that the peasant land-tenure system was a matter of public law). He denounced this reactionary policy in the strongest terms and his criticism of different idealizations of the commune became even more forceful than before. He indicated, among other things, that the notorious 'unanimity principle', so extolled by the Slavophiles, was in fact pure fiction, confusing unanimous agreement with the fatal habit of passive obedience and inability to defend one's interests and rights.[97] While never advocating an administrative dissolution of the commune, he insisted that all efforts to prolong its existence be abandoned, that a strong class of individual landholders be allowed to emerge and that the peasants should be transformed, at last, into fully-fledged citizens, endowed with civil rights and equal before the law.[98] This would have entailed the final abolition of the corporate privileges of the nobility. In Chicherin's view this was the only way to complete

[96] B. Chicherin, 'Prakticheskie vyvody kniazia Vasil'chikova', in *Voprosy politiki*, p. 244. The article quoted was first published in V. Ger'e and B. Chicherin, *Russkii diletantizm i obshchinnoe zemlevladenie*, Moscow, 1878.

[97] B. Chicherin, *Voprosy politiki*, p. 47.

[98] B. Chicherin, 'Peresmotr zakonodatel'stva o krest'yanakh', in *Voprosy politiki*, pp. 54–69.

the transition from universal serfdom to universal citizenship and, thence, to political freedom.

After the revolution of 1905 a very similar programme was realized by the energetic prime minister P. Stolypin. It seems legitimate to assume that Chicherin, had he still been alive, would have supported his agrarian reform. It is certain, however, that he would have been satisfied neither with Stolypin's authoritarian and bureaucratic methods nor with the policy of the Kadet party. The Kadets, as is known, refused to support Stolypin and sided in the Duma with the left-wing defenders of the peasant commune. I do not agree with the view that in this they were bewitched by 'the spell of the commune';[99] they knew well enough what the commune really was and how incompatible with liberal principles. A simpler and more convincing explanation is that Stolypin was a symbol of bloody counter-revolution whom the Kadets dared not appear to support, at whatever cost to their principles. To say this is not to blame them: it was a revolutionary time and the dominant mood was such that no liberal party could support the government without committing political suicide. This, indeed, was precisely what Chicherin had in mind when he wrote about the dangers of legalizing open political struggle on a national scale before completing the transition to the rule of law under a strong but constitutionally limited government. He was aware that in a backward country liberal reforms had no chance of success in the midst of a struggle for power, let alone in revolutionary times, and this was the main reason why he was so cautious in his approach to the problem of political freedom in Russia.

4   Law and freedom

My presentation of Chicherin's legal and political philosophy cannot explore the details in depth; he wrote so much and on so many topics that a detailed analysis of his views would require a separate book. It seems better, therefore, to concentrate on his basic ideas concerning the proper understanding of law, its meaning and its function.

Basically, Chicherin saw law as a system of general rules of conduct protecting and limiting individual freedom. He agreed with Kant that universal reciprocal coercion, characteristic of law, serves no other purpose than the creation of conditions 'under which the will of one person can be conjoined with the will of another in accordance with a

---

[99] See D. W. Treadgold, *Lenin and his Rivals*, p. 269.

universal law of freedom'.[100] He was aware, painfully aware, that many theorists defined law as a means of realizing moral, social, or political aims, but he treated such views as symptomatic of a deep crisis in legal culture, as sad evidence of the growing obfuscation of legal consciousness.[101] He repeatedly stressed that law is not merely an instrument for specific purposes but has a value of its own, its own autonomous sphere; that it deals with the boundaries of individual freedom and therefore must be concerned with the rules to be observed by free individual agents rather than the moral or utilitarian aims of their activity. Law, he held, is inseparable from freedom. He defined law (*pravo*) as freedom determined (or limited) by rules.[102] Law in the subjective sense, namely, law as right, is the legally sanctioned freedom to do something, or to demand something; law objectively considered is the system of rules setting necessary limits to the freedom of action.[103]

To appreciate the full weight of these definitions it is necessary to explain what is meant by freedom. According to Chicherin freedom can be conceived either as external, as the scope of individual freedom in a given society, or as inner, moral freedom.[104] In the first sense it is negative, a freedom from constraints, independence from the arbitrary will of other men; in the second sense it means rational and moral self-determination. In his discussion of the first kind of freedom Chicherin quoted Locke, emphatically agreeing with his view that 'the question is not proper, whether the Will be free, but whether a Man be free'.[105] Freedom in this sense pertains not to the will but to the agent, since the lack of external constraints has nothing in common with the *liberum arbitrium*. Freedom in the second sense means the capacity to control one's will, to subordinate man's natural will to a higher, moral will, a will free of natural determinations and subject only to universal reason; it is, therefore, the freedom of will, and not merely the external

---

[100] Cf. I. Kant, *The Metaphysical Elements of Justice* (Part I of *The Metaphysics of Morals*). Translated, with an Introduction, by J. Ladd, Indianapolis–New York–Kansas City 1965, p. 34.

[101] Cf. B. Chicherin, *Voprosy politiki*, pp. 115–16.

[102] See B. Chicherin, *Filosofiia prava*, Moscow, 1900, p. 84: 'Pravo est' svoboda opredelënnaia zakonom'. This definition is very difficult to translate into English, since it is clear that *zakon* in this context is neither 'law' nor 'statute'.

[103] B. Chicherin, *Sobstvennost' i gosudarstvo*, vol. 1, p. 34.

[104] Ibid., pp. 3–9.

[105] J. Locke, *An Essay Concerning Human Understanding*. P. H. Nidditch (ed.), Oxford, 1975, p. 244 (Book 2, Ch. xxi). Cf. B. Chicherin, *Sobstvennost' i gosudarstvo*, vol. 1, pp. 4–6.

freedom of action. Such a freedom is conceivable only if man is treated as a metaphysical being, meaningfully related to the divine Absolute.[106] The idealist philosophers of Germany, chief of whom was Hegel, understood this, conceiving of human freedom as a striving for the Absolute by means of unceasing efforts of rational and moral self-creation. Chicherin recognized Hegelianism as the best, most fully developed philosophical argument against determinism and declared his entire agreement with it.[107] He stressed that Hegel's conception of freedom was much loftier and nobler than Locke's: after all, Locke's freedom was something which men could share with animals (cf. the common-sense distinction between a 'free' wild animal and the same animal in a cage),[108] while the Hegelian conception pertained to the highest capacities of man, to man as a truly divine creature.

However, the further development of Chicherin's thoughts led to rather unexpected conclusions. External freedom, he argued, is an indispensable condition of the higher freedom and therefore it should never be renounced for moral or other reasons. It is, in a sense, a necessary foundation for the entire edifice of freedom. It is a lower freedom, to be sure, but if the higher freedom is absolutized at the expense of the lower, the entire structure breaks down, as the case of Fichte demonstrates.[109] The higher, moral freedom is the freedom of the good; morality, however, cannot be institutionalized by force, therefore the freedom of the evil, within certain limits, must likewise be permitted and protected. Morally neutral, external freedom—freedom to be either moral or immoral[110]—is a precondition of freedom as self-determination and self-perfection. The socially acceptable limits of this external freedom are set by the law. The law, therefore, deals with the sphere of external freedom, with freedom in the Lockeian sense and not with the higher freedom of Hegel.

Despite appearances, this turn of thought was not a radical departure from Hegelianism; on the contrary, it could find justification in Hegel's own 'radical separation between the political and the legal order'.[111] For Hegel the proper sphere of law was civil society,

---

[106] B. Chicherin, *Filosofiia prava*, pp. 47–8.

[107] See ibid., pp. 44–6 and *Sobstvennost' i gosudarstvo*, vol. 1, pp. 8–9. Cf. B. Chicherin, *Istoriia politicheskikh uchenii*, vol. 4, Moscow, 1877, pp. 578–82.

[108] B. Chicherin, *Sobstvennost' i gosudarstvo*, vol. 1, p. 7.   [109] Ibid., p. 13.

[110] Ibid., p. 14. In his *Philosophy of Law* (*Filosofiia prava*, pp. 50–2) Chicherin defined 'licence' (*proizvol*), or 'freedom to be evil' as a necessary element of freedom.

[111] E. Bréhier, *The History of Philosophy*, vol. 6 *The Nineteenth Century: Period of Systems, 1800–1850*, London, 1968, p. 186.

conceived as a battlefield of individual private interests and sharply contrasted with the state, seen as 'the actuality of the ethical Idea'.[112] He regarded civil society as a sphere in which abstract rights, rights which accrue to human beings as such, and not yet as citizens of states, are transformed into laws; he stressed that laws deal only with the external relations of persons to each other, protecting their freedom and personality, and he made it clear that the subject-matter of laws is the relations of persons through property, contract, right, wrong, crime, marriage, etc.[113] Thus it is misleading to say that Hegel saw law as 'the embodiment of the ethical idea emanating from the state'.[114] He did not at all conceive of public law emanating directly from the state as law proper, law *par excellence*, law in the narrow and specific sense of the term. What he identified as law was private law, the law of civil society,[115] law whose function was for him to limit the external freedom of pursuing one's interests, not at all to embody 'the ethical Idea', thus realizing the 'higher freedom'. He never claimed that freedom as protected by law, the freedom of 'individuals in their capacity as burghers', could be anything but freedom from external constraints, that is to say, Lockeian freedom. He contemptuously criticized this conception of freedom as characteristic of the so-called 'philosophy of reflection', of the standpoint of the atomizing and abstract understanding (*Verstand*).[116] But this very standpoint was in his view a correlate of the abstract individualism of juridical thinking, which mirrored the dominant pattern of interpersonal relations in the *bürgerliche Gesellschaft*.

Chicherin accepted the essential points of Hegelian theory but differed from Hegel (sometimes more than he was prepared to acknowledge) in his value-judgements. Like Hegel, he saw private law as the purest expression of the idea of law, as law *par excellence*. Like Hegel, he conceived of civil society as a sphere of conflicting private interests, that is, as a sphere of economic freedom, individualism and privacy, or, in his own words, 'the aggregate of private relations between free individuals'.[117] Finally, he agreed with Hegel on the

---

[112] *Hegel's Philosophy of Right*. T. M. Knox (trans.), Oxford, 1953, p. 155.
[113] Cf. W. T. Stace, *The Philosophy of Hegel: A Systematic Exposition*, London, 1924, pp. 382 and 418–21.
[114] See C. J. Friedrich, *The Philosophy of Law in Historical Perspective*, 2nd edn., London, 1963, p. 237.
[115] Cf. E. Bréhier, *The History of Philosophy*, vol. 6, p. 186.
[116] Cf. Hegel's *Philosophy of Right*, pp. 27–8, 124.
[117] Chicherin, *Kurs*, vol. 1, p. 87.

inseparability of civil society and law, treating civil society as a 'juridical association', situated between the family and the state. But he attributed a far greater value to this juridical sphere of life and to the kind of freedom bound up with it than Hegel did. The extent of his agreement with Hegel and also the above-mentioned difference are made clear in the following quotation:

The full expression of juridical principles, an expression devoid of any extraneous admixture, is private law, civil law. Here man is a free, independent person, placed in certain material conditions and standing in specific juridical relationships to other people. By the very nature of these relationships it is a sphere of individualism; *it is here where the main centre of human freedom is to be found.*[118]

The italicized words express Chicherin's deepest conviction. He repeatedly stressed that 'individualism *is* human freedom', that it is inseparable from the free, rational personality and that the struggle against it, if successful, can only result in degrading human life to the level of animal existence.[119] That Hegel would not have subscribed to this apologia for individualistic freedom Chicherin was well aware. In the *Philosophy of Law* he pointed out that anti-individualism was a peculiar feature of German social philosophy and that Hegel was not immune from this unhealthy tendency.[120] He accused him of reducing the human individual to 'a transitory manifestation of general spiritual substance', which objectifies itself in institutions, stressing that 'institutions exist for men, and not the other way round'.[121] He also opposed the instrumental treatment of individuals in the Hegelian philosophy of history, declaring firmly: 'The importance of the human individual is not confined to his role as an organ of the universal historical process. As the bearer of an absolute principle man has absolute significance in himself'.[122]

At the same time Chicherin presented Hegel as a thinker whose attitude towards individualism was inconsistent rather than simply negative.[123] After all Hegel fully acknowledged the necessity and relative autonomy of civil society; he was inclined to deify the state but he respected the dignity of man and gave it a metaphysical sanction.

---

[118] Chicherin, *Sobstvennost' i gosudarstvo*, vol. 1, pp. 88–9.
[119] Chicherin, *Kurs*, vol. 2, p. 149.   [120] Chicherin, *Filosofiia prava*, p. 227.
[121] Ibid., pp. 224–5. Cf. Zor'kin, *Iz istorii*, pp. 35, 131.
[122] Chicherin, *Nauka i religiia*, 2nd edn., 1901, p. 132. Quoted from V. V. Zenkovsky, *A History of Russian Philosophy*, p. 616.
[123] Chicherin, *Filosofiia prava*, p. 227.

The real danger to individualism was seen by the Russian thinker to lie in the anti-individualistic tendencies of sociology, especially those of the organicist school, whose followers (for instance Schäffle) denied the very existence of individuals by treating them as mere cells of a supra-individual social organism.[124] Furthermore, the very emergence of sociology as a discipline, the fact that the word 'society' was no longer associated with the private sphere, as in the theory of 'civil society', was for Chicherin an unwelcome development. In the preface to his *Property and State* he wrote:

Now a new monster has risen above the state: it is called 'society'. Earlier, society was conceived as an aggregate of free forces, now it has been transformed into a certain mysterious entity, swallowing both the state and the private sphere; an entity directing everybody and everything, making impossible all independent manifestations of life. In fact it is a new name for the state, but this time it is a state with much broader prerogatives.[125]

Chicherin was of course aware that his earlier writings gave an impression that he was a staunch advocate of a strong centralized state. In his view this was perfectly compatible with the advocacy of individualistic freedom since both centralism and individualism were legitimate in their proper spheres: centralism in the theory of the state, individualism in the theory of civil society.[126] He conceded, however, that his emphasis on individualism was bound up with a shift in the thematic scope of his work, because this shift was itself a response to a striking change in the general intellectual climate. In the 1850s the dominant trend of thought, both in the West and in Russia, was so strongly, so one-sidedly anti-centralist that it was necessary to resist it by dwelling on the historically progressive role of the centralized state. In the 1870s, however, the contrary was the case: public opinion increasingly favoured state intervention, a broadening of the scope of government powers, thus making the state virtually omnipotent.[127] This drastic change was accompanied by the development of anti-

[124] Cf. ibid., pp. 27–8 and *Kurs*, vol. 2, pp. 5–6.
[125] Chicherin, *Sobstvennost' i gosudarstvo*, vol. 1, pp. xix–xx. Chicherin was right: in the classical liberal conception of the public and the private civil society belonged entirely to the private sphere (see S. I. Benn and Gerald F. Gauss, 'The Liberal Conception of the Public and the Private', in *Public and Private in Social Life*, S. I. Benn and G. F. Gauss (eds.), London, 1983). This conception is to be found also in Hegelianism, quite irrespective of Hegel's attitude to classical liberalism. In Hegel's view civil society was 'a system of private ends'. (Ibid., p. 51.)
[126] Chicherin, *Filosofiia prava*, p. 259.
[127] Chicherin, *Sobstvennost' i gosudarstvo*, vol. 2, p. xix.

individualistic sociological theories, on the one hand, and by the growing influence of socialist or semi-socialist ideologies, on the other. But its main cause was extra-intellectual: it was the process of political democratization.[128] Freedom conceived as participation in political decision-making was bound to foster a tendency to widen the scope of political decisions and, by the same token, to restrict the private, non-regulated sphere of life. In this way political freedom, freedom in the public sphere, was gradually swallowing up individual, non-political freedom. Political democracy, conceived earlier as an institutional safeguard for individual freedom, was becoming an end in itself, fully revealing its essentially collectivist ethos. While struggling against authoritarian political structures it was growing more and more committed to the idea of increasing government regulation, more and more inclined to endow democratic governments with unlimited power and thus more and more inimical to classical liberal values.

This pessimistic diagnosis did not entail any change to Chicherin's view of political freedom. He had always seen it as the final stage of normal historical development. In his book *About Popular Representation* he presented parliamentary government as a natural consequence of the coming of age of each nation and as the final stage in the political development of mankind; he repeated this judgement in his *Course of Political Science*;[129] in *Property and the State* he added an additional argument for political freedom in Russia—the danger of 'democratic Caesarism'. In each case, however, he meant political freedom within a constitutional monarchy which he saw as the best form of mixed government limited by law. Democracy as simple majority rule was in his view the sheer rule of force, absolutely incompatible with law and justice.[130] In his philosophy of history he accepted Benjamin Constant's distinction between 'ancient freedom' (i.e. freedom in the public sphere) and 'modern freedom' (freedom in the private sphere), and concluded from this that the task to be accomplished was the combining of the first with the second.[131] His political ideal was a state based upon modern civil society, that is protecting freedom in the

---

[128] Chicherin, *Kurs*, vol. 1, p. 339. A similar observation was made a hundred years later by F. A. Hayek: 'I have belatedly come to agree with Josef Schumpeter who 30 years ago argued that there was an irreconcilable conflict between democracy and capitalism' (F. A. Hayek, *New Studies in Philosophy, Politics, Economics and the History of Ideas*, London, 1978, p. 107).

[129] Chicherin, *O narodnom predstavitel'stve*, p. 175 and *Kurs*, vol. 1. p. 180.

[130] Chicherin, *O narodnom predstavitel'stve*, p. 75.

[131] Chicherin, *Sobstvennost' i gosudarstvo*, vol. 1, pp. 32–3.

private sphere, and crowned by representative government, exercising freedom in public life.

The new element in Chicherin's political views was his growing realization that political authority as such must be qualified and restricted, and that therefore he could no longer support the Hegelian doctrine of the unlimited sovereignty of the state. He never identified this doctrine with legal positivism but stressed that in Hegelianism the state was conceived as a 'metaphysical being', as the embodiment of a universal ethical idea, and not merely as an organized power.[132] He had to concede, however, that sociology had succeeded in demonstrating the dependence of the state on different particular interests and that the Hegelian idealization of the modern state had thus become untenable. Therefore it was necessary to make law, and the sphere of freedom protected by it, more autonomous in relation to the state than it was in the Hegelian philosophy of right.

This characteristic change is clearly marked in Chicherin's attitude towards human rights.[133] In his book on popular representation he firmly rejected natural-rights liberalism, which conceived of human rights as being natural, pre-political and inalienable.[134] In reality, he argued, people could have rights only as members of a certain body politic; such rights were a product of historical development and attempts to make them absolute could only bring about the institutionalization of anarchy. Fifteen years later, in *Property and the State*, this emphasis on the political foundation and framework of all legal rights was replaced by emphasis on the essentially non-political features of civil law and on the 'natural' character of its basic principles, such as the inviolability of the person and private property, freedom of contracts, performance of promises, and so forth. True, Chicherin did not claim that these principles (above all the basic principle of formal equality before the law) had always been embodied in positive laws, or that they did not need to be sanctioned by the highest political authority. He stressed, however, that there are certain 'eternal principles of law', which are 'written in the hearts of men' and serve as an ideal norm for the historically developing systems of positive law.[135] He emphasized that such norms could only be formal,

---

[132] Chicherin, *Kurs*, vol. 2, p. 9.

[133] This was noticed by P. Struve (*Na raznye temy*, p. 543, n.), although he was quite wrong in treating Chicherin's earlier views as representing sociological and legal positivism.

[134] Chicherin, *O narodnom predstavitel'stve*, p. 481–1.

[135] Chicherin, *Sobstvennost' i gosudarstvo*, vol. 1, p. 96.

---

that their concrete content, and the extent to which they are embodied in positive laws, depended on historical development. It may be argued that in this he anticipated Stammler's conception of natural law with changing content.[136]

In his *Philosophy of Law* Chicherin agreed with Kant that all the natural rights of man can be reduced to one: 'Freedom (independence from the constraint of another's will), in so far as it is compatible with the freedom of everyone else in accordance with a universal law, is the one sole and original right that belongs to every human being by virtue of his humanity'.[137] In his earlier works Chicherin preferred to define freedom not as an innate right of man but rather as man's innate potential for being a right-holder.[138] But even this cautious formula made it absolutely clear that in his view law and freedom were inseparable. Freedom, he never ceased to stress, was the eternal source of law; thus it constituted an ever-present element of law, although its legally sanctioned limits might change in relation to historical and social conditions. And it must be remembered that in Chicherin's view the degree of socially permissible freedom was the main criterion of historical progress.

Another defence of the non-relative, unchangeable character of the basic principles of modern civil law was provided by the Hegelian concept of the 'end of historical development'. According to Chicherin this was precisely what had happened with the law: its historical development had reached the highest stage, all ideal norms inherent in the notion of law had at last been revealed and explicitly formulated. 'It is impossible to go further in this sphere. The ideal has been attained.'[139]

The implications of this were obvious. It meant that the power of the government should be *limited* by civil law, by the rights of individuals and, also, by the rights of different associations, such as business companies, churches, and so forth. In other words, respect for law demands that the authority of the government should not be extended to the sphere of non-political ('private') inter-personal relations.[140] In themselves civil rights are not something 'natural' and inalienable;

---

[136] See Zor'kin, *Iz istorii*, p. 37.
[137] I. Kant, *The Metaphysical Elements of Justice*, p. 43–4. Cf. Chicherin, *Filosofiia prava*, pp. 105–7.
[138] Cf. Chicherin, *Istoriia politicheskikh uchenii*, vol. 3, Moscow, 1874, p. 122.
[139] Chicherin, *Kurs*, vol. 2, p. 424.
[140] Cf. Chicherin, *Sobstvennost' i gosudarstvo*, vol. 2, p. 214.

nevertheless, at a certain stage of historical development *they should be made inalienable.*

Of course, it was not always easy to draw a line between the civil and the political spheres. In his approach to those rights which could assume a directly political significance he remained very cautious; because of this he never championed the freedom of the press in Russian conditions. He was firm, however, that freedom of conscience, freedom of thought and inviolability of the person must not be encroached upon.[141] This was enough to make him a resolute opponent of the reactionary policies (associated with his former friend, K. Pobedonostsev) of persecuting religious minorities, instigating anti-semitism, and russifying the so-called 'borderlands'. Unlike the majority of nineteenth-century Russian liberals, he was even bold enough to defend the national rights of the Poles.[142] To him the Jewish and Polish questions had not only legal but also moral significance for the Russians. I shall be returning to this point later, in connection with the problem of law and morality.

On the whole, Chicherin's view on the proper relation of civil to political rights can be epitomized in one general principle, which he formulated clearly and applied consistently. Civil rights, he held, should have priority over political rights; civil freedom, freedom from political control, was more important than political freedom, freedom as political participation, and, therefore, civil rights should always be broader in scope than political rights.[143] It followed from this that to broaden the scope of political (public) freedom at the expense of civil (private) freedom must destroy the very foundation of freedom. From this perspective authoritarian dictators did not pose the greatest threat to freedom; much more dangerous were the democratic socialists, or semi-socialists, who wanted to democratize the process of political decision-making, while at the same time subjecting the private and above all the economic sphere to constantly increasing political regulation.

Under Russian conditions the chief priority of the civil rights issue was, of course, that of extending full civil rights to the peasants and thus abolishing the village commune. This shows once more how remarkably consistent Chicherin's thought was.

---

[141] Cf. Chicherin, *Filosofiia prava*, pp. 107–16.
[142] See Chicherin, *Polskii i evreiskii voprosy*, Berlin, 1901 (2nd edn.).
[143] Chicherin, *Sobstvennost' i gosudarstvo*, vol. 2, p. 305.

5 Law and purpose

If the law is inseparable from individual freedom, it follows that it should not be concerned with the aims of human activity. Its proper function consists in laying down general rules of action, and not in furthering any special ends. Its rules should be 'purposeless', aim-independent, negative, because the choice of the purposes, of the positive aims of any activity, should be left to individuals themselves. The law sets up the necessary limits for individual freedom, but within these limits individuals should have full freedom to pursue their own aims. The law, therefore, cannot be seen as an instrument for purposive collective activity. The 'idea of law' demands that laws should protect the autonomy of persons, their freedom of choice, and precisely because of this laws should never be used to steer society or to engineer a certain 'social policy'.

The struggle against instrumentalization of the law, against all attempts to interpret the law as a means for the realization of certain preconceived positive aims—political or social, utilitarian or moral—was a leitmotif of Chicherin's philosophy of law. We should remember, however, that he meant only 'law proper', that is private law. In the sphere of public law the general interest of the state is of paramount importance and individual freedom should be subordinated to the public good.[144] It deals not with individual freedom but with public duties and, therefore, cannot be aim-independent: a private citizen must be allowed to pursue his own, freely chosen aims, but an official must not use his position for his private ends. Government regulations are necessarily purposive and, therefore, in the sphere of public service there is always a tension between respect for general rules and the carrying out of specific policies.[145] Chicherin found the same tension between general abstract rules and the solution of concrete practical problems in the entire field of public law. It comprised laws which were more or less general, more or less stable, in a word, more or less 'law-like'. According to Chicherin some government regulations did not deserve the name 'law' at all, even at the most metaphorical level. These included specific commands, dealing with single events or specific practical problems, as well as different kinds of administrative regulations (*Verordnungen, règlements*), and so forth.[146]

[144] Chicherin, *Sobstvennost' i gosudarstvo*, vol. 1, pp. 90–1.
[145] Chicherin agreed that purposiveness is the leading principle of politics (see *Kurs*, vol. 3, p. 17).
[146] See Chicherin, *Kurs*, vol. 1, pp. 299–306.

From the classical liberal point of view 'private law is the heart of all law, with public law as a narrow protective frame laid around private law and especially private property'.[147] Although a specialist in the field of public law, Chicherin, as indicated, fully subscribed to this view. When he spoke about law as such he meant exclusively private law. Public law was in his eyes something more and something less than law proper: something more, because, like Hegel, he saw the state as the highest social union; something less, because, again like Hegel, he saw not the state but civil society as the proper sphere of pure, uncontaminated juridical principles. At first glance it may seem that his Hegelian emphasis on the importance of the state distinguished him profoundly from classical liberalism, especially its Anglo-Saxon variety. On closer examination, however, Chicherin proves to have largely reinterpreted Hegelianism in the spirit of classical liberalism. Sometimes he openly rejected Hegelian metaphysical impersonalism, resorting instead to the metaphysical personalism of Kant.[148] Let us take, for instance, the following quotation from his *Property and the State*:

> Metaphysics, seeing in law the expression of freedom, must acknowledge that the true source of freedom is not the universal impersonal spirit but the individual person, his inner self-determination. Therefore it cannot allow the swallowing up of private law by public law. From the metaphysical point of view private law is the true sphere of freedom; public law is erected upon it as a higher sphere, but not to destroy it, rather to protect it from infringement.[149]

In this manner the inviolability of private law, that is, of the law proper, was 'metaphysically' sanctioned. By the same token, the power of the government was 'metaphysically limited'. It followed that to make the state omnipotent and omnipresent would contradict the very 'idea' of the state, that the sovereign political power should not encroach upon the autonomy of civil society and that the swallowing up of private by public law was 'metaphysically' forbidden.

In spite of this statement Chicherin was aware that metaphysical idealism was by no means immune against such temptations. On the contrary, he emphasized that the decisive steps towards the theory of an omnipotent state, which regarded law as a mere instrument for realizing the purposes of government, were taken by metaphysical

[147] G. Radbruch, 'Legal Philosophy', in *The Legal Philosophies of Lask, Radbruch, and Dabin*, Cambridge, Mass., 1950, p. 153.
[148] See Zor'kin, *Iz istorii*, p. 35.
[149] Chicherin, *Sobstvennost' i gosudarstvo*, vol. 1, p. 90.

idealists. This, he explained, was because the idealist world-view was naturally bound up with the idea of a lofty general purpose, which created the danger of absolutizing this purpose at the expense of the autonomy of the private spheres of human life.[150]

As might be expected, he illustrated this thesis by pointing to Plato. The Platonic vision of the ideal state was to him an instructive and terrifying example of the consequences of sacrificing individual freedom to an imaginary collective purpose; an example showing that a consistently 'purposive' view of the state leads inevitably to the total enslavement of individuals, who are regarded as the property of the state, and to the subjection of their entire life to humiliatingly minute control and regulation.[151] A complete contrast to this gloomy utopia had been offered by Aristotle, whose *Politics* Chicherin held to be 'the most remarkable political treatise of all time',[152] an inexhaustible source of political wisdom. The Russian thinker wholeheartedly subscribed to a number of Aristotle's ideas, such as the theory of mixed government, the conception of politics as the art of moderation and, last but not least, his view of the middle classes as the social basis of freedom and observance of the law in the state. The spirit of Aristotelian political philosophy was in his view very close to Hegelianism, properly understood, and to the modern theory of constitutional monarchy.[153]

In modern times the danger of idealist absolutization of collective purpose became especially conspicuous in the writings of two German idealists: Fichte and Krause. For Fichte freedom meant not the negative freedom of the individual but the positive freedom of the species: the rule of the universal human ego over the non-ego, the victory of the subjectivity of the human world over the objectivity of nature. Because of this it was quite natural that what he meant by law was not 'a formal principle' securing external freedom of action; he wanted to give law a positive content and, therefore, saw it as a means of attaining 'truly human' purposes. In this way he embraced the 'positive' conception of freedom, which turned out to be perfectly compatible with the ideal of 'the closed state', regulating all spheres of individual life.[154] More than that: the omnipotent rational state could be seen from this perspective as a powerful instrument of freedom—an instrument of the collective ego, which controls and determines itself,

---

[150] Ibid., p. 47.
[151] Chicherin, *Istoriia politicheskikh uchenii*, vol. 1, Moscow, 1869, pp. 50–4.
[152] Ibid., p. 57.   [153] Ibid., p. 66.   [154] Ibid., vol. 3, p. 435.

subjects itself to laws, and thereby liberates itself from the humiliating power of the blind necessity which governs the world of things. A less well-known German idealist, C. C. F. Krause, saw the purpose of human life not in the increase of man's power over nature but, rather, in the fulfilment of all truly human needs. Defining law in relation to this purpose led him to proclaim a new human right—the right to the fulfilment of all man's reasonable needs. On the other hand, however, realizing that there could be no rights without corresponding duties, he proclaimed the right of the wealthier and the stronger to place under their benevolent tutelage those members of society who were not able to satisfy their needs themselves.[155] In this way what seemed to be an immense extension of the sphere of human rights turned out to be achieved at the cost of man's basic right: the right to individual freedom and autonomy.

An equal danger to law and freedom appeared from another quarter: from a thinker who, unlike Fichte or Plato, was, in Chicherin's view, completely devoid of any philosophical capacity.[156] This man, Jeremy Bentham, 'recognized only practical aims in human actions and thus completely eliminated the very notion of law'.[157] He was right in rejecting the eternal tenets of natural law, especially the innate rights of man, but he rejected also man's innate potential as a right-bearer (*pravosposobnost'*) which amounted to an outright denial of man's dignity.[158] Chicherin attributed his remarkable reputation to the low level of philosophical culture in England,[159] but had to agree that his influence was enormous. It was also especially dangerous because of its strong appeal to common sense and its apparent closeness to certain currents within the liberal tradition. Therefore, Chicherin strongly urged the necessity of resisting it and recommended for this the works of Kant and Humboldt. In his view Humboldt's idea of a state founded upon and strictly limited by law was a most welcome counterweight to Bentham's concept of an unrestrained government, pursuing utilitarian aims and disregarding aim-independent general rules.[160]

The dangers of utilitarianism reappeared in Germany in the guise of Ihering's 'jurisprudence of interests'. His energetic fight against conservative-romantic historicism, that is, against the uncritical

---

[155] Ibid., vol. 4, p. 103–4.　　　　　　[156] Ibid., vol. 3, p. 256.
[157] Ibid., p. 280.　　[158] Ibid., p. 294.　　[159] Ibid., p. 289.
[160] Ibid., pp. 374–97. According to Chicherin, focusing on the problem of the *limits* rather than the *forms* of state activity was an invaluable merit of Humboldt's work, *Idee zu einem Versuch die Gränzen der Wirksamkeit des Staats zu bestimmen* (1792).

acceptance of unconscious 'organic growth', his enthusiasm for Roman law, his vindication of the role of consciousness, and of the teleological element in law-making, appeared consistent with the rational individualism of the Enlightenment and with the liberal approach to legislation. Chicherin, however, emphasized the utter impropriety of replacing general rules of justice by purposes, interests and other practical considerations. He firmly associated Ihering's name with the crisis of liberalism and with the general obfuscation of legal consciousness. He pointed out that to derive law from interests amounted in practice to deriving right from might.[161] He was horrified by Ihering's view that the binding force of contract was of less importance than the purpose of law; he stressed that interests and purposes had nothing in common with law—the interests of debtors might be socially more important than the interests of creditors, but, nevertheless, the law must take the side of the latter.[162] In the first pages of his *Philosophy of Law* he attacked Ihering's views as completely incompatible with a philosophical approach to legal theory: the philosophy of law, he claimed, could not base itself upon the 'practice of life', its true task was to evaluate this practice and provide norms for it.[163]

However, Chicherin's most sweeping criticism was levelled at the general assumptions of the doctrine of legal positivism, of which Ihering's theory was a particular variant. If law, as claimed by the legal positivists, is a coercive command flowing from the sovereign political power, the division of law into private and public does not make sense. Private law, protecting individual freedom, is swallowed up by public law, directly subordinated to the purposes of the body politic. Everything becomes a matter of public concern, that is to say subject to control from the point of view of the public good and public morality, which amounts to the denial of individual freedom in its innermost sphere.[164] Civil society becomes part of an all-embracing political organization and thus loses its autonomous existence.[165] Where the

---

[161] Chicherin, *Sobstvennost' i gosudarstvo*, vol. 1, p. 48.
[162] Ibid., pp. 176–82.   [163] Chicherin, *Filosofiia prava*, pp. 1–4.
[164] Chicherin, *Sobstvennost' i gosudarstvo*, vol. 2, p. 212. Identical reasoning is to be found in Hayek, who saw legal positivism as the forerunner of socialist and totalitarian ideologies. See F. A. Hayek, *Law, Legislation and Liberty*, vol. 1, *Rules and Order*, London, 1982, pp. 133–4.
[165] According to Chicherin, Ihering's work *Der Zweck im Recht* was a theoretical justification of state interventionism in the economic sphere. Cf. B. Chicherin, *Sobstvennost' i gosudarstvo*, vol. 2, pp. 172–3.

private sphere is, nevertheless, not encroached upon, it is not for reasons of principle, but merely a matter of convenience, expediency, or other practical consideration.

In this manner, according to Chicherin, legal positivism paved the way for various attempts to use law for socialist purposes. When private law was firmly entrenched as the 'law proper', socialists had no choice but to proclaim their opposition to law as such. With the advent of legal positivism they recognized the possibility of using public law against private law in order to further their own aims, first of all the cause of distributive justice. This possibility was fully exploited by the German 'professorial socialists' who thus greatly contributed to the growing obfuscation of legal consciousness in Europe, especially in their own country. The most fatal result of this obfuscation was the social legislation of Bismarck. Chicherin saw it as the first step towards state socialism and commented: 'State socialism is not a proper means to use in the struggle against revolutionary socialism . . . When conservatives, out of hatred towards liberals, stretch out their hands to socialists, the social order is threatened at its very foundations.'[166]

One can safely say that in his principled hostility to socialism Chicherin had no equal among nineteenth-century Russian thinkers. He defined socialism as a system combining the greatest oppression with the greatest inefficiency;[167] a system in which everybody is transformed into an official of the state;[168] a system in which everything is based upon the principle of command and which is, therefore, absolutely incompatible with freedom. Such a system contradicted not only his view of law but also his view of society and his view of the state. Society as a sphere of interaction between independent persons would cease to exist and the state would be transformed into a kind of super-state, directly managing all the affairs of the population. This immense extension of state activity would entail a drastic departure from the very idea of the state: the modern state as the highest form of unity in multiplicity would be replaced by a form of primitive unmediated unity, incompatible with the autonomy of its constituent parts. In Chicherin's eyes this would mean a' disastrous retrogression—a relapse into a kind of unity characteristic of the earliest stages of social development, preceding the differentiating work of historical progress.[169]

---

[166] Ibid., p. 243. [167] Chicherin, *Kurs*, vol. 2, p. 193.
[168] Chicherin, *Sobstvennost' i gosudarstvo*, vol. 1, p. 434.
[169] Chicherin, *Kurs*, vol. 2, p. 30.

It sometimes seems that Chicherin saw the paramount danger in peaceful, reformist forms of socialism, and not in its revolutionary variety. For him every step in the direction of 'social policy' was a small but irreversible victory for socialism—even if it was not part of a consciously formulated socialist programme.[170] He was fully aware that such steps were often necessitated not by economic or other utilitarian reasons, but by the growing force of the moral ideal of social justice. No wonder, therefore, that he devoted a lot of energy to the problem of the proper relationship between morality and legislation, morality and the state.

6 Law and morality

In Chicherin's view the retrogressive tendency of socialism manifested itself with special strength in its strange but essential similarity to theocracy. Both socialism and theocracy made no distinction between the legal and the moral and accepted the use of the coercive power of the state for the realization of moral aims. According to Chicherin this could only lead to 'the worst imaginable tyranny'.[171] He thought (in accordance with the '*Gesellschaft* -paradigm' of law) that law should be sharply distinguished from morality, that any confusion of juridical law and moral law leads inevitably to the decrease of freedom and thus to the undermining of the very foundation of both morality and law. He disagreed with Leibniz's view that law is 'minimum morality', agreeing instead with Thomasius that morality flows from love and is absolutely incompatible with juridical coercion.[172] Law is concerned with the external behaviour of people, not with the salvation of their souls. Morality which tries to institutionalize itself by legal means becomes an instrument of immoral and lawless oppression.[173] The same happens if the law tries to extend its proper scope and ignores the boundary dividing it from morality; the 'moralizing jurists', advocating legislation on matters of morality, contribute willy-nilly to the destruction of the autonomy of the personality, the cornerstone of both morality and law.[174] Juridical law defines the exernal limits of liberty whereas moral law defines the inner dictates of moral duty. The legal definition of the limits of liberty does not destroy the individual's autonomy but—on

---

[170] Chicherin, *Sobstvennost' i gosudarstvo*, vol. 1, p. 160 ('Social policy' is here called 'a thoughtless servant of socialism').
[171] Chicherin, *Mistitsizm v nauke*, Moscow, 1880, p. 60.
[172] Chicherin, *Istoriia politicheskikh uchenii*, vol. 2, Moscow, 1872, pp. 195–210, 229.
[173] Chicherin, *Mistitsizm v nauke*, p. 95.   [174] Chicherin, *Filosofiia prava*, p. 87.

the contrary—demarcates a certain sphere where the individual is not subject to interference of state or society; a sphere in which he can be either moral or immoral. A legal definition of moral duty, on the other hand, is incompatible with freedom of conscience and therefore morality. It is incompatible with true law as well, since freedom of conscience is inherent in the very 'idea' of law. Chicherin paid homage to freedom of conscience even in his early book on popular representation—a book most strongly critical of the 'absolute rights of man'. Freedom of conscience, he wrote there, 'is a fundamental right of man, a right which is independent of man's social relations'.[175] It was always obvious to him that morality is a matter of conscience and not of any kind of external regulation. The law, backed by coercive powers, decides what is permitted and what is not permitted; morality, on the other hand, decides what is positively recommendable and desirable, but must refrain from resorting to coercion.[176] Even organized moral pressure was seen by Chicherin as destructive of morality because incompatible with freedom of conscience and with the ideal of love. Morality, he stressed, should not imitate law in trying to enforce its rules; it should realize its aims by example, not by creating an atmosphere of compulsory conformism.

These arguments were directed against many different thinkers, both Russian and non-Russian. In his *Mysticism in Science* Chicherin levelled them at Soloviev's utopia of a 'free theocracy'; we may suppose, however, that he also had in mind the Slavophiles' ideal of community and their criticism of the law as an 'external truth'. In his other books he criticized the Slavophiles explicitly, pointing out that their contemptuous attitude towards law did not serve the cause of morality; on the contrary, the notorious lack of legal culture in Russia was a correlate of the 'moral rottenness' of Russian life and only the Westernizing legal reforms of Alexander II succeeded in partially improving this sad situation.[177] In a sense Chicherin's emphasis on the need of separating law from morality served also as a warning against conservative interpretations of Hegelianism. He stressed in this connection that the state is not a supra-individual organic whole: it is a 'union of wills', an organism in the moral sense, composed of free persons, and not of mere organs, a form of unity embracing all spheres

---

[175] Chicherin, *O narodnom predstavitel'stve*, pp. 490–1.
[176] Chicherin, *Filosofiia prava*, pp. 314–15.
[177] Chicherin, *Kurs*, vol. 3, pp. 405–6.

of life without destroying their autonomy.[178] Moreover, he claimed that this highest form of human unity also contains some definitely inorganic elements—primarily civil and political freedom, which by its very nature represents an 'inorganic principle'.[179] This amounted to a radical rejection of the conservative tradition in German idealist political philosophy. Even more radical, and much more contemptuous, was Chicherin's criticism of biological organicism in sociology.

It is obvious, however, that the Right was not Chicherin's main target. He recognized the greatest, most serious danger as lying in socialism: in the socialist contempt for law, often arising out of misplaced ethical maximalism, and in the idea of 'social justice'. In the socialist state, he argued, law would become a mere instrument for the realization of social aims, and economic activity would be transformed into a kind of duty.[180] This would result in the total bureaucratization of life and in the creation of a kind of oriental despotism.[181] Morality would gain nothing from it, since moral virtues could not flourish under tyranny. Equality, implicit in the idea of social justice, could be realized only at the expense of human dignity and freedom, because distributive justice (in contrast to commutative justice which is the proper concern of law) always implies hierarchical subordination and arbitrary commands. Chicherin's memoirs ended with a foreboding that the victory of socialism was imminent in Europe, that it would bring about the 'all-embracing despotism of the masses' and a complete destruction of civilization.[182] The spread of socialist ideas proved fatal for Europe, including Russia, even before this final victory. Socialism had already created a deep moral crisis in the West and the greatest obstacle to freedom in Russia.[183] Marx, Chicherin claimed, should be held morally responsible for this sad result.[184]

Chicherin's own approach to the problem of social justice placed him on the extreme right wing of Russian liberalism. He repeatedly stressed that it was not the business of the state to interfere in economic activity.[185] The solution of social problems should come

[178] Chicherin, *Sobstvennost' i gosudarstvo*, vol. 2, p. 180.
[179] Ibid., pp. 181–2.   [180] Ibid., p. 172.
[181] Ibid., vol. 1, pp. 410–11.   [182] Chicherin, *Vospominaniia*, 4, p. 301.
[183] Cf. Chicherin, *Sobstvennost' i gosudarstvo*, vol. 2, p. 373 and *Kurs*, vol. 2, p. 119.
[184] Chicherin, *Kurs*, vol. 2, p. 119.
[185] V. D. Zor'kin (*Iz istorii*, pp. 118–21) tries to present Chicherin as a precursor of the theory of state interventionism in economic affairs. In reality, however, the opposite was true. For Chicherin state interventionism was not something normal and superior to classical *laissez-faire* economy; on the contrary, he saw it as an extremely dangerous practice, paving the way to socialism. He conceded only that state intervention could be

about as part of the improvement of individual moral standards; the rich had a moral duty to help the poor, but the poor were not legally entitled to demand such help. Chicherin conceded that the state could also help the poor, but only exceptionally and as a matter of philanthropy. It must never institutionalize this help as a matter of legal rights, not could it demand for this purpose additional funds from the taxpayers.[186]

Thus, we may conclude that Chicherin consistently opted for a clear separation of law and morality, and that in this respect he was closer to Kant than to Hegel.[187] However, this is not the entire truth. The above conclusion applied only to the sphere of law proper, that is to private law. It could not apply to public law because Chicherin, like Hegel, saw the state as the highest, all-embracing stage of 'objective spirit' and, therefore, could not treat it as a purely juridical union. As the highest form of unity, the state had to embrace the moral sphere of human life as well.[188]

Chicherin differed from Hegel on several points, among them in claiming that four stages, not three, should be distinguished in the dialectical process: primary unity, giving rise to the opposites of abstract universality and abstract particularity (the second and third stages), followed by their ultimate unity on a higher plane (the fourth stage).[189] In his philosophy of objective spirit this meant the replacement of the Hegelian triad of (1) family, (2) civil society, and (3) the state, by the following model:[190]

---

helpful in conditions of economic backwardness: the more backward a given country was, the greater could be the role of its government in promoting economic modernization. See Chicherin, *Kurs*, vol. 3, pp. 419–20.

[186] Chicherin, *Kurs*, vol. 2, pp. 181–6.

[187] Cf. W. Friedmann, *Legal Theory*, London, 1967, pp. 159, 167 n.

[188] Chicherin, *Kurs*, vol. 1, p. 49.

[189] Chicherin was convinced that this modification of the Hegelian dialectic was a discovery of outstanding importance, bringing the dialectic into line with the Aristotelian theory of four types of causes. The stage of primary unity (creative force in the Absolute) corresponded to Aristotle's active cause; abstract universality and abstract particularity (Reason and matter in the Absolute) coresponded to his formal and material causes; and the new and higher unity (the Spirit) corresponded to the final cause.

A fuller account of Chicherin's philosophy is contained in Walicki, *A History of Russian Thought*. See also V. V. Zenkovsky, *A History of Russian Philosophy*, pp. 606–20.

[190] Chicherin, *Sobstvennost' i gosudarstvo*, vol. 2, p. 194. For an application of this scheme to the history of political and legal thought see Chicherin, *Istoriia politicheskikh uchenii*, vol. 4, p. 596.

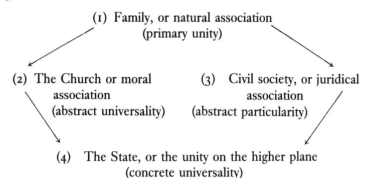

(1) Family, or natural association
(primary unity)

(2) The Church or moral
association
(abstract universality)

(3) Civil society, or juridical
association
(abstract particularity)

(4) The State, or the unity on the higher plane
(concrete universality)

This scheme enabled the Russian thinker to preserve the Kantian separation of law and morality (i.e. of the second and third stages) while overcoming it at the fourth stage. The separation and autonomy of each sphere of life within the state was for him the most important guarantee of liberty; he insisted, therefore, that law proper, and civil society as a juridical association, should be separated from morality and its institutionalization in the Church. This separation, however, could not be preserved in the sphere of public law, regulating relationships between citizens and the state.

It did not follow from this that the state is 'the absolute, final and true embodiment and actualization of the ethical idea'.[191] Chicherin did not discuss this Hegelian theory and was apparently not prepared to accept it literally. His own view of the state in relation to ethics was both more modest and more Christian. The state, he held, being among other things organized coercion, therefore could not pretend to embody the highest moral ideal—that of love. The highest moral law—the law of love—is absolutely incompatible with the use of force, and the ideal of love is infinitely more sublime than anything the state could achieve.[192] The state, therefore, should not try to use its coercive powers for the realization of a moral ideal, which because of human shortcomings and even more because of human freedom cannot be realized on earth.[193] On the other hand the state should not be immoral; its coercive power should serve moral ends by creating conditions in which morality is possible. It should not interfere with the private morality of citizens but should respect moral rules in its

[191] See W. T. Stace, *The Philosophy of Hegel*, p. 426.
[192] See Chicherin, *Kurs*, vol. 1, pp. 24–5 and vol. 3, p. 24–39.
[193] Chicherin stressed that this view was in accordance with the teaching of the Church. See his *Filosofiia prava*, p. 221–2.

own activity. Public law, as the direct instrument serving the public good, should include a moral element. The state should not interfere in the sphere of private relations on behalf of morality; it should not restrict the freedom of contract, but, in exceptional cases, it should refuse to enforce the fulfilment of drastically immoral agreements.[194] Public law, and especially its highest expression, state law, is, therefore, a peculiar combination of the juridical and the moral.[195] Chicherin summed up his views on this relationship as follows:[196]

1. State law distributes rights and obligations whereas moral law imposes obligations without giving rights.
2. Moral law cannot be backed by coercion.
3. Moral obligations are boundless and not strictly defined whereas the demands of the state must be limited and defined in detail.
4. Moral obligations embrace the entire sphere of human life whereas state law deals only with the obligations of men as citizens.
5. Morality strives for perfection whereas state law is concerned with material interests as well.
6. Both morality and law are historically changing; the moral *ideal*, however, is eternal and absolute, whereas in state law, which strives for the welfare of the people in constantly changing historical conditions, everything must be flexible.

It should be added that Chicherin laid special emphasis on the necessity for moral rules in international relations. He condemned the rule of pure force in politics and the immorality of Bismarck's doctrine of 'reason of State'.[197] He stressed that a purely practical foreign policy, neither bound by moral rules nor guided by moral ideals, was always short-sighted and unlikely to realize even its own aims; that, therefore, it should be rejected even from the point of view of rationally conceived, long-term national interest.[198] As an example of an immoral political act which had not benefited its perpetrators he instanced the partitioning of Poland,[199] and advocated a 'moral' solution of the Polish question, by which he meant giving political autonomy to the Kingdom of Poland and cultural autonomy to the Polish population of the Ukraine, Belorussia, and Lithuania. He was

---

[194] Chicherin, *Sobstvennost' i gosudarstvo*, vol. 1, pp. 196–7.
[195] Ibid., pp. 89–91.   [196] Chicherin, *Kurs*, vol. 1, pp. 25–6.
[197] Cf. Chicherin, *Vospominaniia* 4, p. 300.
[198] Cf. Chicherin, *Kurs*, vol. 3, pp. 27–33.
[199] Ibid., pp. 27–9 and Chicherin, *Pol'skii i evreiskii voprosy* (quoted ed.), pp. 10–17.

morally indignant over the Russian treatment of the Poles which, he felt, fully justified the Polish hatred of Russia; he even declared that a policy of reconciliation with Russia could only appeal to 'mean souls' in Poland.[200] He was especially concerned, however, to prove that the subjugation of Poland was detrimental to the properly conceived national interest of Russia. The suppression of Poland could be achieved only at the cost of enormous effort, not remunerative in terms of material benefits. It diverted public attention from necessary reforms in Russia and strengthened reactionary chauvinism. Finally, it totally demoralized an entire army of Russian officials in the Kingdom of Poland, and so greatly contributed to the growing demoralization of Russian society as a whole.[201] Thus, the cause of internal progress in Russia was presented as inseparable from a satisfactory solution of the Polish problem.

Chicherin's attitude to the Poles was bound up with his general view of the principle of national self-determination. He was inclined to support this principle as the only means for achieving internal stability in the states and for securing international peace.[202] He accepted it also for moral reasons: the right of national, not necessarily political, self-determination could not be denied without denying freedom of conscience, and freedom of conscience as we know, was for him an absolute human right. In this sense he condemned the policy of national oppression as denying 'those rights which are inherent in the very nature of man'.[203]

Chicherin recognized the Jewish question as yet another problem of paramount importance. It could not be subsumed under the question of nationality since the Jews were a non-territorial religious and ethnic minority, demanding only full civil rights. Chicherin supported this demand with great energy and moral conviction. He saw the Jews as 'a tribe from which mankind has received its entire moral legacy and to which, therefore, eternal gratitude is due'.[204] He rejected the widespread view that the Jews were economically damaging to Russia, stressing at the same time that all discussion of their role in the

---

[200] Chicherin, *Pol'skii i evreiskii voprosy*, pp. 39–40.

[201] Ibid., pp. 41–2.

[202] Cf. Chicherin, *Kurs*, vol. 3, pp. 68–71, 80, 343–51 and *Filosofiia prava*, pp. 335–6. In this respect the progressive evolution of Chicherin's thought is clear: at first he rejected the principle of national self-determination (cf. *O narodnom predstavitel'stve*, pp. 402–3), later he gave it qualified support and finally, in his *Philosophy of Law*, he embraced it as a general rule.

[203] Chicherin, *Pol'skii i evreiskii voprosy*, p. 62.   [204] Ibid., p. 46.

Russian economy was totally irrelevant to law. 'The category of people detrimental to the state', he wrote in this connection, 'cannot be admitted in a well-ordered society. It has been introduced by revolutionary or despotic governments.'[205] Certain actions must be legally forbidden, but a state must not discriminate between its citizens on grounds of religion or ethnic background. Any transgression of law must be punished but no citizen should be held responsible for the deeds of other citizens in the same religious or ethnic category.

Let us return now to the sphere of private law, 'the law proper'. We have seen that Chicherin's postulate of the separation of law from morality should be applied only to this sphere, and not to public law. Even in the case of private law, however, Chicherin's interpretation of this postulate was in fact much less radical than that set forth by the legal positivists. This was because, unlike the latter, he did not reject the central idea of natural law—the idea of a just law, a law which is higher than positive law; he rejected natural law as a system of norms which could juridically nullify existing positive law, but accepted it as a philosophical ideal to which positive law ought to conform as far as possible in existing historical conditions.[206] He stressed that the law must defend man's freedom to be immoral, but never intended this to signify approval of laws which contradicted the idea of justice. Such laws he rejected on moral grounds. An element of moral indignation is clearly visible in his struggle against all forms of legal positivism: to derive a law from interests and to identify might with right were seen by him as contradictions of justice and, therefore, as symptoms of dangerous immorality in juridical thinking.

Was this attitude inconsistent with the postulate of a strict demarcation between the juridical and the moral? From the positivist point of view it certainly was, but from Chicherin's it was not. In Chicherin's interpretation the separation of the juridical and the moral was not meant to sanctify unjust positive laws, or to eliminate moral considerations from juridical thinking. He rather wanted to say that justice, that is, the moral component of legal consciousness, should not be confused with the ideal of morality proper—the ideal of love. He made this clear in his important discussion with D. I. Shipov, claiming that Shipov's criticism of his views was based upon a fundamental misunderstanding:

---

[205] Ibid., p. 59.
[206] For the distinction between these two interpretations of natural law see W. Friedmann, *Legal Theory*, p. 96.

He [Shipov] has not made it clear to himself what law really is and has therefore completely misunderstood my words. For him there is no other law except the positive, but I had in mind a different kind of law when I wrote of the relationship between law and morality. It was not concerned with the opposition between positive law and the higher demands of justice, which provide the philosophical foundation of law; I was concerned with the relationship between these demands and the law of love. I am not in the least inclined to treat law as an expression of interests; on the contrary, I see it as as a manifestation of the eternal principles of justice, which should serve as a guide to legislators and jurists. . . . I think, however, that the law of justice, which requires that everyone be given his due, should not be confused with the law of love, which demands sacrifices for the sake of one's neighbour; such confusion has always led mankind into the most fatal error.[207]

This difference between the law of justice and the law of love corresponded to the difference between legal and moral obligations, or between the negative virtue of blamelessness and the positive one of moral effort. The law, on this interpretation, should, for moral reasons, not strive to make men morally virtuous, as freedom would thereby be destroyed and without freedom morality is impossible. In other words, the law must be morally neutral in order to be moral; it must refrain from imposing morality because the legal enforcement of morality would be deeply immoral.

It is justifiable to conclude that Chicherin's separation of law and morality was essentially Kantian and, therefore, had little in common with the seemingly similar separation in legal positivism. Legal positivists rejected the ideal of a 'just law', setting against it the Hobbesian view that *ius est quod iussum et*; by contrast, Chicherin fully accepted the ideal of justice (and in this sense the concept of 'natural law'), insisting only on its negative character and carefully distinguishing it from a positive moral ideal. His conception was based on the same distinction which had caused Kant to divide his metaphysics of morals into the metaphysical principles of justice and the metaphysical principles of virtue. Chicherin, like Kant, held that the former, being the foundation of law, involve only respect, while the latter involve love of one's neighbour, which cannot be legally enforced.[208] The only important difference between the two thinkers was that Kant made the common ethical foundation of law and morality explicit in his famous

[207] Chicherin, *Voprosy politiki*, pp. 113–14.
[208] See I. Kant, *The Metaphysical Principles of Virtue* (Part II of *The Metaphysics of Morals*), J. Ellington (trans.), with an Introduction by W. Wick, Indianapolis–New York 1964, pp. 112–13.

'categorical imperative', whereas Chicherin did not try to present law as a species of ethics. From the point of view of formal logic he recognized the *genus proximum* of morality and law not in the broader notion of morality but in that of law. The moral and the juridical law were in his view two species of a common genus: law in the sense of a system of norms determining and limiting human freedom.[209] The task of legal norms consisted of determining the limits of external freedom from the standpoint of an ideal of justice; in contrast to this, morality provided the norms for inner freedom, freedom as positive self-determination, freedom of man as a moral being, trying to realize the ideal of love.

Thus Chicherin corrected Kant by rescuing his conception from the fatal error of confusing the law of justice with the law of love. Additional reasons for his modifications can probably be found in his commitment to Christianity on the one hand, and to Hegelianism, on the other. Despite his 'cold outward rationality' Chicherin was a genuine Christian,[210] probably more so than Kant, and his Christianity was less compatible than a rationalist Protestantism with the legalistic spirit. It is likely, therefore, that the contrast between the coldness of mere justice and the warmth of Christian love seemed sharper to him, and the Kantian 'categorical imperative' too legalistic to serve as a bridge between morality and law. If so, he should have been readier to stress the opposition between morality and law, to keep them, as it were, in different compartments, rather than to look for their common ethical denominator. In addition, he shared the Hegelian belief in the dialectical development of spirit and from such a perspective the primary common ground of morality and law was much less important than the higher dialectical unity which both could share without trespassing on each other.

7   Chicherin's place within the liberal tradition

Let me conclude this chapter with some remarks on Chicherin's place in the history of European and Russian liberal thought.

The classification of Chicherin's views on economy and civil society is the easiest: there can be no doubt whatsoever that he was a consistent economic liberal, faithful to the classical liberal doctrine of economic freedom. He was unrelentingly critical of German social legislation in the years 1870 to 1890; in his *Property and the State* he

[209] Cf. Chicherin, *Filosofiia prava*, pp. 83–5, 91.
[210] Cf. V. V. Zenkovsky, *A History of Russian Philosophy*, p. 611.

devoted much attention to countering the ideas of Schäffle, Wagner, and other 'professional socialists' (or 'socialists of the chair') whose influence had inspired Bismarck's reforms or prepared public opinion to accept them.[211] From the same point of view he criticized the legal positivists, arguing that any attempt to play down the distinction between public and private law would inevitably lead to the publicization of private law and thus to the justification of state intervention in economic affairs. Ihering's famous book *Der Zweck im Recht* was in his eyes a sad example of the deep abasement of juridical thought brought about by such misguided commitment to a purposeful social policy.[212]

As a defender of economic liberalism Chicherin was not an original thinker. He was original, however, in his historical diagnosis: in his claim that the greatest danger to economic freedom should be recognized not only in socialism but in the general politicization of life, namely, in the inevitable consequences of the growing strength of political democracy. In this respect he was anticipating the views later developed by such famous economists as Schumpeter and Hayek.[213] The main reason for this was the Russian context of his thought. He was painfully aware that most of the Russian intelligentsia were deeply prejudiced against economic freedom; it is no wonder that this awareness led him to visualize the future Russian parliament (irrespective of the number of convinced socialists among its members) as a resolute champion of state interventionism.

More complicated is the problem of Chicherin's political liberalism. From the standpoint of the liberal-democratic tradition, as understood and carried on today, he was certainly too tolerant of absolute monarchy, too Hegelian in his glorification of the modern centralized state and generally too authoritarian in his emphasis on the need for a strong government. This is one reason why Aileen Kelly, a recent interpreter of Chicherin's thought, refused to call him a liberal.[214] This sweeping conclusion, however, is unjustified, both as resting on a very one-sided reading of Chicherin's texts and, more importantly, as concentrating on Chicherin's early writings while ignoring the further evolution of his thought, an evolution which, as I have tried to show,

---

[211] See Chicherin, *Sobstvennost' i gosudarstvo*, vol. 1, pp. 155, 160, 186–9, 434.

On the influence of 'professorial socialists' on Bismarck see H. J. Braun, 'Political economy and social legislation in Germany, *ca.* 1870–1890', *History of European Ideas*, vol. 4, no. 1, 1983.

[212] Chicherin, *Sobstvennost' i gosudarstvo*, vol. 1, pp. 51–6.

[213] See n. 128.   [214] See above, n. 18.

led him to an extended defence of local self-government in Russia and, finally, to an explicit demand for constitutional rule.

I fully agree that even these considerations do not make Chicherin a liberal democrat, but, historically at least, liberal democracy and liberalism were two different things. Chicherin was not a liberal democrat, but he was a liberal none the less. Liberal democracy, with a tendency to broaden the scope of political regulations, is not compatible with an authoritarian style in politics. The reverse, however, is true of classical liberalism: authoritarianism as a psychological feature was a well-known and typical feature of Victorian liberalism. Chicherin was the same kind of liberal as Benjamin Constant, a liberal for whom freedom in the public sphere, extolled by Rousseau, was less important than private (including economic) freedom;[215] for whom non-political individual freedom under an authoritarian but limited government was greatly preferable to freedom of political participation (i.e. democratic freedom) without safeguards for the individual rights of men as men, not of men as citizens. Accordingly, it was quite natural for him to see liberal values as threatened not only by monarchic absolutism but also by democratic absolutism, and to take as his highest priority the rule of law, which would limit the scope of political power independently of its source, whether democratic republic or hereditary monarchy.[216] Like many European nineteenth-century liberals he feared the so-called 'despotism of the masses' and treated the principle of simple majority rule as a potential justification of dictatorship. All these features of his thought were not deviations from liberalism but characterize him as a rather typical liberal of an epoch when liberalism and democracy were not yet blended together and could even be opposed to each other. True, to the very end of his days he remained more apprehensive of democracy than most Western liberals at the turn of the century, but this difference is readily understandable in view of the general backwardness of Russia and the almost total domination of Russian democratic thought by explicitly anti-liberal, populist trends.

From the perspective of the present book Chicherin's place in the

---

[215] In his *Philosophy of Law* Chicherin criticized Rousseau for sacrificing individual (private) freedom to collective (public) freedom (*Filosofiia prava*, p. 308).

[216] For a better understanding of this position we may recall the words of Isaiah Berlin: 'The answer to the question "Who governs me?" is logically distinct from the question "How far does the government interfere with me?" ... The connexion between democracy and individual liberty is a good deal more tenuous than it seemed to many advocates of both'. (See I. Berlin, *Four Essays on Liberty*, Oxford, 1969, pp. 130–1.)

history of the liberal view of law is of course of paramount significance. Since it is not possible to trace here the entire history of liberal ideas on law we must somewhat arbitrarily decide on an ideal model of the liberal conception of law. We find such a model in Hayek's study of liberalism.[217] Other contemporary theorists may find it controversial but to a historian of European thought it seems entirely convincing. In any case, it will serve as a frame of reference for classification of Chicherin's views.

For classical liberals, argues Hayek, the law proper, law as the indispensable safeguard of freedom, was 'only those rules of just conduct which constitute private law and criminal law, but not every command issued by the legislative authority'.[218] Such rules must be general, 'applicable to all alike in an unknown number of future instances, defining the protected domain of the individuals, and therefore essentially of the nature of prohibitions rather than specific commands'.[219] Their function is 'not to organize the individual efforts for particular agreed purposes, but to secure an overall order of actions within which each should be able to benefit as much as possible from the efforts of others in the pursuit of his own ends'.[220] Therefore, they cannot serve as means for realizing preconceived collective aims, political, utilitarian or moral; they are conducive to the formation of a spontaneous, self-generating order, the order of a rule-connected open society (as opposed to the end-connected order of a tribal or socialist society).[221] The freedom they protect is negative, individual freedom, which 'implies a rejection of the idea of *any* unlimited or sovereign power'.[222] They are concerned with commutative justice and not with what is known as distributive or social justice; this is so, because distributive justice necessarily presupposes 'a common unitary hierarchy of ends' and requires that individuals must 'do what is needed in the light of an authoritative plan of action'.[223] In other words, liberalism refrains from defining social justice, insisting instead that 'the rules of the game, by which the relative positions of the different individuals are determined, be just (or at least not unjust)'.[224]

---

[217] See F. A. Hayek, 'Liberalism', in his *New Studies in Philosophy, Politics, Economics and the History of Ideas* (see above, n. 128; hereafter referred to as 'Liberalism').

[218] Ibid., p. 134.   [219] Ibid., p. 135.   [220] Ibid., p. 136.

[221] Cf. F. A. Hayek, *Law, Legislation and Liberty* (see above, n. 164), vol. 2: *The Mirage of Social Justice*, pp. 38–9.

[222] F. A. Hayek, 'Liberalism', pp. 138–9.

[223] Ibid., p. 140 (cf. Chicherin, *Filosofiia prava*, pp. 100–3).

[224] Ibid., p. 141.

It is committed to the idea of formal equality, that is, equality before the law, while rejecting the idea of material equality as incompatible with freedom. It should not be confused with democracy because democracy is concerned with the question of 'who is to direct the government' while liberalism revolves around the problem of the limitation of all political power, including the power of a democratically elected government.[225] Since democracy tends to become unlimited, it gradually abandons such liberal principles as it has previously embraced. This process is destructive of both liberalism and democracy because it seems inevitable that under unlimited government 'effective powers will devolve to a bureaucratic apparatus increasingly independent of democratic control'.[226]

It is obvious that socialism must be enemy number one of a liberalism so conceived. But it is important to add that, in the field of legal theory, Hayek saw legal positivism as the first fatal deviation from liberal principles, quite without reference to the more or less liberal political views of its representatives. 'Liberal theory', he claimed, 'is indeed in conflict with legal positivism with regard to the latter's assertion that all law is or must be the product of (essentially arbitrary) will of a legislator'.[227] Legal positivism blurs the fundamental distinctions between private and public law, between rules and commands. It sees the function of law as serving certain known purposes, a view which contradicts the very idea of law, since a system of rules cannot be reduced to a purposive construction. In his other works Hayek often mentions Ihering in this connection, entirely agreeing with Kant's emphasis on the 'purposeless' character of rules of just conduct and firmly opposing 'the Utilitarians from Bentham to Ihering' who regard purpose as the central feature of the law.

It is truly remarkable how close Chicherin's thought came to this ideal model of the liberal conception of the law. The only discernible

[225] 'The difference between the two principles stands out most clearly if we consider their opposites: with democracy it is authoritarian government; with liberalism it is totalitarianism. Neither of the two systems necessarily excludes the opposite of the other: a democracy may wield totalitarian powers, and it is at least conceivable that an authoritarian government might act on liberal principles.' (Ibid., p. 143.)

Classical liberals did not, of course, know the term 'totalitarianism': so, we should remember that 'totalitarian' is used here as a synonym of 'unlimited'. With this reservation, we may conclude that classical liberals, Chicherin among them, were opposed to both authoritarian and democratic variants of totalitarianism, the former being exemplified for them by 'oriental despotism', the latter by ancient democracy, as understood by Constant.

[226] Ibid., p. 144.   [227] Ibid., p. 140.

difference concerns the problem of sovereignty. As a Hegelian, Chicherin saw the state as endowed with unlimited sovereignty; as a constitutionalist, he supported the limitation of political authority. But he conceived this as itself an act of political authority and could not accept the view that sovereignty as such is limited by laws which are not 'made' but 'discovered', that there are eternal rights to which a legal appeal can be made against the state. He emphasized these views in his works dealing with public law, such as his book on popular representation and his course on state law.

At first glance this may seem a very substantial difference, but on closer examination it turns out not to be so. For the state to which Chicherin attributed unlimited sovereignty was the Hegelian state, that is a state whose very idea presupposed freedom of conscience, the autonomy of civil society and the inviolability of private law. As 'the actuality of the ethical idea' it was also immune against immorality; it had to pursue moral aims in its own actions but, unlike theocracy, without encroaching upon the moral freedom of its citizens. All these benefits were guaranteed, so to speak, by the metaphysical essence of the state. But with the advent of positivism metaphysics no longer existed; the state which the legal positivists entrusted with a monopoly of legal commands was nothing but government, the rule through power of a specific group of people. Simultaneously a tendency, strongly supported by legal positivists, towards state interventionism and social legislation developed; a tendency which, in Chicherin's eyes, contradicted both the liberal and the Hegelian ideas of the state. All these factors powerfully moved Chicherin to a considerable shift of emphasis in his conception of the state. Unlike T. H. Green, who used Hegelianism to support the new trend towards interventionism, he concentrated on proving that the state should remain faithful to its idea, as revealed by Hegel, and not interfere in economic life. In this respect he clung to the old liberal tenets and used Hegelianism as a philosophical ally. He stressed Hegel's view that the state must respect 'subjective freedom' and private law,[228] and that civil society constitutes an autonomous sphere not subject to political regulation. This evolution of thought sometimes led him beyond Hegelianism. At many points he moved closer to Kant than to Hegel. The general ethos of his philosophy became more Kantian, further removed from the spirit of the Hegelian dictum that 'what is real is rational'. He in part revived

---

[228] For instance: 'The state is obliged to recognize private law'. (*Sobstvennost' i gosudarstvo*, p. 153.)

the Kantian dualism of *Sein* and *Sollen*, stressing that positive law was often very unjust and should not be the only frame of reference for jurists (as demanded by legal positivists); that it should be made as consistent as possible with 'philosophical', 'natural' law.[229] In this way he helped to pave the way for a revival of natural law, an intellectual movement which emerged at the end of the nineteenth century, both in the West and in Russia, as a reaction to legal positivism.[230]

His most remarkable contribution to the struggle against legal positivism was, however, his insistence that it was not enough to interpret existing laws but that a philosophy of law was also necessary and that the only philosophy which could save the true meaning of law was metaphysical idealism. In the light of his own intellectual development this was nothing new, since he had never thought otherwise. What was new was contextual. At the end of the nineteenth century the dominance of legal positivism had already been challenged, by Petrażycki in Russia and by Stammler in Germany.[231] The need to revive a philosophical approach to law was felt more and more widely, and because of this Chicherin's *Philosophy of Law*, published in 1900, appeared not as the work of an epigone but, rather, as a milestone on the new road. It was indeed such a revival of the old philosophical idealism, which took account of new trends in philosophy and the theory of law, and could therefore be treated as representing a neo-idealist current in legal philosophy.

Chicherin's main concern was the destructive influence of empiricism, an influence resulting in the dominance of psychologism, sociologism and other forms of relativism and of a nihilistic attitude towards absolute values. In this sense he may be said to have been concerned with essentially the same problems which were worrying Husserl; his views on the contemporary intellectual crisis anticipated to a certain extent the famous Husserlian diagnosis of the destruction of European culture, although the theoretical assumptions of Chicherin's idealism were different from Husserl's and rather old-fashioned.[232] The positivist rejection of metaphysics, he argued, resulted in complete

---

[229] Cf. Chicherin, *Filosofiia prava*, pp. 1–4, 94–102.
[230] Cf. W. Friedmann, *Legal Theory*, pp. 132 and 152–6.
[231] See below, Ch. IV, 6.
[232] Cf. L. Kolakowski, *Husserl and the Search for Certitude*, London 1975, pp. 16–24. The similarity between Chicherin and Husserl is limited to a common diagnosis of the cultural dangers of empiricism and positivism. Husserl, however, saw the remedy for these dangers in the notion of transcendental truth while Chicherin was concerned mainly with the metaphysical status of the human individual.

relativism and thus in the total denial of reason.[233] The development of empiricist epistemology brought about a deontologization of the subject; empirical phenomenalism reduced it to an 'empty receptacle' and Avenarius's attempt to do away with the dualism of subject and object destroyed it altogether.[234] Similar results were achieved by psychological and sociological interpretations of the personality. This was because only metaphysics could defend personality as an ontologically grounded spiritual entity, endowed with free will and dignity.[235] Empirical studies of human beings had destroyed the theoretical basis for treating people as autonomous persons, bearers of rights, and Chicherin therefore concluded that the restoration of metaphysics was vital for overcoming the crisis in legal consciousness.

An apt summary of Chicherin's metaphysical personalism is contained in the following words:

An individual person is not simply a transitory phenomenon, but a definite and permanent *essence* which recognizes as its *own* the acts which flow from it—in the past and in the future. But this defines the individual personality as a metaphysical principle. The *rights* and *obligations* of the individual become the *sheerest nonsense* if we do not recognize the unity of the individual person, if we reduce personality to a series of shifting states ... Personality is a unitary essence. It is not a universal essence diffused in many individuals, but an essence concentrated in itself and separate from others—an independent centre of energy and activity.[236]

It is obvious from this that the personalist aspect of Chicherin's metaphysics was much closer to Kant than to Hegel. Since neo-Hegelianism in legal philosophy is usually associated with demands for 'the almost unqualified abandonment of the individual to the state',[237] it would be misleading to see Chicherin's *Philosophy of Law* as belonging to this current. But it would be equally misleading to treat this book as neo-Kantian. The neo-Kantian legal philosophers generally adopted 'Kant's theory of knowledge but not his moral and legal philosophy',[238] while in Chicherin's case the reverse was true; they tended to develop Kantianism in the direction of pure formalism, while Chicherin was interested not in forms but in objective values. It

---

[223] Chicherin, *Filosofiia prava*, p. 28.
[234] Ibid., pp. 30, 39. (Cf. L. Kolakowski, *The Alienation of Reason. History of Positivist Thought*, Garden City, NY, 1968, p. 113.)
[235] Ibid., pp. 53–5.
[236] Ibid., p. 54 (quoted from V. V. Zenkovsky, *A History of Russian Philosophy*, p. 618).
[237] W. Friedmann, *Legal Theory*, p. 175.   [238] Ibid., p. 177.

seems better to see Chicherin in a wider historical perspective and to stress his main intention: his intransigent struggle against the debasement of the law and his insistence on the destructive effect of positivism on liberal legal theory and on modern 'legal culture in general.

Seen from this angle, Chicherin's ideas are not merely a page in a closed book but are relevant, or should be relevant, today. After the total collapse of legal culture in the totalitarian states we are more sensitive to criticism of the positivist worship of authority and more aware of the inherent contradiction of combining liberalism with the positivist claim that (as Hans Kelsen put it) 'every state is a *Rechtsstaat*'. An excellent example of this awareness is the book by John H. Hallowell, writen in the aftermath of the horrors of World War II.[239] It substantiates the suspicion that liberalism was not murdered, as is often said, but rather committed suicide. The author sees the inner degeneration and destruction of liberalism as deriving from positivist views and attitudes, such as the definition of law according to its coercive powers rather than its content, the abandonment of the belief in objective values, an excessive formalism, the tendency to identify rights with interests (as exemplified by Ihering), and so forth.[240] If we add to this the postulate that metaphysics be restored and the belief in transcendent truth revived,[241] the parallel with Chicherin becomes complete.

To sum up. Chicherin's legal philosophy, based upon a liberal interpretation of Hegelianism, was formed early but underwent a certain evolution in the last decades of the century. This evolution was the result of confronting two problems: that of the transition from the old liberalism to the new, socialized liberalism, on the one hand, and that of the positivist interpretation of law, on the other. These two problems were interconnected because legal positivism was fully in accord with the tendency to see law as an instrument of social policy. Chicherin was equally hostile to legal positivism and to the socialization of liberalism: he wanted to remain faithful to the old, true liberalism and repeatedly warned that its betrayal would bring about the most fatal results. Historical hindsight, however, allows us to distinguish two different aspects of his thought. Let me call them the two faces of Chicherin as a legal philosopher.

---

[239] J. H. Hallowell, *The Decline of Liberalism as Ideology*. London, 1946, p. ix. Critical references to Kelsen's statement are to be found on pp. x, 97.

[240] Ibid., pp. 11–19, 53–6, 69–86.   [241] Ibid., pp. 9–10, 53–4, 65–9.

The first face was turned to the past and is the face of a man who stubbornly refused to acknowledge any need to move towards state interventionism and social legislation, a man whose principled position degenerated sometimes into an impractical dogmatism and who gave every excuse for accusations of lack of compassion towards the underprivileged. Quite irrespective of one's political or economic opinions, it is difficult to deny that from this point of view Chicherin was a thoroughly nineteenth-century figure, anachronistic even by nineteenth-century standards, although Struve's labelling him 'a literary fossil' is scarcely just.

Chicherin's other face is much more attractive. It is the face of a lonely thinker, who was deeply concerned with saving the idea of law, who saw with exceptional clarity the dangers of legal positivism and whose defence of the old liberalism was at the same time a struggle for a deepening and clarification of the liberal conception of law. The word totalitarianism was not known in his day, but he may justly be said to have predicted totalitarian dangers and done everything to resist them. In this sense his second face was turned not towards the past, but towards the future.

Chicherin's successors in Russian liberal legal philosophy shared his utterly negative view of legal positivism while at the same time accepting the new, social liberalism and making considerable efforts to combine it with anti-positivist philosophies of law. Most of them did not try to develop Chicherin's view of the need for a metaphysical foundation of law; even Soloviev, the greatest metaphysical idealist in Russia, thought that morality and law could and should be entirely autonomous and distinct both from religious beliefs and from metaphysical theories. An important exception to this was Pavel Novgorodtsev, a leading theorist of social liberalism who followed Chicherin in basing legal philosophy on the metaphysical conception of the personality.

III

Vladimir Soloviev: Religious Philosophy and the Emergence of the 'New Liberalism'

1 Introductory Remarks

The vindication of law in Chicherin's work was consistent with his entire intellectual background: with his indebtedness to Granovsky, his programmatic Westernism and his uncompromising hostility towards both the Slavophile and the populist versions of legal nihilism. Vladimir Soloviev was nurtured in a very different intellectual tradition. His metaphysical idealism was linked not to Hegelianism but to the anti-Hegelian 'positive philosophy' of the later Schelling; his mysticism, gnosticism, and Messianism were severely criticized not only by positivists but also by Chicherin. He began his philosophical career with wholesale criticism of all Western philosophy from a distinctively Slavophile standpoint, and the first outline of his own views developed the ideas of Ivan Kireevsky.[1] In addition he was a personal friend and admirer of Dostoevsky. Thus, his ideas were rooted in the mainstream of Russian religious anti-Westernism and he might easily have become yet another Russian critic of Western rationalism, invididualism, and legalism. This was precisely what his Slavophile friends, and others in the conservative camp, expected of him. In fact, however, his thought developed in a different direction. In the field of law he entirely left behind the tenets of religiously inspired legal nihilism and may be credited with the elaboration of a philosophy of law which contained the main ideas of neo-liberalism and greatly influenced Russian liberal thinkers. Pavel Novgorodtsev, otherwise much closer to Chicherin in his philosophical views, saw Soloviev as the first and greatest representative of social liberalism in Russia. In spite of the profound differences between Chicherin's and Soloviev's

---

[1] For a detailed analysis of the relationship between Soloviev's thought and Slavophilism see Walicki, *The Slavophile Controversy*, ch. 15.

ideas, their names were often linked, as the two great founding-fathers of the Russian tradition in legal philosophy.[2]

Unlike Chicherin, whom he called a 'Pythagoras without Pythagoreans',[3] Soloviev did not stand alone in Russian philosophy. On the contrary, L. M. Lopatin expressed a widespread opinion when he compared Soloviev's role in the history of Russian philosophy to Pushkin's in the history of Russian poetry.[4] It is difficult to endorse this view without qualification but it cannot be denied that an entire generation of Russian metaphysical idealists and religious thinkers was schooled in Soloviev's philosophy. This, however, does not apply to his philosophy of law. As a rule, Russian religious philosophers remained rather cool towards or sceptical of this part of his universal philosophical synthesis. As a legal philosopher Soloviev did not create anything resembling a school of thought; some of his ideas, most notably that of the 'right to a dignified existence', exerted considerable influence, but, as a rule, they influenced people who distanced themselves from his philosophical views as a whole. The only work to be obviously and deeply influenced both by his philosophy of law and by his metaphysics of All-Unity was written fifty years after his *Justification of the Good* and still remains unpublished.[5]

There were indeed good reasons for the relative neglect of Soloviev's philosophy of law among people who recognized his greatness in the realm of religious philosophy. The idea of the autonomous value of law, combined with an emphasis on the liberal values protected by it, seemed contrary to the spirit of all-unity and the striving for universal reintegration. On closer examination, however, it transpires that Soloviev's philosophy was deliberately aimed at a synthesis of *heterogeneous* elements,[6] that, unlike Slavophilism, it was not rooted in a coherent, socially-conditioned *Weltanschauung* and so lacked a monolithic quality.[7] In fact, Soloviev's universal synthesis is syncretic rather than organic. As we shall see, he himself came to the conclusion that the entire sphere of ethics, including law defined as a

[2] Cf. G. Gurvitch, 'Die zwei grössten russischen Rechtsphilosophen: Boris Tchitcherin und Wladimir Solowjeff', in *Philosophie und Recht*, vol. 2 (1922–3), pp. 80–102.

[3] V. S. Soloviev, *Sobranie sochinenii*. Phototype edition. Brussels, 1966, vol. 8, p. 673.

[4] See S. M. Soloviev, *Zhizn' i tvorcheskaia evolutsiya Vladimira Solovieva*, Brussels, 1977, p. 407.

[5] See below, Ch. VII, 6.

[6] Cf. V. V. Zenkovsky, *A History of Russian Philosophy*, vol. 2, p. 484.

[7] Cf. Walicki, *The Slavophile Controversy*, pp. 576–7.

'compulsory minimum of morality', should be completely divorced from religion and metaphysics. This autonomization of ethics, paralleled by the autonomization of epistemology, provided an explanation of and justification for the differences between the reception of his religious metaphysics on the one hand, and his views on morality and law on the other.

2 *Biographical note*

It is tempting to see a partial explanation of the syncretic character of Soloviev's philosophy in the heterogeneity of his inherited cultural background. In particular, Soloviev's favourite idea of Christian unity—which for him meant, above all, the reconciliation of the Catholic and the Orthodox Churches—seems to be significantly related to his links with the so-called 'Western borderlands' of Russia, lands which had belonged earlier to the Polish–Lithuanian Commonwealth and had been exposed to strong Catholic cultural influences.

Vladimir Soloviev (1853–1900) was the son of Sergei Soloviev, a leading westernizing historian and professor at Moscow University. His maternal grandmother (née Brzeska) came of an aristocratic Polish family, settled in the Ukraine and related to the famous religious philosopher, the 'Ukrainian Socrates', Gregory Skovoroda.[8] His paternal grandfather, Michael Soloviev, was an Orthodox priest who had been educated in a theological school modelled on the Theological Academy in Kiev, using Latin as the language of instruction and strongly influenced by Catholic scholasticism. Such theological schools still flourished in Russia even up to the early nineteenth century. Father G. Florovsky explained this in terms of Spenglerian 'pseudomorphosis', a process resulting in 'distorted forms, crystals whose inner structure contradicts their external shape'.[9] He further commented:

In Kiev in the early seventeenth century this method [teaching all subjects in Latin] might be considered normal, since in Poland Latin was the official language of education and even of the courts. When, however, the system was extended to Great Russia, the situation became abnormal. And this is what happened. All the theological schools were established on the Kiev model, and until the early nineteenth century all theological education was given in Latin, which was neither the language of public worship nor the spoken language of the worshippers.[10]

[8] S. M. Soloviev, *Zhizn' Vladimira Solovieva*, pp. 31–4.
[9] G. Florovsky, *Collected Works*, vol. 2 *Christianity and Culture*, Belmont, Mass., 1974, p. 181.   [10] Ibid., p. 186.

Whether or not we agree with this, a younger kinsman of the great philosopher, Father S. M. Soloviev, a Catholic priest who suffered persecution in Soviet Russia, obviously saw it in a different light—as a fruitful cultural osmosis. In his monograph on Vladimir Soloviev he proudly mentioned his personal treasure: Michael Soloviev's Latin Bible, bearing the inscription 'Ex libris Michael Soloviovus.'[11]

Young Vladimir was brought up by his mother in an atmosphere of strict piety. When he was fourteen he experienced a crisis of faith that turned him into a 'total materialist . . . a typical nihilist of the sixties'.[12] He now professed a somewhat chiliastic atheism linked to a burning faith in the total transformation of the world. (We may add that to the end of his life he saw this faith as a positive element in the Russian revolutionary movement.) At seventeen he enrolled in the history and philosophy faculty of Moscow University, although, influenced by Pisarev, he soon transferred to the science faculty instead. However, he continued to read the philosophical works of, among others, Spinoza, Schopenhauer, Kant, the later Schelling, Fichte, and Hegel. As a result of his reading and his own reflections and experiences, he gradually regained his faith in God and in the profound philosophical significance of Christianity. By 1872, at nineteen, he was once again a convinced Christian. He gave up his scientific studies and devoted himself entirely to philosophy under the guidance of the philosopher and theologican P. D. Yurkevich, also attending lectures at the Moscow Theological Academy.

Soloviev's master's thesis, *The Crisis in Western Philosophy: Against the Positivists* (1874) was basically a development of the main argument of Ivan Kireevsky's dissertation 'On the Necessity and Possibility of New Principles in Philosophy'. It revolved around the Slavophile conception of 'integral wholeness', which was to counteract the destructive effects of rationalism. Kireevsky's name was only once mentioned but the parallels with his views were self-evident. K. Mochulsky sums them up as follows:

> Soloviev has absorbed Kireevsky's view of the world *in toto*. His thesis is not an independent piece of work: its basic concepts—the synthesis of philosophy and religion, the view of Western philosophy as the evolution of rationalism, the idea of the integral unity of life, of metaphysical cognition, the emphasis on

[11] S. M. Soloviev, *Zhizn' Vladimira Solovieva*, p. 31. S. M. Soloviev was the son of Mikhail Soloviev, the younger brother of the philosopher.

[12] L. M. Lopatin, 'Filosofskoe mirovozzrenie V. Solovieva', in *Folosofskie kharakteristiki i rechi*, Moscow, 1911, p. 123.

the need to combine Western philosophy with the speculative wisdom of the East—all these were previously put forward by Kireevsky. His work, too, suggested to Soloviev the framework of his thesis, which starts with criticism of scholasticism and proceeds via Descartes, Spinoza and Leibniz to Schelling and Hegel. The closing passage of the thesis [pointing out the philosophical and moral significance of the ancient traditions of Eastern Christianity] is a reasonably accurate repetition of the conclusions of Kireevsky's article. Soloviev's own contribution is the unsatisfactory substitution of Hartmann for Schelling: for Kireevsky the final stage in the evolution of Western Philosophy was Schelling's 'positive philosophy', whereas for Soloviev it was reached in the teaching of Hartmann.[13]

In fact Soloviev's enthusiasm for the metaphysical pessimism of Schopenhauer and Hartmann, in whom he saw the most profound awareness of the moral and intellectual crisis of the West combined with a hope for salvation from the East, proved to be short-lived, while the importance of Schelling's 'positive philosophy' grew more and more evident to him. A few years later he had come to see it as the first word of the 'New Christianity' and as a stepping stone for his own philosophy.[14]

Having defended his thesis Soloviev began lecturing at St Petersburg University. After one year, however, he went to England to study in the British Museum library. He immersed himself in the history of mysticism, especially the cabbalistic and Neoplatonic tradition, Boëhme and Swedenborg, Franz Baader and the theosophical ideas of German romanticism. A sudden impulse led him to undertake a journey to Egypt, which very nearly ended in tragedy. Dressed in the clothes he normally wore in London, he set out one day on a walk through the desert in search of a tribe that was believed to have kept alive the ancient cabbalistic traditions. Seeing his long black coat and tall black hat, nomad Bedouin took him for an evil spirit, and he barely escaped with his life.

The real reason for Soloviev's journey to Egypt was a mystical vision of *Sophia*—the Divine Wisdom, which he identified with the World Soul or 'eternal womanhood'. *Sophia* appeared to him three times, first in his childhood, when he was suffering from unrequited love for a little girl of nine; secondly in the British Museum, when he was told to go to Egypt; and for a third time in the desert, after the adventure with the Bedouin. Twenty years later Soloviev, who was also a poet,

---

[13] K. Mochulsky, *Vladimir Soloviëv: Zhizn' i uchenie*, Paris, 1951, p. 54.
[14] Cf. S. M. Soloviev, *Zhizn' Vladimira Solovieva*, pp. 121, 188.

described the three visions in his lighthearted autobiographical poem 'Three Meetings'.

After his return to Russia, in the summer of 1876, Soloviev established close relations with Slavophile and Panslavic circles (chiefly Ivan Aksakov) and also with Dostoevsky, whom he very deeply impressed. (This is reflected in Dostoevsky's last novel, where Alosha Karamazov is modelled on Soloviev, whose ideas are obvious in the theocratic utopia of Ivan Karamazov.)[15] The climax of Soloviev's specific version of Slavophilism came in 1877, the year of the Russo-Turkish war 'for the liberation of the Slavs'. The outbreak of this war stimulated Soloviev to give a public lecture entitled 'Three Forces'. The first force he saw in the Moslem East, the second in Western civilization, and the third in Slavdom. The first represented a fossilized and despotic unity in which all spheres of life were subordinated to religion, thus turning man into the passive tool of an 'inhuman God'. The second set 'godless man' against an 'inhuman God'; its last word is universal egoism and atomism. To save humankind from the threat of destruction was the mission of the third force, capable of achieving a synthesis of 'unity' and 'multiplicity', of making God human and turning man towards God, the reconciling East and West. Such a mediator had to be entirely free from all exclusivity and one-sidedness. These features, Soloviev concluded, were typical of the tribal character of the Slavs and especially of the Russians.

Soloviev found the philosophical foundation for this vision of a reconciliation between the divine and the human history in the idea of 'Godmanhood', the innermost meaning of Christianity. In 1878 he gave a series of extremely successful lectures in St Petersburg on this concept, the earthly realization of which he defined as 'free theocracy'. Its first outline was contained in his *Philosophical Principles of Integral Knowledge* (1877); a more detailed version was presented in his doctoral thesis, entitled *A Critique of Abstract Principles* (1877–1880).

After his brilliant defence of this thesis (in 1880) Soloviev received the title of 'Dozent' and resumed his lectures at the university and at higher courses for women. His academic career, however, was very short. The assassination of Alexander II prompted him to give a public lecture in which, while condemning the revolutionary terrorists, he

---

[15] Cf. Mochulsky, *Vladimir Soloviev*, p. 80. According to S. Hessen Soloviev's influence penetrated the entire construction of Dostoevsky's *Brothers Karamazov*. See S. Hessen, 'Der Kampf der Utopie und der Autonomie des Guten der Weltanschauung Dostoewskis und Solowjows', in *Die Pädagogische Hochschule*, Baden, 1929, no. 4.

also appealed to the new emperor to spare their lives. As a result he was forbidden to lecture in public and shortly afterwards was forced to resign from the university.

The next milestone in Soloviev's intellectual development, his break with the epigones of Slavophilism, was completed in 1883, when he stopped publishing in Aksakov's *Rus '* and instead—to the indignation of his right-wing friends—became a contributor to the liberal and westernizing *European Messenger (Vestnik Evropy)*. This marked the close of the first phase in his intellectual evolution and the beginning of the second, which Prince Eugene Trubetskoi (his disciple and the author of a fundamental book on his life and work) has called his 'utopian period'.[16]

There were two reasons for Soloviev's break with the Slavophiles. For an outside observer they seem very different, having little in common with each other; for Soloviev, however, they were closely interconnected. The first was Soloviev's messianic heterodoxy, bound up with his growing sympathy for Catholicism. The Slavophiles were religious fundamentalists, seeing truth only in the Orthodox Church and full of prejudices against other Christian churches; the ecumenical idea, let alone that of a 'new, regenerated Christianity', was completely alien to them. Soloviev, on the other hand, strove for the unification of all Christians, to be followed by the establishment of a messianic Kingdom of God on earth. His vision of the future had, in order to evade Russian censorship, to be expounded in books published abroad, such as *The History and the Future of Theocracy* (in Russian, Zagreb 1887), *L'Idée russe* (1888) and *La Russie et l'Église Universelle* (1889). Mankind's crowning fate on earth was there defined as spiritual unification under the Pope and political unification under the Russian emperor. Soloviev attempted to win the Croatian bishop Josip Strossmayer to this cause, and through him Pope Leo XIII. Strossmayer, engrossed in dreams of Pan-Slavic unity, greatly admired Soloviev; Pope Leo XIII, too, agreed that the Russian philosopher's ideal was a beautiful one, but thought that only a miracle could make it come true.[17]

[16] E. N. Trubetskoi, *Mirosozertsanie V. S. Solovíeva*, Moscow, 1913, vol. 1, pp. 87–8. Trubetskoi divides Soloviev's intellectual evolution into three periods: (1) the preparatory period, to 1882; (2) the 'utopian' period, 1882–*c*.1894 (Mochulsky suggests that this period ended in the early 1890s); and (3) the 'positive' period, in which Soloviev no longer believed in the possibility of realizing his utopian vision. Some authors also distinguish a final apocalyptic phase—the last year of Soloviev's life.

[17] See Mochulsky, *Vladimir Soloviev*, p. 185.

The second reason was, paradoxically, Soloviev's growing sympathy with liberal political ideas, such as civil liberty, religious tolerance and, above all, the rule of law. He combined this with his ideal of a 'free theocracy' by increasingly emphasising the adjective 'free' and, in fact, it was on behalf of this ideal that he attacked all forms of national egoism—which he sharply distinguished from patriotism—religious particularism, and persecution of national and religious minorities. (His articles on this subject, published in the *European Messenger*, were later collected under the title *The Nationalities' Problem in Russia*). He also shared with the liberals their belief in 'bourgeois progress' which aroused the particular ire of his ultra-reactionary admirer Konstantin Leontiev. He was fully aware that his religious philosophy could not be shared by the editors of the *European Messenger* but he refused to treat the lack of 'metaphysical unanimity' as an obstacle to political alliance.[18] It had a certain symbolic significance that he became especially close to Włodzimierz Spasowicz, the famous liberal barrister of Polish descent who was so deeply hated by Dostoevsky.[19] We know from Spasowicz that he gave him his *The Nationalities' Problem in Russia* with the following characteristic inscription: 'hoping to find a practical, if not theoretical, agreement'.[20]

The two reasons which alienated Soloviev from Slavophilism, his liberalism and his heterodox Messianism, were linked in his treatment of the Polish and Jewish question in Russia. His bold and noble defence of Russia's Jews and Poles was not only part of his commitment to combating anti-Semitism and the policy of russification; it was also part of his theocratic utopia. The Jews, the Poles, and the Russians were in his eyes 'theocratic nations', the only ones which had not abandoned the messianic hope that religious truth would some day be realized in political and social life.[21] He attached great significance to the fact that the bulk of the world's Jewry—indeed the most orthodox part—lived in Poland and in Russia, on the territories which had earlier belonged to Poland and later became incorporated into the Russian empire.[22]

[18] Cf. his letter to M. M. Stasulevich (1888) quoted in Mochulsky, *Vladimir Soloviev*, p. 190.
[19] See above, Ch. I, 5.
[20] W. Spasowicz, 'Włodzimierz Sołowjew', in W. Spasowicz, *Pisma*, vol. 7, SPb 1899, p. 231.
[21] Soloviev, *Sobranie sochinenii*, vol. 4, p. 172 ('Evreistvo i khristianskii vopros').
[22] Ibid. The same view of the Jews was incorporated into the messianic teaching of the great Polish poet, Adam Mickiewicz (see Walicki, *Philosophy and Romantic Messianism:*

The possible contributions of these two groups, the Jews and the Poles, to the establishment of a 'free theocracy' he characterized as follows. The Jews—the nation of Biblical prophets, teachers of law and, recently, of industrialists and merchants—represent the principle of materialistic (*vel* naturalistic) and activist individualism; therefore it will be appropriate for them to play the leading role in the economic life of a future theocratic kingdom.[23] Because of the strong naturalistic elements in their religion their economic activity will not consist in the ruthless exploitation of nature but will rather establish a harmonious relationship between humankind and nature, based upon mutual love. Such a re-direction of economic activity was seen by Soloviev as a necessary condition for the universal regeneration of the world, both of humankind and of nature, which was to be brought about by his 'free theocracy'.

At the time of writing, however, Soloviev saw as the most important task the unification of Eastern and Western Christianity; in essence the Russian acknowledgement of the spiritual authority of the Pope. In this he conceived the possible role of the Russian Poles to be extremely important. The mission of the Poles, reasoned Soloviev, had always been to serve the noble cause of Catholicism among the Slavs.[24] But the subjugation of Poland had created conditions in which a Polish initiative could no longer be expected. If, however, the Russian Emperor and the Russian Church should decide to acknowledge the authority of Rome, the Poles could resume their role as a bridge between the Slavs and the Western world. Religious reconciliation would bring with it political reconciliation between the two leading Slavonic nations to the great advantage of both. In contrast to the Russians, the Poles had always lacked a strong government, while the Russians, unlike the Poles, had lacked a strong and independent upper class. Reconciliation with Rome would make the Russian Tsar

The Case of Poland, Oxford, 1982, pp. 265–7). It seems worthwhile to note that Soloviev knew both Mickiewicz's poetry and his messianic ideas, as set forth in his Paris lectures on Slavonic literature (1840–4). In 1898, in a lecture given on the occasion of the centenary of Mickiewicz's birth, he interpreted Mickiewicz's Messianism as the victory of spiritual freedom over the external authority of the Church and, at the same time, the overcoming of nationalism by the subordination of the national cause to the cause of the universal regeneration of humankind. (Cf. Soloviev, *Sobranie sochinenii*, vol. 9, pp. 257–64.) Mochulsky has rightly observed that the same could be said about Soloviev himself (*Vladimir Soloviev*, p. 247).

[23] Soloviev, *Sobranie sochinenii*, vol. 4, pp. 184–5 (cf. Soloviev, *Istoriia i budushchnost' teokratii*, ibid., p. 433).

[24] Ibid., p. 182.

acceptable to the Poles and the Polish gentry would fill the place of the public-spirited upper class that Russia herself lacked.[25] The moral satisfaction of the Poles would automatically cause the disappearance of Russian revolutionary 'nihilism' which Soloviev (together with the Slavophiles and Katkov) called 'a mere mask for the Polish question'.

It seems worthwhile to add here that Soloviev was very interested in the Uniate Church—a church created in the old Polish–Lithuanian Commonwealth, subordinating its members to the authority of Rome without abandoning the liturgical and cultural distinctiveness of Eastern Christianity.[26] Another touching testimony to Soloviev's constant search for bridges between Catholic Poland and Greek-Orthodox Russia was his attitude towards the Black Madonna of Częstochowa, the symbolic 'Queen of Poland'. He stressed that this most famous miraculous picture of the Virgin Mary in Poland was in fact a Byzantine ikon whose cult was shared by the members of the Orthodox Church.[27]

At the beginning of the 1890s Soloviev became disillusioned with theocratic utopianism and as a result drew even closer to the liberals. The main work in this new stage of his intellectual evolution was an elaborate system of ethics entitled *A Justification of the Good* (1897, 2nd edn. 1899). The greater part of this major study was devoted to law, to its social significance and its defence against the 'abstract moralism' of Tolstoy. An important supplement to this book was published separately under the title *Law and Morality: Essays on Applied Ethics* (1897). It was officially dedicated to Spasowicz stressing the warmth of their friendship and their intellectual unity 'in necessary essentials'.[28]

The secularization of Soloviev's thought did not weaken his commitment to the reconciliation of Eastern Christianity with Rome. In February 1896 he decided to receive the eucharist from the hands of a Uniate priest N. A. Tolstoy (who had himself become a Uniate under the influence of Soloviev's ideas).[29] The interpretation of this act is a matter of dispute. Some authors see it as merely an expression

[25] Ibid., pp. 179–81.
[26] He was even reading Uniate theological treatises in Polish (S. M. Soloviev, *Zhizn' Vladimira Solovieva*, p. 236).
[27] Soloviev, *Sobranie sochinenii*, vol. 9, pp. 69–70. Another miraculous picture of the Madonna, greatly revered by Catholics in the Lithuanian part of the ancient Polish–Lithuanian Commonwealth, was the ikon of Ostra Brama (Pointed Gate) in Wilno (Vilnius). After Soloviev's death a copy of it was put on his grave, side by side with an Orthodox Christian ikon. (See Mochulsky, *Vladimir Soloviev*, p. 268.)
[28] See Soloviev, *Sobranie sochinenii*, vol. 8, p. 519.
[29] S. M. Soloviev, *Zhizn' Vladimira Solovieva*, p. 346.

of Soloviev's belief that intercommunion between the Catholic and Orthodox Churches was possible and theologically valid; others go further, seeing it a practical application of the view that membership of the Orthodox Church was compatible with membership of the Catholic Church, since on the deeper level the two Churches had never really been separated.[30] Still others, mainly Catholics, stress the fact that the act was preceded by reading aloud the Catholic creed (as established by the Council of Trent) and thus amounted to a conversion to Catholicism.[31]

In the last year of his life Soloviev's views apparently underwent another change. His optimistic faith in liberal progress and his confidence that even secularization was essentially part of the ultimate process of salvation through Christ began to give way to a mood of pessimism. An expression of this was the philosophical dialogue *Three Conversations* (1899–1900), and especially the *Tale of Antichrist* appended to it.

Soloviev's personality is well described in Trubetskoi's book. His sensitive features gave him a rather otherworldly look, so that simple people often took him for a priest and knelt down in front of him. At the same time he was not without a sense of humour and in his poems often poked gentle fun at himself. His nature was childlike and trusting, and he tended to see everything in spiritual terms, as a 'reflection of the invisible world'. He fell in love easily, and his romantic mysticism was undoubtedly a sublimation of his erotic feelings, although it cannot be dismissed as merely displaced eroticism. He led an untidy life, often sleeping during the day and working at night, and showing little concern for the future. It was well known that he found it impossible to send away beggars, and was likely to hand over all the money he had with him or even to give away his boots. He strongly disliked Tolstoy—his single-minded 'abstract moralism', his anarchism, unconditional pacifism and the wrathful thunderings as of a patriarchal prophet. He abhorred one-sidedness and steadfastly sought out aspects of the many-sided universal truth.

[30] See, for instance, G. Florovsky, *Christianity and Culture*, p. 231.

[31] This is, of course, the position of S. M. Soloviev. From the strictly Orthodox point of view the most important thing about Soloviev was the patently heretical character of his views. According to S. Bolshakoff Soloviev, together with Skovoroda, belonged to the category of 'lonely thinkers professing a curious blend of theosophic and pantheist theories'. To the Russian Orthodox monks, he wrote, 'their treatises were simply unknown and when known, abhorrent'. (S. Bolshakoff, *Russian Mystics*, London, 1977, p. 107.)

3   The philosophy of All-Unity

It is not necessary to set out here Soloviev's philosophical system as a
whole—this I have done elsewhere.[32] Some parts of it, or themes in it,
although otherwise interesting and important, have little or no direct
relevance for the proper understanding of Soloviev's philosophy of
law.

The most important in the present context is Soloviev's conception
of All-Unity—a conception which underlies his entire system and also
typifies the peculiarities of his dialectical method of thinking. It was a
conception which tried to reconcile the absolute with the relative,
integrality with autonomy. As a method of thinking it was an effort to
avoid both atomism and holism—to see all things as parts of a great
unity, but a unity of a dialectical type, that is, compatible with the
autonomy of its constituent parts, or 'moments'. Such a unity did not
dissolve differences but only made them relative. It was incompatible
with the notion of absolute autonomy, autonomy as separation and
isolation; on the other hand, it legitimized and presupposed the
relative autonomy of the different spheres, or grades, in the
hierarchical structure of the universe.

The following is a brief summary of the most general outline of
Soloviev's philosophy. Conceiving the world as the divine Absolute in
the process of becoming, he distinguished in it three moments,
corresponding to the three persons of the Holy Trinity: the moment of
a static, undifferentiated unity, the moment of individuation and
differentiation and, finally, the highest moment of a free, differentiated
unity. The idea of such a unity in the cosmos—*Sophia* or the World
Soul—had once fallen away from the divine *Logos*, plunging the world
into a chaotic struggle of hostile elements. The second act of this
cosmic drama was the appearance of man. Since then *Sophia*, having
identified herself with the 'ideal humanity', began to ascend to a
renewed unity with God in Godmanhood. The union of *Logos* with
Sophia, of God with man, had been accomplished in Jesus. It
remained, however—in order to achieve the total regeneration and
transfiguration of the world—to reconcile West and East, to unite the
Christian Churches and realize in history the Kingdom of the Holy
Ghost.

The first outline of Soloviev's system, *Philosophical Principles of
Integral Knowledge* (1877), bears a title harking back to the notion of

---

[32] See Walicki, *History of Russian Thought*, ch. 17, pp. 371–94.

'integral wholeness' (*tsel'nost'*) which was the kernel of Kireevsky's philosophical work. The general scheme of cosmic development—from primitive unity through atomism towards reintegration on a higher level—is here applied to human knowledge and history. In the evolution of humankind, Soloviev argues, the first phase—that of substantial monism—was represented by the Eastern world (including nineteenth-century Islam), and the second phase (atomism) by Western European civilization. During the first phase the three spheres of human activity—the spheres of creativity, knowledge, and social practice—were entirely subordinated to religion. In the sphere of creativity, technology (the first, material grade) was fused with art (the second, formal grade) and mysticism (the highest, absolute grade) in an undifferentiated and mystical creativity—in other words, in what Soloviev called a *theurgy*. In the sphere of knowledge, positive science (the material grade) was fused with abstract philosophy (the formal grade) and theology (the absolute grade) in an undifferentiated whole that might be called *theosophy*. In the sphere of social practice, the economic society of producers or *zemstvo* (the material grade) was fused with the state (the formal grade) and the church (the absolute grade), forming a homogenous and *theocratic* whole. In the second evolutionary phase, represented by Western Europe, the different grades within each sphere strove for absolute autonomy and mastery over one another. In the resulting struggle matter conquered spirit: the final outcome of Western civilization was materialistic socialism (the true scion of capitalism, as Soloviev saw it) in the social sphere, positivism in the sphere of knowledge, and utilitarian realism in the sphere of creativity. But now the time had come for the third phase—that of *free unity*—in which the separate spheres and grades of human creativity, knowledge, and social practice would once more be united, but without losing their distinctiveness. In the three spheres of life this renewed unity would express itself as a *free theurgy*, a *free theosophy*, and a *free theocracy*. The mission of inaugurating this universal regeneration and reintegration of human life was allotted by Soloviev to the Russians.

In the sphere of knowledge Soloviev distinguished three types of philosophy—naturalism (empiricism), rationalism, and mysticism. Empiricism and rationalism, he suggested, take different paths to arrive at the same result—the denial of the substantial reality of both the external reality and the knower himself. Following the elderly Schelling and the Slavophiles he saw Hegelianism as the last word in rationalism. He accused Hegel of creating a merely 'negative' philosophy, that is, a philosophy dealing only with the notion of things, their pure essences, while ignoring everything truly actual and existent, positively given. Like Schelling, he set against this a programmatically 'positive' philosophy, rehabilitating 'the given'. It involved, above all, a 'rehabilitation of nature' (as a *manifestation* of the divine Absolute, and not, as Hegel preferred to see it, as an *alienation* of it) and, also, a lively interest in the philosophical interpretation of the 'positively given' content of the Christian revelation.[33]

Soloviev's reinterpretation of Christianity revolves around the concept of Godmanhood (*Lectures on Godmanhood*, 1877–81). He used the idea of Godmanhood to overcome the dualism between the divine and the temporal, characteristic of traditional Christian theology, without falling into pantheism. The concept of 'God made Man', Soloviev asserted, does not assume either a dualistic belief in the transcendence of God, or a pantheistic belief in His immanence in the world. God is both transcendent and immanent, and the mediating principle that allows the world to become transfused by the Divine spirit—the link between the Creator and created matter—is Man. The ultimate purpose of the universe is the synthesis of the temporal and the divine—universal reintegration in a living All-Unity. The whole of nature tended towards Man, and humanity harboured the God-Man within its womb. The incarnation of God in Jesus Christ was thus the central event in the entire cosmic process. Even this, however, was only the beginning of the redemptive process, the completion of which would be achieved only with the universal regeneration of earthly life.

The concept of Godmanhood in Soloviev's work is closely linked to the idea of *Sophia*. Soloviev saw *Sophia* both as the World Soul and as an ideal Humanity, whose role is to mediate between God and the world. As the word made flesh or divine matter, it epitomizes the passive, receptive principle and is therefore feminine. Thus the concept of *Sophia* served the cause of a mystical rehabilitation of nature.[34] Soloviev's theory of love shows, however, how different was this mystical naturalism from ordinary biological naturalism: he claims that the real significance of love consists not in procreation but in

---

[33] Cf. H. Dahm, *Vladimir Solovyev and Max Scheler: Attempt at a Comparative Interpretation*, Dordrecht–Boston, 1975, pp. 106–7.

[34] Cf. E. Munzer, *Solovyev: Prophet of Russian–Western Unity*, London, 1956, pp. 20–4.

man's striving for the likeness of God in a restored androgynous unity. A comparison between *Philosophical Principles of Integral Knowledge* and *Lectures on Godmanhood* shows a certain change in Soloviev's attitude towards the West. In the first he wholeheartedly subscribed to Slavophile anti-Westernism, stating unequivocally that any kind of monism was superior to atomism and concluding therefrom that 'the Moslem East was superior to Western civilization'. In the second he emphasized the development and perfection of the divine truth through man and from this perspective Western progress, developing the human side of Godmanhood, had to be seen as the means whereby the truth of Christ perfects itself in history. Konstantin Leontiev indignantly rejected this view; having read Soloviev's article 'On the Decline of the Medieval World-View' (1891) he denounced his former friend as a tool of the Antichrist. He was obviously not aware that his reaction was overdue since Soloviev had already imparted a divine meaning to 'liberal and egalitarian progress' in his *Lectures on Godmanhood*. Let me quote from the concluding chapter of this book:

Had history included only the Byzantine Christianity, the truth of Christ (Godmanhood) would have remained imperfect, in the absence of a (developed) human element of free initiative and activity necessary for its perfection. As it is, however, the divine element of Christianity, preserved by the East, can now reach its perfection in mankind, for now it has the material upon which it can act, in which it can manifest its internal force: namely, the human element which has been emancipated and developed in the West. And this has not only an historical, but also a mystical, meaning.[35]

A similar shift of emphasis can be detected by comparing *Philosophical Principles of Integral Knowledge* with Soloviev's doctoral dissertation, the *Critique of Abstract Principles*. At first glance the two works seem very similar: each systematizes Soloviev's ideas in the spheres of epistemology, ethics, and social philosophy, each criticizes the state of disunity and chaos into which human knowledge and social life has been plunged, and finally, each postulates a reintegration through 'free theosophy' and 'free theocracy'. On closer examination, however, it turns out that the second work deals much more with the legitimate, though relative, autonomy of the different spheres of human activity, seeing them as parts of the All-Unity which should fully develop their proper characteristics and warning more emphatically against fusing them together in an undifferentiated

[35] V. Soloviev, *Lectures on Godmanhood*, London, 1948, p. 206.

whole. This was, surely, one of the reasons why Soloviev abandoned the Slavophile term 'integral wholeness'.

It should be added that the germ of such a development was already contained in *Philosophical Principles of Integral Knowledge*. Unlike the Slavophiles, the young Soloviev did not idealize the unity of the past. The first stage of development, for him, was a stage of merely *external unity*. Historical Christianity expressed no such unity; on the contrary, its progressive role was to break it up and replace it with the dualism of Church and State, by separating the 'profanum' from the 'sacrum'. Thus, the historical significance of Christianity lay not in representing the principle of integrality, as the Slavophiles had believed, but, rather, in sanctifying the principle of dualism, which was the price of freedom.[36] This dualism led to the separation of the economy and politics from religious morality. Unlike Kireevsky, for whom this separation was merely a symptom of decline, characteristic of the West, Soloviev was prepared to justify the relative autonomy of the economic (material) and political (formal) spheres of social life. We may conclude therefore that Soloviev, contrary to Mochulsky's opinion, had not in his early works absorbed Kireevsky's world-view *in toto*. True, in the earliest stage of his intellectual evolution, he was heavily influenced by Slavophilism, but even then the inner logic of his thought led him away from the backward-looking conservative Romanticism of his Slavophile teachers.

Soloviev's theory of development was derived from the ancient neo-Platonic idea of self-enriching alienation—an idea which underlies not only the entire neo-Platonic tradition in Christian mysticism, but also Hegelianism and even Marxism.[37] It provided a pattern of thinking in accordance with which self-enrichment can be achieved only through self-alienation, namely, through the destruction of the primordial unity. The different potential capacities of the divine or human spirit must become external (and thus alienated) in order to develop; they must develop separately, autonomously, in order to unfold fully and to become reintegrated on a higher level. The emphasis, of course, could be placed differently: either on the misery of alienation and a longing

---

[36] Soloviev, *Sobranie sochinenii*, vol. 1, p. 267. The same view of Christianity was developed earlier, in the messianic historiosophy of the Polish romantic philosopher, August Cieszkowski (see my *Philosophy and Romantic Nationalism*, pp. 298–300). Nicolai Berdyaev suggested that a comparison of Soloviev's philosophy of history and Cieszkowski's ideas would be interesting (N. Berdyaev, *The Russian Idea*, London, 1947, p. 212).

[37] Cf. L. Kolakowski, *Main Currents of Marxism*, Oxford, 1978, vol. 1, ch. 1.

for Paradise lost, or on the hope of reintegration and the glory of Paradise regained. Soloviev, a future-oriented Messianist, from the very beginning committed himself to the second of these interpretations.

4 The liberal philosophy of law and theocratic utopianism

The first comprehensive presentation of Soloviev's views on law, as a part of his philosophy of ethics, is to be found in his *Critique of Abstract Principles*. It is, in fact, a well-rounded outline of legal philosophy. Its originality, however, consists not so much in what Soloviev said about legal matters, which was very little indeed, but rather in his views on the place of law in the entire structure of things human and divine.

His starting point was the distinction between two kinds of principles: (1) The 'substantial' religious principles which are given to us directly, in our inner experience or as positive facts of divine revelation, and (2) the 'abstract principles', those which we discover for ourselves, unaided, by critical, scientific thought, divorced from divine inspiration. The first are either mystical or traditional; the second are either empirical or rational.

In morality the highest empirical principle can be deduced from the universal fact of compassion which unites each individual with others and, to a lesser extent, with all sentient beings. Schopenhauer formulated it in the words: 'Neminem laede, imo omnes, quantum potes, juva'. The first part of this formula ('do not harm anybody') appeals to the negative virtue of justice (*justitia*), the second ('help everybody, as much as you can') to the positive virtue of charity and love (*caritas*).[38]

Empirical morality, however, is not enough. It deals with humans as empirical beings, suffering animals, but not with humans as autonomous personalities.[39] It can provide practical instructions, but not a universally valid moral law. Because of this the Schopenhauerian formula must be supplemented by the highest principle of rational ethics, namely, by the categorical imperative of Kant. The abstract, rational universality of this imperative might be felt as too cold and formal, but means in practice that each individual must be treated as an end, never just as a means. Thus, only rational morality can elevate man to the status of a person.

Moral aims, however, can not be achieved by virtue of the inner quality of the moral will alone. Soloviev strongly felt that no morality is

---

[38] Soloviev, *Sobranie sochinenii*, vol. 2, pp. 26–9.   [39] Ibid., pp. 47–50.

possible without an organized society, without the minimum objective conditions for realizing moral postulates. Here he had to pass from 'subjective ethics' to 'objective ethics', that is, to the theory of the economic and legal order of society.

Soloviev's economic views are not developed in detail. He saw economic individualism and socialism (collectivism) as equally one-sided and, moreover, as sharing the characteristic of making the economic principle absolute, treating man as merely an economic agent, a bearer of determinate material interests. In the sphere of competing economic interests people have to be treated as means only; therefore the economic order must be subordinated to the legal order, in which people are treated as persons, subject to rights and duties (and not merely interests), thus securing the realization of justice. The most extreme expression of 'abstract economism' is materialistic socialism, and just because of this its followers have shown definite suspicion of, or even outright hostility towards, law. Against the civil and political rights of man, as proclaimed by the French revolution, socialists set the right to material well-being, seeing it as the only right which really mattered. They were right in turning attention to the material side of human existence, but completely wrong in disregarding the formal element of social life, represented by law. In Soloviev's eyes this was 'the greatest untruth and the basic sin of socialism'.[40]

We may safely assume that in passing this judgement on socialism Soloviev had in mind Russian populist socialists who, as we know, represented a peculiarly extreme form of left-wing nihilism. It is obvious, however, that he saw these as epitomizing the fundamental inadequacy of the entire socialist tradition, from the early utopian socialists, who had proclaimed the 'rehabilitation of matter', to the historical materialism of Marx. He also criticized socialism on purely economic grounds, arguing that in the economic sphere unconditional private property, industrial competition and social division of labour must be regarded as necessary conditions of progress,[41] and that the one-sidedness of economic individualism consists not in defending these principles but in making them absolute, at the expense of overall social solidarity.

Thus, socialists absolutize the right to material consumption while economic individualists champion absolute individual freedom in pursuit of material interests. Both standpoints are equally immoral

<hr>

[40] Ibid., p. 144.   [41] Ibid., p. 129.

because both reduce man to *homo economicus*, instead of giving him the status of a person. Capitalist plutocracy exploits the masses for its own benefit, but consistent socialism also 'limits man's fundamental significance to the economic sphere, sees man above all as a worker, a producer of material wealth, an economic actor', in other words, as a potential exploiter or subject of exploitation. And it must be so, because economics as such fosters a narrowly utilitarian, instrumental and exploitative attitude towards everything—both human beings and nature. The objective conditions for recognizing in each individual something inviolable and sacred can be created only in the higher sphere of social existence—that of a political order whose basis is law.

In discussing the genesis of law Soloviev tried to do justice both to the theory of organic development, as represented by the German 'historical school', and to the 'mechanical' theory of social contract. In his view both theories were partially right because law had two sources: the spontaneous, unconscious creativity of the collective mind and the conscious will of individuals. The strength of the first theory lay in explaining the early history of law while the strength of the second consisted in a better understanding of the idea of law and of the inner logic of its development. In its early stages law develops organically from customs and embodies the unconscious collective reason of a nation. This stage of organic community, so idealized by the Slavophiles and other apologists of traditional *Gemeinschaft*, had however to give way to a higher stage in which society becomes 'a free union of free individuals'.[42] Soloviev, in sharp contrast to the Slavophiles, saw this as a universal, irreversible, and basically benevolent historical law. In the higher stage, he thought, organic social ties and plant-like growth must be replaced by the conscious will of the legislator, whose aim is the common good. The two stages, however, and the two corresponding types of law, cannot be neatly separated. Any legal order contains both organic and contractual elements, because both communalism (corresponding to the organic element in law) and individualism (corresponding to the contractual element) are necessary for social life; they struggle with each other, but neither can be completely eliminated.

The social ideal consists in a harmonious reconciliation between communalism and individualism, unity and freedom. In applying this view to law Soloviev stressed that the ideal legal order of the future

---

[42] Ibid., p. 145.

would entail the disappearance of conflicts between the conscious will of individuals and the unconscious collective mind.[43] In contrast to other social dreamers, however, he did not envisage a 'withering away of law'; he thought that a legal order would be needed even at the stage of 'free theocracy'. A theocratic order should not swallow up the relative autonomy of law; otherwise it would become a 'false theocracy', unity without freedom. Before his break with the Slavophiles Soloviev followed their tradition (which included Dostoevsky) in attributing such a false ideal to Catholicism.

Soloviev carefully distinguished the problem of the genesis and development of law from the problem of the essence of law, and historical order from logical order. In his view the true essence of law manifested itself only at the higher stage of legal development; in other words (to introduce the *Gemeinschaft–Gesellschaft* typology) at the stage in which the *Gesellschaft* paradigm of law achieved its maximum logical consistency and became firmly established. In Soloviev's interpretation this applied not only to law in the narrow sense but to politico-legal order as a whole. Only the modern state, fully respecting and guaranteeing the rule of law, was in his eyes an acceptable expression of the ideal essence of statehood.[44]

Law, reasoned Soloviev, defines relationships between free persons, holders of rights; therefore it must recognize, take for granted, as it were, both freedom and equality: the freedom to further ones own interests and equality in respecting the freedom and interests of others. The main concern of law, at the mature stage of its development, is the protection of equal freedom or, to put it differently, the limitation of freedom for the sake of equality. Thus, Soloviev concluded, law can be defined as the 'synthesis of freedom and equality' or as 'freedom conditioned by equality'.[45]

In accordance with the *Gesellschaft* paradigm of law, he hastened to add that he meant only formal, negative equality, equality in what is common to all men—their individual freedom. He also stressed that law serves the cause of morality by enforcing only the idea of justice, that is, only the first, negative part of the Schopenhauerian formula (*neminem laede*). In contrast to morality, law is concerned only with the means of human activity and does not prescribe for it any positive goals. It demands from us giving to everyone his due, but it does not demand that we help each other, let alone that we sacrifice ourselves

[43] Ibid., p. 151.   [44] Ibid., p. 136.   [45] Ibid., p. 153.

for the sake of others. Unlike morality it does not condemn egoism. From the point of view of love we should strive for the good of other people whereas from the point of view of legal justice other people are seen rather as limitations of our freedom in pursuing our own good; therefore the common good as the aim of legislation must be defined in a negative way. Different individuals have different interests, law must protect their equal freedom and therefore cannot support certain interests against others. It should be concerned with the proper 'delimitation' of competing interests,[46] namely, with defining the limits of the legitimate freedom of each individual and with protecting all of them equally.

The same formula, of law as 'delimitation of interests', was used at almost the same time by Nicholas Korkunov, who had succeeded Redkin (Chicherin's teacher) in the chair of Legal Encyclopaedia (general theory of law) in the University of St Petersburg. Like Soloviev he used this formula for distinguishing between legal and moral norms: 'The norms for the delimitation of interests set the boundary between law and not law and constitute "juridical norms".'[47] Like Soloviev he levelled it against the utilitarian view of law, especially against Ihering's theory of the purpose of law (*Zweck im Recht*).[48] This remarkable similarity of views cannot be attributed to mere accident. At the end of the 1870s Soloviev was lecturing at the University of St Petersburg and Korkunov was appointed to the chair there in 1878; so the coincidence of their views might be explained as due to the influence of one (probably Korkunov) on the other; it might also be the result of informal discussions to which each contributed his share. Anyway, it is beyond doubt that each knew the relevant works of the other.[49]

In developing his ideas Korkunov came to the conclusion that the function of law is to mediate between the sphere of economic interests and the sphere of moral values: 'Morality furnishes the criterion for the proper evaluation of our interests; law marks the limits within which they ought to be confined.'[50] Soloviev shared this view,

[46] Ibid., p. 148.
[47] N. M. Korkunov, *General Theory of Law*, W. G. Hastings (trans.), Reprint, South Hackensack, NJ, 1968, p. 52.
[48] Ibid., p. 96.
[49] Korkunov's book contains a reference to Soloviev's conception of law as a 'combining of liberty and equality' (ibid., p. 81).
[50] Korkunov, *General Theory of Law*, p. 52. Soloviev made reference to this formula in his *Justification of the Good* (vol. 8, p. 494).

although, of course, his moral philosophy was very different from Korkunov's. If law does not prescribe the goals, the positive content of our activity, he argued, this content may be either (1) prescribed by our economic interests, or (2) prescribed by morality. Law is characterized by the absolute universalism of its form which does not harmonize with the particular and accidental content of economic interests; it demands, as it were, *absolute* content which can be furnished only by absolute morality. The highest norm of absolute morality is charity or love. It is much more than natural compassion, upon which empirical morality is based, or the cold categorical imperative of rational ethics; it is a gift of divine grace and it demands that man should 'treat his fellows in the same way that God treats him'. In his *Spiritual Foundations of Life* (1882–4) Soloviev formulated these demands as follows:

' "Freely ye have received, freely give". Give your neighbour more than he deserves: treat him better than he deserves. Give to him to whom you owe nothing; require nothing of him who owes to you: That is how the heavenly powers treat us, and that is how we should behave towards one another.'[51]

In contrast to this, law 'stops short at negation: it tells man what he may not do but is silent about what he ought to do';[52] it aims only at a 'reciprocal *limitation*' of conflicting forces.[53] Small wonder, then, that Soloviev so strongly stresses the insufficiency of law;[54] we should rather wonder how it was possible that such a sharp contrast between juridical laws and the law of love did not push him in the direction of Christian anarchism. His formula of the morality of love fits perfectly in to Tolstoy's writings. And yet nothing was more alien to Soloviev than the violent and intransigent legal nihilism of the great writer.

Using the Hegelian terminology, one may say that the fundamental disagreement between Soloviev and Tolstoy concerns their different attitudes towards 'objective spirit', the sphere of *institutionalized* social life. Tolstoy accepted only the quasi-natural institution of family while adamantly rejecting law and the state; Soloviev treated law and state as the foundation of 'objective ethics', without which the very existence of a higher 'subjective ethics' would have been doubtful. He accused Tolstoy of 'abstract moralism' by which he meant divorcing moral

---

[51] V. Soloviev, *God, Man and the Church: The Spiritual Foundations of Life*, D. Attwater (trans.), London [*c.*1930], pp. 70–1.
[52] Ibid., p. 29.   [53] Ibid., p. 71.
[54] Cf. Soloviev, *Sobranie sochinenii*, vol. 2, p. 155 (the title of ch. 20).

postulates from the conditions necessary for their realization. It was logical, he thought, that Tolstoy had come not only to the negation of all states but to the negation of all established churches as well.

In Soloviev's theory, in contradistinction to Hegelianism, the highest manifestation of the institutionalized, objective ethic was not the state but the church. This is why he championed the idea of a new theocracy. But he stressed as strongly as possible that the rule of law, in its proper sphere, must not be endangered in the theocratic society of the future. He constantly repeated that law and the state must be neither swallowed up by morality and the church nor rigidly separated from them. On this ground he rejected both 'false theocracy' and the modern doctrine of the mutual separation of state and church, setting against them his ideal of a free theocracy. False theocracy, he argued, liquidates law as an autonomous sphere, which amounts to the liquidation of human freedom in the name of divine love. On the other hand, the complete, mechanical separation between juridical state and church makes freedom empty and creates a situation in which the moral unity based on love is endangered by the formalism of legal justice which, as is well-known, can easily transform *summum jus* into *summa injuria*.[55] Free theocracy prevents these dangers: it reconciles freedom with love, law with morality, by recognizing the autonomy of the legal sphere while, at the same time, making it relative, a part of the great unity of the divine-human world, and not an absolutized abstract principle.

The social ideal of the Slavophiles was also defined as the reconciliation of unity with freedom—as a 'free unity', as opposed to a 'unity without freedom'. Because of this, even in the early 1880s, the Slavophiles could still see Soloviev as their philosophical ally, if not exactly their follower. In fact, however, this similarity of views was merely formal while the difference in substance was profound. The Slavophiles treated law, except for customary law, with suspicion and only accepted it as a 'necessary evil'. They were especially intransigent in their negative attitude towards what has been called the *Gesellschaft* paradigm of law: rational legislation was in their eyes the main instrument for the pernicious rationalization of social relations and an expression of the growing atomization, the increasing erosion of inner, organic unity. In contrast to this Soloviev insisted on the great and irreplaceable value of law. For him, it was necessary to secure the wide,

[55] Ibid., pp. 163–4.

although relative, autonomy of law in order to safeguard the autonomy of persons, their mutual impenetrability. In other words his defence of law was bound up with the defence of the idea of autonomous personality —an idea which to the Slavophiles was something peculiarly Western and utterly incompatible with the 'integral wholeness' of life.

What distinguished Soloviev from the Slavophiles brought him at times very close to the classical liberalism of Chicherin. Like Chicherin Soloviev thought that the proper function of law was to define the limits of man's 'negative freedom', and not to force people to help each other; that law should be aim-independent, committed to the 'common good' only in a negative way, namely, that it should not serve as a mere tool for the implementation of social policy. He held that law should safeguard unconditional private property and economic freedom but that, on the other hand, it must not try to enforce morality; rather it should defend man's freedom to be immoral, within the limits prescribed by the existing legal order. Finally, Soloviev subscribed to the concept of 'subjective rights', to the idea of the individual as an autonomous right-holder. In short, he accepted the basic principles of modern, *Gesellschaft*-type law and, by the same token, endorsed the main tenets of the legal philosophy of classical liberalism.

In spite of this Chicherin continued to see Soloviev as half-Slavophile and a dangerous enemy of freedom. In his *Mysticism in Science* he accused Soloviev of wishing to establish a coercive control over private morality, intellectual life and economic activity; a control vested in the Church and exercised in the name of a higher morality, drawing upon the most reactionary theocratic medievalism and, at the same time, paving the way for socialism.[56] He was apparently misled by Soloviev's terminology: the word 'theocracy' was so strongly associated in his mind with extreme antiliberal values that he could not pay enough attention to Soloviev's efforts to make liberalism an inseparable part of the theocratic ideal. In the opposite, antiliberal camp the same error was committed by Leontiev: his fascination with Soloviev's philosophical rehabilitation of theocracy was so strong that for a long time it effectively prevented him from recognizing the liberal content of Soloviev's social and legal philosophy.

Nevertheless Chicherin's interpretation was not entirely groundless. There is a perceptible tension, if not an outright contradiction, in

---

[56] B. Chicherin, *Mistitsizm v nauke*, Moscow, 1880, pp. 87–91.

Soloviev's social philosophy: a tension between autonomy and All-Unity, between liberal principles and a striving for the thorough Christianization of political and social life. Soloviev's philosophy of law, as presented in the relevant chapters of his *Critique of Abstract Principles*, is undoubtedly liberal, but we must not forget that it is part of a larger whole, whose character is very ambiguous. When Soloviev passes from 'society as juridical union' to 'society as religious union' the artificiality of his syncretic synthesis becomes more and more evident. It is easy to follow his thought when he argues that social life forms a hierarchical structure, that the economic sphere, in which other people are treated as means only, is subordinate to the juridical sphere, in which other people are a limit to individual freedom, and that both, without losing their independence, are subordinated to a religious morality of love, for which other people are absolute ends.[57] But it is not easy to see how this ideal—of 'society as Church'—was to be realized in practice. It is clear that Soloviev wanted to preserve the autonomy of the lower spheres and, at the same time, to prevent their separation from the highest principle of human conduct, the principle of absolute morality, without which he could not conceive a 'normal' society. It is not so clear, however, how it would be possible, either in theory or in practice, to combine a defence of classical liberalism in legal philosophy with the postulate that legal justice must not be divorced from the demands of Christian love;[58] nor how it would be possible to endorse unconditional private property and economic freedom while, at the same time, subordinating these principles both to the formal demands of justice and to the absolute demands of religious morality.

Chicherin's criticism was therefore partially justified, but only as criticism of the *implications* inherent in the very idea of theocracy. As a critic of Soloviev's alleged *intentions* Chicherin was completely wrong. Quite irrespective of the logical consistency or inconsistency of his views, Soloviev's commitment to the cause of liberalism in Russia was beyond doubt (although it did not entail radical political demands). Even more unambiguous was his commitment to combating all forms of 'legal nihilism', and especially the notorious depreciation of law in the name of morality.

In his *Nationalities' Problem in Russia* and in his various articles published in the *European Messenger* Soloviev declared himself as a resolute defender of the 'idea of law', in full agreement with the

[57] Soloviev, *Sobranie sochinenii*, vol. 2, pp. 166–9.
[58] Cf. ibid., p. 186.

historical views of his father, who, like Chicherin, had strongly emphasized the role of law and state in Russian history.[59] He scorned any depreciation of law and justice in the name of conscience and holiness, and quoted with approval Almazov's satirical poem ridiculing the Slavophile view of law.[60] He was intolerant towards idealization of the lack of 'bourgeois honesty' in Russia and openly declared that, if it was really easier in Russia to find a holy man than to find an honest man, this would indicate a grave social deficiency, and not spiritual superiority.[61] In an article entitled 'The Significance of the State' he extolled the virtues of ancient Rome, as exemplifying a close connection between morality, respect for law, and civic patriotism.[62] In an attack on Lev Tikhomirov, an ex-revolutionary turned reactionary, he energetically defended law and legal justice against both religious and social demagogy.[63] He pointed out that the Christian gospel of love had not lessened the value of law: Christ had come to fulfil the law, not to reject it. The negation of law in the Christian world derives from gnostic antinomianism, an officially condemned heresy.[64] A realization of the universal idea of justice, in the sense of negative justice as the regulative idea of law, is, in fact, part of the moral demands of Christianity and a precondition of moral progress. This was the ground of Soloviev's firm conviction that believers in Russia's Christian mission ought to be aware that such a mission was completely incompatible with contempt for the law.[65]

We may safely conclude that the rule of law without theocracy was acceptable to Soloviev, while the reverse was not. He was completely honest and sincere in assuring his liberal friends that in all practical matters he was with them, not against them.

5 The de-utopianization of Soloviev's thought and his new philosophy of law

The 1880s were the period of Soloviev's closest collaboration with the liberal *European Messenger* and, at the same time, of his greatest commitment to the idea of a new theocratic order to be instituted by the Russian Tsar under the spiritual guidance of the Roman Pope. He saw no contradiction between condemning all forms of Russian

[59] Ibid., vol. 5, p. 313.
[60] Ibid., p. 357. (For the relevant quotation from Almazov's poem see above, p. 38.)
[61] Ibid., pp. 355-8.
[62] Ibid., vol. 12, p. 326.　　　　　　　[63] Ibid., vol. 6, pp. 442-84.
[64] Ibid., pp. 463-4.　　　　　　　　　[65] Ibid., vol. 5, p. 357.

nationalism in his articles on the nationalities problem in Russia and seeing Russia as a chosen nation in his works on the new theocracy. Nationality, he stressed, should not be confused with nationalism, but bears the same relationship to it as 'personality' does to 'egoism'. The Russian nation as a spiritual entity was for him completely different to the Russian nation materially conceived. 'By Russian nationality', he wrote, 'I do not mean an ethnic unit with its natural distinctive features of material interests, but a nation which senses that the universal cause of God stands above all distinct features and interests; a nation prepared to devote itself to this cause, a *theocratic* nation by destiny and duty.'[66]

In spite of all these distinctions Soloviev's utopia was not a liberal utopia. True, it was possible to identify the cause of liberalism with the cause of universal empire, thus combining liberalism with imperialism. But the *Russian* empire was, after all, the most illiberal of all and it was hardly conceivable that the idea of an alliance between the Russian autocracy and the Catholic Church would evoke even the slightest sympathy in liberal circles. The uneasiness in the Russian liberals' attitude towards Soloviev is therefore fully understandable.

According to Trubetskoi Soloviev's disillusionment with the idea of the messianic role of the Russian autocracy was caused, in part at least, by the great Russian famine of 1891—a national disaster which the government could neither prevent nor successfully cope with.[67] This so shocked him that he started to talk of the necessity for representative government in Russia. He soon abandoned this view, but never returned to his former faith in Russian monarchy as the potential 'third Rome'. More generally, he rejected the very idea of a 'sacred monarchy', which amounted in practice to abandoning his idea of a theocracy as the utopian blueprint for the future. 'Free theocracy' was, so to speak, stripped of its millenarian features and reduced to something like a Kantian 'regulative idea' in ethics.

This de-utopianization of Soloviev's thought brought about a marked secularization of his views on ethics. The Church ceased to be for him the visible Kingdom of God on earth, becoming instead merely 'organized piety'. His emphasis on the proper balance between religious unity and the relative autonomy of the spheres of knowledge,

[66] Ibid., p. 74.
[67] Trubetskoi, *Mirosozertsanie, V. S. Solovieva*, vol. 2, pp. 6–7. For Soloviev's criticism of the government's attitude towards the famine see his articles 'Narodnaia beda i obshchestvennaia pomoshch'' and 'Nashi grekhi i nasha obiazannost'' (in vol. 5).

artistic creation, and social practice gave way to outright acceptance of the secularization of these three spheres of human activity.

In 1894 Soloviev started to prepare a new edition of his *Critique of Abstract Principles* but, soon realizing that his ideas on ethics and law had changed too much, decided to write a new book instead. This was the genesis of his comprehensive treatise *A Justification of the Good*. It is widely recognized as the most important Russian contribution to ethical philosophy or, at least, as 'the only complete ethical system' in Russian philosophical literature.[68] With his shorter book, *Law and Morality*, it constitutes an important contribution to the philosophy of law.

The most important innovation in Soloviev's general approach to ethics was his emphatic endorsement of the independence of ethics both from religion and from metaphysics. There is some disagreement over the extent of this: some students of Soloviev's philosophy assume that he was tending toward the total autonomy of ethics, whereas others suggest that this autonomy is in fact only apparent, since it assumes as a necessary precondition the existence of God and the immortality of the soul.[69] The second view is more soundly based. In fact Soloviev's ethics presuppose also a metaphysical conception of man as a potentially divine creature, capable of infinite self-perfectibility and approximating to a God-like image—the state of theosis in the language of mystical theology.[70] More than that, Soloviev often indicated that his ethics, or ethics in general, presupposed a concrete solution to certain metaphysical questions. Thus, for instance, he challenged the widespread view of the central ethical importance of free will (a view shared by Chicherin among others) by insisting that free will, *liberum arbitrium*, is completely incompatible with ethics.[71] Determinism, he reasoned, should not be identified with its mechanist variety, since two other forms of determinism, the psychological, which includes moral elements, and the moral, also exist. If the human will were free, that is purely arbitrary, free from all determinations, it would be free from determination by any moral considerations

[68] Cf. Mochulsky, *Vladimir Soloviev*, p. 232.

[69] For the first view see Mochulsky (p. 229) and Zenkovsky (*A History of Russian Philosophy*, p. 523) who treats this as an 'unexpected paradox'. The second view was set forth by Trubetskoi *Mirosozertsanie V. S. Solovieva*, vol. 2, p. 80. All these authors are strongly critical of this aspect of Soloviev's views. Trubetskoi explains Soloviev's emphasis on the autonomy of ethics as a self-deception stemming, allegedly, from his quest for popularity (ibid., p. 58).

[70] Soloviev, *Sobranie sochinenii*, vol. 8, p. 379.   [71] Ibid., pp. 38–47.

whatever, a situation making moral conduct impossible and moral doctrines utterly superfluous. In fact, Soloviev added, an element of freedom in the human will must be assumed not, as Kant thought, as an explanation of morality but as an explanation of immorality, because only man's choice of evil might be completely groundless.

This being so, what was the real meaning of Soloviev's declaration of the independence of ethics from metaphysics? The best answer to this question was given, I think, by Sergius Hessen.[72] In his view Soloviev did not mean the logical independence of his ethical theory from his metaphysical theories; what he meant was the factual independence of ethical conduct from professing certain theories or dogmas. Ethics is independent from metaphysical theory because people can be good quite irrespective of their theoretical views; because humankind can become more divine without theoretical knowledge of divine matters. In relation to religion Soloviev's new standpoint meant a resolute rejection of ethical heteronomy and instead the proclamation of the full autonomy of ethics from the dogmas of positive religion and the authority of the Church, in fact a break with the ideal of a theocratic state. What remained of this ideal was merely the postulate that the three highest authorities in the moral sphere—the secular sovereign, the religious head, and the divinely inspired prophet—should seek mutual agreement.

Justification of the Good is divided into three parts: (I) 'The Good in Human Nature', (II) 'The Good from God', and (III) 'The Good in the History of Mankind'. In Part I Soloviev tried to give his ethics empirical foundations by deriving them from feelings of shame, compassion, and religious adoration. Shame (whose prototype is sexual shame) expresses man's attitude to what is beneath him: a sense of shame reminds him that he is a spiritual being intended for higher purposes than the world of physical matter. A further development of shame is conscience, whose role is to preserve integrity at the level of man's individual life. Compassion is a social feeling expressing man's attitude to his equals, his fellow men; its role is to transform society into an integral organism, to bring to pass 'the truth of co-essentiality' or 'the real solidarity' of all beings. Finally, religious adoration (*pietas*, *reverentia*) expresses man's attitude to what is superior to him; its role is to restore the wholeness of man's species nature by uniting it with the absolute centre of the universe. The fact that feelings of shame,

[72] In his article 'Der Kampf der Utopie und der Autonomie des Guten . . . ' (see above, n. 15).

compassion, and religious adoration were universal was for Soloviev convincing proof that it was possible to set up a universally valid system of ethics without basing it on revealed religion, let alone theology. At the same time, Soloviev followed Kant in insisting that ethics cannot be founded on psychological data. Universality and necessity are imparted to ethics by reason. It is only possible to speak of ethics when reason deduces the inner ethical content from the natural data and confirms it as a categorical imperative independent of its psychological foundations.

In Part II Soloviev concentrated on the immanent presence of a divine element in human beings as an explanation of both moral autonomy and moral progress. He supported Kant's claim that morality must be autonomous but, in opposition to Kant, treated the existence of God and the immortality of souls as primary data of man's consciousness, and not merely 'postulates of practical reason'. The demand for autonomy, he argued, is grounded in the divine potential of human nature. Man is the image of God and, therefore, the more his will concurs with the divine will, the more autonomous he is. Intellectual and moral autonomy is a precondition of his divine attributes. Maturity, however, is a result of a long process of education. At the stage of childhood and adolescence people (both individuals and mankind as a whole) have to rely on external authority; they need schools to prepare them for mature life and this is the reason for the existence of churches and other institutionalized forms of religion.[73] Moral progress and, by the same token, the meaning of history, consists in the development of man's divine features, in realizing the idea of Godmanhood. This process is logically divided into two parts: (1) the realization of Godmanhood in an individual and (2) the realization of Godmanhood in the collective life of mankind. Jesus Christ was the perfect fulfilment of the first task; at the same time he opened an era whose task—the realization of Godmanhood in the collective life of the human species—still remains unfulfilled.

With this conclusion Soloviev passed to the third part of his ethical system—to 'objective ethics', or the social forms of the historical self-education of humanity. This part of Soloviev's book was directed against the moral subjectivism and 'amorphism' of Tolstoy, but this attack was no longer bound up with a defence of the theocratic ideal. In contrast to his earlier views, Soloviev now proclaimed the need for a

---

[73] Soloviev, *Sobranie sochinenii*, vol. 8, p. 205.

formal separation of church and state, expressing his hostility to state-promoted religious intolerance in Russia. The cause of religious and moral progress, consisting in the Christianization of political and social life, was thereby radically divorced from the ideal of binding together the spiritual power of the church with the coercive power of the state. On the contrary: the realization of the idea of Godmanhood in history was made dependent on man's maturity, on his full moral autonomy, incompatible with any form of tutelage in the spiritual sphere.

The main theme of the third part of Soloviev's 'objective ethics' is the relationship between economics, law, and morality. The guiding idea is always the Kantian principle of the absolute significance of human dignity. There is no possible justification, wrote Soloviev, to treat human beings as means only, to sacrifice them for the benefit of other people, or even for the sake of the common good.[74] In order to be moral, society must be based upon free mutual consent, which means that any social compact must be voluntary and that each member of a given society preserves his inalienable right to secede. On the other hand, society must not be indifferent to the lot of its members: it is its duty to secure to everybody a certain minimum of welfare, that necessary for a 'dignified existence'. Soloviev's definition of this minimum was very broad and surprisingly modern, going much further than the satisfaction of basic physical needs: 'Everybody should have the means of existence and sufficient physical rest secured to him, and he should also be able to enjoy *leisure* for the sake of his spiritual development.'[75]

The peculiarly modern element in this definition of the 'right to a dignified existence'—the stress on 'positive freedom', on providing everyone with the material means for spiritual development—derives not from Kantianism but from Soloviev's own religious philosophy. He freely acknowledged Kant's merit in defending human dignity while still accusing him of formalism and, consequently, of clinging to a narrowly negative conception of justice. This formalistic one-sidedness was absent in the conception of man as potentially divine. Such a conception assumed that each human being had an inherent capacity for self-perfectibility, and this view could be used as an argument for 'positive freedom'. Extreme poverty and other social

[74] Ibid., pp. 296–300.
[75] Ibid., p. 380. This formula, Soloviev added, was intended to define not only the necessary social minimum, but also the *maximum* of legitimate claims (if not based upon special merits).

handicaps, argued Soloviev, could clearly create insurmountable obstacles to the actualization of human capacities. Therefore these obstacles should be removed by providing each person not only with formal freedom but also with the necessary aid in the worthy fulfilment of man's destiny.

It is not surprising that in his treatment of economic questions Soloviev emphasized the need to combat the views of the classical liberals, whom he called 'conservative anarchists'.[76] Economic life, he maintained, could not be free from moral considerations or state intervention. The principles of *laissez-faire* could reign supreme only in epochs of decay, in societies which had become morally dead.[77] Moral progress demanded a marked increase of moral restraint in economic activities and of legal control over the economic sphere as a whole. Such control, exercised by government, should not be considered a violation of economic laws. Like other social laws, the so-called laws of political economy do not possess the objectivity of the laws of nature; in spite of their apparent naturalness they are man-made and can be abolished by an act of human will.[78] Their independence from other regulators of human conduct, including the laws of political economy and moral development, is only relative, since a pure *homo economicus* never in fact existed.

The true meaning of economic activity, Soloviev continued, consists in the 'spiritualization of nature' and should not be reduced to a mere struggle for existence. This was understood, in part at least, by the Saint-Simonians, who proclaimed the idea of the 'rehabilition of matter'—an idea which implied that nature, both human and non-human, has certain rights and should not be treated as a means only.[79] But in the further development of socialist thought this profound idea was completely forgotten; man came to be seen as merely a producer and nature as a mere object for exploitation. Efforts to raise matter to the level of spiritual existence were replaced by the domination of crude material interests over the spiritual life of man. From this point of view Soloviev saw no difference between 'materialist socialism' and 'capitalist plutocracy'.

A comparison of these views with the relevant parts of *Critique of Abstract Principles* shows a number of changes, or shifts of emphasis, in Soloviev's thought. In the *Critique* Soloviev did not mention man's right to a dignified existence nor did he attribute to economic activity

76 Ibid., p. 362.   77 Ibid., p. 363.
78 Ibid., pp. 366–7.   79 Ibid., pp. 368–9.

other aims than exploitation in the interests of maximum productivity. At this stage he saw unconditional private property and unrestrained competition as necessary conditions of economic progress. The idea that increased moral control over the economy might bring about, among other things, an increase of economic productivity, had not occurred to him then.[80]

In *Justification of the Good* Soloviev supported private property differently and for different reasons. He stressed its conditional character and, at the same time, linked it with human freedom and self-determination, emphasizing its moral and not merely economic importance. He pointed out the simple fact that even a man's body is not regarded as his absolute property in the sense of *jus utendi et abutendi*: suicide is morally unacceptable and self-mutilation can even be legally penalized.[81] The absolutization of private property is in fact a quite recent phenomenon. The ancient Romans, in spite of the undeniable individualism of their legal thinking, were not guilty of this, since their definition of private property as a right to use and abuse was followed by the important qualification: 'in so far as the rational interpretation of law allows' (*quatenus juris ratio patitur*).[82]

Another novel element in Soloviev's economic thinking (or, rather, in his philosophical assessment of economic activity) was the postulate restricting the freedom of 'economic man' both in production and in consumption. Anticipating modern ecological movements, he postulated that enterprising individuals should not be given a free hand in conquering and exploiting nature, because the preservation of the natural environment is a necessary condition of a worthwhile human existence.[83] This anthropocentric argument was supplemented by references to the rights of nature as such and to man's duties in relation to nature. Nature, Soloviev argued, is not rightless:

It has a right to our help in its transformation and elevation. Things have no rights, but nature and soil are not mere things . . . The meaning of our work in relation to material nature does not consist in exploiting it to enrich ourselves with more goods and money; it consists in perfecting nature for its own sake . . . *Without the love of nature for its own sake it is not possible to achieve moral organization of material existence.*[84]

Soloviev's thoughts on consumption were directed against the unrestricted and indiscriminate freedom of the capitalist market.

---

[80] Ibid., p. 382.   [81] Ibid., p. 389.   [82] Ibid., p. 393, n.
[83] Ibid., pp. 383–5.   [84] Ibid., pp. 383–4.

Human needs, he reasoned, are different in kind: some are noble, some are not; some are natural, some degenerate or artificially created; the satisfaction of one category of needs is necessary for the fulfilment of man's divine calling while the satisfaction of some others leads to the increasing moral degradation of humankind. Therefore, the indiscriminate satisfaction of all possible consumer needs, or the stimulation of unhealthy needs (such as pornography), is incompatible with morality.[85]

It is easy to see in these thoughts an anticipation of the ideas made fashionable in our times by such radical critics of consumerism as Herbert Marcuse and others. Even more surprising is the fact that they are bound up with other distinctively modern themes, such as the postulation of limited growth and support for the liberation of women. Soloviev saw a close interconnection between the ruthless exploitation of nature through unlimited productivity, unlimited population growth, and the exploitation of women, which he briefly summarized thus: 'The immoral exploitation of the earth cannot cease while the immoral exploitation of women continues.'[86]

We turn now to Soloviev's views on law. These were closely connected with his views on the economy because moral control over economic activities, which he stood for, was to be exercised by means of law. As in his earlier views, developed in the *Critique of Abstract Principles*, the author of *Justification of the Good* saw law as mediating between economic activity and the absolute morality of love. It is obvious, therefore, that his entire philosophy of law had to revolve around the problem of the relationship between law and morality.

Law in Soloviev's eyes was the sphere of the relative, as opposed to the absolute, good. He wanted to defend this sphere against two opposing dangers: (1) the radical denial of the value of law in the name of absolute moral values, and (2) the separation of law from moral considerations and its defence as a sphere of legality, standing completely apart from the sphere of morality. The main representative of the first view, having its roots in the old Antinomian heresy, was Tolstoy; the most consistent and radical upholders of the second view were, of course, the legal positivists.

The relative character of legal values, Soloviev argued, does not consist in their changing, history-bound and culture-bound character. True, actually existing positive laws are always relative in precisely this

<hr>

[85] Ibid., pp. 385–6.   [86] Ibid., p. 395.

sense, but the same is true of actually existing morality. On the other hand, timeless, unchangeable ideals are to be found not only in morality but in law as well. They constitute the sphere of natural law which provides ideal standards for all positive law. Natural law is the inner essence, the inner norm of all law. Legal progress, undeniably existing, consists in the gradual approximation to this ideal.[87]

Thus, the inherent relativity of law, as opposed to the absolute nature of the highest moral standards, must be seen not in the historically conditioned character of all positive law but in the very content of the idea of law. In short, the relative nature of legal ideals consists in their inner imperfection. Law, in contrast to morality, is a sphere of relative values because even its ideals are imperfect and, therefore, unavoidably relative.

The essential differences between morality and law may be reduced to three:[88]

First, purely moral obligations are boundless while legal obligations are always strictly limited. This is because morality is striving for perfection whereas law is concerned only with 'the lower limit, or the definite minimum of morality'.

Second, legal obligations are clearly defined: it is always possible to establish whether they have been fulfilled, or not. In contrast to this moral demands, because of their boundless nature, lack precision and exactness of content and scope: thus, for instance, the commandment 'love your enemies' does not tell us what precisely is to be done and at what point one could say that one has truly fulfilled this demand. Soloviev saw in this a distinctive merit of law. Law guarantees the realization of a certain minimum morality and it is socially better to have a minimum good safely secured to all than to strive for individual moral perfection without due care for the achievement of a minimum of moral conduct on a mass scale, in the lives of average members of society. In other words, morality is subjectivist and élitist whereas law is socially-oriented and, therefore, peculiarly important from the point of view of objective ethics.

Third, morality is incompatible with compulsion whereas law must be backed by force. This distinction, in spite of its practical importance, may seem banal; from the point of view of some later theorists of law (especially Petrażycki) it might even be seen as an unnecessary concession to legal positivism.[89] In fact, however,

[87] Ibid., pp. 403–4.   [88] Ibid., pp. 407–9.   [89] See below, Ch. IV. 5.

Soloviev's interpretation of the point was quite original. By compulsion he meant not only direct but also *indirect* compulsion, thus distancing himself from the legal positivist claim that only those laws are truly laws which are directly backed by the coercive power of the state. On the other hand, he thought that morality, because of the absolute nature of its demands, must be absolutely free, that is, free not only from external physical compulsion but from all kinds of psychic pressure as well.[90] This rather unusual view of morality was explicable by a characteristic feature of Soloviev's conception of what morality really is: the tendency to identify morality with a striving for perfection. This entailed a certain aristocratic disregard for the moral regulation of the prosaic problems of everyday life. It seemed sometimes, incorrectly, that Soloviev left all such problems to legal regulation alone.

The conclusion drawn from these analyses was a new definition of law (law in the sense of *pravo, droit*, i.e. in the sense of legal justice encompassing both objective law and subjective right). It runs as follows: '*Law is a compulsory demand for the realization of a definite minimum of good, or for a social order which excludes certain manifestations of evil.*'[91]

In the *Critique of Abstract Principles* Soloviev, as I have already mentioned, defined law as 'freedom conditioned by equality'. This definition saw the function of law as both protecting and setting necessary limits to negative freedom; thus, it was perfectly in accord with the spirit of classical liberalism. The new definition shifted the emphasis towards ensuring a certain minimum positive good, in fact towards embracing the concept of 'positive freedom'. While the earlier definition was influenced by the liberal theory of the natural rights of man, the new one accorded more with earlier Catholic doctrines of natural law, dealing with the rightness of the objective order of things rather than the subjective rights of the individual, and emphasizing morality rather than freedom.[92] The earlier definition developed in a direction very close to Korkunov's theory of law as a 'delimitation of interests'; the new one, asserting that law was a part of ethics, was firmly placed in the classical tradition of natural law.[93]

True, there existed an influential theory of law which was often

---

[90] Soloviev, *Sobranie sochinenii*, vol. 8, p. 409.   [91] Ibid.

[92] See A. P. d'Entrèves, *Natural Law: An Introduction to Legal Philosophy*, 2nd edn., London, 1970, pp. 48–9.

[93] Cf. ibid., p. 110.

classified as belonging to legal positivism and which, none the less, also treated law as a part of ethics. This was the theory of Georg Jellinek who, in 1878, defined law as an 'ethical minimum'.[94] It seems probable that Soloviev knew his works and was influenced by them but if so, it did not modify his opposition to legal positivism. The similarity between Jellinek's and Soloviev's definitions of law suggests that it may be very misleading to classify the former as a legal positivist. It is not really possible to adhere to legal positivism, sharply separating law from morals, while at the same time defining law as an 'ethical minimum'. It is more justifiable to see Jellinek as one of the founders of the psychological view of law[95] and thus as a precursor of Petrażycki, the sworn enemy of legal positivism. Further, it has been correctly pointed out that Jellinek's psychological theory drew upon Aristotle's ethical view of society and included 'the position of natural law'.[96] It is *this* aspect of Jellinek's views which explains how he may have influenced the Russian thinker. Both theorists agree that command is not the essence of law, which is a part of ethics and thus enforces observance not merely through fear but also *propter conscientiam*, by reason of its intrinsic moral force.

In defining law as the enforceable minimum morality Soloviev was of course endorsing the use of external compulsion by the apparatus of state. In doing so he was consciously challenging Tolstoy's view that moral good is incompatible with the use of force. Without a socially enforceable minimum morality, he argued, all striving towards higher moral values would simply be impossible;[97] the routine enforcement of a certain minimum ethical standard of conduct is a necessary condition of moral progress and, therefore, the negation of law in the name of morality deserves to be condemned as immoral.[98] On the other hand, however, Soloviev stressed that the use of compulsion must be strictly limited. In particular, he agreed with Tolstoy that neither society nor the state have a right to take anybody's life. The public good may justify different kinds of limitation of individual freedom, but not the application of capital punishment. Laws prescribing the death penalty are a denial of the very essence of both morality and law.[99]

---

[94] See G. Jellinek, *Die sozialethische Bedeutung von Recht, Unrecht und Strafe*, 1878.

[95] See F. Berolzheimer, *The World's Legal Philosophers*, R. S. Jastrow (trans.), New York, 1924, pp. 435–42.

[96] Ibid., p. 438.

[97] Soloviev, *Sobranie sochinenii*, vol. 8, p. 411.   [98] Ibid., p. 404.

[99] Ibid., pp. 416–17. Soloviev's views on criminal law are fully developed in his book *Law and Morality, Sobranie sochinenii*, vol. 8, pp. 519–655.

Another absolute limit to the use of compulsion and one which Soloviev saw as inherent in the idea of law was man's spiritual freedom. By its very nature law can control only external conduct; it has no power over the human conscience and human thought.[100] In this respect Soloviev was a faithful disciple of Kant.

Finally, it must be stressed that Soloviev did not see compulsion as the essential characteristic of law. He wrote: 'The *principal* feature of the good which is secured by the legal order of society is not its compulsory character (which is only a possible consequence of the legal order) but the *direct objectivity of the task to be performed*. What is really important is the factual state of affairs—the presence of certain factors and the absence of others.'[101] In his definition of law, that is, the 'demand for *realization*' was emphasized and not its *compulsory* character. In other words, law, as distinct from pure morality, must guarantee the realization of a certain minimum good, and compulsion might if necessary be used to this end. A similar view was formulated by Jellinek who stressed that legal norms are those whose observance is guaranteed, not necessarily those whose observance is backed by physical compulsion.

Thus, law is a socially guaranteed minimum morality. By definition, therefore, it must be moral; if it is not, it contradicts the very nature of law and should be abrogated in a lawful way.

Statute law, according to Soloviev, must be characterized by the following three features: (1) it must be publicly promulgated, (2) it must be concrete, that is, it must make it clear how it should be applied in concrete cases, and, finally, (3) it must be applicable to existing conditions and backed by sanctions in case of non-observance. To secure the observance and improvement of laws organized power (*vlast'*) is necessary.[102] Legitimate power may be defined as 'the real representation of law' or legality in action.[103]

The supreme power, its subordinate offices and a populated territory within its jurisdiction together form the state. For Soloviev the state was above all the 'embodiment of law', the 'objective being of law'.[104] He wrote:

In its simplest practical expression the meaning of the state consists in the subordination, within its boundaries, of violence to justice, arbitrariness to legality, and the replacement of the chaotic and destructive conflict of

[100] Ibid., p. 415.   [101] Ibid., p. 414.   [102] Ibid., p. 419.
[103] Ibid., p. 420.   [104] Ibid., pp. 421, 495.

particular elements of natural humanity by a regular order of existence. Compulsion may be exercised by the state only in the last extremity, its extent must be determined beforehand in accordance with law, and it is legitimized by the fact that it proceeds from a common and impartial authority.[105]

It is easy to see a close affinity between this view of the state and the *Rechtsstaat* liberalism of Bismarck's Germany. Soloviev differed from the German *Rechtsstaat* liberals mainly in his efforts to prove that this conception of the state was perfectly compatible with Christianity, efforts which involved a constant polemic against the Christian anarchism of Tolstoy. He argued, in a somewhat strained manner, that it was unjustifiable to oppose the truth of the Gospel to the spirit of statism, that Christ himself had sanctified military service and that the territorial expansion of the Russian state had been in the interests of Christianity.[106] Christianity, he concluded, does not want to limit, let alone deny, the sovereign authority of the state.[107] It proclaims that the state can achieve its true and fullest significance only by serving the cause of the Kingdom of God on earth; thus, Christianity wants to help the state to develop as completely as possible.[108]

The tasks of the state, in Soloviev's new conception, were both negative and positive. The influence of German *Rechtsstaat* liberalism was combined in his views with a strong sympathy for the German 'professorial socialists' who wanted to subject the economic sphere to legal regulation on ethical grounds. The state, he proclaimed, should guarantee everyone the right to a dignified existence. Therefore it must use its coercive powers 'to ensure to everybody a certain minimum material well-being'.[109] This minimum, he stressed, should be treated as a new right of man, as something legally claimable.

The right to a dignified existence, in Soloviev's interpretation, had no connection with a commitment to egalitarianism. On the contrary, Soloviev highly valued the idea of a hierarchy based upon unequal merit. He came to think, however, that legal justice should not be reduced to a negative notion, that the law should also be concerned to give each individual the minimum positive incentive to do his best and show his or her true merit. But he also opposed the classical liberal view that helping the weak and poor must be left to private charity. He even opposed the view that the poor should be helped in order to make them self-reliant in the competitive struggle for survival, arguing that

---

[105] Ibid., p. 421.   [106] Ibid., pp. 481, 487–8.   [107] Ibid., p. 497.
[108] Ibid.   [109] Ibid., pp. 307, 501.

people who were objectively handicapped and unable to take care of themselves should be provided with the minimum necessary to a worthwhile existence by virtue of their humanity alone, whether or not they could be made self-reliant. He laid this duty on the state because he no longer saw it as an agency concerned merely with the proper delimitation of interests. In his new ethical theory he defined it as 'organized compassion' and assigned it the role of independent mediator between the sphere of material interests, represented by the socio-economic order, and that of higher moral values, represented by the Church.[110]

Of course this new conception of the essence and functions of the state entailed a corresponding change in Soloviev's views on legal justice. He came to reject the Schopenhauerian opposition between the negative ethic of justice (*neminem laede*) and the positive ethic of charity (*omnes quantum potes juva*),[111] emphasizing that justice and charity have a common root in the altruistic principle of compassion. 'Charity', he wrote, 'presupposes justice and justice demands charity.'[112] It seems probable that he was remembering the following words from Dante's *Monarchy*: 'charity gives force to justice, so that the more powerful it is the more force justice will have'.[113] He was very familiar with this classical work by the great Catholic poet and thinker[114] and it is clear that its philosophy, stressing the moral order of the universe and the perfectibility of man, fitted his own views much better than did the Schopenhauerian philosophical pessimism.

Proclaiming the 'right to a dignified existence' accorded with the general evolution of liberalism. In this respect Soloviev's role in Russia might be compared to that of T. H. Green in England. It is significant that a book summarizing this evolution formulated the main tenets of the New Liberalism in words strongly reminiscent of Soloviev: 'the State has the duty to use its powers to help men to live their lives worthily'.[115]

Soloviev was not unaware of this shift in liberal thought, but the

[110] Ibid., p. 499.
[111] Ibid., p. 102. In *Law and Morality* Soloviev's criticism of this opposition is even sharper (see p. 536).
[112] Ibid., p. 102.
[113] Dante, *Monarchy and Three Political Letters*, D. Nicholl (int.), London, 1954, p. 17.
[114] Soloviev was reading *De monarchia* in 1883, at the time when his growing sympathy towards Catholicism caused his break with the Slavophiles. See Mochulsky, *Vladimir Soloviev*, p. 188.
[115] H. Samuel, *Liberalism: An Attempt to State the Principles and Proposals of Contemporary Liberalism in England*, London, 1902, p. 207.

peculiarity of his position consisted in its philosophical and religious foundation. It often happens in the history of ideas that the newest views are derived from much earlier ones and that a programme for the future is justified by reference to the remote past.[116] This was obviously Soloviev's case. His espousal of the neo-liberal position was greatly facilitated by his sympathy with medieval Catholicism. His formula of the 'right to a dignified existence' was not supported by classical natural-rights theory—a theory of 'subjective rights', turning on the problem of individual freedom—but easily found support in the classical Thomist doctrine of natural law, which was linked to the notion of an objective moral universal order, and claimed that all humans, as living beings, have a right to life and its necessities.[117]

It may seem strange indeed that Soloviev's philosophy of law was so close to classical liberalism at the time of his greatest enthusiasm for the utopian vision of Russia as the 'third Rome', and that an emphasis on the moral and social function of law appeared in his thought only after his final disillusionment with this theocratic blueprint. On closer examination, however, it is possible to see a certain logic in such a development. In a social philosophy which proclaimed the ideal of the unification of humankind and saw the crowning unity in a theocratic Empire, law could be given a narrow and strictly limited sphere. Its main task could be reduced to the delimitation of interests because higher tasks—the realization of positive moral goodness—were allotted to the 'sacred monarchy', whose authority was above the law. It was natural, therefore, that disillusionment with the idea of 'sacred monarchy' should lead Soloviev to broaden the scope of legal regulation and to entrust moral and social tasks to an impersonal legal order. In this manner his ideal of a theocratic Empire gave way to the more modest but much more modern ideal of the social *Rechtsstaat*, an ideal anticipating the practice of the democratic welfare states of our own time.

In the last year of his life Soloviev seemed to change his views once more. In his *Tale of the Antichrist* he presented the future triumphs of secular humanitarianism and its successes in improving man's material well-being as the work of the Antichrist. It is difficult to say what this

[116] A pioneer of Marxist sociology in Poland, K. Kelles-Krauz, saw this as a psycho-sociological law: a law of 'revolutionary retrospection'. See K. Kelles-Krauz, 'La Loi de la rétrospection révolutionnaire vis à vis de la theorie de l'imitation', *Annales de l'Institut International de Sociologie*, 1896.

[117] For the distinction between the older theory of natural law and the modern theory of natural rights see d'Entrèves, *Natural Law*, pp. 61–2.

new turn in his thought really signified. Was it a new beginning, or merely an additional warning against divorcing the human from the divine? Many interpretations are possible, but discussion of their relative merits does not fall within the scope of this book.

6   *Soloviev's place in the Russian liberal tradition*

In the preface to *Law and Morality* Soloviev pointed out that, in the light of the debate on the relationship of morality and law, the intellectual situation in Russia presented a most interesting case, for it was here that the two extremes in this debate found their best representatives. On one side, claiming that any connection with law was fatal for morality, stood the greatest of Russian writers, Tolstoy; on the other side, maintaining that connections with morality were, if not fatal, at least unimportant for law, stood Chicherin—the most universal and systematic intellect among Russian scholars.[118]

As I have tried to show,[119] Chicherin's separation of law and morality was essentially Kantian and thus not only different from but in fact explicitly opposed to legal positivism. Chicherin struggled against the moralization of law, but never remotely saw the essence of law as command or claimed that 'law may have any content'.[120] His demarcation between law and morality was not intended as a defence of *ius qua iussum* (law as command) against *ius qua iustum* (law as justice); it actually represented the opposition between the ideals of justice (including 'the higher demands of justice') and love, namely, the same opposition which Soloviev had set forth in his *Critique of Abstract Principles*. Thus Chicherin's position in the debate on the relationship of morality and law was by no means extreme; yet his views may justifiably be seen as diametrically opposed to those of Tolstoy. Legal positivists were much more radical in separating law from morality but for just this reason were simply not interested in such problems as the relationship of the ideals of justice and love. In the case of the two Russian thinkers this was the crux of the matter. Chicherin idealized law and legal justice as 'an absolute and self-sufficient principle',[121] whereas Tolstoy condemned all juridical elements in life outright in the name of evangelical love. He denounced not only law as command but also legal justice: the first he condemned as an anarchist, the second he rejected as a prophet of that

---

[118] Soloviev, *Sobranie sochinenii*, vol. 8, p. 521.   [119] See above, Ch. II, 6.
[120] Cf. H. L. A. Hart, *The Concept of Law*, Oxford, 1961, p. 195.
[121] Soloviev's expression (vol. 8, p. 521).

boundless love which is incompatible with the mere existence of law courts.

In spite of their fundamental disagreements Tolstoy and Chicherin shared—or seemed to share—at least one important ethical tenet, that morality should never be backed by force and coercively institutionalized. Actually this agreement was more apparent than real. Tolstoy thought that all human conduct should be guided by the demands of Christian love alone, whereas Chicherin never denied that certain rules of conduct (such as, for instance, that against stealing) should be backed by coercively implemented laws. If he nevertheless persisted in claiming that morality must not be enforced, it was merely because of a terminological difference, since he reserved the term morality for what Kant had called 'the principles of virtue', as opposed to the negative 'principles of justice'.[122]

Soloviev seems not to have been sufficiently aware of this. For him both Chicherin and Tolstoy, in spite of their contrasting attitudes towards law, stood for the view that morality, unlike the law, must not be enforced. In this respect he was opposed to both: he labelled this view 'moral subjectivism' and declared that without the coercive institutionalization of a certain minimum morality no morality at all would be possible. This institutionalized minimum morality was for him the sphere of law. He thought of it as historically changing and always limited in scope but, on the other hand, refused to acknowledge that certain socially important spheres of life, especially the economic, might be excluded on principle from legal regulation. He broke with Korkunov's view that law is concerned only with the delimitation, not the evaluation, of interests. Delimitation of interests is necessary even in the case of criminal interests, which should be simply suppressed by the law; in fact the law evaluates interests from the point of view of the minimum morality which means that its norms are moral norms.[123] For moral progress legal control over the economy should be extended rather than contracted.

For Chicherin such views were completely unacceptable. In his lengthy review of Soloviev's *Justification of the Good* and *Law and Morality* he did not achieve restraint. When he came to deal with Soloviev's postulate of socially organized morality he burst out, accusing him of being a 'modern Torquemada'. Soloviev, he

---

[122] By contrast, justice for Soloviev was explicitly a moral idea (cf. ibid., p. 398).

[123] Ibid., pp. 494–5. It is obvious that Soloviev here refers to Korkunov, although he does not mention his name. Cf. above, n. 50.

indignantly argued, wanted to use legal coercion to serve the cause of absolute morality, which recalled the practices of the Inquisition.[124] Soloviev's struggle against moral subjectivism was extremely dangerous because morality cannot be given an objective existence by such means as police or prisons.[125] Soloviev in fact, through his theocratic utopianism, wanted to realize morality and to establish the Kingdom of God on earth by force.[126]

Soloviev defended himself by pointing out that he did not want to institutionalize absolute morality but only to give legal backing to a moral minimum; in particular, unlike the Inquisitors, he demanded legal guarantees for absolute freedom of conscience.[127] As proof that he never envisaged a moral state as a state with unlimited power, he recalled his arguments for the abolition of the death penalty. Human life, he had always argued, must be treated as the absolute limit to the punitive power of the state. By contrast, Chicherin had always defended the death penalty as part of the Hegelian theory of retribution. Indeed, on this point their roles could be reversed: Soloviev, this time having Tolstoy on his side, could accuse Chicherin of not sufficiently limiting the power of the state.[128]

Chicherin, in turn, also criticized the libertarian aspect of Soloviev's conception of the state. For him Soloviev's view that society must be based upon voluntary consent, thus guaranteeing the right of secession to each of its members, indicated anarchist leanings, curiously reminiscent of the Golden Freedom of the Polish gentry and their notorious *liberum veto*.[129] This anarchic feature of Soloviev's conception was to him corroboration of the old truth that tyranny and anarchy often go hand in hand and support each other.

Curiously enough, Chicherin's earlier criticism of Soloviev's 'mysticism in science' was less violent than his attack on the book which actually marked Soloviev's abandonment of his theocratic ideal, but the explanation is easy to find. In Soloviev's *Critique of Abstract Principles* the ideal of a free theocracy was combined with a view of law which was acceptable to Chicherin and did not provoke him to attack, whereas in *Justification of the Good* Soloviev insisted on the positive

---

[124] B. N. Chicherin, 'O nachalach etiki', *Voprosy filosofii i psikhologii*, 1897, vol. 39, p. 645.

[125] Ibid., p. 685.　　　　　　[126] Ibid., pp. 646, 685.

[127] Soloviev, *Sobranie sochinenii*, vol. 8, pp. 675–7.

[128] Ibid., pp. 709–13.

[129] Chicherin, 'O nachalach etiki', pp. 647–8. Cf. Soloviev, *Sobranie sochinenii*, vol. 8, pp. 296–8.

function of law and proclaimed a new legal right—the right to a dignified existence. This right, anticipating the so-called social and economic rights of man, differed completely from the classical concept of human rights, and undermined the entire classical liberal conception, which was based upon the idea of negative liberty. For Chicherin such changes were absolutely indigestible and more dangerous than patently utopian dreams.

Quite different was the relation of Soloviev's new ideas to the legal philosophy of the New Liberalism in Russia. This current of thought, flourishing early in this century, was officially embraced by the Kadet Party. It produced a spirited intellectual movement in legal philosophy, thereby contributing to the Silver Age of Russian culture. Its most eminent legal philosophers were Leon Petrażycki in St Petersburg and Pavel Novgorodtsev in Moscow—both formal members of the Kadet party. The latter, widely recognized as the leader of the neo-idealist school in Russian legal philosophy, was directly influenced by Soloviev.

In a public speech on the occasion of Soloviev's death Novgorodtsev unhesitatingly included him among the most eminent defenders of the 'idea of law' in nineteenth-century philosophy.[130] He praised Soloviev for his unceasing struggle against the depreciation of law by the Slavophiles and the outright legal nihilism of Tolstoy; he fully accepted Soloviev's view on the need for a minimum of 'socially organized morality', seeing it, quite properly, as a vindication of the value of law and state within the framework of a religious *Weltanschauung*; he paid homage to Soloviev's commitment to freedom which had led him to a practical alliance with the Westernizing liberals.[131] Furthermore, at the beginning of his speech Novgorodtsev drew a gloomy picture of contemporary legal consciousness, recalling the fact that Chicherin and Petrażycki, the two most outstanding representatives of two generations of Russian jurists, had declared it to be in a state of crisis, and expressed his hope that Soloviev's views on law would help in the effort to overcome this crisis.[132]

It is no exaggeration to say that to overcome the crisis in legal

---

[130] P. Novgorodtsev, 'Ideia prava v filosofii V. S. Solovieva', *Voprosy filosofii i psikhologii*, 1901, vol. 56, p. 112.

[131] Ibid., pp. 116–28.

[132] Ibid., p. 113. Referring to Chicherin and Petrażycki, Novgorodtsev had in mind Chicherin's *Philosophy of Law* (Moscow, 1900) and Petrażycki's article 'Modnye lozungi yurisprudentsii', published as an appendix to his book *Prava dobrosovestnogo vladel'tsa na dokhody s tochki zreniia dogmy i politiki grazhdanskogo prava* (SPb, 1897).

consciousness became the main task, the guiding idea, of Novgorodtsev's intellectual activity, and in his own case at least his prognosis of the role which Soloviev's legal ideas could play in such an effort turned out to be true. Soloviev's right to a dignified existence was proclaimed by him as the most important and necessary supplement to the symbol of faith of modern liberal jurists.[133] His detailed examination of the different schools of socialist criticism of liberalism, especially Marxism, led him to the conclusion that its deepest insights could be reduced to the idea of a dignified existence—an idea, he added, which Marxism, because of its negative attitude to law, had obscured rather than clarified.[134] On the other hand, his examination of the development of liberal thought[135] convinced him that the right to a dignified existence could be seen as a liberal principle, deducible (despite the protests of old-fashioned liberals) from the liberal conception of the rights of man, inherent in the very idea of personality, the metaphysical cornerstone of the liberal view of the world.

We may conclude, therefore, that Soloviev holds an important place in the Russian liberal tradition. His views on the positive tasks of law and on the relationship of law and morality constitute a real watershed between the Old and New Liberalism.

It may seem somewhat paradoxical that the New Liberalism, a thoroughly secular, progressivist movement of thought, owed so much to a religious visionary, whose ideas had originally been strongly connected with Slavophile tradition and who for long had been hypnotized, as it were, by the mystical halo of Russian autocracy. This feeling, indeed, was widely shared by both the rank-and-file members and the leaders of the Kadet party. Historical hindsight has made it perfectly clear that Soloviev's idea of the right to a dignified existence was an extremely important and necessary link in the development of liberal ideas in Russia, but it was by no means clear to everybody in the heyday of Russian liberalism as a political movement. It was rather esoteric knowledge, confined to a few narrow circles.

These circles, however, included some very important people. Novgorodtsev was not only one of the leading legal philosophers in Russia, but also a member of the Central Committee of the Kadet party. Soloviev's monographist, Prince Evgeny Trubetskoi (a legal theoretician and eminent historian of both legal and religious

[133] See P. Novgorodtsev and I. A. Pokrovsky, *O prave na sushchestvovanie*, SPb 1911.
[134] P. Novgorodtsev, *Ob obshchestvennom ideale*, 3rd edn., Berlin, 1921, p. 385.
[135] See P. Novgorodtsev, *Krizis sovremennogo pravosoznaniia*, Moscow, 1909.

philosophy) was also active in the broadly conceived liberal movement. Nor must we forget the whole constellation of religious philosophers inspired by Soloviev who created the so-called religio-philosophical renaissance in Russia. Most of them had little interest in law, some were even very critical of the 'idolization of law' characteristic of the Kadet party, but, politically speaking, they generally supported the liberal programme. I venture to think that this was possible because Soloviev had convinced them that the cause of the spiritual regeneration of Russia, to which all of them were deeply committed, was bound up with the cause of liberal progress. It was Soloviev's merit to undermine, if not completely destroy, the widespread view that liberal values are incompatible with Christianity. This, the general message of his work, had a powerful influence in Russia. It might be questioned but not ignored.

From the point of view of the history of legal philosophy in Russia the importance of Soloviev's ideas does not stop at the formulation of the right to a dignified existence. This main tenet of neo-liberalism became a bone of contention between Soloviev and Chicherin, but this should not obscure the fact that both thinkers energetically opposed the dominant doctrine of legal positivism, thus paving the way for the so-called revival of natural law in Russia. From this point of view Chicherin, Soloviev, Petrażycki, and Novgorodtsev can legitimately be seen as links in a remarkably continuous line of thought. Chicherin, as I have tried to show, rejected the view that natural law invalidates any inconsistent positive law but, nonetheless, fully accepted natural law as the philosophical ideal to which positive law ought to conform as far as was consistent with changing historical conditions. Soloviev set forth a very similar view in his *Critique of Abstract Principles*, retaining it in his *Justification of the Good*. Positive law, he argued, is a historical manifestation of the rational essence of law, which is natural law; thus natural law is 'the general algebraic formula', 'the general logos' and 'the logical *prius*' of all law.[136] Twenty years later a very similar conception was developed by the neo-Kantian legal philosopher, Rudolf Stammler, who coined the famous formula 'natural law with changing content' and is supposed to have inaugurated the revival of natural law in Germany. At the same time the same claim was made, as we shall see, by Leon Petrażycki, whose philosophical background was different, but whose intention was identical—to provide an antidote to

---

[136] Soloviev, *Sobranie sochinenii*, vol. 2, pp. 153–4.

legal positivism. Still later, at the beginning of the present century, the movement for the revival of natural law was in full swing in Russia. The main protagonist of this movement, Novgorodtsev, was initially inspired by Petrażycki but, as a metaphysical idealist, he was even more indebted to both Chicherin and Soloviev. Through him Russian liberalism became aware of the existence of a Russian tradition of legal philosophy—a tradition remarkably rich philosophically, unswervingly anti-positivist, and distinctively Russian in its concentration on the problem of the proper relationship between law and morality.

IV

Leon Petrażycki: A Theory of Legal Consciousness against Legal Positivism

1 Introductory remarks

THE heated discussions between Chicherin and Soloviev can be classified as a controversy within the idealistic school of philosophy of law. However, in the second half of the nineteenth century, idealism was by no means the dominant school in Russian legal thought. N. S. Timasheff wrote:

> As elsewhere in continental Europe Russia's legal philosophy was divided between legal idealism and legal positivism. The idealists tried to locate the law in the world of ideas and took it for granted that, in one way or another, law as idea is reflected in the world of human actions. The positivists were further divided between sociological positivism, emphasizing the place of the law among social phenomena, and legal positivism in the narrow meaning, considering that law was a self-sufficient system of norms to be studied from within, not from 'above', as alleged by idealists, nor from 'without' as done by the sociological jurists.[1]

The above quotation is a good starting point for presenting a more detailed and more diversified picture. The 'idealism versus positivism' dichotomy is certainly an oversimplification. Both categories are much too broad. Within 'idealism' the Hegelian idealism of Chicherin was, of course, very different from the earlier natural-law school; it was in fact much closer to broadly conceived positivism, because, first, it concentrated on actually existing, positive, state-made or state-sanctioned law, and, secondly, saw the law as a part of historically changing social reality. Broadly conceived positivism, on the other hand, should not be equated with sociologism. As a programme for studying law as a real phenomenon, by means of positive, empirical methods—a programme consciously opposed to metaphysical speculations about the abstract 'idea of law'—it could lead not only to

---

[1] N. S. Timasheff, Introduction to L. Petrażycki, *Law and Morality*. H. W. Babb (trans.), Cambridge, Mass. 1955, p. xviii.

sociologism but to psychologism as well. The main representatives of positivistic jurisprudence in Russia—V. I. Sergeevich (1841–1910), S. Muromtsev (1850–1910), and N. Korkunov (1833–1902)—were, indeed, the pioneers of the sociological approach to the study of law; pioneers, it should be added, not only in Russia, but on a European scale. The best known among them, Korkunov, was, however, very close to psychologism. He saw society as 'a psychic union of men', stressing that 'authority has its source in men's consciousness' and concluding from this that the state derives its power not from coercion but from the consciousness of dependence and subordination on the part of the people who consider themselves its citizens or subjects. In this way his socio-psychological theory of law provided him with strong arguments against legal positivism in the juridical sense of the term. 'Positive legislation', he claimed, 'is not the sole course of law', coercion 'is neither a fundamental, nor even a general, attribute of juridical phenomena'. He thought, moreover, that the very idea of the unlimited sovereignty of the state, the cornerstone of classical doctrines of legal positivism, contradicted the socio-psychological analysis of the phenomenon of power. According to his view,

The power of the state exists only to the extent that it is accepted by the consciousness of the citizens, and for this reason the notions which individuals have as to their own freedom and social liberty produce a corresponding restriction upon the state power. Thus, the limitation of power by law arises not only from well-advised representatives of the state's power limiting it by the rights of the citizens, but also and especially from the fact that the idea which the citizens have of their dependence upon the state is never unlimited.[2]

The notion of 'legal positivism' in the narrow sense, as defined by Timasheff, is also somewhat misleading. It covers, in fact, two different, although sometimes overlapping, schools of juristic thought: (1) the traditional analytic, or doctrinal, school, reducing its tasks to the purely immanent ('dogmatic') logical analysis of existing state-made laws, with the aim of establishing their exact, objective meaning (the so-called *Rechtsdogmatik* or *Begriffsjurisprudenz*), and (2) the command theory of law proclaimed by John Austin and widely accepted everywhere in Europe in the second half of the nineteenth century. 'Legal positivism' in this sense was a doctrine identifying law proper with commands and prohibitions whose only source and sanction was

[2] See N. M. Korkunov, *General Theory of Law*. W. G. Hastings (trans.), South Hackensack, N.J. 1968, pp. 90, 96, 321, 352, 375.

in statutes issued by the state and backed by its coercive force; a doctrine leading to the dangerous conclusion that every command properly enacted by the state, however arbitrary it might be, should have the authority and dignity of law, that the test of legality is the force behind laws, in a word, that 'might is right'.

Finally, the 'idealism–positivism' dichotomy ignores the specific features of the so-called 'jurisprudence of interests', represented by Rudolf von Ihering.[3] In his theory of law the tendency of 'legal positivism' (in the narrow sense) to reduce law to state-made and state-sanctioned law was powerfully expressed but, at the same time, combined with a utilitarian approach, interpreting law in terms of material and other interests, equating rights with interests protected and defended by the state. Thus, this theory was opposed to conceptual jurisprudence (*Begriffsjurisprudenz*), since it rejected the very notion of the 'objective' meaning of law and treated law instrumentally, as a means to an end; on the other hand, it introduced into jurisprudence the teleological element, the notion of the consciously chosen purpose, and thus cut itself off from the positivistic tendency ('positivistic' in the broad meaning of the word) to limit the science of law to the causal study of 'the given'.

This is the general background which enables us to perceive and appreciate the creative originality of Leon Petrażycki—a Pole who became 'the most eminent of the Russian legal philosophers of the early twentieth century'.[4] He had nothing in common with speculative

---

[3] Most legal scholars classify Ihering's theory as a variant of legal positivism; some of them, however, oppose this view. G. Radbruch, for instance, wrote that Ihering 'transcends positivism too definitely to be appraised within its framework' (G. Radbruch, 'Legal Philosophy', in *The Legal Philosophies of Lask, Radbruch, and Dabin*, K. Wilk (trans.), Cambridge, Mass. 1950, p. 66).

Petrazycki himself, in chapter 3 of his *Theory of Law and the State*, entitled 'Review and Criticism of the Most Important Contemporary Theories of Law', treated Ihering as representing three theories at the same time: (1) The state theory, identifying law with state-enacted or state-approved laws, (2) The theory of compulsion, and (3) Utilitarian theory, seeing law in terms of 'interests'. The first two points characterized Ihering as a representative of legal positivism.

Law and Morality, the above-mentioned American edition of Petrażycki's works, is an abridged translation of his *Introduction to the Study of Law and Morality* and *Theory of Law and the State*. Unfortunately, it omits many important parts of these works, including the chapter mentioned above.

[4] Timasheff, *Law and Morality*, p. xvii. Most authors spell Petrażycki's name as 'Petrazhitsky' or 'Petrazhitskii'. Babb explained this by referring to the Library of Congress 'whose authority in spelling of Russian names' should be followed (see H. W. Babb, 'Petrazhitskii: Science of Legal Policy and Theory of Law', *Boston University Law Review*, vol. 17, 1937, p. 793).

idealism; on the contrary—if broadly conceived positivism could be reduced to programmatic empiricism plus the acceptance of the basic tenets of evolutionism he could be classified as a 'positivist'. There are, however, strong arguments against such a label. In spite of his commitment to positivistic scientism he was most strongly opposed to the positivistic negation of the 'ideal element' in law and to equating law with the external coercion monopolized by the state. 'Legal positivism' was tantamount in his eyes to 'absolute legal idiotism' since, as he put it, only a man suffering from complete inability to have 'legal experiences', that is, to experience the feeling of having a legal right, or a legal obligation, could suppose that law was only 'a matter of commands laid by the powerful in their own interests upon the weak and defenceless, with appropriate threats in case of disobedience'.[5] He ridiculed attempts to reduce the tasks of legal science to analytical jurisprudence, 'the lawyers' law'; he solemnly proclaimed that a radical emancipation from professional jurisprudence was the first and essential condition for the emergence of a truly scientific theory of law. And yet, at the same time, he resolutely defended the doctrinal study of law (*Rechtsdogmatik*) and conceptual jurisprudence against Ihering's 'realism', which saw the function of law in the defence of 'practical interests' and, consequently, neglected juridical logic, setting against it a pragmatic, instrumental attitude towards existing laws.[6] Nobody went further than he did in emphasizing that law was not a system of abstract norms but a part of social reality which had to be studied causally—and yet nobody was more insistent on the vindication of the deontological, ethical function of law, and nobody was more committed to the idea of a purposeful, conscious law-making. His notion of law was so broad and so different from the usual that he was often accused of representing an anti-juridical approach, dissolving law in the vast variety of socio-psychological phenomena; on the other hand, however, he represented a truly 'pan-juridical world-view', since he saw law as virtually omnipresent in human life and treated the

---

This explanation is self-defeating because 'Petrażycki' is not a Russian name. There is no more reason for transliterating it from Russian than for writing 'Gegel'' instead of Hegel, or 'Tomazii' instead of Thomasius. I decided therefore to disregard this practice everywhere except in the titles of books and articles.

[5] Petrażycki, *Law and Morality*, p. 15.

[6] Cf. the article by A. Peczenik, 'Leon Petrażycki and the Post-Realistic Jurisprudence', in *Sociology and Jurisprudence of Leon Petrażycki*, J. Gorecki (ed.), Urbana–Chicago–London 1975.

science of law as the most important behavioural science.[7] The complexity of his thought made his influence curiously multidirectional. He inspired not only jurists but sociologists as well (G. Gurvitch, P. Sorokin). He was a member of the Central Committee of the Constitutional-Democratic (Kadet) Party, fighting for a liberal *Rechtsstaat* in Russia; among his pupils, however, we find not only *Rechtsstaat* liberals but also advocates of a 'spontaneous, living law' (Gurvitch) and even a Marxist, M. A. Reisner, who after the October Revolution was appointed Vice-Commissar of Justice.

2 Biographical note

In view of the peculiar importance of Petrażycki's theories and of his unique place in the history of Russian legal theory and Russian liberalism as well, a few words should be said about his life and activities.

Leon Petrażycki was born in 1867, to a family of the Polish gentry near the Belorussian town Vitebsk. As a child, he was steeped in Polish patriotic tradition. His father, Józef Petrażycki, had taken part in the Polish uprising of 1863–4 and had been punished for this by confiscation of his estates.[8] Although he died young, his memory was kept alive.

Young Leon studied medicine and, later, law at the University of Kiev. Even as a student he had to his credit an unusual achievement: he translated from German into Russian the famous *Roman Pandects* by Baron, a book which was to become, in his translation, a standard textbook in Russian universities. His teachers thought very highly of him. After graduation he was made a 'professorial aspirant' and sent to Berlin, where the Russian government had organized a special seminar for Russian post-graduate students of law, conducted by the great German Romanist, Professor Dernburg.

During the years of his post-graduate studies German jurists were engaged in preparing the draft of the new civil code, the famous *Bürgerliches Gesetzbuch* promulgated in 1897 and enacted in 1900. This aroused his interest in the German civil law and, more importantly, in the general problems *de lege ferenda*. The performance of German scholars, both Romanists and Germanists, did not satisfy him. He

---

[7] See K. Opałek, 'Teoria Petrażyckiego a współczesna teoria prawa', in *Z zagadnień teorii prawa i teorii nauki L. Petrażyckiego*, Warsaw, 1969, p. 129.

[8] See Babb, 'Science of Legal Policy' p. 793 n. and Giorgio del Vecchio, *Lehrbuch der Rechtsphilosophie*, 2nd edn., Basle, 1951, p. 322.

criticized them sharply and bitterly in the two books which he published in Germany: *Fruchtverteilung beim Wechsel des Nutzungsberichtigten: drei civilrechtlige Abhandlungen* (1892) and *Die Lehre vom Einkommen vom Standpunkt des gemeinen Civilrechts* (2 vols., 1893, 1895). The second of these books contained an appendix entitled 'Civil Policy and Political Economy' in which he outlined a new legal science—the science of legal policy, that is (to use the apt term introduced later by Roscoe Pound) of the general principles of social engineering through law. This appendix he also published in Russian as part of his *Introduction to the Science of Legal Policy*.

The German reception of Petrażycki's books was varied. Some people were shocked by the arrogance shown by the young foreign scholar and even talked about offending against German legal science. In general, however, there was no doubt as to the seriousness of his contributions. One of the leading representatives of German jurisprudence, Leonhard, praised his works as a ´first-rate performance which ensured the author a place in the ranks of the masters in the scientific milieu of German jurists'.[9] The commission preparing the civil code took into account some of his concrete critical remarks and changed the draft accordingly.[10]

Petrażycki's influence on German legal theorists is a separate problem. It undoubtedly existed, but how deep and lasting it was is still a matter of dispute. Petrażycki himself, an ambitious man, was inclined to see it in many quarters but, at the same time, often complained that his alleged impact on German scholarship had not been properly acknowledged. Thus, for instance, he eagerly agreed with A. Lobe, who had indicated the similarity between his ideas and the views of Ofner, Gareis, and Menger, but strongly emphasized his priority.[11] Anton Menger, the well-known 'professorial socialist', was even accused by him of a kind of simple plagiarism.[12] He levelled a similar accusation against Rudolf Stammlcr. The famous neo-Kantian philosopher of law recognized some of Petrażycki's merits and

[9] R. Leonhard, *Die Vollendung des Deutschen Bürgerlichen Gesetzbuches*, Marburg, 1897, p. 7. Quoted from G. S. Langrod and M.Vaughan, 'The Polish Psychological Theory of Law', in *Polish Law Throughout the Ages*, W. J. Wagner (ed.), Stanford, 1970, p. 309.

[10] As reported by Petrażycki in his *Introduction to the Science of Legal Policy*. See L. Petrażycki, *Wstęp do nauki polityki prawa*, Warsaw, 1968, pp. 209–10 (in view of the unavailability of the Russian original I quote from the Polish edition).

[11] Ibid., pp. 233–4. The title of Lobe's pamphlet was: *Was verlangen wir von einem bürgerlichen Gesetzbuch? Ein Wort an den Reichstag.*

[12] Ibid., p. 236.

mentioned him by name in his works. Petrażycki, however, saw Stammler as a mere popularizer of his own ideas on legal policy and wanted him to acknowledge his alleged intellectual debt.[13] It seems that such a claim was exaggerated, to say the least; besides, the question of priority as such, especially if the ideas on legal policy are taken out of context and the obvious differences between the two thinkers are disregarded, is not of primary importance.

After his return to Russia, Petrażycki brilliantly defended his doctoral thesis (on joint-stock companies) and in 1897 was appointed to the chair of the Encyclopaedia of Law at the University of St Petersburg. This chair had earlier been held by Korkunov, who enjoyed great popularity among his students. However, Petrażycki's popularity soon outshone that of his predecessor. In his own words, he 'thought in Polish, wrote in German, and lectured in Russian', translating his thoughts from Polish into German and then into Russian;[14] small wonder, therefore, that his Russian (as his American translator has somewht dryly remarked) was 'not particularly good or typical'.[15] In spite of that, however, the striking originality of his ideas and the strength of his convictions—expressed at the beginning of his lectures in a blunt assertion that only with his works was jurisprudence being raised to the level of a science—enabled him to exercise a truly charismatic influence upon his students. 'From the early 1900's he was easily the most conspicuous figure in the Law faculty. His classes were enormous, overflowing the largest hall (which seated over a thousand students)'.[16] Trying to impress American readers, the author of these words, H. W. Babb, added: 'His annual income, measured in part by student attendance, reached the unprecedented figure of forty thousand roubles'.[17]

Another measure of Petrażycki's influence is the fact that he was one of the very few Russian professors who could be credited with creating his own school of thought.[18] He was able to stimulate an active interest

---

[13] See. L. Petrażycki, *Wstęp do nauki prawa i moralności* (*Introduction to the Study of Law and Morality*), Warsaw, 1959, pp. 20, 123. The Russian original was not available to me and the relevant fragments are not included in *Law and Morality*.
[14] N. S. Timasheff, 'Petrazhitsky's Philosophy of Law', in *Interpretations of Modern Legal Philosophies: Essays in Honor of Roscoe Pound*, P. Sayre (ed.), New York, 1947, p. 736.
[15] Petrażycki, *Law and Morality*, p. xxxix.
[16] Babb, 'Science of Legal Policy', p. 795.
[17] Loc. cit.
[18] See *Sotsiologicheskaia mysl' v Rossii. Ocherki istorii nemarksistskoi sotsiologii poslednei treti XIX–nachala XX veka*. B. A. Chagin (ed.), Leningrad, 1978, p. 22.

in his subject: the circle of students interested in the philosophy of law, organized under his auspices, was the biggest at the University, reaching the impressive number of 500, or even 600, members.[19] His popularity among faculty members was equally great; it was glowingly corroborated when the University was granted autonomous status and he became the first freely elected dean of the Law faculty.

An important chapter in Petrażycki's activities, and in the history of Russian liberalism as well, opened with the establishment of the first Russian newspaper devoted to the struggle for legal culture in the Tsarist Empire. It was founded through the efforts of I. V. Hessen (its future editor-in-chief), his cousin V. M. Hessen and *Privatdozent* A. I. Kaminka,[20] all of them of Jewish origin—characteristically enough, in view of the fact that Jews, along with the Poles, were a minority group most affected by the lack of civil liberty, legal equality, and general respect for law under the Russian Empire. The initiators of the new weekly did not dare, at first, to invite Petrażycki to join the editorial board—he seemed to them too famous, too highly placed and too immersed in pure theory.[21] However, he offered himself and was, of course, joyfully welcomed.

The editorial board met every Thursday and its members (their number gradually increasing) became a closely-knit group of friends holding the same, or very similar, political views. The weekly had a long life and its end was not 'natural'—it liquidated itself after the Bolshevik revolution which left no place for a further meaningful 'struggle for law'. I. V. Hessen later wrote that, in his view, the years devoted to the editing of this militant juridical newspaper were for all the members of the editorial board the most meaningful, most intensive and the happiest period of their lives.[22]

The title of the weekly was *Pravo*—a word which (to quote R. Pound) 'in the Slavonic group stands for both *iustum* and *dextrum*' that is, it means both the objective 'law' and the subjective 'right', both what is 'legal' and what is 'just'.[23] According to I. V. Hessen, this beautiful word soon became 'part of the soul' of all the editors and authors of the newspaper which had chosen it as its title.[24]

[19] Ibid., p. 72.
[20] The name Hessen, in spite of its German origin, is sometimes spelt 'Gessen'. A. L. Kaminka was a relative of Professor Eugene Kamenka mentioned in the Acknowledgements.
[21] See I. V. Hessen (Gessen), *V dvukh vekakh: zhiznennyi otchet*, Berlin, 1937, p. 155.
[22] Ibid., p. 185.
[23] Roscoe Pound, *The Ideal Element in Law*, Calcutta, 1958, p. 80.
[24] I. V. Hessen, *V dvukh vekakh*, p. 152.

The first number of *Pravo*, issued on 8 November 1898, contained an important editorial article, written mainly by I. V. Hessen and A. I. Kaminka. (An alternative article was written by Petrażycki, but it could not be used because of its length.)²⁵ It put forward two postulates: objectivism and the struggle for legal reforms. The first postulate was levelled against the tendency to interpret laws 'freely', not according to their inner logic but according to the moral conscience of the judge. Such a tendency, made popular in juridical circles by the autobiography of a former judge, A. L. Borovikovsky, was seen as too close to the old, Slavophile-inspired legal nihilism and too dangerous in Russian conditions. The second postulate was consonant with, and inspired by, Petrażycki's idea of a scientific legal policy.

In order to avoid returning to this later, it seems proper to emphasize at this point that Petrażycki, although he was so often accused of neglecting the traditional search for the immanent logic of existing laws, fully subscribed to the postulate of 'objectivism'. What was really characteristic of his approach was his emphasis on objectivism understood as following the objective logic of laws and opposed to a mechanical adherence to the 'mere letter' of the law. We find a good example of this in I. V. Hessen's memoirs. After a dinner in Petrażycki's home A. I. Kaminka started to argue with his host about the meaning of a certain paragraph in the Russian civil code. It turned out that Petrażycki's interpretation was corroborated by the text of the paragraph, but Kaminka's interpretation was endorsed by a footnote to it. Petrażycki remained undisturbed and answered quietly: 'But look, I have crossed out this footnote'.²⁶ The meaning of this answer, curious as it might seem, was clear: he felt that the footnote could be disregarded since it contradicted the objective meaning of the law to which it was added.

From the very beginning Petrażycki's contributions to *Pravo* were substantial and important. These included many theoretical articles, always made highly relevant to the existing situation in Russia (for instance, in a series of articles on customary law, 1899). Nor did he avoid directly political, topical questions of the day. In this connection one should mention his study 'Ritual Murders' (1913),²⁷ written against the anti-Semitic campaign stirred up by the notorious Kiev trial of Mendel Beilis, accused of committing a murder on ritual grounds.

²⁵ Ibid., p. 153.   ²⁶ Ibid., p. 157.
²⁷ *Pravo*, 1913, pp. 2403 ff., 2423 ff.

At the end of 1904 the editors of *Pravo* dared to proclaim the incompatibility of autocracy with the rule of law. Soon afterwards the editorial board of *Pravo* became a meeting-ground for the gently-born liberals from the provincial *zemstvo* assemblies and the liberal intellectuals, and was thus instrumental in the emergence of the Kadet party. For Petrażycki, although he was respected and trusted, sometimes even consulted, by the government,[28] this was the beginning of his direct political involvement in the ranks of the liberal opposition. He joined the Kadet party, became a member of its Central Committee, and was elected to the first Duma. As a result he lost not only his position as dean of the Law faculty but also his chair, being demoted to the rank of associate professor. In protest against the arbitrary dissolution of the Duma he signed the famous Vyborg manifesto, which, among other things, appealed to the population to oppose the army draft and to stop paying government taxes. In fact he was against this act, seeing it as unlawful, but did not want to break his solidarity with the other former deputies, members of his party.[29] Like his colleagues, he was tried for illegal propaganda and sentenced to a brief term in prison. When he returned to the University his students wanted to congratulate him on signing the manifesto at a specially organised meeting; Petrażycki however firmly refused to accept this idea, saying that breaking the law was not a good reason for celebration.[30]

Predictably, all the ex-deputies who had signed the Vyborg manifesto were banned from contesting the elections for the Second Duma. Thus the formal pretext for not re-appointing Petrażycki as a full professor (the alleged incompatibility of professorial duties with political activity) was removed. In 1908 the Ministry of Education agreed to consider such a possibility, on condition, however, that the President of the University obtained from Petrażycki a written promise

[28] See the article by Petrażycki's disciple A. Meyendorff, 'The Tragedy of Modern Jurisprudence', in Sayre, *Interpretations*, especially p. 531. In spite of its title this article is devoted entirely to Petrażycki's life and thought.

[29] See A. Tyrkova-Williams, *Na put'iakh k svobode*, New York, 1952, pp. 331–2. Tyrkova attributed this to the influence of her own eloquence (although in retrospect she regretted Petrażycki's decision). According to her account, before signing the manifesto Petrażycki said to her: 'Ariadna Vladimirovna, you are forcing me to commit an act contradicting my juridical logic. I hope that I will never do anything like this in the future. Now I am ready to sign the appeal to the people'. (Ibid., p. 332.)

[30] See Timasheff in Sayre, *Interpretations*, (p. 737) and G. K. Guins, *L. I. Petrazhitskii: kharakteristika nauchnogo tvorchestva*, Harbin, 1931 (written at the time of Petrażycki's death).

to abstain from any activity contrary to the penal law, the civil regulations, and the oath to the crown. Although a refusal to give such a pledge was to result in dismissal, Petrażycki not only refused to comply but explained his position in a letter to the Ministry, arguing that acceptance of this demand would be against his political ethics and personal dignity. The Ministry, in its turn, reminded him that, as a civil servant, a professor had no right to criticize his superiors.[31] However, the threat of dismissal was not carried out. Petrażycki was by then at the height of his fame: his *Introduction to the Study of Law and Morality* was published in two editions (1905 and 1907), his main work—*Theory of Law and the State in Connection with a Theory of Morality*—soon followed (2 vols, 1907, second edition, 1909–10).[32] The Russian government then still had a certain respect for scholarship and did not want open conflict with the academic community. On the eve of the war Petrażycki regained his full professorship and was once more elected dean of the Law faculty.

In spite of his theory emphasizing the importance of non-rational emotions Petrażycki was personally a rationalist and optimist, firmly believing in the possibility of general rational and humanitarian progress. The world war, therefore, was a terrible shock to him. During the Thursday meetings of the editorial board of *Pravo* he often proposed that it should stop editing juridical articles and discuss, instead, means of ending the war. He wanted to explain to the Tsar that the war was destructive for the state, for law, for culture, for everything and everybody, cherishing illusions that the force of rational argument could change the course of history.[33]

However, as time went on, his mood grew more and more pessimistic. After the revolution of March 1917 he was appointed to the Senate but, to the surprise of his colleagues and disciples, he did not take part in its activities. When G. K. Guins asked his reasons for this, he answered: 'What's the use of working when everything is lost anyway'.[34] Within a month of this conversation the Bolshevik revolution took place and the Senate was dissolved.

After the Riga treaty (1921) with a newly-independent Poland, Petrażycki opted for Polish nationality and settled in Warsaw. The

[31] See Langrod, 'Polish Psychological Theory', pp. 313–14 (n. 58).
[32] He also published a book entitled *University and Science* (1907) which, in Timasheff's view, was 'comparable in value to Max Weber's *Wissenschaft als Beruf* which appeared fourteen years later' (See *Law and Morality*, p. xxxi).
[33] I. V. Hessen, *V dvukh vekakh*, p. 345.
[34] See Guins, *L. T. Petrazhitskii*, pp. xxxi–xxxii.

Law faculty of the University of Warsaw offered him a chair; since he wanted to teach sociology, a chair in this subject was created specially for him. In fact he lectured in Warsaw on many subjects, including psychology, general methodology of the social sciences and, of course, the theory of law. He also took an active part in the work of the Polish Committee for Codification. His influence in Poland was considerable and constantly increasing. After his death in 1931 a special Petrażycki Society was established, with the aim of publishing and propagating his works.[35] The reception of his ideas was not confined to jurists; for instance, he also influenced the philosopher Tadeusz Kotarbiński, who was particularly impressed by his vision of applied social science and saw him as a direct forerunner of his own 'praxeology', namely, the science of effective action. When the first edition of Petrażycki's collected works began publication in Poland in the late 1950s Kotarbiński wrote a preface for it and summarized the importance of Petrażycki's thought in the following words:

> The heritage of Petrażycki should be studied not only by every theoretician of law who wishes to become truly competent, but also by every researcher, every thinker who deals with the living problems of methodology in the human sciences, of the theory of civilization, of socio-technique, whether or not he sympathizes with the psychological theory of law, whether or not he adheres to the theses and arguments of this theory.[36]

Petrażycki's death was tragic—he committed suicide. Some Russian authors (Timasheff, Meyendorff) have attributed this to his disappointment at the realities of the Polish situation, such as the anti-Semitism of the right-wing nationalists or Piłsudski's *coup d'état*. There is, however, no evidence to corroborate such a conclusion. No doubt Petrażycki was worried by the growth of anti-Semitism in Poland but he was certainly even more worried by the general state of the world: the world-wide economic crisis, the emergence of totalitarianism, the threat of German Nazism, the Stalinist collectivization in the Soviet Union, and so forth. On the other hand, people who were close to Petrażycki in the last years of his life were inclined to question all 'political' explanations of his suicide.[37] On the basis of the available facts it cannot be established who was right in this controversy.

Many Russian and Soviet scholars treat Petrażycki simply as a

---

[35] The President of this Society was J. Finkelkraut.
[36] T. Kotarbiński, Introduction to Petrażycki's *Wstęp*. Quoted from Langrod 'Polish Psychological Theory', p. 305.
[37] See Langrod, 'Polish Psychological Theory', p. 315, n. 68.

Russian. Polish scholars could easily counter such a view by providing details about Petrażycki's background and by pointing out many cases in which he had shown his Polish national feeling.[38] On the other hand, it cannot, and should not, be denied that before the revolution he was an important figure not only in Russian scholarship but in the broader spectrum of Russian intellectual history as well. Thus we can perhaps agree with Timasheff, who has defined Petrażycki as a 'great Russo-Polish master',[39] and it would be proper to add that in the general intellectual history of Russia he was more important than in the general intellectual history of Poland.

Another question is Petrażycki's 'Polishness', as reflected in his personality and his writings. Timasheff has rightly noted that 'the fact that he was of Polish ancestry and that he belonged to the nobility seemed to have some bearing on the formation of Petrażycki's personality'.[40] This question, however, should not be reduced, as Timasheff has done, to such trivial remarks as that Petrażycki's accent was 'definitely Polish' and that in his German works he used the prefix 'von' before his name. In order to reach a deeper understanding of the importance of Petrażycki's 'Polishness' two other points should be made.

First, Petrażycki's violent reaction to the 'legal idiotism' of narrow legal positivism was deeply rooted in Polish history. Poland has never passed through a period of royal absolutism; the notion of law as a simple command by a legally constituted executive power was completely alien to the Polish 'democracy of the gentry'.[41] W. Goślicki, the sixteenth-century Polish political thinker, expressed a general and deeply-felt conviction when he wrote:

> The King of Poland, in the administration of his government, is obliged to make the law the sole guide and rule of his conduct. He cannot govern according to his own will and pleasure, without the advice and consent of the Senate. He cannot go beyond, or break in upon their decrees, nor exceed the bounds which they and the laws have set him.[42]

[38] For instance, he broke with the Kadet newspaper *Rech* because he was not pleased with the way in which this newspaper attacked an anti-Semitic Polish periodical. See I. V. Hessen, *V dvukh vekakh*, p. 345.

[39] See Petrażycki, *Law and Morality*, p. xxxiii.   [40] Ibid., p. xxi.

[41] The deep inner connection between state absolutism and legal positivism is obvious to many authors. See W. A. Luijpen, *Phenomenology of Natural Law*, Pittsburgh, Pa. 1967, p. 79.

[42] Quoted from: W. J. Wagner, A. P. Coleman, C. L. S. Haight, 'Laurentius Grimaldus Goslicius and His Age—Modern Constitutional Ideas in the Sixteenth Century', in *Polish Law Throughout the Ages* (see n. 9 above), p. 111.

This conviction, we should remember, was given a formalized legal expression: ever since the first 'free election' which took place in 1572 Polish kings had to agree that, in the case of a breach of law on their part, their subjects would be automatically released from obedience. *Non rex, sed lex regnat.* It was the main tenet of the Polish legal consciousness, shared by all 'active citizens' of independent Poland. In the eighteenth century the 'rule of law' was an ideal to which both the conservative champions of 'golden liberty' and the progressive leaders, founders of the Constitution of 3 May 1791, equally subscribed. The famous *liberum veto*, the main cause of the ruinous anarchy characteristic of the last century of the Polish–Lithuanian Commonwealth, was, paradoxically, a much too extreme expression of a legal world-view rejecting all arbitrary legislation, the view that laws should be stable and placed above any act of arbitrary will, even if it happened to be the will of the majority.

Secondly, as we shall see below, a characteristic feature of Petrażycki's legal philosophy was his emphasis on 'rights', on the 'attributive' function of law. He gave his approval to litigiousness, emphasizing that one's right should be treated as a matter of honour, that it was natural for people with strong legal emotions rather to be ruined by litigation than to give up the demands they felt to be right. It may justly be said—indeed, it seems strange that this observation has not previously been made—that such a view of law reflected the traditional mentality of the Polish nobility, proud of their rights and always ready to defend them.

3   The schools of legal philosophy and the tasks of jurisprudence in Russia

In order to place Petrażycki not only in the history of legal theory but also, and primarily, in the intellectual history of Russia, it seems proper to preface any account of his psychological theory of law by an attempted summary of his views on the main schools of contemporary jurisprudence in their relation to what he saw as the historical task, the moral mission, of the Russian jurists: to raise the level of jural culture in Russia, paving the way for the transformation of Russia into a 'rule-of-law' state.

In one of Petrażycki's early books on civil law we find two interesting supplements: (1) 'On the fashionable slogans in jurisprudence', and (2) 'On the duties of jurisprudence in Russia'.[43] The first

---

[43] L. Petrażycki, *Prava dobrosovestnogo vladel'tsa na dokhody s tochki zreniia dogmy i politiki chastnogo prava*, SPb, 1897.

is a devastating critique of Ihering's version of legal positivism. Against conceptual jurisprudence (*Begriffsjurisprudenz*) with its respect for logic, Ihering's school set the defence of 'practical interests'. As a result two basic principles of honest scholarship were lost: (1) the subjective principle of a disinterested search for truth, and (2) the objective principle of sufficient logical justification. Moreover, there was a remarkable similarity between the *Realpolitik* of Bismarck and this 'practical' school of jurisprudence: both extolled the egoism of brute force, both started a crusade against 'humanitarian sentimentality', in fact a crusade against truth and justice; both dangerously poisoned the soul of the German nation. The historical justification for such an attitude to law already occurs in Ihering's book on the spirit of the Roman law: the virtues of the ancient Romans were seen in their strong and shameless egoism, Roman law was interpreted as being based upon egoistic force and, precisely because of this, was presented by the author as a paragon of legal order. In practice, Petrażycki added, Ihering did not go as far as his theory would have allowed, and German jurisprudence, as yet, was not as corrupt as it could be. This was because German jurists still clung to the good traditions of their profession. On theoretical grounds, however, they were not able to defend a more lofty ideal of law. In Petrażycki's eyes it was a symptom of a general cultural crisis, of a general and deep 'obfuscation of minds and hearts'.[44]

Considering himself as founder of a new science of legal policy, Petrażycki was, of course, keenly aware that the law cannot stand still. Ihering's attacks against the purely doctrinal (dogmatic) study of law were seen by him as part of the legitimate effort to make law more sensitive to changing social realities. Nonetheless, he did not recognize any common ground between the demands of legal policy and Ihering's 'practicism'. The 'practical school' limited itself to the ingenious interpretation of existing laws, whereas Petrażycki's programme of legal policy consisted in creating a science which would gradually enable the necessary changes in legislation to be made. 'Practicism', in the sense of disregarding truth and logic, and positivism, in the sense of identifying might with right, would be utterly alien to this science. There would be no conflict between the doctrinal study of law and legal policy since there would be a clear-cut delimitation between them. Even should an attempt be made to

[44] Ibid., p. 420.

subordinate the doctrinal study of law to the demands of legal policy no neglect of, let alone contempt for, logic would ensue: there would be only a transient conflict between the two kinds of logic—the logic of the immanent study of law and the logic of political science, based upon socio-psychological data. Thus, logic would not become the prostitute or slave of particular interests, interpreting laws in a convenient but consciously mendacious way.

The real source of the idea of legal policy was seen by Petrażycki in the school of natural law—the school which for so long seemed completely discredited, buried underneath nineteenth-century historicism and positivism. According to him, the science of natural law represented in fact a discipline devoted to the problem of 'making good laws', and its downfall, resulting in the programmatic elimination of a deontological approach and limiting jurisprudence to the study of existing positive laws, prevented the much earlier appearance of a scientific legal policy.

A few years later, when Russia witnessed the so-called renaissance of natural law, Petrażycki was fond of reminding people that the postulate of reviving the natural-law standpoint had already been set forth by him in the appendix to *Lehre vom Einkommen*, where he wrote: 'the emergence of the science of legal policy can be interpreted as a revival of natural law'.[45] In another place he explained this thought as follows: 'The significance of the science of natural law as an independent, systematic discipline on a level with positive-law jurisprudence consisted precisely in the fulfilment of the lofty and important mission which the future science of legal policy should serve.'[46]

The essay 'On the duties of jurisprudence in Russia' contains a pessimistic diagnosis of the state of jurisprudence and general jural culture in Russia. For many historical reasons, Petrażycki argued, the Russians as a nation did not develop a genuine respect for law; their national soul needed therapy and because of this the principles of lawfulness and legality were to be approached by Russian jurists as something sacred, too important to the Russian national recovery to be treated lightly. In the West Ihering's teachings were not properly

---

[45] *Die Lehre vom Einkommen.* Berlin, 1895, vol. 2, p. 579 ('Civilpolitik und politische Oekonomie').

[46] Quoted from Babb, 'Science of Legal Policy', p. 806. The source of this quotation is Petrażycki's Preface to his *Introduction to the Study of Law and Morality* (not included in *Law and Morality*).

resisted because people do not, as a rule, care for what they possess and take for granted; in Russia, however, they ought to have been resisted as strongly as possible, and the lack of such resistance was an additional proof of an insufficient understanding of the importance of law even among Russian jurists. In the West juridical 'practicism' was not too dangerous, but a country like Russia could not afford to tolerate the 'fashionable slogans' about 'interests' being superior to principles and logic, about the permissibility of interpreting laws in a 'free' and arbitrary way, and so forth. In such a country a strict observance of existing laws, even bad ones, is much better than straining the interpretation of laws in order to further somebody's interests. Without due respect for existing laws and without their strict implementation there is no ground for believing that new and better laws will be respected and observed.

It is interesting to note that in the essay 'On the fashionable slogans in jurisprudence' young Petrażycki, the future founder of a comprehensive theory of legal emotions (impulsions), was very critical of Otto Gierke and other representatives of the 'Germanist' school, emphasizing the role of unconscious emotions in law-making processes and in the legal consciousness. The 'Germanist' school, as we know, was steeped in the tradition of the famous historical school of Savigny and Puchta (although, paradoxically, Savigny was a 'Romanist' in his approach to the history of German law). In the last part of his *Introduction to the Science of Legal Policy* (1896–7) Petrażycki gave a detailed account of his attitude toward, and appraisal of, the tradition of German historicism, and of his view of the relevance of this tradition to the science of legal policy.

Ihering, as is known, set against the historical school the idea of a conscious purpose in law; a purpose, be it added, deriving from interests. Petrażycki, with his ideal of conscious, scientific law-making, could not subscribe to the theory of an organic, unconscious, language-like or plant-like growth of law in the depths of the national psyche. However, he wholeheartedly agreed with Gierke as to the superiority of the historical school over the 'shallow utilitarianism' of the 'jurisprudence of interests'. He shared the view of the founders of the historical school that the development of law *in the past* was, as a rule, not an outcome of rational calculation but, rather, an unconscious and arbitrary growth, the result of gradual changes in the collective legal consciousness. He declared therefore that the theory of the historical school, although far from philosophical truth (from being *vera philosophia*, as he puts it), was nevertheless a genuine philosophy, that is a system of views touching upon genuine problems, providing deep insights and deserving of respect.[47] The basic tenets of legal historicism were partially accepted in Petrażycki's theory. He agreed with the view that law reflects the achieved level of historical development, that premature changes are detrimental, that legislators should avoid haphazard experimentation and, even, that in a conflict between rational blueprints and the collective experience of a nation it is better to show a certain presumption in favour of the *status quo* than to risk creating a deep division between legislation and the juridical conscience of the masses.[48] Unlike the historical school he emphasized, however, that studying the historical roots of existing laws should not be done with the aim of finding in the past the norms for the present; on the contrary, knowledge of the past should help the legislator to understand the historical conditions of the present and to move ahead, slowly but firmly, toward the expected and desired future. Needless to say, he disagreed also with the view that the historical evolution of each nation was predetermined by its allegedly unique and basically unchangeable 'national spirit'.

Another difference between Petrażycki and the protagonists of legal historicism concerned the question of historical relativism. In accordance with his natural-law sympathies Petrażycki often indicated that not everything in law was historically relative, that there were certain postulates, especially in the civil law, which were absolutely, universally valid, 'eternal in time and universal in space and in nationality'.[49] They were absolute, he hastened to add, only under certain conditions: civil law as such is valid only in a decentralized economy based upon private property, which means that it could not be valid, or even exist, before such conditions had been realized or after they had ceased to exist. However, all other historical conditions, and especially national conditions, could and should be treated as irrelevant for civil law. This was the reason, Petrażycki thought, for the universal significance of Roman law. It had developed spontaneously and unconsciously (that is as Savigny, and not as Ihering, saw it), on the basis of accumulated experience, but it had found solutions of civil-law problems applicable everywhere, in every country, irrespective of

---

[47] L. Petrażycki, *Wstęp do nauki polityki prawa*, p. 418.
[48] Cf. Babb, 'Science of Legal Policy', p. 822.
[49] L. Petrażycki, *Wstęp do nauki polityki prawa*, pp. 155–160.

historical epoch, whose economy was based on free contracts and private property. It is no exaggeration, therefore, to see Roman law as a true *ratio scripta*.

The category of 'absolute' legal principles, in Petrażycki's sense, included not only general postulates but also some very concrete, specific rules. For instance, the rule that necessary expenses of a temporary possessor should be returned to him, in order to enable him to behave like a rational *pater familias* and to care for the property entrusted to him. This principle, Petrażycki asserted, was absolute, that is independent of time, space and national character, applicable to all countries with private property and the institution of temporary possession, equally necessary in ancient Rome and in contemporary America.[50]

The historical school and, later, the 'Germanist' school led by Gierke, attributed special significance to customary law. Petrażycki himself was very interested in customary law; he used his knowledge of it as a weapon against the positivistic tendency to identify all law with statute law but, in conscious opposition to Gierke, he never idealized customary law and did not think that it could serve as a guide for conscious, progressive legislation. He pointed out that in contemporary Germany, a country torn by strong economic and social conflicts, customary law in fact supported some most brutal forms of capitalist exploitation. Although the followers of Gierke idealized the *Gemeinschaft*, the old Germanic community, their support for customary law meant in practice a support for *laissez-faire* individualism.[51] Idealization of customary law could not restore the spirit of archaic communalism; it could, however, effectively prevent enlightened legislation in favour of the economically weak.

Under Russian conditions this idealization of customary law, characteristic of the Slavophile trend in Russian thought, led to results as bad, if not worse. Petrażycki dealt with this question at length in his *Theory of Law and the State in Connection with a Theory of Morality*. After the emancipation of the peasants, he argued, the rural population, about three-quarters of the entire population of Russia, was excluded from the benefits of state-enacted civil law, deprived of elementary civil rights, and the reason given for this was the view that the peasantry, in order to preserve tradition, ought to be ruled by their own customary law. The results were deplorable: the majority of Russians

[50] Ibid., p. 248.   [51] Ibid., pp. 203–4.

suffered from the worst kind of arbitrariness, deprived of clear legal rules concerning their property relations, doomed to live in rural communes which could not, and did not even try to, prevent the exploitation of the weak but which effectually hampered productivity, killing any incentive to work by periodical redistribution of land and by the notorious collective responsibility for the gathering of taxes and redemption payments. Such a state of affairs was, in Petrażycki's view, extremely detrimental to economic, legal, and moral progress.

It should be stressed that this position was never officially endorsed by the Kadet party. It was a consistently liberal position, and the Kadets were afraid of being consistent liberals. They were anxious to get support from the left and afraid of being seen as supporting Stolypin's agrarian policy. Petrażycki, however, had the civil courage to raise himself above tactical considerations. From the standpoint of his final ideal he was much closer to socialism than the other Kadets, but, at the same time, in his practical, socio-economic programme for Russia he represented a more consistent liberal position and was not afraid of being placed on the right wing of his party.

As we shall see, one of the most characteristic features of Petrażycki's theory was his emphasis on 'intuitive law'. He is often treated as a champion of intuition in law, although in fact he pointed out many cases of the clear superiority of statute law over 'intuitive law'. An especially striking example of the progressive, educative role of official legislation was found by him in contemporary Russian history. He wrote about it as follows:

Undoubtedly the abolition of serfdom in Russia under Alexander II—a tremendous legal reform, realized under the action of the intuitive law of cultured and advanced personalities headed by the monarch—was far in advance of the development of the intuitive law of the great majority of the population. The intuitive law of this part of the population—of the majority of the squires and most of the peasants—was, at the time when the Emancipation Manifesto was promulgated, the law of master and slave. The squires ascribed to themselves corresponding rights with regard to serfs, while the latter ascribed to themselves corresponding obligations with regard to their masters and corresponding rights to the latter—in general, not merely on the basis that such was the mandate of positive law but also (and independendently thereof) in conscience and according to their intuitive law views. Many did not even conceive that any other law—a law of freedom—was either possible or admissible. The legislative reform produced in this regard a revolution which was extremely swift and radical. Some peasants—chiefly those who were aged—preserved for decades, and to the end of their lives, the earlier intuitive mentality of the law of serfdom and were unwilling to know and to acknowledge the reform, declaring to their former masters that they considered it their sacred duty to serve faithfully and truly for the future also. But the vast majority—especially the young—were liberated very swiftly indeed from their former servile, intuitive law convictions, and the converse reform would have been absolutely unthinkable a year, or even less, after the publication of the manifesto because of the corresponding intuitive law revolution in the national mind. Similar revolutions in the intuitive law mentality of the nation—great and more or less swift revolutions—have occurred in the history of other nations as well under the influence of far-reaching and progressive reforms of like content in the positive law—as, for example, under the influence of the legislative grant and effectuation of political rights.[52]

In Petrażycki's *Theory of Law and the State* there is also an appendix devoted to the existing state of the law in Russia.[53] The author there shows that the Russian Empire was not only a state recognizing a variety of systems of customary law, based upon principles of territory and nationality, but also a country which could be defined as a true 'kingdom of intuitive law'.[54] First, the institution of so-called 'legal expertise' was curiously overdeveloped in Russia. The hypertrophy of such expertise, arbitrarily 'explaining', that is, enlarging or restricting the meaning of existing laws, was, in Petrażycki's view, extremely dangerous in a country where the authority of the law was inadequately grounded, where the objective meaning of statute law was always less important than the opinions of various 'influential people'. Secondly, Russian statute law contained too many references to subjective factors, such as 'good will' or 'conscience', which the judges were to take into account in performing their duties. Thus, for instance, the statute defining the role of courts of conciliation said: 'The court of conciliation gives sentences in accordance with conscience'. Most horrifying of all, however, was the fact that the same formula about 'conscience' was repeated in article 25 of the 'Temporary Rules Concerning the Communal Courts'.[55] Such disregard for 'formal law' in the institution exercising judicial control over the lives of Russian peasants might please the Slavophile critics of 'Western legalism', and was, indeed, in part a result of the influence of their ideas. For

---

[52] *Law and Morality*, pp. 239–40.
[53] Unfortunately, omitted in *Law and Morality*.
[54] L. Petrażycki, *Teoriia prava i gosudarstva v sviazi s teoriei nravstvennosti*, SPb 1907, vol. 2, p. 618.
[55] Ibid., p. 638–9.

Petrażycki, however, no less than for Chicherin, it was a glaring proof that the Great Reforms of the 1860s had not improved the legal conditions in which the majority of Russians had to live. The dangers inherent in such a situation were for him only too obvious.

Petrażycki's essay 'On the duties of jurisprudence in Russia' did not attract the attention of Western language scholars writing on his thought. The same is true of his numerous, important articles published in *Pravo*. Apparently, his books published in Germany and in Russia were considered to be a sufficient basis for the study of his thought; in addition, the annual sets of *Pravo* were not easily available. Moreover, Petrażycki's legacy was being studied, as yet, only by those scholars who were interested in the purely theoretical aspect of his thought, in his contribution to the science of law, and not in the relevance of his ideas to the situation in the Russian Empire on the eve of the revolution. Such an approach to the works of the 'great Russo-Polish master' found a somewhat too radical expression in the abridgement of his two chief books (*Introduction to the Study of Law and Morality* and *Theory of Law and the State*) published in English under the title *Law and Morality*. Almost all references to Russia, including the separate appendix on Russian laws, were carefully and completely eliminated from this book, on the grounds that they were 'important only at a particular time or in a European context'.[56]

The emphasis placed on the purely theoretical context of Petrażycki's thought is neither wrong nor surprising. There is no doubt that Petrażycki was, above all, a great theorist and, as a rule, people who wrote about him were theorists too. The next step, however, should have been made by historians: specialists in Russian history, especially in Russian intellectual history, would have shown him as one of the great intellectuals of the Kadet party, as a theorist actively committed to the cause of the liberal *Rechtsstaat* in Russia.

This next step, however, has not so far been made. In the existing histories of Russian liberalism—by V. Leontovich and by G. Fischer—Petrażycki's name is not mentioned at all;[57] nor has it appeared in later works on this subject.[58] The other legal theorists of the Kadet party—notably P. Novgorodtsev and B. Kistiakovsky—have also been

[56] *Law and Morality*, p. xxxix (Translator's Note).
[57] See V. Leontovich, *Geschichte des Liberalismus in Russland*, Frankfurt am Main, 1957; G. Fischer, *Russian Liberalism: From Gentry to Intelligentsia*, Cambridge, Mass., 1958.
[58] See, for instance, *Essays on Russian Liberalism*. C. E. Timberlake (ed.), Missouri, 1972.

neglected by historians of liberalism in Russia. Even *Pravo* and other juridical periodicals, showing the legal ideas of Russian liberalism in action (i.e. in their application to the changing concrete problems of the day), have not been properly studied and taken into account in the general appraisal of the Russian liberal tradition. For this reason among others the widespread opinion that Russian liberalism was intellectually weak, amorphous, almost non-existent, remained unchallenged.

4 The psychological theory of law and its sociological assumptions

Let us turn now to Petrażycki's theories.

It should be noted that he was fond of using the term 'philosophy of law'. He wrote:

Philosophy is a complex discipline: it is the supreme theory (the theory of being in general) plus the supreme teleology (a teleological discipline concerning the supreme purpose: concerning the meaning of existence and of the corresponding supreme principles of conduct). Philosophy of law is a complex discipline: it is the supreme theory of law plus a supreme teleology: the supreme policy of law.[59]

As we know, Petrażycki started constructing his philosophy of law from its second part, from the policy of law. The logical order, however, was different. From the very beginning Petrażycki repeatedly emphasized that legal policy, in order to be scientific, had to be based upon a comprehensive empirical theory of law.

If we want to present Petrażycki's thought in its logical, and not merely chronological, order we should begin with his general methodological postulate concerning all theories: the postulate of logical adequacy. Any statement which claims to be theoretical should be logically adequate, that is it should refer specifically to the class of objects about which it is stated; in other words, it should be neither too broad, nor too narrow. If the predicate is related to a class which is too broad (as in the case of those sociological theories which attribute 'everything' to the influence of one factor), the theory is 'jumping'; if, on the other hand, the predicate is related to a class which is too narrow, the theory is 'limping', or 'lame'.[60] The latter case, reduced to absurdity, could be exemplified by a statement that all cigars fall to the ground, if neither supported nor suspended. Such a statement,

[59] *Law and Morality*, p. 299.   [60] Ibid., p. 19.

although undeniably true, could not be treated as theoretical because it is true in relation to all material objects, and not just cigars. The concept of adequate theory, as T. Kotarbiński has pointed out, was in fact a rediscovery of an old idea going back to Aristotle. In later times it was revived by Petrus Ramus and Francis Bacon. After Bacon, however, 'the tradition breaks'. The interest in adequate theories disappeared for centuries and reappeared only in Petrażycki's teaching.[61]

The reason behind Petrażycki's interest in logical classes and in the 'adequacy' of generalizations was his strong feeling that prevailing legal theory, reducing all law to the 'lawyers' law', was much too narrow, referring only to some phenomena out of all those which should be covered by a truly scientific theory of law. He was fond of pointing out that in ordinary language the word 'law' (*pravo*) referred to a much broader category than was the case with professional jurists. He was convinced that mere 'lawyers' law' was not a coherent class about which theoretical statements could be made and, therefore, he decided to define law anew, by finding a broader class (*genus proximum*) under which law could be subsumed, and a specific feature (*differentia specifica*) which would enable him to construct a narrower class of legal phenomena—a class which would cover all legal phenomena and only legal phenomena.

In order to achieve this it was necessary to acquire insight into the 'idea of law', into its 'essence'. Petrażycki assumed that the law was to be found in inner experience and that knowledge of it could be achieved by means of introspection. Thus, almost imperceptibly, he abandoned the 'purely logical' method and became committed to 'psychologism'. However, it has been correctly pointed out (by N. Lossky, G. Gurvitch and G. K. Guins) that his method of gaining insight into the inner essence of things had, in fact, very little in common with the methods of empirical psychology and that it would be more proper to emphasize its closeness to phenomenology.[62] In view of the well-known Husserlian 'anti-psychologism' this observation might seem strange; we should recall, however, that the father of phenomenology, Franz Brentano, represented an extreme psychologism and, as such, was rightly placed in the pedigree of

---

[61] T. Kotarbiński, 'The Concept of Adequate Theory', in Gorecki, *Sociology and jurisprudence*, pp. 17–22.

[62] See Guins, L. T. *Petrazhitskii*, p. xxxiii (Lossky's opinion referred to); G. Gurvitch, *Le Temps présent et l'idée du droit social*, Paris, 1931, p. 280; G. Gurvitch, 'Petrazhitsky', *Sovremennye zapiski*, Paris, 1931, vol. 47, p. 480.

Petrażycki's thought.[63] Certain kinds of psychologism, emphasizing introspection and 'descriptive psychology' combined with logical analysis, could provide starting points for developments leading toward a phenomenological method of 'eidetic insight' into the essence of empirically-given phenomena. This was the case with Brentano, whose psychologism, combined with Aristotelian logic, became the philosophical starting point for the line of development leading to Husserl, with Meinong and K. Twardowski as mediating links.[64]

It seems worthwhile to point out the most conspicuous similarities between Petrażycki's and Brentano's psychology. Petrażycki could subscribe to Brentano's thesis that 'vera philosophiae methodus nulla alia nisi scientiae naturalis est'; in both cases, however, this view did not imply commitment to naturalism;[65] on the contrary, both thinkers developed an independent science of 'descriptive psychology', consciously opposed to naturalistic 'experimental psychology' (represented, among others, by Wundt). Brentano 'fully recognized the independent role of impulsive affective-conative processes in human life';[66] Petrażycki did the same in his theory of impulsions. Like Petrażycki, Brentano was greatly interested in ethics and defined the good by reference to 'love'. Both saw psychology as 'the necessary foundation for both philosophy and science'.[67] Finally, Brentano was very close to Petrażycki in regarding psychology as a science especially important for solving practical problems; he treated it as 'the science of the future', namely, as 'the science to which more than to any other theoretical science the future belongs, which more than any other will mold the future'.[68]

In view of this we can safely assume that Petrażycki—whether consciously or not—also accepted Brentano's criterion of truth: self-evidence. What seemed to him 'self-evident' became a stepping-stone for his definition of law.

The first outline of Petrażycki's psychological theory of law appeared in 1900 under the title *Essays on Legal Philosophy*. It described law as a psychic phenomenon, a phenomenon of our spirit; as an inner voice authoritatively prescribing our conduct, telling us what our duties are in relation to others and, even more important, what our rights are,

---

[63] See Babb, 'Petrazhitskii: Theory of Law', *Boston University Law Review*, vol. 18, 1938, p. 571.
[64] Cf. W. Tatarkiewicz, *Historia filozofii* (*History of Philosophy*), vol. 3, Warsaw, 1950, pp. 209–19.
[65] Ibid., p. 217.
[66] A. C. Rancurello, *A Study of Franz Brentano*, New York and London, 1968, p. 63.
[67] Ibid., p. 75.   [68] Ibid., p. 134.

what we can legitimately expect and demand from other people. The proper way to study law is, therefore, through analysis of our inner experiences. To see law as something external, existing by itself, interpreting our 'rights' and 'duties' as something given to us or imposed upon us by higher entities such as 'Nature', 'Reason', 'Popular Will', 'National Spirit', and, especially, 'State' (an abstraction peculiarly favoured by jurists, to the point of idolatry in positivistic philosophies of law), is, thus, nothing less than projecting outside what is really inside, producing 'impulsive phantasmata or projected ideological entities'.[69]

A psychological approach to law as such was nothing particularly new. At the end of the nineteenth century law was seen as a psychic phenomenon by the influential philosopher W. Wundt and by the famous sociologist G. Tarde. Different interpretations of this idea were provided by professional jurists.[70] At the beginning of the nineteenth century historical jurists in Germany interpreted the law as a function of the collective psyche of the nation; later, as we know, this idea was taken over and further developed by the 'Germanist' school of Gierke. In the 1870s Zitelman indicated the necessity of turning to psychology to solve legal questions. Bierling, often seen as Petrażycki's direct predecessor, 'reduced objective law to subjective psychic experiences' and explained the conception of law as something really existing outside us as a psychic illusion.[71] Even Georg Jellinek, one of the protagonists of positivism in legal philosophy, turned to psychology in his later works, seeing the psychological approach as the only scientific way of studying law as a phenomenon of real life and, by the same token, as the only alternative to metaphysical speculation.[72]

And yet, in spite of all these facts, it is widely acknowledged that the first truly comprehensive, systematic and methodologically sophisticated psychological theory of law was created by the 'Russo-Polish master'. His *Essays on Legal Philosophy* were only a first draft, a general outline of this theory, but one in which the main idea was put forward so forcefully and consistently that the deliberate intention of provoking juridical circles might be suspected.

A legal phenomenon, Petrażycki stated, is a state of mind and, as

[69] Cf. *Law and Morality*, p. 41.
[70] Cf. F. Berolzheimer, *The World's Legal Philosophers*, New York, 1924, pp. 431–43; see also Babb, 'Theory of Law', p. 571.
[71] See Babb, 'Theory of Law', p. 573.
[72] See Berolzheimer, *The World's Legal Philosophers*, p. 441.

such, does not presuppose the existence of a state or, indeed, any other form of social organization, issuing commands and backing them by force. To support this thesis the author of the *Essays* gave several most unusual examples. Let us imagine, he wrote, an Earth-man on Mars meeting a creature in human likeness, who takes something from him and does not want to return it: the Earth-man would surely feel that his legitimate right had been violated by this, in spite of realizing that Martians are not bound by any institutionalized legal order existing on Earth. The same is true in our relations with animals: do we not feel that our dogs have certain rights, that what they want us to do can be divided into 'lawful' claims, which we are obliged to fulfil, and 'unlawful' ones, which we can ignore? For the emergence of a sense of legal rights and duties there is no need even of the real existence ('real' in the sense of an external reality) of the other creature: a superstitious person or a madman may contract to sell his soul to the Devil and his experiences, after signing such a contract, would be classified as a legal phenomenon, not substantially different from the experience of rights and duties involved in any other contractual relationship.

The statements quoted, which were repeated (although in a much wider context) in Petrażycki's later works, became the main pretext for accusing their author of 'subjective idealism' or even solipsism. Such accusations, levelled mainly, though not exclusively, by Marxists, are to be found even in the recent literature. In fact, Petrażycki defined philosophy as the supreme knowledge of 'the real', that is of the *two* classes of phenomena into which he would divide 'the real': the class of psychic phenomena and the class of physical (material) phenomena, existing independently of mind.[73] Thus, he might more justifiably be accused of taking the existence of the material world for granted, than of denying it. On the other hand, however, he espoused a standpoint of phenomenalism in epistemology and emphasized many times that the world as we see it is not a 'copy' of the external world but only our psychic image of it, formed to suit the exigencies of our human condition and dominated by our values and norms of conduct, namely, by our 'practical reason'.[74] Unfortunately, there are still people who, following Lenin's *Materialism and Empiriocriticism*, identify such a

---

[73] L. Petrażycki, *Wstęp*, p. 136–7 (In *Law and Morality*, this paragraph was omitted).

[74] Probably because of this in a recent Soviet book Petrażycki has been classified (mistakenly, of course) as a Kantian. See I. A. Golosenko, 'Sotsiologicheskie vozzreniia russkogo neokantianstva', in Chagin *Sotsiologicheskaia mysl'*, ch. 8.

standpoint with outright denial of the very existence of the so-called 'objective world'.[75]

The most important reviews of Petrażycki's *Essays* were by two leading representatives of the idealistic school in Russian philosophy: the Hegelian, Chicherin, and the neo-Kantian, Prince Evgeny Trubetskoi. Both combined sharp criticism of Petrażycki's psychologism with a sympathetic understanding of his anti-positivistic crusade. Chicherin welcomed Petrażycki's attacks in Ihering's view of laws as 'defended interests';[76] Trubetskoi went further because he agreed with Petrażycki's criticism of all 'legal positivism'.[77] Law, he argued, cannot be defined by reference to the state because the state itself is a legal union, thus presupposing law and not being prior to law. Defining law as a set of norms coercively implemented by people in power (not necessarily state power) is even worse because such norms could be arbitrarily chosen and, therefore, unlawful. On the other hand, canon law is law, international law is also law, although there is no organized coercion behind them. (These examples were pointed out by Petrażycki himself.) All theories equating law with officially recognized positive law involve a vicious circle: 'they reduce law to external authority which, in turn, is interpreted as a kind of law'.[78] Petrażycki's view that official positive law is in fact only a peculiar species of law should, therefore, be fully accepted. His *Essays* show the fatal dilemma of contemporary legal philosophy: 'It should either give up all further attempts to define law, which would amount to surrendering its function as philosophy, or look for the criteria of law outside and above positive law. The main merit, and an undoubtedly great merit, of the book under review consists precisely in showing this dilemma and explaining it.'[79]

However, Trubetskoi continued, Petrażycki was not consistent enough. He was not anti-positivist enough, attacking legal positivism without cutting himself off from philosophical positivism. He was afraid of metaphysics and therefore turned to empirical psychology instead of seeking support in speculative ethics. Legal positivists, criticized by him, identified law with the factually existing legal order;

---

[75] See, for instance, G. L. Seidler, *Doktryny prawne imperializmu* (*Legal Doctrines of Imperialism*), 3rd edn., Lublin, 1979, pp. 76–7.

[76] B. Chicherin, 'Psikhologicheskaia teoriia prava', *Voprosy filosofii i psikhologii*, vol. 55; Nov.–Dec. 1900, p. 383.

[77] E. N. Trubetskoi, 'Filosofia prava professora L. I. Petrazhitskogo', *Voprosy filosofii i psikhologii*, vol. 57, 1901, pp. 23–9.

[78] Ibid., p. 28.   [79] Ibid., p. 29.

Petrażycki, on the other hand, identified law with some factually existing psychological phenomena. This was the source of his errors, just as in the case of legal positivism; he looked for norms in the sphere of facts, not being aware that facts as such were radically, epistemologically, different from the sphere of ethical values.

There will be no separate chapter on Trubetskoi in this book and that is one of the reasons why it seemed worthwhile to set out at length his views on Petrażycki's *Essays*. These views were not otherwise very original, but quite typical of the neo-Kantian school in Russian legal philosophy, and this is an additional reason why they deserve our attention. They show both the wide area of agreement between Petrażycki and the neo-Kantian school and the equally wide area of disagreement which, as we shall see, tended to increase as time went on.

In short, like the neo-Kantians Petrażycki wanted to combat all kinds of legal positivism (especially Ihering's variety) but, unlike the neo-Kantians, he wished to defeat them on empirical grounds. He was aware, however, that psychologism as such was not enough to achieve this end. He knew, in particular, that his main foe, Ihering, was, in fact, very close to a psychological interpretation of law, that in his theory law was 'not only teleological but psychological'.[80] The reason for this he attributed to the 'limping' character of traditional psychology, dividing psychic life into cognition, feeling, and will and thus referring to too narrow a group of phenomena. This 'limping' theory of psychic life could not explain disinterested motives of human behaviour and rather supported an image of man as an egoistic, rationally calculating and hedonistic creature. Petrażycki felt strongly that this was not the whole truth and that traditional psychology should be changed to make room for a more adequate, and more lofty, interpretation of the psychological roots of law. He embarked on this task in his *Introduction to the Study of Law and Morality*.

The main contribution of this book was the discovery of a fourth class of psychic phenomena: the class of 'emotions' or 'impulsions'.[81] The other elements of psychic life were unilateral, that is, either purely passive (cognitive and emotional) or purely active (volitional); the distinctive feature of impulsions was their dual, bilateral, passive-active character. Petrażycki described them as 'correlative to the dual

---

[80] R. von Ihering, *The Struggle for Law*. 2nd edn. reprint, Chicago, 1979, p. xxviii.

[81] H. W. Babb consistently uses the term 'impulsions'. See Translator's Note to *Law and Morality*.

centripetal-centrifugal, anatomical structure of the nerve system and to the dual irritant-motor, physiological function of that system'.[82] Precisely because of this he saw them as the most important class of psychic phenomena, as 'the prototype of psychic life in general'. 'In the life of animals and of man', he wrote, 'impulsions act as the principal and directing psychic factors of adaptation to the conditions of life; other (unilateral) elements of psychic life play an ancillary, subordinate, and subservient part.'[83]

A detailed presentation of Petrażycki's theory of impulsions, with all its complicated divisions and sub-divisions, does not fall within the scope of this book. As to its scientific value (a question beyond the competence of a historian of ideas) I shall limit myself to three remarks. First, it was undoubtedly badly constructed, expressed in difficult and somewhat clumsy language. Secondly, critical estimates of it varied—to begin with it was received rather coolly and treated as the least convincing part of Petrażycki's teachings; later, however, N. Timasheff classified it as an important discovery, 'resembling the almost simultaneous discovery of conditioned reflexes by the Russian physiologist, Ivan Pavlov'.[84] Thirdly, irrespective of its scientific value, this theory is much more important for a proper understanding of Petrażycki's system than most of its critics or, even, most of its followers have believed. As we shall see, it provides the key to Petrażycki's sociology, interpreting human behaviour in terms of adaptation and cultural selection.

The peculiar importance of this theory for the philosophy of law lay in providing an answer to the fundamental question: how are legal and moral norms possible? how is it possible to explain human behaviour, not in terms of interests, utilitarian purposes, 'seeking pleasure—avoiding pain' and so forth, but in terms of duty? In other words, the theory of impulsions enabled its author to distinguish a specific class of 'legal impulsions', independent of pleasure, egoistic interest, or calculated utility.

The first important step in this direction was the distinction between special and abstract or blanket impulsions. Timasheff's remark about the parallel between Petrażycki and Pavlov was made in connection with this part of Petrażycki's theory. Let us quote:

According to Petrażycki, in some bilateral experiences such as hunger or sex

[82] Babb, 'Theory of Law', p. 529.
[83] *Law and Morality*, p. 23.   [84] Ibid., pp. xxv–xxvi.

the active ingredient is completely predetermined by the passive ingredient. In other bilateral experiences, for instance, those caused by commands, or connected with aesthetic urges, or the sentiment of duty, the active ingredient is determined by the mental image of virtual action experienced simultaneously with the passive ingredient. The second type of bilateral experiences he called 'abstract', while those of the first type he called 'special'. In terms of contemporary psychology, Petrażycki's 'special' experiences of the bilateral type approximately correspond to conditioned reflexes in which the passive elements (stimulus) brings about the active (response) according to definite laws of learning.[85]

The next step is to be found in Petrażycki's elaborate typology of impulsive motivation. It strongly emphasized that 'the very great majority of human and animal actions are non-purposive in character and are based on other than purposive motivation'.[86] To support this view Petrażycki mentioned the following three types of intellectual-impulsive motivation:

1. Fundamental motivation. By this he meant actions 'because of', as contrasted with actions 'in order that'; actions motivated by ideas concerning the past, and not the future. In all such cases, he stressed, 'an impulsion seeks to evoke a corresponding response without asking whether or not a certain end must be accomplished'.[87]

2. Objective motivation. Petrażycki meant by this 'the most ordinary and widespread species of motivation in human and animal life', that is, a motivational process in which perceptions of certain objects evoke in the mind of the percipient an immediate feeling of strong attraction or repulsion with corresponding bodily movements. It was important for him to stress that in such common behaviour too 'purposive calculations are completely alien'.[88]

3. Action or self-sufficing motivation. This was Petrażycki's main argument against the dominant, hedonistic and utilitarian, view of human nature. Because of the crucial importance of the relevant fragment it seems justifiable to quote it in its entirety:

> Finally, mention must be made of still another species of intellectual-impulsive motivation, which plays an important part in certain fields of human conduct (including moral and legal behaviour): those motivational processes wherein *the images of conduct themselves act as their cognitive components* —which arouse the impulsions evoking various positive and negative actions (abstentions). These may be succinctly termed *action ideas.*

[85] Ibid., p. xxvi.   [86] Ibid., p. 28.
[87] Ibid., p. 29.   [88] Loc. cit.

In an honourable man, invited to commit (for money or other advantage) deceit, perjury, defamation, homicide by poisoning, or the like, the very idea of such 'foul' and 'wicked' conduct will evoke impulsions which reject these acts; moreover, this rejection will be so powerful as not to permit the attractive impulsions (with reference to the promised advantages) and the corresponding purposive motivation to arise, or to crush such motives as they do appear. Other action ideas—such as ideas of behaviour termed 'good' or 'sympathetic' —evoke, on the contrary, attractive impulsions with reference to such behaviour (which is the very reason for their being called 'good').

Motivation wherein action ideas operate—arousing impulsions for or against corresponding conduct—may be termed _self-sufficing motivation_ (self-sufficing in the sense that here no extraneous—purposive or other—cognitive processes are needed: the idea of the conduct is itself sufficient to evoke the impulsions in favour of or against it).

The existence and operation, in our mind, of immediate combinations of action ideas and impulsions (rejecting or encouraging corresponding conduct), may be manifested in the form of judgements rejecting or encouraging certain conduct _per se_—and not as a means to a certain end: 'a lie is shameful'; 'one should not lie'; 'one should speak the truth'; and so forth. Judgements based on such combinations of action ideas with repulsions or attractions we term _normative judgements_; and their content we term the principles of conduct—or norms.[89]

In this way, disregarding the neo-Kantian view that norms and values could not be derived from facts, Petrażycki had managed to create a psychological theory which was to explain the emergence of norms and normative judgments. In his _Theory of Law and the State_ he divided norms (and the corresponding impulsions) into aesthetic and ethical categories. He defined ethics as a special class of normative experiences—experiences of duty, and divided it, in its turn, into two narrower classes: morality and law. The difference between morality and law he saw as lying in the purely imperative character of moral norms and imperative-attributive, bindingly-exigent character of legal norms. Thus both, the _genus proximum_ and the _differentia specifica_ of law had been found: law was defined as a class of psychic phenomena belonging to the wider class of ethics and differing from the other species of ethics, namely, from morality, by the bilaterally-binding, imperative-attributive character of its norms.

Petrażycki's view on the relationship between morality and law is worthy of detailed treatment and analysis, and we shall return to it later. In the present context it seems more important to turn our

[89] Ibid., p. 30.

attention to an aspect of Petrażycki's thought which has often been neglected or completely ignored, but without which his theories cannot properly be understood—the *sociological* aspect of his social philosophy. It may seem strange but it was so: the founder of the 'psychological theory of law', so often accused of methodological 'individualism', 'atomism' or even 'solipsism', in fact represented a deeply *sociological* approach to psychic phenomena.[90]

The awareness of this is more and more pronounced in the literature on the subject, scarce as it is as yet. A book on Petrażycki published in 1975 in the United States has the word 'sociology' in its title.[91] A Soviet book on the history of Russian sociology, which appeared in 1978, contains a chapter on Petrażycki's sociological thought;[92] the author quotes with approval the opinion of an American sociologist, J. S. Roucek, that Petrażycki's role in the development of sociology in Russia 'can be compared to that of Durkheim in France'.[93] In another chapter of this book we read: 'We can say, with certain qualifications, that [in the non-Marxist Russian sociology] there was only one fully-fledged school of 'subjective' sociology, and two half-formed, half-organized schools: that of M. M. Kovalevsky and that of L. J. Petrażycki'.[94]

The reasons for this belated acknowledgement of Petrażycki's contribution to sociology are obvious. Although he had lectured on sociology several times, had stimulated sociological interest among his students and promised to present his sociological views in a separate book, such a book was never published. In Warsaw, where he held the chair of sociology, he left behind three sociological manuscripts, two of them written in Russia. After his tragic death one of his students, Rafał Wundheiler, prepared an abridged presentation of Petrażycki's sociology on the basis of his own notes of Petrażycki's lectures. This typescript, however, was not published either and shared the fate of Petrażycki's manuscripts: all were destroyed during the Warsaw uprising of 1944.

The most important attempt at a systematic reconstruction of

---

[90] According to Eileen Markley-Znaniecki, Petrazycki's theory 'results in the most complete psychological atomization of social systems to be found in the history of social thought'. (*Twentieth-Century Sociology*, G. Gurvitch and W. E. Moore (eds.), New York, 1945, p. 704.) I find this judgement very one-sided and, consequently, untrue.

[91] See Gorecki, *Sociology and Jurisprudence*.

[92] See Chagin, *Sotsiologicheskaia mysl'*.

[93] See J. S. Roucek (ed.), *Contemporary Sociology*. London, 1959, p. 910.

[94] Chagin, *Sotsiologicheskaia mysl'*, p. 22.

Petrażycki's sociology is the long article by his Polish disciple, J. Lande, published in 1952, based not only on Petrażycki's published works but also, like Wundheiler's manuscript, on his lectures (a shortened version of this article is available in English translation).[95] Another important contribution is a book by Petrażycki's friend and disciple, G. K. Guins, published in distant Harbin in 1938.[96]

Let us start, however, from the last chapter of *Theory of Law and the State*, devoted to the relevance of sociology for a truly scientific theory of law. This chapter should be much longer and, in order to prevent misinterpretations, should be placed at the beginning rather than at the end of the book. It contains statements which substantially change the meaning of Petrażycki's 'psychological theory of law', making it clear that it would be more appropriate to call it 'socio-psychological theory', as part of a larger, comprehensive theory of socio-psychic phenomena, their inner structure and development.

The problem of the origin and development of law, Petrażycki maintained, found a much better, much deeper, explanation in sociology than in professional jurisprudence. Two sociological theories were for him of special interest: the Darwinian theory, explaining law and morality as products of the 'subconscious mechanism of adaptation', and the theory of historical materialism. He did not hesitate to declare that his own theory could be seen as presupposing the basic tenets of evolutionism and historical materialism, while concentrating, of course, on specific features of law. He wrote about it as follows:

> Between certain sociological theories (such as the Darwinian, the theory of historical materialism and the like) and the nature of law as special ethical experiences, there is no essential antagonism: one can, on the contrary, follow Darwinism or historical materialism in sociology, and the theory of law as imperative-attributive experiences at the same time. Moreover, the theory of law as imperative-attributive experiences and corresponding dispositions affords some support to both sociological theories. Thus if law is an individual-psychic experience based on corresponding dispositions, it seems from the point of view of the Darwinian theory analogous to various other elements and attributes of the psycho-physical apparatus (the organism), the origin and development of which is explained by this theory. From the point of view of economic materialism, reducing the law to special psychic phenomena

[95] See J. Lande, 'Petrazycki's Sociology', in his *Studia z filozofii prawa* (*Studies in the Philosophy of Law*), Warsaw, 1959. For the shortened English version see Gorecki, *Sociology and Jurisprudence*.

[96] G. K. Guins, 'Pravo i kul'tura. Protsessy formirovaniia i razvitiia prava', in 'Pravo i kultura'. *Izvestia Iuridicheskogo Fakulteta v G. Kharbine*, vol. XXI, Harbin, 1938.

is not unfavorable: legal phenomena appear to be psychic correlates—reflections of social material—and their content changes in history in accordance with changes of social material, as a function of the latter.[97]

However, Petrażycki added, the Darwinian theory

leaves out of view the special processes occurring on the basis of communication and, in general, of the psychic community between members of social groups. Psychic community is, so to speak, mutual psychic infection: not intellectual infection merely but emotional infection as well. Not only the relevant ideas, but also the emotions and impulsions connected therewith in the minds of those so communicating, are communicated and given currency. Against what caused the individual to suffer, negative impulsions—repulsions, antipathies—are developed in individual minds; while in favor of forces which had acted in the opposite direction attractive impulsions—sympathies—are developed. The impulsive-intellectual *social* communion gives rise to definite resultants (shared appraisals) in the life of successive generations.

Such 'average resultants' of emotional interaction in society are achieved, as a rule, at increasingly higher and higher levels, as the impulsions which are better for social life oust and replace those which reflect a lower level of social adaptation.

Such unconscious adaptation, improvement, and development takes place in all spheres of life: in the language itself (the chief instrument of the processes in which we are interested), in the classification of phenomena and objects, in the customs and rules of national hygiene, medicine, agronomy, education, morality, law, and so forth.[98]

The meaning of these all too brief and somewhat enigmatic remarks is made clearer in Petrażycki's lectures. The general category of 'adaptation' was there divided into three different kinds: egocentric, phylocentric, and sociocentric. Egocentric adaptation takes place in the life of an individual man or animal: it consists in the process of subconscious learning through the association in the individual psyche of certain experiences with certain things or actions. Phylocentric adaptation applies to the life of an entire (human or animal) species and is explainable by means of the Darwinian theory of natural selection in the struggle for survival; it is a purely biological process which means that it can be seen in terms of natural evolution only, and not in terms of progress. The last category, sociocentric adaptation, is a purely human phenomenon, being the subject matter of the social

[97] *Law and Morality*, p. 327.   [98] Ibid., pp. 329–30.

sciences. It deals with a new factor: socio-psychological interaction, the transmission of ideas, judgements and impulsions (emotions) by means of movements, facial expressions, language and other forms of 'mutual psychic infection'. It is not a biological struggle for survival but a struggle, a competition, between ideas, judgements, and impulsions, particularly ethical impulsions. It leads to ethical and cultural progress, explains the emergence of law-norms regulating human conduct; among other things, it also explains the peculiar nature of ethical experiences, showing them to be unconscious products of multi-generation social history, which appear to individuals as something 'authoritatively mystic', revealed from above by higher beings.

It was rightly noticed that Petrażycki's theory of 'sociocentric adaptation' led in practice to conclusions 'sharply contrasting with various Social Darwinist notions'.[99] Social Darwinism, as is known, supported the principle 'might is right' whereas Petrażycki's theory tried to explain and advocate the possibility of moral and legal progress, conceived as a process in which individuals overcome their natural, animal egoism and become better and better socialized.

According to Guins, the theory of 'sociocentric adaptation' was in fact a theory of cultural selection, anticipating the respective theories of C. Ellwood and McDougall.[100] In spite of Petrażycki's references to Darwin, his ideas were in reality far removed from the spirit of naturalism. What he really represented, even if he was not sufficiently aware of it, was a peculiar combination of evolutionism with a culture-centred sociology, which concentrated on the emergence and functioning of social norms and values. The contrast between the principle of 'cultural selection', which he had espoused, and the principle of 'natural selection' was, indeed, a sharp one: from the point of view of the latter the old and disabled ought to be eliminated whereas the former principle implied a notion of cultural progress based on increasing socialization, that is, among other things, an increasingly protective attitude toward the physically and socially weak.[101]

There is much to be said in favour of this interpretation of Petrażycki's theory, and this was the view adopted by his best-known Russian disciple, Pitirim Sorokin. He represented a definitely anti-naturalistic, 'culturalist' standpoint in sociology and, at the same time, closely followed Petrażycki in his view on the broad conception of law. In an article entitled 'The Organized Group (Institution) and Law-

[99] J. Gorecki, 'Leon Petrażycki', in Gorecki, *Sociology and Jurisprudence*, p. 11.
[100] Guins, *Pravo i kultura*, p. 299.   [101] Ibid., p. 297.

Norms' he emphasized: 'The subsequent analysis of law-norms follows the brilliant analysis of law by Leo Petrajitsky'.[102]

On the basis of his general sociological assumptions Petrażycki constructed an elaborate theory of the development of law and morality. It is justifiable to call it a theory of progress because it tried to show a puzzling purposefulness governing the subconscious formation of ethical values and bringing mankind closer and closer to the ideal of perfect socialization. Petrażycki was, however, careful to avoid the fallacy of determinism: he repeatedly stressed that ethical progress was not 'guaranteed' by irreversible historical laws, that human history had witnessed many periods of regression, sometimes gradual, sometimes following great catastrophes of civilization. He tried to give a theoretical explanation for such reverses and breakdowns in history by pointing out the unevenness of historical development. Different peoples, he argued, represent very different levels of socio-psychic (i.e. cultural) development and, therefore, contacts between them may bring about not only positive results—as when a nation on a higher cultural level succeeds in raising another, more backward nation to that level—but also results which are deeply detrimental to both sides: as, for instance, when close cultural contact between two different peoples (through colonization, massive immigration, or other means) causes a lowering of the cultural level of the more highly developed group and, at the same time, violates the spontaneous development of the second group, bringing about its cultural disintegration or even its physical degeneration.[103] Such difficulties of mutual adjustment may result in devastating wars or invasions, becoming a catastrophe to all mankind.

Nevertheless, in spite of all these reservations, Petrażycki believed that in any relatively homogeneous society, if left to itself and allowed to develop freely, the changes in ethics, that is, in law and morality, will follow a certain universal pattern of progress. There is nothing 'inevitable' about it, but, even so, in each case the same tendencies of progressive development can be found. In the development of law,

---

[102] See Sayre, *Interpretations*, p. 694. See also Sorokin's account of Petrażycki's theory in his *Contemporary Sociological Theories*, New York, Evanston, Ill., and London, 1928 (repr. 1956), pp. 699–705. In his memoirs (*A Long Journey: An Autobiography*, New Haven, Conn., 1963, p. 73) Sorokin referred to Petrażycki as 'possibly the greatest scholar of law and morality in the twentieth century'.

[103] See L. Petrażycki, *O dopełniających prądach kulturalnych i prawach rozwoju handlu (On Supplementary Cultural Trends and on the Laws of the Development of Commerce)*. J. Finkelkraut (ed. from ms.), Warsaw, 1936.

Petrażycki insisted, three universal tendencies have revealed themselves. First, 'the tendency of increased demands'. The demands of law increase both numerically and qualitatively: for instance, the duties of parents to educate their children. This increase in demand parallels the progressive socialization of men, dependent, in its turn, on man's mastery over external nature.

Secondly, 'the tendency to change incentives'. At more advanced levels of social development, the law produces identical, or better, behaviour, by using higher incentives. Thus, to quote Lande,

the system of serfdom is based on the very primitive motive of fear of physical force. It was succeeded by the individualist system: here, productive work is not compulsory, but motivated by the expectation of gain and security, both for oneself and one's family. This system can work only at those levels of social development where men have achieved the capacity for independent planning, inventiveness, and an inclination to work. The next level, the socialist order, replaces these motives of private rivalry by the motives of duty and the social good. Parallel changes occur within political structures.[104]

Thirdly, 'the tendency to diminish motivational pressure', or the reduction of both punishments and rewards. The law becomes more humane, torture and cruel punishments are gradually removed; public services are dissociated from great rewards, such as hereditary privileges and so forth; in private law cruelly severe sanctions against debtors, such as 'cutting them up into pieces', are replaced by imprisonment and, finally, by a simple obligation to pay interest—and even this is increasingly conditional, that is, more and more dependent on the debtor's capacity to pay. The list of such examples could of course be much longer.

Petrażycki warned that even the soundest, least disturbed, development is not rectilinear. Thus, for instance, a change of incentives (second tendency) is not paralleled at the beginning by diminished motivational pressure (third tendency); on the contrary, new incentives have to be, initially, very strong to exert their educational influence. This was the case at the beginning of the individualist system when the threat of coercion had to be replaced by different, but very strong, motivational pressure—by threats of starvation on the one hand, and opportunities for accumulating unlimited wealth on the other. Later, however, when new motives of economic conduct became internalized,

[104] See J. Lande, 'The Sociology of Petrażycki', in Gorecki, *Sociology and Jurisprudence*, p. 30.

transformed into stable dispositions and rooted in the national character of popular masses, there emerged the possibility of diminishing the pressure of both threats and temptations. As a result, some important reforms were carried out (social security, progressive taxation and so on) and the individualist system, without abandoning its basic principles, became more humane, better socialized.

It should be remembered that the above theory—in accordance with Petrażycki's psychological definition of law—applied not only to positive law, as demanded by legal positivists, but to all kinds of imperative-attributive experiences regulating human behaviour in all spheres of life. Even positive law was defined quite differently by Petrażycki than by the legal positivists. It is necessary, therefore, to present here—without dwelling on details—a general scheme of the inner divisions within the broad class of phenomena to which Petrażycki gave the name of 'law'.

The most important of the many divisions and sub-divisions of law which we find in Petrażycki's books is the division into intuitive and positive law. Challenging the legal positivists, Petrażycki claimed that the main characteristic of positive law was not the fact that it was 'posited' by the state: the scope of positive law was for him much broader, and what made it 'positive' was its heteronomous nature, its necessary reference to 'normative facts'. These 'normative facts' could not be reduced to statutes or judicial practice or customs approved by the state. There are many other sorts of 'normative facts', such as religious books, *communis opinio doctorum*, the law of the sayings of religious-ethical authorities, the law of religious-authoritative models of conduct, the law based on acknowledgement, and so forth. Petrażycki classified 'normative facts' under fifteen headings and, in dealing with each of them, deliberately played down the role of the state. He insisted that even statutes were not necessarily state-enacted statutes; there were also ecclesiastical, communal or, even, family statutes ('legalized' by the heads of families), some of them recognized by the state and thus made 'official', some of them not.[105]

In contrast to positive law, intuitive law is characterized by the absence of these ideas of 'normative facts'.[106] It is, therefore, autonomous, diverse and individual in content, growing spontaneously and easily adaptable to the changing conditions of life. Usually, though not necessarily, it is more progressive than the positive law and exerts a

---

[105] See *Law and Morality*, p. 259.   [106] Ibid., pp. 225–6.

constant pressure on it; in the case of a sharp conflict between the norms of intuitive law, recognized by the masses, and the existing legal order a revolution might reasonably be expected. However, there are also cases in which enlightened legislation 'from above' is more progressive than the average level of legal consciousness among the people. Petrażycki supported such progressive legislation, but only to a certain extent: he warned that legal reforms should not go too far ahead of dominant notions of 'justice'. He defined 'justice' as intuitive law[107] and emphasized that the sense of justice, dominant at a given time among the masses, should not be arbitrarily violated by legislators. Premature changes in the legal order could either be nullified in practice or bring about quite unexpected and undesirable results.

These considerations, as we shall see, were of fundamental importance for Petrażycki's conception of a scientific 'legal policy'.

Equally 'anti-positivistic' was Petrażycki's division of law into 'official' and 'unofficial'. By 'official law' Petrażycki meant not only that part of positive law which was enacted or officially recognized by the state, but also a part of intuitive law—if acknowledged by state courts and other organs of state authority. The last category, intuitive official law, referred to such cases as *judicia bona fidei* in ancient Rome, equity justice in England and 'conscience' justice in Russian courts. Petrażycki pointed out that in the first two cases the process of 'positivization' had taken place:

Thus, in English courts of equity intuitive law was to a significant degree ousted, in the final analysis, by prejudicial law: by law referred to previous decisions in accordance with justice. In the *bonae fidei judicia* of Roman law intuitive law was gradually replaced by positive law, in consequence of the development of the law of learned jurists through interpretation of what is usual according to justice or good conscience, and the elevation of suitable opinions of jurists to the rank of normative facts.[108]

As for Russia, as we already know, officially recognized intuitive law was, in Petrażycki's eyes, not a useful supplement to official positive law but, rather, an officially approved sphere of judicial arbitrariness, a sad testimony to an insufficiently developed legal culture. Therefore, in the Russian case, the 'positivization' of official intuitive law was not only something to be expected but also something to be desired for the sake of elementary standards of lawfulness.

The main and most 'anti-positivistic' conclusion from this theory

[107] Ibid., p. 241.   [108] Ibid., p. 294.

was that official law of all kinds embraced but a small fraction of the vast sphere of legal phenomena. Law is to be found everywhere. Bandits and other criminals have their own quite elaborate and scrupulously implemented laws; the dead, animals and, sometimes, even material things are treated as subjects of rights and obligations. Economic activity is always dependent on laws, whether officially recognized or not. Religion and family relations, seen by the Slavophiles as ruled by 'love' only and completely immune from the impact of a formalistic legal mentality, are in fact deeply permeated by the legal, imperative-attributive consciousness: every family is a complicated legal system,[109] the Old Testament was nothing but a kind of legal contract between man and God. Law, therefore, has very little in common with the state and, also, cannot be defined by reference to coercion. There are, for instance, very definite legal rules of etiquette (returning somebody's greeting is a 'duty' for one person and a 'right' for the other, and so forth), but none of these rules, of course, can be implemented by force.

Thus we have come full circle: starting from Petrażycki's definition of law we finally come back to this definition. It remains, however, to answer the question: what were the reasons behind Petrażycki's choice of so broad and so unusual a definition of law?

Petrażycki's conception of 'adequate theories' implied that 'the formation of ideas scientifically correct from the point of view of pure logic is the first, rather than the last, link in the chain of scientific knowledge'.[110] He seemed to believe that there was nothing arbitrary in his definition of law, that 'the lawyers' law' could not be the subject of a properly constructed scientific theory and that the 'adequate' character of his own theory could be proved by reference both to empirical evidence and to the logical rules of classification. This, however, was really an illusion. There was, of course, an arbitrary, a priori, element in Petrażycki's approach to law and, consequently, in his definition of law.

---

[109] It seems worthwhile to quote a paragraph describing the 'legal status' of children in an upper-class family: 'At every step small children ascribe to themselves with reference to other children, servants, and so forth—and to others in reference to themselves—various rights with regard to what 'father directed', or 'mother said', or the 'nurse allowed', or 'aunt decided', and the like (statute law). Thereafter, arrangements established in the house, customs (customary law), court decisions of elders where children have quarrelled (with each other or with a servant), the matter is handed over to the judgment of domestic authorities, and certain other facts possess juridically normative significance for children' (*Law and Morality*, p. 70).

[110] Babb, 'Theory of Law', p. 524.

This element is to be found in the sphere of values. It is widely recognized by philosophers—in Petrażycki's time it was a favourite theme of the neo-Kantians—that values predetermine cognition, that there are no ready-made facts, because what we call 'facts' are not something 'given'; in a sense, 'facts' are created by values because it is the values which give direction to our cognitive processes, introduce order into the chaotic mass of direct experiences, and so enable us to construct 'facts'. What we see as a 'fact' is, in reality, a product of cognitive efforts strained toward achieving certain aims and thus inseparable from the values which had predetermined these aims. This explanation, even if not entirely convincing, can be accepted, I think, as a comment on the 'arbitrary element' in Petrażycki's theory.

There are at least two value judgements which predetermined Petrażycki's image of what is law. First was a deep, ineradicable conviction that law cannot be identified with the existing legal order, that what is lawful cannot be decided by power and that every legal order needs a justifying ground and a critical norm. From this point of view Petrażycki's struggle against legal positivism was, as he himself had stressed, a commitment to the ethical and critical approach to law, represented throughout history by different schools of natural law.

The struggle between legal positivism and the theory of natural law, writes a contemporary philosopher of law, 'can be traced back from our time to far into antiquity'. This struggle 'imposes itself as an existential dilemma on all those who are concerned with humanity. No humanity is possible without positive law, but positive law itself must be supported by a foundation and subject to a critical norm. It is the merit of the defenders of the natural law that they saw this necessity'.[111] We may add to this that it was the merit of Petrażycki that he already recognized this necessity at the end of the nineteenth century, when legal positivism reigned supreme among professional jurists.

Another value judgement which influenced Petrażycki's theory and, in particular, his terminology, was his high estimation of individual freedom. This was not the same thing as 'individualism': Petrażycki conceived of the latter as being merely a phase in the historical education of mankind. Law was for him not a means of protecting egoistic, individual interests; on the contrary, he saw its mission, its goal (we shall return to this later) as helping to bring about the perfect socialization of man. If 'individualism' is understood as 'atomism', he

---

[111] Luijpen, *Phenomenology of Natural Law*, p. 44.

does not fall into this category either: despite his phenomenalism, sometimes expressed in an exaggerated way, his psychological theory of law was in fact based on sociological assumptions and proved that the content of the individual psyche is radically social. Nevertheless it is significant that he chose to call this theory 'psychological', and not 'socio-psychological', which would certainly have been more correct. His intentions seem to be clear: he wanted to emphasize that 'the social' did not exist 'outside' or 'above' the individual, that socialization, in order to be genuine and effective, had to take place inside the individual psyche, to be internalized, and not merely imposed on men as an external force. Very probably he consciously opposed his 'psychologism' to Durkheim's 'sociologism'. Interpreting 'social facts' as something external and 'thing-like' (to use Durkheim's expression) was in his eyes too close to a servile attitude toward 'projected ideological entities' and, by the same token, incompatible with the individual freedom and dignity of man.[112]

5   Law and morality

A peculiarly interesting part of Petrażycki's theory of law was his interpretation of the relationship between the two species of ethics: law and morality. It was especially impressive and challenging in Russian conditions. As I tried to show in the first chapter of this book, the traditions of legal nihilism—both left-wing legal nihilism (populism, anarchism) and right-wing nihilism (Slavophilism)—were much stronger in Russia than elsewhere in Europe. At the beginning of this century the most crude and uncompromising of nihilistic attitudes toward the law was represented by the Christian anarchism of Tolstoy. Most of the Russian intelligentsia had by then overcome such an attitude, but even so the tradition of regarding the law as something soulless, merely formal, easy to manipulate and infinitely inferior to morality was still firmly established. It held sway even over the minds of people who thought themselves completely free from underestimating the importance of law. They were prepared to embrace the idea of a 'rehabilitation of law'; some, mainly political radicals, accepted this idea by adhering to Plekhanov's view on the necessity of bourgeois constitutionalism in

[112] Cf. Lande's comment on the relationship between Petrażycki and Durkheim: ' . . . Durkheim, in *The Determination of Moral Facts*, gives a very similar analysis of 'moral' experiences. He also proclaims the social origin of 'morality', but his unclear and inconsistent notion results in a naive reification of society, as if it were a person separate from individuals, with its own mind, capable of giving orders to individuals' (Gorecki, *Sociology and Jurisprudence*, p. 36).

Russia while others, mainly religious people, reconciled themselves to the law by, like Soloviev, seeing in it a necessary 'minimum of morality'. Petrażycki, however, went much further: he considered law to be socially superior to morality, more important for the historical education of mankind. Such a view was shockingly unfamiliar in Russia. No wonder, therefore, that it evoked strong reactions—both for and against.

The strongest negative reaction, as was to be expected, came from Tolstoy. He was not directly acquainted with Petrażycki's books, but his famous 'Letter to a student concerning law', quoted above, was written in connection with Petrażycki's lectures. One of Petrażycki's students, I. Krutik, a follower of Tolstoy, was so impressed by Petrażycki's conception of law and morality that his Tolstoyan faith was shaken. Confused and hesitating, he decided to write to Tolstoy asking him for advice, both for himself and for his colleagues. Among other things, he wrote: 'I am standing on the verge of an abyss, because if Professor Petrażycki is right, I should break all threads which bind me to the teaching of Tolstoy.'[113]

Tolstoy's answer, analysed in the first chapter of this book, was merely a brilliant summary of his views on law and, therefore, completely missed the point as far as Petrażycki's theory was concerned. He concentrated on attacking law as an instrument of state coercion, apparently unaware that Petrażycki conceived of law in a completely different way. Yet Krutik was right that Petrażycki's views on morality and law were utterly incompatible with Tolstoy's teaching. We can agree with G. Radbruch who, in his *Rechtsphilosophie*, commented on this eposide as follows:

> ... it is no accident that the juridical approach is attacked in the very person of Petrażycki by Tolstoy in the last of his writings, when Tolstoy wants in a purely moral way to found all human relations upon the spontaneous overflowing fullness of love and not the compelling pressure of a claim.[114]

The most positive responses to Petrażycki's challenging conception were found, of course, among members of the Kadet party, deeply committed, as they were, to the idea of transforming Russia into a liberal *Rechtsstaat*. Very typical in this respect was B. Kistiakovsky, for

---

[113] Quoted in B. Eichenbaum's commentary on Tolstoy's 'Letter', in L. N. Tolstoy, *Polnoe sobranie sochinenii*, vol. 38, Moscow, 1936, p. 501.

[114] *Legal Philosophies*, p. 81. I have changed one word in this quotation, using 'moral' instead of 'ethical' (since 'ethical' in Petrażycki's terminology refers both to morality and law).

whom the chapter on morality and law was the best part of Petrażycki's *Theory of Law and the State*. Let us quote his words:

Pages devoted to this question are distinguished by an almost classical perfection. If, following the example of Justinian, new Pandects were to be compiled in our times from the fragments of modern juridical writings, these pages from Petrażycki's work should be given a place in them. At the same time, they should be included in every anthology of psychological and pedagogical literature.[115]

Petrażycki's conception of morality versus law was based, as already mentioned, upon the distinction between the purely imperative and imperative-attributive impulsions, with their respective norms. Moral impulsions are impulsions of duty—unilaterally binding, non-exigent, whereas legal impulsions are bilaterally binding, exigent, inseparably connecting duties with corresponding rights, obligations with claims. The classical example of the contrast between law and morality is provided by the famous words from the New Testament, so often quoted by Tolstoy: 'You have heard that it was said, "An eye for an eye and a tooth for a tooth". But I say to you, Do not resist injuries, but whoever strikes you on the right cheek, turn to him the other as well.' (Matth. 5:38–9). It meant: you have a duty to do good, you have a duty to refrain from doing evil, but you have no right to enforce upon others the same duties toward yourself. Moral consciousness, as epitomized in this passage, is therefore peaceful and undemanding while legal consciousness, by contrast, is demanding, militant, and vengeful, evoking powerful indignation when somebody's (not only one's own!) 'indubitable' and 'sacred' rights are contested or trampled underfoot.

In law, according to Petrażycki, the attributive function is of primary and decisive significance. Precisely because of it, law exerts a more powerful pressure on conduct than does the purely imperative moral consciousness. Active motivation, that is, motivation starting from awareness of our right (or the duty of another), is stronger and socially more 'educative' than passive motivation, starting from the pure consciousness of duty. It is the consciousness of one's own rights which makes one a citizen, feeling one's own worth; it has also a decisive influence on economic efficiency. It brings about visible, positive changes in man's deportment—'raised head, a resolute tone of voice, and so forth', and even some physical changes: 'the action of the

---

[115] B. A. Kistiakovsky, *Sotsial'nye nauki i pravo: ocherki po metodologii sotsial'nkh nauk i obshchei teorii prava*, Moscow, 1916, p. 285.

heart and lungs is heightened, the pulse strengthened, the flow of blood livelier, the breathing deeper'.[116] The pride of a citizen of ancient republican Rome—*Civis Romanus sum!*—was something diametrically different from and infinitely superior to the 'servile souls' (*anima servilis*) of the inhabitants of despotic countries. For the formation of strong character, law, with its exigent nature, is a better school than pure morality.

The consequence of education 'without law' is that there is neither firm ethical ground nor assurance against the temptations of life; and with special reference to the relationship to human personality—the personality of others and one's own—such upbringing naturally produces a 'slavish spirit' and a lack of respect for another's personality: despotism and stupid willfulness.[117]

It is law which

communicates the firmness and the confidence, the energy and initiative, essential for life. A child brought up in an atmosphere of arbitrary caprice (however beneficent and gracious), with no definite assignment to him of a particular sphere of rights (although of a modest and childish character), will not be trained to construct and carry out the plans of life with assurance. In the economic field, particularly, he will be deficient in confidence, boldness, and initiative: he will be apathetic, act at random, and procrastinate in the hope of favourable 'chances', help from another, alms, gifts, and the like.[118]

Let us now set out Petrażycki's conception in more detail. He discusses the differences between law and morality under the following headings.[119]

First, 'Fulfilment of the Requirements of Law and Morality'. Petrażycki summarized the respective differences as follows:

1. Law, in contrast to morality, allows the fulfilment of obligations by third parties. This is because morality is concerned with the duty of the obligor (with the 'salvation of his soul', as the Gospels put it), whereas law emphasizes the rights of the obligee.

2. Moral obligations, in contrast to legal ones, cannot be fulfilled by people representing the obligor, acting in his name; he must fulfil them himself.

3. Fulfilment of moral obligations must be voluntary, whereas the legal psyche is ready to resort to compulsion if a person's rights (that is, the duties toward him of somebody else) are not voluntarily observed.

4. For morality the intentions of the obligor are of decisive

[116] *Law and Morality*, p. 96.   [117] Ibid., p. 99.
[118] Ibid.   [119] Cf. ibid., pp. 100–37.

importance, whereas for law what matters is only the fulfilment of his duties; if a man fulfils his obligations unintentionally, by chance, absent-mindedly or mechanically, the moral duty is not fulfilled, but the legal duty is.

5. Finally, law, in contrast to morality, is indifferent to the motives behind the fulfilment of its requirements. Whether the obligor acts under compulsion, even whether he fulfils his duty from a wish to humiliate and destroy the obligee, is completely immaterial from the legal point of view. The same point was made, it may be remembered, by K. Aksakov, who stressed that even the most evil man could behave lawfully. However, the scope of this agreement was very limited and the conclusions very different: the Slavophile thinker concluded from this that the law was not interested in improving the inner quality of men, whereas Petrażycki, as we shall see, saw it as a powerful means of educating people, of raising them to a higher level of ethical development.

Second, 'Nonfulfilment of Moral and Legal Obligations'. The respective points are these:

1. In contrast to morality, law demands that the effectuation of a right be attained independently of the desire of the obligor.

2. The militant character of the legal psyche, as opposed to the peaceful character of morality. Legal consciousness reveals a 'repressive' tendency, in the sense that it tends toward the forcible securing of its 'just claims', and to repressive action in case of non-fulfilment.

Third, 'The Unifying Tendency of Law', with the following subdivisions:

1. The tendency to develop a single pattern of norms. This is most readily achieved through positive law, which explains why in law the positive element is more developed than in morality.

2. The tendency of legal concepts toward precision and exactness of content and scope. Morality, on the other hand, limits itself to pointing out the general trends of recommended conduct. There is also another side to this: legal duties are strictly limited while moral duties, in principle at least, are boundless.

3. The tendency of law to rely on relevant facts susceptible of verification and proof, a tendency 'completely foreign to morality in consequence of its purely imperative nature'.[120]

4. The tendency of law toward the unification of actual and specific legal relationships in order to avoid conflicts and the institution of the

---

[120] Ibid., p. 118.

court. In the case of a conflict, the legal psyche, in contradistinction to the moral psyche, feels the need to resort to third persons for a decision and this explains the genesis of courts.

Finally, the social function of law. Law, Petrażycki claimed, has a peculiarly significant *social* role to fulfil. Moral experiences, if strong, are individualistic and élitist, important mostly for the further self-perfection of the best, whereas 'legal experiences' are of decisive importance for the masses. Law is the main means of 'unconsciously successful *mass* psychic adaptation',[121] and, therefore, it is more important than morality from the point of view of historical progress. Its social function is twofold: (1) distributive and (2) organizational. First of all, however, it is law which generates co-ordinated social systems of conduct, differing from each other by the nature of the relevant rights and obligations and by the relative weight given either to the distributive, or to the organizational function of law. H. W. Babb summarized this part of Petrażycki's conception as follows:

> The laws or tendencies of the legal psyche and of its development result in a firm *coördinated system of social conduct evoked by law, a stable and precisely defined order*, with which separate individuals and masses can and should conform, on which we may rely and reckon, in the province of economic and other plans and enterprises and, in general, in organizing life. In the psyche of the public and of jurists is a firm association of the two ideas—'law' and 'order' (*Rechtsordnung*). Morality creates no coördination of conduct. Its motivation is unilateral, unstable, untrustworthy.[122]

What should be added, perhaps, to this otherwise excellent summary is Petrażycki's contention that every such system is psychologically possible only as long as the belief in its legitimacy continues to exist among the people benefited by it. The belief of the privileged upper classes in the legitimacy of their 'rights' was, in Petrażycki's eyes, more important for the functioning of a given social system than the corresponding belief in the legitimacy of their 'duties' among the exploited lower classes.[123] This was the logical consequence of the view that active ethical motivation (consciousness of right) is socially more important than passive ethical motivation (consciousness of duty).

Petrażycki's insistence on the value of the 'militant' character of the legal psyche brought him quite close, if only in this respect, to Rudolf

---

[121] Babb, 'Theory of Law', p. 556. [122] Ibid., p. 558.
[123] Cf. *Law and Morality*, p. 97.

Ihering—the legal theorist whom he otherwise so strongly disliked. In his famous little book *The Struggle for Law* (translated into Russian as early as 1874). Ihering proclaimed the principle that struggling for one's rights is a duty, and tolerating their violation is moral cowardice, indeed, in the case of total surrender, moral suicide.[124] Rights should be defended even at the cost of material interests becuse nothing less than the honour of their possessors is at stake. If an Englishman, a citizen of the country representing the highest level of legal culture, is being duped by innkeepers on the Continent, he is ready to fight for a few shillings, unlawfully demanded from him, with a manfulness which seems strange and laughable in the eyes of less litigious people. But, Ihering commented, it would be better if these people understood him: 'For, in the few shillings which the man here defends, Old England lives'.[125]

I. V. Hessen, the editor-in-chief of *Pravo*, wrote in his memoirs about the strong influence exerted by this part of Ihering's teaching on the Russian, populist-inspired revolutionary movement (in which he himself took part in his youth). According to him, the revolutionary populists who decided to fight not only for 'the welfare of the people' but also for political ends were inspired, among other things, by Ihering's maxim: 'By struggling shalt thou obtain thy rights'.[126]

It seems probable that Ihering's identification of the struggle for one's rights with the defence of one's 'honour' influenced Mikhailovsky's ideas about 'honour' and 'conscience'. A man of wounded conscience, Mikhailovsky argued, feels guilty in the sight of others, 'undeserving', whereas the man of wounded honour feels that he is 'deserving' and others are guilty toward him. In other words, 'conscience corresponds to the feeling of duty, honour to the feeling of having rights'.[127] Russian revolutionaries who took part in the 'going to the people' movement felt guilty in the sight of 'the people' and did not demand any rights for themselves; they even agreed to be flogged, because 'the peasants were also being flogged'.[128] However, by the end of the 1870s, this mood had changed; the members of the 'People's Will' decided to struggle not only because of their duty toward the peasants, but also in the name of their own 'honour'.

Using Petrażycki's terminology we can describe this change as a

---

[124] R. von Ihering, *The Struggle for Law*, pp. 30 and 32.   [125] Ibid., p. 66.
[126] I. V. Hessen, *V dvukh vekakh*, p. 47. Cf. Ihering, *The Struggle for Law*, p. 138.
[127] N. K. Mikhailovsky, *Sobranie sochinenii*, SPb 1896–7, vol. 5, p. 115.
[128] Ibid., vol. 4, p. 152.

shift from merely imperative moral consciousness to attributive legal consciousness. The attitude expressed in the quotation on flogging is a good illustration of what Petrażycki meant when he wrote that without an imperative-attributive foundation 'healthy ethics are lacking, and character is disfigured by deformities, some of which are repulsive'.[129]

In the Russian original these words were followed by a paragraph referring directly to Russia and, characteristically, omitted in the abridged English translation. It ran as follows:

> Society usually treats law as something inferior to morality, something less valuable, less respectable. There are even theories (like the teaching of Tolstoy, various anarchic doctrines, and so forth) which adopt an outright negative attitude toward the law. Such views, as we can see from the above, stem from a complete ignorance of the nature and significance of law and morality as the two branches of ethics.[130]

There can be no doubt that Petrażycki's views on law and morality were felt by his audience and by his readers as extremely relevant to Russian conditions. They were directed against the long-established Russian tradition of 'legal nihilism', still surviving dangerously in the extreme left-wing of the Russian revolutionary movement and in the Tsarist illusions of the masses (which could easily be transformed into uncritical acceptance of other kinds of arbitrary leadership) and directed also against the right-wing Slavophile myth claiming that legal guarantees were superfluous and even detrimental in Russia, in view of the 'humility' and other Christian virtues of the Russian people. Perhaps the most original aspect of Petrażycki's conception was his insistence that this notorious 'humility', so glorified by various Russian moral prophets, was no more than a rather repulsive symptom of the extreme underdevelopment of attributive ethics, of a legal mentality proudly aware of its subjective rights. In Russia, as Berdyaev put it, 'humility was the only form of inner discipline. It was better to indulge humbly in sinning than to perfect oneself proudly'.[131] Petrażycki fully realized that this 'slavish spirit', not yet eradicated in Russia, created psychic grounds for believing in force rather than in lawfulness and, thus, could only result either (usually) in blind obedience, or (occasionally) in desperate outbursts of anarchic rebellion. Prophetically, he pointed out the grave dangers involved in such an underdevelopment

[129] *Law and Morality*, p. 100.   [130] Petrażycki, *Teoriia prava*, vol. 1, pp. 146–7.
[131] N. A. Berdyaev, *Sud'ba Rossii: optyty po psikhologii voiny i natsional'nosti*, Moscow, 1918, p. 74.

of human dignity: tolerating (sometimes even enjoying) arbitrariness, lack of self-confidence or self-reliance, and economic inefficiency.

6   Social ideal and legal policy

Let us turn now to the 'teleological' part of Petrażycki's philosophy of law—to his ideas on 'legal policy'.

The first outline of Petrażycki's programme of a new science called 'legal policy' was elaborated, as mentioned earlier, in connection with discussions stirred up by the draft of a new civil code in Germany. It was published in an appendix to *Die Lehre vom Einkommen* (1895), reprinted later as a part of a larger work in Russian—*Introduction to the Science of Legal Policy*, which appeared, as a series of articles, in 1896–7. Thus Petrażycki's science of legal policy preceded, chronologically, his psychological theory of law: the latter was developed in order to provide legal policy with a solid theoretical foundation explaining law as a part of empirical reality, in terms of causal relations. In later years Petrażycki returned to the problems of legal policy in an important article entitled 'On the Social Ideal and the Revival of Natural Law';[132] this article, published in 1913 in connection with Novgorodtsev's study on the revival of natural law,[133] made it clear that scientific legal policy was Petrażycki's favourite idea not only at the beginning of his scholarly career but also later, after his psychological theory of law took final shape. If so, it is the more deplorable that none of Petrażycki's works devoted to legal policy exists in English; even his important Preface to the *Introduction to the Study of Law and Morality*, containing a good summary of the author's ideas on this subject, was omitted in the abridged English translation of this book.

The best presentation of Petrażycki's science of legal policy in English is still the study by H. W. Babb, unfortunately not easily available. It is much more detailed and much more systematic than later works which, sometimes, draw on it too extensively. Its content justifies the conclusion which reads: 'He [Petrażycki] has opened entirely new and original lines of investigation, to the end of creating a conscious legal policy (general, civil and criminal) *de lege ferenda*, the importance and necessity of which have been demonstrated in our own times more forcibly than ever before in history'.[134]

---

[132] Published in *Iuridicheskii vestnik*, vol. 2, 1913.
[133] P. Novgorodtsev, 'Sovremennoe polozhenie problemy estestvennogo prava', *Iuridicheskii vestnik*, vol. 1, 1913. (Cf. Ch. V. 2.)
[134] Babb, 'Science of Legal Policy', pp. 828–9.

From the point of view of philosophy of law—conceived as a part of philosophy—Petrażycki's essay 'Civil Policy and Political Economy' (the appendix to *Die Lehre vom Einkommen*) constituted a breakthrough. It should be remembered that it was a time when legal philosophy was completely eliminated by legal positivism, that is, by the historical and positive-dogmatic (doctrinal) study of existing laws. Any attempt to look for the 'right law', to philosophize about the extra-legal and supra-legal aims of law, to think in terms of 'what ought to be' (*Sollen*), and not only in terms of 'what is' (*Sein*) was rejected, in Germany at least, as a relapse into the errors of the natural law school, which seemed to be completely discredited and survived only among Catholic jurists.[135] According to G. Radbruch, 'the reëstablishment of legal philosophy, the restoration of an independent view of legal value beside the investigation of legal reality',[136] was due to the neo-Kantian thinker, Rudolf Stammler; and, be it added, after decades of inaction, Stammler was for a long time the only man who 'held the banner of legal philosophy aloft'.[137] Petrażycki, however, had some justification for claiming that the merit of re-establishing legal philosophy was also his. After all, together with Stammler, he was the first legal theorist writing in German who dared to proclaim the need for a return to the dualistic division of legal science into the science of existing positive law and the science of so-called natural (rational, philosophical) law, arguing that his own idea of legal policy was, in a sense, a 'revival of natural law'. This was, undeniably, an outspoken challenge to legal positivism and a call to philosophize about the 'ideal' of law.

Moreover, in his first works on legal policy, Petrażycki was fond of using Kantian terminology, sometimes flirting with it, as it were (which led some scholars to conclude, quite erroneously, that, like Stammler, he himself was a follower of Kant).[138] He defined the highest good, the highest criterion of moral and legal progress, as complete dominance of active love in social life, and emphasized that this was an 'axiom of practical reason'.[139] As such, it needs no proof nor even to be supported by reference to other values: every effort to prove the rightness of the ideal of love would be self-contradictory, assuming, as it were, that goodness is good not in itself but because of some other quality, like utility, and so forth. Ethics, Petrażycki insisted, is not a means to practical ends. Defining love as the *summum bonum* is, and

---

[135] Cf. E. Lask in *Legal Philosophies*, p. 7.
[136] Ibid., p. 68.   [137] Ibid., p. 48.   [138] See above, n. 74.
[139] L. Petrażycki, *Wstęp do nauki polityki prawa*, p. 25.

should remain, axiomatic. It would be disgraceful if it allowed of argument—just as disgraceful as to discuss a view that a piece of sausage is of more value than a beautiful symphony.[140]

Thus Petrażycki firmly defended the standpoint of ethical absolutism as far as the ultimate values were concerned. At the same time, as witnessed by his theory of progress, he was fully aware that concrete realizations of absolute values were time-bound, historically relative; in this sense he was certainly a historical relativist, but to ascribe to him 'a deep relativism' in ethics would have been utterly mistaken.[141] In fact, he was deeply concerned with the general relativization of values and tried to resist this process. A similar tendency, that is a tendency to vindicate some absolute standards while, at the same time, fully acknowledging the relativity of man's historical achievements and the impossibility of achieving an 'absolute' solution of contemporary problems, was manifested by Stammler. It was precisely this tendency which led both thinkers to revive the natural law point of view, while fully aware that there could be no return to the naïve rationalist standpoint of the seventeenth and eighteenth centuries. Both agreed that absolute values could not be embodied in a system of rationally deduced and allegedly immutable and perfect state-enacted laws; they therefore conceived of absolute standards as 'regulative ideas' or 'postulates of practical reason', that is they did not ascribe absolute value to anything historically given. There was a tension in their thinking between absolutism and relativism, sympathy for the natural law school of thought and acceptance of the discoveries of historicism and evolutionism. Stammler found a solution of this dilemma in his famous formula: 'Natural law with a changing content'.

Petrażycki, as already mentioned, attached much importance to being the first to express such ideas. He repeatedly pointed out that the appendix to his *Lehre vom Einkommen* was published before Stammler's book *Wirtschaft und Recht* (1896), in which the idea of a 'Wiedergeburt des Naturrechts' was set forth. He used to quote a paragraph from Stammler's book, suggesting the possibility that its main theme had already been voiced by another, and interpreted these words as referring to himself in reluctant acknowledgement of his priority. Whether he was right is difficult to say and, in view of the inevitable relativity of priority rights in the history of ideas, not of great concern.

---

[140] Ibid., p. 36.
[141] Such a mistake is to be found in Langrod, 'Polish Psychological Theory', p. 324.

Much more important is the relationship between the relevant ideas of the two thinkers.[142] In his *Recht der Schuldverhältnisse* (1897) Stammler quoted Petrażycki's definition of the 'social ideal' and conceded that it was analogous to his own idea of the final end of law and the state, defined as 'a community of men willing freely' (*Gemeinschaft frei wollender Menschen*). He explained that by 'men willing freely' he meant not the impossible freedom from causal laws, but moral freedom, freedom from subjective egoism, that is something very close to Petrażycki's 'love'. Petrażycki, however, was not satisfied and did not agree with this statement. He continued to accuse Stammler of plagiarizing his idea of a conscious legal policy, directed by a non-relative social ideal, but, at the same time, pointed out many important differences between Stammler and himself. His article 'On the Social Ideal' has been called, not unjustly, 'the most serious interpretation of Stammler's conception'.[143]

First, Petrażycki indicated, Stammler's ideal of a community of 'men of free-will' was too narrow, one-sidedly negative, too rational and thus unable to embrace the entire rich content of the ideal of 'active love'.

Secondly, Stammler wrote of mutual love among members of the same legal community (*der Zustand der Liebe der Rechtsgenossen zu einander auf*), whereas what was really important was universal love, knowing neither Greeks not Jews, as demanded by the Gospels. Mutual love limited to a given legal community, Petrażycki felt, was a peculiarly dangerous phenomenon, a breeding-ground for the most brutal national egoism; in this respect men were inferior to animals, because animals of the same species were not divided into separate communities, or, at least, did not make war on each other and kill each other. The great moral teachers of mankind—Christ and Buddha—had concentrated on preaching love of one's neighbour, but the ultimate ideal was to extend this love, to achieve a single love embracing all mankind.

Thirdly and finally, Stammler wrote of the dominance of love (equated with a lack of egoism) within a legal community which implied that legal order and a legal mentality would exist, and be

---

[142] Cf. M. Szyszkowska, *Neokantyzm. Filozofia społeczna wraz z filozofią prawa natury o zmiennej treści (Neo-Kantianism: Social Philosophy and Philosophy of Natural Law with a Changing Content)*, Warsaw, 1970, pp. 129–32.

[143] Ibid., p. 129.

needed, even at the highest stage of ethical progress. Petrażycki completely disagreed with this. His own vision of the social ideal was extra-legal and supra-legal, although the way to its realization was seen, above all, in progressive legal evolution. 'Love' was for him not only extra- and supra-legal, but extra- and supra-moral as well. Morality and law, Petrażycki explained, are symptoms of insufficient adaptation and, simultaneously, the means of achieving perfect adaptation, that is a state when moral and legal pressures would no longer be necessary. In other words, having fulfilled their tasks morality and law would wither away. They would live on in the memory of men only as a remembrance of barbaric times when human spontaneity had to be held in the grip of ethics.

Several comments are called for at this juncture.

What was the relationship between this ideal and Marx's and Engels's view of the future 'withering away of law'? According to Babb, the similarity was very superficial and insignificant. In Petrażycki's view, he pointed out, law will lose its reason for existence 'not in the sense of the Marx–Lenin dogma that Law (like the State) as a purely historical phenomenon and temporary instrument of class struggle or proletarian dictatorship will finally die out, and society operate by purely technical norms of expediency transformed into habit, but because the existence of law will then be psychologically inappropriate. This is not incompatible with the establishment of general plans of action and their voluntary fulfilment by all without any 'psychological pressures'. The ultimate goal of legal development is the inculcation of 'autonomous' social conduct (established by inner consciousness and will) so that society shall attain a harmonious condition of cooperation in social serving.[144]

We must agree with this: true, the differences were well marked and quite important. And yet, from a broader perspective, we can also see a similarity which should not be too easily dismissed. In both cases the vision of the 'withering away of law', together with the idea of a final aim and end of history, was a relic of millenarianism—a thoroughly secularized millenarianism, to be sure, but millenarianism none the less. Many great social doctrines and philosophies of history were permeated by some elements of millenarianism: in the case of Marxism such elements were often pointed out, in Petrażycki's case they should be recognized as well. He was as far removed as possible

---

[144] Babb, *Science of Legal Policy*, p. 810.

from that revolutionary impatience which is typical of many (though not all) forms of millenarian thinking, but he was unexpectedly close to millenarian hopes.[145] His vision of the final stage of the historical education of mankind resembled the millenarian 'Kingdom of God on earth'—a state of eternal bliss, a reign of grace and love.

Of course, the genesis of Petrażycki's ideal of love cannot be derived directly and exclusively from the millenarian tradition. Even less can it be explained by his alleged 'Russianness'. Yet such a claim has been made at least twice—by Novgorodtsev and, after him, by Timasheff. The latter wrote:

According to Petrażycki, 'active love' must guide the efforts of the legislator in his search for better law. This was a truly Russian version of the doctrine of progress, as well as an original expression of the then incipient movement aiming at the revival of natural law. Strangely enough, it was so uniquely Russian that Novgorodtseff, himself an enthusiastic adept of the natural law movement, called Petrażycki's version fantastic, sentimental, and almost unintelligible to a Westerner.[146]

It is clear what Novgorodtsev and Timasheff had in mind: the idea of Christian love, as opposed to the soulless formality of 'mere law', was well entrenched in nineteenth-century Russian intellectual history. They overlooked, however, Petrażycki's emphatic rejection of such a contrast; he embraced 'love' as the ultimate ideal while insisting that at any given stage of cultural development, whether in Russia or elsewhere, the first essential was education through law. Law was more important than morality, and 'love,' which was not only supra-legal but supra-moral as well, could replace law only in the remote future, when legal education would have fulfilled its mission. The gist of his legal policy was precisely the idea that the psychic pressure exerted by law could be decreased only when the psychic development of the people was sufficiently advanced and that this pressure should be progressively reduced in proportion to the successes achieved by law.

Curiously, the other fact overlooked in this case was the obvious one that adoption of the ideal of 'love', both as the highest criterion of legislation and as the ultimate end of social progress, was in itself

[145] For an analysis of the peaceful, 'gradualistic' type of millenarian thinking (in its religious form) see G. Shepperson, 'The Comparative Study of Millenarian Movements', in *Millennial Dreams in Action*, Sylvia L. Thrupp (ed.), The Hague, 1962.

[146] *Law and Morality*, p. xxiii. Timasheff refers to Novgorodtsev's article 'Über die eigentümlichen Elemente der russischen Rechtsphilosophie', *Philosophie und Recht*, vol. 2, p. 61.

nothing peculiarly Russian. In contradistinction to the above-mentioned Russian authors, Babb was fully aware of this. He wrote:

As early as 1692 Chr. Thomasius sought to put at the foundation of policy the principle of love (in Petrażycki's sense of love united with reason). Leibniz subordinated law and truth to the principle of love and asserted that truth is nothing but *caritas sapientis*. Comte put the principle that love is the highest criterion of social life at the foundation of his formula of practical positivism.[147]

For a more exact knowledge of Petrażycki's forerunners in this view of the final end of legal progress, two groups of thinkers, both inspired by millenarian ideas, should be added to this list: the French socialists of the early nineteenth century (Saint-Simonians and Fourierists, Buchez, Leroux) and the Polish Romantics, especially the philosopher August Cieszkowski and the great Messianic poets, Mickiewicz, Słowacki, and Krasiński.[148] One of the main ideas of all these thinkers was that Christ's mission had been limited, that He had influenced only relations between individuals, whereas the most important task of the future was to extend the reign of love to inter-group and international relations. This idea was close to Petrażycki's view of the limited character of Christ's real achievement and that of the other moral teachers of mankind. In view of the fact that every patriotic Polish family was steeped in the Polish Romantic tradition, and that a postulated 'ethicization of social and political relations' was central to this tradition, it might have been more appropriate to speak of a certain 'Polishness' of this particular aspect of Petrażycki's historical and ethical philosophy.

'Axiomatic' knowledge of the ultimate task of law was, in Petrażycki's eyes, only a part of the science of legal policy; another was empirical knowledge of the law, that is, knowledge of the nature of law as a reality and knowledge of the relations of 'cause and effect' governing the sphere of legal phenomena. Legal policy, he argued, should be able to foresee the effects of recommended legislation. The difference beween scientific and arbitrary legal policy consists precisely in the ability of the former to take into account actual conditions, such as the level of the average legal consciousness of the masses, and to make use of the laws of causality, thus avoiding unexpected and undesirable results. A truly scientific legal policy would make possible the replacement of laws developed through unconscious adaptation to

---

[147] Babb, 'Science of Legal Policy', pp. 813–14.
[148] Cf. Walicki, *Philosophy and Romantic Nationalism*, part III.

existing conditions by a deliberately directed legal progress, in fact by a conscious making of history. The same idea, as we know, was espoused by Marxists. The latter saw, as a necessary precondition of the conscious steering of history, a truly scientific knowledge of economic reality, of the existing level and general direction of economic development, whereas Petrażycki stressed the necessity of knowing the existing level and general direction of psychic development. This difference, important as it is, can be minimized and relativized if we realize that (1) Petrażycki's use of the term 'law' was much broader in scope than the Marxists', and (2) that law, for Petrażycki, was closely bound up with economics—so closely that, in most cases, they were two aspects of the same thing.

Another similarity between Petrażycki and Marxism—especially the moderate, social-democratic Marxism of the Second International—consisted in a common conviction that science can discover definite tendencies of progressive development and scientific policy should therefore renounce all attempts to change the direction of development and concentrate, instead, on accelerating its pace, removing obstacles, preventing malformations, anomalous changes, and so forth. Certainly Petrażycki referred only to 'developmental tendencies' and, unlike Plekhanov, was not committed to the idea of objective historical necessity. Nevertheless his attitude to these developmental tendencies closely resembled Plekhanov's, both in his positive recommendations and in his warnings against the disastrous effects of premature changes. He wanted 'to lead mankind consciously *in the same direction* which it had been following hitherto by means of unconscious, empirical adaptation, and thus to bring about quicker and more perfect progression toward the great radiant ideal of the future'.[149] Plekhanov could certainly subscribe to this view.

To sum up: Petrażycki firmly believed that there are two necessary conditions for success in the conscious realization of the final ideal, first, adherence to the general tendency of progressive development and secondly, the need to make one's goals dependent on the achieved level of development, to move forward 'through stages' and not try to accelerate progress too much, by omitting a necessary phase in the historical education of humanity. It should be added that the word 'necessary' means in this context not the impossibility of making such historical 'leaps' but a 'teleological' necessity, that of passing through

---

[149] Preface to *Introduction to the Study of Law and Morality*. Quoted from L. Petrażycki, *Wstęp*, p. 16.

phases in sequence if the desired ends are to be achieved. Belief in necessity conceived in this way—the necessity of gradualism in the process of adaptation—was derived by Petrażycki not from speculations about 'historical inevitability' but from empirical knowledge of the human psyche.

Petrażycki was very consistent in applying his ideas to political practice—even more consistent and logical than Plekhanov. The 'Father of Russian Marxism' came to the conclusion only at the end of his life, that it had been too early 'to begin the propaganda of Marxism in backward, semi-Asiatic Russia'.[150] In contrast to this, Petrażycki wholeheartedly supported the cause of liberalism in Russia, although liberalism as such was not his ideal. He is reported to have declared: 'In Germany I was an academic socialist (*Kathedersozialist*), in Russia I am a moderate liberal, and I see England as a country which is already ripe for socialism'.[151]

As we remember, Petrażycki himself pointed out that his psychological theory of law was compatible with Marxism and could even be made supplementary to Marxism. It seems more correct to say that a combination of historical materialism and psychologism was indeed possible, provided that the former was suitably reinterpreted. An interesting and very instructive attempt at constructing such a theory was made by an eminent Polish thinker (writing also in French), Edward Abramowski.[152] A brief outline of his main ideas may throw additional light upon the possible points of contact between Marxism and sociologically oriented 'psychologism' (including Petrażycki's variety of it).

Like Petrażycki, Abramowski wanted to apply to the social sciences the methodological principle of 'phenomenalism', that is of reducing the phenomena of social life to individual psychic experiences. The same principle, he thought, could be applied in a more up-to-date reinterpretation of Marxism. The unmystified content of historical materialism is the thesis that economic needs, which (according to Abramowski) are nothing more than a kind of psychic experience, determine man's productive capacities and undergo a process of objectification, giving birth to political institutions and social structures. The

---

[150] Quoted from A. Besançon, *The Intellectual Origins of Leninism*, Oxford, 1981, p. 186 (cf. E. Kuskova, 'Davno minuvshee', *Novyi zhurnal*, 56, 1958, p. 139).

[151] Reported by J. Finkelkraut.

[152] He was a theorist of what was known as 'stateless socialism' and of the Polish co-operative movement. At the beginning of his career he considered himself a Marxist.

so-called economic laws are therefore psychic in nature and depend on the psychic life of human individuals. To bring about a certain line of conduct, economic facts must first become part of human souls and produce corresponding changes in them; since such processes repeat themselves on a massive scale, they mould the average conscience of the masses and result in a corresponding mass behaviour. In Abramowski's eyes this was the real meaning of the Marxian view of economic changes as prime movers of history.

What Abramowski meant by the 'average conscience' of the masses was very close to Petrażycki's 'average resultant' of the processes of psychic adaptation. A further similarity between the two thinkers was a warning against premature, purely mechanical and external changes—against the creation of political institutions and economic structures which have no roots in human souls. The same attitude can readily be found in Plekhanov's condemnation of 'Jacobinism' and 'Blanquism', although, like other Marxists, he tended to think in terms of 'levels of economic development', leaving aside the problem of psychic development. Petrażycki and Abramowski, in their turn, emphasized the importance of the level of psychic development, and psychic preparedness for the desired changes. It seems clear, in retrospect, that there was much truth in their recommendations and warnings: there are very many countries in which revolutionary changes have proved to be a failure because of insufficient psychic adaptation of the masses. Abramowski is often too easily dismissed as a utopian prophet of 'moral revolution'; in fact, however, his preaching of 'moral revolution' was levelled against the dangers of utopian radicalism and its belief that radical reforms could be imposed on people 'from above', without considering the existing level of the national psyche. Like Petrażycki, Abramowski did not believe that 'normal progress' was guaranteed by historical necessity; he did not, for instance, exclude the possibility that a communist revolution might succeed in a country whose population was not prepared for it. He warned, however, that this would be a very dubious victory, that the communism established in such psychic conditions would be 'a social monster', worse than anything hitherto known in history.[153]

This attitude to social change was the only one which could be combined with Petrażycki's idea of a conscious and scientific legal policy. Rigid determinism, bound up with a belief in 'automatic

---

[153] E. Abramowski, *Filozofia społeczna* (*Social Philosophy*), Warsaw, 1965, p. 180.

progress', left too little room for conscious policy and in fact rendered it superfluous; on the other hand, 'voluntarism' (in the Marxist sense) neglected the causal laws governing social and psychic phenomena and thus left too much room for arbitrary decisions, for believing that 'everything is possible to us', that is, for a view which, in Petrażycki's (and Abramowski's) eyes, was not only deeply erroneous, but extremely dangerous as well.

In order to understand the theoretical framework of Petrażycki's legal policy it is necessary to return to the problem of the species of law. To the division of law into intuitive and positive, cutting across the distinction between official and unofficial law, we should add the division of law into public and private. Unlike the legal positivists, Petrażycki saw this division as of fundamental importance; he did not hesitate to call it 'the highest division of law and jurisprudence'.[154]

In thus dividing law into public and private Petrażycki formally followed the well-known definitions of Roman jurists. In fact, however, he was constructing new notions, or, rather, a new typology. Significantly enough, in this case he abandoned his favourite method of logical classification, striving instead, like Ferdinand Tönnies or Max Weber, to create typological concepts, having both a synchronic and a diachronic dimension. In the synchronic dimension private and public law, in Petrażycki's view, corresponded to 'two types of the action of the legal mentality upon human conduct';[155] in the diachronic dimension they corresponded to two different phases of historical progress.

For an easier understanding of this twofold typology it seems better to begin from its historical aspects. There are, Petrażycki asserted, two basic types of socio-economic and legal systems. The first is based upon (a) the obligation of all able-bodied members of a social group to contribute to the common welfare, and (b) the right of each member of the group to subsistence and to the satisfaction of his other needs by sharing in the collectively produced common property. Following Morgan, and the Marxist writers influenced by him, Petrażycki believed that such a system appears both at the earliest and at the latest stage of the historical cycle, both in the primitive tribal society and in the socialist system which he saw as the legitimate successor of capitalism.

[154] *Law and Morality*, p. 298. A separate chapter on public and private law was added by Petrażycki to the 2nd edition of his *Theory of Law and the State*.
[155] Ibid., p. 299.

The other system—the 'individualistic system'—was fully developed in ancient Rome and reappeared in modern Europe. Its essential features were reduced by Petrażycki to four points:[156] (1) the private ownership of the means of production, understood as absolute property, that is, *jus utendi et abutendi*, (2) the inalienable law of inheritance, (3) the responsibility for bringing up children resting with the parents, and not the social group, and (4) the absence of obligatory productive tasks and the recognition of relationships based upon free contracts and the sanctity of the principle *pacta sunt servanda*.

Needless to say, in this typology private law was seen as flourishing, in its most classical form, in the individualistic, decentralized system, whereas public law, although also existing in the individualistic system, was to reach its full development, and to swallow private law, in the centralized, socialist system of the future. When these divisions coexist, as they do in individualistic systems, they can be defined and separated by means of logical classification. Petrażycki did not question such logical distinctions; he felt a need, however, to build upon them a classification (or, rather, a typology) of law which would be 'independent from terminological habits and other traditions'[157] and which would apply not to different laws within one legal system, but to different legal systems, defining the nature of each in accordance with the role played in it by the general principles of public and private law. He defined the general principle of private law as 'individual (free) law' while the opposite principle of public law was 'the law of social service'.

There is no need, in the present context, to dwell upon the details of Petrażycki's elaborate conception of the differences and mutual relationship between private and public law. Let us concentrate instead on the relevance of this 'highest division of law' for collective 'education through law' and, by the same token, for legal policy.

Petrażycki's main assumption was that legal policy must be consistent with the nature of the legal system which it wants to improve (except in cases of revolutionary legislation). In the individualistic system dominated by private law, in which public law has its own, separate and strictly limited sphere, the basic motivation of human conduct is ego-altruistic, or 'ego-family-centric'.[158] In such a system the most valuable pedagogic function of law is to promote a love of labour, economic efficiency, thrift, self-reliance combined with due

[156] Ibid., pp. 304–5.　　[157] Ibid., pp. 312–13.
[158] Cf. Babb, 'Science of Legal Policy', 816 n.

care for one's family (an 'altruistic' motive), individual initiative and responsibility, and so forth; in other words, law should promote those qualities of character which are necessary for a good head of a family, *bonus pater familias* in the language of Roman jurists.[159] This was precisely the pedagogic function of private law, although its wisdom in this respect was usually naïve and unconscious; the same pedagogic function would be performed by conscious civil policy in the countries which still remain at the 'individualistic' stage of development.

It is worth noting that Petrażycki's conception of ego-altruistic motivation was levelled against the view, so often embraced by simple-minded socialists, according to which motives of conduct in a free market economy could be reduced to pure egoism. If it were so, Petrażycki observed, everybody would behave in accordance with the saying 'après moi la déluge', the social system would lack the necessary stability and long-term national education through law would hardly be possible. In fact the puritan virtues, so essential for a successful capitalist development, represented a combination of self-reliant individualism with a deep attachment to family values, even a severe patriarchal authoritarianism. Contemporary legal policy, in Petrażycki's view, ought of course to break with this puritan severity (especially in the field of criminal law), but should not encourage a lack of care for the fate of one's progeny. It should for instance respect the law of inheritance and not try to limit the respective rights of partners and children.

Each global legal system was conceived by Petrażycki as a dynamic structure, that is as a system developing historically, having both an inner structural-functional logic and a developmental logic as well.[160] Progress toward the better socialization of men—in accordance with the aforementioned general tendencies—was seen, therefore, as possible within each of these systems. Within the framework of an individualistic system such progress was evident in growing public control over private property and private contracts, and in the increase of state intervention, in other words, in a broadening of the sphere of public law and in the growing importance of the ethos of social service bound up with it.

Petrażycki's image of socialism had nothing in common with the dreams of Herzen, Mikhailovsky, and Lavrov, for whom socialism was

---

[159] *Law and Morality*, p. 309.
[160] Cf. H. M. Johnson, 'Petrażycki's Sociology in the Perspective of Structural-Functional Theory', in Gorecki, *Sociology and Jurisprudence*.

to be a free federation of self-governing communes. He conceived of socialism as a 'centralized regime of production', in which 'there would be none of free of independent legal motivation of an ego-altruistic character'.[161] There would be 'a single general economy with a single complex organization, a single plan, guidance and management, a single guiding and directing centre, and a complex and numerous hierarchy of subordinate organs'.[162] People's conduct would be directed by two kinds of motivation: (1) by immediate legal motivation, that is, by a legal duty of social service, and (2) by auxiliary economic motivation, striving for the satisfaction of economic needs (differing from economic motivation in the individualistic system because bereft both of its centrality for human conduct and of its independent character). Economic motivation would be especially important in the lower stages of socialist development.

It certainly was not a very attractive vision. It should be remembered, however, that for Petrażycki socialism was not the embodiment of the social ideal but merely a further step toward it. His ideal was a reign of love incompatible with law, whereas socialism was, in his eyes, a very rigid legal system. A system, be it added, whose virtue consisted in inculcating the national psyche with the ethos and discipline of social service, thus paving the way for complete freedom from legal pressure.

As far as his final ideal was concerned, Petrażycki undeniably belonged to the utopian visionaries in the field of the social sciences. At the same time, however, he was very sober-minded and utterly devoid of utopian illusions in his view of human nature and in his conception of legal policy. He accepted the desirability of socialism but he was as far as possible from believing that the adaptation of the human psyche to the requirements of a socialist order would be a quick and easy process. A particularly good illustration of this was his view of the relationship between socialism and social equality. He wrote about it as follows:

. . . the usual combination of the idea of social equality with the ideas and aspirations of socialism is a misunderstanding since it assumes such perfection of character in the national masses that the presence of law suffices, without sanctions of any kind, for the relevant legal order to operate successfully, and presupposes that merely pointing out to each his obligations, distributing work, and so forth will suffice to cause all—or almost all—to manifest the corresponding zeal and industry; that everybody will work conscientiously and

---

[161] *Law and Morality*, p. 311.   [162] Ibid., p. 310.

energetically, although laziness, carelessness, egoism, or, even, dishonest and cynical attitudes towards social interests are not punished and energetic, diligent and highly useful work is not well rewarded. If such a high level of the development of national psyche is not yet achieved, associating, or identifying, of socialism with the idea of social equality is a grave psychological and legal mistake . . . Social inequality is a legal correlate of social imperfection, of the insufficiently high cultural level of the masses.[163]

This was in accordance with the general rule of Petrażycki's legal policy, which proclaimed that further steps in progressive education through law may only be made if earlier lessons have been learned and not forgotten. It followed from this that socialism should not be introduced until the masses of a given country and thoroughly assimilated the results of legal education in the individualistic system. In view of Petrażycki's pessimistic assessment of the existing level of legal culture in Russia, it is only too obvious that attempts to build socialism on the ruins of the Russian monarchy were, in his eyes, 'psychologically and legally mistaken', inviting a historical disaster.

7   *The reception of Petrażycki's thought*

Petrażycki's contemporaries had no doubts that he was one of the major figures in Russian social science. They were not sure, however, where to place his ideas in the intellectual history of the Russian intelligentsia or even whether he deserved such a place at all. Perhaps he was too narrowly academic, too 'professorial', detached from the topical problems of the day?

I have tried to show that this was not so, although this is not to deny that his works were rather difficult and their deep relevance to topical Russian problems was not easy to grasp. A negative factor in addition was his imperfect command of Russian: Petrażycki could neither speak nor write in a smooth, 'elegant' way, although he was in love with everything 'elegant' and the adjective 'elegant' was one of his favourite words.[164] But this circumstance, important as it was for some people, cannot be treated as a sufficient reason.

A more adequate explanation may be derived from an analysis of the relevant paragraph in Ivanov-Razumnik's *History of Russian Social Thought*. The young author came across Petrażycki's ideas, dimly realized their importance, mentioned Petrażycki's name but finally

---

[163] Cf. ibid., p. 311. In the Russian original the quoted footnote is longer than in *Law and Morality*.
[164] See I. V. Hessen, *V dvukh vekakh*, p. 156.

decided to dismiss him in two phrases and to dwell, instead, on the ideas of Novgorodtsev (although the latter could also be seen as a purely academic figure). The reasons for such a decision were understandable although the decision itself was, I think, unjust and too easily taken.

Petrażycki's importance for the general intellectual history of Russia was seen by Ivanov-Razumnik to be in the fact that, together with Novgorodtsev, he was the first Russian scholar to put forward the idea of a 'revival of natural law' and thus legitimize the dualism between _Sein_ and _Sollen_. In Ivanov-Razumnik's eyes this was an original contribution to the typically Russian debate between 'subjectivists', thinking in terms of 'what ought to be', and 'objectivists', preaching that the individual should 'humble himself before the objective course of events'; a debate which can be traced back to Belinsky's 'reconciliation with reality' and which, quite recently, culminated in the controversy between Populists and Marxists. For Ivanov-Razumnik —a neo-Populist who sympathized with 'subjective sociology' but was aware of the need to give it a more modern foundation—the vindication of natural law was welcome as an antidote to historicism, positivistic evolutionism, and the Marxist concept of historical necessity; in his view this was the only link between Petrażycki's thought and the mainstream of Russian thought. The neo-Kantians, as represented by Novgorodtsev, seemed to him much more important; they were part of a broad neo-idealist movement of thought, their dualism between facts and values could be seen (despite their intentions) as a rehabilitation of the main idea of 'subjective sociology', and their insistence on the trans-empirical value of personality was, undoubtedly, a new way of defending the 'personality principle', so dear to people claiming to be the heirs of Herzen, Mikhailovsky, and Lavrov. By contrast, Petrażycki's psychological theory of law seemed dry and abstract. Ivanov-Razumnik therefore decided that 'the latter [Petrażycki] represents the standpoint of psychological individualism and not the standpoint of critical philosophy and ethical individualism; because of this we shall omit his otherwise interesting theory'.[165]

Characteristically, it did not occur to Ivanov-Razumnik that Petrażycki's significance for the history of Russian thought might lie elsewhere, in his struggle to implant legal culture in Russia, in his defence of the idea that law is prior to the state and not _vice versa_ and in

[165] Ivanov-Razumnik, _Istoriia russkoi obshchestvennoi mysli_, 2nd edn., SPb 1908, vol. 2, p. 476.

his stubborn opposition to legal positivism, which identified the
Rechtsstaat with any state which observed its own laws.

The reception of Petrażycki's thought among pre-revolutionary
Russian jurists may be described as of three kinds: (1) its strongly
critical, sometimes utterly negative reception by representatives of a
narrowly conceived jurisprudence, adhering mostly to legal positivism,
(2) its somewhat ambiguous reception by representatives of an
idealistic legal philosophy and (3) its influence on his disciples,
sociologists as well as jurists.

The first category does not fall within the scope of this book; the
reaction to Petrażycki's thought among professional representatives of
'lawyers' law' was understandably purely defensive and quite without
interest in a broadly conceived history of ideas. The second category
has already been mentioned in connection with reviews of Petrażycki's
Essays on Legal Philosophy by Chicherin and Trubetskoi. However,
Chicherin's views on Petrażycki's legal philosophy deserve a closer
examination.

In spite of his endorsement of Petrażycki's criticism of Ihering,
Chicherin saw both Ihering and Petrażycki as representative of the
crisis in legal ideas, expressing in their theories two different variants
of the 'obfuscated legal consciousness'.[166] In fact he found a common
denominator between Ihering's view of law as 'defended interest' and
Petrażycki's treatment of law as an instrument of social policy: in both
he saw an attempt to link law to aims and thus a complete
misunderstanding of the aim-independent, 'purposeless', negative
nature of legal rules. He accused Ihering of a tendency to subordinate
law to the egoistic interests of the stronger side while in Petrażycki he
recognized the danger of that altruistic utopianism which sees the
ultimate taste of law as bringing about the perfect socialization of men
in the kingdom of 'active love'. Thus both thinkers undermined the
classical liberal view that law should be concerned not with aims,
whether utilitarian or moral, but with freedom. Petrażycki's image of
law was loftier than Ihering's but, none the less, equally distorted and
dangerous. Freedom, Chicherin maintained, is incompatible with the
legal (that is coercive) imposition of social goals; to treat law as a means
for the realization of the ideal of 'active love' would destroy freedom
without serving the cause of 'love', since legal coercion cannot teach
people to love one another and subordinate their private aims to the
public good.[167]

---

[166] See B. Chicherin, *Filosofiia prava*, Moscow, 1900, pp. 4, 127.   [167] Ibid., p. 209.

Chicherin's fears about Petrażycki's idea of 'legal policy' found spectacular confirmation in the latter's view of the socio-economic and legal system of the future, in which economic relations would be regulated by public law and, in addition, subject to a single directing centre. In Chicherin's eyes this commitment to socialism, even though stressing that its realization lay in some distant time, was incompatible with a proper understanding of the nature of law. Petrażycki's vision of a social ideal, he argued, represented 'a completely distorted view of all economic and juridical ideas', a view stemming from a confusion of society and the state, and leading to the replacement of a free interaction of individuals by a hierarchical organizational order.[168] In such a system there was no place for law properly conceived, since law by its very nature was inseparable from individual freedom. Petrażycki's endorsement of the ideal of the 'withering away of law' was therefore entirely consistent.

Other representatives of the idealistic school in legal philosophy softened this harsh verdict. This was especially true of Bogdan Kistiakovsky and Sergius Hessen, the two theorists of rule-of-law socialism. Their attempts to reconcile the growing socialization of the economy with a liberal conception of law as the guardian of individual autonomy can be seen as mediating between Chicherin's defence of individual freedom and Petrażycki's view of law as an instrument of social policy. As we shall see,[169] both paid much attention to Petrażycki's thought, stressing its importance in the struggle against legal positivism, while at the same time trying to overcome its one-sidedness and presenting it as a phase, or aspect, of a continuous liberal tradition in searching for the true meaning of the rule of law.[170]

Paul Novgorodtsev, a neo-Kantian who saw himself as the main theorist of the 'New Liberalism' in Russia, was even more ambiguous in his assessment of Petrażycki's ideas. His so-called 'Moscow school' of legal philosophy became, indeed, the main rival of Petrażycki's 'Petersburg school'.

At the beginning, however, Novgorodtsev's attitude towards Petrażycki was very positive: he emphasized Petrażycki's great merits and sought support for his own views in Petrażycki's works. In his article 'Ethical

---

[168] Ibid., pp. 265–6.   [169] See below, Ch. VI, 3 and Ch. VII, 6.

[170] At the same time Kistiakovsky made it clear that this view was not shared by Petrażycki, who was inclined to see himself as 'beginning everything anew' and therefore deserved to be accused of a nihilistic attitude towards existing traditions in legal philosophy. See B. Kistiakovsky, *Sotsial'nye nauki i pravo*, Moscow, 1916, p. 266.

Idealism in Legal Philosophy' (1903) he referred to Petrażycki's *Introduction to the Science of Legal Policy* and credited him with being the first to rehabilitate natural law. He fully agreed with Petrażycki in rejecting such dominant standpoints in contemporary legal philosophy as the positivist identification of law with commands backed by the force of the state or Ihering's utilitarian theory defining laws as 'defended interests'. He also shared Petrażycki's relatively high estimate of the purely analytical study of law (*Begriffsjurisprudenz*), seeing it as an attempt to interpret law as a logically coherent system of norms and not merely a convenient instrument of the powerful. Conceptual jurisprudence was for him the first stage in the development of the normative principle in law, the second stage of which he saw in Petrażycki's empirical analysis of the psychic content of law. The next stage, he held, should be to pass from Petrażycki's psychologism to an 'ethical theory of law', based upon philosophical idealism.[171]

In later years, naturally enough, what the two theorists had in common came to be felt as less important than the differences dividing them. In an article published in 1913 under the title 'Contemporary State of the Problem of Natural Law' Novgorodtsev conceded that the merit of proclaiming the need for a revival of natural law belonged to Stammler and Petrażycki; at the same time he tried to show that neither had in fact succeeded in reviving natural law properly conceived. Stammler's conception of 'natural law with a changing content' was self-contradictory; Petrażycki, on the other hand, referred to natural law only in connection with his idea of legal policy. In addition, he then happened upon the psychological theory of law and devoted all his energy to its development. Thus, by implication, the real merit of reviving the idea of natural law in Russia belonged to the author and to the Moscow school centred on him. To dispel all possible doubt Novgorodtsev hastened to declare that his own early defence of natural law had not been inspired either by Petrażycki or Stammler, and that in his later works he went his own way and never agreed with Petrażycki's conclusions.

Petrażycki's answer to this article was his study 'On the Social Ideal', explaining the relationship between the idea of natural law and the science of legal policy. It contained no comment on Novgorodtsev's possible indebtedness to the author; although, as we have seen it

[171] P. Novgorodtsev, 'Nravstvennyi idealizm v filosofii prava', in *Problemy idealizma*. P. Novgorodtsev (ed.), Moscow, 1903, p. 280.

devoted much attention to Stammler, who was accused of plagiarism and distortion of the author's ideas.

Novgorodtsev, in his turn, published an important article entitled 'The Psychological Theory of Law and the Philosophy of Natural Law'.[172] While complimenting his colleague and rival, he made it clear that what divided them was of fundamental importance: legal science should be normative, and not causal, transempirical, and not empirical; 'the philosophy of natural law is a deontological, not a causal science'.[173] By this statement he completely ignored Petrażycki's distinction between a psychological theory of law, which should be empirical, and a knowledge of the social ideal, which should be 'axiomatic' and not derived from empirical facts. He categorically denied not only Stammler's indebtedness to Petrażycki but even the existence of any important link between the two theories. In addition he tried to show that Petrażycki's theories were methodologically old-fashioned, inspired by early positivism, especially the ideas of Comte, whom Petrażycki resembled in combining a cult of the natural sciences with sentimentality and chiliastic dreams.[174]

In the same year and in the same periodical appeared a whole series of articles severely criticizing Petrażycki.[175] He saw this as a campaign deliberately organized against him by the Moscow school and reacted by himself developing an anti-Kantian obsession. In order to undermine the philosophical foundations of the Moscow school of jurists he embarked on a study of Kant, finally coming to rather strange conclusions: the great sage of Königsberg became in his eyes a second-rate thinker, even a shameless plagiarist, stealing ideas from Maupertuis and from an unjustly forgotten J. N. Tetens.[176]

---

[172] P. Novgorodtsev, 'Psikhologicheskaia teoriia prava i filosofiia estestvennogo prava', *Iuridicheskii vestnik*, vol. 3, 1913.

[173] In Russian: 'Filosofiia estestvennogo prava est' nauka dolzhnykh otnoshenii, a ne prichinnykh sviazei' (ibid., p. 15).

[174] Ibid., pp. 23–4.

[175] Such as E. V. Spektorsky, 'Filosofiia i iurisprudentsiia' (vol. 2) and N. N. Alekseev, 'Osnovnye filosofskie predposylki psikhologicheskoi teorii prava L. I. Petrazhitskogo' (vol. 4). Kistiakovsky's programmatic article 'Nashi zadachi' (vol. 1) also contained a polemic against Petrażycki's views.

[176] What remains of Petrażycki's long manuscript in Russian, devoted to the fight against Kantianism, was published in Polish by J. Finkelkraut. See L. Petrażycki, *Szkice filozoficzne* (*Philosophical Essays*), Warsaw, 1939. According to the editor, Petrażycki wanted to publish this book in Germany. He also wanted to publish, in Petersburg, a special juridical journal in German, propagating an empirical approach in the social sciences and combating neo-Kantianism, including the Moscow school of philosophy of law. None of these plans materialized, because of war and revolution.

Let us turn now to Petrażycki's disciples representing the 'Petersburg school' in Russian legal philosophy. They can be divided into two groups: the one developing (in different directions) Petrażycki's ideas on intuitive law, the other concentrating on the sociology of law, particularly problems of cultural selection.

The main contribution of Max M. Laserson was the division of intuitive law into two branches: (1) individually adapted intuitive law, and (2) socially adapted intuitive law, which, for ideological reasons, has usually been termed natural or inborn law. Individually adapted intuitive law undergoes a process of socialization and socially adapted intuitive law, in its turn, sooner or later becomes positive law. Each stage of this process corresponds to a certain level in the increasing motivation of conduct: the lowest level is represented by individually variable intuitive law, a much higher level of motivating power is held by socially adapted intuitive law and the highest degree of all is attained in positive law—on condition that its content coincides with the dominant legal consciousness, that is, with socially adapted intuitive law.[177]

Laserson believed that his distinction between the two kinds of intuitive law was made 'in clear contrast to Petrażycki';[178] in fact, however, Petrażycki was perfectly aware that individual intuitive law usually (though not always, as, for example, in the case of a madman) stems from psychic adaptation to socially typical conditions and is transformed into the intuitive legal consciousness of the masses—he only omitted to introduce the appropriate terminology. It seems fair to say that the whole of Laserson's theory was contained in Petrażycki's works and that Laserson's own contribution lay mainly in presenting the relevant views of his teacher in a more systematic, better articulated way.

Another of Petrażycki's disciples, the well-known sociologist of law Georges Gurvitch, interpreted his teacher's theories in the spirit of the German school of 'free law' (*Freirecht*) and, at the same time, in accordance with the French legal theorists (F. Gény, F. Lambert, and the theorist of syndicalism Maxime Leroy) who championed the cause

For an analysis of Petrażycki's *Philosophical Essays* see A. L. Zachariasz, 'Leona Petrażyckiego krytyka filozofii transcendentalnej I. Kanta', in *Studia filozoficzne*, no. 5, Warsaw, 1981.

[177] For a good summary of Laserson's view see his article 'Positive and "Natural" Law and their Correlation', in Sayre, *Interpretations*, pp. 434 ff.

[178] See *Twentieth-Century Sociology* (as above, n. 90), p. 675 (chapter on Russian sociology by Laserson).

of a 'spontaneous, living social law', as opposed to a rigid and formal state law. He saw in Petrażycki's theory of intuitive law powerful support for these two movements and indicated, among other things, that E. Jung, one of the theorists of 'free law', was directly influenced by Petrażycki's ideas (the fact that Petrażycki himself did not sympathize with the 'free law' movement was passed over in silence).[179] He did much to popularize Petrażycki's theory of intuitive law in France and, having modified it in some points, made it part of his own legal philosophy. His main modification consisted in denying that intuitive law, as opposed to positive law, could be defined as 'autonomous'.[180] According to Gurvitch, every law is 'positive' in Petrażycki's sense, that is, it refers to a 'normative fact'; the distinctive feature of intuitive law is not its alleged autonomy but its mode of existence as something 'immediately given'. For the opposition between intuitive and positive law, therefore, should be substituted the distinction between intuitive law on the one hand, and the formal law of the state on the other.

On the occasion of Petrażycki's death Gurvitch published an article in French entitled 'Une philosophie intuiviste du droit'. In it he tried to show that Petrażycki, whom he called 'le plus grande philosophe du droit contemporain de Russie et de Pologne',[181] was a staunch opponent not only of legal positivism but also of philosophical positivism. Petrażycki, he argued, tried to overcome the opposition between empiricism and spiritualism by creating an experimental metaphysics based upon the immediate data of intuition; in doing this he unknowingly paralleled the similar efforts by Bergson and the German phenomenologists—Husserl and Scheler.[182] Petrażycki's psychology, according to Gurvitch, could be defined as a psychology 'compréhensive de sens métaphysique' or, in German, as 'verstehende, sinndeutende Psychologie'.[183] Petrażycki's ideal of rational love, already propounded in his early German works, made it clear that, like Scheler, he in fact believed in objective, absolute values and that,

---

[179] G. Gurvitch, *Le Temps présent et l'idée du droit social*. Preface de Maxime Leroy, Paris, 1931, p. 279. (Chapter entitled: 'La théorie du "droit intuitif" et de la multiplicité infinie des sources du droit positif du savant russe Léon Petrasizky'.) See also Gurvitch's article in Russian (referred to in n. 62) and his study 'Une philosophie intuitiviste du droit', *Archives de philosophie de droit*, 1931, pp. 403 ff.

[180] Ibid., pp. 291–3.

[181] G. Gurvitch, 'Une philosophie intuitionniste du droit', *Archives de philosophie de droit*, 1931, p. 403.

[182] Ibid., p. 404.　　　　[183] Ibid., p. 407.

therefore, his apparent 'subjectivism' was not consistent with the deepest, although not fully realized, meaning of his thought.[184] The most interesting aspect of the reception of Petrażycki's theory of intuitive law was undoubtedly its reinterpretation from a Marxist standpoint. This was done by M. A. Reisner (or Reussner) who in 1908 published in Petersburg a booklet entitled *The Theory of Petrażycki: Marxism and Social Ideology*.[185]

In contrast to other Marxists who, in the spirit of legal positivism, saw law as merely an instrument of the coercive power of the state and, therefore, emphasized the idea of the 'withering away of state and law', Reisner, a staunch opponent of legal positivism, treated law as an important part of social ideology, having its roots in the psychology of class and serving the aims of the class struggle. He therefore insisted on the necessity of fighting against the bourgeois legal consciousness and replacing it by the legal consciousness of the working class. Petrażycki's theory of intuitive law was in his eyes a good explanation for the emergence of a proletarian legal consciousness under the class rule of the bourgeoisie and, by the same token, a 'legal' justification for social revolution. He stressed, of course, the necessity of combining Petrażycki's theory with Marxian teaching about the class nature of all kinds of ideological superstructure, a mission he himself undertook. He was not inclined to belittle this task and consequently claimed the merit of having overcome the alleged 'individualism' of Petrażycki's doctrine, a merit more relative than he was ready to concede. It is necessary to remind ourselves at this juncture that Petrażycki himself at times came very close to the Marxist thesis about the class nature of consciousness, including legal consciousness; he pointed out, for instance, that differences in understanding what law is depend on differences in class position and that ideas of justice 'possess a different content in different classes of society'.[186] He usually referred to 'different classes of people', an ambiguous expression, but he in fact meant social classes. This is evident, for instance, from the following paragraph:

[184] Ibid., p. 408. Gurvitch quoted with approval Petrażycki's criticism of German jurists who 'have forgotten that after the Roman law the Gospel of love had appeared' (*Die Lehre vom Einkommen*, part I, p. 340) and Petrażycki's statement that 'the entire human civilization in its positive achievements is a crystallization of love' (ibid., part II, p. 477; cf. Gurvitch, 'Une philosophie intuitionniste du droit', pp. 404–5).

[185] English translation in *Soviet Legal Philosophy*. H. W. Babb (trans.), Cambridge, Mass., 1951.

[186] Cf. *Law and Morality*, p. 245 (translation corrected).

They [differences in law as a psychic phenomenon] may be connected with the class structure of a population—the typical domestic law prevailing in the well-to-do and rich strata is distinguished from the same law in the spheres of those who are not well-to-do and of proletarians, while the typical domestic law of the peasants is different from that of the businessman and the aristocrat.[187]

As a Marxist, Reisner was naturally eager to find materialistic elements in Petrażycki's thought. He was, therefore, prone to discover similarities between Petrażycki's views and the ideas of Ludwig Knapp, a German materialist disciple of Feuerbach who had developed a psycho-physiological theory of legal consciousness.[188] In the entire literature devoted to Petrażycki's legacy the only scholar to comment on this is H. W. Babb. His reaction, sharply negative, is expressed as follows:

It seems a downright cruelty on the part of Professor Reisner to have disinterred Knapp of Erlangen, a 'long forgotten materialist and pupil of Feuerbach', and to charge him with having, more than fifty years ago, 'made an attempt analogous to that of Petrażycki to reform jurisprudence and to destroy the old juridic phantasmata which choked the bright and conscious development of law'. This method of legal philosophy is said to have included the examination of the psychological tendencies necessarily inherent in the psychological origin of law and creating legal phantasms (the chief of them being the acknowledgment of superhuman legal imperatives). As a matter of fact there is no true analogy of principle in the two theories. Knapp's reappraisal of legal ideology is based on the old materialistic understanding of human nature, then fashionable, which sought to reduce all spiritual activity of man to simple physiological functions, whereas Petrażycki created an entirely new and independent discipline, as the cornerstone for the entire structure of the psychological theory of law and emotional sociology. The only similarities between them are that they use some words in common (e.g. 'motor' and 'muscular stimuli') and have a dual system of ethics ('renunciation' and 'demand' in Knapp, 'imperative' and 'attributive' in Petrażycki). Both speak of phantasms, but Knapp does not mean thereby emotional projections, as Petrażycki does, but everything immaterial (that is, not muscular). For Petrażycki law is certainly not Knapp's physiology of organs of thinking. For Petrażycki law is generally distinct in principle from constraint as such. Knapp has the physiological point of view of a materialist. Petrażycki's point of view is pure psychologism.[189]

[187] Ibid., p. 68.
[188] See *Soviet Legal Philosophy*, pp. 76–80.
[189] Babb, 'Theory of Law', pp. 571–2.

There is much truth in these remarks, but the similarities between Petrażycki and Knapp cannot easily be dismissed. If the essence of Knapp's theory was the 'unmasking of all hypostases and fictions',[190] destroying all 'legal phantasms' and thus liberating man from the idols which he had created and which had enslaved him, then it cannot be denied that a similar motivation may be found underlying Petrażycki's psychologism. Moreover, in this respect there is also a similarity between Petrażycki and Knapp's teacher, Ludwig Feuerbach: Knapp's and Petrażycki's fight against 'legal phantasms' can be legitimately compared to Feuerbach's struggle against the idols of theology (God) and idealistic philosophy (the Absolute)—a struggle waged by reducing these metaphysical entities to externally projected and deified images of man's inner nature.

Having said this, it is necessary to point out differences which remained unnoticed by both Reisner and Babb. The first of these is the anti-hedonism of Petrażycki's psychology, in sharp contrast to Feuerbach's, and Knapp's, aim of rehabilitating man's 'sensuality', of seeing man as a primarily 'sensual' creature (which was for them the essence of 'anthropological materialism', as opposed to idealistic anthropology, which sees man's essence in 'spirit' or 'mind'). The second difference is Petrażycki's gradualism, as opposed to the Feuerbachian belief in the possibility of liberating man from his self-created idols by revolutionary means and the conviction that this overthrowing of idols would immediately endow actually existing men with god-like attributes. Petrażycki, as we know, also believed that man could be liberated from all kinds of pressure, including moral pressure, and, in this sense, become 'god-like'; he repeatedly stressed, however, that this final liberation of man could only be achieved after the total historical and legal education of mankind had been completed.

After the Bolshevik Revolution Reisner, as already mentioned, was appointed Vice-Commissar of Justice. In this capacity, as reported by Timasheff, he used Petrażycki's theory of intuitive law 'to persuade his superior, the Commissar of Justice, that it was possible to abrogate *uno actu* the legislation of the Tsarist regime and of the Provisional Government, since a substitute already existed in the form of the intuitive law of the working class. Reisner's advice was embodied in the decree *On Courts* (7 December, 1917), according to which the new courts had to render decisions on the basis of the enactments of the

---

[190] G. Radbruch in *Legal Philosophies*, p. 71.

'Workers' and Peasants' Government' and of the revolutionary
consciousness of the judges which was supposed to coincide with the
ideas on justice held by working men. Since, at that time, the
enactments of the new government were scarce and unsystematic, the
other source, revolutionary consciousness had to prevail'.[191]

Needless to say, the decree *On Courts* contradicted all the principles
of Petrażycki's legal policy and its results, as might have been expected,
were deplorable. Reisner himself soon came to be regarded as a
theorist having little in common with Marxism. Nevertheless, he did
not easily surrender: in 1925 he published a book, *Our Law, Foreign
Law, General Law*, in which he referred to Petrażycki's views on the
importance of legal motivation and attacked the nihilistic attitudes to
law by then prevalent among Soviet jurists.[192] He did not repent of
his influence upon the decree *On Courts*, but rather related with pride
how he had managed—'with the citation of certain scientific materials'
—to convince Lunacharsky, the powerful Commissar of Education,
that revolutionary government had to rely on the legal consciousness of
the revolutionary masses and how Lunacharsky in turn had succeeded
in gaining the support of Lenin for this view.[193] By this somewhat
enigmatic reference to 'certain scientific materials' Reisner meant
chiefly the relevant paragraphs from Petrażycki's works. This is clear
from Lunacharsky's article 'The Revolution, Law and the Courts',
written in connection with the decree *On Courts*.[194] Petrażycki, along
with Knapp, was here praised for describing in detail how new legal
ideas grow among the masses and for not being afraid to justify
revolutions. To add more weight to his views on intuitive law he was
presented as a man 'in whom official Russian science takes pride as
one of the greatest authorities in Europe'.[195]

The other current in the Russian reception of Petrażycki's thought
was represented mainly by G. K. Guins and, in a much wider context,
by Sorokin. Guins's interpretation of Petrażycki's theory is identical
with the reconstruction of Petrażycki's views on cultural selection,
presented above; it is therefore sufficient to stress that the merit of
interpreting Petrażycki in such a way is his and that his book *Law and
Culture* (unfortunately not easily available) clarifies many points in

---

[191] *Law and Morality*, p. xxxii.   [192] *Soviet Legal Philosophy*, p. 88.
[193] Ibid., pp. 86–7.
[194] See *Soviet Political Thought: An Anthology*. M. Jaworskyj (ed. and trans.), Baltimore,
Maryland, 1967, pp. 52–56.
[195] Ibid., p. 55.

Petrażycki's theory of socio-psychic adaptation. It seems proper to add that from the point of view of this anti-naturalistic interpretation the similarities between Petrażycki and Pavlov, indicated by Timasheff, appear more superficial and less important.

Petrażycki's influence on Sorokin is a topic in itself. It was multi-directional and should not be reduced to Petrażycki's impact on Sorokin's theory of the role of law-norms in the creation of a culture. Sorokin's campaign for 'creative altruism', launched at the end of his life, may also be seen as inspired, to a certain extent, by Petrażycki, or more exactly by Petrażycki's view of 'active love' as the social ideal.

Petrażycki's influence in Poland is also a separate topic. It has been rightly noted that 'his Polish compatriots and former students in St Petersburg and those who were in turn taught by them formed the most lasting group of disciples, spreading and interpreting Petrażycki's thought with an enthusiasm that is seldom stimulated by legal studies'.[196] The most outstanding of them was Jerzy Lande who produced the best reconstruction of Petrażycki's sociology. As already mentioned, Petrażycki's ideas influenced not only Polish jurists, but some philosophers and sociologists as well. It is interesting to note that Polish scholars have been particularly interested in the 'teleological' part of Petrażycki's theory, trying to derive from it some general rules of 'praxeology' (T. Kotarbiński) or socio-technics.[197] This may in part be explained by the fact that a strong interest in different kinds of 'philosophy of action', that is, in creating a theory which might serve as a guide for historical and social praxis, has characterized Polish thought since the early nineteenth century.[198]

The year 1981 marked the fiftieth anniversary of Petrażycki's tragic death. Poland was the only country to commemorate this date. The Polish Philosophical Association organized a modest conference and a special number of *Philosophical Studies*,[199] devoted to Petrażycki's legacy, was published.

[196] Langrod, 'Polish Psychological Theory', pp. 341–2. For more information concerning Petrażycki's Polish disciples see ibid., pp. 341–6.

[197] See especially the works of Adam Podgórecki.

[198] The Polish philosopher, August Cieszkowski, was the first post-Hegelian thinker to propose a programme of 'philosophy of action', by which he meant a philosophy which could serve as a guide to the conscious creation of history (A. Cieszkowski, *Prolegomena zur Historiosophie*, Berlin, 1938). Another Polish philosopher, B. Trentowski, in 1843 invented the term 'cybernetics' as a name for a new science which was to provide the rules for a conscious direction of political developments. See A. Walicki, *Philosophy and Romantic Nationalism*, part II.

[199] *Studia filozoficzne*, No. 5, 1981.

Finally, a few words are called for on the fate of Petrażycki's ideas in the West. The planned translation of his major Russian works into German did not materialize because of the First World War. After the war the legal sciences were dominated by Kelsen's 'pure theory of law', a theory consistently eliminating from the science of law the two main concerns of Petrażycki's thought, namely, both the interest in suprapositive law and the interest in causal laws governing human conduct. Petrażycki's Russian disciples, forced to emigrate to the West, tried to counteract this trend. The psychological theory of law later reappeared in Sweden. The leader of the so-called Uppsala school, Karl Olivecrona, in rejecting Kelsen's normativism and proposing instead the study of 'law as fact' came close to Petrażycki; he recognized this but preferred to stress the differences between his and Petrażycki's understanding of law.[200] In America Petrażycki's ideas were presented in detail in the two articles by H. W. Babb, so often quoted above. Roscoe Pound, a leading American legal philosopher, took some interest in them, and probably because of this, the important collection of essays in his honour, entitled *Interpretations of Modern Legal Philosophies*, contains four contributions devoted to, or inspired by, Petrażycki's thought.[201]

In spite of these and other efforts,[202] Petrażycki still remains largely unknown in the West. The too-heavily abridged English translation of his two major works is not a good guide to the meaning and value of his legacy; it gives almost no idea of his legal policy, of his criticisms of different legal philosophies (the relevant chapter has simply been omitted), or of the importance of his ideas for the practical problems of contemporary society. The legacy of the 'great Russo–Polish master' deserves, I think, to be critically assimilated by Western scholars, but for this to be possible a new, complete, and unabridged edition of his works in English and a detailed, historical and analytical monograph on his views are badly needed.

[200] Cf. Timasheff, *Law and Morality*, pp. xxxiv–xxxv. Olivecrona's criticism of Petrażycki's thought was published in *Theoria*, vol. 14, 1948, pp. 168–81.

[201] By M. Laserson, A. Meyendorff, P. Sorokin, and N. Timasheff. See above, n. 14.

[202] The most outstanding of these is undoubtedly the collection of articles published by Gorecki (see above, n. 6).

V

Pavel Novgorodtsev: Neo-Idealism and the Revival of Natural Law

1 Introductory remarks and biographical note

PAVEL Novgorodtsev (1866–1924), head of the so-called Moscow School of Russian jurisprudence and one of the main representatives of the neo-idealist current in Russian thought, has already been mentioned in this book in connection with Chicherin, Soloviev, and Petrażycki. In spite of the great differences and sharp disagreements between these three thinkers he rendered each his due, seeing clearly that their rejection of legal positivism helped to undermine its dominant position in legal philosophy and paved the way, more or less consciously, for a revival of natural law, a movement with which he himself was identified. He defined his own task as giving this movement firm foundations in German idealism, thereby helping to overcome the crisis in legal ideas. He wanted to rehabilitate the category of 'oughtness' and therefore preached a return to the Kantian dualism of *Sein* and *Sollen*. At the same time he was very conscious of the necessity of modernizing natural law, making it immune against the errors and illusions of unhistorical, abstract rationalism. In this respect he did not forget what he had learned from Hegelianism.

In his warm obituary tribute to Chicherin, Novgorodtsev made it clear that his own neo-idealism was a direct continuation of the last phase of Chicherin's thought, whose *Philosophy of Law* was, he declared, an 'unquestionable step forward by comparison with Hegel' in its 'consistent development of the individualistic principle, which was lacking in the Hegelian system'.[1] He wrote:

> Hegel fully recognized the demands of human personality as a bearer of spirit, but saw it merely as a transient manifestation of general spiritual substance, finding expression in objective laws and institutions. Boris Nikolaevich protested against this, rightly insisting that 'the true manifestation of spirit should be seen not in formal and dead institutions but in the living

---

[1] P. I. Novgorodtsev, *Boris Nikolaevich Chicherin*, Moscow, 1905, pp. 7–8.

person, endowed with consciousness and will. Because of this it is one-sided to define the social principle in human life as a system of institutions. Human societies are not institutions, but unions of persons.' Chicherin's tremendous achievement lay in properly justifying and developing this view. In recognizing this merit the followers of Boris Nikolaevich agree with his critics. Of all his works, his *Philosophy of Law* is obviously the most widely approved. To the inherent value of this work we should add the fact that it is the only comprehensive, systematic statement of the foundations of legal philosophy in the Russian language.[2]

Although in his tribute Novgorodtsev did not mention what he saw as the weakest point of Chicherin's legal philosophy, namely, his stubborn defence of the dogmas of Old Liberalism, in his books he did not try to conceal his disagreements with the man whom he otherwise considered as his spiritual father. He rejected Chicherin's view that law must not be concerned with helping the weak and poor, but should leave this task to morality. He forcefully opposed Chicherin's opinion that social inequalities are something natural and that the rule of law demands only equality before the law, not equality of opportunity. Social inequalities, he argued, are different from truly natural inequalities; they derive from man-made institutions, and institutions (unlike the laws of nature) should be constantly improving in accordance with progressive ideals.[3] As the standard for legal progress, marking the transition from the Old Liberalism to the New, he took Soloviev's 'right to a dignified existence'.[4] We can say therefore that as the chief representative of neo-idealism in Russian legal philosophy he was a disciple of Chicherin, but as a theorist of the New Liberalism he was inspired by Soloviev.

The relation between Novgorodtsev and Petrażycki is complicated by their entirely different attitude towards the legacy of German idealism and also by the element of rivalry between Novgorodtsev's 'Moscow School' and Petrażycki's 'Petersburg School' in Russian legal theory. Novgorodtsev was perfectly right in emphasizing that Petrażycki treated law as a fact of individual and social psychology, whereas the neo-idealist approach to law was transempirical and non-causal.[5] Yet, in spite of this contrast, in the early stages of his intellectual evolution Novgorodtsev was greatly impressed by Petrażycki's science of legal

[2] Loc. cit.
[3] P. I. Novgorodtsev, *Krizis sovremennogo pravosoznaniia*, Moscow, 1909, pp. 317–18, 337–8.
[4] See above, Ch. III, 5.   [5] See above, Ch. IV, 6.

policy. He saw it as a rehabilitation of the category of 'oughtness' (*Sollen*) in legal thinking, agreeing with Petrażycki that this was a vindication and modernization of the old natural law viewpoint; he even seemed to recognize Petrażycki's claim to have been the first to put forward the idea of a revival of natural law. His programmatic article, 'Ethical Idealism in Legal Philosophy', begins with a reference to Petrażycki, whose ideas are interpreted as an important stage in the development of the normative principle in law.[6] According to this interpretation the first stage was so-called conceptual jurisprudence, that is, the purely immanent, 'dogmatic' analysis of the normative content of positive law. The next stage, going beyond the limits of existing laws, was Petrażycki's analysis of the psychic content of the idea of law. The final step would be the ethical theory of law, based upon philosophical idealism. The first stage developed within legal positivism but the second, Petrażycki's own theory, placed the normative principle beyond 'lawyers' law'. Thus analysis of the normative content of *existing* law was replaced by a normative approach towards law, which implied a renewed concern with metajuristic justice, and in this sense was a return to the standpoint of natural law.

This return, however, was incomplete and methodologically imperfect. Novgorodtsev wanted to go much further, as he himself put it: 'We need a revival of natural law with its a-prioristic method, its idealistic yearnings, its recognition of moral autonomy and its normative approach.' Such a mode of thought, he added demands a radical overcoming of relativism, it needs 'a halo of absolute oughtness'.[7] Petrażycki's psychological theory of law could not supply such absolute standards. With the passage of time it became clear that it was closely tied to sociological evolutionism and thus inevitably committed to a form of historical relativism.

Novgorodtsev's biography has not yet been written,[8] nor did he, like Chicherin, write his memoirs. He took part in political events, but his role was not important enough to attract the particular attention of historians. By nature he was not a public man, preferring privacy and quiet academic work;[9] his commitments were intellectual rather than

---

[6] P. I. Novgorodtsev (ed.), *Problemy idealizma*. Moscow, 1903, pp. 236, 279–80.

[7] Ibid., p. 250.

[8] In the recent monograph by George F. Putnam biographical information is very scarce. See G. F. Putnam, *Russian Alternatives to Marxism: Christian Socialism and Idealistic Liberalism in Twentieth Century Russia*, Knoxville, Tenn., 1977 (the book deals with the ideas of Novgorodtsev and Bulgakov).

[9] Cf. Putnam, *Russian Alternatives to Marxism*, pp. 35–6.

directly political. But he lived in times when a man of his calibre could hardly avoid political involvement.

He was born in Bakhmut, a small town in the Ekaterinoslav province of Ukraine. After graduating from the Ekaterinoslav gymnasium he entered the law faculty of Moscow University. He was a brilliant student and his teachers recognized this: he finished his Moscow Studies in 1888 as candidate for a professorial post. From 1888 to 1896 he continued his studies in France and Germany, mainly in Freiburg, where he was strongly influenced by the Baden School of neo-Kantianism. In 1897 he defended his master's dissertation *The Historical School of Jurists, Its Genesis and Fate* (published in 1896) and began lecturing at Moscow University. In 1901 he published a monograph *Kant and Hegel and Their Teachings on Law and the State* which he defended the following year as a doctoral dissertation. Soon afterwards he received a professorial position at Moscow University. An excellent university teacher, he was very popular among his students and also lectured to the higher women's courses and at the newly founded Moscow Institute of Commerce, of which he was director.

Novgorodtsev's involvement in the Russian liberal movement began early: while still a student in Moscow he was associated with a circle of Constitutionalists organized by the veteran of gentry liberalism, Ivan Petrunkevich. From 1901 to 1902, he was active in organizing the Liberation Movement. He took part in the joint meeting of *zemtsvo* liberals and Moscow liberal intellectuals which approved the idea of publishing abroad an illegal constitutional newspaper *Osvobozhdenie* (*Liberation*)[10] and he was one of the founding members of the Union of Liberation, the germ of the future Constitutional Democratic Party (Kadets). In 1903 he took part in an important meeting of constitutionalist leaders at Schaffhausen, a Swiss city near Lake Constance. Like other liberal-radical intellectuals he opposed the views of the right-wing, Slavophilc-inspired *zemstvo* liberals led by Dimitry Shipov, who criticized Western constitutionalism as a potential breeding ground for international power struggles and set against it the idea of a representative advisory body modelled on the Land Assemblies of Old Russia. In 1904 he was among the liberal leaders who prepared a draft constitution, known as the 'Union of Liberation Constitution',[11] a

---

[10] Shmuel Galai, *The Liberation Movement in Russia, 1900–1905*, Cambridge, 1973, p. 116.

[11] G. Fischer, *Russian Liberalism: From Gentry to Intelligentsia*, Cambridge, Mass., 1958, pp. 170–2.

document more moderate than later liberal programmes but, firmly demanding a constituent assembly and 'four-strand' suffrage (universal, direct, equal and secret). In 1904 he became an important figure in the Union of Professors and in the following year revolutionary events made him a leader of the academic unions in the Union of Unions,[12] an organization trying to emancipate civil society in Russia and to give expression to the popular will. After the emergence of the Kadet party he contributed to the final elaboration of its programme and in 1906 became a member of its Central Committee. In the same year he was elected by his native province of Ekaterinoslav to the First State Duma.

As is known, there were many jurists among the leaders of the Kadet party, among them Petrażycki, V. D. Nabokov, Vladimir Hessen and Iosif Hessen (the editor of *Pravo*), A. Kaminka, V. Maklakov, the Jewish leader M. M. Vinaver, the famous Polish barrister A. Lednicki, and others. Some of these, especially Maklakov and Petrażycki, found it very difficult, if not impossible, to combine political struggle with the defence of law. They were aware that in a revolutionary situation legal considerations must, as a rule, be subordinated to political tactics, but nevertheless felt very uneasy about the growing radicalism within the party and the contempt for formal legality it displayed. While not wanting to weaken their party by a too active moderation of its policies, they feared that lack of moderation might play into the hands of right- and left-wing extremists and thus endanger the frail foundations of constitutionalism. In other words, they were torn between their loyalty to the party and their idea of the rule of law; between the political advantages of yielding to the pressure of an increasingly radical public opinion and the view that the true task of Russian liberalism was to bring about 'the peaceful transformation of the autocracy into a constitutional monarchy'.[13] We have not sufficient evidence to claim that Novgorodtsev was as conscious of this painful dilemma as Petrażycki, but it is difficult to imagine that he was quite unaware of it. He started out in the Duma as an advocate of reasonable compromise: it was he who prevented the escalation of conflict over the way in which the Duma's Address to the Monarch should be presented.[14] But his last act as a member of the Duma was a romantically provocative

---

[12] Putnam, *Russian Alternatives to Marxism*, p. 122.
[13] Cf. V. A. Maklakov, *The First State Duma*. M. Belkin (trans.), Bloomington, Ind., 1964, p. 11.
[14] Cf. A. N. Healy, *The Russian Autocracy in Crisis*, Hamden, Conn., 1976, pp. 187–8.

gesture, the signing of the famous Vyborg Manifesto. We do not know what his attitude was towards Petrażycki's arguments against this move, but we may safely assume that, like Petrażycki, he yielded to majority pressures in spite of his juridical convictions. He must have known that to urge people not to pay taxes and to resist military draft was equivalent to abandoning legal grounds and committing political suicide.

Like other signatories of the Vyborg Manifesto, Novgorodtsev was not only imprisoned for three months but, more importantly, made ineligible for membership of future Dumas. He resumed his teaching duties and concentrated on scholarly work, which after all was where his real preference lay. But in these difficult years he could not shut himself up in an ivory tower; he could not escape the consequences of the politicization of academic life and the hard choices bound up with this. Tolstoy's death, on 7 November 1910, gave rise to a wave of student disturbances, work stoppages, and mass meetings in memory of the great writer, followed by revolutionary demonstrations. The repressive measures taken against the revolutionaries, especially some brutal incidents in the prisons, added fuel to the flames and transformed limited unrest in the universities into a storm of student protest. Novgorodtsev later wrote this concise account of what followed:

The Christmas vacations brought a natural pacification. But before work was resumed, a decision of the Council of Ministers was published forbidding all meetings in the universities except those held for purely academic purposes. With a complete disregard of university autonomy and existing traditions, the police were thenceforth allowed to enter on university premises, without being summoned by the university authorities, on the slightest suspicion that students' meetings were being held. To this decision the students almost everywhere replied by violent demonstrations, and even went to the length of proclaiming a strike, which was to last throughout the term. The conflict assumed a particularly violent character in the University of Moscow. As usual, the declaration of the strike by the students was strongly resented by professors, and the University Council was prepared to adopt extreme measures to combat it and to insist on the continuation of work. But the University authorities were placed in a quite novel position by the order of January 11, 1911. The police might now come into the University building without their knowledge and act upon instructions from their chiefs. The result was that after the first appearance of the police in the University, the Rector, Professor Manuilov, and his two deputies, Professor Menzbir and Professor Minakov, resigned, asserting that the right given to the police to enter on university premises 'was creating an absolutely inadmissible division of power'. The Minister of Education regarded this as a new anti-Government demonstration and dismissed all three professors. Upon this, twenty-one professors and over eighty other members of the faculty resigned in their turn. At the same time students were expelled *en masse* from Moscow and other universities.[15]

As might have been expected, Novgorodtsev was among the professors who felt it necessary to resign. He was firmly opposed to student disturbances, let alone political strikes and revolutionary demonstrations, nor did he see Tolstoy as the highest moral authority in the land, or sympathize with his anarchism and he could not regard the symbolism of his death as a sufficient reason for disturbing the normal work of the universities. He condemned the revolutionary extremists for having no regard whatever for the universities.[16] But he felt exactly the same about Stolypin's government and had, therefore, no choice but to resign.

He returned to his university after the March revolution of 1917, but concentration on academic activities alone was no longer possible for him. In May 1917 the Eighth Congress of the Kadet Party elected him to the Central Committee of the party. He was by then a leading figure of 'the party's far right',[17] firmly opposed to any coalition with the moderate socialists and, on the whole, more intrested in preserving the purity of liberal ideals than in participating in political power.[18] At the Ninth Kadet Congress (July 1917) he strongly supported the view that the Orthodox Church was an 'institution of public-legal [*publichno-prævovoi*] character' and as such, had a right to state aid, a view indignantly rejected by the left-wing Kadets, as a violation of the principle of the separation of church and state.[19] After the Kornilov affair he clearly recognized the dangers of the Bolshevik seizure of power and advocated a consolidation of all anti-Bolshevik forces. Not surprisingly, the October Revolution was in his eyes a national disaster. Although the victorious Bolsheviks outlawed the Kadets and arrested many of their leaders, he decided to take part in the preliminary session of the Constituent Assembly on 28 November.[20] After the

[15] P. I. Novgorodtsev, 'Russian Universities and Higher Technical Schools During the War', in *Russian Schools and Universities in the World War* (*Economic and Social History of the World War*, Russian Series), New Haven, Conn., 1929, pp. 149–50.

[16] Ibid., p. 151.

[17] W. G. Rosenberg, *Liberals in the Russian Revolution: The Constitutional Democratic Party, 1917–1921*, Princeton, 1974, p. 190.

[18] Ibid., pp. 175, 200–1. [19] Ibid., p. 204. [20] Ibid., p. 278, n.

disbanding of the Assembly on 18 January 1918 he devoted himself to the activities of the so-called 'Right' or 'Moscow' centre of the Kadets. He was the chief speaker at their May conference in Moscow and the main author of its policy guidelines.[21] In 1919 he became the head of the Ekaterinodar Kadet party office and in this capacity collaborated closely with General Denikin. Among other things he was instrumental in persuading Denikin to acknowledge Admiral Kolchak as Supreme Commander of the combined anti-Bolshevik forces. (The decisive arguments for this step were provided by Peter Struve who was then in Paris and recognized that Kolchak was much more acceptable to the West.)[22]

Novgorodtsev's political position was then quite straightforward, free of characteristic liberal hesitations and scruples. As he put it:

If nothing remains of our democratism, then it is an excellent thing, since what is needed now is a dictatorship, a force for creating authority . . . There is now no 'Kadetism' or 'democratism', there is only the task of national unification. The party's own responsibilities derive from this . . . It is a question of the Nation and the Russian State, and not of the party . . . Established party dogmas must be done away with; free thinking on these matters is absolutely essential.[23]

After Denikin's defeat Novgorodtsev was forced to emigrate. At first he settled in Berlin and helped I. V. Hessen and A. I. Kaminka to edit the *émigré* Kadet newspaper *Rul*. Later, like many other Russian *émigré* scholars, he decided to settle in Prague. He became founder and elected dean of the Russian Faculty of Law—a kind of *émigré* school of law affiliated to the Charles University of Prague. In fact it was much more than a school of law, since its staff included such eminent philosophers, theologians, historians and sociologists as G. Gurvitch, N. Lossky, N. S. Timasheff, S. Vernadsky, S. Bulgakov, G. Florovsky, and P. Struve.[24]

Novgorodtsev himself was not only a jurist, but also a philosopher, historian of ideas, and latterly a religious thinker. According to Gurvitch he was 'the founder and universally recognized head of the newest idealist school in Russian jurisprudence', 'one of the greatest

[21] Ibid., pp. 289–96.
[22] R. Pipes, *Struve: Liberal on the Right, 1905–1944*. Cambridge, Mass., 1980, pp. 276–7.
[23] Quoted from Rosenberg, *Liberals in the Russian Revolution*, p. 410.
[24] P. E. Kovalevsky, *Zarubezhnaia Rossiia*, Paris, 1971 (Collection Études Russes, vol. 3), p. 97.

thinkers of the New Liberalism' and, above all, a great historian of legal philosophy, whose knowledge in this field was 'unparalleled both in Russia and in the West'.[25] The scope of his scholarly interests was immense but, in spite of this, the inner unity of his *œuvre* is readily apparent. His thought always centred on the problem of relativism and absolutism, of relative and absolute values. He was deeply aware of the dangers of historical and cultural relativism, as destroying the very notion of objective truth, and thus depriving people of the will to change their social life in accordance with objective, supra-historical standards of justice. But he was equally sensitive to the dangers of an absolutization of relative values, in the shape of overconfident dogmatism and social utopianism. In his earlier career he wanted to strengthen the will for change and for a healthy self-confidence among the advocates of liberal reform; he therefore concentrated on combating relativism and vindicating the absolute standards of natural law. In his later years after the disappointing experiences of 1905–7, he changed his position to criticize the zealots of radical change and concentrated on exposing the 'false absolutes' of socialism. The final solution of the problem of relativism versus absolutism he found in religion, coming to view Christianity as providing an absolute ethical standard while, at the same time, warning against the millenarian heresy and against all attempts to conceive the Absolute in terrestrial form and to realize it in history.

2 Idealism and natural law

To give full account of Novgorodtsev's works in the history of legal ideas is not an easy task; happily, it does not fall within the scope of this book. Instead of presenting his historical explanations, of trying to establish the degree of originality of his approach, or the truth of his historical findings, I shall concentrate on those aspects of his historical works directly related to his own views, which can be treated as part of his own legal philosophy.

In the introduction to his *Kant and Hegel*, Novgorodtsev himself justified this method of analysis, distinguishing clearly between the two equally legitimate methods, historical and philosophical, of dealing with the history of ideas.[26] The historical method is genetic and functional,

[25] G. D. Gurvitch, 'Prof. P. I. Novgorodtsev, kak filosof prava', *Sovremennye zapiski*, vol. 20, Paris, 1924, pp. 389–90, 392.

[26] Novgorodtsev, *Kant i Gegel' v ikh ucheniiakh o prave i gosudarstve*, Moscow, 1901, pp. 1–25.

although not necessarily sociological. Ideas may be explained by their social context, but their historical life cannot be reduced to the social history of the epoch in which they emerged and became influential. Great thinkers are not only products of their own times but also inheritors of earlier traditions; therefore, it is methodologically justified to separate the history of ideas from social history by stressing autonomous logic in the development of different ideological traditions. In other words, genesis and function must not be identified with *social* genesis and function; the recognition of purely intellectual genesis and function is also important and, therefore, the autonomous history of ideas is a legitimate field of historical research.

In the case of philosophical method, problems of genesis and function are of secondary importance. What really matters is the inherent meaning of the given ideas or doctrines. Philosophical interest in the ideas of a thinker of the past involves (a) a *systematic* analysis of his views, (b) a criticism of them from the point of view of the timeless standards of objective truth and, finally, (c) the 'dogmatic interest', the need to explain the contemporary significance of the ideas in question and their relevance to the views of the researcher. The main task consists in explaining the given system of ideas not as a reflection of its times, but as a 'logical construction, important for us'.[27] The legitimacy of such an approach Novgorodtsev defended as follows: 'The logical scope of a doctrine, as a system of abstract notions, is wider than [the meaning of] the direct real causes which called it into being. Because of this we can discuss it without reference to its historical preconditions.'[28]

Novgorodtsev recognized Chicherin's history of political doctrines and Gierke's history of natural law[29] as excellent examples of this method. His own works, we may add, were even more instructive in this respect, since, unlike Chicherin, he expressed his views almost exclusively as philosophical analysis of the ideas of other thinkers.

Novgorodtsev's first book, *The Historical School of Jurists, Its Genesis and Fate*, tries to find a compromise solution to the conflict between the natural law tradition and nineteenth-century historicism. There he defines natural law as the 'sum total of ideal, moral notions about law', and explains it as the reaction of moral consciousness against positive law and thus as an attempt to restore the primordial bond between law

---

[27] Ibid., p. 24.
[28] Ibid., p. 20.
[29] Ibid., p. 24.

and morality.[30] At the same time, from the philosophical point of view, natural law is a form of rationalism: of rational reflection raising the individual above 'natural immediacy' and enabling him to adopt a critical attitude towards the 'positivity' of the given. As is known, the German historical school attacked this inherent rationalism of natural law and set against it the idea of organic growth, the spontaneous, 'plant-like' development of the national spirit. Its criticism of the natural law school may be reduced to three main points:[31]

1. Of seeing the origin of positive law in conscious legislation only while ignoring unconscious organic growth;

2. Of trying to find a universal system of norms, thereby ignoring the specificity of different historical epochs and the distinctive features of different nations;

3. Of a tendency to treat subjective legal ideals as legally binding norms, thus ignoring the demarcation line between abstract notions and real history.

Novgorodtsev does not deny the weight of these accusations. His strategy consists rather in showing that the opposition between natural law and historicism may be interpreted as relative rather than absolute. In his book he presents F. C. von Savigny, the greatest representative of the historical school, as a thinker who in fact shared many of the assumptions of the natural law school, believing that true law was not 'made' but 'discovered'. One might even say that he broadened the application of this thesis since he claimed that even positive law must be 'discovered' in the legal consciousness of the nation, and not arbitrarily invented. Like the theorists of natural law he opposed the command theory of law and energetically defended the view that law must stem not from any individual will but from objective standards of justice. He sought to overcome the dualism between moral conscious-ness and legal obligation in the notion of organic growth, but realized that organic growth was an ideal norm rather than a universal feature of historical development. His philosophy of law, therefore, had a definite normative standard, far removed from the uncritical acceptance of all officially state-promulgated laws. While he historicized the criteria of 'just law' by making them dependent on the living historical consciousness of the nation, this should be seen not as abandoning

---

[30] Novgorodtsev, *Istoricheskaia shkola iuristov, eë proiskhozdenie i sud'ba.* Moscow, 1896, p. 9.

[31] Ibid., p. 2.

natural law but, rather, as transforming it into the 'natural law of the
historically real'.[32] In any case, Novgorodtsev concludes, Savigny
treated legal consciousness and the living customs of the nation as 'a
kind of natural law' which should be 'inviolable and sacred to the
rulers'.[33]

In the case of the historical school and other forms of conservative-
romantic thought this combination of historicism and natural law was
achieved at the cost of rationalism. But another development was also
possible: namely, the historicization of rationalism, best exemplified by
Hegelianism. To raise rationalism to a higher level demanded a more
critical attitude towards rationalist criticism of the given, and this was
the great achievement of Hegel. In his philosophy abstract rationalism
was transformed into historical rationalism, uniting reason and history
in the idea of rational development.[34] This synthesis, however, proved
to be unstable. There was a tension between historicism and
rationalism, since the first demanded a reverence for history while the
second aspired to judge historical processes and pass verdicts upon
them, and this split the Hegelian legacy between conservative and
radical thinkers.

In the last part of his book, dealing with the fate of historicism in the
legal philosophies of the second half of the century, Novgorodtsev tries
to argue that the legacy of natural law was in part revived in the
'teleological theory' of Ihering. This is a rather unexpected conclusion,
since Ihering was famous for his purely utilitarian and positivist
approach to law, for his emphasis on the practical purposes of law and
disregard for its moral content. Novgorodtsev, however, is undoubtedly
right in contrasting his views with the theory of organic growth and in
seeing in them a revival of the rationalist approach to legislation,
characteristic of the natural law school. He quotes with approval
Ihering's words that law is the creation of purpose (*Zweckschöpfung*), of
rational reflection and practical calculation, that historical progress is
not an unconscious and spontaneously harmonious process but the
outcome of the struggle between different conscious forces, motivated
by rational self-interest; that history as a whole is not an organic
process, independent of human consciousness and will, but the result
of conscious and purposeful human activity.[35] He sees in all this not

[32] The quotation is from Max Weber. See *Max Weber on Law in Economy and Society*.
Max Rheinstein (ed. and int.), New York, 1954, p. 288.
[33] Novgorodtsev, *Istoricheskaia shkola*, p. 101.
[34] Ibid., p. 12.   [35] Ibid., pp. 143, 152–8.

only a rehabilitation of rationalism but also due acknowledgement of the role of the individual in history. He even shares Ihering's sympathy for state socialism, treating it as proof of the 'progressiveness' of his doctrine.[36]

In the conclusion Ihering's legal philosophy is presented as a dialectical return to the standpoint of eighteenth-century natural law: 'The disintegration of the historical school brought about a certain revival of natural law doctrine. The latest form of historicism, as expressed in the teaching of Ihering, assimilated the critical-progressive tendencies of idealism and in this respect drew nearer to the philosophy of the previous century.'[37]

Many years later, in his article 'The Contemporary State of the Problem of Natural Law' (1913), Novgorodtsev mentioned his book on the historical school as an early appeal for a revival of natural law; an appeal completely independent of Petrażycki and Stammler, to whom he conceded the merit of strongly proclaiming such an appeal.[38] At first glance this claim seems very modest but on closer examination it turns out to be exaggerated. In fact the young Novgorodtsev wrote his master's thesis with no intention of proclaiming a revival of natural law; he simply stated that Ihering's doctrine represented such a revival, and expressed his sympathy with this development. It did not occur to him that he was saying something new about natural law; on the contrary, he stressed his agreement with what he called 'the contemporary view of the natural law problem', according to which natural law was not a higher law, invalidating any positive law inconsistent with it, but merely an ideal of law, to be found in the progressive development of positive law. He referred to the 'brief and good' formulation of this view in Chicherin's *Property and State* and refrained from adding anything to it.[39]

The choice of Ihering as the main representative of the movement for the revival of natural law was, indeed, rather unfortunate. According to Max Weber, natural law is the purest type of the value-rational (*wertrational*) attitude towards law, and it is quite obvious that Ihering was perhaps the most consistent advocate of a different, purposively rational (*zweckrational*), consciously instrumental approach

---

[36] Ibid., p. 160.
[37] Ibid., p. 218.
[38] Novgorodtsev, 'Sovremennoe polozhenie problemy estestvennogo prava', *Iuridicheskii vestnik*, vol. 1, 1913, pp. 21–2, n.
[39] Novgorodtsev, *Istoricheskaia shkola*, p. 20.

to law.[40] It seems probable that Novgorodtsev only fully realized this fundamental difference after the devastating critique of Ihering's utilitarianism in Petrażycki's early works and in Chicherin's *Philosophy of Law*. As he himself acknowledged, Chicherin and Petrażycki— 'the most prominent representative of the older Russian jurists and the most prominent representative of the young'[41]—were at one in declaring that contemporary legal consciousness was in a state of deep crisis, a diagnosis he entirely agreed with, without objecting to the negative view of Ihering which was an important part of it.

Novgorodtsev's next book, *Kant and Hegel and Their Teachings on Law and the State*, is an attempt to resist the historicist and positivist negation of the normative approach, to vindicate the validity of the unbridgeable dualism of *Sein* and *Sollen*, and to do so on the basis of transcendental idealism. The philosophy of Kant was, of course, of central importance, especially his conception of moral autonomy, and the analysis of Hegelianism was only a convenient means of showing up certain weak points of the Kantian position.

According to Kant, law—or rather, positive law—was merely a mechanism of external coercion, *Maschinenwesen der Polizei*,[42] a view which severed the link between morality and law. It was restored, however, in the Kantian idea of natural law, that is, in the notion of the categorical imperative,[43] whereby the highest criterion of morality became purely formal and thus immune to absolutization of specific, empirical content of moral demands. In other words, Kant gave powerful support to the view that there is an absolute element in morality (and in *Recht*), but stressed that it could be found only in its form, and never in its concrete content.[44] This, as Novgorodtsev commented, was a radical reversal of the old idea of natural law, and replaced it with a completely new approach to the natural law problem. Kant agreed with the theorists of natural law claiming that there is an eternal, timeless standpoint enabling us to judge the changing content of empirical morality; he emphasized, however, that this absolute yardstick is purely formal, demanding only that our deeds be consistent with the universality of reason and with the principle of moral autonomy.

[40] Cf. *Max Weber on Law*, pp. 8–9.
[41] Novgorodtsev, 'Ideia prava v filosofii V. S. Solovieva', *Voprosy filosofii i psikhologii*, 1901, vol. 56, no. 1. p. 113, cf. above, pp. 209.
[42] Novgorodtsev, *Kant i Gegel'*, p. 112.
[43] Ibid., p. 147.   [44] Ibid., p. 148.

In this way Novgorodtsev discovered in Kant Stammler's idea of 'natural law with changing content',[45] which for many years seemed to him the only acceptable solution of the natural law problem and which he propagated in his works.[46] But he always stressed his direct debt to Kant, never considering himself particularly indebted to Stammler, whose conception he saw as merely a 'direct consequence of Kant's ethical formalism' and thus contained, *in nuce* at least, in Kant's work.[47]

He recognized another important interpretation of Kant's teaching in Paul Natorp's *Sozialpädagogik* (1899) where Natorp used Kant's ethical formalism to criticize eudaemonistic dreams of realizing a state of universal happiness in history. Practical tasks, he argued, are always empirical and finite, but for this very reason no practical task, no matter how radical or grandiose, should be absolutized and treated as final. Moral will demands ceaseless striving, ceaseless self-improvement, and unlimited development.[48]

Novgorodtsev wholeheartedly agreed with this and, as we shall see, developed the idea in an original way in his later works, adding a religious dimension and directing it against the millennial dreams of radical socialists.

In contrast to Kant, Hegel concentrated on the historical conditions of moral progress, on *socially organized* ethics. Because of this, his teaching on the 'objective spirit' was, in Novgorodtsev's eyes, a useful antidote to the danger of one-sided subjectivism. In arguing for this view Novgorodtsev repeated Soloviev's argument on the insufficiency of moral subjectivism and the necessity for 'objective ethics'. It seems, however, that for him the opposite danger—that of one-sided 'objectivism', annihilating the autonomy of the moral subject—was more important and more threatening. Hegel, Novgorodtsev asserted, was guilty of anti-individualism as Chicherin had correctly pointed out.[49] He subordinated human individuals to a supra-individual Spirit, reducing them to the role of obedient and most unconscious instruments of a deified history. This anti-individualism characterized not only his metaphysics but also his method, since it implied the treatment of individuals as mere links in objective, impersonal processes. This historicist error was inherited by the sociological evolutionism of the second half of the century.[50]

[45] Ibid., p. 150.
[46] See, for instance, his article, 'Pravo estestvennoe', in *Entsiklopecheskii slovar'*, Brokgaus i Efron (eds.), vol. 48, SPb 1898, pp. 885–90.
[47] Novgorodtsev, *Kant i Gegel'*, p. 150.
[48] Ibid., p. 149.   [49] Ibid., p. 223.   [50] Ibid., p. 225, and n.

Nevertheless Novgorodtsev tried to do justice to Hegel. He defended his philosophy against accusations that it was an apologia for the reactionary status quo in Prussia, and (following Chicherin) presented him as one of the great theorists of the modern constitutional state.[51] In the final summing-up he contended that in legal philosophy Kantianism and Hegelianism were not mutually exclusive, but rather complementary.[52]

As he himself confessed, Novgorodtsev had written his book on Kant and Hegel to contribute to the solution of the problem which had been 'the subject-matter of the exceptionally interesting controversy between Chicherin and Soloviev': whether morality should be purely subjective, as Chicherin maintained, or also 'socially organized', as Soloviev argued. This controversy, in Novgorodtsev's words, 'had not been brought to a conclusion and, therefore, it seemed to me desirable to approach this problem through an analysis of the respective doctrines of Kant and Hegel, in which the opposition between subjective and objective ethics was expressed with a force and depth worthy of the classics.'[53]

Novgorodtsev's views on Kant and Hegel were also closely linked to the situation in German legal philosophy described by John H. Hallowell:

Positivism severs finally the realm of the *Sein* from the realm of the *Sollen*. In consequence of this separation, towards the turn of the century, two schools of jurists arose: the Neo-Kantians who restricted themselves to the realm of the *Sollen* and rejected all substantive criteria of law, and the Neo-Hegelians who restricted themselves to the realm of *Sein* and rejected all normative criteria of law. The theories of the former led to irresponsibility on the part of the individual and those of the latter to irresponsibility on the part of the state.[54]

It is plain that Novgorodtsev had conciliatory intentions but equally plain that he wholeheartedly sympathized with the neo-Kantians. He embraced the cause of the *Sollen*, linked it to the cause of the revival of natural law, and saw it as the only way out of the moral and legal crisis. In a speech delivered in 1902 at Petersburg University, he declared war on historicism, positivism, naturalistic evolutionism, and pan-sociologism, defending idealism, the moral autonomy of the individual and a normative approach. He condemned practical, utilitarian

---

[51] Ibid., p. 235. [52] Ibid., pp. 244–5.
[53] P. Novgorodtsev, 'Moral' i poznanie', *Voprosy filosofii i psikhologii*, 1902, vol. 64, no. 4. pp. 833–4.
[54] J. H. Hallowell, *The Decline of Liberalism as an Ideology*, London, 1946, p. 69.

considerations in law-making, calling instead for the derivation of laws from the 'powerful and incontestable authority' of the moral consciousness.[55] The restoration and preservation of 'the ideal meaning of law, its moral foundations', he proclaimed to be the main task of modern philosophy of law.

The programme was part of the antipositivist upheaval and the corresponding shift towards idealism which began in Russia at the turn of the nineteenth century. In his preface to Berdyaev's book on Mikhailovsky (1900)[56] Peter Struve, the former leader of the 'legal Marxists', who a few years earlier had advocated extreme 'objectivism' in the social sciences and had treated the individual as a *quantité négligeable*, in a complete *volte-face* hailed the return to idealism; he welcomed the revival of Kantian transcendental idealism but wanted to go further and revive the openly metaphysical, transcendent idealism of the great post-Kantian philosophers. He accompanied this change of front by an espousal of the liberal conception of human rights, which he derived from the notion of 'absolute right'—a notion in which he saw 'the essence and eternal content of liberalism'.[57] Among professional jurists the same tendency took the form of a revival of natural law. In 1902 V. M. Hessen published an excellent, detailed analysis of all the symptoms of this revival in Germany and in Russia.[58] He emphasized the merits of Petrażycki's 'psychological theory of law', while arguing that the mainstream of the movement was linked to the revival of philosophical idealism represented by men like Novgorodtsev and Struve. The tone of his article was optimistic, elevating and exhilarating. Philosophical idealism and the return to a moral, normative approach to law were for him the harbingers, or even first symptoms, of a great progressive change in political and social life.[59]

Soon after this there appeared an important book, *The Problems of Idealism* (1903). Its authors included S. Bulgakov, N. Berdyaev, and S. Frank, all former legal Marxists who had passed from Marxism to idealism and were now passing from philosophical idealism to religious philosophy. The book also included an anonymous contribution by

---

[55] P. Novgorodtsev, *O zadachakh sovremennoi filosofii prava*, SPb 1902, pp. 7–8.

[56] See N. A. Berdyaev, *Sub''ektivizm i individualizm v obshchestvennoi filosofii. Kriticheskii etiud o N. K. Mikhailovskom.* SPb 1900.

[57] See P. Struve, *Na raznye temy.* SPb 1902, pp. 538–9. Interestingly enough, Struve tried to combine liberalism so conceived with a Slavophile-inspired Russian nationalism.

[58] V. M. Hessen (Gessen), *Vozrozhdenie estestvennogo prava*, SPb 1902, originally published in *Pravo*.

[59] Ibid., pp. 42–3.

Struve and an article by Prince E. N. Trubetskoi, the disciple of and writer on Soloviev. It was edited by Novgorodtsev, who wrote the preface and the article 'Ethical Idealism in Legal Philosophy', mentioned above. The preface declared that the authors were looking for 'absolute commandments and absolute principles' and that they all believed in the absolute value of the personality: 'The new forms of life do not now appear as the demands of simple expediency; they appear rather as the categorical commands of morality which attribute paramount importance to the principle of the unconditional significance of the personality.'[60]

The Problems of Idealism marked the completion of the revolt against positivism in Russian thought and the beginning of the so-called 'religio-philosophic renaissance' of the early twentieth century. Its authors were unanimous in condemning positivism, naturalism, and Marxism (which they considered to be a form of sociological evolutionism); they opposed relativism, determinism, and materialism, seeing their common denominator in the capitulation of moral consciousness before the mere facticity of the given. Bulgakov passionately attacked the idolatry of progress, interpreting it as a 'theodicy of mechanicism', a poor substitute for religion. Berdyaev rejected the evolutionist concept of adaptation, demonstrating its affinity with hedonism and claiming that true ethics should have metaphysical foundations. Trubetskoi criticized historical materialism; Askoldov, representing spiritualist monadism, assailed the different forms of relativism, concentrating mainly on Mach, Avenarius, and Simmel; Frank extolled the ideas of Nietzsche, and Struve presented Russian neo-idealism as the culmination of the development of philosophical thought in Russia.[61]

Novgorodtsev's article, one of the best in the book, outlined the conception of three stages in the development of the normative principle in law (to which I referred above),[62] and proclaimed the transition to the last and highest phase of this process—the phase of ethical idealism. In this connection he urged the necessity of reviving natural law and wanted to base it upon the Kantian categorical imperative, which he saw as excluding both ethical conservatism and the radical utopia of an earthly paradise.[63] At this stage, however, his

---

[60] *Problemy idealizma*, pp. viii–ix.
[61] The other authors of *The Problems of Idealism* were B. A. Kistiakovsky, A. S. Lappo-Danilevsky, S. F. Oldenburg and D. E. Zhukovsky.
[62] See above, p. 293.   [63] *Problemy idealizma*, p. 288.

main enemy was conservatism. The tone of his article recalled V. M. Hessen's article, to which he referred with warm approval.[64] Both authors felt that a great and progressive change was imminent, both were positively excited by this prospect and presented their ideas as paving the way for its realization.

Many people on the left shared this view and interpreted the neo-idealist movement in the same way. Of course, this did not apply to the Marxists, who were too committed to materialism to see anything positive in the revival of idealist philosophy. But the attitude of the Socialist Revolutionaries was different: they were responsive to new trends and found in the new idealism a welcome ally, rehabilitating the normative approach of populist 'subjective sociology' and supporting the populist struggle against the idea of historical inevitability. This attitude found expression in the pages of Ivanov-Razumnik's *History of Russian Social Thought*. The author of this influential book, one of the most outstanding ideologists of the neo-populist movement, devoted much attention to *The Problems of Idealism* and treated Russian neo-idealism as a philosophically sophisticated expression of ethical individualism, constituting, in his view, the most precious tradition of the Russian intelligentsia.[65]

Two misunderstandings were involved in this positive appraisal. First, the vindication of subjectivism by Russian neo-idealists had little in common with the 'subjective sociology' of Lavrov and Mikhailovsky. Novgorodtsev, Berdyaev, Kistiakovsky, and Struve tried to make clear, by stressing that the transcendental subject of idealist philosophy and the merely empirical subject of sociology are two different things, that the populist theorists dealt with the latter and that therefore their 'subjectivism' was incapable of overcoming positivist scientism; it was merely a form of relativism, or a defence of arbitrary moral choice, or both. Second, in their further intellectual evolution, the chief authors of *The Problems of Idealism* moved sharply to the right, becoming highly critical of the entire tradition of the progressive Russian intelligentsia, so dear to Ivanov-Razumnik's heart. *The Problems of Idealism* led directly to the famous *Landmarks (Vekhi*, 1909), a book which marked a radical break with the legacy of the intelligentsia (in the specifically Russian sense of this term) and which was in turn severely condemned not only by the Socialist Revolutionaries and Marxists, but by

[64] Ibid., p. 246.
[65] See Ivanov-Razumnik, *Istoriia russkoi obshchestvennoi mysli*, 2nd edn., SPb 1908, vol. 2, pp. 453–85.

310 *Pavel Novgorodtsev*

mainstream liberals as well. Struve, Bulgakov, Berdyaev, Frank, Kistiakovsky, and Askoldov were its authors; Novgorodtsev was not, but he sympathized with many of the ideas in *Landmarks* and gave this book a cautious, qualified support.[66] He became more outspoken after the Bolshevik revolution, deeply regretting that the Russian intelligentsia had failed to understand the message of *Landmarks* and to change its ways in accordance with that message.[67]

Let us now return to pre-revolutionary times and to Novgorodtsev's views on idealism and natural law. It is a striking fact that Novgorodtsev did not develop his own theory of natural law, but limited himself to declarations on the necessity of its revival and to the endorsement of the neo-Kantian idea of 'natural law with changing content'. His views were very important culturally, as part of a wider phenomenon: the revolt against positivism in Russian thought and the corresponding changes in literary and artistic life (this was commented on by V. M. Hessen, who stressed the link between philosophical neo-idealism and poetic symbolism).[68] The theoretical content of these views was, however, rather thin.

To give Novgorodtsev his due, it is necessary to point out that in a more detailed analysis of the relation between law and morality—'the crux of all natural law theory'[69]—he went beyond general declarations. His early article 'Law and Morality' (1899) was a valuable theoretical contribution, while not attempting to create a new natural law theory. Stressing the link between morality and law, it yet showed the growing autonomy of law and explained this process as part of the individualization of men, a result of replacing unreflective traditionalism by rational reflection and individual autonomy.[70] Following Chicherin, the author agreed that law should not strive to become 'entirely moral' because such strivings would bring about the extinction of individual freedom. Law, he argued, must be thoroughly rationalized, that is, well-defined, codified, and formal, leaving substantive considerations to morality.[71] It must be backed by force, but the use of force should

---

[66] Cf. Putnam, *Russian Alternatives to Marxism*, pp. 148–9.

[67] See P. Novgorodtsev, 'O put'iakh i zadachakh russkoi intelligentsii', in *Iz glubiny. Sbornik statei o russkoi revolutsii*. Paris, 1967 (reprint), pp. 251–68. The entire article is devoted to the propriety and significance of *Landmarks*.

[68] See V. M. Hessen, *Vozroshdenie estestvennogo prava*, p. 40.

[69] Quoted from A. P. d'Entrèves, *Natural Law: An Introduction to Legal Philosophy*. London, 1970, p. 79.

[70] In this respect he repeated the ideas of Kavelin and the liberal Westernizers of the 1840s.

[71] P. Novgorodtsev, 'Pravo i nravstvennost'. In *Sbornik po obshchestvenno-politicheskim naukam*, S. Gambarov (ed.), SPb 1899, pp. 122–3.

not be its distinctive feature; its essence should consist rather in strictly *limiting* the use of force in social life.[72] The boundary between morality and law is a fluid one, as purely legal demands become internalized and thus made moral, while moral demands become enforceable and thus made legal. Nevertheless, the demarcation line should always be present and should not be effaced. Therefore, it was not enough to say, as Soloviev did, that law is the enforceable minimum morality. Novgorodtsev corrected this formula by defining law as the enforceable minimum of *social* demands and by stressing that social demands are not necessarily or exclusively moral.[73] In the light of this article Novgorodtsev appears more cautious and historically minded, more relativist as it were, than in his appeals to the 'absolute demands of moral consciousness.'

My final remarks in the present context concern the development of Novgorodtsev's views on the natural law problem. In his important article 'The Contemporary State of the Problem of Natural Law', quoted above, he abandoned Stammler's idea of 'natural law with the changing content,' declaring it to be 'an eclectic attempt to reconcile Plato's ancient insights with the data of empirical history',[74] and concluded:

In the revival of natural law it is necessary to go beyond Kant, to return to Hugo Grotius, or even to Socrates. It is necessary to reject Stammler's eclectic and indecisive formula, to restore the old truths of unalterable natural law. We must only remember that the question is not one of an unchangeable system of legal norms, which might at some future time replace a changing positive law, but of an unchangeable ideal, or principle of law, which has always directed, and will continue to direct the development of positive law.'[75]

In the light of others of Novgorodtsev's works the meaning of this train of thought is clear enough. It was an attempt to overcome the crisis in legal ideas by putting an end to the constant reinterpretation of the concept of law in radical and socialist thought. In a sense Novgorodtsev returned to Chicherin's position, for he wanted to make the idea of law narrower and more immune to historical change, less liable to increasingly 'social' interpretations of the nature and functions of the legal order. In Marxist language it could be described as an effort to defend and eternalize at least some features of the classical 'bourgeois-liberal' ideal of law.

[72] Ibid., p. 131.   [73] Ibid., p. 117.
[74] See Putnam, *Russian Alternatives to Marxism*, p. 135.
[75] Novgorodtsev, 'Sovremennoe polozhenie', p. 22.

3 Law and the state

In 1904, when Russia was waging its unsuccessful and unpopular war
with Japan and the liberal Liberation Movement was in full swing,
Novgorodtsev decided to translate his ideas into more directly political
language. The result was the long article 'Law and the State'. It was
not written for the general reader, but the leaders of the Union of
Liberation could not doubt that it was meant as a theoretical
justification of constitutionalism.

The article begins by establishing a sharp contradiction between
legal consciousness and legal theory.[76] Contemporary legal consciousness strongly demanded a definite limitation of state power through
the rights of the individual—rights which should be inalienable and
inviolable. Simultaneously the dominant legal theory, legal positivism,
derived all laws from the unlimited sovereignty of the state, making the
state virtually omnipotent. In this way contemporary legal theorists,
many of them liberals, in fact endorsed the reactionary, illiberal theory
of K. L. Haller, which claimed that the state stands above the law and
derives its authority from sheer force.[77] The positivist modernization of
this theory essentially combined it with the pedantic formalism of
conceptual jurisprudence, which did not make it more attractive. No
wonder, commented Novgorodtsev, that this view of law helped to
discredit law as such and to make it repulsive to morally sensitive
people.

To illustrate this point Novgorodtsev referred to the 'exceptionally
interesting protest against formal jurisprudence' in the works of the
late Slavophile, Ivan Aksakov.[78] Jurisprudence, wrote Aksakov, teaches
that 'there is nothing in the world except the dead mechanism of the
state, that everything is, and should be, accomplished in the name of
the state and through the agencies of the state, quite irrespective of the
forms in which the power of the state manifests itself, so long as it
bears the stamp of external legality'.[79] Novgorodtsev quoted these
words with approval, implying that they were directed against the
positivist view of law, and could not apply to the anti-positivist view,
which aimed at restoring the moral foundations of law. He obviously
hoped in this way to influence the right wing of the *zemstvo* liberals,

---

[76] P. Novgorodtsev, 'Gosudarstvo i pravo', Part I, *Voprosy filosofii i psikhologii*, 1904,
vol. 74, no. 4, p. 397.
[77] Ibid., pp. 404–5.   [78] Ibid., p. 400, n.
[79] See ibid., p. 405. Quoted by Novgorodtsev from I. S. Aksakov, *Polnoe sobranie
sochinenii*, vol. 2, Moscow, 1886, p. 17.

among whom Slavophile ideas, including criticism of the law, were still alive and widely accepted.

Novgorodtsev distinguished two great schools within a broadly conceived legal positivism: the command theory of law, which had developed mainly in England, and conceptual jurisprudence, which was dominant in Germany. The spiritual father of the English school was Thomas Hobbes, with his view of the state as the embodiment of an Absolute Sovereign Will and a corresponding belief that *ius est quod iussum est*. Nineteenth-century legal positivists, such as Austin and Bentham, Pollock and Bryce, abandoned the idea of royal absolutism but remained faithful to the doctrine of state absolutism, transforming it into a doctrine of unlimited sovereignty, according to which the state irrespective of its form, is the only source of law, wherefore its power cannot be legally limited. It is usually limited in practice, by the balance of forces or by the power of tradition, but not by the rights of the individual; the Bill of Rights is only a declaration of principles which an omnipotent parliament can suspend or change at any time, if the external situation allows such change.[80] Every command issued by the sovereign legislative power is a law; therefore, if the British parliament were to demand that all babies with blue eyes be killed this absurd and monstrous demand would have the binding force of law.[81] In this way English jurists constructed a consistent and complete system of legal despotism.

Novgorodtsev hastened to add that such a system could have emerged only in a country in which the practical danger of despotism did not exist.[82] English jurists could afford to ignore the problem of the legal limits of state power, because the power of the British government was limited by the facts of life and nobody felt threatened by it.[83] Nevertheless, theories have their own autonomous logic and the logic of the English variety of legal positivism has been extremely dangerous and destructive.

The German version of legal positivism shared the view that law is a product of the state and that right is identical with positive law. German jurists, however, were acutely aware of the difference between

[80] Ibid., p. 412.
[81] Ibid., p. 411. This shocking illustration of the view *ius est quod iussum est* was not invented by Novgorodtsev, but taken from A. V. Dicey, *Introduction to the Law of the Constitution*.
[82] Ibid., p. 113.
[83] In fact it was not quite so. Herbert Spencer, for instance, frequently pointed out the dangers inherent in unlimited parliamentary power.

the arbitrary exercise of power and power exercised in accordance with the law, hence their emphasis on legal formalism and on the immanent analysis of existing laws by independent professional lawyers. They wanted to ensure that the rulers of the state respected their own laws, but carefully refrained from making value-judgements on these laws. For them, the 'oughtness' point of view was necessarily subjective and incompatible with science. This produced peculiarly sterile results, since the analysis of existing law on its own terms could, of course, give only analytical judgements (in the Kantian sense), which could not increase the knowledge of law as a fact of life. Kant had complained that jurists had not defined law, to which Novgorodtsev added that jurists *qua* jurists would never produce such a definition, because in order to define law it is necessary to go beyond it, to look at it from the outside.[84] It followed from this that conceptual jurisprudence was unphilosophical and unscientific: unphilosophical, because the philosophy of law demands a metajuristic standpoint;[85] unscientific, because a scientific approach to law involves studying it as a part of social reality, that is, resorting to history, sociology, or psychology.[86]

The greatest German representative of broadly conceived legal positivism, Georg Jellinek, was aware of the limitations of conceptual jurisprudence; he also wanted to overcome the crudeness of the English school. In his view laws were not arbitrary commands of the sovereign, but derived from his autonomous (as opposed to arbitrary) will, which meant a self-limitation of sovereign power. The notion of autonomy, reasoned Jellinek, contains the notion of *nomos*, which means that the autonomous will must be law-abiding, respecting its own laws and limited by them. For Novgorodtsev this reasoning was not sufficiently convincing. Jellinek, he argued, had misunderstood Kant's notion of autonomy,[87] according to which the autonomy of the human will was made possible by unconditional moral law, inseparable from the nature of man as a rational being, whereas Jellinek's interpretation of autonomy simply meant giving laws to itself, namely, limiting the will of the state by the will of the state, and not by a higher, absolute principle.[88] A true theoretical limitation of the power of the state, concluded Novgorodtsev, could not be achieved without introducing the notion of legal norms above the state, the norms of natural law.

[84] Novgorodtsev, 'Gosudarstvo i pravo', p. 419.
[85] Ibid., p. 403.
[86] Ibid., p. 419.   [87] Ibid., p. 431.   [88] Ibid., pp. 431–5.

With this the Russian legal philosopher had returned to his favourite theme: the need for a revival of natural law. He devoted much space to proving that Jellinek, like many other outstanding jurists, could not in practice dispense with natural law norms and unconsciously invoked them. Thus, for instance, he interpreted Jellinek's conception of a supra-legal norm inherent in the very nature of the state as, in fact, a natural law conception. Similarly, he explained Jellinek's attempts to explore the psychological foundations of law as demonstrating that the main law-generating factor is the human image of 'oughtness' and saw this as a powerful argument for the natural law position.[89]

In the second part of his treatise Novgorodtsev concentrated on the genesis and meaning of sovereignty. In the Middle Ages, he argued, the notion of unlimited sovereignty was unknown: all power was divided, decentralized, and the public sphere was not separated from the private. The other side of this was the dominance of private interests, centrifugal tendencies and legally sanctioned universal inequality, in other words the lack of statehood in the modern sense of this term. The gradual emergence of the modern state was seen, in this perspective, in the centralization of political power and the simultaneous replacing of closed estates with a civil society in which all individuals were equal before the law. Here Novgorodtsev agreed with Chicherin that the historical task of the modern centralized state consisted in paving the way for the society of 'universal citizenship'.

His own important contribution was the explanation of the concept of sovereignty which had emerged in the early stages of this historical process. It was, he explained, a militantly polemical and transitional notion, directed against medieval particularism.[90] Its principle was one of uniting social forces on the basis of universal state law and thus presupposed equality before the law and at least a minimum individual freedom. Its proper meaning did not contain the idea of unlimited, omnipotent government but rather referred to the *unity* of the state, the *undivided* character of its power, and its monopoly of legislation and law-enforcement. Unlimited sovereignty described a situation in which the authority of the government of a given state was unchallengeable and undisputable, irrespective of its nature. This explained why the idea of unlimited sovereignty could be used both by the ideologists of absolute monarchy (Bodin) and by the ideologists of

---

[89] Ibid., p. 449.
[90] Ibid., part II, no. 5, pp. 523–4.

democracy (Rousseau), why, in fact, it was Rousseau who 'had completed the work of Bodin'.[91]

It followed from this that the idea of unlimited state sovereignty did not necessarily imply unlimited power of government over individuals which would have been tantamount to a complete denial of inalienable human rights. As a rule the reverse was true: Bodin wanted to limit the power of the monarch by natural and divine laws, and even Rousseau devoted one chapter of his *Social Contract* to the 'limits of sovereign power' (*Des bornes du pouvoir souverain*).[92] Nevertheless it was also plain that unlimited sovereignty could be interpreted as justifying state absolutism. For this reason, Novgorodtsev stressed that only natural law gave a firm theoretical foundation for a logically consistent construction of the inviolable subjective rights of the individual members of the state. In his view the idea of the sovereignty of the state had outlived its time and should be replaced by a subordination of the state to higher laws, originating in the depths of human nature. It had helped materially in breaking medieval particularisms and paving the way for modern civil society, but it should now be transformed into a 'mere symbol of unity'.[93] It should not be used against decentralizing tendencies because, in conditions created by the equality of all citizens before the law, such tendencies were no longer dangerous but, on the contrary, expressed a legitimate need for the free self-determination of different social forces.

It is striking that Novgorodtsev did not dwell on the differences between the absolutist and the democratic versions of the ideal of the sovereign state. He concentrated on natural, pre-political human rights and seemed to be saying that, from this point of view, the difference between Bodin's absolute monarchy and Rousseau's sovereignty of the people was not very important. He wanted to derive a just law and, thereby, the limitation of state power, from the very idea of the human personality and was keenly aware that the idea of the sovereignty of the people could be used to justify something very different, the unlimited power of the state. He wanted to defend the absolute moral standards of natural law and refused to recognize the sovereign will of the people as the only source of law. His *bête noire* was legal positivism, which was, of course, fully compatible with the doctrine of popular sovereignty, while his own theory was not.

There was also a political aspect in this. Novgorodtsev, had tried to

---

[91] Ibid., p. 520.
[92] Ibid., part I, no. 4, p. 429.   [93] Ibid., part II, no. 5, p. 523.

woo the *zemstvo* Slavophiles, but did nothing to conciliate the radicals, who demanded active participation in political power. His article was a theoretical defence of constitutional guarantees of human rights, not a theoretical justification of the struggle for parliamentary democracy. In contrast to the Slavophiles, he demanded legal reforms, not merely an improvement of the moral relationship between the tsar and the people; in spite of this, however, he placed himself on the right wing of the Liberation Movement.

The theoretical content of 'State and Law' is rather disappointing. It shows once more that Novgorodtsev's strength lay in analysing other people's ideas, not in original theoretical construction. As a neo-Kantian he should have been more discriminating in his attempts to derive law from human nature. In fact, however, while enthusiastically supporting Jellinek's efforts to explore the psychological foundations of law, that is, its 'subjective side', he did not care to point out the fundamental distinction between the empirical subject of psychology and the transcendental subject of idealist philosophy. He was eager to find support for natural law anywhere, even at the cost of the theoretical coherence of his views.

The element of psychologism in Jellinek's views encouraged Novgorodtsev to conclude that law was rooted 'in the depths of the psychic world of the individual'.[94] He triumphantly presented this view as powerful support for the natural law position, but failed to mention in this connection that a more elaborate theoretical basis for this conclusion could be found in Petrażycki's psychological theory of law, a theory which, unlike Jellinek's doctrine, broke definitively with legal positivism and consciously aimed at a revival of natural law. This strange omission must have been deliberate, since other, lesser representatives of the movement for the revival of natural law in Russia, such as V. M. Hessen, M. A. Reisner and Prince E. Trubetskoi, were carefully mentioned in the article.[95] A year before, in his article in *The Problems of Idealism*, Novgorodtsev discussed Petrażycki's theory, presenting it as an important stage in a return to the natural law standpoint. Whereas Jellinek tried to give a psychological explanation of law without abandoning legal positivism, Novgorodtsev wanted to

---

[94] Ibid., part I, no. 4, p. 450.
[95] Ibid., part II, no. 4, p. 510. All these names are mentioned in a footnote in which Novgorodtsev approvingly referred to the popularity of the natural law revival among Russian scholars. In such a context the omission of Petrażycki's name was indeed strange.

show the anti-positivist implications of the psychological approach to law, so the very logic of his argument demanded a reference to Petrażycki's theory.

It is difficult to believe that the lack of such reference was merely accidental: an explanation in terms of personal rivalry seems more probable. In 1904 Russian liberalism became an organized social movement, with very promising prospects, and Novgorodtsev must have felt the temptation to become its main theorist. He was not widely accepted in this role, but not because of the greater influence of Petrażycki. In fact both of them were ill-fitted for such a role because of the rapid radicalization of the movement.

4   The crisis of the juridical world-view

Novgorodtsev's reaction to the revolutionary events of 1905–6, including his own experiences in the First Duma, may be found in his book *The Crisis in the Modern Legal Consciousness* (published in 1906–8 in the journal *Problems of Philosophy and Psychology*). With his later book *On the Social Ideal*, it undoubtedly belongs to his best achievements. It is regrettable that it has not been translated and remains undeservedly neglected in the West.

I have already referred to Engels's conception of the 'classical world-view of the bourgeoisie', namely the 'juridical world-view'.[96] Novgorodtsev's book may be described as a comprehensive, historical, and critical analysis of this world-view, its emergence, development, and crisis. As such, it is truly unique without equivalent or counterpart in the scholarly output of other legal philosophers, whether in Russia or elsewhere.

In the introduction to his book Novgorodtsev quotes Tolstoy's criticism of the liberal movement on the eve of the 1905 revolution. Liberals, Tolstoy argued, wanted a constitution and representative government, not realizing that a mere change of external, political, and legal forms can never bring about a genuine improvement. What is really needed is religious and moral regeneration and the only means to achieve this is individual self-perfection.[97]

As might be expected, Novgorodtsev saw this as not only very wrong but also socially harmful, especially in the Russian situation. But he also recognized in it a somewhat crude expression of a general disappointment in merely political changes and of an increasingly

---

[96] See above, Ch. I, 2.
[97] Cf. P. Novgorodtsev, *Krizis sovremennogo pravosoznaniia*, Moscow, 1909, p. 3.

pessimistic view of law, characterizing contemporary legal consciousness. People, he stressed, no longer believed in the miraculous power
of legislation, they no longer saw law as a powerful instrument of social
regeneration.

It was quite different in the eighteenth and early nineteenth
centuries, when the ideal of the rule-of-law state held sway over
people's minds. The French Revolution was inspired by an ardent
faith in the miracles of republicanism, 'tous les miracles de la
république', as Robespierre put it.[98] The credo of the progressive
bourgeoisie was firmly based on three tenets:

1. A belief in the salutary force of political institutions,
2. a view of law, i.e. just law, as the crowning achievement of cultural
   progress, or, for Kant, as the final aim of universal history,
3. a view of the law-abiding state as the highest form of social unity, a
   'terrestrial God', in Hegel's phrase.[99]

Now however, this optimism had given way to a general disenchantment.
Law and the state were seen as instruments of oppression in the hands
of the privileged and powerful, as cold monsters (Nietzsche), or
necessary evils.[100] Even among legal philosophers the classical view of
law was being replaced by such completely new ideas as that of
solidarity. All these significant shifts in attitudes towards law and the
Rechtsstaat should, Novgorodtsev maintained, be treated as symptoms
of a deep crisis in the legal consciousness, which could no longer be
ignored.

He developed his views on the nature of this crisis by analysing two
conceptions which lay at the foundations of the modern rule-of-law
state: that of popular sovereignty and that of the rights of man. He
shared the view (put forward, among others, by Jellinek) that these two
conceptions were in fact incompatible, mutually exclusive: the absolute
sovereignty of the popular will would not tolerate the inalienable rights
of the individual, and a consistent doctrine of human rights would not
allow any unrestricted sovereignty of will—whether of the monarch, or
of the collective democratic majority.[101] But the peculiar feature of the
classical juridical world-view was precisely that it ignored this,
attempting to treat democracy (the principle of the sovereignty of the
people) and liberal individualism (the theory of human rights) as two
parts of the same anti-absolutist and anti-feudal programme. This

[98] Ibid., pp. 6–7.   [99] Ibid., pp. 8–9.
[100] Ibid., p. 12.   [101] Ibid., p. 65.

attitude, expressed in the French Declaration of the Rights of Man and the Citizen, was historically justified, since the two conceptions were indeed natural allies in the struggle against the ancient regime in politics and feudalism in social relations. On the theoretical plane, however, they contradicted each other and with the passage of time this contradiction became increasingly evident.

In accordance with this general view Novgorodtsev's book was divided into two parts, dealing with the two main components of the modern legal consciousness: the conception of the rule-of-law state, deriving its legitimacy from the popular will, and the theory of human rights, expressing the world-view of liberal individualism.

The classical theoretical formulation of the first was, of course, Rousseau's *Social Contract*. The attraction and lasting influence of this theory no doubt lies in its simplicity. In fact, however, the questions involved were not simple at all and Rousseau himself was aware of this. That is why he made a sharp distinction between the 'general will' and the 'will of all', and why he so strongly insisted that genuine democracy needed special conditions, such as a small state, a lack of deep social conflict and a patriarchal simplicity of life.

It was not true, Novgorodtsev stressed, that the French Revolution had realized the doctrine of Rousseau; while paying lip service to it, it had in fact changed it significantly. From the very beginning the ideologists of the French Revolution, especially Sieyès took it for granted that the French people did not already have a definite view of the different legislative proposals that, in other words, the popular will was not something ready-made and given, something prior to parliamentary debate, but rather something to be shaped, created as it were; not a fact to be reflected but a task to be achieved.[102] It followed from this that the parliamentary deputies should interpret their electors' wishes and not merely act as their mouthpiece, which meant in practice that their freedom in performing their representative function ought not to be restrained by any binding instruction, or by the threat of revocation by their electors. In this way the sovereign will of the people operated only as a very remote source (*fons remota*) for the will of the representative body, and the idea of a juridical expression of the popular will gave way to the quasi-mystical notion of the emanation of this will.[103] This was no modification, but a

---

[102] Ibid., p. 44.
[103] Ibid., pp. 111–12.

fundamental change, replacing the idea of the sovereignty of the people by the idea of representative government.[104]

The thorough transformation of Rousseau's doctrine was achieved by fusing it with the teachings of Montesquieu. The author of *The Spirit of Law* did not believe in direct manifestations of the popular will, holding that the common people were always either too passive or too active to become legislators. He recognized the possibility of conflict between the popular will and human rights, and emphasized that the ideal of justice in which he grounded the rights of man was entirely objective, natural, and independent of either the will of or acceptance by the populace. He was favourably impressed by British political institutions which Rousseau severely condemned, and his impact on the legacy of the French Revolution was in fact, and happily, greater than the impact of the latter.

In its subsequent evolution the idea of popular sovereignty was interpreted less and less literally; what remained of it in the final result was only a kind of regulative idea, a symbolic legitimation of political democracy. It became obvious that public opinion is usually passive and must be awakened, shaped and organized.[105] Both the theorists and the practitioners of political democracy understood that this was a task for political parties, which meant, of course, a complete break with Rousseau. It was recognized that politics consists in the active interpretation, shaping and direction of the popular will, and not merely its expression, that the decisions of representative bodies are the result of struggle between different forces, of transient compromises, and not a reflection of a stable and firm general will.[106] J. S. Mill concluded that the so-called popular will could not even be identified with the will of the majority, but merely with the will of those politicians who successfully posed as representatives of the majority.[107] James Bryce has shown that representative government rests upon passive acceptance rather than active support and Moisei Ostrogorski has exposed that role of the 'electoral machine' and of political oligarchies in the democratic system.[108] People who tried to counter such oligarchies by restoring the elements of direct democracy, such as referendums or extra-parliamentary legislative initiatives, could not succeed. The representative system proved well entrenched and the

---

[104] Ibid., pp. 96–9, 110.   [105] Ibid., pp. 122–9.   [106] Ibid., p. 131.
[107] Ibid., p. 130.
[108] Novgorodtsev often referred to James Bryce's *The American Commonwealth* and to Ostrogorski's *Democracy and the Organization of Political Parties* (London, 1902).

addition to it of some features of an archaic democracy could not change its essence.

Novgorodtsev concluded from this that in contemporary politics the will of the people was in fact nothing but the will of the organs of the body politic, although it remained the supreme concept to which everybody appealed.[109] He was careful to add, however that the 'despotism of the politicians' was confined to the narrow sphere of politics and presented no threat to the civil rights of individuals. Parliamentary government, he maintained, was indeed in a state of crisis, but constitutionalism was not, and a return to absolutism was not possible.[110]

In applying these ideas to Russian conditions one might easily conclude that constitutionally guaranteed civil rights were a more significant Western achievement than representative government and that the Russian liberals should therefore concentrate on defending the principles of constitutional monarchy, without necessarily trying to introduce the parliamentary system as well. In fact everything indicates that this was indeed what Novgorodtsev wanted to suggest. It implied a criticism of his own party, because the Kadets, as Maklakov has aptly put it, 'intentionally, as a matter of tactics, confused two completely different conceptions: the constitution and parliamentarianism'.[111]

Ostrogorski's book on democracy and political parties in Britain and the United States served the same purpose. The great merit of this pioneering book, written by a Russian liberal of Jewish background, consisted in its revelation of the darker aspects of the workings of suffrage democracy. According to S. M. Lipset, Ostrogorski was the first political analyst to demonstrate forcefully that 'party organizations are not democratic reflections of the popular will, but powerful instruments for dominating the electorate, for imposing officials, opinions, and policies on the public. As he, and later Michels, noted party functionaries have interests of their own and use their control of the party apparatus to further them.'[112] Novgorodtsev was in full agreement with Ostrogorski's view that the popular will, on which political democracy was supposed to rest, was mostly a product of manipulation, but in saying so he deliberately went against the main

---

[109] Novgorodtsev, *Krizis*, p. 207.   [110] Ibid., pp. 167–9.

[111] V. A. Maklakov, *The First State Duma*, p. 101.

[112] S. M. Lipset, 'Moisei Ostrogorski and the Analytical Approach to the Comparative Study of Political Parties', in S. M. Lipset, *Revolution and Counterrevolution: Change and Persistence in Social Structures*. New York, 1968, p. 404.

current of liberal thought. The mainstream Russian liberals were not pleased with Ostrogorski's findings and used their influence to prevent publication of his book in Russia. According to Max Laserson, 'they did not wish to stir up criticism of Western democracy and the Anglo-American state order at a time when the old autocratic Russian regime was challenged by world opinion and the country was on the verge of establishing a Western type of administration based on a large parliamentary representation.'[113] Novgorodtsev, however, thought otherwise. For him Ostrogorski's pessimistic view of political democracy was a useful reminder that the core value of liberalism was, and should be, human rights and not participation in political power.

Having shown that the popular will cannot be treated seriously as a solid foundation for political order, Novgorodtsev proceeded to the philosophical criticism of the doctrine of popular sovereignty. There was nothing inevitable, he argued, about the identification of the popular will with the will of the majority; on the contrary, the course of history had shown that everywhere the introduction of the majority principle was preceded by a belief that only unanimous decisions deserved to be treated as a true *vox populi, vox dei*. Nor was there anything inevitable in the treatment of the *vox populi* as the highest tribunal of justice; on the contrary, a single individual might be morally right and the collective might be totally wrong, the enslavement of one by all was as unjust as the enslavement of all by one.[114] In fact the only

---

[113] Max M. Laserson, *The American Impact on Russia—Diplomatic and Ideological—1784–1917*, New York, 1950, p. 390. Ironically, a shortened version of Ostrogorski's book later appeared in the Soviet Union (M. Ostrogorski, *Demokratiia i politicheskie partii*, 2 vols. Moscow 1927–1930, with a preface by E. Pashukanis). In the preface to this edition Pashukanis wrote:

> The author, according to his views, unquestionably stood on the average platform of the liberal Russian society of that time. Yet notwithstanding all this, that is despite the fact that the representatives of this society exercised an almost complete monopoly in literature and science and despite their enthusiastic propagandizing of the ideas of constitutionalism and democracy, the work of Ostrogorski, brilliantly and skillfully describing the political regime of the two most outstanding bourgeois democracies, never appeared in Russian translation . . .
>
> It may be that a fortuitous coincidence of circumstances prevented the translation of this work of Ostrogorski's into Russian. But behind this fortuitousness there is undoubtedly a more general hidden cause: The work of Ostrogorski contains a pitiless revelation of the real core of bourgeois democracy; it unmasks the true mechanism of the parliamentarian state ruled by bourgeois political pressure groups, and shows the ugliness behind this mechanism which tries to put on the deceptive face of 'national sovereignty', 'the will of the majority', etc.

(Quoted from Laserson, *The American Impact on Russia*, pp. 391–2.)

[114] Novgorodtsev, *Krizis*, p. 225.

consistent justification of the sovereignty of the people was provided by Bentham, who simply defined the good as the benefit of the greater number and thus completely eliminated any appeal to objective justice. In this way the principle of popular sovereignty was saved at the cost of its moral significance. Henceforth it could be defended as a matter of expediency, but not in the name of higher justice.[115]

The new turning point in the history of popular sovereignty was marked by the works of Tocqueville and J. S. Mill. They returned to the notion of human rights, placing these rights above any positive law and pointed out the dangers inherent in the unlimited power of the democratic majority.[116] Their views influenced even those liberal thinkers who, like Jellinek, were otherwise committed to legal positivism.[117] It became widely acknowledged that the popular will must be constrained by the rights of the individual, that the majority principle was not an equitable norm but merely a means of securing a relatively stable consensus, and that it might degenerate into a form of collective subjectivism and arbitrariness. In order to avoid such an outcome it was necessary to subordinate the collective will to a higher unconditional norm, which could serve as the moral foundation of society and the ultimate sanction of its legal order. Such a norm, Novgorodtsev concluded, could be found only in the 'principle of personality', the cornerstone of liberal individualism.[118]

This conclusion led naturally to the second half of the book, devoted to the history of modern liberal individualism and its present crisis. Lack of space makes it impossible to present here a summary of Novgorodtsev's historical analysis. But it is necessary to refer, at least, to his conception of the different stages in the development of individualism. It is tempting to treat them rather as different types of individualism, but this would contradict the author's intention: he specially stressed that he meant not different types, having no common denominator and therefore involving different principles, but different successive stages of one and the same principle.[119]

In its first stage, represented by the French Enlightenment, individualism was conceived as the participation of each individual in shaping the popular will. Thus individualism was inseparable from political democracy. The very notion of the individual was political: individuals were seen as active citizens, as members of state. The potential conflict between this theory and another individualistic

---

[115] Ibid., pp. 228–32.   [116] Ibid., pp. 233–5.   [117] Ibid., p. 236.
[118] Ibid., pp. 237–8.   [119] Ibid., p. 249.

theory, that of inalienable human rights based upon natural law, was either unnoticed, or deliberately ignored.

In classical German philosophy, especially in the philosophy of Kant, the individual was conceived as a 'species notion' (*rodovoe ponyatye*), that is, as a representative of universal human nature, a bearer of universal human rationality.[120] This notion of individualism was opposed to the inevitable particularism of different, historically determined forms of collective life. Individualism so conceived stood for universalism and therefore contributed to freeing men from dependence on closed estates or ethnic groups. At the same time, however, it was always ready to sacrifice living people to the cause of abstract humanity; thus Hegel reduced human individuals to the role of mere instruments in the history of the species, while for Marx the true individual, as opposed to the egoistic individual of bourgeois civil society, was a 'species being', a *Gattungswesen*.[121]

Yet another form of individualism—economic individualism—developed mainly in Britain. It was opposed to the *étatist* implications of the principle of popular sovereignty, preaching instead the supremacy of the individual will and the greatest possible depoliticization of life. But it was just as abstract as Rousseauan or German philosophical individualism. All these forms of individualism differed in their definitions of the true self, but all defined it in abstract terms—as *homo politicus*, *homo economicus*, or *homo universalis*.

In Novgorodtsev's view an appreciation of the truly individual, unique, distinctive features of each concrete personality was the result of a process of 'development of the principle of freedom within individualism'. What he meant was freedom of individualization, freedom to assert one's own unique personality, namely, something more than political or economic freedom; a truly *individualized* freedom, as opposed to a freedom to perform certain social roles, predetermined by the nature of the political or economic system. In this context he analysed the work of many different thinkers, such as Constant and Humboldt, who defended freedom in the private rather than the political sphere, Tocqueville, who pointed out the anti-libertarian aspect of democratic equality, J. S. Mill who saw individual freedom as endangered less by the state than by different social pressures, and Nietzsche, with his dream of superman and his hatred of the weak and mediocre. He even referred to the Russian ultra-

---

[120] Ibid., p. 259.   [121] Ibid., p. 271.

reactionary thinker, Konstantine Leontiev, who treated the rise of modern liberal individualism as a process of levelling down and was deeply hostile to everything peculiar, distinctive, different, and thereby destroying the individuality of persons, provinces, and nations.[122] Novgorodtsev recognized the existence of a certain conflict between the development of individuality and democratic equalization, but refused to see it as absolute incompatibility. Following Simmel's work *Über die Soziale Differenzierung* he distinguished two aspects of the atomic process of equalization: on the one band the destruction of the anti-individualist traditionalism of closely-knit social groups which created conditions for the emancipation of the individual, and, on the other hand, the subordination of newly emancipated individuals to the anonymous mechanisms and alienated social forces of large-scale society.[123]

In the next chapter, entitled 'The Development of the Principle of Equality Within Individualism', Novgorodtsev passed to directly political problems: to the transition from the Old to the New Liberalism, as it occurred in England. Unlike Chicherin, he did not question the view that the Old Liberalism had 'died and been buried',[124] but entirely agreed with the British liberal leader, former Home Secretary H. H. Asquith, who stated:

Liberty (in a political sense) is not only a negative but a positive conception. Freedom cannot be predicated, in its true meaning, either of a man or of a society, merely because they are no longer under the compulsion of restraints which have the sanction of positive law. To be really free, they must be able to make the best use of faculty, opportunity, energy, life. It is in this fuller view of Liberty that we find the governing impulse in the later developments of Liberalism in the direction of education, temperance, better dwellings, and improved social and industrial environment; everything, in short, that tends to national, communal and personal efficiency.[125]

These words are taken from Asquith's preface to a book on liberalism by H. Samuel which developed the view that 'the state has the duty to use its powers to help men to live their lives worthily'.[126] Novgorodtsev was fully prepared to accept this formula, since he had

---

[122] Ibid., pp. 296–7.   [123] Ibid., pp. 304–5.
[124] Ibid., pp. 313–14.
[125] See H. Samuel, Liberalism, *An Attempt to State the Principles and Proposals of Contemporary Liberalism in England.* (Introduction by H. H. Asquith) London, 1902, p. x. Novgorodtsev quoted these words in *Krizis*, pp. 315–16.
[126] Ibid., p. 207.

earlier embraced and developed Soloviev's 'right to a dignified existence'.[127] He traced the evolution of English liberalism in much detail and with great sympathy, pointing out that a similar evolution had taken place in Germany and France, and concluding that the New Liberalism marked 'a new stage in the development of the rule-of-law state'.[128] But he also posed a crucial question about the capacity of the rule-of-law state to cope with the new tasks, predicting that it would not be easy, that social tasks would multiply *ad infinitum*, and the difficulties involved would prove to be one of the main sources of the crisis in legal ideas.[129]

His last two chapters dealt with the situation in France. Unlike England, where the evolution from negative to positive freedom took place within a liberal tradition, in France this important change brought about a partial revival of some distinctively non-liberal ideas: backward-looking utopias, the preaching of a return to the harmony of the past organic epochs, nationalist anti-individualism, playing with the idea of a collective national soul, or dreams of restoring the 'moral unity of the country', reminiscent of Rousseauan anti-individualism.[130] There was, however, also a positive side to this. French thinkers, less committed to the mechanicism and atomism characteristic of British thought, proved more able to break the narrow confines of law and politics, to approach the new problems from historical, sociological, and moral perspectives. They were more aware of the inadequacy of legal change alone, of the need to create support for the new legal order in the new social morality.

A *sui generis* summing-up of these new ideas could be found, Novgorodtsev held, in the doctrine of 'Solidarism', inspired by Durkheim, developed by L. Duguit and popularized by L. Bourgeois, although his own attitude to this doctrine was undoubtedly ambiguous. He sympathized, of course, with its rejection of legal positivism, its emphasis on social duties and even with the view that private property should be treated as a social function rather than an inalienable right. He was not prepared, however, to follow Duguit in claiming that '*L'État est mort*' nor in rejecting the distinction between private and public law; he could not accept Duguit's attacks on the natural law tradition and his condemnation of the 'individualist theory of law', in opposition to which the Solidarists set a conception of 'social law'. Nevertheless, Novgorodtsev was inclined to treat the idea of solidarity

---

[127] See above, Ch. III, 6.
[128] Novgorodtsev, *Krizis*, p. 340.
[129] Ibid., p. 342.
[130] Ibid., pp. 362–4.

as an extension, and not an annihilation, of the liberal idea of personality. He stressed the differences between Duguit and anti-liberal thinkers, as for instance, in Duguit's rejection of quasi-mystical hypostatizations of collective will, and tried to prove that in practice French Solidarism was the equivalent of English New Liberalism.[131] In socio-political terms, he thought the essential content of both trends could be reduced to a demand for legal guarantees of the right to a dignified existence.[132]

This was in harmony with the final conclusion to the entire book. The idea of the rule-of-law state, Novgorodtsev argued, was based upon two theories, the theory of the sovereignty of the people and the theory of individualism, which had both undergone severe crises. The crisis in the idea of popular sovereignty found expression in a general disillusionment with formal, purely political democracy, that is, with the mechanisms of representative government; the crisis in individualism manifested itself in a movement towards positive freedom, towards an increasingly 'social' interpretation of democracy. The result of the first was growing criticism of the state, while the second produced a tendency to endow the government with new functions and to broaden the scope of its control over social life.[133] The dangers implicit in such a diagnosis were obvious, yet Novgorodtsev believed that they could be avoided. In spite of his severe criticism of the conception of popular sovereignty he wanted to preserve it at least as a 'regulative idea', if only to resist the positivist conception of absolute sovereign power of *any* state; in spite of his awarenes of the crisis in individualism he held firmly to the view that the idea of personality, that all people are persons endowed with certain inalienable rights, was the only possible foundation for a morally acceptable social and legal order. He saw no basic incompatibility between classical human rights and the new, social rights epitomized in Soloviev's concept of the right to a dignified existence, but stressed that the struggle for these new rights must not give rise to dangerous, destructive illusions of establishing a paradise on earth.

5 Law, socialism, and religion

Novgorodtsev's next book, *On the Social Ideal*, was first published in 1911–16 in the pages of *Problems of Philosophy and Psychology*, but appeared in book form only after the March revolution. It was devoted

---

[131] Ibid., p. 377.   [132] Ibid., p. 378.   [133] Ibid., pp. 392–3.

to the dangers of the utopian belief in a paradise on earth, to the common nature and most influential forms of this belief, and finally, to its present crisis.

Utopianism, Novgorodtsev explained, is a belief in an ideal society, a belief that the absolute ideal can take earthly form and be realized historically. It is secularized millenarianism, because the chiliastic heresy itself is the dream of a terrestrial realization of the Kingdom of God.[134] The fundamental error in such thinking is a disregard for the transcendent nature of the Absolute. Infinite, absolute content cannot be forced into finite forms and, therefore, any attempt at the immanentization, or terrestrialization, of the Absolute creates false Absolutes and encourages the mortal sin of idolatry. There is no immanent meaning in history, no definite direction, and no final goal. In this respect Novgorodtsev was in full accord with Herzen's book *From the Other Shore*, while disagreeing with Herzen's pessimistic conclusions. A rejection of the Hegelian historical theodicy did not, in his eyes, inevitably lead to the view that history is ruled only by the blind forces of nature, that everything in human life is relative, accidental, and meaningless, and that in his search for meaningful progress man is left without any guidelines and is doomed to eternal improvisation.[135] There *is*, Novgorodtsev claimed, a meaningful relationship between the Absolute and historical processes. The Absolute is above history but manifests itself in the unceasing, infinite striving for perfection, which is the source of all true progress. Every achievement of historical progress is necessarily relative, limited and transient, but, nevertheless, the Absolute is not completely absent in history; it can never take an earthly form, but it is always present in the striving for absolute values. History is neither divine, nor Godless.

In this way Novgorodtsev used the Kantian idea of a ceaseless, infinite striving for perfection to counter the idolatrous cult of false Absolutes while at the same time avoiding historical relativism. In religious terms it was a defence of the idea of a transcendent Kingdom of God, as opposed to an early millennium.[136]

To understand the genesis, function, and direct political relevance of this conception it is necessary to place it in the context of Russian

---

[134] P. Novgorodtsev, *Ob obshchestvennom ideale*. 3rd edn., Berlin, 1921, pp. 9–10, 20–1.

[135] Ibid., pp. 13–14, 34.

[136] Novgorodtsev acknowledged his intellectual indebtedness to the critique of utopianism in E. Trubetskoi's book *Mirosozertsanie V. S. Solovieva* (ibid., p. 144).

Pavel Novgorodtsev

thought after the revolution of 1905. Different combinations of secular
utopianism with religious, or quasi-religious, millenarianism and
messianism were an extremely characteristic feature of the intellectual
climate of that time. On the one hand Dmitry Merezhkovsky, the chief
ideologist of the so-called 'New Religious Consciousness', came out as
a prophet of a new revelation, a new religious dispensation which would
replace outworn 'historical Christianity', rehabilitate the flesh by
divinizing matter, and establish on earth a Messianic Kingdom of God
in the form of an anarchist theocracy. On the other hand a group
of Bolshevik intellectuals, who became known as 'God-builders'
combined religious messianism with Marxism. In contrast to the so-
called 'God-seekers', they preached, not a genuine belief in God, but a
Feuerbachian Religion of Humanity, in which God was conceived as
the collective creation of humankind; they sought collective salvation
on earth, not individual salvation in Heaven, and were really trying to
use religious enthusiasm in support of the millennial dreams of
communism. In 1908 the future Bolshevik Commissar, Anatoly
Lunacharsky, published his *Religion and Socialism* which presented
Marx as the last and greatest Jewish prophet, and the working class as
the new Messiah, whose sufferings would usher in the social
emancipation of all oppressed people and the total regeneration of
earthly life.[137] It is clear that to emphasize the eschatological dimension
of socialism and anarchism was by no means the monopoly of the
critics of these movements. True, most of the Russian intelligentsia
remained faithful to the tradition of the 'Enlighteners' of the 1860s,
but it was no longer possible to ignore the close affinities between the
old millenarian patterns of thoughts and the modern 'religion of
progress'.

Interestingly enough, the issue of millenarianism is still alive today;
in fact we are witnessing an unprecedented revival of the idea of
collective salvation on earth. In many under-developed countries
Christianity has been burdened with the task of earthly salvation, an
interpretation most radically and consistently developed in the Latin-
American 'theology of the liberation', but which can also be found in
the influential philosophy of Pierre Theilhard de Chardin. To make
use of religious sympathies in the cause of revolutionary socialism
became very common; left-wing scholars, including Marxists, produced a
vast literature idealizing all forms of millenarianism, especially in

[137] Cf. A. Lunacharsky, *Religiia i sotsializm*, SPb 1908, vol. 1, pp. 72, 101–2, 145–8,
188–9, vol. 2, ch. 8.

Third World countries.[138] On the other hand, the horrors of our
century have also produced books in which millenarian hopes are seen
as paving the way for totalitarian dictatorships.[139]

One of these books deserves special attention in the present context:
Karl Löwith's *Meaning in History*, which might be read as a precious
theological counterpart and supplement to Novgorodtsev's *On the
Social Ideal*. In spite of religious, philosophical, and other differences,
Löwith, a Protestant theologian and outstanding representative of
Christian existentialism, in fact developed the same argument as the
Russian scholar. He stressed that 'what the Gospels proclaim is never
future improvement in our earthly condition but the sudden coming of
the Kingdom of God in contradistinction to the existing Kingdom of
man'.[140] Consequently, he condemned the chiliastic vision of Joachim
of Floris and defined all forms of millenarianism as a fatal transition to
the 'irreligion of progress'—'a sort of religion, derived from the
Christian faith in the future goal, though substituting an indefinite and
immanent *eschaton* for a definite and transcendent one'.[141] Primitive
Christianity was permeated by millenarian expectations, but the great
Fathers of the Church led the way in rejecting them and reaffirming
the fundamental distinction between redemptive events and profane
happenings, between *Heilsgeschehen* and *Weltgeschichte*.[142] 'The Christian
doctrine from Augustine to Thomas had mastered history theologically
by excluding the temporal relevance of the last things. This exclusion
was achieved by the transposition of the original expectations into a
realm beyond historical existence.' But it is the tragedy of the Christian
world that the temptation to see eschatology in a terrestrial form
proved ineradicable, that attempts to fulfil history by and within itself
have not been abandoned and, finally, that 'the third dispensation of
the Joachites reappeared as a third International and a third *Reich*'.[143]

Norgorodtsev developed the same ideas in the language of Kantian

[138] See especially such works as E. J. Hobsbawm's *Primitive Rebels*, P. Worsley's *The
Trumpet Shall Sound*, or V. Lanternari's *The Religions of the Oppressed*. There is also a
dictionary of messianism and millenarianism, stressing the affinities between archaic
millenarianism and modern radicalism, messianic religions and the belief in progress:
H. Desroche, *Dieux d'hommes: dictionnaire des messianismes et millénarismes de l'ère
chrétienne*, Paris, 1968.

[139] See, for instance, N. Cohn, *The Pursuit of the Millennium*, London, 1957, and J. L.
Talmon's *The Origins of Totalitarian Democracy*, London, 1952, and *Political Messianism*,
London, 1960.

[140] K. Löwith, *Meaning in History: The Theological Implications of the Philosophy of
History*, Chicago, 1949, p. 112.

[141] Ibid., p. 114.   [142] Ibid., p. 203.   [143] Ibid., p. 159.

philosophy. He placed the absolute ideal not at the end of history, but above history, thus replacing a 'horizontal' vision of man's relation to the Absolute by a 'vertical' vision. He opposed temporalization of the Absolute and the idolatry of progress connected with it, setting against them the conception of a transcendent Absolute and the idea of the human personality as an end in itself and the only foundation of moral law.[144]

He saw the main threat in the absolutization of social ideals, as opposed to political ones. In the nineteenth century, as he had shown in his previous book, faith in politics was so deeply undermined that nobody any longer believed in the 'miracles of the republic'; on the contrary, it had become necessary to defend the ideal of the rule-of-law state, to resist disillusionment and to combat negative or cynical attitudes towards law and the state. But faith in the miraculous power of political change was replaced by an even more irrational faith in social change. The old idea of paradise on earth was revived in socialist and anarchist eschatology.

The main theoretical error in the very notion of the social ideal, Novgorodtsev contended, was the belief in the possibility of perfect harmony between the individual and society. A non-utopian social philosophy should abandon this assumption, and should acknowledge the inevitable lack of harmony between the individual and society: it should cease to oscillate between individualist and collectivist visions of social harmony, drawing instead a clear distinction between the individual and the social sphere.[145] The two spheres are united only on the higher plane of the absolute ideal, which can never be realized in history.

Almost half of Novgorodtsev's book is devoted to Marxism, the highest form of socialism and, in spite of its intention to abandon utopianism, the most influential utopian teaching of the nineteenth and twentieth centuries. The third edition in 1921 was enriched by penetrating remarks on Lenin and the October Revolution. On the whole, all chapters devoted to Marxism show Novgorodtsev at his best, as a historian of ideas capable of deep analysis and sharp criticism. His writings on Marxism were probably the first serious contribution to

---

[144] Novgorodtsev, *Ob obshchestvennom ideale*, pp. 139–41.

[145] Ibid., p. 142. The conception of history as an eternal oscillation between individualism and collectivism was developed, in response to the earlier edition of Novgorodtsev's book, by I. V. Hessen, the former editor of *Pravo*. See I. V. Hessen (Gessen), *Iskaniia obshchestvennogo ideala*, 2nd edn., Berlin, 1922.

'Marxology' (as distinct from Marxism) produced by a Russian scholar. In the present context, however, we must confine ourselves to a general outline of Novgorodtsev's conception, leaving aside his interesting and detailed presentation of the evolution of Marx's views, and even his concrete analyses of Marx's major texts.

Marxism, in Novgorodtsev's view, is the most perfect modern specimen of a religion of collective salvation in history, a religion of the immanent divinity of humankind, devoid of all yearnings for transcendence, because in a perfect earthly paradise all needs must be fulfilled while a yearning for infinity can never be satisfied.[146] It is a religion of absolute collectivism, or, rather, a religion of the species, conceiving salvation as reuniting individuals with the species, raising them to the level of species beings.[147]

In the Golden Age of Marxism, the epoch of the Second International the notion of man as 'species-being' (*Gattungswesen*) was almost completely ignored. This was, we are often told, because the most important works of the young Marx were then unknown. But this is only a partial explanation. More important is the fact that the dominant interpretation of Marxism was strongly coloured by positivist evolutionism and scientism, deeply hostile to all essentialism, and from this point of view the notion of man's species essence seemed a glaring contradiction of the spirit of 'scientific socialism'. It was only the so-called 'Western Marxism' of our times which rediscovered this notion and restored it to its central position in Marx's thought.[148] Novgorodtsev's achievement in anticipating this important shift in the interpretation of Marxism is therefore quite impressive. It must be stressed, however, that his conclusions were entirely different. Unlike later Marxologists and Western Marxists he did not try to use the concept of man as species-being to show Marx as a great humanist, deeply concerned with individuality and freedom; on the contrary, he presented him as an ardent advocate of a complete fusion of the individual and the species in a paradisiac state of grace, excluding individuality and freedom in the normally accepted meaning of these terms.[149]

---

[146] Ibid., pp. 154–7.   [147] Ibid., pp. 150–1.
[148] See, for instance, the chapter on 'The Human Essence' in A. W. Wood, *Karl Marx*, London, 1981, pp. 16–30. Wood is very consistent in interpreting Marx as a classical essentialist. In his 'Concluding Remarks' he stresses: 'Both his (Marx's) dialectical method and his concept of humanity are based more or less openly on the Aristotelian notion that things have essences and that the task of science is to understand the properties and behaviour of things in terms of these essences' (p. 235).
[149] Novgorodtsev, *Ob obshchestvennom ideale*, p. 198.

Novgorodtsev attributed crucial importance to Marx's early article 'On the Jewish Question', especially to the way in which it linked a vision of the future disappearance of political alienation (the state) to the disappearance of egoistic individuals composing civil society. He referred mainly to the following quotation:

Political emancipation is the reduction of man to a member of civil society, to an *egoistic independent* individual, on the one hand and to a *citizen*, a moral person, on the other. Only when actual, individual man has taken back into himself the abstract citizen and has become a *species-being* in his everyday life, in his individual work and his individual circumstances, only when he has recognized and organized his own powers as social powers so that social power is no longer separated from him as *political* power, only then is human emancipation complete.[150]

In Novgorodtsev's view these words described a utopian vision in which the state was unnecessary because people had become completely socialized. Marx was right in asserting that modern law and the rule-of-law state (*pravoe gosudarstvo*, in the terminology of Russian liberals) had sanctioned individualism. Indeed, the idea of law, as distinct from mere command, presupposes a limitation of freedom for the sake of equal freedom for others, thus securing the existence of a 'system of freedom', just as the modern idea of the state presupposes the existence of a sphere of life not regulated by public law, that is, the sphere of a free civil society. But just because of this the separate existence of the political sphere is a necessary precondition of individuality and freedom.[151] Man as species-being, that is, man directly and totally socialized, is no longer an individual right-holder. He may be better morally, if he has overcome his egoism, and more powerful, if he has succeeded in embodying in himself the capacities of the species, but he is no longer individualized and independent. In other words, the idea of personality and the idea of man as species-being are mutually exclusive.

In Marx's eyes, Novgorodtsev continued, individual freedom protected by the rule-of-law state was nothing more than the unworthy egoism of atomic individuals. This might have been true, or partly true, at an early stage in the development of the rule-of-law state, but it was foolish to mistake an early stage for the last stage, to confuse the birth-pangs of a new social order with its agony.[152] The subsequent

[150] See ibid. Quoted from *The Portable Karl Marx*, E. Kamenka (ed.), Penguin 1983, p. 114.
[151] Novgorodtsev, ibid., p. 200.   [152] Ibid., p. 199.

development of the rule-of-law state demonstrated its capacity to promote realistically conceived socialization. Nevertheless, Marx was right in claiming that the total socialization of man made law and the state superfluous or, to put it more strongly, that in the struggle between modern individualism, as exemplified by bourgeois civil society, and the tendency towards total socialization law and the state were definitely on the side of the former. Novgorodtsev agreed with this, while radically disagreeing with Marx's value-judgement—he used Marx's diagnosis to *justify* law and the state, to prove that the idea of a 'withering away of law and the state' must be rejected in principle, as identical in fact with the idea of a 'withering away' of autonomous personality.[153]

In making this claim Novgorodtsev carefully distinguished between Marx's view of law and the state, as an alienated political sphere whose existence was the other side of modern civil society, and the later, cruder conception, developed mainly by Engels, according to which law and the state were simply instruments of the will of the ruling class.[154] This conception, a particularly unsophisticated version of legal positivism, was in his view totally wrong. Law and the state, he argued, are the instruments of the public-legal regulation of social life, the exercise of which may be socially neutral and the need for which will not disappear with the disappearance of class divisions. Many socialist leaders, especially Lassalle, have grasped this truth and changed their views accordingly.

The Critique of the Gotha Programme, another important document for the understanding of Marx's attitude towards law and the state, was directly connected with his quarrel with Lassalle. In analysing it, Novgorodtsev agreed with Marx that 'right by its very nature can consist in the application of an equal standard' and, therefore, that every right is inevitably 'a right of inequality',[155] words which he saw as both an expression of the realistic side of Marx's world-view and also an additional explanation of the radical incompatibility between the juridical point of view and Marx's utopianism. On the one hand Marx had acknowledged that individuals were unequal—'they would not be different individuals if they were not unequal'.[156] On the other hand he

---

[153] Ibid., p. 229.
[154] Ibid., p. 200. The same distinction has recently been made by E. Kamenka in his article 'Law' in *A Dictionary of Marxist Thought*, T. Bottomore (ed.), Oxford, 1983, pp. 274–6.
[155] Ibid., p. 224 (Marx's words are quoted from *The Portable Karl Marx*, p. 540).
[156] *The Portable Karl Marx*, p. 540.

had envisaged that in a higher phase of communist society 'the narrow horizon of bourgeois right' would be crossed and the application of an equal standard, labour, would be replaced by the principle: 'From each according to his ability, to each according to his needs'. If so, Novgorodtsev commented, the passage to the higher stage of communism meant in practice that producers would cease to feel themselves as different individuals, becoming instead 'species-beings', renouncing any appeals to right and justice, wholly identifying themselves with the supra-individual life of the species.[157]

Novgorodtsev did not forget that the realization of this ideal was made dependent on the previous achievement of a high level of productivity and affluence. Taking into account other works by Marx and Engels he came to the conclusion that their criticism of law and the state was diametrically opposite to that of Stirner, whose anarchism consisted in a rejection of law and the state in the name of complete freedom for the irrational egoism of the individual.[158] Unlike Stirner, Marx and Engels criticized law and the state as institutions sanctioning egoistic individualism and therefore creating obstacles to a complete rationalization of social life. They conceived of freedom as the maximum rational control over the conditions of life and development of the human species. Their ideal of freedom was utterly collectivist and rationalist: collectivist, because they were concerned not with individual freedom, but with the creation of optimum conditions for the free development of humankind; rationalist, because they saw freedom as freedom from the accidental and irrational, that is, as rational planning and a perfect rational order eliminating all irrational spontaneity.[159] They were blind to the fact that administration over things is impossible without ruling over people and therefore the maximum rationalization of society cannot be achieved and maintained without increasing the role of compulsion in social life.[160]

This naturally led to Marx's attitude towards democracy. Novgorodtsev agreed with Bernstein that Marxism was compatible with both democracy and dictatorship, explaining this by the lack of sharp contrast between these two notions in Marxist theory.[161] According to Marx, democracy is a form of dictatorship, perhaps even a preferable form, but form is always less important than class content and, therefore, there can be no doubt that non-democratic dictatorship by a

---

[157] Novgorodtsev, *Ob obshchestvennom ideale*, p. 225.
[158] Ibid., p. 227.   [159] Ibid., p. 229.   [160] Ibid., p. 230.
[161] Ibid., pp. 216–18.

progressive class is always better than democratic dictatorship by conservative forces. On this question Novgorodtsev sided with Trotsky and Lenin.[162] Marxism, he wrote, may be combined with support for democracy, but only when such support is seen as conducive to the realization of its final ideal; if it is not, all other means are acceptable and sanctified in the name of the forward march of history. Everything depends on concrete conditions and, therefore, Kautsky's criticism of Lenin is completely groundless: Lenin's conception of proletarian dictatorship as the application of naked force by a revolutionary minority is no less Marxist than the democratic methods of proletarian struggle advocated by the elderly Engels and the German Social Democrats. The real difference between Bolshevism and genuine Marxism consists not in the Bolsheviks' contempt for democracy but in their disregard for the problem of economic preconditions to proletarian dictatorship.[163]

Lenin's book *State and Revolution* was for Novgorodtsev the best systematization of the anarchist motifs in Marx's thought.[164] But it was obvious to him that it was a rather pseudo-anarchism, based upon self-delusion, and that Bakunin came close to the truth in seeing Marxism as a form of state socialism.[165] The socialist state, burdened with the tasks of organizing production and distribution, would have to be stronger and more pervasive in its control over social life than all non-socialist forms of state power.[166] Its future withering away depended, in Marxist theory, on the prior achievement of a thorough rationalization of socio-economic conduct; such a rationalization, however, was impossible and, therefore, the need for state control over the totality of social life would never disappear. Further, this control would be exercised with a self-confidence and ruthlessness stemming from faith in the absolute social ideal.

Novgorodtsev accounted for the strength of this religious faith by instancing its peculiar combination with the spirit of positive science. Marxism notoriously pretended to be a purely scientific theory of history, based upon a knowledge of necessary and objective laws of social development and deriving its social ideal from these laws, and not from subjective feelings and utopian dreams. It rejected a normative approach, ridiculed ethical considerations, and presented historical processes as the 'objective course of things', completely independent of human consciousness and will. In Novgorodtsev's view

---

[162] Ibid., pp. 218, 210–11, n.   [163] Ibid., pp. 219–20.
[164] Ibid., p. 230, n.   [165] Ibid., p. 231.   [166] Ibid., p. 221.

this theory of history resembled Marx's theory of commodity fetishism, since in both cases man's products were endowed with a capacity for living a life of their own, independent of men and subjugating them.[167] On the other hand, however, Novgorodtsev detected in Marx strong, although hidden, ethical convictions, a passionate faith, an attempt to discover in history a deeper meaning, a theodicy, and not mechanical determinism;[168] he recognized that Marx's 'objectivism' coexisted with the powerful appeal of seizing control over historical forces and thus liberating man from the tyranny of things, making him master of his fate. There was no contradiction between 'objectivism' and activism, since history itself was believed to prepare conditions for the great leap from the 'kingdom of necessity' to the 'kingdom of freedom'. In this way optimistic fatalism changed mere hope into a scientific certainty.

Novgorodtsev's remarks on dialectics deserve attention as a definite break with the dominant interpretation, which saw dialectics as a general scientific theory of development. Anticipating to a certain extent the views of the young Lukács, Novgorodtsev pointed out that dialectics, properly conceived, was a method of thought and could only be given an ontological meaning in Hegelian panlogism, which identified thought and being.[169] Marx and Engels should have rejected its ontological interpretation, but the temptation to transform it into a scientific theory of development, guaranteeing the victory of their ideal, proved too strong. In this way the theory of so-called 'dialectical materialism' came into being.[170] The systematic exposition of this theory was the work of Engels who, in fact, transformed dialectics into a kind of positivist evolutionism.[171] He emphasized, of course, the importance of revolutionary changes but, nevertheless, could not properly justify the notion of an absolute change. Relativism, inherent in scientific evolutionism, was incompatible with the absoluteness of the final ideal, while materialism badly fitted the Hegelian legacy. Because of this Marxism as a systematic world-view could not escape contradictions and eclecticism. It combined materialism with idealism, scientism with utopianism, fatalism with pragmatism, absolutism with relativism, economism with eschatological vision.[172]

For a long time this could be seen as a pattern of dialectical tensions

---

[167] Ibid., p. 167. The same observation was made by the young Lukács in his *Geschichte und Klassenbewusstsein*. Lukács, however, concluded that Marx's theory of history is in fact a theory of the reification of historical processes, characteristic of capitalism; in other words, a theory of something which can and should be abolished.

[168] Ibid., pp. 163–70.   [169] Ibid., p. 172.

[170] Ibid., p. 176.   [171] Ibid., pp. 172–4.   [172] Ibid., pp. 177–8.

within a higher, well-constructed whole. It was a source of strength to the Marxist world-view, the reason for its appeal to a wide variety of people. But the application of Marxism to the solution of practical problems brought about its inevitable disintegration. Different thinkers took different parts of the Marxian synthesis. Bernstein took scientific evolutionism, Sorel inherited the irrationalist spirit of activism, and both made a conscious decision to go beyond Marxism.[173]

The last chapters of Novgorodtsev's book are devoted to German Social Democracy and French Syndicalism. The development of Social Democracy was shown as a process of consistent and irrevocable de-eschatologization of Marxism. In his presentation of French Syndicalism Novgorodtsev stressed not only its uncompromisingly negative attitude towards the state, but also its 'realistic and vital side', namely its increasingly positive attitude towards law.[174] He meant by this the Sorelian idea of the syndicates as a source of new juridical principles, new *social* law, independent of the state, an idea inspired by Proudhon who rejected the sovereignty of the state and the 'government of the will', but freely acknowledged the authority of the law.[175] Like some other Russian liberals,[176] Novgorodtsev treated these views as a symptom of the growth of positive attitudes towards law within socialism and, at the same time, as welcome support for his own criticism of the idolatry of the state in legal positivism.

The conclusion of the book was well balanced. Marxism, Novgorodtsev argued, had split into reformist and revolutionary currents; the former had already abandoned the utopia of ultimate salvation on earth, the latter was still under its sway, but sooner or later the utopian ideal would become either discredited or rejected. This would be tantamount to the death of Marxism, which as a total world-view is inseparable from the absolute ideal. But everything valuable in Marxism would be saved by democratic socialism and assimilated by

[173] Ibid., pp. 181–2.   [174] Ibid., pp. 339–40.
[175] See especially Sorel's article 'The Socialist Future of the Syndicates', in J. L. Stanley (ed.), *From George Sorel: Essays in Socialism and Philosophy*, New York, 1976. Cf. J. Stanley, *The Political and Social Theories of George Sorel*, Berkeley, 1981, pp. 114, 206–12.
Proudhon has been characterized as the best representative of the strain of anarchist theory which was able to support the Aristotelian model of political association—a model based upon 'the profoundest *respect* for law.' See Lisa Newton, 'The Profoundest Respect for Law: Mazor's Anarchy and the Political Association', in J. R. Pennock and J. W. Chapman (eds.), *Anarchism*, (Nomos 19), New York, 1978, pp. 160, 164.
[176] Especially Gurvitch with his theory of 'social law' and Hessen (see Ch. IV, 7 and Ch. VII, 4).

the modern rule-of-law state. The 'deepest intuitions of Marxism' could be reduced to the idea of man's right to a dignified existence. There was nothing specifically socialist in this principle; it was formulated in the process of the organic development of liberal thought and Marxism had obscured rather than clarified it. Nevertheless, Novgorodtsev conceded, 'we must recognize that Marxism marks a point after which moral consciousness cannot return to the past, after which the modern rule-of-law state had radically to change its views on the tasks of politics, on the nature of law, and on the principles of equality and freedom'.[177]

In exile, having survived the ordeals of the revolution and civil war, Novgorodtsev returned to the problem of the social ideal in a directly religious context. He wrote an article on the Russian religious consciousness in which he developed a Slavophile-inspired conception of Catholicism, Protestantism, and Orthodox Christianity.[178] The Catholic Church, he claimed, had always been inclined to treat itself as the visible embodiment of the Kingdom of God, thus succumbing to the temptation of seeing the absolute ideal realized on earth. Protestantism represented the opposite tendency, towards subjectivist interiorization of religious life, concentrating on the Kingdom of God within individual souls and leaving the organization of social life to the mercy of the secular authorities. The Orthodox Church believed that the Kingdom of God, conceived as the ideal of collective salvation, would be fully realized only at the end of time and did not see itself as its representative in the present; none the less, it also believed that people should always be guided in their social life by the invisible light of the divine ideal. In this manner, according to Novgorodtsev, Orthodox Christianity avoided the errors of both Catholicism and Protestantism. It was the tragedy of the Russians that they proved unable to learn from their Church and to apply its teaching in their striving for the realization of the social ideal.[179]

In his obituary tribute to Novgorodtsev, G. Gurvitch presented Novgorodtsev's peculiar 'Slavophilism' as the expression of a deep spiritual crisis which seemed to lead him to break almost completely with his former views, but added, that this was rather a dialectical phase in Novgorodtsev's spiritual development, and that in his last

[177] Novgorodtsev, ibid., p. 385.
[178] P. Novgorodtsev, 'Sushchestvo russkogo pravoslavnogo soznaniia', in *Pravoslavie i kul'tura*. V. V. Zenkovsky (ed.), Berlin, 1923.
[179] Ibid., pp. 22–3.

days Novgorodtsev had begun to reconcile his new ideas with his liberal Westernism.[180]

In the light of my analysis the problem is simpler. The idealization of the Orthodox Church was indeed something new in Novgorodtsev's world-view, but it entailed no change in his view of the social ideal, or on the relationship between the relative and the absolute in human life. On the contrary, he simply concluded that the Orthodox Church was close to his own position. The absolute ideal, he thought, should be neither immanent, because this would mean deification of the world and absolutization of the relative, nor absolutely extramundane, because this would sever all links between the relative and the absolute. The proper solution was to conceive the ideal as transcendent while, at the same time, making it a 'regulative idea', always present in our activities and imparting a higher meaning to them. In his article on the Russian religious consciousness Novgorodtsev said nothing new on this matter, but merely expressed his views in religious language and even in the language of Russian popular mythology. The idea of Kitezh Grad, hidden on the bottom of a deep lake, but nevertheless, guiding true believers in their search for truth and justice,[181] impressed him not as a new solution of the problem of the absolute ideal, but, rather as confirmation of his own conception.

[180] Gurvitch, 'Prof. P. I. Novgorodtsev', pp. 392–3.
[181] Novgorodtsev, 'Sushchestvo', p. 22.

VI

Bogdan Kistiakovsky and the Debate about the Intelligentsia

1 Introductory remarks and biographical note

BOGDAN Kistiakovsky (1868–1920), the author of the classic article on the Russian disrespect for law,[1] was born to a Ukrainian family which had deserved well of its country.[2] His father, Alexander Kistiakovsky, was professor of criminal law at the University of Kiev and president of the Legal Society in Kiev, which he founded and provided with a programme advocating liberal legal reforms.[3] As a criminologist, he was well known for his resolute opposition to capital punishment, his advocacy of more humane treatment for juvenile delinquents, his attacks on severe administrative penalties, and his popularization of the theories of progressive foreign criminologists. He also wrote on the history of law in Ukraine and was involved in the movement for the Ukrainian national awakening. He was the co-editor of the short-lived journal *Osnova*—the first socio-political and cultural Ukrainian journal, published in Petersburg in 1861–2. This journal, devoted to the study of Ukraine and the promotion of Ukrainian literature, numbered among its contributors the greatest Ukrainian poet, Taras Shevchenko, and the two famous historians and ideologists of Ukrainian nationalism, N. I. Kostomarov and P. A. Kulish.

In spite of his deep involvement in the rise of the Ukrainian national awakening movement Alexander Kistiakovsky had also close links with Russian culture. The young Ukrainian intelligentsia was never sufficiently numerous or strong enough to dominate the intellectual life of its country, and the draconian measures of Russification introduced in 1876 threatened its very existence. The language of

---

[1] See above, p. 13.
[2] The Ukrainian spelling of his surname is 'Kistiakivs'kii'. I am using the Russianized form 'Kistiakovsky' because he himself used it in his publications.
[3] See *Russkii biograficheskii slovar'*. Reprint, New York, 1962, vol. 8, pp. 720–5.

education was Russian, most publications in Ukrainian were prohibited, the culture of the upper classes was, as a rule, either Russian or Polish. This created a situation in which even the members of the Kistiakovsky family were not assured of their national identity, but had to rediscover and struggle for it. In an open letter to P. B. Struve (published in 1911) Bogdan Kistiakovsky described his case thus:

As for myself, I was born in one of the biggest and, therefore, Russianized Ukrainian cities; the family into which I was born was highly educated and, therefore, to a considerable degree, also Russianized. I know not only Russian and Polish but also foreign languages, I can even write in them; and till now I have not ceased to curse my fate for not being educated in a native [Ukrainian] school; I curse it for the fact that as a child I rarely heard the songs and melodies of my country, that my imagination was not being moulded by native fairy-tales, that my first acquaintance with literature was not in my native language, in a word, that I was alien to the people among whom I lived, alien to my own nation. Only as an adolescent did I embark on serious study of the Ukrainian language, become acquainted with Ukrainian songs, literature and poetry, come to love Ukrainian theatre; and I have always thought, and continued to think, that only then did I begin to be an educated and cultured man. Emotional experiences of that period of my life greatly broadened my perceptive capacity. Only then did I become deeply responsive to the irresistible force of Russian and European lyrical poetry, only then did I suddenly penetrate the essence of dramaturgy and elaborate a completely new view of literature. You maintain that Ukrainian culture does not as yet exist; perhaps you are right. But is it not strange that the elements from which this culture is to be or is already being composed, made me an educated and cultured man? This paradox has been created by life itself.[4]

This letter makes it clear, once for all, that Kistiakovsky felt himself Ukrainian, not Russian. Although addressed personally to Struve, it was written in the form of an article entitled 'On the Issue of an Independent Ukrainian culture'; it was signed 'a Ukrainian' and left no doubt that its author wholeheartedly supported the cause of Ukrainian cultural independence.

True, Kistiakovsky cut himself off from Ukrainian political separatism and criticized the extreme forms of Ukrainian nationalism. At the same time, however, he accused Russian society, as well as the Russian government, of an extremely 'egoistic' attitude towards Ukraine, by which he meant its chauvinistic policy of Russification;[5] he made the

---

[4] See [Kistiakovsky], 'K voprosu o samostoiatel'noi ukrainskoi kulture. Pis'mo v redaktsiiu', *Russkaia mysl'*, 1911, no. 5, p. 142.

[5] Ibid., p. 133.

same accusation against Struve, to whom the mere idea of the Ukrainian language in high schools and universities seemed bizarre and unacceptaแ 'e. Kistiakovsky recognized the 'overwhelming greatness' of Russian culture but refused to conclude from this that an independent and original Ukrainian culture had no chance to develop.[6] Neither overconfident nor dogmatic, he saw both the future and the past of Ukrainian culture as a great enigma. 'I am completely unable', he confessed, 'to give a more or less satisfactory explanation of how it was possible for Ukraine in the nineteenth century, in spite of horrible conditions, to produce more than eighty poets, novelists and playwrights.'[7] He was inclined to believe that this phenomenon was not explicable in rational terms, but just for this reason he saw the Ukrainian cultural awakening as testimony to the irrational and indestructible vitality of the Ukrainian will to exist. He wrote:

It should be recognized that the Ukrainian people is endowed with a separate will, or a certain mystical force, which prompts it to assert its independent national individuality . . . Of course, this is not a solution, only a different formulation, of the historico-cultural riddle.

In any case, if the Ukrainian striving for an independent culture is a divine cause, it cannot be defeated by earthly forces. The words of Gamaliel, in the Acts of the Apostles, about the newly emergent Christianity, may be applied to all cultural movements. Every genuine cultural movement is a manifestation of the divine spirit in man; therefore it is sacred, and to do violence to it is a sin.[8]

It is evident from this that Bogdan Kistiakovsky, however moderate, however ready to subordinate the Ukrainian national cause to the cause of freedom throughout the state as a whole, was a committed Ukrainian cultural nationalist. Therefore it is hardly accurate to call him simply 'a Russian sociologist and jurist'.[9] On the other hand, it is.

---

[6] Ibid., p. 143.   [7] Loc. cit.

[8] Ibid., p. 146. Kistiakovsky refers here to the following words of 'a Pharisee named Gamaliel': 'So I advise you to keep away from these men [Christians] and leave them alone; for should this plan or movement be merely human, then it will go to pieces; but if its source is God, then you will be unable to crush them. You might even find yourself fighting against God' (Acts of the Apostles, 5:34–9).

[9] Cf. G. Gurvitch, 'B. A. Kistyakovsky', in *Encyclopaedia of Social Sciences*, New York, 1932, vol. 8, pp. 575–6. Alexander Vucinich, who devoted an entire chapter to Kistiakovsky in his *Social Thought in Tsarist Russia* is somewhat inconsistent in this matter: he stresses Kistiakovsky's Ukrainian background but, nevertheless, calls him 'a typical Russian sociologist'. (See A. Vucinich, *Social Thought in Tsarist Russia: The Quest For a General Science of Society, 1861–1917*, Chicago and London 1976, p. 125.) In a recent Soviet presentation of Kistiakovsky's thought his Ukrainian background is not mentioned at all. (See B. A. Chagin (ed.), *Sotsiologicheskaia mysl' v Rossii:*

undeniable that he took an active part in Russian intellectual life and contributed to Russian thought. In this respect his case is similar to Petrażycki's: both were non-Russians but deserve a place not only in the history of social science in Russia but also in Russian intellectual history, broadly conceived.

Let us turn to the biography of this remarkable man.[10] The available data are scarce but significant, closely related to his intellectual activities.

As a high school student Bogdan Kistiakovsky resisted Russification by his active participation in various circles devoted to the study of illegal works on Ukrainian history and culture. He was punished for it by expulsion and changed schools several times, even moving to other Ukrainian cities. The same pattern was repeated at university level: he enrolled at Kiev University, then moved to Khar'kov, and finally had to leave his native Ukraine by moving to the University of Dorpat (Tartu). In Dorpat he joined a Marxist circle but did not abandon his interest in the Ukrainian national revival. He spent his summer vacations preaching a combination of Marxism and Ukrainian cultural nationalism to the Ukrainian population of Volhynia, which led to his arrest and imprisonment in 1892. On his release in 1893 he was under police surveillance for a further two years, after which he decided to continue his studies in Germany.

Kistiakovsky's time abroad proved very fruitful. He studied in Berlin under Georg Simmel, in Heidelberg, in Paris and, finally, in Strasbourg where he attended the seminars of Wilhelm Windelband and completed his doctoral dissertation, 'Society and the Individual'. This was published in book form (*Gesellschaft und Einzelwesen*, Berlin) in 1899, and marked his final break with Marxism. In it, he combined some of Tönnies's and Simmel's ideas with the sophisticated methodology of the neo-Kantians; he severely criticized some sweeping sociological generalizations, especially Paul Lilienfeld's organicist theory, and elaborated a more precise conceptual apparatus for the social sciences. For example, he distinguished between 'the state in the juridical sense' and 'the state in the sociological sense', which corresponded to his distinction between the normative and the sociological approach. This aspect of his work was discussed at length

Ocherki nemarksistskoi sotsiologii poslednei treti XIX—nachala XX veka, Leningrad, 1978, pp. 260–4.)

[10] In my account of Kistiakovsky's life I rely almost entirely on Vucinich, *Social Thought in Tsarist Russia*.

in Hans Kelsen's *Der soziologische und juristische Staatsbegriff* and influenced Kelsen's theory of the 'juridical' and 'sociological' attributes of the state.[11] Kistiakovsky's début was well received in Germany. Apart from Kelsen, it favourably impressed such eminent scholars as Georg Jellinek, Alfred Vierkandt, and Max Weber,[12] and influenced the American Sociologist R. E. Park, who was then studying in Berlin.[13] Thus, like Petrażycki, he first won recognition in Germany, a big asset to an academic career in Russia. But thereafter Kistiakovsky's fate differed markedly from Petrażycki's. He was not a professorial candidate, but was treated with suspicion as a potential enemy of the state. Having defended his doctoral dissertation, he returned to Russia, where shortly afterwards his wife was arrested and exiled for her work in the Ukrainian democratic-nationalist movement. In consequence Kistiakovsky returned to Germany and embarked on political activity there. He helped Struve to edit the *émigré* journal *Liberation*, took part in organizing the Union of Liberation and was present at the meeting of constitutionalist leaders in Schaffhausen.[14] In the pages of *Liberation* he set out his views on the Ukrainian question, which he saw as subordinate to the cause of pan-Russian liberation, and expressed his belief that victory for constitutionalism in the Russian empire would automatically bring about a satisfactory solution to the problems of subject nationalities. (In later years he became painfully aware that this was an illusion.)[15] He also took an active part in publishing the political works of M. P. Dragomanov, whom he regarded as the most important ideologist of the non-chauvinist, democratic element in the Ukrainian nationalist movement.

His main scholarly achievement at that time was the long article 'The Russian Sociological School and the Category of Possibility in Solving Socio-Ethical Problems', published in Novgorodtsev's

[11] Cf. Hans Kelsen, *Der soziologische und der juristiche Staatsbegriff. Kritische Untersuchung des Verhältnisses von Staat und Recht*, Tübingen 1962, pp. 106–13 and *passim*.
[12] Cf. Vucinich, *Social Thought in Tsarist Russia*, p. 126. Vierkandt's review of Kistiakovsky's book appeared in *Zeitschrift für Socialwissenschaft*, 10, 1900, pp. 748–9.
[13] See L. A. Coser, *Masters of Sociological Thought*, 2nd edn., New York, 1977, pp. 368, 374–5.
[14] See above, p. 294.
[15] See [Kistiakovsky], 'K voprosu o samostoyatel'noi ukrainskoi kul'ture', pp. 133–4. Kistiakovsky referred in this context to the fact that his early articles in *Liberation* were strongly criticized by Ukrainian nationalists and implied that his critics were not entirely wrong (ibid.).

symposium *The Problems of Idealism*. Max Weber took notice of this and used some of its ideas in constructing his own theory of 'objective possibility'.[16]

The revolution of 1905 and the return of his wife, who was released from exile in 1904 and allowed to join him in Germany, gave a new stimulus to Kistiakovsky's interest in the Ukrainian question and brought him closer to Ukrainian nationalist organizations. This did not, however, prevent him from working with the Russian liberals and, later, joining the newly formed Kadet party.[17] He viewed revolutionary events from a pan-Russian liberal perspective and his knowledge of them was impressive. Max Weber chose him as his main guide in writing his book *Zur Lage der bürgerlichen Demokratie in Russland* (1906).[18]

After the October Manifesto Kistiakovsky returned to Russia. He was appointed to a teaching position at the Institute of Commerce and, after 1909, also taught as *Pravotdozent* at Moscow University. In 1911 he joined the group of liberal professors who resigned from the University in protest against the repressive measures of the government.[19] Almost immediately he accepted an offer from the Demidov Lycée in Jaroslavl to teach the philosophy of law and political science there. In 1912 he became editor-in-chief of the revived *Juridical Messenger*, the prestigious organ of the Moscow Juridical Society, previously edited by S. A. Muromtsev. He contributed to many journals and in 1916 published a collection of his articles under the title *The Social Sciences and Law*. This book of seven hundred pages is rightly considered his *magnum opus*. According to A. Vucinich, who concentrated on its sociological aspects, 'no Russian sociological work of pre-Soviet vintage matched Kistiakovsky's *magnum opus* in the compass of examined problems, the depth of epistemological analysis, and the logical elaboration of methodology'.[20]

This high assessment, made many years later, was not widely shared in Kistiakovsky's lifetime. He was undoubtedly underestimated and did not occupy a central place in Russian political and intellectual life.

[16] Cf. Vucinich, *Social Thought in Tsarist Russia*, pp. 136–7.

[17] See R. Pipes, *Struve: Liberal on the Right, 1905–1944*, Cambridge, Mass. 1980, p. 107.

[18] See R. Pipes, 'Max Weber and Russia', *World Politics*, vol. 7, no. 3, 1955, pp. 380–1.

[19] See above, pp. 296–7.

[20] Vucinich, *Social Thought in Tsarist Russia*, p. 128.

Politically he was probably too involved in the Ukrainian question and, at the same time, too disappointed by the Kadets' attitude towards it, to become influential in the Kadet party. Intellectually too he was isolated, because he consciously distanced himself from the three main currents in Russian social philosophy, populist 'subjective sociology', Marxism, and metaphysical idealism. While the same was true of Petrażycki, he could compensate for this disadvantage by the striking originality of his theories and by the influence he exerted on his many students and disciples. In other words, Kistiakovsky was perceived as the author of many respectable academic works, but not as a mainstream thinker.

There was, however, one important exception to this. Among Kistiakovsky's many articles, one stirred up all thinking Russians and became the subject of debate throughout the nation. This was his contribution to *Landmarks*, entitled 'In the Defence of Law; the Intelligentsia and Legal Consciousness'. From all points of view, in form, content, and historical significance, it was and remains a classic in its field. It is the best introduction yet written to the problem of Russian 'legal nihilism', and an extremely important contribution to the controversy about law in Russian intellectual history.

The last years of Kistiakovsky's life were bound up with his native Ukraine. After the March revolution he was appointed to the chair of law at the University of Kiev. In 1919 he was elected to the Ukrainian Academy of Sciences, which he had helped to found and which (to quote A. Vucinich) 'symbolized the unity of revitalized Ukrainian national identity and the world of modern scholarship'.[21] In the following year, however, he died suddenly and this, though premature, saved him from the inevitable disappointments which would otherwise have fallen to his lot in the future.

2 Scientific idealism

Kistiakovsky defined his philosophical position as 'scientific idealism': that is, he did not see idealism and scientism as mutually exclusive. He took part in the revolt against positivism but did not interpret it as a revolt against science; on the contrary, he saw neo-Kantian idealism as a rigorously scientific philosophy, providing the social sciences with a sophisticated methodology and solid epistemological foundations. He

[21] Loc. cit.

wanted to overcome naturalism and relativism but without indulging in metaphysical fancies, let alone religious mysticism.

These features of his thought were clearly present in his article on the Russian sociological school, in Novgorodtsev's symposium *The Problems of Idealism*. Unlike Struve,[22] he opted only for transcendental idealism, carefully avoiding the metaphysics of a transcendent idealism. In his view the so-called 'subjective sociology' of Lavrov and Mikhailovsky was not an early attempt to resist positivism and to vindicate the metaphysical value of personality,[23] but rather a product of the relativist degeneration of the scientific spirit. The two populist sociologists defended 'subjectivism' against 'objectivism', 'possibility' against 'necessity'; their programmatic 'subjectivism' implied the independence of ethical values from facts, which could be interpreted as acceptance of the Kantian view of *Sein* and *Sollen*. In Kistiakovsky's opinion, however, such an interpretation was not only superficial but basically wrong. Science, he stressed, cannot dispense with the category of necessity, and ethics cannot be based upon subjectivism. Neo-Kantian idealism tries to establish the objective existence of values and sees inner necessity in moral duty; therefore, its dualism between *Sein* and *Sollen* has nothing in common with the opposition between 'objectivism' and 'subjectivism'. There is no contradiction between necessity and duty, because the idea of duty contains within itself the idea of necessity, and both ideas are equally opposed to 'subjectivism, relativism, and arbitrary choice between different possibilities.[24] Populist 'subjective sociology' was based upon the discovery that human knowledge is socially pre-determined and therefore cannot pretend to neutrality and objective validity; thus, it was a form of sociological relativism. It was also a form of ethical relativism because it saw moral values as something desirable and dependent on subjective choice, instead of treating them as objective and obligatory. As such, 'subjective sociology' should not be seen as an attempt to overcome the cultural crisis brought about by positivism; it was rather a part of this crisis. Marxism, with its defence of objective truth and its attempts to derive the *ought* from the *is*, was far superior and its victory

---

[22] See P. Struve, 'K kharakteristike nashego filosofskogo razvitiia', in P. Novgorodtsev (ed.), *Problemy idealizma*, Moscow, 1903, p. 90.

[23] This was Struve's view, see ibid., pp. 83–5.

[24] B. Kistiakovsky, *Sotsial'nye nauki i pravo: ocherki po metodologii sotsial'nykh nauk i obshchei teorii prava*, Moscow, 1916, p. 119.

over 'subjective sociology' was both fully deserved and historically and theoretically justified.[25]

Kistiakovsky's opinion of Marxism was combined with an original interpretation of it and sharp criticism of some of its aspects. He developed it mainly in his early article 'The Categories of Necessity and Justice in Studying Social Phenomena' (1900), in which he explained the reasons for his break with Marxism. In his view Marxism was valuable not as a system of materialist metaphysics, a world-view, or even a theory of history, but only as a set of methodological proposals for the social sciences,[26] proposals which, though not always formulated with sufficient precision and clarity, should nevertheless not be ignored. This lack of precision, leading sometimes to grave misunderstanding, stemmed from a confusion of Hegelian dialectics with positivist evolutionism and from treating evolutionism as a method—although, unlike dialectics, the theory of evolution was just a description of certain facts, not a method of thought.[27] The results of this were two. On the one hand, the legacy of idealist dialectics, unduly concerned with the vision of an all-embracing totality, gave rise to such sweeping generalizations as the thesis concerning determination of the superstructure by the base, a thesis which was clearly untenable and had consequently to be reduced to the vague and unscientific idea of determination 'in the last instance'.[28] On the other hand, scientific laws became identified with laws of development which led to a general and fundamental confusion about the nature of scientific laws as such. Science, Kistiakovsky argued, deals with isolated causal relations, because only an isolated relationship can be truly causal, that is, characterized by absolute necessity.[29] Historical materialism, therefore, has scientific value only as a methodological device for explaining isolated, artificially abstracted series of facts, but not as a general philosophy of history. Secondly, the notion of the laws of development (or laws of evolution) is a contradiction in terms because scientific laws must be truly necessary and generally valid, not dependent on temporal and spatial variables.[30] Applying this point of view to Marxism, Kistiakovsky

---

[25] Ibid., p. 73.

[26] Ibid., p. 133.

[27] Ibid., p. 144. Kistiakovsky's view of Marxism was almost certainly influenced by Plekhanov, whose philosophy best exemplifies materialist metaphysics and the confusion of dialectics with evolutionism.

[28] Ibid., pp. 138–9.

[29] Ibid., p. 140.

[30] Ibid., p. 149.

came to the conclusion, rather uncommon in his time, that the most valuable part of Marx's theory was to be found in the discovery of certain generally valid, supra-temporal economic laws, such as the laws of commodity exchange, the relation between value and price, surplus value and profit, and so forth. By these discoveries, he believed, Marxism would pave the way for the revival of classical political economy.[31]

To understand Kistiakovsky's position we must always remember that, as a neo-Kantian, he did not conceive of facts and relations between facts as something given, ready-made, independent of the human mind. On the contrary, causality was for him one of the fundamental categories, or pure concepts of the understanding, something *read into* experience, and not *read out* of it. The category of causal necessity, he explained, is in us, not outside us; it is a prism through which we perceive things, or, more precisely, a means of constructing activity for the knowing subject.[32] He stressed that the knowing subject of Kantianism is the transcendental subject, consciousness in general, and not the knowing subject in the empirical, psychological sense.[33] He also agreed with Kant that the unity of transcendental consciousness demanded an ordering of empirical data according to universally valid and necessary laws.

It followed from this that necessity was not to be found in the world of empirical phenomena and, therefore, that the positivists (and orthodox Marxists, like Plekhanov) were wrong in opposing 'what is' to 'what ought to be'. In the social sciences, Kistiakovsky asserted, there is no need to give up the ideal of justice for the sake of objective study of necessary processes; on the contrary, for the social scientist the category of causal necessity and the category of justice complement each other as two different ways of transforming the chaotic world of empirical phenomena into the ordered universe of science. Both are brought into the world of phenomena, not discovered in it, but ordering empirical data by means of categories has nothing in common with subjectivism; otherwise the natural sciences, which eliminate the category of justice, would have been just as 'subjective' as the social sciences, in which the category of justice plays an important part. Categories of the understanding are objective in the sense of

---

[31] Ibid., pp. 150–1.
[32] Ibid., p. 172.
[33] Ibid., p. 132.

imprescriptibility and universal validity (*Allgemeingültigkeit*) and from this point of view 'justice' is no less objective than 'necessity'.[34]

In this way Kistiakovsky increased the list of Kantian categories of the understanding by adding to it the category of justice—a category to be used only in the social sciences, but along with the category of necessity. This solution stressed the difference between the natural and the social sciences, thus supporting the anti-naturalist tendency in humanities, characteristic of the Baden school of neo-Kantianism. At the same time Kistiakovsky distanced himself from anti-scientism and the more extreme forms of anti-naturalism; after all, he treated social knowledge as a science, and emphasized that the category of causal necessity must be used there just as in the natural sciences, and not confused with the 'laws of development', as in evolutionism and Marxism. A vindication of the role of the normative element in the social sciences was thus achieved without abandoning the rigours of objectivism and scientific methodology.

This peculiar combination of causality ('necessity') and normativism ('justice') proved very inspiring for the study of law. Kistiakovsky saw law as the final product of the social processes and as a perfect combination of the form of necessity, modelled on the laws of nature, with normative content. Consequently, he attached particular importance to the science of law, often referring to it when arguing for the use of both the causal and the normative approach in the social sciences.[35]

The Problems of Idealism was a challenging, self-confident manifesto of the neo-idealist revival in Russian thought. Very soon, however, it became clear that Russian neo-idealism was divided into two different streams whose alliance became increasingly difficult. The title of Kistiakovsky's article, 'In Defence of Scientific-Philosophical Idealism' (1907), is self-explanatory. Russian idealism, he declared, was divided between the broad and fashionable metaphysical tradition, developing in the direction of religious mysticism, and the scientific tradition, much narrower, quantitatively weak and almost completely unknown to the general public.[36] The first tradition derived from such great nineteenth-century figures as Soloviev and Chicherin, while the second, allied to the Baden school of neo-Kantianism, had no

---

[34] Ibid., p. 186.
[35] Ibid., p. 188.
[36] Ibid., pp. 189–90.

antecedents in Russian philosophy.[37] The leaders of the first group were not mentioned by name but it was obvious that they included Berdyaev, Bulgakov, Frank, and other thinkers who had passed from Marxism to idealism in transition to an openly religious philosophy. It was equally obvious, although modestly passed over in silence, that the chief candidate for intellectual leadership in the second group was Kistiakovsky himself.

The two streams shared a common origin: both derived from a recognition of the independence of ethics, from the newly acquired awareness that 'what ought to be' is independent from 'what is'. Both rejected naturalist sociology and Marxism, setting against them the view that oughtness is neither subordinate to nor derivative from necessity. From this point, however, most neo-idealist thinkers went on to conclude that the solution of ethical problems is dependent on metaphysics which in turn must be based upon religious faith.[38] Kistiakovsky sharply disagreed with this position and tried to promote a healthy confidence in science. He wished to make the Russian neo-idealists aware of the scientific character and tremendous scientific importance of their task. Science, he stressed, should not be confused with the natural sciences. The core of the ethical problem is beyond the grasp of the natural sciences, but not beyond the grasp of scientific knowledge. Ethics can be treated as the subject-matter of purely scientific study and its problems can be solved scientifically.[39]

In making this bold claim Kistiakovsky, of course, leant on the authority of Kant. He distinguished between ethical principle and ethical system, maintaining that the first, as formulated in Kant's 'categorical imperative', is unconditional and unchangeable while the second is also a product of human history. Thus, the relation between the ethical principle and the ethical system is similar to the relation between transcendental forms of thought and the empirical sciences.[40] Ethics must be based upon the highest ethical principle but cannot be derived from it, because the 'ethical system, like science, is being

---

[37] A few years later Kistiakovsky was happy to note that scientific idealism in Russia had been strengthened by the appearance of the Russian–German philosophical journal *Logos*, edited by F. Stepun and S. Hessen (ibid., p. 190, note cf. below, Ch. VII, 2), to which he contributed his important study 'The Reality of Objective Law' (ibid., pp. 257–337).

[38] Ibid., p. 191.

[39] Ibid., p. 192.

[40] Ibid., p. 248.

created by the whole of humankind in its historical development'.[41] In order to avoid concessions to historical relativism Kistiakovsky added that historical creativity has nothing in common with the unconscious, spontaneous evolutionary process, determined by various blind natural forces or by quasi-natural social evolution. In his view historico-ethical progress was 'a product of fully conscious ethical actions accomplished in the name of the categorical imperative'.[42] The moral message behind this view was clear enough: people should feel responsible for their history, and not seize on it as an excuse.

This emphasis on absolute ethical standards and individual responsibility was nevertheless combined with a resolute rejection of that disregard and disrespect for social and political institutions which characterized Tolstoy and other ethical anarchists. Individual self-perfection, Kistiakovsky stressed, is not enough. A system of ethics is the product of a particular culture; it must be based upon and supported by a complicated structure of economic life, educational system, medical and sanitary institutions, and so forth. It is unthinkable without absolute ethical principles but its social and cultural existence is inconceivable without law and the state.[43]

A striking similarity is obvious between this argument and Soloviev's justification of 'objective ethics'. Soloviev's name has not been mentioned in this context but it is highly probable that his thought exerted some influence: his vindication of law and the state through his criticism of Tolstoy's 'moral subjectivism' was widely known and justly regarded as a milestone in the Russian debate on morality and law.

With the passage of time the differences between Kistiakovsky's scientific idealism and the metaphysical idealists became increasingly sharp. For instance, Kistiakovsky's article, 'The Problem and Task of Social-Scientific Knowledge' (1912), was not just a defence of scientific philosophy but more than that. It was an appeal for the liberation of the social sciences from the tyranny of social philosophy, for their redirection along the road of purely scientific knowledge—the same road which had been chosen long ago by the natural sciences.[44] In other words, social philosophy was defined as the pre-scientific stage in the knowledge of society and compared in this respect to the anachronistic philosophy of nature. A preoccupation with the crisis of

[41] Ibid.
[42] Ibid., p. 249.
[43] Ibid.
[44] Ibid., p. 24.

positivism gave way to a diagnosis emphasing the dangers of some forms of revolt against positivism, as undermining confidence in science. The differences between the natural and the social sciences, consisting in the presence of a normative element in the latter, were not overlooked, but stress was laid on the features common to all sciences, on a defence of the scientific spirit against the cultural decadence manifest in the rejection of the search for objective truth and in different forms of revolt against reason.

Characteristically enough, Kistiakovsky did not agree that the natural sciences were in a state of crisis. He was full of enthusiasm for their achievements; the so-called crisis in physics, challenging the dominance of a mechanistic model of the universe, was in his eyes epistemological rather than substantive.[45] He saw universal relativism as the real crisis, leading to a rehabilitation of irrationalism and fideism. From this perspective he readily found a common denominator for William James's pragmatism and the openly mystical philosophy of Berdyaev.[46] He was keenly aware, however, that relativism emerged *within* scientism and had its representatives among scholars deeply committed to the rigorous standards of scientific enquiry; in this context he pointed out the relativist and even solipsist implications of psychologism, mentioning Petrażycki in this connection.[47] As a remedy against all these dangers he proposed his conception of three fundamental categories in the social sciences: generality, necessity, and oughtness.[48] By emphasizing the first two categories he opted for the view that the social sciences, like the natural sciences, must be nomothetic, and thus distanced himself from the idiographism of the Baden school; by adding the category of oughtness he remained faithful to the neo-Kantian revolt against positivism.

The originality of Kistiakovsky's position consisted in his ability to combine the struggle against relativism with an acknowledgment of the relative value of many different methods in social sciences. He did not pretend to have discovered one, universal method; on the contrary, he stressed the autonomy of the different spheres and dimensions of human existence and so championed the cause of a self-conscious methodological and gnoseological pluralism.[49] Particularly interesting in this respect was his four-faceted general theory of law.

---

[45] Cf. Vucinich, *Social Thought in Tsarist Russia*, p. 129.
[46] Kistiakovsky, *Sotsial'nye nauki*, pp. 4–11.
[47] Ibid., p. 25.
[48] Ibid., p. 28.   [49] Ibid., p. 13.

3 *Towards a general theory of law*

In the scarce literature dealing with Kistiakovsky's ideas he is usually described as a sociologist.[50] It should be clear from the foregoing that he was also deeply interested in the neo-Kantian philosophy of values. As a sociologist he was especially concerned with law, seeing it as society's main means of control over the individual.[51] But law was equally interesting for him from the point of view of a philosophy of values. It could be seen, he stressed, both as the final product of social processes, subject to causality, and, at the same time, as the social embodiment of certain objective, supra-historical values.[52] Thus it occupied the central place in the sphere of culture, that is, the sphere mediating between the quasi-natural dimension of social life and its spiritual dimension.[53] A general theory of law would therefore be the keystone of a general philosophy of culture. It would be both the crowning achievement of social science and an important contribution to philosophy.[54]

According to Kistiakovsky, such a general theory of law had never yet existed. In his view the existing theories of law were not based upon a theory of culture as a whole and were therefore incomplete, although justified and supplementing one another as different methodological approaches. He singled out four approaches to law, as corresponding to the four concepts of law:

1. The analytical approach, characteristic of conceptual jurisprudence and corresponding to the positivist concept of law;

2. The sociological approach, corresponding to the concept of law as a form of social relationship;

3. The psychological approach, corresponding to the psychological concept of law; and finally

4. The normative approach, corresponding to the axiological concept of law.[55]

For Kistiakovsky all these approaches were of equal value for the scientific study of law.[56] A general theory of law should, however,

---

[50] Cf. Vucinich, *Social Thought in Tsarist Russia*, and the pages devoted to Kistiakovsky in *Sotsiologicheskaia mysl' v Rossii*.

[51] Kistiakovsky, *Sotsial'nye nauki*, p. 258.

[52] Ibid., p. 188.

[53] Ibid., pp. 258–9.

[54] Ibid., p. 384.

[55] Ibid., pp. 321–4.   [56] Ibid., pp. 331–2.

stress the one-sidedness and consequent inadequacy of each, considered independently. It should reject the above four *concepts* of law as inadequate and mutually exclusive while at the same time accepting the four methodological *approaches* as corresponding to the four facets of law as a complex cultural phenomenon.

Kistiakovsky's attitude towards the first approach was ambivalent. As we shall see, he was a staunch opponent of the command theory of law but he appreciated the merits of conceptual jurisprudence in the logical analysis of existing legal norms and in the scientific study of the organizational side of legal systems. He stressed that the positivist view of law was too narrow, excluding customary law, unless sanctioned by the state, and international law, if not protected by force. On the whole, he assumed that the *étatist* approach to law was taken for granted by professional jurists and required no special justification. He often criticized its basic assumptions, but in a political, not a methodological, context.

His view of the practical achievements of conceptual jurisprudence was, understandably, much more positive than his attitude towards that main tenet of legal positivism, the absolute sovereignty of the state. He was greatly impressed by its logical precision and by the sophisticated structure of its arguments, and liked to point out that in this respect conceptual jurisprudence provided a model for Hermann Cohen's ethics.[57] He saw this as

the most significant fact in the history of legal science . . . Here for the first time scientific knowledge, produced by a branch of jurisprudence, has provided material for the construction of part of a philosophical system. In principle this attempt is very important, although its realization is far from successful. Heretofore it has been the science of law which has tried to base itself upon philosophy, but now philosophy has become aware of the need to look for support in the scientific knowledge provided by a branch of legal science.[58]

Kistiakovsky found typical examples of other approaches to law in Russian juridical thought. S. A. Muromtsev—a well-known liberal jurist, professor of law at Moscow University from 1877 to 1884 and the chairman of the First State Duma[59]—had, in his view, pioneered

---

[57] Ibid., pp. 396–404.   [58] Ibid., p. 403.

[59] In 1884 Muromtsev was dismissed from Moscow University for political reasons. From 1878 he edited *Iuridicheskii vestnik* (*Juridical Messenger*), journal of the Moscow Juridical Society, of which he became President in 1880. In 1892 publication of the journal was suspended as a result of intensified censorship. It was resumed in 1912

the sociology of law as a distinct discipline, dealing with the social genesis and development of law.[60] Kistiakovsky considered this to be wholly legitimate and necessary for the general education of jurists, pointing out that the sociology of law, unlike the dogmatic study of law (i.e. conceptual jurisprudence), shows the dynamics of law and concentrates on both written and unwritten laws. It analyses law as a social fact, its social functions, its relation to the interests of different groups and to the general progress of society. It limits itself to the study of causal relationships but yet serves the ideal of justice by making jurists more conscious of the shortcomings of existing laws and of the need to change them.[61] In short, its findings are indispensable to the elaboration of a correct legal policy.[62]

Other merits of the sociological approach to law were shown by Kistiakovsky in an interesting study 'The Rational and the Irrational in Law' (1911). The difference between this study and his article 'Law as a Social Phenomenon', devoted mainly to Muromtsev's views, is quite striking: the latter treats the sociological study of law as a version of positivist evolutionism, whereas the former deals with the problems characteristic of the anti-positivist currents in sociology inspired not only by the Neo-Kantian philosophy of values but also by the openly anti-rationalist *Lebensphilosophie*.

Law, Kistiakovsky argued, has both an objective and a subjective dimension, and an objective and a subjective mode of existence. Objective law consists of norms which, like logical notions, are rational, characterized by generality, universality and abstractness; in contrast to this, subjective law, law as a fact, law as it appears in life, is a multiplicity of legal relations characterized by concreteness, uniqueness, and individuality. Consequently, 'from the point of view of its logical nature subjective law is diametrically opposed to objective law. Objective law is a totality of the rational products of man's spiritual life while subjective law is a totality of the legally significant facts of life. In its individuality, peculiarity and uniqueness each of these facts is *something absolutely irrational.*'[63] Identifying legal norms with law as the totality of legally significant facts is therefore a juridical fiction.

Conceptual jurisprudence, Kistiakovsky continued, specializes in studying the purely rational, logical side of law, but other currents in

under the editorship of Kistiakovsky who was proud thus to become Muromtsev's successor.

[60] Kistiakovsky, *Sotsial'nye nauki*, pp. 338–9.
[61] Ibid., p. 355.   [62] Cf. ibid., p. 325.   [63] Ibid., p. 360.

jurisprudence pay due attention to its irrational, subjective side. Even in ancient Rome some jurists had emphasized law as a fact of life and its priority over legal norms; according to Paulus 'non ex regula ius sumatur, sed ex jure quod est, regula fiat'.[64] A powerful protest against an abstractly rationalist approach to law found expression in Hegelianism. In recent times the psychological theory of law has characteristically treated law as a phenomenon of life and emphasized its origins in the irrational depths of the human psyche.[65] But Kistiakovsky found the deepest understanding of the irrational aspect of law in the representatives of the sociological approach to law. He wrote:

> Thinking about law and making juridical decisions not only on the basis of legal norms, but also on the basis of law as it appears in life, belongs to the very essence of the sociological method in jurisprudence. The difference between these two constitutive parts of the legal order is not only clearly realized but also specially emphasized by the advocates of this method. They directly point out, moreover, that this is the difference between the general or rational and the individual or irrational.[66]

Thus, Kistiakovsky, in fact, recognized many merits in the sociological approach to law. Nevertheless, despite his own interest in sociology, his attitude towards this approach remained somewhat ambivalent. He was aware that the sociological study of law was often used and abused for the purpose of 'unmasking the class content' of law, thereby contributing to the depreciation of law as such and providing arguments for 'legal nihilism'.[67] He was equally aware of the danger of methodological pan-sociologism, denying the autonomy of different spheres of social life. He rejected the thesis that legal phenomena cannot be isolated from social life as a whole, setting against it his resolute defence of the view that the method of isolating certain facts is a prerequisite of science and that the study of law should develop as a separate, fully autonomous discipline.[68]

In discussing the third approach to the study of law—the psychological approach—Kistiakovsky concentrated, of course, on Petrażycki's theory. He devoted much attention to it in many of his articles, but his most comprehensive treatment occurs in the long study entitled 'The Reality of Objective Law' (1910). This study, published in Hessen's

---

[64] Ibid., p. 361.
[65] Ibid., pp. 369–70. Kistiakovsky mentions in this context the names of Petrazycki and E. R. Bierling.
[66] Ibid., p. 363.
[67] Ibid., pp. 322–3.   [68] Ibid., pp. 342–3.

Logos,[69] analyses both the psychological theory and the normative theory of law and presents them as two different ways of denying the reality of objective law. To understand it properly, it is necessary to realize that the term 'objective law' was here used in a different sense to that of the article 'The Rational and Irrational in Law': it referred not to the objective logical meaning of legal norms, as opposed to the alogical and subjective character of legal relations in real life, but to institutionalized law, as opposed to law as an element of consciousness. From this point of view the psychological and normative approaches to law could be seen as sharing a neglect for the external reality of law as represented by the institutionalized legal order.

Kistiakovsky, while admiring Petrażycki in some respects, was generally very critical of him. He strongly criticized his nihilist attitude towards existing legal science and the legacy of the past, stressing the continuity in the development of legal thought and pointing out that even Petrażycki's psychological theory had many predecessors and was not as original as he claimed. In this context he specially emphasized the achievements of E. R. Bierling, the author of what he considered the best psychological interpretation of objective law,[70] while acknowledging that Petrażycki's theory was the most comprehensive and consistent, that he alone had most fully developed the psychological approach to law.[71]

The shortcomings with which Kistiakovsky reproached Petrażycki were numerous and not always convincing. In my view Kistiakovsky was right to accuse Petrażycki of exaggerating the methodological importance of formal logic for the social sciences, of paying too much attention to formal classifications, and of overestimating the value and novelty of his own theory of 'adequate notions' (a theory which in fact could be traced back to Aristotle).[72] He correctly pointed out many weaknesses in Petrażycki's theory of emotions (impulsions) but was less convincing in his accusations of naturalism, since Petrażycki's psychology is really closer to the tradition of non-empirical descriptive psychology, as accepted and developed by some of the leading rebels against naturalism in the humanities. In fact Kistiakovsky himself acknowledged Petrażycki's merits in this field when he called him a great master of descriptive as opposed to theoretical psychology.[73] In

[69] See below, p. 408.
[70] Kistiakovsky, *Sotsial'nye nauki*, p. 260.   [71] Ibid., p. 297.
[72] Ibid., p. 272. The same point was later made and developed by T. Kotarbiński (see above, Ch. IV, n. 61).   [73] Ibid., p. 284.

The Debate about the Intelligentsia

his criticism he concentrated on the early version of Petrażycki's theory, which dealt only with the individual psyche, and overlooked or underestimated Petrażycki's transition from a purely psychological theory of law, as presented in *Essays in Legal Philosophy*, to a socio-psychological theory whose foundations were laid in his *Theory of Law and the State*. Though vaguely aware of this change, Kistiakovsky saw it as due to the unacknowledged influence of the Russian sociological school in jurisprudence, and not as an organic development in Petrażycki's thought. On the whole, he looked at Petrażycki through the prism of *Essays* and because of this tended to reduce his theory to one of individual legal experience. From this perspective Petrażycki's typology of socio-economic and legal systems seemed unconnected and inconsistent with the basic assumptions of his theory.

To Kistiakovsky psychologism by definition typified the negation of the objective element of culture. For theory of law he saw such a negation as not only methodologically wrong, but also socially harmful. Petrażycki's position, he argued, reduced institutions to a number of concrete individual persons and explained the phenomena of power and obedience as attributes of individual men and women. In this connection Kistiakovsky went on to develop his sharpest political argument against Petrażycki's theory as a justification of personal power. 'In contemporary cultural states', he wrote, 'power belongs to institutions, not persons . . . One can ignore the law which has become objective and embodied in institutions only at the price of ignoring the entire legal culture of modern times. To a considerable extent this applies to Petrażycki's case.'[74]

Strong words, but stemming, basically, from a misunderstanding. There is nothing in Petrażycki's view to justify power in terms of the personal charisma of particular individuals or to deny the importance of institutions. He markedly differentiated between law and commands, both personal commands and those issued by institutionalized bodies, but there can be no possible doubt that legally institutionalized power was incomparably better in his view than purely personal power. He did not neglect institutions but was, rather, concerned about the *proper* institutionalization of social life. This was, after all, the primary objective of his 'science of legal policy'; his elaboration of a psychological or socio-psychological theory of law, claiming that only those institutions which are rooted in an historically shaped social

[74] Ibid., p. 296.

psychology (and through it in the legal psyche of each individual) can be really good and efficient, had the practical aims of providing a sound basis for institutional changes.[75] His theory of 'legal impulsions', too, irrespective of its scientific value, was an attempt to make law independent of fear and egoistic interests; in other words, it was an attempt to interpret law psychologically while preserving its autonomy from the utilitarian motives of pleasure-seeking and pain-avoidance favoured by traditional psychology.

Kistiakovsky summed up his criticism of Petrażycki by saying that his theory of law was too broad in one respect and too narrow in another:[76] too broad, because it dealt with a multiplicity of psychic phenomena beyond the scope of jurisprudence, and too narrow, because it did not deal with institutionalized, objective law. In fact, he contended, Petrażycki's theory was not a theory of law, but a theory of legal consciousness, or legal mentality.

Kistiakovsky readily acknowledged, however, that Petrażycki's theory had great scientific value.[77] As mentioned above, he was peculiarly impressed by Petrażycki's view of the differences between the legal and the moral psyche[78] and thought that his treatment of the problem of morality and law was the best part of his work, distinguished by 'an almost classical perfection' and deserving inclusion 'in every anthology of psychological and pedagogical literature'.[79] It is evident that his enthusiastic agreement with this part of Petrażycki's theory was politically motivated. Both wanted to combat legal positivism and, at the same time, to overcome the legacy of Russian 'legal nihilism', which so often depreciated law in the name of morality. Both wished to strengthen the 'militant' traits in Russian legal consciousness, to extirpate the slavish spirit of unconditional obedience and replace it with firmness and a self-confidence, born of a proud awareness of one's rights and a readiness to defend them.

The fourth approach to law—the normative one—was very close to Kistiakovsky's heart. In Russia it was led by Novgorodtsev, with whom he had both scholarly and personal ties; in Germany it was represented by the two currents of neo-Kantianism—the transcendental-empirical

---

[75] Vucinich completely ignores this when he writes: 'The psychological orientation, particularly as elaborated by L. I. Petrazhitskii, was the most notable academic adaptation to the government's determination to suppress the study of the concrete social and political attributes of law in general and Russian law in particular'. See Vucinich, *Social Thought in Tsarist Russia,* p. 143.

[76] Kistiakovsky, *Sotsial'nye nauki,* p. 289.   [77] Ibid., p. 283.

[78] See above, Ch. IV, 5.   [79] Kistiakovsky, *Sotsial'nye nauki,* p. 285.

Baden school and the transcendental-rationalist Marburg school,[80] both of which contributed to his education and retained his high esteem. Nevertheless he found none of the existing variants of the normative approach to law satisfactory, even within the limits of its own premises. He criticized Novgorodtsev, for instance, for concentrating only on ethical norms and disregarding logical norms.[81]

To Kistiakovsky the most general and fundamental shortcoming of the normative approach was essentially the same as that of the psychological approach. Normativism, he argued, deals with transcendental consciousness, not with consciousness in the psychological sense, but both these streams (normativism and psychologism) concentrate on law in consciousness while neglecting the objectified, institutionalized existence of law. To illustrate this thesis he drew on an article by I. A. Ilyin, Novgorodtsev's disciple, entitled 'The Notions of Law and Force'. Law, Ilyin reasoned, should not be thought of in terms of force, since the two notions, law and force, have no common dimension: law exists only on the logical plane while force has ontological significance. Purely juridical theory of law should therefore consciously avoid ontology and dispense with the category of the real. All attempts to interpret law ontologically and to create different versions of 'realistic jurisprudence' would inevitably lead to a view of law as a force, a grave theoretical error entailing dangerous practical consequences.

On this Kistiakovsky commented: 'To divorce the logical notion of law from the reality of law in this way leads easily and quite naturally to a kind of scholastic Platonism.'[82]

Thus, after a careful examination of the four main approaches to law, Kistiakovsky came to the conclusion that, while all could be fruitful, none of them deserved special preference at the cost of the others. This conclusion served him as an argument for methodological pluralism but did not undermine his belief in the possibility of an all-embracing general theory of law. In the natural sciences he saw no need for such general theories: natural phenomena can be studied from the points of view of different, separate disciplines, without attempting to use their findings for the construction of a general theory. In the cultural sciences, on the other hand, synthetic theories

---

[80] Ibid., p. 299.
[81] Ibid., pp. 300–1.
[82] Ibid., p. 308. Ilyin's article (originally called 'Poniatiia prava i sily. Opyt metodologicheskogo issledovianiia') appeared in *Voprosy filosofii i psikhologii*, 101, 1910.

were, in his view, of vital importance.[83] He hoped, therefore, that a synthetic theory of law, making use of all four methodological approaches while mastering their respective shortcomings, would be possible in the future and of course saw his own analyses as paving the way for such a synthesis.

4 The theory of the rule-of-law state

It is very characteristic that in his typology of the main theories of law Kistiakovsky passed over in silence one of the most influential, the command theory of law. He paid much attention to legal positivism in the form of conceptual jurisprudence but completely ignored its cruder version, which claimed that laws are merely commands of political power.

The explanation of this lies, I think, in a tendency to separate the theory of law from the theory of the state. For Kistiakovsky the command theory of law was part of the theory of the absolute sovereignty of the state. Its basic assumption was a certain view of the state rather than of law and, therefore, its importance was political rather than legal. As a rule it was linked to the analytical approach to law but it could also be combined with the sociological approach. Hence it was possible to treat it, from a juristic point of view, as lacking a distinctive methodology of its own.

In political philosophy the view of the state as the sovereign political power, the source of all laws and therefore standing above law, was, for Kistiakovsky, the perfect expression of the conception of the state as organized force, in contrast to the view of the state as the embodiment of an idea.[84] The first conception, deriving from Hobbes' *Leviathan*, concentrated on the 'bestial face' of the state;[85] its dominant position in political science greatly contributed to the growing hostility towards the state by adding fuel to the anarchist doctrine of the state as merely an organization of violence. The second conception, characteristic of German idealism, emphasized the noble, moral or even divine aspect of the state. It conceived of the state as inseparable from and limited by law. Thus the first conception was incompatible with the ideal of the rule-of-law state while the second one was, explicitly or implicitly, inseparable from it.

[83] Ibid., pp. 327–8.
[84] Ibid., pp. 552–5. (Chapter entitled 'Gosudarstvo i lichnost''. Its first, shorter version appeared in *Voprosy filosofii i psikhologii*, 85, 1906, under the title 'Gosudarstvo pravovoe i sotsialisticheskoe'.)
[85] Ibid., p. 553.

Kistiakovsky was convinced that as an explanation of the origin of law the command theory of law was completely wrong. Its basic premiss, the notion of the unlimited sovereignty of the state, was in fact a relatively recent concept. Originally law and the state existed quite independently of each other. With the passage of time the state became increasingly interested in law. At first it figured as protector and executor of existing laws; later it began also to interpret them, to determine which rules were laws, and which were not, and, finally, to create completely new laws. This development of legislative activity paved the way for the emergence of absolute monarchy under which the abrogation of old laws and the creation of new ones became the exclusive prerogative of the state. But law, although it had subordinated itself to the state, had not become the obedient tool of the rulers; on the contrary, its importance steadily increased and in the final result it succeeded in establishing its rule over the political authorities. At first the state simply found it convenient to achieve its ends by means of law but it soon became evident that the creation of a legal order was not merely a convenience, but a necessity, stemming from the very nature of the state. On the other hand, it is of the nature of law that it never renders service without a corresponding claim; everybody who makes use of law must subordinate himself to it.[86] Thus a new cycle of development began: law, having strengthened the state, started to extend its authority and finally established its rule over the state. In this way the highest type of state—the rule-of-law state—came into being.[87]

An important watershed in this development, Kistiakovsky continued, was, of course, the transition from absolutism to constitutionalism, which, however, would be gradual rather than abrupt.[88] Pure absolutism closely resembles Bakunin's image of the state as such: it is a wholly alienated political power, standing above all classes of the population and denying them their freedom in all spheres of life.[89] But the first significant step in the direction of the rule of law—the introduction of independent courts—could be made under absolutism, as happened in the case of Russia.[90] Similarly the fully developed

[86] Ibid., pp. 593–5 (in the chapter entitled 'Gosudarstvo i pravo').
[87] Ibid., p. 556.
[88] Ibid., p. 559. By stressing the gradual character of this transition Kistiakovsky was criticizing the views of V. M. Hessen, who simply identified the rule-of-law state with the constitutional state. Cf. V. M. Hessen (Gessen), 'Teoriia pravovogo gosudarstva', in *Politicheskii stroi sovremennykh gosudarstv*, SPb 1905, vol. 1, p. 135.
[89] Ibid., p. 563.   [90] Ibid., p. 597.

constitutional state is a rule-of-law state, but there are also transitional forms as in Russia after 1906.[91] Even a genuinely constitutional, as opposed to a semi-constitutional, state tries to preserve some forms of 'free' (i.e. arbitrary) exercise of power and thus resists the permeation of all spheres of life by the rule of law. But this process is irresistible; the rule of force is doomed to give way to the rule of law, the interests and aims of the state must be determined by, and subordinated to, its legal order.

Kistiakovsky was aware that this would not happen of its own accord, that the final victory of law depended on strenuous cultural efforts and a resolute, conscious struggle against all remnants of arbitrary power.[92] He was equally aware that the pure rule-of-law was only an ideal type in Max Weber's sense and that ideal types cannot assume empirical reality.[93] Yet these qualifications did not impair his surprising optimism. He had no doubt that in the long run the establishment of a universal rule of law would overcome all opposition and firmly believed in its ultimate supremacy both nationally and internationally.[94] It is not surprising, then, that he warmly welcomed and strongly supported H. Krabbe's theory, claiming that the principle of the unlimited sovereignty of the state had become obsolete and should be replaced by a higher principle of the sovereignty of law.[95]

The ideal of the rule-of-law state (*pravovoe gosudarstvo*) was shared by all Russian liberals, though they were not all equally consistent in defending it, and some openly sceptical voices could be heard amongst them. For example, the liberal jurist S. A. Kotlarevsky thought it necessary to warn his colleagues of the dangers of 'juridical fetishism', 'juridical fanaticism' and 'juridical utopianism'.[96] In his book *Power and Law* he put forward the view that both power and law should be seen as essential, equally important, and irreducible elements of the state. Law, he argued, is not the creation of power and should not be treated as a mere instrument of power. But the converse is equally true: power is not the creation of law and neither can nor should be totally subordinated to law, reduced to the role of a mere instrument in realizing the rule of legal norms.[97]

---

[91] Ibid., pp. 598–9.　　　　　　[92] Ibid., p. 598.
[93] Ibid., p. 558.　　　　　　　　[94] Ibid., p. 596.
[95] Ibid., p. 611. Kistiakovsky referred in this context to Krabbe's book *Die Lehre der Rechtssouveränität: Beitrag zur Staatslehre*, Groningen, 1906.
[96] Ibid., p. 606, n. Cf. S. A. Kotlarevsky, *Vlast' i pravo. Problema pravovogo gosudarstva*, Moscow, 1915, pp. 383, 386, 387–9.
[97] Ibid., pp. 602–4.

Kistiakovsky took Kotlarevsky seriously and tried to refute his arguments. He pointed out that Kotlarevsky's views originated with Lassalle, who claimed that the state had always been, and would remain, an 'organized force', whose submission to the rule of law could only be relative and limited. He also referred to Georges Sorel's *Réflexions sur la violence*, seeing their hostility to parliamentary government and their eulogy of violence as proofs that the victory of the rule-of-law principle in people's minds was not yet complete and that a relapse to earlier ways of living and thinking was still possible.[98] But he refused to recognize this as a serious danger and felt that the growing acceptance, among German Social Democrats, of the principles of the rule-of-law state represented the dominant tendency. He steadily argued that no theoretical refutation was possible of the view that, in principle at least, power can be entirely permeated by law and thus transformed into a phenomenon of law.[99] He also remained convinced that the future would belong to the rule-of-law state and that other types of state represented mere remnants of a closed and doomed historical past.[100]

Kistiakovsky's theory of human rights formed an important part of his theory of the rule-of-law state. He insisted that the rule of law involved not only substitution of rule by impersonal norms for rule by individuals, but also the definite limitation of state-enacted regulations by inalienable human rights. These rights, he stressed, must be recognized *de iure*, and not merely *de facto*. From this point of view the eighteenth-century declarations of rights, especially the French Declaration of the Rights of Man and the Citizen, were a real breakthrough in the development of modern legal consciousness. True, for a long time their interpretation to some extent justified their treatment as a 'Gospel of the bourgeoisie'.[101] But this harsh judgement, typical of the socialist and anarchist critique of law, failed to distinguish between the social function of law in given historical conditions and its normative content. The normative content of the Rights of Man and the Citizen was not class-bound; as legal principles they set standards of universal and absolute significance.[102]

Kistiakovsky agreed with the natural rights theory that human rights are not created by the state: they are 'natural', that is, pre-political, belonging to people as human beings, and not as members of a body politic.[103] Nevertheless, to be respected, they must be recognized and

---

[98] Ibid., pp. 609–10.   [99] Ibid., p. 606.   [100] Ibid., p. 593.
[101] Ibid., p. 490.   [102] Loc. cit.   [103] Ibid., p. 560.

safeguarded by the state in the sphere of both private and public law. In this respect Kistiakovsky differed markedly from Chicherin for whom the most important thing was freedom in the private sphere, guaranteed by the autonomy of civil society, in the Hegelian sense. Unlike Chicherin, Kistiakovsky did not believe that absolute rule was reconcilable with true respect for law or genuine autonomy in the private sphere of human existence. Respect for law can only take firm root in a state dealing not with mere subjects but with citizens, endowed with legal rights not only in their relations with each other but also in their relations with the instruments of state. This is not the case under an absolute monarchy and therefore all efforts by absolute monarchs to instil into their states a respect for law are doomed to failure. In the absence of rights legality is impossible; in such conditions only administrative arbitrariness and police violence can blossom.[104]

This reasoning, strongly supported by the Russian experience, led Kistiakovsky to embrace Jellinek's theory of public-legal subjective rights,[105] according to which subjective private rights were the province of the legally allowed while subjective public rights were the province of the legally claimable. The first defined the scope of natural freedom while the second provided individuals with legal support in realizing their rights, thus increasing their capacity for pursuing their rightful aims. The first dealt only with private-legal relations while the second established people in full possession of their rights *vis-à-vis* the state. Jellinek concluded from this that the modern individual, the individual as a holder of legal rights, was a 'public-legal phenomenon', a creation of the state. This view accorded with legal positivism in deriving all laws and rights from the state but at the same time showed how the state had limited itself and how the rule-of-law state had come into being.[106]

Kistiakovsky shared the optimistic belief that historical development consists in continuous growth and enlargement of individualism[107] and readily accepted Jellinek's theory of legal progress, which recognized four successive stages in the changing relations of individual and state. The first stage was state serfdom, in which individuals were no more than servitors of the state. In the second stage at least some individuals

---

[104] Ibid., p. 562.
[105] As developed by Jellinek in *System der subjektiven öffentlichen Rechte*, Freiburg i/B, 1892.
[106] Kistiakovsky, *Sotsial'nye nauki*, pp. 515–31.   [107] Ibid., p. 527.

secured for themselves a private existence, free from state interference. In the third stage this negative freedom was supplemented by a passive version of positive freedom, the right to claim certain services from the state. Finally came the development of an active positive freedom, that is, the right to participate in the activities of the state. As Kistiakovsky sums it up:

In the beginning the individual, wholly obedient to the state, is deprived of individuality, as it were; later he is given a sphere of activity free from state interference; later still the state itself assumes an obligation to act for his benefit; finally, the individual is allowed to participate in the exercise of state power or even to become a constituent part of this power.[108]

The difference between this conception of the progress of individualism in modern history and the classical liberal doctrine is quite marked. Unlike Chicherin and other classical liberals, Kistiakovsky did not see *laissez-faire* capitalism as providing optimum conditions for the development of individualism; consequently, he had reservations about the *Gesellschaft* paradigm of law, with its emphasis on private law and negative freedom. He criticized some Russian liberals, especially the eminent civilist I. A. Pokrovsky, for exaggerating the positive value of private-law individualism and ignoring, or neglecting, the growing importance of public-law individualism.[109] Nor was he afraid of the extension of the sphere of public law at the expense of private law. For him public law was not inevitably an instrument of 'legal despotism', increasing government control over people's lives and so reducing individual freedom; it could also serve the cause of freedom by endowing individuals with a positive juridical capacity to act in pursuit of their freely chosen aims.

From this angle, the problem of socialism appeared in a light very different to Chicherin's pessimistic diagnosis. Kistiakovsky agreed with Chicherin that the idea of the withering away of law and the state could not be taken seriously, that socialism would in fact entail a vast increase in state prerogatives and the public-law regulation of social life. Nevertheless the conception of public-law subjective rights of citizens enabled him to foresee the socialist state as fully compatible with individual freedom and representing a new and higher phase of the rule-of-law state. He devoted to this problem an interesting study

---

[108] Ibid., p. 529.
[109] Ibid., pp. 541 n., 585–6.

published in 1906 and included in a revised and enlarged version of his *Social Sciences and Law*.[110]

The rule-of-law state, Kistiakovsky argued, was often called bourgeois and set against the ideal of the socialist state. Such a view, especially strong in Russia, was both politically harmful and theoretically wrong, arising from a terminological confusion.[111] True, the modern rule-of-law state was based upon the socio-economic relations of capitalism, but it did not therefore follow that its juridical nature was wholly determined by or inseparable from this system, or that the rule-of-law state could not be part of a non-capitalist structure. On the contrary, Jellinek's conception of public-law subjective rights had shown that the existing rule-of-law state was laying the foundations of a future socialist state just as the existing capitalist economy was laying the foundations of a socialist economy.[112] To see capitalism as paving the way for socialism was the great merit of Marxism.[113] It was regrettable that the false idea of the withering away of law and the state had prevented the elaboration of a Marxist conception of the socialist rule-of-law state of the future.

This glaring gap in socialist theory, Kistiakovsky continued, had been partly filled by an Austrian 'professorial socialist' Anton Menger who in 1903 published an important book *Neue Staatslehre*. (The Russian translation of this, edited by Kistiakovsky, appeared in 1905.)[114] In his earlier works, especially in *Das Recht auf dem vollen Arbeitsertrag in geschichtlicher Darstellung* (1886), Menger developed the idea of a new right—the right to full compensation for work done. He hoped to shed more light on the history of socialism from a 'legal-philosophical point of view' and to contribute to the elaboration of a juridical conception of socialism, which he saw as 'the most important task of legal philosophy of our time'.

Kistiakovsky's view of Menger's theory is very interesting and instructive. He quite agreed with the thesis that socialism or, in Menger's own words, 'the popular Labour-State' of the future, would greatly extend the sphere of public-law regulation, but rejected the prediction that private law would entirely disappear, making the

---

[110] B. Kistiakovsky, 'Gosudarstvo pravovoe i sotsialisticheskoe' (see above, n. 84).

[111] Kistiakovsky, *Sotsial'nye nauki*, pp. 570–1.

[112] 'The recognition of socialist rights as part of the rights of man and the citizen', Kistiakovsky maintained, 'is a natural consequence of the system of public-legal subjective rights', as elaborated by Jellinek. (Kistiakovsky, 'Gosudarstvo pravovoe', p. 504, n.)

[113] Kistiakovsky, *Sotsial'nye nauki*, p. 574.   [114] Cf. ibid., p. 578, n.

distinction between public and private affairs juridically irrelevant. He defended his position not only against Menger, who saw such developments as desirable and beneficial, but also against I. A. Pokrovsky who, while accepting Menger's thesis, used it as an argument against socialism. Private law, he argued, could not disappear under socialism because the nationalization of the means of production would not entail the liquidation of purely personal property and the abolition of class conflicts would not end conflicts between individuals.[115]

Another weakness in Menger's theory, for Kistiakovsky, was his one-sided conception of the nature of public law and of its future extension. Menger's *Neue Staatslehre* appeared ten years after Jellinek's *System der subjectiven öffentlichen Rechte* (1892), but took no account of Jellinek's theory. Because of this Menger failed to see that the future extension of the scope of public law would increase not only the prerogatives of the state but also the rights of individual citizens.[116] He stressed the necessity and desirability of state control in the economic sphere, but failed to recognize that such a limitation of individual freedom would be balanced by its increase in the public sphere, that, in other words, the curtailment of individual freedom from state control (private-law individualism) would be accompanied by a marked increase of freedom within the state, that is, by the increased capacity of each individual to take part in public affairs and to exert influence on political decision-making (public-law individualism).

Finally, Kistiakovsky agreed with Menger that a future socialist state would secure to everybody a 'right to exist', but criticized him for failing to formulate this right in precise juridical language. The right to exist, he reasoned, should be given a clearly defined public-legal status, otherwise concern for the necessary conditions of human existence might be confused with charity, which would confer on the government an aura of benevolent paternalism, incompatible with the spirit of individual dignity.

The importance which Kistiakovsky attached to this point can be seen in his controversy with I. A. Pokrovsky. In his essay 'The Right to Existence' (published together with Novgorodtsev's 'Right to a Dignified Existence') Pokrovsky supported Menger's demand for the creation of legal safeguards to secure the right of existence for all and claimed that this would be possible without changing the existing

---

[115] Ibid., pp. 578–9.
[116] Ibid., pp. 579–80, 583.

socio-economic system.[117] Kistiakovsky attacked this view as an insufficient commitment to the cause of social reform. He suspected Pokrovsky of wanting to solve the problem of the right to existence within the framework of private law, but himself preferred to formulate this right more strongly, in Soloviev's phrase, the 'right to a *dignified* existence'.[118] He utterly rejected, however, Soloviev's attempt to deduce this right from the ethics of compassion and from the nature of the state as 'organized compassion'.[119] He wanted to see the right to a dignified existence as a public-law subjective right and treated this as the next step in the evolution of the rule-of-law state.[120]

Engels and Kautsky, in a very interesting article entitled 'Juridical Socialism',[121] criticized Menger's programme for translating socialist ideas into 'sober juridical language', as set out in his *Das Recht auf den vollen Arbeitsertrag*, and a brief outline of this detailed criticism may be helpful for a better understanding of Kistiakovsky's views on law and socialism.

Leaving aside unnecessary insults and unfounded allegations,[122] Engels's and Kautsky's charges against Menger may be summed up as follows.

First, they accused Menger of advocating legal reforms instead of revolutionary action, a line of criticism both obvious and uninteresting in the present context.

Secondly, they derided Menger for what they saw as his anti-historical approach to social problems, for his view that 'the privileged classes obtain their income without an equivalent social contribution'. They stressed that 'in the course of their development the ruling classes have quite definite social functions to fulfil and become rulers for that very reason'.[123] Marx, they claimed, 'understands the historical inevitability, or justification, of ancient slaveholders, of feudal lords in the Middle Ages, and so forth, as the necessary conditions of human development for a limited historical period; he also recognizes the historical and textual justification for exploitation, the usurpation of

[117] See I. A. Pokrovsky, 'Pravo na sushchestvovanie', in P. I. Novgorodtsev and I. A. Pokrovsky, *O prave na sushchestvovanie*, Moscow, 1911, pp. 45–7.

[118] Kistiakovsky, *Sotsial'nye nauki*, pp. 584–5.

[119] Ibid., pp. 587–8.   [120] Ibid., p. 589.

[121] 'Juristen-Socialismus', *Die Neue Zeit*, 1887, No. 2. See F. Engels and K. Kautsky, 'Juridical Socialism', Piers Beirne (trans.), *Politics and Society*, 7, No. 2, 1977, pp. 199–220. Cf. above, pp. 18–19.

[122] Such as calling Menger an 'ignorant lawyer' whose 'real aim was to dismantle Marx' and whose book 'is read only because it deals with Marx'. Ibid., pp. 211–12.

[123] Ibid., p. 209.

the work proceeds of others'.[124] They contrasted this facet of Marxist theory with appeals to abstract justice, characteristic, as they saw it, of the very essence of the 'juridical world-view'. Scientific socialism, for them, was based upon the discovery of the laws of economic development, and not merely on proclaiming that certain principles were unjust;[125] therefore 'the goal of the socialist movement consists not in transforming socialist ideas into sober legal phraseology, but in studying the underlying forces of social development'.[126] In other words, they saw the juridical approach to the problems of social change as linked to a peculiarly naïve and unscientific form of historical idealism.

Thirdly, Engels and Kautsky suspected Menger of a juridical and legalistic approach to politics. They distanced themselves from the 'legal nihilism' in the form of the anarchist hostility towards legal demands, but were not prepared to see law as anything more than an instrument of political struggle. They wrote:

The demands emerging from the common interests of a class can only be realized when that class gains political power and can give its demands universal validity in the form of legislation. Every struggling class must therefore formulate its demands as legalistic demands within a program. But the needs of every class alter during the course of social and political change; they differ in every country according to its characteristics and its degree of social development. Correspondingly, the legalistic demands of individual parties cannot be the same for all peoples in all times, despite general consensus as to the end goal. They are a variable element and are revised from time to time, as can be observed in the actions of socialist parties of different countries. Such revisions are actually reflections of real circumstances; however, no existing socialist party has thought of making a new legal philosophy of its program, and this will not happen in the future. What Mr. Menger has perpetrated in this area can only serve as a warning.[127]

Kistiakovsky's views on the problems posed by Menger were completely different. Unlike Engels and Kautsky he stressed the continuity between the existing forms of *Rechtsstaat* and the future socialist state; he did so, indeed, more forcefully than Menger, since the latter underestimated the value of civil and political rights for the working class and quite explicitly reduced legal questions to questions

[124] Ibid., pp. 212–13.
[125] Ibid., p. 213.
[126] Ibid., p. 219.
[127] Ibid., pp. 219–20.

of might.[128] Kistiakovsky could not agree that law depended entirely on economic and political forces, but emphasized its autonomous value and the autonomous character of jurisprudence. Most importantly, he did not see law as a mere instrument in the struggle for power, or simply a means of consolidating political power. His conception of the rule-of-law state led him to postulate the priority of law over politics and the subordination of force to law. Like Menger, he accepted a gradual transition to socialism; he thought of socialism in juridical terms and preferred legal forms of social change. But, unlike Menger, he held strongly to the liberal values which he saw as inseparable from the true spirit of law. Liberalism and democratic socialism—which, while not then existing, he saw as the coming social system—were for him the two stages of the modern rule-of-law state. His socialism, therefore, should be called 'rule-of-law socialism', and not just 'juridical socialism'.[129]

5 The Russian intelligentsia and the spirit of law

We have now reached a point from which to judge Kistiakovsky's famous article in *Landmarks*. The article itself fits neatly into Kistiakovsky's conception of law as a cultural value, to which it adds a significant time-and-place-bound dimension by showing its relevance for the practical problems of pre-revolutionary Russia. But, at least at first glance, this excellent article does not seem to fit at all well into the theoretical position of *Landmarks*. Two points may be made in this connection.

First, Gershenzon's preface to *Landmarks* defined the 'common platform' of its authors as a belief in 'the theoretical and practical preeminence of spiritual life over the external forces of community: in the sense that the individual's inner life is the sole creative force of human existence and that it, and not any self-sufficient principle of political order, is the only firm basis for any social construction'.[130] How could Kistiakovsky agree with this? He was a thinker who

---

[128] As Berolzheimer writes, 'For the masses the prime consideration is the question of bread. Menger does not allow that the state exists for itself, and considers only the ends towards which the authorities work. Right is might: legal questions are questions of might'. See F. Berolzheimer, *The World's Legal Philosophies*, R. S. Jastrow (trans.), New York, 1924, p. 301.

[129] Cf. Vucinich, *Social Thought in Tsarist Russia*, p. 152. To translate the term *pravovoe gosudarstvo* as 'legal state', as Vicinich does here, rather than 'rule-of-law state', is also very misleading.

[130] See *Landmarks: A Collection of Essays on the Russian Intelligentsia*, B. Shragin and A. Todd (eds.), M. Schwartz (trans.), New York, 1977, p. 1.

stressed the importance of 'objective law', of the 'external forms of community'; he was a theorist of the rule-of-law state, namely, a supporter of a definite 'principle of political order'. Consequently, his agreement with people like Gershenzon could only be partial. What was the real basis of this partial agreement?

Second, the authors of *Landmarks* represented the extreme right wing of Russian liberalism. Their criticism of the Russian 'progressive intelligentsia' was directed not only against radicals, but also against liberals. The Kadet leader, Pavel Miliukov, saw them as representative of 'decadent attitudes to politics' and described their position as a return to the favourite Russian reactionary formula: 'Not institutions, but people; not politics, but morals.'[131] This opinion was shared by almost all members of the Kadet party. The judgement of moderate socialists was even harsher, differing little from that of Lenin, who called *Landmarks* 'an encyclopaedia of liberal renegacy';[132] Martov, for instance, labelled *Landmarks* as evidence of a rapprochement between Russian liberalism and the right: 'Liberalism is attempting to become on principle monarchist, nationalist and anti-democratic in its political conceptions, counter-revolutionary in its legal views, strictly individualistic in the sphere of economics and national-soil in its attitude to the State and the Church.'[133] The accuracy of this diagnosis seemed confirmed by the fact that the right-wing Archbishop Antonii of Volhynia welcomed *Landmarks* as a 'great and beautiful feat'.[134] But Kistiakovsky plainly cannot be described as a right-wing 'liberal renegade'; on the contrary, his theory of rule-of-law socialism placed him on the left wing of Russian liberalism, among people gravitating towards moderate democratic socialism. Then why did he associate with those who had definitely broken with socialism and whose rapprochement with the right, irrespective of its motivation, could not be denied? Why did he fail to distance himself from them when their isolation from all 'forces of progress' became evident?

An answer to these questions is reached by concentrating on those views of the *Landmarks'* authors which, in the light of later events,

---

[131] See P. Miliukov, *Political Memoirs, 1905–1917*, A. P. Mendel (ed.), Ann Arbor, 1967, p. 3.

[132] Lenin, *Collected Works*, vol. 16, 1963, p. 124.

[133] Quoted from C. Read, *Religion, Revolution and the Russian Intelligentsia 1900–1912: The Vekhi Debate and Its Intellectual Background*, London, 1979, p. 150.

[134] See J. Brooks, '*Vekhi* and the *Vekhi* Dispute', *Survey*, vol. 19, no. 1 (86), 1973, p. 43.

turned out to be prophetic, exhibiting 'mature wisdom'.[135] This view of *Landmarks* became widespread among Russians who had witnessed the victory of the Bolshevik revolution. After World War II it spread further, to Western students of Russian history. Today it seems likely to win recognition among Western intellectuals who are aware of the similarities between the mentality of the pre-revolutionary Russian intelligentsia and some attitudes of contemporary Western radicals, above all those of the New Left, although the phenomenon is certainly wider.[136]

To begin with, we must forget Gershenzon's words on the 'common platform' uniting the authors of *Landmarks*. His formula was particularly unfortunate and misleading: unfortunate, becuse somewhat naïvely expressed, misleading, because it drew attention away from a more important common platform uniting the authors, and exposed the book to easy criticism. We can even say that it was simply wrong, because some authors of *Landmarks* clearly distanced themselves from it: Izgoev did so in a rather enigmatic footnote while Kistiakovsky, in the second edition of the book, added an explanation of his position which showed very plainly how limited his agreement with Gershenzon really was.[137]

The common platform of the seven authors of *Landmarks* was in fact their sharp, unrelenting criticism of the Russian intelligentsia, of its enshrined traditions and its still dominant mentality. This criticism centred on three problems: (1) the intelligentsia's attitude towards cultural-spiritual values and creativity, (2) its attitude towards economic wealth and productivity, and (3) its attitude towards the state and law. From this point of view Kistiakovsky's contribution to *Landmarks* was of central importance, and his conclusions were in harmony with the conclusions of the other authors.

The opening essay—Berdyaev's 'Philosophic Truth and the Moral Truth of the Intelligentsia'—deals with the first of these problems. The Russian intelligentsia, Berdyaev asserted, subordinated all spiritual-cultural values to 'the exclusive and despotic sway of a utilitarian moral standard' and to 'the equally exclusive and oppressive "love for the people" and "love for the proletariat".'[138] It was always much more

[135] Cf. L. Schapiro, 'The *Vekhi* Group and the Mystique of Revolution', *Slavonic and East European Review*, vol. 34, 1955, p. 68.
[136] Cf. Shragin's 'Introduction' to *Landmarks*, pp. lii–liii, see above, n. 130.
[137] See *Landmarks*, p. 111 n. Kistiakovsky's explanation is quoted below, p. 388.
[138] Ibid., p. 4.

interested in the distribution and equalization of cultural values than in their creation.[139] The thirst for pure knowledge and pure art was morally condemned, treated as something reactionary. The culmination of this 'populist obscurantism' came in the 1870s, but the negation of the independent importance of scholarship, philosophy, the enlightenment and the universities, their subordination to political interests, remained a permanent feature of the world-view of the intelligentsia.[140] Their 'almost maniacal tendency' to judge everything by political and utilitarian standards, combined with their 'love for an equalizing justice', produced a nihilist attitude towards truth and cultural values.[141] A typical Russian *intelligent* is not interested in philosophic truth, or, rather, his interest in it, often intense, is purely instrumental: he looks to philosophy for instruments in the eternal struggle for social justice, for tools in pursuing the class interests of the proletariat or peasantry; hence he does not bother about truth but concentrates instead on the real or alleged socio-political function of ideas, dividing them into 'reactionary' or 'progressive', 'bourgeois' or 'proletarian'. His attitude towards scientific truth is the same: the Russian intelligentsia embraced the cause of scientific positivism, not because it was interested in the pursuit of truth but because it identified the scientific spirit with political progressiveness and social radicalism.[142] In this way the Russian intelligentsia 'yielded to the temptation of [Dostoevsky's] Grand Inquisitor who demanded the rejection of truth in the name of the people's happiness'.[143]

Sergei Bulgakov, an ex-Marxist who was to become a priest and an Orthodox Christian theologian, attacked the intelligentsia's worship of the people as a form of self-worship, of seeing themselves as 'saviours of mankind or at least of the Russian people'.[144] He accused them of 'heroic maximalism', of exhibiting 'symptoms of ideological mania, of self-hypnosis . . . shackling thought and producing a fanaticism deaf to the voice of real life'. Their attitude towards the people, he contended, was in fact élitist, patronizing and even arrogant—'an arrogant attitude toward the people as a minor, unenlightened (in the intelligentsia's sense of the word) object of its crusade dependent on a nursemaid to be nurtured to "consciousness"'.[145] He saw this as the sad result of the deep cleavage between the Russian intelligentsia and the Russian people, a cleavage brought about less by education than by the

---

[139] Ibid., p. 5. [140] Ibid., pp. 5–6. [141] Ibid., pp. 9–10.
[142] Ibid., p. 12. [143] Ibid., p. 10. [144] Ibid., p. 36.
[145] Ibid., p. 55.

intelligentsia's atheism and cosmopolitanism. This phenomenon was unknown in the West where the educated strata remained national and where even economic progress (as shown in recent studies on the significance of Puritanism for capitalist development) was rooted in a religious world-view.[146] By cutting itself off from the ancient wisdom of the Christian and national traditions, the Russian intelligentsia fell into a kind of self-congratulatory, conceited immaturity, rejecting the ideal of the Christian saint and replacing it with the image of the revolutionary student.[147] Russian students, because of 'the physiology and psychology of their youth, the inexperience of life and scientific knowledge, so easily replaced by passion and self-confidence', came to be regarded as the natural leaders of the intelligentsia, whence arose 'spiritual pedocracy', the greatest evil of Russian society.[148]

This theme was developed in detail in Izgoev's essay 'On Educated Youth', which described Russian students as living in a 'unique infant culture', despising 'bourgeois' science, stubbornly committed to a number of 'progressive' dogmas and intolerant of inner freedom. A certain student, quoted by Izgoev, complained: 'It's a horrible thing not to think as our student crowd think! They make you into an exile, accuse you of treachery, consider you an enemy.'[149]

In Bulgakov's interpretation the mentality of the Russian intelligentsia also had its positive side. He saw it as unconscious religiosity—perverted, to be sure, but capable of recovery if returned to its Christian source. He wrote:

Alongside the anti-Christ aspect of this intelligentsia, one senses higher religious potential, a new historical flesh waiting to be spiritualized. This intense search for the City of God, this desire to execute the will of God on earth as in heaven, are profoundly distinct from bourgeois culture's attraction to solid worldly prosperity. The intelligentsia's abnormal maximalism with its practical unfeasibility is the result of religious perversion, but it can be conquered through the recovery of religious health.[150]

Semyon Frank, another ex-Marxist moving through idealism to religious philosophy, categorically rejected this position. In his view the Russian intelligentsia was not religious because 'religiosity is incompatible with the ascribing of absolute significance to worldly, human interests or with the nihilistic and utilitarian reverence for the

---

[146] Ibid., p. 32. Bulgakov was referring primarily to Max Weber's study *The Protestant Ethic and the Spirit of Capitalism.*
[147] Ibid., p. 41.
[148] Ibid., pp. 40–1.   [149] Ibid., pp. 100–1.   [150] Ibid., p. 62.

outward blessings of life'.[151] In his view the intelligentsia's *Weltanschauung* could best be described as a peculiar combination of nihilism and moralism, nihilism in substance, moralism in form, 'the lack of faith and the fanatic severity of moral requirements'.[152] He conceded, however, that his disagreement with Bulgakov was to some extent semantic, and himself described the classic Russian *intelligent* as a militant monk of the religion of earthly salvation.[153] He agreed that the fanatical faith in a future paradise on earth, which characterised the Russian intelligentsia and which was so well analysed as a general phenomenon by Novgorodtsev, was a form of secularized millenarianism, that is a substitute for genuine religion. He insisted, moreover, that a thoroughly secularized millenarianism, that is, faith in a terrestrial millennium without faith in an Absolute Being, was a peculiarly dangerous form of nihilism, and not a symptom of religiosity in an acceptable sense of this term.

A major part of Frank's essay was devoted to the second of the three problems mentioned above—the problem of the intelligentsia's attitude toward material wealth and economic productivity. He defined the pseudo-religion of the Russian intelligentsia as a religion of social justice or, more precisely, of distributive justice, a religion of the equal distribution of material and cultural goods, permeated by a spirit of ascetism and by a deeply-rooted hostility to the principle of productivity, whether cultural or material. The same point was made by Berdyaev, who stressed that the intelligentsia's attitude to economic production closely paralleled its treatment of philosophical creation. 'The intelligentsia', he wrote, 'has always been willing to accept any ideology in which the central place is given over to the problems of distribution and equality, and in which all creation is kept in check.'[154]

Frank develops the same thought, but with more emphasis on economic productivity. It seems worthwhile to quote his own words:

The Russian intelligentsia does not love wealth. In the first place, it does not value spiritual wealth or culture, the ideal force and creativity of the human spirit that impels it to master and humanize the world and to enrich life with the values of science, art, religion, and ethics. And what is most remarkable of all, it even extends this dislike to material wealth, instinctively recognizing its symbolic link with the general idea of culture. The intelligentsia loves only the just distribution of wealth, and not wealth itself; rather, it even hates and fears that wealth. In its soul, love for the *poor* becomes love for *poverty* . . . Its ideal is

---

[151] Ibid., p. 160.
[153] Ibid., pp. 159, 179.
[152] Ibid., p. 163.
[154] Ibid., p. 5.

more the innocent, pure life than it is the truly rich, abundant, and powerful life.[155]

This is why socialism, understood as an ideology whose moral pathos is focused on the idea of distributive justice, is in a sense a natural world-view for the Russian *intelligent*, and why too the Russian intelligentsia, in spite of its intentions, has been unable to promote its declared aim of 'people's welfare'. It has been guilty of 'a philosophical error and a moral sin', of exalting political struggle at the expense of productive labour.[156]

This argument sounds like a harsh indictment:

Neglecting production in the name of distribution, the spirit of socialist populism—taking this neglect not only to the point of total indifference but even to outright hostility—in the final analysis undermines the people's strength and perpetuates its material and spiritual poverty. Expending the enormous forces concentrated within it on the unproductive political struggle guided by the idea of distribution, and not participating in the *creation* of national property, the socialist intelligentsia remains barren in the metaphysical sense; and despite its proclaimed and most valued aspirations, it leads a parasitic existence feeding off the nation's body.[157]

It is interesting that both Berdyaev and Frank stressed some positive features of Marxism, in this way explaining *ex post* their early commitment to Marxist theory. Marxism, wrote Berdyaev,

sees the essence of human history in the creative process of vanquishing nature in the economic creation and organization of productive forces. The entire social structure with its inherent forms of distributive justice, all the subjective attitudes of social groups, were subordinated to this objective principle of production. It should be said that there was a healthy seed in Marxism's objective-scientific aspect, a seed which was affirmed and developed by the most cultured and scholarly of our Marxists, Petr Struve.[158]

Frank's view of Marxism was very similar:

With the appearance of Marxism, motifs alien to the intelligentsia conscious-ness were heard for the first time—respect for culture and raising productivity (material as well as spiritual). For the first time it was noted that the moral problem is not universal, in a certain sense is even subordinate to the problem of culture, and that the ascetic self-renunciation of higher forms of life is always evil, not good. But these motifs could not dominate intelligentsia

---

[155] Ibid., pp. 176, 179.
[156] Ibid., p. 175.
[157] Ibid. [158] Ibid., p. 14.

thought for long; the victorious and all-consuming populist spirit swallowed up and assimilated Marxist theory.[159]

Berdyaev made the same point. He complained that,

> on Russian soil economic materialism lost its objective character: the productive-constructive factor was pushed into the background and the subjective class-oriented aspect of social democracy stepped out into the foreground. Marxism underwent a populist degeneration here, and economic materialism turned into a new form of 'subjective sociology'. Russian Marxists were seized by an exceptional love for equality and an exceptional belief in the proximity of the socialist objective and in the possibility of achieving this end in Russia even sooner than in the West. The element of objective truth was completely eclipsed by the subjective element, the class point of view, and class psychology.[160]

The third problem—the intelligentsia's attitude towards the state and law—was the main concern of the remaining authors of *Landmarks*. All agreed that after the Manifesto of 17 October 1905, the intelligentsia's crusade against the government should cease and revolutionary struggle should be replaced by constructive forms of activity. But each approached this problem in his own way and from a different angle to the others.

Gershenzon, in my opinion, had a particular talent for compromising the common cause of the authors of *Landmarks*. His essay, entitled 'Creative Self-Cognition', condemned revolutionary activity in general, and not just its continuation after the October Manifesto. It was permeated by a fear of the masses and by an exaggerated, hysterical feeling of the intelligentsia's isolation among the common people of Russia. The author saw the Russian people as filled with a passionate hatred for the intelligentsia, which he attributed to a 'metaphysical discord' and 'unconscious mystical horror'.[161] His conclusion comes as no surprise: 'Not only can we not dream about fusing with the people, but we must fear them worse than any punishment by the government, and we must bless that authority which alone with its bayonets and prisons manages to protect us from the popular fury.'[162]

The intelligentsia's 'alienation from and hostility towards the state'[163] is the theme of Struve's essay 'Intelligentsia and the Revolution'. Like Gershenzon, Struve strongly protested against the

[159] Ibid., p. 166.
[160] Ibid., p. 14. (I have slightly modified the translation of this passage.)
[161] Ibid., p. 80.   [162] Ibid., pp. 80–1.   [163] Ibid., p. 141.

politicization of 'all of spiritual life' and demanded 'the subordination
of politics to the idea of education'.[164] But the main thrust of his essay
was elsewhere. Unlike Gershenzon, Struve did not condemn past
revolutionary struggle but made it clear that revolutionary methods of
struggle before the October Manifesto were justified because 'the state
of affairs was intolerable from [both] the national and governmental
viewpoint'.[165] The novelty of this approach lay in his emphasizing that
the fight against autocracy was necessary not only for the sake of the
people, but also for the sake of the state, since it was deeply
detrimental to the state to keep its development within prearranged
boundaries. But Struve was firmly convinced that 'the revolution ought
to have been formally concluded by the act of October 17th'.[166] In this
respect he differed sharply from most of the Kadet party, not to
mention the more left-wing Russian parties. He was bitterly critical of
the fact that after 17 October 'the struggle against traditional Russian
statehood and against the "bourgeois" social order was conducted with
even greater passion and greater revolutionary intensity than it had
been before October 17th', a fact he tried to explain by accusing the
intelligentsia of introducing into the struggle 'a virulent fanaticism, a
murderous logic of conclusions and constructs'.[167]

Frank's unpublished memoir of Struve contains a good commentary
on his thought at that time. According to Frank, Struve wanted to
change the consciousness of the intelligentsia in such a way as to make
it responsible for and not just critical of the state. He wanted to
overcome its estrangement from the state—an estrangement which
commonly found expression in the all-too-familiar habit of dividing
people into 'us' and 'them'.

State power was 'they', a strange and inaccessible compound of court and
bureaucracy, pictured as a group of corrupt and mentally limited rulers over
the real 'national and public' Russia. To 'them' were opposed 'we', 'society',
the 'people', and above all the 'caste' of the intelligentsia, concerned for the
welfare of the people and devoted to its servcice, but by reason of its lack of
rights capable only of criticizing the government power, of arousing
oppositional feelings, and secretly preparing a revolt.

Struve, Frank continues, 'had within him and displayed from the very
first, the embryo of something quite different . . . He always discussed
politics, so to say, not from "below", but from "above", not as a

164 Ibid., p. 151.   165 Ibid., p. 146.
166 Ibid.   167 Ibid., p. 148.

member of an enslaved society, but conscious of the fact that he was a potential participator in positive state construction.'[168]

Struve displayed this attitude not only in private but in public as well. In his articles published after 1907 in *Russian Thought* (*Russkaya Mysl'*) he repeatedly stressed that the Russian state and the Russian nation must 'grow organically into one',[169] and also that such a fusion of state and nation was not compatible with autocracy. Unlike Miliukov and the official Kadet line—although he was still, nominally, a member of their central committee—he did not demand an immediate transition to parliamentary government. He insisted, instead, on respect for the Fundamental Laws and condemned 'the unprincipled attitude toward the law' of both the revolutionary left and the counter-revolutionary right. He expressed this unpopular position as follows:

> The unprincipled attitude toward the law of the part of the revolution found expression in the formula: every action is allowable if it is useful to the revolution. As the consequence of a thoughtlessness well known to logical theory, everything harmful to the government was equated with useful for the revolution. And so, a morally monstrous premise was linked with a factually absurd assumption. With what real content history has filled this logic it is sufficiently well known.
>
> The unprincipled attitude toward the law on the part of the counter-revolution finds expression in the formula: every administrative action is allowable if it harms 'sedition' (*kramola*) . . . This paves the way not for the pacification of the country, but for the revival, with renewed vigour, of an identical formula with a revolutionary emblem.[170]

Kistiakovsky's position was basically the same. In spite of all the philosophical and political differences which divided him from the other authors of *Landmarks*,[171] he shared their views on the autonomous value of culture, on the priority of production over distribution, and on the need for *constructive* work within the framework of the newly introduced Fundamental Laws. He thought, that is, that the constitution of 1906 created conditions in which the revolutionary struggle against the state could and should be replaced by cultural, economic,

---

[168] Quoted from Schapiro, 'The *Vekhi* Group and the Mystique of Revolution', p. 58.

[169] See P. Struve, *Patriotica. Politika, kul'tura, religiia, sotsializm. Sbornik statei za piat' let (1905–1910)*, SPb, 1911, pp. 92–3.

[170] P. Struve, 'Gipnoz strakha i politicheskii shantazh', *Slovo*, 338, 23 Dec. 1907, reprinted in *Patriotica*, pp. 164–72 (see above, n. 169). Quoted from Pipes, *Struve: Liberal on the Right*, pp. 80–1.

[171] These differences included the attitude of the other authors of *Landmarks* (especially Struve) to the Ukrainian question.

and legislative activity within the state. He had enough civil courage to propagate his views without trying to flatter public opinion, and was not afraid to subscribe to unpopular views held by other people, if they happened to coincide with his own convictions. This provides, I think, a sufficient explanation of his willingness to associate himself with the *Landmarks* group.

There is no need, I think, to explain why Kistiakovsky's essay deserves a detailed presentation in this book. It is obvious that almost every sentence in it is relevant to our central theme: the problem of law in the Russian cultural and intellectual history of the nineteenth and early twentieth century.

Spiritual culture, Kistiakovsky argues, consists of content values and formal values. The most developed and concretely tangible cultural form is law. 'Social discipline can be created only by law: a disciplined society and a society with a developed system of law are identical concepts.'[172] At the same time the most essential element of law is freedom. True, law is concerned only with external freedom, relative and socially conditioned. This outward freedom, however, is the necessary foundation of more absolute, spiritual freedom. Unfortunately, this has never been properly understood by the Russians. 'The Russian intelligentsia consists of people who are neither individually nor socially disciplined. This is related to the fact that the Russian intelligentsia never respected law and never saw any value in it. Of all the cultural values, law was the most suppressed.'[173]

This sad state of affairs, Kistiakovsky continues, is reflected in the amazing fact that the Russians have not produced a single study of law capable of attracting public attention. In other words, legal ideas played no role in Russian spiritual development. The recent efforts of some Russian thinkers have not succeeded in changing this. In Kistiakovsky's opinion 'neither Chicherin nor Soloviev ever created anything of particular significance in the realm of legal ideas. And what good work they produced proved almost fruitless: their influence on our intelligentsia was negligible—their legal ideas most of all.' Equally sceptical was Kistiakovsky's view of the possible influence of 'the resurrected idea of natural law' and Petrażycki's idea of intuitive law. He thought that Novgorodtsev's and Petrażycki's works lacked 'the external form, the definite formula that usually gives ideas their elasticity and aids in their dissemination.' And he asked rhetorically: 'Where is our *L'esprit des lois*, our *Le contrat social?*'[174]

[172] *Landmarks*, p. 112.   [173] Ibid., p. 113.   [174] Ibid., p. 115.

The lack of such books in the Russian cultural heritage cannot be explained by the possibility of borrowing the ideas of freedom and the rights of the individual from the West, that is, by the absence of any need to develop these ideas independently. Legal ideas cannot simply be 'borrowed', they 'acquire their own unique nuances and their own shading in the consciousness of each separate people.'[175] Even if it were possible to borrow them in a ready-made form, it would not be enough: 'at a certain moment of life it becomes necessary to be wholly possessed by them . . . But the consciousness of the Russian intelligentsia has never been wholly possessed by ideas of the individual's rights or of the rule-of-law state; the intelligentsia has never fully experienced them.'[176]

More than that: the lack, or extreme weakness of legal consciousness became an object of idealization. To illustrate this Kistiakovsky quotes from both right-wing and left-wing Russian thinkers, the Slavophiles and Herzen, Leontiev and Mikhailovsky. He stresses the fact that even K. D. Kavelin, a typical Russian liberal, 'paid attention only to the social nature of constitutional government', and for this reason 'objected to constitutional plans because at that time [the 1860s] a national constitutional assembly would have consisted entirely of noblemen'.[177] His position here was similar to that of Mikhailovsky, who rejected constitutional government as bourgeois; both 'totally lost sight of the legal nature of the constitutional state'. They were not aware that

if we are to examine and clarify the nature of the constitutional state's legal organization, we must refer to the concept of law in its pure form, that is, its genuine content, not what is borrowed from economic or social aspects. It is not enough to indicate that law delimits interests or creates a compromise between them; it must be insistently stressed that there can be law only where there is freedom for the individual. In this sense the legal order is a system of relationships in which all persons of a given society possess the greatest possible freedom of activity and self-determination. But, defined as such, it is impossible to oppose the legal order to the socialist order. On the contrary, a more profound understanding of both leads to the conclusion that they are tightly linked to each other, and from the juridical point of view the socialist order is only a more strictly consistent legal order.[178]

Given the general poverty of the Russian intelligentsia, even such leaders as Kavelin and Mikhailovsky could not understand that a

[175] Ibid., p. 116.   [176] Ibid., pp. 115–16.
[177] Ibid., p. 120.   [178] Ibid., p. 122.

constitutional order serves the cause of democracy and socialism *irrespective* of the character of power relationships in the state.

Kistiakovsky's assessment of the role of Marxism in Russia is very similar to the views of Berdyaev and Frank. Marxism, he maintains,

> began to refine somewhat the Russian intelligentsia's legal consciousness . . .
> Our intelligentsia understood at last that any social struggle is a political
> struggle; that political freedom is a necessary condition for a socialist order;
> that the constitutional state, despite the bourgeoisie's supremacy in it, gives the
> working class room in which to struggle for its own interests . . . that the
> struggle for political freedom is the primary and most urgent task of any socialist
> party; and so forth.[179]

Unfortunately, all these changes proved to be too superficial to inspire the intelligentsia with a genuine respect for law. As time went on, it became evident that the Marxist intelligentsia had no real commitment to the cause of legal order in Russia, and gave it only half-hearted and partial support. The Second Congress of the Russian Social-Democratic Workers' Party (1903) made it clear that even Plekhanov, the Marxist leader who had done more than anyone to fight populist prejudice against political freedom, was not prepared to recognize the rule of law as an autonomous value and too readily subordinated it to 'the idea of the supremacy of force and the seizure of power'.[180]

Further proofs of the weak and warped character of the intelligentsia's legal consciousness were provided with the emergence of political parties at the beginning of the twentieth century. According to Kistiakovsky, all exhibited a tendency towards the detailed regulation of all social relations by means of written laws—a tendency characteristic of the police state, as opposed to the rule-of-law state.[181] This showed that the Russian bureaucracy was the scion of the Russian intelligentsia, which itself was 'thoroughly permeated with its own bureaucratism . . . It could be said', he concluded, 'that our intelligentsia's legal consciousness is at the police-state stage.'[182]

Kistiakovsky's illustrated this thesis by reference to the decisions of the Second Congress of the Social-Democratic Party. He agreed with Martov that the Congress had legalized within the party 'the state of

---

[179] Ibid., p. 123.
[180] Ibid., pp. 124–5. Kistiakovsky was referring to Plekhanov's 'Jacobin speech' at the Second Congress of the Russian Social-Democratic Workers' Party, in which 'The Father of Russian Marxism' proclaimed that 'the success of revolution is the highest law'. (See Ch. I, 6.)
[181] Ibid., pp. 128–9.   [182] Ibid., p. 129.

siege with its exceptional laws against individual groups', quoting Lenin's answer: 'With regard to unstable and wavering elements we not only can but must create a "state of siege",'[183] but also noted that the charter, with this clause, had been adopted by a majority of only two votes. Yet he insisted that 'faith in the omnipotence of statuses and the force of compulsory rules' was also shared by such liberal organizations as the Union of Liberation. Even the liberal intelligentsia perceived law 'not as a legal conviction but as a compulsory rule'.[184]

The last part of Kistiakovsky's essay is devoted to the problem of the Russian intelligentsia's attitude towards the law courts. This problem was of crucial importance to him in answering the question: 'How capable is our intelligentsia of participating in the legal reorganization of the state, the conversion of state power *from a power of force* into a *power of law*.'[185] Its examination led him to very pessimistic conclusions.

The reorganization of Russian courts introduced by the Judicial Reform of 1864, he argued, had been based on judicial principles fully consonant with the rule of law but, in spite of this, Russian courts remained bad and the prestige of judges low. True, it was hard to make the best possible use of judicial reform under existing political conditions; indeed Kistiakovsky had earlier thought that it was simply impossible.[186] But later experience led him to put more emphasis on 'subjective factors', on the intelligentsia's collective guilt and collective responsibility. 'Political conditions alone', he wrote, 'cannot be blamed for our bad courts; we too are guilty. Under exactly analogous political conditions the courts of other nations still upheld the law. The saying "there's a judge in Berlin" dates from the late eighteenth and the first half of the nineteenth centuries, when Prussia was still an absolute monarchy.'[187]

What were the reasons for this striking difference between Russia and Prussia? In the first place Kistiakovsky mentions the subordination of legal justice to political and ethical considerations. The intelligentsia was hypnotized, as it were, by the political role of the new courts, whose main value it saw as the possibility of defending political revolutionaries; at best, it saw trial by jury 'as a court of conscience, in the sense of passive humanitarianism'.[188] Moreover, the intelligentsia

---

[183] Ibid., p. 130.   [184] Ibid., p. 131.
[185] Ibid., p. 132.   [186] See above, p. 368.
[187] *Landmarks*, p. 137. A few years earlier Kistiakovsky had treated such views as 'an idealization of the Russian autocracy'. See his 'Gosudarstvo pravovoe i sotsialisti-cheskoe', p. 477 (cf. n. 84).
[188] Ibid., p. 134.

displayed a profound and amazing indifference to such prosaic problems as the rationalization of the civil legal system and the functioning of the criminal courts. Thus it was useless in upholding legal standards or creating an active legal sense among the people.[189] Finally, the lawyers themselves were unduly obsessed with the struggle for new laws and often forgot 'the interests of formal law and law in general'. In the end, they 'sometimes rendered "new law" itself poor service, as they were guided more by political than by legal considerations'.[190]

Kistiakovsky did not share Gershenzon's inclination to stress the 'pre-eminence of spiritual life over the external forms of community', nor did he neglect the influence of external conditions. On the contrary, he himself stressed that the 'dulled legal consciousness' of the Russian intelligentsia was 'the result of a chronic evil—the lack of any kind of legal order in the daily life of the Russian people.'[191] But he still felt that the intelligentsia must recognize its moral responsibility, and not too easily excuse itself on the ground of external conditions. He felt that to use social determinism to explain away one's own guilt while condemning one's enemy in purely moral terms, was logically inconsistent and morally wrong. One must choose either consistent determinism which would leave no place for a concept of moral responsibility, or moral judgement which would then apply also to ourselves. In the second edition of *Landmarks* he added to his essay a footnote clearly explaining his position. He wrote:

Many feel that it is unfair to blame our intelligentsia for its weak legal consciousness, since the guilty party is rather the external circumstances—that arbitrariness that predominates in our life. The influence of these circumstances is undeniable, and I have noted it in my essay. But all the blame cannot be laid on them . . . If we recognize this evil then we can no longer be reconciled to it; our conscience cannot be at peace, and we must struggle within ourselves against this corrupting principle. It is not worthy of thinking people to say: we are corrupted and will continue to be corrupted until the cause of our corruption is eliminated. Every man is obliged to say: I must not be corrupted any longer, since I have recognized what it is that is corrupting me and where the source of my corruption lies. We must harness all the force of our thought, our emotion, and our will in order to free our consciousness from the perilous influence of these inauspicious circumstances. This is why

[189] Ibid., pp. 134–5.
[190] Ibid., p. 136.
[191] Ibid., p. 116.

the current task is to awaken the Russian intelligentsia's sense of law and to summon it to life and action.[192]

6 The spirit of law and the Kadet party

The publication of *Landmarks* unleashed a storm of debate and protest. The book was almost universally condemned as a shameful betrayal and vilification of the most sacred progressive traditions of Russia.[193] It was indignantly rejected not only by the representatives of all shades of secular progressivism but also by those Russian intellectuals who espoused the cause of the 'new religious consciousness' and were afraid that 'landmarkism' would compromise the idea of religious regeneration in Russia.[194] Although all the authors of *Landmarks* were Kadets, the Kadet party, as already mentioned, hastened to disown them. The party leader, Pavel Miliukov, undertook a lecture tour criticizing *Landmarks* as a dangerous deviation from liberal orthodoxy.[195] Soon afterwards the Kadets published *The Intelligentsia in Russia*—a collection of articles discussing and severely condemning the ideas of *Landmarks*.[196]

In Lenin's opinion this was merely a tactical move. The very fact that Struve remained a member of the Central Committee of the Kadet party proved, for Lenin, that the differences dividing Struve from Miliukov were simply the greater 'practicality' of the latter. The Bolshevik leader was convinced that 'not a single politically thinking person will say that Mr. Miliukov seriously struggles with the *Vekhi* [*Landmarks*] crowd when he 'argues' with them, pronounces them "thoughtless", and at the same time works with them politically hand in hand. Everyone admits that by this Mr. Miliukov proves his hypocrisy without denying the fact of his political solidarity with the *Vekhi* crowd.'[197] The true essence of the Kadet party was expressed, in Lenin's view, in Gershenzon's words about the bayonets and prisons of the regime protecting the intelligentsia from the popular fury. Lenin wrote,

[192] Ibid., p. 137, n.
[193] See C. Read, *Religion, Revolution and the Russian Intelligentsia*, p. 161.
[194] See D. S. Merezhkovsky, 'Sem' smirennykh. O Vekhakh', in D. S. Merezhkovsky, *Polnoe sobranie sochinenii*, vol. 12, SPb–Moscow, 1911, pp. 69–81.
[195] Cf. Pipes, *Struve: Liberal on the Right*, pp. 107–9.
[196] There were two other collections of liberal articles against *Landmarks: Po Vekham*, Moscow, 1909, and *V zashchitu intelligentsii*, Moscow, 1909. See Brooks, *Vekhi*, p. 44.
[197] Quoted from T. Riha, *A Russian European: Paul Miliukov in Russian Politics*, Notre-Dame–London, 1969, p. 174. Cf. Lenin, *Collected Works*, vol. 16, p., 138.

This tirade is good because it is frank: it is useful because it reveals the truth about the real essence of the policy of the whole Constitutional Democratic Party throughout the period 1905–9. This tirade is good because it reveals concisely and vividly the whole spirit of *Vekhi*. And *Vekhi* is good because it discloses the whole spirit of the *real* policy of the Russian liberals and of the Russian Kadets included among them. That is why the Kadet polemic with *Vekhi* and the Kadet renunciation of *Vekhi* are nothing but hypocrisy, sheer idle talk, for in reality the Kadets collectively, as a party, as a social force, have pursued the policy of *Vekhi* and *no other*.[198]

It is impossible to agree with this. Both the philosophical and the practical political differences dividing Miliukov and the mainstream Kadets from the *Landmarks* group were profound. Struve's position on the Kadet Central Committee did not mean that he had any real influence on the party's political line, nor that a significant part of the Kadet leadership endorsed the ideas of *Landmarks*. After the appearance of *Landmarks*, on the contrary, Struve's reputation, to quote Pipes, 'was finished, even in the ranks of the liberal party'.[199]

In his long controversial article 'The Intelligentsia and Historical Tradition', Miliukov disagreed with *Landmarks* on almost every point. He conceded it the merit of raising fundamental issues and that 'its provocative value is very great', but insisted on the necessity of strongly resisting its influence. 'The seeds which the authors of *Landmarks* are sowing', he wrote, 'are poisonous seeds, and the work which they are doing, independently, of course, of their actual intention, is dangerous and harmful work.'[200] It was necessary, he urged, not to break with the tradition of the Russian intelligentsia but to continue it, fully assimilating the positive experience of the 'last earthquake' (the revolution of 1905–7), without making any concessions to its enemies and without rejecting any part of its heritage.[201] In spite of his polite, though insincere, acknowledgement of the 'good intentions' of the authors, he accused them of welcoming the defeat of the revolution and reiterated his firm conviction that the revolution must be carried through, and with the active participation or at least moral support of the liberals. In his view this was the only way to a truly constructive development of the state, while the message of *Landmarks*, which he reduced to an appeal for collective repentance and the replacement of

[198] Lenin, *Collected Works*, vol. 16, pp. 130–1.
[199] Pipes, *Struve: Liberal on the Right*, p. 114.
[200] P. Miliukov, 'Intelligentsiia i istoricheskaia traditsiia', in *Intelligentsiia v Rossii. Sbornik statei*, SPb, 1910, p. 187.
[201] Ibid., pp. 91, 187.

political struggle by individual self-perfection, amounted in practice to a middle way between Slavophile anarchism and the anarchism of Tolstoy.[202] The other authors of *The Intelligentsia in Russia* sometimes went even further than Miliukov. Thus, for instance, Ivan Petrunkevich, the pioneer of *zemstvo* constitutionalism and one of the greatest moral authorities of the liberal movement in Russia, condemned the authors of *Landmarks* morally, for striking at the defeated and for embracing the reactionary Archbishop Antonii.[203] M. I. Tugan-Baranovsky, who had become a liberal while remaining a 'legal Marxist', developed a theory claiming that the intelligentsia's gravitation towards socialism was a phenomenon deeply rooted in Russian history, that an anti-capitalist intelligentsia was also emerging in the West and that, therefore, the authors of *Landmarks*, in trying, as he saw it, to transform the Russian intelligentsia into an ally of the ruling class in a monarchical-capitalist Russia, were simply swimming against the tide.[204] The Kadet party thus confirmed its willingness to remain a classless party, supporting the revolutionary forces, both 'bourgeois-democratic' and socialist, and categorically rejecting 'shameful compromises' with the historical regime.

The practical policy of the party was close enough to this self-image. Because of this Leonard Schapiro concluded that the Kadets were in fact radicals, not liberals. 'The great service of *Vekhi* ', he wrote, 'was to illuminate this fact for the first time, even if the illumination came too late, and the message fell on deaf ears. But, as well as being pioneers, the *Vekhi* group also symbolized a return to a tenuous but more truly liberal Russian tradition, which recognised that when once a major change in society has been accomplished, the more important ally of liberalism is conservation, and not revolution.'[205] This 'more truly liberal Russian tradition' was typified, for Schapiro, by Chicherin. Russian liberals, he thought, should have supported the October Manifesto and the constitution of 1906 in the same way as Chicherin

[202] Ibid., p. 146.

[203] See I. I. Petrunkevich, 'Intelligentsiia i *Vekhi*. Vmesto predisloviia', in *Intelligentsiia v Rossii*, pp. xii–xiii.

[204] M. I. Tugan-Baranovsky, 'Intelligentsiia i sotsializm', ibid., pp. xii–xiii in *Intelligentsiia v Rossii*, pp. 235, 256–7. A similar point was made by Miliukov, who insisted that the intelligentsia was not a specifically Russian phenomenon. In his view the Russian intelligentsia had a close equivalent in the English Fabians. (See Miliukov, 'Intelligentsiia i istoricheskaia traditsia', pp. 92–3.)

[205] Schapiro, 'The *Vekhi* Group', p. 76.

had supported the liberal reforms of the sixties.[206] We may or may not agree with this view, but it is undeniable that the Kadets were neither willing nor able to follow such advice.

The debate about *Landmarks* is a topic too vast to be covered in this book. However, some contributions to this debate are directly relevant to a proper understanding of Kistiakovsky's peculiar position among its authors. It is proper, therefore, to pay attention to them in the present context.

First of all let us further consider Miliukov's article, cited above. The Kadet leader's attitude to Kistiakovsky's essay was one of genuine bewilderment. He wrote:

There is one essay in *Landmarks* with which one could fully agree, except for its terminology and a few sentences at the beginning and end, by which it is stitched on, rather artificially, to the rest of the book. But this essay (independently of its author's intention) contains the most vicious criticism of the fundamental idea of *Landmarks*: the idea of the 'preeminence of spiritual life over the external forms of community'. Its author, Mr. Kistiakovsky, has chosen to elaborate the theme of 'the external forms of community'. Nor is he confused by this. He explains, excusing himself as it were, that he ought to defend a 'relative value'—law, while the other authors defend 'absolute values' . . . He begins with a statement that 'the Russian intelligentsia never respected law' and therefore 'could not have hoped to develop a sound legal consciousness'. But this is very good, from the point of view of *Landmarks*. And Mr. Kistiakovsky hastens to add that 'there is no reason to reproach our intelligentsia for ignoring law. It has aspired to higher and more absolute ideals, and on its way could neglect this secondary value'.[207]

Characteristically enough, Miliukov had difficulty in understanding the ironic sense of these words. He confessed, humourlessly, that the irony became obvious to him only after reading further in Kistiakovsky's essay, where he criticized the Slavophile view of law and quoted from Almazov's satirical poem about 'Russian natures broad and wide, seeking truths eternal'.[208] But this only increased his general confusion. How could Kistiakovsky criticise the Slavophiles while the other contributors to *Landmarks* saw them as their ideological predecessors? How could one reconcile Kistiakovsky's defence of law with the emphasis on 'truths eternal', characteristic of other authors of the book? How could it be explained that Berdyaev, otherwise known as a

---

[206] Ibid.
[207] Miliukov, 'Intelligentsiia', pp. 134–5. Cf. *Landmarks*, p. 112.
[208] Ibid., p. 135. For the relevant quotation from Almazov's poem see above, p. 38.

religious anarchist, and Kistiakovsky, a staunch enemy of all forms of anarchism, had agreed to publish their essays under the same cover? Novgorodtsev, another legal theorist and member of the Kadet party, also contributed to Miliukov's bewilderment. Miliukov knew and valued Novgorodtsev's *Crisis in the Modern Legal Consciousness*, entirely agreeing with Novgorodtsev's formula that 'institutions grow together with people, and people perfect themselves together with institutions'.[209] But he also knew that Novgorodtsev sympathized with the *Landmarks* group and could not understand Novgorodtsev's ideological sympathy with people who, as he thought, openly declared their indifference towards the struggle for a better institutional framework of social life.

The main source of Miliukov's confusion was, of course, Gershenzon's awkward preface to *Landmarks*. The Kadet leader overlooked the fact that the 'common platform' of the seven authors was in fact something quite other than a defence of 'higher spiritual values', as opposed to the struggle for the improvement of 'external conditions of life'. What really united this group, as I have tried to show above, was the opposition to further revolutionary struggle and the excessive politicization of all values. Miliukov simply could not understand that the political struggle, to which he had become totally committed, could be seen as not only *different* from the struggle for law, but, in a sense, as *creating obstacles* for the development of a 'sound legal consciousness' among Russians. He thought of everything, and of law in particular, in political terms, and it did not occur to him that his own party could be criticized for a lack of due respect for the 'spirit of law'.

A somewhat similar confusion about Kistiakovsky's essay found expression in *Landmarks as a Sign of the Times* — a collection of articles published by the Socialist Revolutionary party. It includes a long article by Ia. Bechev, entitled 'Legal Ideas in Russian Literature', which contains a close critical analysis of Kistiakovsky's views. This analysis, however, is unexpectedly polite in tone and moderate in substance. It begins: 'Kistiakovsky's essay "In the Defence of Law" differs favourably from the reactionary noise of *Landmarks* by its pithiness, correctness of style and serious tone. But it is not merely these external qualities, but also its inner content, which put it in a rather peculiar position in the symposium.'[210]

[209] Ibid., pp. 171–3.
[210] Ia. Bechev, 'Pravovye idei v russkoi literature', in *'Vekhi' kak znamenie vremeni*, Moscow, 1910, p. 174.

Bechev went on to point out that Kistiakovsky dissociated himself not only from the religious phraseology favoured by his fellow-authors but also from their hostility towards socialism. He quoted with approval Kistiakovsky's opinion that the rule of law should not be opposed to socialism because 'from the juridical point of view the socialist order is only a more strictly consistent legal order'.[211] He was inclined to see Kistiakovsky being used by the *Landmarks* group though in fact alien to it. He even defined Kistiakovsky as an alien plant in Russian soil (probably an allusion to his Ukrainian nationality), a good legal scholar, who had, however, not experienced the historical heritage of the Russian intelligentsia from within and, therefore, could not form a right judgement of it.[212]

Bechev's quarrel with Kistiakovsky revolved mainly around historical fact. Like Miliukov, he wanted to prove that Kistiakovsky took an oversimplified view of the Russian intelligentsia, whose disrespect for law usually expressed its attitude towards the existing legal order rather than towards the 'idea of law' as such. In fact, he argued, even the law-despising revolutionaries had been motivated by legal consciousness and their victory would have resulted in the establishment of a socialist system combined with the rule of law, so dear to Kistiakovsky's heart. Thus, his disagreement with Kistiakovsky concerned facts rather than principles. He disagreed with Kistiakovsky about the Russian intelligentsia, while accepting his emphasis on the rights of man and the rule of law, thereby distancing himself from the populist tradition, which treated constitutionalism as a mere instrument of bourgeois domination. Significantly enough, he supported his most important theoretical objection to Kistiakovsky's views by reference to legal theory; in his opinion, Kistiakovsky was too much influenced by Merkel's view that law-making is the art of compromise and ignored Jellinek's view that the history of law also includes revolutionary upheavals.[213]

The most interesting part of Bechev's article is entitled 'The Juridical Ideas of Socialism', in which he focuses his attention on Marxism and distinguishes in it two approaches to law: that of historical relativism, best expressed by Engels, and the standpoint of 'positive creation of law', to be found, above all, in Marx's early article 'On the Jewish Question'.[214] Marx, he argued, rejected the subordination of public man, man as *citoyen*, (*der öffentliche Mensch*) to man as private

---

[211] Ibid., p. 175. [212] Ibid., p. 176.
[213] Ibid., p. 260. [214] Ibid., p. 231.

individual, an egoistic member of *bürgerliche Gesellschaft*. He also postulated the reverse relationship, the subordination of the egoistic individual to man as 'species-being', in other words the subordination of the private to the public, of private law to public law, and, finally, the disappearance of the private/public dichotomy.[215] This was precisely what Anton Menger, the theorist of 'juridical socialism', came to define as the main legal task of socialism, thus paying an unconscious tribute to Marx (whom he elsewhere accused of ignoring legal problems) as, in a sense, a legal thinker.[216]

Under the heading 'Legal Ideals', Bechev next took up the problem of the revival of natural law. He briefly discussed the ideas of Petrażycki and Novgorodtsev, agreeing with Kistiakovsky that their practical influence was very limited, but also stressed, supporting his view by another quotation from Jellinek, that revivals of natural law occurred regularly in revolutionary periods and characterized the legal consciousness of revolutionary classes. In contemporary Russia, he continued, the 'new natural law', finding expression in such legal postulates as the right to a dignified existence, the right to work and the right to full compensation for work, derived from the legal consciousness of the revolutionary working class, whose strength was the only safeguard of its victory.[217]

Bechev's article, significantly, contained no wholesale condemnation of the Russian liberals, but compared and contrasted the two kinds of Russian liberalism: the democratic liberalism of Kavelin and the gentry liberalism of Chicherin. This harmonized well with the opening contribution by Iu. Gardenin, in which a similar distinction was applied to the Kadet party. The Kadets, said Gardenin, had to choose between two alternatives: they had either to collaborate with the government in forming a cabinet, as proposed by Witte, and help the regime to arrive at a peaceful solution to Russia's problems, or they must ally themselves consistently with the revolution and thus become fused with the revolutionary masses. The Kadets, however, remained a 'professorial party', too dependent on the traditional outlook of the intelligentsia to choose the first alternative and yet too afraid of the revolutionary masses to opt for the second one.[218] This ideological indecisiveness sealed their fate. After the victory of the counter-revolution the Kadet party (quite naturally, in Gardenin's view) tried to adopt the first way,

[215] Ibid., pp. 233–5.   [216] Ibid., p. 236.   [217] Ibid., pp. 244–6.
[218] Iu. Gardenin, '*Vekhi* kak znamemie vremeni. Vmesto predisloviia', ibid., pp. 19–21.

but all its steps in this direction were too late, inconsistent and timid. They were enough to discredit the party in the eyes of the left but not enough to rehabilitate it in the eyes of the right, to convince the right of the sincerity of this approach. The converse had happened earlier, at the time when the revolutionary wave was building up: then the Kadet party had moved to the left, but all its steps in this direction were too late, inconsistent and timid, thus contributing to discredit it in the eyes of the right without establishing its trustworthiness in the eyes of the left.[219]

The first, consistently anti-revolutionary option was advocated by Maklakov and Struve, Kadets who were faithful in this to Chicherin's type of liberalism. But the mainstream of the party did not follow their advice: 'The traditions of the intelligentsia prevented this'.[220]

As we can see, this analysis was diametrically opposed to Lenin's view that the real essence of 'Kadetism' was revealed in *Landmarks*. In their analysis of *Landmarks* and in their view of the Kadets, the ideologists of the Socialist Revolutionaries proved less prejudiced and incomparably more sophisticated than the Bolshevik leader.

In many respects Kistiakovsky might have subscribed to Gardenin's analysis of the situation in the Kadet party. Where he differed was in his definition of the nature of the two options which were open to the Russian liberals: for him the choice was not between collaboration with the government and alliance with the popular masses. He criticized the revolutionary intelligentsia not because he was a rightist, sympathizing with the propertied classes or with the ruling political élite, but because he was convinced that historical compromise would facilitate the introduction and stabilization of the rule of law in Russia, while further political struggle would not. He wanted the newly created legislative body, the Duma, to be a place for constructive legislative work, and not a convenient forum for radicalizing public opinion by means of political speeches, symbolic gestures, and so forth. For this reason his criticism of the Russian intelligentsia was directed also against his own party. He accused the Kadets of sacrificing the spirit of law to short-sighted political imperatives, thereby contributing to the further polarization of Russian society and thus condemning the cause of liberalism in Russia to inevitable defeat. The modern constitutional state, he argued, is founded on compromise; it presupposes a 'strongly developed consciousness of legal rectitude', capable of suppressing and

---

[219] Ibid., p. 21.
[220] Ibid., p. 20.

controlling 'socio-psychological emotions'. The Russian intelligentsia, however, was 'unprepared for compromise'; it consisted of 'people of principle', incapable of openly accepting the necessity of compromise in social life, preferring rather such compromise as is 'concealed and founded exclusively on personal relationships'.[221]

The same point was made by Maklakov. He wrote:

Out of the conflict of interests of different professions, out of the duality of human nature as from every antinomy, there is one issue, their synthesis; that is, a compromise between them which would be acceptable to both. Every struggle ought to end in peace. But peace is an agreement between two former antagonists. On what basis can it come about in spite of diversity of interests? Not by the victory of the 'strongest' and the forced submission to him [of the conquered]; not by the capricious 'will' of the 'majority'. Voluntary agreement of former opponents can be based only on the recognition of the mutual interests of both, i.e. on justice.[222]

These words were part of Maklakov's criticism of Miliukov's line within the Kadet party, which he summed up thus: 'The Kadet leaders rejected that which constituted the essence of liberalism: voluntary submission to a legal order, work within the framework of the law, and respect for the rights of others.'[223]

Maklakov's position has sometimes been explained by his rightist sympathies and by his close social contacts with bureaucratic circles.[224] But this explanation can hardly be applied to Petrażycki, whose views on the 'social ideal' placed him on the left wing of the Kadets, yet who always defended the priority of long-term interests of law over short-term political considerations—as was demonstrated, for example, by his ardent opposition to the Vyborg Appeal, although he finally submitted to the will of the majority.[225] The same is true of Kistiakovsky: his espousal of the ideal of rule-of-law socialism placed him on the left wing of the Kadet party, although his criticism of the intelligentsia (including the Kadets) was seen, of course, as criticism from the right. The resulting confusion is such that it seems proper to

---

[221] Kistiakovsky, 'In the Defense of Law', *Landmarks*, p. 131.
[222] V. A. Maklakov, Iz vospominanii, New York, 1954, pp. 381–2. Quoted from S. R. Tompkins, *The Russian Intelligentsia: Makers of the Revolutionary State*, Oklahoma, 1957, pp. 242–3.
[223] V. A. Maklakov, *The First State Duma*, M. Belkin (trans.), Bloomington, Ind., 1964, p. 243.
[224] Cf. A. Levin, Foreword to Maklakov, *The First State Duma*, p. ix.
[225] See Maklakov, *The First State Duma*, pp. 228–9.

ask whether the right-wing–left-wing dichotomy is really helpful for a better understanding of his case.

An alternative explanation of Kistiakovsky's position (and of its similarity to Maklakov's and, to a lesser extent, Petrażycki's views) can be provided by stressing the inevitable differences, sometimes even contradictions, between the interests of law and of politics. Maklakov, Petrażycki, and Kistiakovsky were professional jurists, deeply committed to the ideal of the rule of law, while Miliukov, as a political leader, was concerned above all with political power, political influence and, not least, his own political reputation in the eyes both of his followers and of the left-wing allies of his party. He certainly supported the cause of the rule of law, but often confused it in practice with the cause of parliamentary government. In other words, he was more politically than legally minded, while in Kistiakovsky's case the reverse was true.

The overwhelming majority of the Kadets were not only overpoliticized but more than that—they were subject to political emotions, often indistinguishable from moral feelings. They lacked both a strong legal consciousness and the ability to treat politics as a cool, rationally calculated game, to approach it (using Max Weber's distinction) not from the point of view of 'ethics of principle' but rather from that of 'ethics of responsibility'. Hence their political behaviour was often difficult to explain even in terms of purely practical rationality. In crucial moments they were guided neither by legal consciousness, nor by political wisdom. The main reason behind their rejection of Witte's proposal to form a Kadet ministry was their irrational fear of governmental responsibility and an even greater fear of spoiling their reputation in the eyes of their 'allies on the left'.[226] Their reaction to the dissolution of the First Duma—the famous Vyborg Appeal—was a romantic gesture, indefensible from a legal point of view and devoid of real political significance. Their opposition to Stolypin's agrarian reform was too dependent on their attitude to Stolypin himself, whom they saw as a counter-revolutionary henchman, and their refusal to condemn revolutionary terrorism (which led to the dissolution of the Second Duma) was a typical example of political emotions running riot. Important things were at stake here: in exchange for their condemnation of 'political murders and violence', the Kadets hoped to obtain from Stolypin the official re-legalization of their party and a

---

[226] Cf. A. B. Ulam, *Russia's Failed Revolutions: From the Decembrists to the Dissidents*, New York, 1981, pp. 192–3.

position from which to demand the liquidation of military field-courts. Miliukov was almost ready to make this 'sactifice' (provided that the article condemning terrorism would appear without his signature), but Petrunkevich, the patriarch of the movement, prevented this by exclaiming: 'No, Never! Better the party be sacrificed than ruined morally . . .'[227]

The result, in Miliukov's own account, was, sadly, the dissolution of the Duma and the increased political influence of the Black Hundreds and the reactionary nobility.[228]

Seen against this background Kistiakovsky's position appears not so much as support for the right, but rather as a desperate effort to defend truly liberal values, such as rational compromise and, above all, the rule of law. His stubborn and consistent 'defence of law' could not please Stolypin's government. It was Stolypin, after all, who had stated bluntly that 'Juridical considerations must not stand in the way of the higher interests of the state'.[229]

Kistiakovsky's contribution to *Landmarks* should be read together with his programmatic article in the *Juridical Messenger* entitled 'The Road to the Rule of Law (The Task of Our Jurists)'.[230] The two articles complement one another in clarifying Kistiakovsky's views on the problem of implanting 'the spirit of law' in Russia.

'The Road to the Rule of Law' begins with a sad paradox: the introduction of a semi-constitutional regime had not contributed to an increase in the authority of law in Russia. The Fundamental Laws of 1906 had, for the first time in Russian history, drawn a clear demarcation line between laws and administrative rules or commands, insisting that the latter must be consistent with laws, but in spite of this the authority of the law in Russia had visibly fallen.[231] The reason for this, Kistiakovsky argued, was the excessive politicization of life, the all-pervasive atmosphere of political struggle,[232] in which the law could not be regarded as a set of norms regulating the conduct, political or otherwise, of all individuals and groups within the state. On the contrary, people tended to regard the law as a political device, as an instrument for the defence of specific interests, whether of the government, the opposition, the economically strong, or the economically

---

[227] Miliukov, *Political Memoirs*, pp. 151–2.

[228] Ibid., pp. 156–7.

[229] Quoted from Ulam, *Russia's Failed Revolutions*, p. 208.

[230] *Iuridicheskii vestnik*, 1913, no. 1. Reprinted in Kistiakovsky, *Sotsial'nye nauki i pravo*.

[231] Kistiakovsky, *Sotsial'nye nauki*, pp. 245–8.   [232] Ibid., p. 651.

weak, or others.[233] The courts had become less independent than before, owing to the devastating political pressures exerted, both by the government and, more efficiently and openly, by public opinion, the Duma, or by individual political parties, upon the judges. The Kadets, although, as a party, deeply committed to the idea of the rule of law, were not blameless in this matter. They too had been guilty of subordinating the cause of law to the political game, or even to personal likes and dislikes. For instance, their hatred of the counter-revolutionary government prevented them from seeing that Stolypin's agrarian reform, quite apart from its political aims, was worthy of liberal support at least for its legal aspect, as a reform which, by extending the principle of equality before the law to the peasants, emancipated them from the commune and made them full citizens of the state.[234]

An instrumental attitude towards law, Kistiakovsky continued, is common to all countries with weak and underdeveloped legal cultures.[235] It takes time to recognize law as an independent value, to emancipate it from politics and short-term utilitarian considerations, to appreciate its normative importance. In order to strengthen the authority of the law existing laws must be taken seriously, enforced impartially and changed in accordance with legal procedure. Jurists should therefore be immune to changing political moods; they may, in a private capacity, belong to different political parties but professionally they should remain strictly impartial,[236] representing the independent interests of the law and legal culture, resisting all attempts to reduce law to a mere tool of economic or social policy-making, let alone an instrument of political struggle. It is also important that they defend the autonomy of law on a theoretical plane; in particular, although taking account of the sociological and psychological facets of law, they must combat the legal claims of sociologism and psychologism and their attempted infringements of the legitimate autonomy of juris-prudence.[237] Nor need they be afraid of being accused of treating law as an end in itself, for it is their professional mission to make people aware that a recognition of the autonomous value of law is a necessary precondition for further material and spiritual development and that

[233] Ibid., p. 647.
[234] Ibid., p. 650. Because of this Stolypin's reform was said to have started 'the second emancipation' of the Russian peasants. See D. Atkinson, *The End of the Russian Peasant Commune, 1905–1930*. Stanford, 1983, pp. 41–3.
[235] Ibid., p. 652.   [236] Ibid., p. 655.   [237] Ibid., p. 658.

the rule of law, based on such autonomy, even brings purely political gains, by greatly increasing the political weight, general prosperity, and respectability of the state.[238]

Petrażycki (in spite of his psychologism) and Novgorodtsev wholeheartedly agreed with this view and I believe that this explains why they both so often felt they had to dissociate themselves from the practical policy of their own Kadet party and why, in spite of their membership of the Central Committee, they failed to exert a significant influence on this policy. It was inevitable because, as professional jurists, they understood the special mission of Russian jurists essentially as Kistiakovsky did. In a time of revolutionary and counter-revolutionary violence they were condemned to be the proverbial voices crying in the wilderness.[239]

From a political-historical point of view this proves their relative isolation and lack of historical importance. It is arguable, however, that historians of ideas are entitled to disagree with this verdict. The legal philosophies of the three outstanding Kadet jurists—Petrażycki, Novgorodtsev, and Kistiakovsky—provide a unique insight into the way in which the Kadet ideology might have developed if the party's main political aim, the introduction of parliamentary government into Russia, had been realized. The leaders of the Kadet party were, naturally enough, all intensely political, and the conditions created by the revolution of 1905–7, and by the counter-revolutionary measures which followed, fostered political passions. The Kadets certainly committed many political errors, but it must be remembered that it was extremely difficult to strike the right balance between the long-term interests of law and the immediate demands of the political struggle. To put it simply, it was extremely difficult, if not impossible, to play a political role in revolutionary, or counter-revolutionary, times, while at the same time defending the law, including the new Fundamental Laws of the Empire, against excessive politicization. The consistent subordination of practical political issues to the liberal ideal of the rule of law required a unique kind of detachment and legal scholars within the ranks of the Kadet party could exert significant political influence only at the cost of betraying their cherished vision of the proper road to

---

[238] Ibid., p. 659.

[239] A. Tyrkova-Williams in her memoirs wonders why Petrażycki, whom she considers politically more clear-sighted than Miliukov, had so little influence on the policy of the Kadet party. What I have said above may be taken as a partial answer to this question. (Cf. A. Tyrkova-Williams, *Na put' akh k svobode*, New York, 1952, p. 285.)

the rule of law. Petrażycki, Novgorodtsev, and Kistiakovsky were among those who were unwilling to pay this price.

The Kadet party as a political movement was the high point in the history of Russian liberalism. It demonstrated the strength of liberalism and its attractiveness for the educated classes of Russian society. It also showed up its weaknesses and contradictions, the result of the lack of a strong base in society and of the inherited traditions of the intelligentsia, leading to over-dependence on its allies of the left. The relative unimportance of the Kadet legal philosophers in shaping the practical policy of the party was compensated for by their importance in the history of liberal thought in Russia. A certain discrepancy between the liberal movement and liberal thought was inevitable at a time when the old regime in Russia was in a state of crisis and different political parties, anticipating its final breakdown, vied with each other in the struggle for popularity with the politicized masses (which entailed, of course, frequent recourse to demagogy). In such conditions the political influence of Petrażycki, Novgorodtsev, and Kistiakovsky could not be great. This does not, however, diminish their importance as liberal theorists. It is no exaggeration to say that the entire history of liberal thought in Russia revolved around the problem of the rule of law and the rule-of-law state, and it is obvious that from this point of view the contribution of these three was extremely significant. Each in his own way continued Chicherin's struggle against legal positivism and fully shared his view of the autonomous, irreducible value of law. They did, however, move away from Chicherin's conception of law and freedom by increasingly emphasizing positive freedom and the corresponding extension of the responsibilities of the rule-of-law state. Thus Novgorodtsev completed his transition from the Old to the New Liberalism and Kistiakovsky outlined a vision of rule-of-law socialism, producing an elaborate theory of the different stages in the developent of the rule-of-law state. Petrażycki laid its foundations in his conception of the two basic types of socio-economic and legal systems, which corresponded to two different phases of historical progress. Novgorodtsev developed Soloviev's conception of the right to a dignified existence and Kistiakovsky attempted to derive democratic socialism from the inner development of the liberal idea of rule of law. After the revolution of 1917 the idea of rule-of-law socialism was further elaborated by Sergius Hessen, whose views are discussed in the next and last chapter of this book.

Kistiakovsky's place in the history of Russian liberal thought is, I think, more important than is usually acknowledged. He was not a mainstream figure but he was able to use his relatively marginal position as a vantage point for making sound judgements, as a kind of cognitive privilege enabling him to preserve a certain critical distance both from the official leadership of the Kadet party and from the *Landmarks* group. Although, in his contribution to *Landmarks*, he criticized the Russian intelligentsia (including the liberals) from a right-wing position, as it were, he was still the first theorist of Russian liberalism to put forward the idea of rule-of-law socialism, and this placed him on the left wing of the liberal movement. This neatly demonstrates the dangers of an uncritical use of the right–left dichotomy and of trying to explain away problems instead of coming to grips with them.

VII

Sergius Hessen: A Post-Revolutionary Synthesis

1 Introductory remarks

THE last chapter of this book differs from the rest. In the first place, it deals with a man whose intellectual evolution does not fall within our chronological scope—whose most impressive works came into existence after the revolution and in exile. Moreover, this man was my first teacher[1]—a fact which, I hope, justifies a certain personal touch in this chapter.

However, the decision to present the ideas of Sergius Hessen here was not motivated by personal reasons alone. It is the inner logic of our topic which makes such a decision justifiable, if not imperative. Hessen's 'rule-of-law socialism' is the last link in the development of the legal philosophy of Russian liberalism, as analysed in the second part of this work. He transcended Chicherin's classical liberalism while preserving its 'eternal truth', drew all consequences from Soloviev's 'right to a dignified existence', critically assimilated Petrażycki's views on the essence of law and on legal policy, endorsed Novgorodtsev's social liberalism and, like Kistiakovsky, went beyond it. In addition to this, Hessen's general philosophy of law offers the possibility of a reconciliation between the liberal tradition of 'the struggle for law' and those Russian thinkers whose ethical maximalism culminated in the various kinds of 'legal nihilism', as described in the first chapter of the present book. Its main concept—that of the 'two faces of law'—provides both a justification for the criticism of law from the point of view of higher spiritual values and a rationale for a resolute commitment to the rule of law, for seeing law as the most effective means of 'spiritualizing' the social sphere of human existence.

The incorrigible optimism of Hessen's philosophy of universal reconciliation was bound up with a certain calm stoical heroism.[2] It was

[1] See below, n. 16,
[2] Hessen was aware that his historiosophical optimism was sometimes excessive and spoke about it with remarkable self-criticism.

his way of withstanding the catastrophic moods which were, otherwise, so well-grounded in his lifetime, especially in Eastern Europe. In his mature years Hessen lived through the first world war, the revolution and civil war in Russia, and the horrors of the Nazi occupation in Poland; he saw the breakdown of the Russian Empire, the rise of totalitarian regimes and, finally, the end of the 'old world' in East-Central Europe. Catastrophic temptations surrounded him from his youth. The great flowering, on the eve of the revolution, of Russian philosophical and literary culture, to which he contributed in his early works, was permeated by conscious or unconscious catastrophic forebodings. Many Russian intellectuals of this time accepted the imminent catastrophe as a meaningful Providential event—a punishment for old evils and a precondition for messianic regeneration. An excellent expression of such moods is Briusov's poetic welcome to 'the coming Huns':

> Oh, where are you, Huns, who are coming?
> As a cloud you swell over us here.
> I can hear iron footsteps a-drumming
> On the yet undiscovered Pamir.
> . . .
> Past tracking, may be, it will perish
> What alone of the living we knew;
> But the death that you bring me I cherish,
> And my hymns give a welcome to you![3]

Hessen was very far from such suicidal ecstasies. I vividly remember his fascination with another poem (Tiutchev's 'Cicero'), expressing a very different attitude to catastrophic events. He recited this poem on many occasions, taking special delight in its last stanza. In the English translation (far from rendering the beauty of the original) it runs as follows:

> The orator of Rome did speak
> Amid alarms and civil wars:
> 'I rose late and on my way
> Was overtaken by Rome's night.'
>
> That we know. But bidding farewell
> To the glory of Rome, from the Capitoline
> Hill you saw its bloody star
> Setting at last in all its grandeur.

[3] V. Briusov, 'The Coming Huns', C. M. Bowra (trans.). Quoted from *A Book of Russian Verse*, C. M. Bowra (ed.), London, 1947, pp. 95–6.

Blessèd be the visitor
Of this world in its moments of destiny:
He is one the gracious gods
Have bid to the company of their feast.

He has witnessed their exalted pageants,
He has been admitted to their council,
And drunk immortality from their cup,
A dweller in Heaven while still alive.[4]

What fascinated Hessen in this poem was the unique combination of
an acute feeling of historical crisis with a vision of earthly perturbations
from the viewpoint of imperturbable eternity—a viewpoint from which
death turns out to be an illusion while immortality becomes real. He
who has come to this world 'in its moments of destiny' is in a truly
privileged position: he can clearly distinguish what is relative and
doomed to extinction from what is absolute and indestructible.

Let us be more specific. In Hessen's case we find combined an
acute feeling of deep crisis in European civilization, manifesting itself,
among other things, in the crisis of European liberalism, together with
absolute confidence that the 'eternal truth' of this civilization,
including the 'eternal truth' of liberalism, will be saved, because it
belongs to the realm of objective values which 'glow' through history
and make it meaningful. This attitude of mind distinguished him both
from naïve liberals, refusing to concede that the crisis of their world
was a deep structural crisis, and from disappointed liberals, indulging
in gloomy prophecies or taking refuge in eschatological dreams. To the
end of his days he remained a Russian European, free from *émigré*
complexes and obsessions, not allowing himself to be so overwhelmed
by Russia's tragedy as to become insensitive to the problems of the rest
of the world. His deep attachment to the European liberal heritage was
bound up with a conviction that in order to save the truth of liberalism
it is necessary to go beyond it, to transcend it, in the sense of the
Hegelian *Aufhebung*. Because of this his diagnosis of the crisis was not
an additional element of that crisis, as it was with the so-called
'prophets of doom'. We can safely say that all his works on law,
pedagogy, and political economy were conceived as 'applied philosophy'
and that this term meant to him an effort to realize values and thus to
overcome all possible crises. Philosophically speaking, it was always a

---

[4] F. I. Tiutchev, 'Cicero'. Quoted from *Poems and Political Letters of F. I. Tiutchev*.
Jesse Zeldin (trans. and int.), Knoxville, Tenn., 1973, vol. 1, pp. 38–9.

struggle against relativism and subjectivism on the one hand, and against false Absolutes on the other.

2 Biographical note

Sergius Hessen was born in 1887 in the small North-Russian town of Ust-Sysolsk (now Syktyvkar, the capital of the autonomous region of Komi), the illegitimate son of Iosif Hessen, a student of law who was to become the editor of *Pravo*.[5] His father, born to a Yiddish-speaking (though not very orthodox) Jewish family in Odessa, was deported to Ust-Sysolsk for his activities in a populist revolutionary circle; his mother belonged to the local Finno-Ugrian tribe of Komi. Returning from exile, Iosif Hessen took his son to Odessa and put him in the care of his fiancée, a divorcée with three sons of her own. To legitimize Sergius, he became a convert from Judaism to the Orthodox Church and went through a Christian Orthodox marriage.[6] This also removed the formal obstacles to his entry into state service and he soon got a job in Petersburg, in the Ministry of Justice.

Young Sergius received a very good education. He was admitted to the First Gymnasium, one of the best schools in the Russian capital. As a boy of ten he devoured not only classical Russian literature but also the classics of historiography, for instance A. Thierry, whose works were recommended to him by no less a person than P. Miliukov. Soon afterwards, influenced by Renan and Tolstoy, he underwent a crisis of religious belief and, subsequently, became interested in Marxism.[7] He helped his father regularly by proof-reading *Pravo*, which greatly influenced his developing interest in law and his general world-view. His father's flat, next door to the editorial office of *Pravo*, was frequently visited by members of the editorial board and leading contributors to the journal, such as V. Nabokov, P. Miliukov, L. Petrażycki, A. I. Kaminka, and others.[8] Naturally Sergius greatly benefited from meeting and talking with these men. Apart from his father, he owed a

---

[5] The following account of Hessen's life is based upon his autobiography written, in Russian and in Polish, in 1947. It was printed, with some modifications, in Italian. See S. Hessen, *Autobiografia. La pedagogia russa del XX secolo*. L. Volpicelli (ed.), Roma, 1956.

[6] See I. V. Hessen, *v dvukh vekakh*, Berlin, 1937, p. 106. The first chapter of this book gives a colourful description of Iosif Hessen's childhood in the Jewish quarter of Odessa.

[7] He was impressed, above all, by Engels's *Origins of Family, Private Property and State*.

[8] All these names occur in the Russian and Polish versions of Hessen's autobiography. The Italian version retains only two: A. I. Kaminka and L. Petrażycki (see *Autobiografia*, p. 11).

special intellectual debt to his uncle, Vladimir Hessen, a gifted legal scholar and shortly afterwards a prominent member of the Kadet party.

In his political views Sergius was to the left of his father and tried to find a middle way between liberalism and socialism. In 1904 he joined a revolutionary circle—a branch of the 'Northern Union of Gymnasium Students', for which he was briefly arrested and expelled from school.[9] Happily, the affair was hushed up and he was allowed to take the final examinations.

In 1905, having received his secondary-school certificate, he decided to devote himself to philosophy and to study it in Germany. In Heidelberg and Freiburg in Baden he attended lectures and seminars by the most eminent scholars of the day: Windelband, Jellinek, Lask, Meinecke[10] and, above all, Heinrich Rickert who exerted a decisive formative influence on him. Apart from the Baden neo-Kantians he made a thorough study of Husserl's phenomenology and the Marburg branch of neo-Kantianism (Cohen, Natorp, Cassirer); to the latter he owed his deep interest in Plato, strengthened later by his studies of the neo-Platonic sources of some religious ideas of Eastern Christianity. At the end of 1908 he finished his doctoral thesis *Individuelle Kausalität*—highly praised by Rickert, defended the following year *summa cum laude* and published in *Kantstudien*.[11]

On his return to Russia, he embarked on an ambitious and very successful project: the editing, with F. Stepun, of a Russian–German philosophical journal *Logos*. In this position he established close relations with the Petersburg philosophers—A. Vvedensky, N. Lossky, J. Lapshin, S. Frank—and also with philosophizing writers, mainly Symbolists, such as A. Belyi, D. Merezhkovsky, Z. Hippius, and V. Ivanov. Being politically close to the left wing of the Kadet party he frequently contributed to the newspaper *Rech '*, edited by his father and P. Miliukov. Primarily, however, he was preparing himself for a university career, that is for passing the so-called Master's examination

---

[9] Cf. I. V. Hessen, *V dvukh vekakh*, pp. 189–90.

[10] Hessen's study on the political ideas of the Girondins was, originally, a paper presented at Meinecke's seminar. See S. Hessen, 'Politicheskie idei zhirondistov', *Russkaia mysl '*, Moscow, 1917.

[11] See S. Hessen, *Individuelle Kausalität. Studien zum transzendentalen Empirismus.* Berlin, 1909 (*Kant-studien. Ergänzungshefte* no. 15). A bibliography of Hessen's works is added to his two posthumous books in Polish: S. Hessen, *Studia z filozofii kultury.* A. Walicki (ed. and int.), Warsaw, 1968 and *Filozofia, Kultura, Wychowanie.* M. Hessenowa (ed.), Wrocław, 1973.

at Petersburg University. He took this task very seriously, dividing his time between Russia and Germany where he continued his studies with Cohen, Natorp, and N. Hartmann. After three years, in 1913, he finally passed the required examination and began to lecture as *Privatdozent* at Petersburg University. He also taught in high schools which aroused his keen interest in education. In Russian philosophical circles he was, by then, highly respected and regarded as one of their most talented representatives. Among Russian jurists he was widely known and appreciated as the author of a long study on 'The Philosophy of Punishment' (*Logos*, 1912).

A new chapter in Hessen's life was opened by the February revolution in Russia. Still teaching in high school and University, he now also engaged in political activity. His political choice—Plekhanov's group 'The Unity' (*Edinstvo*)—was very characteristic: wishing to place himself to the left of the Kadets, between liberals and socialists, he chose a group which, because of its extremely right-wing position within the social-democratic movement, was virtually isolated and entirely helpless as a real political force. Plekhanov, who made Hessen his personal secretary and often talked with him into the small hours,[12] was by then the only one of the leading Russian Marxists to persist in the once common belief that the aim of a Russian revolution ought to be nothing else than a consistent bourgeois-liberal westernization of Russia. In later years Hessen became aware of the doctrinaire character of this view, of the fact that consistent Westernism did not suit the realities of the revolution and was simply unworkable as a practical socialist programme. In his autobiography he wrote about it as follows:

In spite of my Kantianism I felt myself, as in earlier days, closer to the law-accepting Marxism of Plekhanov[13] than to the ideas of the revolutionary socialists. The cause of it was, I think, my incorrigible Westernism and my democratic liberalism, treating with suspicion all symptoms of populism. Such a state of mind could not be fruitful in hard revolutionary times. My articles in

---

[12] Plekhanov, Hessen recalls, 'was a charming interlocutor. Thanks to my conversations with him I thought over, once more, the philosophical foundations of Marxism and became acquainted with an important aspect of his personality—an aspect which was something of a surprise to me. In his works Plekhanov was a fanatical fighter, one-sided and unobjective in his judgements. In our conversations, however, he was a sage, arousing my admiration for the breadth of his horizons and for his desire for a deep understanding of his opponent.' (S. Hessen, *Autobiografia*, p. 23.)

[13] Hessen meant by this Plekhanov's view of the necessity of modern constitutionalism in Russia.

Edinstvo (*Unity*) were a perfect model of abstract theorizing and impotent attitudes . . . My brochure *Liberty and Discipline*, published in several thousand copies, was equally anaemic and boring . . . Even worse were my speeches at mass meetings. Being a good, experienced speaker to audiences composed of students or teachers, I could not cope with huge crowds of workers whom I often put out of all patience . . . During a meeting in Tsarskoe Selo I irritated my audience to such a degree that I had to escape by the back door, since the workers rushed at me with clenched fists.[14]

When the Bolshevik revolution broke out, Hessen was already in Tomsk where he was given a professorial position. He went to Tomsk in the hope of finding relatively quiet conditions for scholarly work and was not disappointed. He worked there very intensively, lecturing on logic, ethics, the history of philosophy and philosophy of law. It was in Tomsk that he drafted the first outlines of his conception of 'rule-of-law socialism' and of his masterpiece *The Foundations of Pedagogy*. He contributed also to the organization of university life and was elected dean of the Faculty of Humanities.

Despite its remoteness from the main theatre of civil war even Tomsk could not escape from political passions and the hardships of war communism. Hessen was then still trying to find a middle way between reaction and Bolshevism. In the last years of his life he came to the conclusion that these attempts had been futile because the third way had never existed and the Russian people had already made their choice. He attributed this result to the lack of respect for law among the Russians—a characteristic feature of the Russian people which, as he conceded, had been rightly emphasized by nineteenth-century Russian Slavophiles and Populists. In drawing this conclusion he criticized Russia, but also himself as being alienated from the Russian nation and unable to understand its collective psyche.[15] This self-criticism was part of his effort to understand in order to forgive and thus become reconciled with the cruel course of history.

After four years in Tomsk Hessen returned to European Russia and, seeing little prospect of intellectual freedom, decided to emigrate. In taking this difficult decision and in realizing it he was helped by his father, who had settled in Berlin as the editor (with A. I. Kaminka) of the *émigré* Kadets' newspaper *Rul'*. He did not intend to leave Russia for ever and, therefore, for many years led an unsettled life abroad. During his first two years as an *émigré*, which he spent in Germany, he

---

[14] Hessen, *Autobiografia*, pp. 21–2.
[15] Ibid., p. 27.

wrote and published his *Foundations of Pedagogy*. From Germany he went to Prague, by invitation from the newly established Russian Pedagogical Institute. He was to live in Prague for ten years. Apart from the Pedagogical Institute he was active in the famous Linguistic Circle whose moving spirit was Roman Jakobson and in the two scholarly circles attached to the German University of Prague (where he also taught Russian language): the Slavonic Circle and the Philosophical Circle in which he engaged in long discussions with Carnap. In the last year of his stay in Prague he contributed to the organization of a multi-national philosophical association in which Czechs worked together with Germans and Russians. From time to time he lectured in other countries: in Germany, England, Lithuania, and Poland. However, in spite of many successes, it was a difficult period in his life. Although he mastered the Czech language and made some good Czech friends (such as the phenomenologist Jan Patočka) he never felt that he had a settled abode in Prague. His financial position was very insecure: the Russian Pedagogical Institute was closed after four years and its professors had to live on a modest stipend from the Czechoslovak government. Therefore, the invitation from the Free University in Warsaw which offered him the chair of philosophy of education was for Hessen a very attractive proposal.

Thus, in 1935 Hessen settled in Poland—in a country which was to become his second fatherland.[16] Thanks to the friendly atmosphere and above all to his new marriage, he very quickly became acclimatized in Poland. He systematically studied Polish literature and scholarship: his progress in Polish was so quick that he was soon able to lecture and to write in this rather difficult language. He had many Polish disciples and was greatly respected not only in academic circles but also in the broader milieu of schoolteachers. For his part, he was very impressed by the intellectual and moral qualities of the best representatives of the Polish intelligentsia, such as Helena Radlińska, the founder of a new discipline of 'social pedagogy', and the philosopher Tadeusz Kotarbiński whom he described as 'the most noble type of Polish and European intellectual'. In his autobiography he mentioned Kotarbiński's staunch

---

[16] At the beginning he boarded with my mother, Anna Walicka-Chmielewska, who was then an assistant professor at the Free University in Warsaw. He married my mother's friend, Maria Niemyska, a disciple of Professor Helena Radlińska. Thus he knew me from my early childhood. In post-war years he was happy to introduce me to philosophy and Russian culture. He treated me, in fact, as his youngest disciple and wanted to look after my University studies, unfortunately, he died at the end of the first year of my studies at the University of Łódź.

atheism and commented: 'Kotarbiński does not love God, but God loves him'.[17]

During the tragic years of war Hessen fully shared the experiences and activities of his Polish colleagues. He continued his scholarly pursuits and, at the same time, took active part in the underground university courses, organized in private flats under constant threat of arrest and the concentration camp. Twice he barely escaped and another time he was arrested but quite unexpectedly released after a few days because the Gestapo officer who interrogated him knew his works or had been among his German students in Prague. He taught not only at the university level: he also lectured to teachers, social workers, and underground boy scouts. Short popular summaries of his views on modern democracy appeared on the pages of the underground *Newspaper of the Young* (*Pismo młodych*), published for the young soldiers of the Home Army. He added to the dangers of his life by giving shelter to a young Jew who was later killed, arms in hand, in the ranks of the Warsaw insurgents of 1944.

In the Warsaw uprising Hessen himself miraculously escaped death at the hands of infuriated Vlasovtsy, the Russian soldiers fighting on the side of the Nazis. His works, however, could not avoid destruction. Among the mass of manuscripts burned in the flames of Warsaw were his cherished works written during the German occupation: the detailed draft of 'Philosophy of Education', a long study on Dostoevsky's religious philosophy, a full-length book on 'The Real and Illusory Overcoming of Capitalism' and a volume entitled 'The Downfall and the Regeneration of Democracy'. The last two were based upon Hessen's lectures in underground university courses.

After the German invaders were expelled from Polish soil, with Warsaw in ruins, the Free University of Warsaw was made a foundation of the newly created University of Łódź. Hessen at last resumed his normal professorial duties. At first it seemed that he would be able to reconstruct and publish his destroyed works and to contribute to the education of new generations of Polish students. Soon, however, Poland passed through a period of enforced 'Stalinization'. After 1948 Hessen, in spite of all his hoping against hope, could no longer have any illusions: it was obvious that the new political climate left no place for people like himself in Polish intellectual and educational life. The attacks against him, led by some of his former

[17] S. Hessen, *Autobiografia*, pp. 61–2.

disciples, were an ill omen. In order to prevent being cut off from all contact with students he voluntarily withdrew from teaching philosophy and pedagogy, becoming instead a teacher of Russian in the newly established, and strongly supported, School of Russian Philology. However, even as a teacher of Russian he did not cease to be a philosopher. He considered the wisdom and beauty of the language and his linguistic analyses, especially etymological and semantic, were interwoven with masterly philosophical digressions.

It is difficult to avoid the impression that the coming of Stalinism to Poland, combined with bitter disillusion as to possible post-war developments in the USSR, may have precipitated Hessen's death. He desperately sought consolation in the eternal values of philosophy, poetry, and religion. Before his death on 2 June 1950, he expressed his wish to be given an Orthodox Christian burial, and this was done. He was buried with all religious ritual at the Orthodox Christian cemetery in Łódź. The main speech at his grave was delivered by the atheist philosopher, Kotarbiński. I remember his words: 'A sage has left us, a genuine sage.'

3   Philosophy of values and dialectical method

With the important exception of Italy, where an impressive number of Hessen's works have been published in the post-war period,[18] Hessen's thought is virtually unknown in the West. He himself was partly responsible for this: a German translation of his *Foundations of Pedagogy*, suggested by Rickert, had already been made but was not published because of his perfectionist desire to introduce some changes, which he failed to do.[19] A similar fate befell his series of articles on 'rule-of-law socialism', published in the Russian *émigré* journal *Sovremennye Zapiski* (*Contemporary Notes*) in 1924–8: the editors wanted to publish them as a separate book but the author did not consent.[20] If he had, his legal thought would probably be better known, at least to specialists.

In English, the only account of Hessen's thought is to be found in

[18] See the bibliography of Hessen's works mentioned in n. 11.
[19] The book was to be published by the Mohr und Siebeck Verlag in Tübingen. See S. Hessen, *Autobiografia*, pp. 32–3.
[20] See S. Hessen, *Autobiografia*, p. 40. In the memoirs of M. V. Vishniak, the former editor-in-chief of *Sovremennye zapiski*, Hessen's articles on 'The Problem of Rule-of-Law Socialism' are recognized as a very important although 'insufficiently appreciated' contribution. (M. V. Vishniak, *Sovremennye zapiski'. Vospominaniia redaktora*, Indiana University Publications, Slavic and East European Series, vol. 7, 1957, p. 106).

Zenkovsky's *History of Russian Philosophy*.[21] This account, although otherwise quite good and very sympathetic, is, necessarily, too short. In addition, it is incomplete and onesided: Zenkovsky based it almost entirely on the *Foundations of Pedagogy* while ignoring Hessen's other works and being unaware of the further development of his philosophy. It is necessary, therefore, to present here a general outline of the main themes in Hessen's philosophical views.

The main concern of Hessen's articles on 'rule-of-law socialism' was the crisis of liberalism. A more developed *philosophical* explanation of this crisis was offered later—in his first Polish book entitled *On Contradictions and Unity in Education* (1939). This book throws much light on the basic assumptions of Hessen's philosophical pursuits.

The crisis of liberalism, Hessen argues, stems from the undermining of the belief in the objectivity of truth and in the objectivity of values; from the crisis of scientism on the one hand, and from a moral crisis on the other. Empiriocriticism, pragmatism, historical materialism, and different currents of *Lebensphilosophie* destroyed truth in a transcendental sense, reduced it to a mere instrument of 'life'—a biological or social, individual or collective, instrument, but always making truth relative to man's practical needs. The undeniable cognitive advantage of this was the possibility of exposing thought's rootedness in life, of being aware of the vital links between philosophical theories and a theoretical *Weltanschauungen*. But its cost—relativism and subjectivism —was too great, unacceptable both philosophically (as surrendering truth) and for practical reasons (as destructive of morality and culture). The main questions, therefore, could be formulated as follows: how to overcome relativism and the cultural–moral crisis without returning to naïve, scientific and moral dogmatism? how to overcome the political crisis without returning to the naïvely rationalistic illusions of classical liberalism?

Let us recall briefly the intellectual context of these questions. Philosophical aspirations to objective theoretical validity were undermined by Wilhelm Dilthey, who initiated the anti-positivist upheaval in the humanities. Philosophy's only source, he claimed, is life, all possible solutions of philosophical problems depend on an unreflective

---

[21] See V. V. Zenkovsky, *A History of Russian Philosophy*. G. L. Kline (trans.), London, 1953, vol. 2, pp. 697–702. Zenkovsky classified Hessen as belonging to those Russian neo-Kantians who expressed basic problems of transcendentalism in the purest form; in his view, Hessen was 'the most brilliant and philosophically gifted of this group'. (Ibid., pp. 697–8).

act of choice, predetermined by an atheoretical *Weltanschauung*. Nietzsche and some other representatives of *Lebensphilosophie* added to this praise of irrationalist activism and contempt for the disinterested search for truth. Sometimes, as in the case of G. Sorel, this activism could be bound up with support of the workers' movement; usually, however, it appeared as a component of right-wing nationalism, rejecting the liberal legacy and glorifying instead the power and beauty of irrational forces. Among the people who saw a great danger in this three thinkers are of special interest. First and most important was E. Husserl, who shared Dilthey's conviction of the bankruptcy of positivist scientism but, at the same time, resolutely rejected *Weltanschauungsphilosophie* and defended philosophy in the classical sense, treating philosophers as 'functionaries of mankind' and seeking the foundations of universally valid philosophical knowledge. Secondly, Julien Benda in his *Trahison des clercs* (1927) accused European (and especially German) intellectuals of betraying the ideal of pure, disinterested thought and set against this the attitude of a *clerc*, a non-committed intellectual, guardian of enlightened rationalism and supra-temporal moral standards. Finally, K. Mannheim in his sociology of knowledge fully accepted and developed the view that thought is rooted in, and determined by, historical and social life. Having made this decisive concession to relativism he looked, none the less, for the possibility of a rational mediation between different social world-views and of overcoming their respective limitations by confronting them with each other and trying to find a partial truth in each. As is known, he allotted this task to the 'socially unattached intellectuals'.

Hessen can be credited with providing another original solution.[22] He accepted not only Dilthey's basic conception of a *Weltanschauung* but also (although in a modified, historicized form) this typology of *Weltanschauungen*; at the same time, however, he defined the calling of philosophy as overcoming its underlying *Weltanschauung* by striving for objectivity and universality. *Weltanschauung*, that is, a pre-reflective unity of the image of the world, value-judgements and commands of will, is grounded in the personality and in the existential/historical situation of its bearers; it is philosophy's bond with 'life', a bond without which it would have become an empty and lifeless abstraction. But 'anchoring philosophy in life' is only one function of a *Weltanschauung*; its other function consists in a constant striving to overcome

---

[22] See the first chapter of his book *O sprzecznościach i jedności wychowania* (*On Contradictions and Unity in Education*), Lvov–Warsaw, 1939.

its dependence on existential/historical conditions, to transcend itself, as it were, in objective and universal philosophy. Every genuine philosophy is born of a dialectical tension between its anchorage in existence, through a *Weltanschauung*, and its striving for a supra-existential, transcendental truth. The philosophical search for a universal validity is grounded in the dialectic of the inner life of *Weltanschauungen*, which have to strive to overcome their particularisms in order to prevent their degeneration into ossified 'ideological stand-points'. There are, therefore, two dangers: a danger that a *Weltan-schauung* may degenerate into 'ideology', if it abandons the effort to transcend existential determinations in philosophy, and the danger that philosophy may degenerate into a lifeless 'neutral' knowledge, a caricature of universality, if it loses its existential roots. In this way, dialectics enabled Hessen to reconcile the conception of *Weltanschauung* as a vital source of philosophical reflection with Husserl's view of the universalist mission of philosophy.

In a similar way, Hessen tried to resolve the conflict between historicism and belief in objective supra-historical values. History, he argued in *Foundations of Pedagogy*, creates tradition, but tradition, inheriting the legacy of the past, its enrichment and transmission to future generations, would be impossible if human existence were to be reduced to pure history.[23] The phenomenon of tradition could emerge only because people strove throughout their history to realize supra-temporal 'value tasks', because they went beyond the satisfaction of their transient temporal needs to embody eternal cultural values in their works. Thus, history is possible only in culture and within culture. The personality of an individual can be formed only by the effort of realizing supra-personal values; in the same way 'historical individualities' are shaped only by working at the realization of supra-historical cultural tasks. Relativism is in fact a denial of historicism because if everything were 'history-bound' historical continuity would have been unthinkable. Cultural values cannot be fully realized in historically existing cultures but this does not mean that their objectivity is an illusion; the unattainability of values is rather a consequence of their inexhaustibility, of their 'infinity rising above all things finite'. Culture grows out of history but, at the same time, history transcends itself in culture. Because of this only those human

---

[23] See S. Hessen, *Osnovy pedagogiki: vvedenie v prikladnuiu filosofiiu*, Berlin, 1923, Introduction. Cf. the Polish translation in *Filozofia, Kultura, Wychowanie* (as above, n. 11), pp. 27–38.

works are truly historical in which a supra-historical infinite value-task
has become, to a certain extent, actualized in the finite world of human
temporal existence.

As we see, in his efforts to overcome the cultural crisis Hessen made
use of a peculiar variant of dialectical method. He attributed its
discovery to Plato. In Hegelian dialectics he fully appreciated the
distinction between the 'true' dialectic of ideas and the 'evil' dialectic,
namely, the dialectic of their distortions; following Hegel, he
emphasized also that dialectical negation is not a mere destruction
(*Vernichtung*) but an 'overcoming' (*Aufhebung*), that is, negation and
preservation at the same time. His understanding of dialectics was
opposed to those interpretations which stressed the moment of
negation or relativism. For him, dialectic was a means of combating
relativism and saving values from destruction: it enabled him to detect
continuity and permanence in historical change, to see in the realm of
the relative a reflection of absolute values. 'Dialectical comprehension'
of the meaning of values was to him a combination of the historical
approach with phenomenological 'eidetic insight',[24] and the ontological
foundation of dialectics was, in his view, the Neoplatonic idea of 'All-
Unity'—an idea which, thanks to Soloviev, became strongly embedded
in the mainstream of Russian religious philosophy.

Apart from dialectics an important component of Hessen's philosophical method was structuralism. In the 'principle of structure'
which he closely related to the 'principle of concrete wholeness', he
saw a manifestation of the spirit of the time, foreshadowing an
imminent overcoming of cultural crisis. His concept of structure was
composed of three elements: (I) the idea of wholeness reconciling
unity with plurality, an idea which, although levelled against nineteenth-
century atomism, differed fundamentally from simple monism, that is
from a totalitarian distortion of unity; (2) the idea of a 'hierarchy of
layers', levelled against genetic reductionism; and finally (3) the idea of
autonomy, levelled against naturalism and psychologism.[25] All these
components were combined in a dialectical relationship which

---

[24] An excellent example of this combination of dialectical method with phenomenological insight is Hessen's study on Platonic and evangelical virtues. It was written in
I940 in Russian and in Polish and appeared first in Italian translation (S. Hessen, *Le
virtù platoniche e le virtù evangeliche*, Roma, I952). The Polish version was published
posthumously in S. Hessen, *Studia z filozofii kultury*. Hessen's knowledge of
phenomenology was deepened by his personal contacts with Husserl.
[25] See ch. I2 of Hessen's *O sprzecznościach i jedności wychowania*. Reprinted in *Studia z
filozofii kultury*, pp. 89–I05.

prevented the distorting isolation and absolutization of any, thereby removing the danger of interpreting wholeness as totalism and autonomy as autarchy. In this way they turned out to be inseparable from dialectics, inherently contained in it. The linguistic structuralism of the Prague Circle was used by Hessen as an additional argument for this philosophical method originated by Plato.

Hessen's dialectical method, like his entire philosophy, vindicated the objective and universal status of values. Although having no physical existence, values, he claimed, have 'universal validity' (*allgemeine Geltung*); therefore, their mode of being is independent both from the individual psyche and from the supra-individual collective consciousness. Their objectivity and universality consists in their 'inner quality' which can be neither deduced from social conditions nor made dependent on their subjective recognition by a social group. In contrast to the norms of social life, cultural values act not by means of pressure but by means of 'appeal'—an appeal directed to men as free spiritual beings or personalities. The world of values is a hierarchical, multi-layer structure; values are dialectically related to each other and permeate each other; the higher values 'glow through' the lower ones and the lower values are both negated and preserved (*aufgehoben*) in the higher. History is a process of realizing values but the 'inner quality' of values is independent of changing historical situations. Philosophy is the self-consciousness of man as a value-realizing or—which means the same thing—a culture-producing being. (Every culture is nothing other than a pattern of spiritual values realized in history.) The practical application of philosophy is pedagogy, or the science of education.

We can understand now why Hessen's pedagogical works are of crucial importance for his philosophy, and why his philosophical pedagogy, levelled against both naturalism and sociologism in education, has been defined as the 'pedagogy of culture'.

What has been said above, however, requires a qualification at this juncture. Hessen accepted the term 'pedagogy of culture' as an adequate characterization of his *Foundations of Pedagogy*, but in his later philosophical development he tried to transcend this standpoint. In his 'Philosophy of Education', destroyed in the Warsaw uprising, he developed the idea of a supra-cultural and supra-spiritual level of human existence in describing which he involved religious terminology. The first outline of his conception appeared in his book *On Contradictions and Unity in Education* in which we read: 'Thus, man exists, as it were, on four levels of being, with four corresponding levels of education: as a psycho-physical organism, as an individual in society, as a personality forming part of a cultural tradition and as a member of the Kingdom of spiritual beings.'[26] This 'Kingdom of spiritual beings', it was explained, was equivalent to the 'Kingdom of God' in the conception of such religious philosophers as August Cieszkowski and V. Soloviev.

The entire scheme of Hessen's new philosophy of man looks as shown in the diagram.[27]

Basic Correlation	Grades of Love	Grades of Immortality	Grades of Education	Grades of Happiness
1. *The Level of Biological Existence*				
Organism–Species —Heredity	Sexual Desire	Immortality in Progeny	Care and Training (*Pflege* and *Dressur*)	Sensual Pleasure
2. *The Level of Social Existence*				
Individual–Group —Authority	Appetitus Socialis	The Continuity of Group Life in Time, social tradition	Breeding (*Zucht*)	Success
3. *The Level of Spiritual Culture*				
Personality– Spiritual Community —Value	Eros	Immortality in Culture, historical tradition	Self-realization of Personality (*Bildung*)	Satisfaction from fulfilling one's task
4. *The Level of Grace*				
Human Soul– Kingdom of God —God	Caritas	Personal Immortality	Deliverance (*Erlösung*). The super-spiritual process of freeing one's soul from Evil	Joy

The appearance of a religious perspective in Hessen's thought resulted from his deep interest in Russian philosophy, inspired above all by Soloviev and Dostoevsky. From Soloviev he took the idea of 'All-

[26] S. Hessen, *O sprzecznościach i jedności wychowania*, p. 236.

[27] This scheme was reproduced in Hessen's autobiography (see *Autobiografia*, pp. 43–4). In the Russian text the highest grade of education was called *spasenie* (salvation), but the English equivalent of this word, chosen by the author, was 'deliverance'. An interesting supplement to the above scheme was the table of contents of 'Philosophy of Education', also reproduced in Hessen's autobiography. See Appendix 4.

Unity' which he set against both atomistic pluralism and ossified
monism and from which he derived his dialectic-structural method;
his criticism of isolating and absolutizing certain elements of a
dialectical whole was directly related to Soloviev's criticism of 'abstract
principles'. Dostoevsky was for him the greatest Russian thinker,
whose works deserved to be called a true 'guide to life'. He saw *The
Brothers Karamazov* as the formulation and intuitive solution of the
deepest problems of modern ethics. 'This book teaches us to forgive',
he used to say.

Hessen's fascination with Soloviev's and Dostoevsky's ideas was a
telling testimony to his closeness to the so-called Russian philosophical
renaissance of the early twentieth century. Russian thinkers who had
undergone evolution, in Bulgakov's phrase, 'from Marxism to idealism',[28]
were so deeply impressed by Dostoevsky and Soloviev that many, after
their encounter with these two writers, entered a new phase of
intellectual development, this time 'from idealism to religion'.
Dostoevsky's influence was very strong but usually (with some major
exceptions, like L. Shestov) mediated by Soloviev whose philosophy of
Godmanhood and reintegration provided a convenient categorization
for Dostoevsky's ideas. As I have put it elsewhere,[29] it is no
exaggeration to say that an entire generation of Russian philosophers
and religious thinkers was schooled in Soloviev's philosophy and, by
the same token, profoundly influenced by Dostoevsky.

Seen in this context, Hessen's thought occupies a peculiar place of
its own among the philosophies inspired by Soloviev. In his
interpretation of Soloviev's views Hessen was a resolute Westernizer:
he minimized the importance of Soloviev's theocratic utopianism,
stressing, instead, the presence of Kantian motives in his philosophy,
crediting him with vindication of the Kantian 'autonomy of the Good',
and thus with overcoming utopian tendencies.[30] Similarly, Hessen saw
in Dostoevsky not a messianic utopian but rather a profound critic of
utopianism, a thinker who, in his 'Legend of the Grand Inquisitor',
powerfully and prophetically foretold the inevitable totalitarian consequences of utopian thinking.[31]

In his own article on 'the breakdown of utopianism' Hessen defined

[28] Cf. S. N. Bulgakov, *Ot marksizma k idealizmu*, SPb, 1904.
[29] Cf. Walicki, *A History of Russian Thought*, p. 392.
[30] See S. Hessen, 'Bor'ba utopii i avtonomii dobra v mirovozzrenii F. Dostoevskogo i
Vl. Solovieva', *Sovremennye zapiski*, Paris, vol. 45–6, 1931. French transl. in *Le Monde
Slave*, vol. 1–3, 1930, German transl. in *Pädagogische Hochschule*, Baden, 1929, no. 4.
[31] Loc. cit.

the essence of utopianism as absolutizing a certain value task, leading inevitably to the nihilistic rejection of historical tradition and to a purely instrumental attitude towards its legacy.[32] In connection with Dostoevsky and Soloviev, Hessen developed and deepened this conception by adding to it a criticism of the millenarian/messianic aspect of utopianism.[33] The Kingdom of God, he argued, is not a kingdom in the sense of an earthly state; it belongs to an entirely different dimension of being, having nothing in common with the 'horizontal', historical dimension. It shines from above through all forms of human historical existence and precisely because of this no single form of earthly life can legitimately claim to be treated as its final realization, as the perfect embodiment of absolute values in earthly life. In the utopian-millenarian interpretation, terrestrializing the Kingdom of God, the idea of the Kingdom of God becomes dangerously distorted. On the one hand, it means making the infinite finite, substituting the absolute for the relative and, thus, attributing absolute significance to relative values, or, even, to fortuitous features of some forms of earthly existence; on the other hand, it creates a situation in which the false absolute engulfs everything, depriving all different spheres of culture of their relative but legitimate autonomy. Hence, in particular, the nihilistic and purely instrumental attitude towards law, so characteristic of utopian mentality.

In this way Hessen tried to overcome relativism while simultaneously defending the autonomous significance of relative values. It was the defence of those values above all which constituted the legacy of European liberalism. Because of this Hessen should not be identified with the typical Russian followers of Dostoevsky and Soloviev. Slavophile motives, romantic criticism of industrialization, messianic and eschatological ideas are not to be found in his thought. In contradistinction to Bulgakov, Berdyaev, Frank, Lossky, Karsavin, and many other *émigré* thinkers, Hessen never became a religious philosopher *stricto sensu*. Though often on the threshold of religious metaphysics, he never surrendered the autonomy of philosophical reasoning.

The ideas of the Kingdom of God, of personal immortality and of

---

[32] S. Hessen, 'Krushenie utopizma', *Sovremennye zapiski*, vol. 19, 1924. German transl., 'Der Zusammenbruch des Utopismus' in *Festschrift für Masaryk*, Prague, 1927. A similar conception was developed by Novgorodtsev (see above, pp. 329–34), but his name does not appear in Hessen's article.
[33] See his 'Bor'ba utopii' (as above, note 30).

deliverance were a part of Hessen's philosophical anthropology, the applied form of which was his philosophy of education. In this interpretation the Kingdom of God was the ideal of an absolute, personalized spiritual community, embracing all mankind and the whole of nature; it was a supra-cultural ideal, personalizing the sphere of objective spirit, overcoming Platonic Eros, that is the love of objective values, with Christian Caritas, the concrete, personal love of one's neighbour. Personal immortality, in its turn, was conceived not as the 'substantial and natural, as it were, indestructibility of soul', but as the victory of the personality over the 'tentacles of death' (Freud's term for humiliating complexes). The third idea—that of deliverance or salvation—was defined as 'the awakening of the inner forces of life, the overcoming of the lethal nuclei, the release from loneliness to which death-doomed souls stubbornly cling, and entering the spiritual community of love.'[34] This way of translating religious ideas recalls Erich Fromm's views on the therapeutic function of the humanistic elements in religion. Additional support for this observation is provided by the fact that Hessen highly valued psychoanalysis, which he treated as 'a secular theory of salvation'.[35]

The fundamental ambiguity of the religious aspect of Hessen's philosophy came out very clearly in my private conversations with him. At the end of his life Hessen was greatly interested in the problem of alienation. Trying to explain it to me he said once: 'I am not an atheist, I am a Feuerbachian. God exists, although he is not the creator of man; on the contrary, man has created Him.' True, this declaration should not be understood literally. For Feuerbach the creation of God by man was the alienation of man, making man poorer by depriving him of his divine attributes, whereas for Hessen it was a truly creative act, bringing about an incomparable self-enrichment of humanity; Feuerbach wanted to liberate men from religion while Hessen's Feuerbachianism was a justification of religion, an argument for its indispensability in the world of man. In addition, it is obvious that Hessen, following Dostoevsky, resolutely rejected the Feuerbachian religion of 'Mangodhood' and that Feuerbach's naturalism was an obsolete philosophical standpoint in his eyes. However, in spite of this—or, rather, precisely because of this—it is worth stressing that Hessen agreed with Feuerbach that the key to theology is anthropology,

[34] Cf. S. Hessen, *O sprzecznościach i jedności wychowania*, pp. 230–2.
[35] Cf. n. 27, table of contents of 'Philosophy of Education'.

and not vice versa. The state of grace was for him one level—the highest one—in the complicated structure of the human world.

4 'Rule-of-law socialism' versus Marxism

Let us turn now to the first book-length exposition of Hessen's legal and political views which bears the title: 'Problema pravovogo sotsializma'.[36]

The problem of the proper translation of this title is linked to the problem of the proper understanding of Hessen's basic thought. Although the Russian word *pravovoi* means, literally, 'legal' or 'juridical', it would be completely wrong to translate this title as 'The Problem of Juridical (or 'Legal') Socialism.' In order to understand Hessen's intention it is necessary to link his work with the great debate on *pravovoe gosudarstvo* (*Rechtsstaat*) in Russian liberal thought. As I have shown earlier in this book, for the Russian liberals the term *pravovoe gosudarstvo* meant 'the state respecting the rule of law', or 'state limited by law', and thus could be used (as was done by Bogdan Kistiakovsky)[37] not only as a description of liberal states but also as a name for a liberal variety of socialism. It seems therefore that the correct rendering in English of the title in question should be: 'The Problem of Rule-of-Law Socialism'.

The correctness of such a terminological decision is corroborated by at least two additional circumstances.

First, it was Hessen's explicit desire to cut himself off from the juridical socialism of Anton Menger. On the very first page of his work he made it clear that Menger's juridical socialism, along with other conceptions of state socialism, had nothing in common with his views.[38] And in fact Menger's views and Hessen's views were diametrically opposed. Menger proclaimed the complete abolition of private law which would be replaced under socialism by the bureaucratic-administrative regulation of a democratic Labour-State. In contrast to this, the Russian thinker saw as the very essence of law the safeguarding of subjective rights and the protection of legally delimited spheres of privacy, including that of economic freedom. One may say that Menger wanted to replace the *Gesellschaft* paradigm of law by the bureaucratic-administrative paradigm[39] and, thus, to break with

---

[36] See above, n. 20.   [37] See above, ch. VI, 4.

[38] S. Hessen, 'Problema pravovogo sotsializma (Krizis liberalizma)', *Sovremennye zapiski*, Paris, vol. 22, 1924, p. 257.

[39] See above Introduction, p. 3.

the liberal tradition of *Rechtsstaat*, whereas Hessen's intention was to defend the liberal 'rule of law' (and, thus, the *Gesellschaft* paradigm of law) while acknowledging the need for an increase of bureaucratic-administrative regulation.

Secondly, Hessen saw a further essential function of law in limiting the power of the state and resolutely rejected all kinds of legal positivism, including, of course, all forms of state socialism. In his autobiography he emphasized that the originality of his politico-legal conception consisted in the idea of *law-regulation, as opposed* to state-regulation[40] of the economy. In contrast to the utopians, who advocated either the abolition of law or its transformation into a mere instrument of their will, he saw law as part of a great historical tradition and attributed a peculiar significance to the view that the function of law was to protect the 'impenetrability' of each person (*ograzhdenie nepronitsaemosti litsa*).[41] He was deeply committed to liberal-individualist values and would have wholeheartedly agreed that 'the political expression of that culture, with which genuine individualism is intimately bound up, is *not the state but law* [my italics], law not as the arbitrary will of the sovereign, or as a great inchoate flood of legislative acts "reforming" this or that, but law as a live and continuing tradition, based on the belief in justice and maximum individual sovereignty.'[42] It is evident, therefore, that he was for the classical idea of the rule of law, and not for the 'juridicization' of life in the sense of regulating everything by a multitude of detailed rules.

By the 'impenetrability' of person Hessen meant, of course, the classical-liberal notion of an area of personal inviolability. However, he enriched this notion by discussing it not only as a problem of limiting state activity but also as one of limiting the scope of social and moral pressures. Human personality, he insisted, contains a 'supra-social kernel' impenetrable for the group;[43] if this 'impenetrability' is broken, personality itself no longer exists, becomes a mere particle of a collective whole. The same process of depersonalization occurs when subjective rights, which ought to be protected by law, are surrendered to a higher morality. Hessen's discussion of this question was directly related to the controversy between Chicherin and Soloviev. He tried to

---

[40] S. Hessen, *Autobiografia*, pp. 57–8. In the Russian original Hessen used the words *ogosudarstvlenie* and *opravovlenie*.

[41] S. Hessen, 'Problema', *Sovremennye zapiski*, vol. 22, p. 279.

[42] A. Ehr-Soon Tay, 'Law, the citizen and the state', in E. Kamenka *et al.* (eds.), *Law and Society: The Crisis in Legal Ideas*, London, 1978, p. 6.

[43] S. Hessen, 'Problema', *Sovremennye zapiski*, vol. 30, 1927, pp. 383–4.

mediate in this by recognizing a certain truth in Soloviev's definition of law as 'the minimum of morality' while at the same time wholeheartedly supporting Chicherin's view that law constituted a separate and distinct sphere not to be confused with morality. Following Chicherin he regarded such a confusion as typical of the socialist tradition, and pointed out that it was not only theoretically mistaken but extremely dangerous as well, since it could be used to justify the worst excesses of tyranny.[44]

Encouraged by the editors of *Sovremennye zapiski*, Hessen made some effort to prepare a separate edition of his studies on 'rule-of-law socialism.' He gave them the general title, 'Rule-of-law state and socialism' (*Pravovoe gosudarstvo i sotsyalism*), somewhat modifying the inner sub-divisions and added as prologue his article on the breakdown of utopianism. Bound together and preceded by a detailed table of contents the offprints of his articles from *Sovremennye zapiski* are in fact a well composed and comprehensive book.[45] Apart from the prologue, this book consists of three parts: (1) The crisis of liberalism; (2) The evolution of socialism; and (3) Rule-of-law socialism and the New Middle Ages. Let us briefly summarize them.

In Hessen's eyes the crisis of liberalism was at the same time the crisis of communism. The latter had inherited the dead elements of the liberal legacy—the cult of unbounded industrial productivity—while rejecting the 'eternal truth' of liberalism, that is its idea of law. In contrast to this, European socialists had buried the obsolete part of the liberal heritage while preserving its eternal truth. They realized that the idea of the rule of law cannot be reduced to its anachronistic nineteenth-century form, that it can and should be raised to a higher level, because its content is not limited and history-bound but infinite and inexhaustible. They understood that the main problem today is not the economic problem of exploitation but the legal problem of protecting freedom and equality against excessive centralization of economic power; that exploitation as such should not be reduced to an economic phenomenon but should rather be seen in Kantian terms, as treating other men as mere instruments, and not ends in themselves; that what is at stake is not so much the material welfare of the workers

---

[44] Ibid., vol. 22, pp. 267–8 and vol. 26, p. 384. In Hessen's view, Chicherin's book *Property and State* was 'one of the best-grounded and most profound expressions of the doctrine of orthodox liberalism' (ibid., vol. 22, p. 267).

[45] This book, of which unfortunately only one copy exists, is in my possession. For its table of contents see Appendix 1.

but rather their human dignity, constantly threatened by depersonalization and reification.[46]

This awareness, however, was something new, often barely emergent.
The earlier socialists did not believe that their problems could be
solved by law; the same was the view of the classical liberals, although
their practical conclusions were entirely different. The socialist
conclusion was, usually, that law as such is worthless, while the
liberals, in turn, held that socialist ideas are incompatible with the rule
of law and, therefore, have to be rejected. Only relatively recently has
this stage of thought been transcended. On the liberal side the so-
called new liberals, or social liberals, recognized the importance of
socialist problems; on the socialist side the democratic socialists
recognized the value of law and, thus, completed their break with
utopianism.

In the next chapters Hessen analysed in detail a multitude of
differences between the legal doctrines of the Old and New Liberalism.
It seems possible, however, to reduce his analysis to three main
problems: (1) the new conception of freedom; (2) the new attitude
towards democracy; (3) the new interpretation of property.

In contradistinction to the old freedom the new freedom is not
merely negative but positive. It consists not only in the negative right to
be free, in the private sphere of life, from anybody's interference but
also in the positive right to be helped by others; it demands from the
state not only the safeguards guaranteeing every individual the security
of his private activities but also providing everybody with the minimum
of material means indispensable to secure the free development of his
personality. Translated into the language of law the new freedom
amounts therefore to Soloviev's 'right to a dignified existence'. Hessen
was very fond of using this apt term and paid tribute to Soloviev for
coining it.[47]

In explaining the relationship between the old and the new freedom
Hessen opted for the view that the latter is an extension of the former.
He was aware, of course, that the two freedoms could be opposed to
each other: after all, the new freedom, in sharp contrast to the old, was
bound up with a considerable broadening of the responsibilities and
activities of the state. He nevertheless argued that the New Liberalism,
in contrast to state absolutism or utopian socialism (including

---

[46] Instead of the word 'reification' Hessen used a longer expression: *fakticheskoe
prevraschchenie cheloveka v veshch'* (*Sovremennye zapiski*, vol. 22, p. 268).

[47] S. Hessen, 'Problema', *Sovremennye zapiski*, vol. 23, p. 336.

communism), remained faithful to the spirit of law in the sense of protecting personal impenetrability'.[48] Neo-liberal positive freedom was in his eyes simply the old 'negative freedom' understood more broadly. It was so because the neo-liberal state preserved 'the hegemony of Law over Good', refusing to commit itself to any specific vision of the good and to reduce law to a mere means to good ends. It remained the guardian of Law, although, in contrast to the Old Liberalism, becoming aware that legal rights are empty if not supported by a legally guaranteed minimum of Good.

In more simple words: the neo-liberal state, as seen by Hessen, does not prescribe what is good for its citizens, does not subordinate law to any specific image of the good; it only removes economic obstacles which in fact restrict the legal freedom and equality of each person. It does not try to decide what is good and to impose this decision on its population; it tries only to create conditions in which everybody can freely choose what is good for him. It provides the needy with a necessary minimum not in order to free them from personal responsibility for their lives but in order to prevent situations in which economic privation makes a mockery of personal responsibility and freedom.

In this way the contrast between negative and positive freedom has, as it were, been transcended. A similar process occurred with another opposition, formulated by such spokesmen of classical liberalism as Benjamin Constant: the opposition between the liberal idea of limited government and the democratic principle of the sovereignty of the people. In contradistinction to classical liberalism, the New Liberalism ceased to be afraid of the masses and became unequivocally committed to democracy, returning, as it were, to the original belief in the essential correspondence of individual rights (rights of man) with political rights (rights of the citizen). It did not return, however, to the naïve belief in the reality of the 'popular will' and to the conception of democracy as an autocracy of the people, the unlimited power of the majority. In Hessen's view, the New Liberalism achieved a synthesis of liberalism and democracy by becoming aware of such truths as that the 'popular will' is a mere fiction, not an empirical fact, although it remains an important reality as a task, as a 'regulative idea'; that all political power, irrespective of its source, has to be limited because nobody can claim a monopoly for the popular will; or again that

[48] Ibid., vol. 22, p. 287.

sovereignty rests with law, not with any transient and fortuitous majority representing 'the people';[49] that the state is a complicated laboratory in which the 'popular will' is being created by means of necessary compromises and that a genuine compromise stems not from the opportunist considerations but from the respect which all participants in a political community show for human dignity.

Finally, the question of property. According to Hessen, the neo-liberal conception of property was characterized by a growing acceptance of certain forms of socialization together with a growing insistence on individualization. The ancient Roman rigid definition of property—*jus utendi et abutendi*—had been abandoned; dogmatic belief in absolute private property had been replaced by the notion that private property is justifiable only as a means of exercising personal freedom, that is, as an individualized and active relation between men and things. Formal entitlement had become less important than actual possession, that is, a personalized and creative relationship. In this sense the new concept of property, directed against monopolists and rentiers, could be called more individualized, less alienated. Lassalle was perfectly right in claiming that in the classical bourgeois world 'das Eigentum is Fremdtum geworden' (property has become estranged); now, however the individualized character of property was being restored and the estranged forms of property were being eliminated.[50] It can be seen as a dialectical movement, as a return on a higher level to the pre-bourgeois view preserved in the etymological meaning of the word *Eigentum* : property as an extension of personality.

In spite of all its merits the New Liberalism could not in Hessen's view be treated as an adequate solution to contemporary problems. It had not overcome the old mechanistic conception of society and, consequently, did not sufficiently recognize the reality of collective persons; its conception of property, although theoretically correct, had been so interpreted in practice as to create artificial obstacles to the process of further socialization;[51] most importantly, however, the new liberals neglected the problems of depersonalization and reification of men under the impersonal rule of capitalist commodity production. The last problem, analysed in detail by Sombart, had been posed both by socialists and anarchists and by thinkers criticizing capitalism from a conservative or religious standpoint. Among the latter Hessen mentioned Soloviev and all his followers in Russia.[52]

---

[49] Ibid., pp. 288–92.
[51] Ibid., p. 317.
[50] Ibid., vol. 23, p. 319.
[52] Ibid., p. 336.

The second part of Hessen's book, entitled 'The Evolution of Socialism', begins with a short discussion of Novgorodtsev's views. Novgorodtsev was right in pointing out that socialism as a utopian search for paradise on earth had undergone a mortal crisis; he was wrong, however, in asserting that what remained of socialism could be reduced to the right to a dignified existence, as proclaimed by the neo-liberals.[53] Indeed, in sharp contrast to communism, modern socialism has drawn nearer to liberalism and absorbed both its eternal truth (the idea of law) and the results of its recent development. But the degree of convergence between democratic socialism and social liberalism should not be exaggerated. Socialism in its last phase is not transforming itself into neo-liberalism; it goes beyond liberalism, inaugurating a new state in the development of the rule of law state.

Hessen divided the entire history of socialist thought into several phases, often further sub-divided into different parallel currents.

He defined the first phase as 'Utopian socialism as the abstract negation of capitalism'. Utopian socialism was born as a reaction against the juridical world-view of the French Revolution. It rejected the rule of law state as legalized anarchy, accused the law of sanctifying social atomization and set against it the principle of the Good. According to Saint-Simon and his disciples law is necessarily subjectivist, pluralist, and purely formal whereas the Good is objective, monist, and has a concretely definable content.[54] Socialism, therefore, was conceived not as yet another political system, yet another legal order, but as an organic industrial system in which political power is replaced by the administration of things and law, as a means of delimiting subjective, egoistic interests, gives way to organic social ties.

Saint-Simon's ideas were developed by Comte who gave them a distinctively conservative flavour and paved the way for such right-wing criticisms of liberal-capitalist order as, for instance, the 'Prussian socialism' of Spengler. Saint-Simon, like other utopian socialists, had absorbed many ideas from earlier conservative thinkers.[55] Small wonder, therefore that Spencer saw socialism as rejuvenated Toryism.[56] But there was an important difference. The conservative critics of capitalism saw the Good as transcendent whereas utopian socialists demanded its realization on earth; the first denied the autonomy of law, by making law a mere instrument of the historically given state, whereas the latter denied the law and the state as such.[57] At the same

---

[53] Ibid., vol. 27, pp. 382–5.　　[54] Ibid., pp. 385–8.
[55] Ibid., pp. 388–90.　　[56] Ibid., p. 388.　　[57] Ibid., pp. 390–4.

time, in contrast to conservatism, socialism interpreted the objective
Good not in religious and nationalist terms but in terms of the
economic welfare of each individual, thus preserving in itself an
element of liberal thinking.

The second phase of socialism—that of classical Marxism—was
described as a real negation of liberal-capitalist order. It was real, and
not merely abstract, because of the scientific character of Marxian
analyses of the real contradictions of capitalist development. However,
this scientific, or relatively scientific, side of Marxism coexisted with a
strong strain of utopianism, culminating in the idea of the 'withering
away of state and law'. Because of this Marxism represented in fact a
shaky equilibrium between scientifically oriented reformism and
radical revolutionary utopianism.[58] The first tendency got the upper
hand in old Engels, the second gained an absolute victory in Leninism.

The Marxian radical rejection of law and state stemmed from the
assumption that what really counts in history is only the power, and the
will, of the ruling classes. The 'rule of law' is a bourgeois hypocrisy,
trying to conceal existing injustices and, therefore, worse than the
openly arbitrary rule of an absolute monarch;[59] the so-called popular
will is a fiction because only social classes could have a will of their
own. The function of law and state is to oppress the other classes; the
working class whose final aim is to abolish all classes and, by the same
token, all forms of class rule, has to use these instruments of
oppression in a transitory period but wants them to wither away in the
ideal society of the future. In this sense the final aims of communism
and anarchism are the same, as Lenin correctly observed.

In contrast to Kautsky, Hessen did not believe that utopianism is
alien to the true spirit of Marxism. The very structure of Marxian
thought was to him profoundly utopian and anti-historical. Reducing
cultural and political values to the role of transitory superstructures
Marx, in fact, reduced historical continuity to the development of

[58] Ibid., p. 403. A very similar generalization is to be found in Schorske's book
on German Social Democracy: 'Marxism made possible a reconciliation of the
revolutionary rancor engendered in the Social Democratic rank and file during the
persecution, and the need for a reformist tactic in a fundamentally non-revolutionary
period'. (C. E. Schorske, *German Social Democracy 1905–1917*, Cambridge, Mass.,
1955, p. 4).

[59] Ibid., p. 406. It should be pointed out that here Hessen's interpretation of Marxism
was obviously incorrect: in fact Marx and Engels had no doubt that political freedom was
better than absolutism. The view that Hessen here ascribed to Marxism is more
characteristic of the conclusions drawn from Marxism by nineteenth-century Russian
Populists (cf. above, Ch. I, 4).

productive forces and self-confessedly treated all pre-communist history as a pre-historical stage in the life of the human species. He saw the passage to communism as a millenarian breakthrough, an entirely new beginning, introducing a qualitatively different dimension to human existence. Some elements of the superstructures created by class societies of the past were to be completely abolished (law and state) while others—like art, morality, philosophy and science—were to gain, for the first time, autonomous status and become ends in themselves. Thus, history was split into two halves having little in common with each other.

It was not clear what, according to Marx, would happen to the economy in the ideal communist society. In approaching this question, Hessen, following H. Cunow, paid special attention to the three key-concepts of the Marxian theory of economic formations: (1) productive forces (*Produktionskräfte*), (2) the mode of production (*Produktionsweise*) and (3) the relations of production (*Produktionsverhältnisse*). The economy, he argued, deals with the relations of production, and not merely the mode of production, let alone naked technology; economics is a social science. If so, the economy mediates between technology and law which is a necessary component of the relations between people in a productive process. It follows from this that the disappearance of law would necessarily entail the disappearance of the economy, or, to be more precise, the replacement of the economy by the purely technical scientific organization of labour.[60]

It must be remembered that this conclusion was shared at that time by many Marxists. Rosa Luxemburg, for instance, identified political economy with the science of economic processes in a non-regulated, non-planned society and proclaimed that it would disappear under socialism; a similar view was held by the young Lukács and, more importantly, by the overwhelming majority of Soviet economists of the first decade after the revolution. It was strongly represented among the lawyers as well. Evgeny Pashukanis, the most influential of the Soviet legal scholars of the 1920s, developed a theory according to which law emerges and disappears together with commodity production. Under socialism the economy is being replaced by economic policy, by 'conscious regulation of economic processes'.[61] Such a regulation cannot be exercised by means of law:

[60] Ibid., pp. 411–16.
[61] E. Pashukanis, *Selected Writings on Marxism and Law*. Pierce Beirne and Robert Sharlet (eds.), London, 1980, p. 239.

Regulation with the help of law alone, regulation establishing only the general forms in which the economic activity of entirely autonomous entities proceeds . . . is not regulation. True regulation begins where the activity of the state replaces the so-called economic motive, i.e. the motive of individual profit, the egoistic interest of the isolated economic subject.[62]

Although Hessen did not discuss Pashukanis's theory, it is very instructive to juxtapose their respective views. Pashukanis wanted to abolish law for the same reason which led Hessen to see it as 'eternal truth'. In Pashukanis's eyes the law presupposed and protected the autonomy of isolated private subjects,[63] that is, the existence of a certain sphere of economic freedom. Hessen's view was essentially the same, although his value-judgements were diametrically opposed: the 'impenetrability of person', personal autonomy, was for him one of the highest values, whereas for the Soviet theorist it was tantamount to an atomizing bourgeois individualism, which presupposed man as 'egoistic economic subject' and thus incompatible with socialism.[64] It was logical, therefore, that Hessen should want to develop a theory of socialism in which the economy would be regulated, 'bridled', by law alone, while Pashukanis preached 'the full merger of administration and economy', the replacement of regulation by law with state regulation characterized, as he put it, 'by the preponderance of the technical and organization aspect'.[65]

Thus Hessen accused Marxism of subordinating its scientific side to utopian ends, presupposing not only the abolition of law and state but of the economy as well. The Marxian concept of historical necessity, Hessen argued, only masks its utopian anti-historicism.[66] Moreover, the Marxian negation of liberalism does not go beyond the mechanical conception of society characteristic of classical liberalism. The profound mechanicism of Marxism is most conspicuous in the Marxian theory of value, which completely disregards the qualitative aspect of work and assumes that the value of products can be measured by the number of working hours, by units of mechanical 'clock time'.[67]

Hessen found in Russian revolutionary communism the quintessence of Marxian utopianism together with the degeneration of the 'real negation' of capitalism into pure destructiveness. Its inner nature, as Trotsky had frankly conceded, was revealed by 'war communism', that

[62] Ibid., p. 267.
[63] Ibid., p. 101.
[64] Ibid., pp. 102–3.
[65] Ibid., pp. 267–9.
[66] S. Hessen, 'Problema', *Sovremennye zapiski*, vol. 27, pp. 428–9.
[67] Ibid., pp. 424–5.

is, the subordination of all spheres of life to the militarized control of those in power; consequently, the failure of war communism could be seen as additional proof that extreme statism provides no solution to economic and social problems. The degradation of law in the Soviet state revealed another aspect of revolutionary communism, namely its striving by all possible means to realize an arbitrarily defined and absolutist ideal of positive Good. What distinguished communism from other currents of socialist thought, including classical Marxism, was its interpretation of this Good not in terms of the welfare of individuals but, rather, in terms of a supra-individual whole, closely resembling the conservative-theocratic ideal of the Church. In this sense Bolshevism was a crude imitation of conservatism and Lenin could have called his party 'a Jesuit order with proletarian content.'[68] Therefore, Hessen concluded, it was incorrect to say that Bolshevism was paving the way for reaction—its victory was itself a triumphant success for reaction.[69]

The following chapter of the book is devoted to those currents of socialist thought, both non-Marxist and Marxist, in which the negation of capitalism was not only 'real', that is, derived from the analysis of the real contradictions of capitalism, but also 'transforming' and 'constructive'. All these represented different 'moments' (dialectical phases) of the process by which the socialist Good was permeated by the principle of law. The compatibility of such a process with the Marxist tradition in socialism was provided, in Hessen's view, by the Marxian view that in the history of each class there is a period in which it represents the cause of general justice, and not merely its class interest. Applying this view to the contemporary working class in Europe could result in a rehabilitation of the idea of law and a restoration of belief in legal justice. Since the proletariat was supposed to put an end to all forms of class rule, it was possible to believe that its legal consciousness would provide conditions for an absolutely just legal order, an order in which law would for the first time become truly autonomous, an 'end in itself' in the Kantian sense.[70] Hessen ardently wanted to believe that such a unique historical chance really existed. This belief sometimes brought him very close to a peculiar 'legal utopianism'.

The 'idealistic motive' in Marxism, which supported such beliefs, was immeasurably strengthened by Lassalle. In the history of German

[68] Ibid., vol. 28, 1926, p. 322.   [69] Ibid., p. 324.   [70] Ibid., pp. 324–8.

Social Democracy Hessen saw the victory of Lassalle's spirit over that of Marx. The former greatly contributed to the vindication of the idea of law by his fight for progressive legislation; in France a similar vindication of law was achieved, less directly, by Proudhon, who did much to rehabilitate, within the socialist tradition, the idea of the autonomous law-regulated (as opposed to state-regulated) economy.[71]

The spiritual heirs of Lassalle were the German revisionists while the heirs of Proudhon were, of course, the French syndicalists. Hessen completely disagreed with Novgorodtsev who, influenced by Sorel, depicted syndicalism as representing a tendency diametrically opposed to that of social-democratic revisionism.[72] True, revisionists supported the democratic state while syndicalists deeply distrusted political democracy but, in spite of this difference both currents of thought were equally committed to the idea of law: the first by opting for parliamentary methods of struggle, the second by promoting the so-called 'social law', to be applied to industrial relations, and by defending the autonomy of the economic sphere. In fact the syndicalists, just because of their hostility towards the state, made an especially important contribution to the new socialist understanding of law. They considerably broadened the scope of regulation by law without abandoning economic freedom, indeed resolutely resisting all kinds of 'statism'. Of equal importance was their rejection of legal positivism which led in practice to a breaking of the state's monopoly of legislation.

By way of digression, it should be added that there was a potential contradiction between Hessen's idea of the rule of law and the growing power of the trade unions. Hessen, while seeing and welcoming the positive aspects of syndicalism, failed to appreciate that it might be desirable, or indeed necessary, to bring under the rule of law not only the power of the state, but the power of the unions as well. Extolling law as a factor which limited political power, he did not then envisage the necessity of limiting the unions' right to strike: as for instance, in cases where abuse of this right threatens to disrupt essential services to the population, such as medical services, or where a particular group of employees uses its crucial, monopolist position in the industry to impose its will on all others, both as producers and as taxpayers. Even so, however, such conclusions could easily be deduced from his

[71] Ibid., pp. 330–1.
[72] Ibid., pp. 323–3. Hessen means, of course, the respective pages of Novgorodtsev's book *Ob obshchestvennom ideale*.

principles; after all, he wanted to 'bridle' by law all kinds of power, both political and economic, and was especially apprehensive of all monopolist dictates.

Hessen saw in British guild socialism the highest stage so far reached of a reconciliation of socialism and law.[73] In his view, guild-socialism had fully overcome the negative phase and entered the positive phase of construction, in which a mechanical conception of democracy had been replaced by an organic one, union-aggregates had given way to union-communities, and class struggle was seen as the self-organization of the workers for the realization of the general good.[74] Another important contribution of guild socialism was the restoration of the medieval concept of division of property, and the original combination of state property with corporate property. But most impressive of all in Hessen's eyes was the guild socialists' idea of 'penetrating' both the state and the economy by law, of subordinating both to the sovereign authority of law. Because of this, he thought, guild socialism deserved to be called the first form of a fully-fledged 'rule-of-law socialism.'[75]

The last part of the book bears the title 'Rule of law socialism and the New Middle Ages.' The idea of the coming of the New Middle Ages was made fashionable by Nicholas Berdyaev;[76] it was also proclaimed by the theorist of guild socialism, A. Penty, who, like the Russian philosopher, condemned all post-Renaissance development in Europe. Against this background the originality of Hessen's thought can be properly assessed: he also welcomed the 'New Middle Ages' but stressed that the post-Renaissance heritage, especially 'the truth of liberalism', had to be preserved and treated as of irreplaceable value. Referring to Chicherin, he repeated once more that law should not be confused with morality, as had been done in the 'Old Middle Ages', and assured his readers that in the new medievalism the 'impenetrability of person' and inviolable subjective rights of the individual would be fully respected.[77]

The essence of the new medievalism would consist in the sovereignty of law, in establishing a firm rule of law in the political and economic spheres, and in a plurality of legal orders mutually limiting each other.

---

[73] Ibid., vol. 29, 1926, pp. 323–41. In this chapter Hessen often quotes from G. D. H. Cole (especially *The World of Labour*, 4th edn., 1920) and A. Penty (*The Restoration of the Guild System*, 1906).

[74] Ibid., p. 340.   [75] Ibid., p. 341.

[76] Cf. N. Berdyaev, *Novoe srednevekov'e*, Berlin, 1924.

[77] S. Hessen, 'Problema', *Sovremennye zapiski*, vol. 30, pp. 384–5.

Law would no longer be identified with the official laws of the state; it would be a product of a functionally differentiated society and the state as such would undergo a process of 'devolution'. Having lost its 'universal competence', the state would instead become the 'universal co-ordinator', a unifying factor in a multi-functional civil order, representing the principle of universality in a society based upon principles of 'functional federalism'.[78] Such a state could not be opposed to, or alienated from, society; it would itself be a 'society as community', although 'condensed' into a functionally organized polity.[79] Needless to say, it would be limited by the plurality of legal orders and by subjective human rights, both negative and positive. However, just for this reason, because of the necessity of coping with the task of securing to everybody his 'right to a dignified existence', its activity would be much broader and more vigorous than that of an absolutist, let alone classical liberal state. Social atomization would be abolished, individuals would overcome their mutual isolation by participating in the life of different communities which, however, in contrast to guilds, Church fraternities and other forms of medieval *Gemeinschaft*, would not be all-embracing, 'swallowing' up their members. No such tendency would emerge because each individual would be multi-functional, belonging to various different communities and associations at the same time. Property would lose its estranged character and become personalized, conditional, and divided, like the medieval fiefs. Political sovereignty would also be divided, limited, and conditional. The economy would be 'bridled' by law while preserving its autonomy and its inherent element of 'irrational spontaneity'[80] which would entail (contrary to Menger) the preservation, in a modified form, of a separate sphere of private law.[81] In this way the state and the economy would submit to law without losing their autonomy and separate identity, but rather rediscovering their proper limits and thus becoming truer to their inner essence. Human dignity would gain enormously because being dependent on law, rather than on arbitrary political power or blind economic forces, is not a humiliating relationship.[82] Having recognized law, the economy and the state, each in its proper sphere, socialism would at last fully overcome its utopianism and reveal itself as a new and higher form of 'rule-of-law state'.

As we see, Hessen's conclusions were very optimistic indeed. It is

[78] Ibid., p. 397.
[79] Ibid., p. 403.
[80] Ibid., vol. 31, 1927, pp. 349–50.
[81] Ibid., p. 344.
[82] Ibid., p. 353.

admirable that he refused to yield to despair because of Russia's tragedy; he might legitimately be criticized, however, for underestimating the danger of right-wing and left-wing totalitarianism, for not foreseeing the imminent economic crisis of 1929 and for disregarding the possibility of another world war.

While working on 'rule-of-law socialism', Hessen was in close contact with his colleague and friend G. Gurvitch (mentioned above in connection with Petrażycki)[83] whose interest in French syndicalism and in the movement for 'social law' he fully shared.[84] The trains of thought of these two Russian exiles at that time ran in close parallel, although Hessen was much more engaged in the discussion with Marxism and much more committed to the defence of the 'eternal truth' of liberalism.

Politically, Hessen's views on 'rule-of-law socialism' should be placed between left-wing liberalism, as embodied by P. Miliukov, and right-wing non-Marxist socialism. *Sovremennye zapiski*, in whose pages Hessen's book was printed, was officially a non-partisan journal, although in fact all its editors (Vishniak, Gukovsky, Fondaminsky, and Avksentev) represented the right wing of the former 'socialist-revolutionary party'. The populist tradition in which they were steeped and which was rather alien to Hessen's intellectual pedigree did not prevent them from appreciating Hessen's work as a remarkable theoretical achievement nor from accepting, in principle, its main political conclusions.[85] Their sympathy towards Hessen can be explained by, among other things, his desire to bring together in a higher synthesis individual autonomy and communalism, the genuine values of *Gesellschaft* and those of *Gemeinschaft*—an idea which, as I have tried to show elsewhere, figures prominently in such populist thinkers as Herzen and Mikhailovsky, and which, in its variants, became a characteristic component of the intellectual tradition of the Russian intelligentsia.[86]

Equally characteristic of this tradition, however, was the stubborn,

---

[83] See above, Ch. IV, 7.

[84] Cf. G. Gurvitch, *Le temps present et l'idée du droit social*, Paris, 1931.

[85] In his memoirs the editor-in-chief of *Sovremennye zapiski* included Hessen, with Gurvitch, among those authors whose political views were especially 'akin and close' to the views of the editors of the journal (M. V. Vishniak, *Sovremennye zapiski*, p. 106). Another fragment of his memoirs makes it clear that sometimes Hessen's position was to the left of editorial policy: thus, he was horrified by the fact that they accepted a 'reactionary' short story for publication. (Ibid., p. 183).

[86] Cf. Walicki, *A History of Russian Thought*, pp. 165–70, 263, 285.

conscious or unconscious refusal to admit that the only safeguard of individual autonomy is law; not certainly any positive law, but law as conceived by the ancient Romans and by the modern liberal theorists of *Rechtsstaat*. The belated acknowledgement of this truth found acute expression in Hessen's work.

5 The development of the 'rule-of-law state' and the changing content of human rights

This fascination with guild socialism and with the idea of the 'New Middle Ages' marked a peculiar phase in the evolution of Hessen's views on the development of the 'rule-of-law state.' There is a remarkable continuity in this evolution, but some discontinuities can be found in its as well.

The first outline of Hessen's conception of the genesis and development of the rule of law in modern history was formulated in his pamphlet *Political Freedom and Socialism*, written in the revolutionary year 1917. The principle of the rule of law was there conceived as protecting individual freedom, of which the first and most important form was freedom of conscience. The very essence of modern law consisted of respecting a 'supra-social kernel' in man, of treating man as something more than a member of a given polity. Therefore the rule of law was seen as directed against state absolutism and incompatible with it.

In its characterization of 'old' and 'new' liberalism *Political Freedom and Socialism* was very close to the more elaborate views presented ten years later in Hessen's articles in *Sovremennye zapiski*. It showed Russian Kadets as representing a left-wing 'social liberalism' and paving the way for profound social reforms.[87] Socialism, in turn, was presented as facing a choice of two alternatives: either to become a new version of state absolutism, in which case it would be doomed to failure, or to develop into a new and higher form of the 'rule-of-law state'.[88] The author believed that the second alternative, in spite of many difficulties which would have to be removed, was realizable in Russian conditions.

In *Sovremennye zapiski* Hessen characteristically expressed no views on the future of socialism in Russia, but limited himself to analysing its failure. In later years, however, new problems arose. What was the meaning of the victory of Stalinism in Russia? How should German

---

[87] S. I. Gessen (Hessen), *Politicheskaia svoboda i sotsializm*, Petrograd, 1917, p. 24.
[88] Ibid., p. 34.

Nazism be explained and what was the relation between Nazism and Stalinism? Was there any significance in the fact that Stalinist Russia fought against Hitler's Germany on the side of liberal democracies? It is no wonder that in the last decade of his life Hessen embarked once more on developing a conception of the different historical forms of the 'rule-of-law state', of their successes and their failures. During the war, as pointed out above, he wrote two books on this topic, of which, unfortunately, only three chapters have survived. One of these, entitled 'Modern Democracy', has appeared posthumously, in Italian and in Polish.[89] After the war he was invited by the UNESCO Committee on the Philosophic Bases of Human Rights to contribute to the preparation of the Universal Declaration of Human Rights which the General Assembly of the United Nations was to issue on 10 December 1948, in Paris. Having received a detailed questionnaire, he wrote the article on 'The Rights of Man in Liberalism, Socialism and Communism'. This article, together with contributions by such thinkers as J. Maritain, Mahatma Gandhi, H. J. Laski, B. Croce, Teilhard de Chardin and others, was selected for publication by UNESCO in the important volume entitled *Human Rights, Comments and Interpretations*.

The short Note added to this volume explains that some texts presented in it differ from the final conclusions of UNESCO, but have nevertheless been included as 'stimulating in their originality of thought'.[90] It is obvious, however, that Hessen's text does not belong in this category: it perfectly harmonizes with the final result of the UNESCO enquiry,[91] providing it with the most systematically elaborated historical and philosophical arguments, and indeed shares both its merits and its faults or illusions. It seems justified, therefore, to say that the man who embodied the last link in the progressive evolution of Russian liberalism, who was so deeply steeped in the traditions of Russian thought, fully participated in preparing the Charter of Human Rights for our times. The symbolic meaning of this

[89] Italian edition *Democrazia moderna*, Roma, 1957; Polish edition in *Studia z filozofii kultury* (see above, n. 11). There is also an extended but unpublished English version of this study entitled 'Defining Modern Democracy'. The other two chapters from Hessen's book 'The Downfall and the Regeneration of Democracy' survive only in Polish. Their titles are: 'Osłabienie tętna demokracji' (The Weakening of the Pulse of Democracy) and 'O istocie i powołaniu prawa' (On the Essence and Calling of Law). See Appendix 3.

[90] *Human Rights Comments and Interpretations*. A Symposium edited by UNESCO with an Introduction by J. Maritain. New York, 1949, p. 7.

[91] Ibid., pp. 258–72.

should not be exaggerated but neither should it be ignored. It warns us against the view that the whole Russian tradition is totally different from that of the West and that the gap between the two is unbridgeable.[92]

The new version of Hessen's conception, as presented in his article for UNESCO and in 'Modern Democracy', distinguishes four main stages in the development of the modern 'rule-of-law state' (or 'State of Law') in Europe: (1) the Absolute, (2) the Liberal, (3) the Democratic and (4) the Socialist State.

Hessen's new assessment of the legacy of absolutism, influenced by the views of M. Reisner,[93] was a definite break both with his earliest conception, as presented in *Political Freedom and Socialism*, and with his later tendency to idealize the pluralism of the legal order of the Middle Ages. According to this new conception, the absolute state should be credited with having proclaimed the principle of security of law in which Montesquieu saw the essence of liberty. It entailed an awareness of the need for unification and codification of law; in terms of rights, it implied the right to equal treatment in law, the right to justice, the inviolability of the individual citizen, his property, and his dwelling. Even in nineteenth-century Russia the ideologists of enlightened absolutism, such as M. Speransky, insisted that the Russian Empire was 'ruled on a firm basis of unshakeable law' and sincerely wanted to remove the existing discrepancy between principle and practice. True, the fundamental relationship in the absolutist state was that of subordination, but the same is true of the structure of Napoleonic governmental bodies. In fact the Napoleonic state, whose contribution to the rule of law in Europe is incontrovertible, revealed in 'almost ideal form' the inner structure of the absolutist state.[94]

By application of his dialectical method, Hessen tried to show that each state in the development of the rule of law contained the germs of the next stage and, conversely, that the higher stages could be discovered 'glowing' through the lower. In this way the absolutist principle of security of law contained in itself the seeds of the liberal 'negative freedom'. These seeds, however, would never bear fruit without additional factors of an economic and ideological nature. From

[92] Cf. for instance, Tibor Szamuely, *The Russian Tradition*, London, 1974.

[93] See S. Hessen, *Studia z filozofii kultury*, p. 315, n. Hessen referred to Reisner's articles on absolutism in *Vestnik prava* 1910–11.

M. Reisner, who was both a Marxist and a disciple of Petrażycki, was mentioned above in Ch. IV, 7.

[94] 'Defining Modern Democracy' (typescript), pp. 4–6.

the point of view of the dialectic of ideas the most important of them was the Puritan conception of man 'as a spiritual being, who is not only the subject of an earthly state but also a member of a higher, spiritual community—the Kingdom of God'.[95] The Enlightenment conception of pre-social, natural rights was only a rationalist interpretation of this profoundly religious image of the human individual.

Under the influence of natural-law individualism the absolutist principle of security of law was transformed into the liberal principle of limited government. This transition was so smooth and seemed so natural that Montesquieu—the author of the ideal model of the rule of law under absolutism—was accepted as an authority by the Founding Fathers of the first liberal state—the United States of America. Liberal civil rights safeguarded the existence of a sphere of privacy in which the individual was free from state interference and 'impenetrable' by society. In the classical liberal state the scope of this sphere, historically changing, was so broadened as to reduce the state, in Lassalle's famous words, to the role of a night-watchman (*Nachtwächter*). Its model was a company of individuals, each pursuing his own greatest profit and contracting in order to guarantee the security of his own personality, property, and individual or combined activity. Such a state was neither able nor even willing to solve burning social problems. Therefore it had to be transformed into a new type of 'rule-of-law state', that is, a democratic state, gradually broadening the scope of its activity, respecting 'negative freedom' but supplementing it with, or limiting it by, 'positive freedom'. This 'new freedom', however, as W. Wilson and L. Hobhouse correctly emphasized, was not mere negation of the 'old freedom'—but rather its further development. The merely negative and static conception of equality, bound up with the liberal concept of freedom, was replaced by the principle of 'equalization of chances', namely, by a positive and dynamic conception. This change, however, was necessary to universalize the 'old freedom', to remove the obstacles making it merely a privilege of the few. In this sense only the democratic state fulfilled the promises of liberalism. The close interdependence of the negative and positive rights of man had already been understood by some thinkers at the threshold of the liberal epoch. Thus, Condorcet for instance claimed that the right to education is involved in the civil liberties formulated in the Declaration of 1789, in just the same way as the right to justice.[96] As the actual

[95] S. Hessen, 'The Rights of Man', in *Human Rights*, p. 110.
[96] Ibid., p. 115. In the Polish edition of 'Modern Democracy' Hessen referred in thi⌐

author of the Declaration of Rights voted by the French Convention in June 1793 he went even further, adding to the list of human rights the right to work or, in the case of disability, to a pension.

The modern democratic state, which appeared as the final result of this development, could be called an 'insurance state'. Its model, Hessen wrote, 'is an insurance co-operative dividing the costs of insurance according to the value of property insured, but administered by all members on lines of complete equality, on the basis of mutual aid and co-ordination, and not that of subordination to a remote authority'.[97]

In characterizing the main components of this model, Hessen paid special attention to the idea of solidarity (concretization of 'fraternity'), as put forward by L. Duguit and the French 'solidarists', who set against the individualist fiction of 'social contract', with its abstractly universalist counterpart in the 'general will', the concept of 'social debt', based on the concrete fact of social solidarity. They replaced the mechanistic, Newtonian interpretation of the unity of society as primarily a market, bound by ties of competition rather than of co-operation (i.e. by ties negative in their essence), with an ideal of organic social unity, based upon positive social ties of mutual aid and co-operation, thus providing theoretical justification for welfare policies which supported compulsory education, full employment, and different kinds of social insurance.[98] Hessen, however, was fully conscious that such a welfare policy could also be pursued by totalitarian states, completely defying the whole heritage of the liberal state. Therefore, in order to make a sharp distinction between totalitarianism and democracy, he proclaimed the principle of the priority of freedom: 'The most characteristic feature of the modern democratic state is, indeed, the fact that even pursuing the welfare of its citizens it means first and foremost their freedom.'[99] What distinguishes democracy from orthodox liberalism is not its attitude towards individual freedom but its overcoming of formalist and static interpretations. In democracy freedom is seen as 'an inner potential force inherent in every human being that may grow and come to flower, but may also shrink and degenerate in miserable conditions of life.'[100] Thus, the aim of a welfare policy is not to feed and educate (indoctrinate) the slaves of the

---

context to his early study on the political ideas of the Girondists (see above, n. 10).

[97] 'Defining Modern Democracy', p. 33.
[98] Ibid., pp. 32–3.   [99] Ibid., p. 27.   [100] Ibid., p. 28.

state in order to make them reliable tools of the will of their rulers; on the contrary, it consists in removing the most obvious impediments and thus 'helping everybody in his efforts towards the self-realization of his personality'.[101]

This explanation did not claim to demolish the possible contradiction between 'securing the rights of positive freedom' and 'safeguarding negative liberties'. Hessen saw this problem as a dialectical antinomy of modern democracy: an antinomy which might result in creative tension between different but compatible tasks but which might also degenerate into a threat to the democratic polity. Democracy is 'an equilibrium between the principle of equality, liberty and solidarity';[102] in order to maintain it all these components should be preserved but none of them should be made absolute and allowed to swallow the rest.

Hessen recognized another serious threat in the interpretation of democracy as naked majority rule. Referring to Rousseau's distinction between *volonté générale* and *volonté de tous* he refused to accept majority rule as the essence of democracy: majority rule, he asserted, is not a principle but only a technique of decision-making, practised in different types of state.[103] It is not enough to combine majority rule with the extension of the franchise to all adults because the unlimited power of the majority would contradict the basic principles of the rule of law no less than other forms of unlimited government. As a matter of fact, the mechanical method of counting heads, together with the modern party system, was not advocated by Rousseau and not inherent in the democratic ideal; it was rather a product of liberalism whose institutions were inherited by the modern democracies.[104] The essential feature of democracy is not a mechanical method of solving conflicts by a majority vote but rather the unceasing effort to bridge different interests in a creative compromise, to ensure the victory of reason over sheer force of numbers, thereby contributing to the growing cohesion and solidarity of society.[105]

---

[101] Ibid.   [102] S. Hessen, 'The Rights of Man', p. 118.
[103] 'Defining Modern Democracy', pp. 38–9.   [104] Ibid., pp. 18–19.
[105] Ibid., p. 38. An additional argument for this view can be found in the Polish 'democracy of the gentry'. In the parliament of the Polish–Lithuanian Commonwealth the demand for unanimity combined with the threat of veto served the cause of 'creative compromise'. It prevented the polarization of opinions in the Diet, strengthening instead the will for mutual understanding, the awareness that it was in the interests of all deputies to reach agreement through compromise. Thus the Diet could not be divided into organized parties, struggling with each other; it was not a 'machine for voting' but rather a complex laboratory in which the 'general will' was being produced. No wonder

An interesting addendum to these thoughts is to be found in the un-published study 'The Weakening of the Pulse of Democracy'—another surviving chapter from Hessen's book 'The Downfall and the Regeneration of Democracy'. It contains an elaborate diagnosis of the deep crisis of the liberal and liberal-democratic understanding of freedom. For the Puritan fathers of liberalism individual freedom was inseparable from duty, from hard work conceived as a divine calling, from responsibility and creativity. In sharp contrast to this attitude, contemporary theorists of liberal democracy present freedom as a problem of leisure and recreation.[106] In Hessen's eyes this was a decadent view, typical of the gravediggers of a historical epoch and perfectly compatible with totalitarianism: after all, the system of Dostoevsky's Grand Inquisitor consisted in depriving people of their personal responsibility and giving them instead not only bread, but also free time and childish recreation. The idea of the sovereignty of the people underwent a similar process of secularization and degeneration. The Puritans interpreted it as the rule of divine truth on earth, now, however, it came to be interpreted as merely a technique reaching a compromise between conflicting interests; not a creative compromise resulting from mutual respect in a common search for truth, but a compromise assuming the relativity of all values, abandoning the search for objective truth, and striving not for a balance of arguments, but merely for a balance of forces.

This state of mind was reflected and justified in the relativist theory of Kelsen. In the 1920s Hessen held a more favourable view of it: he himself thought then that relativism—in politics, not in philosophy—constituted the 'eternal truth' of democracy.[107] Later, however, influenced by the war and all the horrors brought about by the German 'revolution of nihilism',[108] he came to the conclusion that 'to justify democracy by denying the existence of objective values means to bury it. Kelsen's doctrine of democratic relativism, in spite of the apologetic intentions of its author, is in fact a funeral oration for democracy'.[109]

that Rousseau, the theorist of the 'general will' as opposed to the 'spirit of parties', was so sympathetic towards the institutions of ancient Poland. (Cf. C. Backvis, 'Wymóg jednomyślności a wola ogółu', *Czasopismo prawno-historyczne*, vol. 27, no. 2, 1975.)

[106] Hessen referred in this connection to B. Shaw, *The Intelligent Woman's Guide to Socialism, Capitalism, Sovietism and Fascism*.

[107] Cf. *Sovremennye zapiski*, vol. 22, p. 290 and vol. 23, p. 334.

[108] Cf. H. A. R. Rauschning, *Die Revolution des Nihilismus*, Zürich, 1938.

[109] S. Hessen, 'Osłabienie tętna demokracji' ('The Weakening of the Pulse of Democracy', typescript), p. 198. The same view was put forward by J. H. Hallowell, who

This diagnosis makes it clear that, in Hessen's view, the crisis of European culture was not something which occurred in spite of European liberal-democratic tradition; it was rather a result of the inner weakening and disintegration of this tradition. From this point of view totalitarianism was by no means the only symptom or the only result of this crisis. Hessen was keenly aware of other dangers as well, such as the prevalence of consumerist attitudes, the special kind of tolerance stemming not from respect for persons but from indifference towards truth, the peculiar infantilism of what was later called 'mass culture', and so forth. The outspokenly 'anti-Puritan' ethos of all these phenomena was, in Hessen's eyes, a dangerous symptom of the further deepening of destructive processes. It seemed to him that the overcoming of such a crisis could be expected only from an overall regeneration: from religious revival on the one hand and from socialist reconstruction on the other.

This was the reason for the remarkably parallel development of two tendencies in Hessen's views: his increasingly positive interest in religion and his growing acceptance of the basic tenets of socialist planned economy. He did not wait to draw his conclusions until socialism was imposed on Poland. Even during the war he was teaching in underground university courses that the industrialized world was facing an inescapable alternative: either socialist planning (to be exercised, to be sure, through law and not through arbitrary decisions) or a relapse into barbarism.[110]

At this point we come to the most controversial part of Hessen's legacy: his views on socialism, as presented in his UNESCO article. While trying to express the claims of Socialism in terms of the 'rights of man' Hessen distinguished three kinds of such rights. The first group, very close to, indeed sometimes overlapping, the rights of positive freedom in the democratic state were those rights which could be realized by a comprehensive system of social insurance (the right to a job, to education, etc.). The second group consisted of so-called

claimed that belief in the objectivity of values is a necessary condition of healthy liberalism. He wrote: 'When men abandon the belief in transcendental standards, when the idea of objective truth and value is destroyed, liberalism becomes degenerate'. (J. H. Hallowell, *The Decline of Liberalism as an Ideology*, London, 1946, p. 10). Hallowell, like Hessen, saw in Kelsen's doctrine the perfect model of 'degenerated liberalism'. (Ibid., p. 19.)

[110] Hessen developed this view in his book 'The Downfall and the Regeneration of Democracy'. For a relevant quotation see Walicki, Introduction, in Hessen's *Studia z filozofii kultury*, p. 41.

economic rights, that is the rights of man as producer and consumer. They derived, in Hessen's view, from the more comprehensive and specifically socialist principle of freedom from exploitation, or, in other words, 'the right of man to be treated in economic life as a human being, not as a mere commodity'.[111] The list of these rights was rather bizarre, including, for instance, the right to a decent home along with freedom of consumption, the right to a free choice of commodities and the right freely to save one's income—all protected by means of a planned economy.[112]

Hessen insisted that the national economy ought to be planned 'in a democratic way, from below, and not in a bureaucratic way, from above'.[113] He demanded also the preservation of money, as the only guarantee of freedom of consumption. He called his socialism 'liberal socialism', by which he meant that a limited degree of economic freedom would be preserved because the economy would be regulated by legal rules and not by commands. He was impressed by the vision of British Socialism proclaimed by some Labour ideologists. He agreed with Harold Laski that the right to strike should be used only in extreme cases and, on the other hand, he abandoned his earlier sympathy for the syndicalist ideal of industrial democracy in which workers as well as consumers control industry.[114] The socialist state, in his view, was to be a 'co-operative association based on co-partnership in a common task, and not the office that was the model of the absolutist State, nor the liberal joint-stock company, not even the mere insurance co-operative, the model of the modern democratic State'.[115] He made it clear, however, that co-partnership would not mean the handing over of factory-management to workers' councils, and that managers would not be elected, as in a democratic state organization. These caveats stemmed from his concern to preserve the relative autonomy of the economic sphere, although in more limited confines.

The third group of rights derived from the communist principle, to each according to his needs. In dealing with them Hessen contrasted absolute communism and relative communism: the first he dismissed as utopian, the second he treated as not an alternative to but rather a constituent of liberal socialism.[116] If a park or beach can be used freely by all, he reasoned, if in a country like Britain everybody receives freely according to his needs the services of doctors and nurses, there is

[111] S. Hessen, 'The Rights of Man', p. 123.   [112] Ibid., pp. 121–3.
[113] Ibid., p. 125.   [114] Ibid., pp. 123–4.   [115] Ibid., p. 125.
[116] Ibid., p. 127.

nothing inherently impossible in the idea that at some future time everybody will have a right to three decent meals a day. In his *Manifeste du personnalisme* Emmanuel Mounier envisaged 'a state of things where everybody will have his elementary needs satisfied by the free distribution of a minimum of commodities and services indispensable for a decent life'. And indeed, Hessen commented, one need not be a Communist in the political sense of the term to see such development as possible and desirable.[117]

In the history of Soviet communism Hessen observed a most encouraging phenomenon: the overcoming of its initial utopianism, the vindication of a relative autonomy in the economic sphere; the restoration of law and an increasingly positive attitude towards the historical heritage. In the first years after the Bolshevik revolution communism had not only an heroic but also an eschatological character. Religion, law, the cultural heritage of the past, both national and universal, were to be destroyed as mere tools of the class enemy; the economy was militarized and completely subordinated to politics. This stage found its best spokesman in Trotsky who conceived the proletarian dictatorship on purely military lines. Fortunately, the other communist leaders decisively defeated this utopian radicalism, Lenin by the daring introduction of his New Economic Policy and Stalin by proclaiming a programme of 'building up Socialism in one country'. Stalin's contribution was especially important, showing 'a great deal of courage, perseverance, sagacity and patience'.[118] He introduced into the new state-owned industry the principles of economic calculation, based upon the business autonomy of single enterprises, the responsibility of the management and clearly defined property rights. Following Lenin, he strongly supported the new, affirmative attitude towards historical tradition. Above all, he restored law, which signalled a decisive break with the utopian spirit of radical communism.

The few pages devoted by Hessen to Stalin's Constitution of 1936 are surprising and depressing indeed. No mention is made of the glaring discrepancies between the text of the Constitution and the actual practice of Stalin's Empire. The Constitution, we are told, gave Soviet citizens all possible rights of positive freedom as well as such rights of negative freedom, as freedom of speech and the press, freedom of association, the inviolability of the individual, his home and correspondence, etc., etc. It especially mentioned freedom to save and

[117] Ibid.   [118] Ibid., p. 135.

implied freedom of consumption. In a word, it created an 'atmosphere of security'.[119] On its promulgation Stalin declared: 'We need the security of law now more than ever'. These words are quoted in Hessen's article without any reference to the reign of terror which immediately followed them.

Was this *naïveté* or hypocrisy? Neither. Hypocrisy was entirely out of the question, though *naïveté* was not. There *was* an element of *naïveté* in Hessen, stemming from his goodness, his ardent desire to deny hatred, to see the better side of everything, to find everywhere symptoms of the inevitable triumph of the Good. But *naïveté* did not blind him to the facts, did not protect his inner comfort by wilful ignorance of the cruel reality.[120] The yawning discrepancy between words and deeds, law and reality, was one of his major concerns. Precisely because of this he loved to repeat the famous 'Prayer' from Tuwim's poem 'Polish Flowers', especially the following words:

> But above all we beg Thee
> To help us to give shufflers the lie,
> And to restore the true meaning
> To our words:
> Let law mean nothing but law,
> And justice nothing but justice.[121]

In order to understand Hessen's attitude to Stalin and to Soviet Russia, it is necessary, I think, to be aware of the different aspects, different dimensions, of this problem. Firstly, from the perspective of a law-centred conception of socialism Stalin appeared as a great suppressor of rampant legal nihilism. Hessen was generous enough to call utopian communism 'an admirable expression of hope'.[122] In spite of this, however, there can be no doubt that revolutionary utopianism, and especially its idea of the withering away of law, was in his eyes the greatest danger to culture, the surest way to barbarism. Being conscious of the discrepancy between Stalin's Constitution and reality he could still think that similar discrepancies, although usually on a lesser scale, had occurred many times before throughout history and

---

[119] Ibid., p. 138.
[120] In his book 'The Real and Illusory Overcoming of Capitalism' Hessen described the Soviet economy under Stalin as an 'illusory' overcoming of capitalism, strengthening the negative features of capitalism instead of removing them. One chapter of this book was entitled: 'Intensification of the degeneracy of capitalism in the Soviet economic order'. See Appendix 2.
[121] T. Tuwim, *Dzieła*, vol. 2, Warsaw, 1955, p. 106.
[122] 'The Rights of Man', p. 129.

that even a hypocritical tribute to law promised better for the future than an idealistic commitment to the struggle against law. He emphasized Stalin's words about the security of the law; since this was in his view the historical achievement of state absolutism it seems justifiable to conclude that he wanted to see Stalin as an enlightened despot. At the end of his article he expressed his hope for 'a growing actualization of the Rights of Man' in the Soviet Union,[123] making clear thereby that at that moment he saw these rights as merely proclaimed and not realized in practice.

Secondly, the years immediately after the war were characterized by a widespread belief that the war-time alliance between the Western democracies and the Soviet Union, if enough effort were made to preserve it, would create conditions for a convergence of the two systems. Such a hope was also voiced by Hessen and the closing pages of this article were an attempt to justify this optimistic conclusion. We may treat it as an expression of wishful thinking but we should remember that this vision was strongly suggested and encouraged by the UNESCO Committee on the Theoretical Bases of Human Rights. In the 'Memorandum and Questionnaire Circulated by UNESCO on the Theoretical Bases of the Rights of Man', the document which accompanied Hessen's invitation to participate in the project, the idea of reconciling the Western conception of human rights with the Soviet view was explicit. A suggestion was even made that Marxist dialectics ought to be used to this end: 'One of the major tasks immediately ahead of us is thus clearly to find some common measure for the future development of the two tendencies, or in the terms of the Marxist dialectic to effect a reconciliation of the two opposites in a higher synthesis.'[124]

Thirdly, similar hopes were widespread at that time among Russian *émigrés*, most of whom felt proud of and elated by Russia's heroic contribution to the victory over Nazism. The former Menshevik leader, F. Dan, recalled in this connection Herzen's view that the West and Russia were bound to reach the same goal, although moving towards it from opposite ends: the West was going 'through freedom to

[123] Ibid., p. 142.

[124] *Human Rights*, p. 254. The contributors included some who criticized this aim from a Marxist standpoint (John Lewis, ibid., pp. 58–9). In one article we find the curious statement that Stalin and Molotov assimilated the ideological stock-in-trade of the Russian intelligentsia, as represented by Bakunin, Kropotkin, Herzen, Tolstoy, and Dostoevsky (Boris Tchechko, 'The Conception of the Rights of Man in the U.S.S.R.', ibid., p. 165).

socialism' while Russia's road lay 'through socialism to freedom'.[125] Nicholas Berdyaev, the most influential Russian philosopher in exile, emphasized the uniqueness of the Russian destiny but carried wishful thinking about Russia's future even further.[126] Thus, Hessen's case was far from singular.

Finally, Hessen realized that post-war Poland had in fact become a kind of Soviet protectorate and that its future was bound up, to a greater or lesser extent, with Soviet Communism. This awareness confronted him with a new, vitally important question: how should one behave in these conditions, how define one's place in the new reality? For the liberal-democratic intellectuals it was a very difficult problem. In contrast to the Communists, who represented only a small minority in Poland, they could not identify themselves with the new Polish state but, unlike nationalist hard-liners, they could not simply reject it either. It was not like the Nazi occupation which mobilized everybody to active resistance without creating any moral dilemmas, being incapable of exercising ideological influence, let alone of exerting interiorized ideological pressure. The coming of communism to Poland was something else. Even if it was seen as catastrophe, it had to be taken seriously, as the irreversible verdict of History, as the beginning of a new world which could not simply be overthrown; even if this new world was felt to be evil, its evil could be treated as the price of progress or as punishment for the multiple evils of the pre-communist political/social order. This attitude was characteristic of Hessen and of many people around him. It is understandable, therefore, that he did not think of actively resisting the new rulers; he chose rather to influence them, which presupposed, naturally, a concentration on their good side, minimizing or passing over in silence the differences and trying instead to discover common values. Hessen's conscious choice of this strategy explained the new emphasis in his interpretation of Marxism: his attempts to counterpose Marxism to the totalitarian ideologies by stressing Marx's individualism (the idea of the full emancipation of man as an individual) and universalism, especially Marx's view that under Communism moral and cultural values would become truly autonomous and universal. This strategy explains also the awkward passages on Stalin in Hessen's article on the Rights of Man.

[125] F. I. Dan, *Proiskhozhdenie bol'shevizma*, New York, 1946.
[126] Cf. N. Berdyaev, *Russkaia ideia*, Paris, 1946.

6 *General philosophy of law*

Let us turn now to the general philosophy of law elaborated by Hessen in the last years of his life.

The last part of Hessen's book, 'The Downfall and the Regeneration of Democracy', was entitled 'On the Essence and Calling of Law'. Its Polish version escaped destruction and in the years 1946–7 was used as a basis for Hessen's lectures on the philosophy of law at the University of Łódź. In fact it is a separate, book-length study (182 typescript pages), subdivided into the following chapters:

1. Law and morality
2. Social existence and spiritual life
3. Law and spiritual life
4. Law and social existence
5. Attributes and grades of law
6. The antinomic character of law
7. The development of law and its function in 'spiritualizing' (personalizing) social existence.[127]

In the following pages I do not attempt a summary of this excellent study, but rather aim to show its importance to the controversy about law in Russian intellectual history. It was, I think, a remarkable effort to transcend this controversy by rendering to each part its due. As such, it can be seen as making possible an intellectual reconciliation between the two most general views on law which have found often forceful expression in the history of Russian thought: the view that law is of very limited value, held by the vast majority of Russian thinkers, some of whom, like the anarchists, even went so far as to proclaim that law is evil and, on the other hand, the view that law is absolutely necessary, proclaimed and boldly defended by the liberal minority.

In the first chapter Hessen traces the problem of morality versus law back to antiquity. He starts with his favourite philosopher, Plato, then passes on to Aristotle, the Stoics, Plotinus, neo-Platonists, and so forth. The most important conclusion derived from this lengthy historical digression seems to be the assertion that the sharp distinction between morality and law has its roots in early Christianity. That was so because the Christian virtues of hope, faith, and love of one's neighbour were absurd from the point of view of intellectual knowledge, especially that of Roman Law. In the beginning the law was simply held in contempt

[127] A typescript copy of this book was kindly given to me by Hessen's widow, Maria Niemyska-Hessenowa.

among Christians and rejected for the sake of love. Later, the scholastic reception of ancient philosophy restored the intellectual approach to morality, characteristic of Plato and Aristotle. The new turn was due to Kant, whose moral philosophy can be seen as the beginning of the modern stage in the history of the problem. As is known, he counterposed 'morality' to 'legality', treating the first as interior, autonomous, and independent of theoretical knowledge. However, in his own theory of morality he succumbed to intellectualism by rationalizing and schematizing moral categories, that is, by modelling them on the categories of law.

Hessen in his theory tried to mediate between the three conceptions which he saw as the most precious legacy of the Russian philosophy of law: Petrażycki's conception, which defined law and morality as two different species of ethics—the former more important socially, Chicherin's conception, treating law as completely distinct from morality and dealing with the proper delimitation of freedom, not with ethical duty; and Soloviev's conception, which saw in law 'the minimum of morality'.

Hessen very broadly agreed with Petrażycki. He emphatically supported the latter's view that coercion is not the essence of law and that the sphere of legal phenomena is much broader than official state law. Petrażycki's distinction between the attributive-imperative character of law and the purely imperative character of morality belonged, in Hessen's view, to that rare class of original ideas, fortunate in being immediately accepted by the *communis opinio doctorum*. Likewise, Hessen's method of 'phenomenological insight into the essence' is reminiscent of those aspects of Petrażycki's psychological method in which G. Gurvitch correctly recognized a certain closeness to phenomenology.[128] Nevertheless Hessen's conception was not a development of Petrażycki's views: it absorbed and critically digested a great deal from them but started from different philosophical assumptions and had a different focus.

Chicherin's conception, typical of classical liberalism, saw the legal as compared to moral norms, as essentially negative in character; thus, it agreed with Schopenhauer's dictum that the principle of morality is *omnes, quantum potes, iuva* while the principle of law is merely *neminem laede*. The development of law, however, has refuted such views: all kinds of positive freedom secured by law are in fact different forms of

---

[128] See above, Ch. IV, n. 62.

positive help (*iuvare*), which indicates that the difference between negative and positive obligations is not as sharp as classical liberals once thought. In spite of this, Hessen conceded, there was an important element of truth in Chicherin's view. In contrast to morality, positive freedom, as conceived by law, does not claim that self-development is imperative nor does it provide individuals with positive stimuli for developing their resources. It consists only in removing economic and social obstacles which prevent some groups of people from fully developing their capacities—provided that they really want to develop them. Thus it can be seen as a broader interpretation of negative freedom and might be derived from the principle of *neminem laede*.

From Soloviev, Hessen took the conception of law as the minimum of morality but interpreted it differently. By the minimum of morality he did not mean that the scope of law is less; on the contrary it is broader because many laws, such as traffic rules or different administrative regulations, are morally indifferent. Soloviev's definition is true if minimum is understood not as lesser scope, but as lesser intensity. Moral obligation is maximalist by nature, demanding always the greatest efforts, recommending selfless sacrifice and heroism; by contrast, legal obligation is mild and reasonable, demanding only *average* efforts and thus is truly 'minimalized' in intensity. Unlike morality, the law does not inspire people with love for values (Eros)—it satisfies itself with a cold respect for values. Moral values act upon man as an appeal for creativity whereas in law creativity shrinks, as it were, to mere 'possession'. Morality belongs to the sphere of spiritual culture while the essence of law consists in a peculiar 'lessening' or minimalization of spiritual values.

Following Bergson and Scheler, Hessen pointed out yet another difference between morality and law: the atheoretical, anti-intellectual nature of the former. Legal norms are theoretically justifiable and subject to deliberation while moral norms stem from the vision of the heart and from the intuition of the will; the first can be known but not recognized while knowledge of the second, just because of its non-rational nature, is equivalent to a recognition of their validity. Law imitates the repetitive and necessary character of the laws of nature, as conceived by positivist scientism; morality resembles rather the flow of free creativity as described by Bergson.

The final conclusion of these analyses was as follows. The attributive character of law, discovered by Petrażycki, was explained by

Hessen as deriving from the intellectualized nature of law—from the fact that legal duties had, as it were, been sifted through the prism of a theoretical, conceptual knowledge. Only obligations which are rationalized, logically defined, and schematized can be attributive, that is, treated not as individual creative acts but as something to be possessed, something which can be claimed from others as a due right.

At the end of the chapter on morality and law Hessen recognized the relative truth in the Marxist view that law had always been used as the instrument of class domination.[129] He insisted, however, that law had never been reduced to this function alone and claimed, as in his earlier works, that Marx himself had implied this by pointing out that there were periods of history in which progressive classes transcended their class egoism and legislated in the interests of all.

The next three chapters dealt with the location of law in Hessen's conception of the levels of human existence, the scheme of which is reproduced above in connection with his philosophy of man.[130]

In order to understand law, Hessen maintained, it is necessary to go beyond the purely descriptive phenomenology of law. A legal philosopher should answer the question of the calling of law and thus offer a philosophical justification of law. This requires a clear view of the position of law in relation to the two levels of human existence in which theorists have usually placed legal phenomena: that of social existence and that of spiritual/cultural life. In other words, the philosophy of law should answer the question: is law merely a mechanism of social adaptation or can it be treated as something more—as a part of the realm of Objective Spirit in the Hegelian sense of this term.

It was obvious to Hessen that the level of social existence cannot be reduced to, or derived from, biological existence. He was concerned rather with proving that the higher level—that of spiritual/cultural life—has an autonomy of its own and cannot be reduced to man's social existence. His point of departure was an interesting comparison between Durkheim, as the most consistent representative of sociologism, and Marx, the result of which sounded paradoxical. In spite of his

---

[129] This chapter of Hessen's work was published in Polish but without the pages on Marxism. See S. Hessen, 'Prawo i moralność', *Mysl Współczesna*, 1948, no. 2/3, reprinted (also without the last pages) in *Studia z filozofii kultury*. There is also a French translation of this study (in Actes du XIème Congrès International de Philosophie, vol. 9. Philosophie sociale juridique et politique, Amsterdam, 1953) and a separate Italian edition, *Diritto e morale*, Rome, 1958.

[130] See above, p. 419.

sociologism Durkheim ignored the most important element in social life, the constant struggle for power; Marx, with his theory of class struggle, penetrated much more deeply the essence of social existence. On the other hand, in spite of his widely misinterpreted dictum about social existence determining consciousness, Marx clearly distinguished between the social and the spiritual/cultural level of man's life. This distinction was implied both in treating cultural phenomena as a separate superstructure and, more significantly still, in the view that communism would emancipate culture from its dependence on socio-economic struggles, thus allowing art to be simply art, philosophy simply a disinterested search for truth, and so forth. Of course, this forecast did not apply to law: Marx saw law together with the state as a lower part of the superstructure, serving the class struggle in a direct way and therefore destined to wither away in the classless society of the future.

In Hessen's own view, there is an essential difference, between the social and the spiritual/cultural level of human existence. Social existence does not produce history but only tradition as mere heredity, holding sway over men, constantly restoring but unable to transcend itself. The social group exerts a pressure on its members while cultural and moral values, constituting a spiritual community, act upon men by means of erotic appeal (in Plato's sense); their necessity is not that of *Müssen* but of *Sollen*, something completely different from both the determinism of nature and coercion by those in power. Because of this only on the spiritual/cultural level does man exist as a personality, as a free, creative and self-transcending being.

In law the appeal of moral values is replaced by commands,[131] universal validity (*allgemeine Geltung*) is replaced by the social fact of universal recognition (*allgemeine Anerkennung*). Instead of attraction we have pressure, instead of autonomy, heteronomy. Eros and Caritas are no longer there: their active love has been 'lessened', 'minimized', reduced to a cold respect (*Achtung*) for moral and other values. Respect for values does not demand creativity: and indeed, the law is concerned not with creativity itself but rather with securing the conditions for it. This minimalization of the spiritual life in law occurs because the law serves as a means by which the social level of man's life acts upon the higher spiritual/cultural level. Marx was perfectly right in claiming that the spiritual life is necessarily based upon social

[131] But Hessen distinguished commands of law from direct commands of the executive power, even if properly legislated.

life. The relative truth of the Marxist theory of law consists in
emphasizing, however exaggeratedly, the negative influence exercised
on law by the struggles for domination characteristic of man's social
existence.

However, if we look at legal phenomena from below, from the social
level of existence, and not from above, from the spiritual/cultural level,
we discover a quite different face of law. Seen from this perspective
law reveals itself as a means whereby the spiritual life may influence its
existential basis. This was in Hessen's view the true calling of law:
'spiritualizing' the social existence of men, making it more and more
similar to a spiritual/cultural community.

In his analysis of how law realizes its calling Hessen made the
following points.

1. Concerning social groups: the more a given group is permeated
by law, the less 'closed' it is. It becomes open to various aliens,
establishes tolerance, a respect for values which makes possible an
'erotic' attitude towards them, and, finally, it imitates a spiritual
community by enabling all its members to take active part in its life.

2. Concerning individuals: under the rule of law individuals cease to
be merely members of different social groups. The law recognizes in
each individual an extra-social kernel impenetrable by the group.
True, the legal principles of liberty, equality, and fraternity (solidarity)
weaken and diminish active love but they also enable individuals to rise
above the social level of their existence, to personalize themselves, and,
above all to do so not by escaping from society but as active members
of it.

3. Concerning authority: political authority which is subject to law is
no longer naked power. It becomes power in the service of moral
values because the principles of its legitimacy, that of the general will
in the original Rousseauan conception, is nothing less than the voice of
moral values which can be heard in the soul of each member of the
polity 'when the passions are silent.'

The two faces of law are paralleled by two types of legal theory,
which isolate and absolutize different sides of legal phenomena.[132]

Some legal philosophies see only the face of law which is turned

---

[132] A similar typological dichotomy was recently presented by a phenomenologist
philosopher of law, W. A. Luijpen: see his *Phenomenology of Natural Law*, Pittsburgh,
1967, pp. 43–4. For Luijpen, however, the opposite of 'legal positivism' (broadly
conceived) is 'natural law' whereas Hessen, as we shall see below, did not accept this
term.

towards and influenced by social existence. The best known of these is legal positivism whose main idea may be summarized in Hobbes' words *ius est quod iussum est*. This view is fully shared by social theorists who, like Durkheim or Marx, reduce law to certain facts of social life, seeing it as a system of coercive regulation exercised in a given society by its rulers, quite irrespective of whether the rulers themselves represent a minority, or a majority.

The opposite type of legal philosophy concentrates on that face of law which is turned towards higher spiritual values; consequently, it sees law not as authoritarian commands but rather as a means of limiting political power, irrespective of its source. Representatives of this view of law include in antiquity Aristotle, in the Middle Ages Thomas Aquinas and many other schoolmen, in early modern times Grotius and the natural-law school, and today many theorists of modern liberalism and democracy. It was also defended by Proudhon who, far from being a simple anarchist, was in fact the spiritual father of the syndicalist conception of social law. Hessen, understandably, emphasized in this context the contributions of the Russian liberal theorists of the 'revival of natural law', including Petrażycki.

Hessen wholeheartedly sympathized with the second type of legal theory, while at the same time recognizing the relative truth of the first. In his view, law mediated between the social and spiritual/cultural levels of human existence. From this point of view, it might seem, the two types of legal theory were equally true, or, rather, equally untrue, equally one-sided. But this was not so. Hessen interpreted law not only with reference to its place in the hierarchical structure of the human world but also, and chiefly, with reference to its calling. And it is obvious that from this point of view he could accept only representatives of the second type of legal theory and credit only those with fruitful insights.

The next chapter, 'The Attributes and Grades of Law', revolves around the problem of authority. Authority, as distinct from domination or power, was for Hessen a necessary foundation of law. The problem was what kind of authority conformed to the idea of law.

First, legal authority should not attempt to mould the inner life of man in a positive way or to prescribe positive goals for society. It must be repeated that for Hessen law is essentially negative: it can secure positive freedom but only in the sense of removing obstacles, not in the sense of predetermining the positive content of men's lives. Thus, law should not be used, as in totalitarian states, to mould the 'new man'.

On this point Hessen fully agreed with Chicherin: to prescribe a definite moral content by means of law amounted, in his view, to a combination of the worst features of the modern secular state and the ugliest aspects of theocracy.

Secondly, there are different sources of authority, of which the state is only one. There are religious and secular authorities, official and unofficial, personal and social ones. Petrażycki and Gurvitch (who in this respect was Petrażycki's disciple) were perfectly right in pointing out that there are many normative or authoritative facts, which might be treated as sources of law: judicial precedents, customs, opinions of learned jurists, pronouncements of religious authorities, the declarations and practice of political and social organizations, and so forth. Law, unlike morality, must at all times invoke a certain authority and, in this sense, remains heteronomous. Petrażycki's conception of an autonomous intuitive law is unacceptable because the appeal to authority is constitutive of law, inherent in its essence, as opposed to the essence of cultural and moral life, which is based upon the appeal of values. In Hessen's view the same was true of natural law: a law which directly invoked the 'divine will', 'reason', or 'the natural sense of justice', instead of seeking support in a certain socially recognized authority, could not strictly be called law. It is important to distinguish between officially binding, organized law and law which is not yet binding, not yet organized, existing only as a postulate; even the latter, however, if it really deserves to be called law, must derive from the authority of historically created 'normative facts.'

Another difference between Petrażycki and Hessen concerned the problem of legal consciousness as a source of law. Hessen agreed that the consciousness of a revolutionary group might constitute a law for its members, or a germ of law for post-revolutionary society, but resolutely rejected the notion of a 'bandit law'. In his view a necessary attribute of law was mediating between social groups and the supra-social realm of universally valid values; values which could not be realized by means of law but which should nevertheless 'glow' through it and justify its existence. Obviously, this attribute would not be found in the laws of criminal organizations.

The heteronomous nature of law, together with its 'intellectualized' character, constituted for Hessen the main difference between law and morality but not a sharp division. Hessen conceded that law could be more or less precise, more or less 'intellectualized', and the social authority upon which it was based more or less organized, or even not organized at all. It followed from this that there were many different grades of law, many intermediate links between pure morality and pure law. Social morality (*Sitten*), invoking the authority of socially accepted norms, was already a kind of law; even more so were the moral codes of professional organizations since, as a rule, these were more 'intellectualized' and invoked the authority of organized associations; then came unorganized social law, that is, law which was postulated but not yet binding; the next grade was organized social law such as trade-union law and, finally, the official law of the state.

In the concluding part of these considerations Hessen pointed out a certain similarity between his conception and the theory set forth by Bergson in *Les deux sources de la religion et de morale*. It was, however limited to the contrast between open morality, based upon creative intuition and active love, and closed or social morality, formulated in ready-made, stiff, intellectualized norms. Law had no place of its own in Bergson's conception; it was in fact equated with social morality and its supra-social aspect was ignored. In addition Bergson, in Hessen's view, failed to distinguish between the two levels of supra-social, spiritual life, that of spiritual/cultural values and that of grace. These two levels of human existence had moral equivalents in the morality of Eros, stemming from the love of values, and the morality of Caritas, based on active love of one's neighbour. According to Hessen's study of the ancient classical and Christian virtues, the first had been attained in antiquity while the second was peculiar to Christianity.[133]

The title of the following chapter, 'The antinomic character of law', is somewhat misleading. In fact it deals rather with overcoming the antinomies of law, transcending them, preventing situations in which different components of law are opposed to each other in a seemingly irreconcilable way. The central notion is that of 'equilibrium', borrowed from the dialectics of Proudhon. Hessen's debt to Proudhon was even greater, because he also accepted his view that the task of law is to balance the different principles of social life.

Hessen defined the regulative idea of law, or simply the idea of law, as a balance of three principles: equality, liberty, and solidarity (fraternity).[134] The most common antinomies of law result from deranging this equilibrium, as for instance when the principle of liberty is absolutized and set against the principle of equality, or the other way

---

[133] Cf. Hessen's study on the ancient classical and Christian virtues (see above, n. 24).
[134] Thus, the definition of the ideal of law was identical with the definition of the ideal democracy.

round. Another very common antinomy arises from the split between the subjective rights of the legal person and the rightful claims of legal union. This antinomy between the 'individualistic' and 'socialistic' principles in law should not be allowed to take the form of rigid opposition, and the struggle between them should be transformed into a creative tension. In putting forward this view Hessen took issue with a pessimistic brochure by his father, in which the history of mankind was presented as an endless repetition of the eternal struggle between individualism and socialism.[135]

Among the other more specific antinomies which have been exposed and analysed in the book under discussion, the most important are the historically changing antinomic relationship between private and public law, that between the individual and the social aspect of private property, a similar one in criminal law—punishment as the subjective right of the criminal and punishment as society's self-defence, and finally, the antinomies made possible by the tensions between individualist, transindividualist and transpersonal values.[136] In each case establishment of an equilibrium is recommended as the best solution.

The last chapter, dealing with the development of law, poses the question of the progress of law. This progress, Hessen maintains, can be measured by different criteria, such as: (1) the degree of perfection attained by a given legal system, (2) the closeness to the final ideal of law, and, finally (3) the degree in which social life is permeated by law.

In the first sense there is no progress in law. The perfection of a given legal system depends on how well it fits the needs of a given society and, of course, it can easily happen that a less developed society has a better adjusted, more perfect, legal order than a more highly developed society.

In the second sense progress in law cannot be denied, although one should not expect the final ideal of law to be fully realized in history. Even more unrealistic are the expectations that law, having fulfilled its mission, will simply wither away. In this connection Hessen submitted to detailed criticism Petrażycki's view that the final aim of law is to

---

[135] Cf. I. V. Gessen (Hessen), *Iskaniia obshchestvennogo ideala*, 2nd edn., Berlin, 1922. This pamphlet was dedicated to the author's sons.

[136] The conception of the three alternative kinds of world outlook, the individualist, the transindividualist and the transpersonal, was formulated by G. Radbruch. (Cf. *The Legal Philosophies of Lask, Radbruch, and Dabin*. K. Wilk (trans.), Cambridge, Mass., 1950, pp. 94–7). Hessen sympathized with Radbruch's view but accused him of yielding to the temptations of relativism.

make itself unnecessary and to be replaced by active love. Similar criticism could be applied to other theories of the withering away of law, especially Marxism. This time, however, Petrażycki was a much better target for Hessen; both men were equally committed to the same Christian ideal of love (Caritas) and for this very reason it was necessary to make clear what divided them.

Hessen readily conceded that all theories of the withering away of law contain an important grain of truth. This is the clear realization that law feeds on the imperfection of man and on the shortcomings of society. In Petrażycki's case the area of agreement was even greater because, like Hessen, he emphasized that man is not merely a social animal and treated the ideal of love as supra-social or, even, supra-moral, 'jenseits des Guten und Bösen'. Nevertheless Hessen, in line with his criticism of the millenarian interpretation of Christianity, did not expect the kingdom of love ever to be realized in history. Absolute values 'glow' through all forms of man's historical existence but these forms will never become perfect; thus, the need for mediation between the social and spiritual levels of existence, the need for law, will never disappear.

Approaching Petrażycki's theory in its own terms, Hessen pointed out that the Russo-Polish master had not given sufficient grounds for his conclusions. In his view law was a symptom of insufficient adaptation and a means toward more perfect adaptation; true, but it did not follow from this that the state of perfect adaptation, in which legal pressures could be completely dismissed, would ever be attained. On the contrary: unless we assume that history itself will end, we must envisage a constant need for adjusting people to changing conditions and, thus, a constant need for law. Petrażycki was perfectly right in indicating that many laws had been interiorized and could therefore be eliminated from legal codes; he was not sufficiently aware, however, that the growing complication and spiritualization of social life would require the extension of legal regulation to areas which in earlier times were outside the scope of legislation. In accordance with Petrażycki's 'legal policy' law would become more subtle, more flexible, increasingly permeated by higher, supra-social values, but it would never die out.

Moreover, Hessen's conception of the progress of law in the third sense showed that in reality the scope of legal regulation was constantly widening and that the law penetrated the different spheres of life more and more deeply. This applied, above all, to the economy. Once completely autonomous and uncontrolled, the economy was now either 'conquered' by the state, or permeated by law. The first tendency, represented by state imperialism, created the terrible danger of a union of political and economic power, reducing law to a mere instrument of naked force. The second, characteristic of modern democracy and/or liberal socialism, increasingly limited political power, eliminating all arbitrary decisions and establishing a rational control of the economy, while preserving its legitimate autonomy, and thereby inaugurated the highest stage in the development of the rule-of-law state.

In the 1920s Hessen called this stage 'rule-of-law socialism'; in his books written (and destroyed) during the war he preferred to call it 'regenerated democracy', while after the war he decided on the term 'liberal socialism'. Despite these terminological changes his basic idea remained the same. In the last paragraphs of his book on the essence and calling of law he forcefully condemned totalitarianism as lacking faith in man: totalitarian rulers, like Dostoevsky's Grand Inquisitor, do not believe that man is a spiritual being, created in the likeness of God and responsive to the appeal of higher values.

7 Instead of conclusion

The above presentation of Hessen's philosophy of law justifies, I hope, what I said at the beginning of this chapter.

Hessen's attempt to reconcile liberalism with socialism was the last link in the development of Russian liberalism, and not only in a chronological sense; it was also the last phase of the inner logic of this development. All legal philosophers of Russian liberalism, while recognizing the relative truth of Chicherin's classical liberalism adopted the principle of the new, democratic liberalism and tried to absorb as much as possible from social democracy, social-democratic 'revisionism' and 'professorial socialism'. Petrażycki, Novgorodtsev, and Kistiakovsky represent on this view the intermediate stages between Chicherin and Hessen; Novgorodtsev deserves a special place, resembling Hessen as he does in his criticism of socialist millenarism and in his interest in the syndicalist conception of social law. With the exception of Petrażycki, all were inspired by Soloviev's idea of the right to a dignified existence; some, like Hessen—especially E. Trubetskoi and, to a lesser degree, Novgorodtsev—drew inspiration from Soloviev's religious philosophy as well, although, again like Hessen, dissociating themselves from his utopian theocratic leanings. Hessen was emphatically aware and proud of this remarkable continuity. He fully shared his father's pride in *Pravo* and liked to recall his own frequent contributions to this newspaper. He often referred to the works of Russian liberal jurists, not only those mentioned above, but also lesser figures, such as his father, his uncle V. M. Hessen, I. Pokrovsky, N. Alekseev, and others. In other words, he felt strongly that Russian liberalism, although short-lived in active politics, had successfully created a tradition of its own in legal philosophy; he saw himself as belonging to this tradition and did all in his power to enrich it philosophically and to transcend its limitations.

A characteristic feature of Hessen's thought was its constant dialogue with Marxism, due both to his genuine life-long fascination with Marxian ideas and to the tremendous, indeed formidable, importance of these ideas in Russian history. Hessen treated Marxism as an integral part of the European and Russian intellectual tradition and never cherished the arrogant illusion that he could afford to ignore it. He wanted, on the contrary, in accordance with his favourite principle of *Aufhebung* to transcend it in a positive way, which presupposed not only a thorough knowledge of it but also the capacity to understand its relative truth. He was certainly able to understand Marxism much better than the great majority of Marxists. Faced with the aggressiveness of a vulgarized, politicized, and brutalized Marxism he reacted not aggressively but by reminding people of the conveniently forgotten, humanitarian aspects of Marxism and by providing his own interpretation of the relevance and significance of the Marxist legacy. He was undoubtedly able to learn from Marxism and to utilize what he had learned in his own theories. Thus, for instance, his theory of law as a mediation between the two levels, social and spiritual, of human existence, seems to be influenced to a certain extent by the Marxian conception of law as a mediation between an economic base and an ideological superstructure. It is significant, almost symbolic, that at the end of his life he became deeply interested in the newly discovered, or rather rediscovered concept of alienation.[137] He saw this concept as an important bridge between Marxism and the great tradition of philosophical idealism, a tradition which he saw as derived from deep religious sources.[138] He was happy to find that the idea of the future

[137] I vividly remember Hessen's comments on this problem, made in connection with an article by A. Cornu and a book by H. Lefebvre.

[138] This interpretation was correct. We have recently been reminded that the Hegelian concept of alienation—that alienation of the spirit which goes out of itself, becoming something different from and alien to its essence—dates back to the

disalienation of culture corroborated his own interpretation of the final aim of Marxism, in which the classless society of the future would liberate culture from its humiliating dependence on material interests, making cultural values ends in themselves and thus restoring them to their true essence.

Hessen's hostility to relativism had nothing in common with dogmatic intolerance and one-sidedness. It was, on the contrary, combined with a deliberate striving for universal understanding and reconciliation. This was the cherished aim of his dialectics: to reconcile different standpoints by transcending them, that is, by overcoming their respective one-sidedness and, at the same time, paying attention to the element of truth which each contained. He used this method not only to reconcile liberalism with socialism; even more impressive was his ability to combine a wholehearted commitment to the rule of law with the discovery and emphasis of important elements of truth in the entire Russian tradition of legal nihilism. It was part of his moral effort towards reconciliation with Russia. For a long time, like other liberal Westerners, he saw the Russian people as lacking even a rudimentary legal culture and worse, treating this lack as a virtue; he was especially critical of the Russian intelligentsia who idealized this attitude and indulged in different kinds of legal nihilism. With the passage of time, however, he himself became inclined to believe that the Russian contempt for law, sometimes at least, did indeed stem from a kind of virtue—from a kind of moral maximalism, so much extolled (and not without reason) by Russian thinkers both of the Left (like Herzen) and of the Right (the Slavophiles). His reasoning was as follows:

Russian 'legal nihilists' were one-sided but not entirely wrong. They saw only one 'face of law'—law as a function of the social level of human existence; they erred in denying the more lofty aspect of law, but they were right in refusing to idolize law and in stressing that the social face of law had some very ugly features. In their attitudes

---

theological concept of *kenosis* (A. Schaff, *Alienation as a Social Phenomenon*, Oxford 1980, pp. 25–8). 'St. Augustine, quoting St. Paul's Epistle to the Philippians, interprets the Incarnation as Christ emptying himself of divine properties. The Greek text uses the verb *ekenosen* which the Vulgate translates as *exinavit* while Luther in German has *hat sich geäussert* (literally 'emptied' himself). Hegel's *Entäusserung* is a noun borrowed from Luther's translation'. The concept of *Entäusserung* can be distinguished from that of *Entfremdung* (alienation) but 'the difference between these concepts is not very clear in Hegel, and in Marx, who in his later writing used the concepts interchangeably, it is lost completely'. (Ibid., p. 25.)

towards law there was, as a rule, something just and valuable. Thus the Russian anarchists were right in claiming that freedom as delimited by law should not be equated with freedom as such; the Russian populists were equally right in arguing that equality before the law, or even constitutional freedom, could not solve painful social questions; both groups were not mistaken in seeing law as a powerful instrument of exploitation and oppression. Even more justified were Russian religious thinkers—the Slavophiles, Tolstoy, and Dostoevsky—who were repelled by the intellectual coldness and formalism of law and proclaimed the infinite superiority of Christian love. Hessen himself subscribed to this view. In his study on the ancient classical and Christian virtues he wrote: 'The vigilance and fortitude in the struggle for law is only a pale reflection of this tireless moral creativity which characterizes the true love of one's neighbour'.[139]

And yet, the meaning of Hessen's legal philosophy may be adequately summarized in the words: *justification of law*. Law has another face, turned towards the realm of universal objective values; it is a necessary mediation between the social level of human life, with all its antagonisms and brutalities, and the higher spiritual sphere; it cannot replace cultural and moral values but is indispensable in creating the necessary conditions for their victory. It safeguards that impenetrability of person, which is a precondition of higher forms of personal self-realization. It should not be mistaken for the principle of the Good, neither should it be identified with everything which serves the good cause. For modern man it is a true anchor of salvation, since it shows him how to escape totalitarian temptation, both in its demonic form and in the form of benevolent tutelage, whose totalitarian nature was exposed in Dostoevsky's 'Legend of the Grand Inquisitor'.

---

[139] S. Hessen, *Studia z filozofii kultury*, pp. 265–6, note.

[*See p. 466 for Appendices to Chapter VII.*]

Appendix 1

Table of Contents of Hessen's 'The Rule-of-Law State and Socialism'[1] (original title: 'The Problem of Rule-of-Law Socialism')

Prologue: The Breakdown of Utopianism

PART I: THE CRISIS OF LIBERALISM

Chapter 1. The Problem of Socialism

Chapter 2. New Liberalism

Chapter 3. New Freedom and Old Freedom

Chapter 4. The Limits of Liberalism

PART II: THE EVOLUTION OF SOCIALISM

Introduction: The Problem of Rule-of-Law Socialism

Chapter 1. Utopian Socialism as the Abstract Negation of Capitalism

  a) The principle of the Good and the principle of law

  b) Socialism and conservatism: the individualist principle in socialism

  c) Utopian socialism as the abstract negation of law and economy. Its illusory 'positivism'

Chapter 2. Marxism as the Real Negation of the Liberal-Capitalist Order

  a) Scientific and utopian varieties of socialism: the theory of class struggle, its positive and negative character

  b) The utopian aspect of Marxism: the negation of law. State and economy.

  c) Marxism as a mechanistic conception of society. Its fatalism. Real negation as an unstable equilibrium between destruction (*Vernichtung*) and transformation (*Aufhebung*)

---

[1] Translated from Russian

Chapter 3. The Degeneration of Real Negation into Pure Destruction: Communism as the Absolute Negation of Law

a) Nationalization (*ogosudarstvlenie*) of the means of production: disintegration of property, society, and personality

b) The dictatorship of the proletariat: adopting the mask of conservatism and degenerating into reaction

Chapter 4. Regenerating Real Negation into a Transforming (Constructive) Negation

a) The idealistic motive in Marxism. Lassalle and Proudhon

b) Restoration of the idea of the state: reformism

c) Restoration of the idea of economy: syndicalism

d) Guild-socialism as the first attempt to create a positive model of rule-of-law socialism

PART III: RULE-OF-LAW SOCIALISM AND THE NEW MIDDLE AGES

a) The broadened idea of law

b) State and society

c) The autonomous economy

d) Law as an instrument of spirit

Appendix 2

Table of contents of Hessen's 'The Real and Illusory Overcoming of Capitalism'[1]

PART I: THE DEFORMATION OF CAPITALISM IN TOTALITARIAN ECONOMIES

Chapter 1. The Two Capitalisms: Classical and Monopolist. Truth and Error in Marx's Forecasts Concerning Capitalist Development

Chapter 2. The Change in the Inner Structure of Capital in the Second Half of the Nineteenth Century

§1. Unwieldy capitalism (changes at the level of productive forces)

§2. Financial capitalism (changes at the level of relations of production)

§3. Vanishing of the principle of profit

---

[1] Translated from Polish

§3. A state-regulated economy

§4. Corporatism as the illusory overcoming of capitalism

Chapter 8. The Nazi Economy

Appendix 3

Table of Contents of Hessen's 'The Downfall and the Regeneration of Democracy'[1]

[1] Translated from Russian

Appendix 4

Table of Contents of Hessen's 'Philosophy of Education'[1]

Part I: Education as a biological process (*Pflege, Dressur*)
   1. Categories of biological life and education in the animal world
   2. Biologism (naturalism) in the theory of education
      a) Behaviourism   b)Montessori
   3. Care and training in the education of man

Part II: Education as a social process (*Zucht*)
   1. Categories of social life and the education of primitive man
   2. Sociologism in the theory of education
      a) Durkheim   b) Marxism   c) E. Krieck
   3. Education as a social function

Part III: Education as a spiritual process (*Bildung*)
   1. The categories of spiritual life
      a) Value   b) Personality   c) Tradition   d) Cultural goods
   2. Education as the cultivation of culture
   3. Humanism in the theory of education
      a) Humboldt   b) G. Gentile

Part IV: Education as deliverance (*Erlösung*)
   1. Psychoanalysis as a secular theory of salvation
   2. The dogmatism of religious pedagogy
   3. The reality of the Kingdom of God and the resurrection of man

[1] Original in Russian and in Polish

Index